W9-BDY-903

The Architect
At Mid-Century

EVOLUTION
AND ACHIEVEMENT

VOLUME TWO OF THE ARCHITECT AT MID-CENTURY IS

CONVERSATIONS

ACROSS THE NATION

EDITED BY FRANCIS R. BELLAMY

The Architect
At Mid-Century

EVOLUTION

AND ACHIEVEMENT

EDITED BY

TURPIN C. BANNISTER

VOLUME ONE OF THE REPORT OF THE

COMMISSION FOR THE SURVEY

OF EDUCATION AND REGISTRATION OF

THE AMERICAN INSTITUTE OF ARCHITECTS

Reinhold Publishing Corporation   New York

This report was made possible by funds granted by Carnegie Corporation of New York. That Corporation is not, however, the author, owner, publisher, or proprietor of this publication, and is not to be understood as approving by virtue of its grant any of the statements made or views expressed herein.

THE COMMISSION FOR THE SURVEY

OF EDUCATION AND REGISTRATION

PUBLICATION OF THIS SURVEY REPORT
WAS ADMINISTERED BY

THE DEPARTMENT

OF EDUCATION AND RESEARCH

OF THE AMERICAN

INSTITUTE OF ARCHITECTS

WALTER A. TAYLOR, DIRECTOR

THE COMMISSION 1949–1954   Edwin S. Burdell, Chairman

Turpin C. Bannister	Ernest J. Kump
Clinton H. Cowgill	Sidney W. Little
George B. Cummings	Fred L. Markham
B. Kenneth Johnstone	Walter T. Rolfe
Roy Childs Jones	Walter A. Taylor
Walter H. Kilham	Ralph Walker

Andrew Fraser, Consultant

LETTER OF TRANSMITTAL

May 1, 1954

Mr. Clair W. Ditchy, President
The American Institute of Architects
The Octagon, 1741 New York Avenue, N.W.
Washington 6, D. C.

My dear Mr. President:

We have the honor to transmit herewith the report of the Commission for the Survey of Education and Registration appointed by your predecessor Ralph Walker in 1949.

This document is the first major attempt to describe, on the basis of statistical data interpreted by the collective judgment of professional men, the nature of the current practice of architecture and the evolution as well as the present educational methods to prepare youth for that practice.

Sincerely yours,

Edwin S. Burdell, Chairman

Turpin C. Bannister	Ernest J. Kump
Clinton H. Cowgill	Sidney W. Little
George B. Cummings	Fred L. Markham
B. Kenneth Johnstone	Walter T. Rolfe
Roy C. Jones	Walter A. Taylor
Walter H. Kilham, Jr.	Ralph Walker

Contents

Foreword

It so happens that the first fifty years of this century and my life and interest in the architectural profession are nearly parallel. I have been a keen observer of the many changes—the revolutionary changes—which have taken place. I have seen the architect develop from an artist practicing what was chiefly an art into an all-around man of professional stature; requiring in his education, as well as in his experience, a knowledge of the many facets of modern engineering. The latter, especially, have changed things from a point where they represented practically nothing in the cost of building to a point where, often, they represent the largest combined factor of building expenditure. Like all other things, building has been affected by a change in philosophy. The great destruction of effort brought about by two major wars and the rise of the common people to positions of authoritative demand upon the world economy, have produced a need for more—indeed *complete* management—in effecting possible savings in building costs. The world no longer thinks of architecture as a symbol either of faith or of wealth, but rather as the practical shelter needs for everyone. Housing, schools, factories, all have become necessitous problems, each urgent in its immediate demands.

Architecture is changing its characteristics: for centuries it had, within the eclecticism possible, a large choice of ideas inherent in the knowledge of the great past; present indications are merely a stereotype growing out of the experience of these fifty years. Certainly there has been an increasing demand for standardization, not only in structure but also in panelized exteriors. Buildings of all classes have come to look more alike and this trend, apparently, is but in its beginnings.

In some parts of the world architects are already fearful that industrialization in building will affect them adversely; that the builder and the manufacturer will take over the design of these stereotype buildings. Here in America there is a growing concern in relation to the "package building" in which design is merely a minor part of the complete building construction services.

The architect in private practice may tend to disappear. In England, I understand, the greater proportion of the members of the R.I.B.A. are working for a governmental agency of one kind or another.

Yet stereotyped as the construction and appearance may be, the need for an understanding of the many factors which make up the essentials of life in modern shelter requires that the architect gain a wide knowledge of human aspirations as well as material wants. There is also everywhere in evidence a need for the over-all designer who takes the many parts and successfully molds them into an efficient whole. But there is a danger that the architect may attempt to revert to the mere artist concept, letting others do the coordinating and eventually losing control of the way the building itself is constructed.

The complications of modern life as lived here in America make it very difficult for any concept of a master-builder to develop except in very small building operations. There is, however, a great need for the master-designer fully conversant with construction requirements who can take leadership not only in production of architectural and engineering design but also in guiding the actual building in the field. In America there has developed, over the last fifty years, a recognition by the building industry as a whole that the architect, properly trained and ripened in experience, should take this position of leadership.

These circumstances and factors have important implications for the education of an architect, both in his beginnings at an architectural school and later as a trainee. They require that instead of the use of a few simple design motifs, without precision, comparable to childish playing with Erector sets, he must be developed and encouraged to a comprehension that the disciplines inherent in the practice of architecture are so serious and so extensive as to warrant his full attention. Only thus may he gain at the very start an experience in which trained curiosity will be enlarged throughout his life. He must be guided away from the blind admiration of clichés into self-critical analysis.

The architect at the half century seems to be enjoying the esteem of the American people and an increasing number have found gainful employment. In truth, however, the influence of the architect upon American society does not appear to be as great and as beneficial as it might be. The architects at the mid-century do not seem to be as great, or as beneficial, a force in city planning as was McKim, for example, and others at the beginning of the century. The appearance of cities has worsened; the character of all architecture has lost some of the joy of life which was everywhere to be found just prior to the first World War. Modern architecture is more tricky; it seeks always to be novel and has apparently failed, even while generally producing a characteristic style, to create the qualities of aesthetic well-being.

The architect, in the next half century, has the opportunity of using the revolution in engineering forms and technologically-made comforts (to which fundamentally he, the architect, has contributed little either in invention or in development) as a step toward healthy progress in human betterment in its largest aspects. Indeed, he may find that unless he achieves more and wider variations in cultural unity, he will remain resting on an interminable plateau of small progress.

To achieve what he needs to do, the education of the man who is to become and remain an architect must develop along the lines of a continuous quest. As he leaves the hands of his teacher, he should have acquired an understanding that "the object of any education (preliminary or life long) is to break up man's dogmatism and to place himself at a universal point of view." He must continually appreciate that "it is not what happens that matters, but why it happens."

The future of our profession lies not in the creation of more and more gadgets but in attaining, as they are assimilated, a quality of community and social aesthetics—that quality which attains a calm appearance, a sense of variety in unity, and, at the same time, an ever-widening horizon for human aspirations and ideals.

Ralph Walker

New York, May, 1954

Introduction to the Report

The architectural profession in the United States has distinguished itself in many ways but, to the outsider looking in, the most impressive evidence of its vitality is its recurring urge to examine its state of well-being by penetrating surveys. Beginning with the Bosworth-Jones report published in 1932, these periodic examinations have included the investigations of the Joint Committee on Practice of Architecture (1933–38) and the Young-Goldsmith Report in 1939. Across the seas our British cousins in the Royal Institute of British Architects published a report in 1943 in the midst of World War II. A resolution submitted by the Chicago Chapter and adopted at the Houston Convention in 1949 authorized Ralph Walker, as President of The AIA, to appoint a Commission, which met in the latter part of that year at the University of Illinois at Urbana and began this latest study.

This *Survey* is unique in that the conception and execution were accomplished by the collective thought and action of ten members of the profession. The original intention was to have three educators, three practitioners, three State Board men, and one representative of the Accrediting Board; but because architects are versatile people several of them "doubled in brass."

Among the school men were Roy Jones, former head of the Department of Architecture at the University of Minnesota, who also represented the Accrediting Board; Turpin Bannister, former head of the Department of Architecture at the University of Illinois; Sidney Little, Dean of the School of Architecture and Allied Arts at the University of Oregon; Kenneth Johnstone, former Dean of the College of Fine Arts at Carnegie Institute of Technology; and Clinton H. Cowgill, Head of the Department of Architecture at Virginia Polytechnic Institute and also a State Board man.

Among the practicing professionals were Walter Rolfe of Houston, Texas; George Cummings of Binghamton, New York; Walter Kilham of New York City; Ernest Kump of San Francisco and Fred Markham of Provo, Utah. Both

Mr. Cummings and Mr. Markham are also State Board men. Mr. Walker and Walter A. Taylor were members *ex officio*. It was my good fortune to work with these practitioners, teachers, and licensing experts as a member of their team—a rare and rewarding opportunity for one trained as an engineer and sociologist. They devoted a wealth of talent to the *Survey*. As the statistical material came to light, conclusions were drawn on the basis of their broad experiences. To draw upon architecture for a simile, there was no "ivory tower" remoteness of the past in their deliberations. Neither, I hasten to add, is there any crystal ball gazing at the future to be found in this report. For the first time, facts about the architect himself and how he practices his profession are available for examination and evaluation.

The function and place of the architect in this mid-century were examined by the Commission. The nature of architectural practice and the principal aptitudes and skills necessary to perform them effectively were analyzed statistically and qualitatively. The problems of registration and the period of training between graduation and the call to the licensing examination were warmly debated. Finally the role of The AIA in professional education and preparation for practice was assessed. Definite recommendations on all of these points are submitted herewith.

Delays occurred in this final production only because so many of the members of the Commission are key people in the profession. Their responsibilities toward their private practice and toward their national and international commitments have interposed barriers to continued concentration on their deliberations and reports.

The relationship of education to practice has long been a concern of the leaders in all professional fields. It is a good omen that the title "architectural education" is giving way to the longer but more significant term "education for professional practice of architecture." The latter implies a professional rather than classical or academic orientation. The notion of art for art's sake or the study of architecture for the sake of architecture devoid of the social, economic, and technological content no longer satisfies the schools, the practitioners, or the consumers.

The need to produce a well-rounded candidate for practice in the short period of five years has forced a revolutionary change in the curricula of schools of architecture. The large proportion of time formerly devoted to teaching and exercises in drafting and rendering has had to be drastically reduced in order to provide an introduction to the humanities, to social studies, and to a more comprehensive grasp of technology. The products of the schools of architecture today may be less technically skilled but they are more professionally knowledgeable. The practitioner today must accept more of a burden than heretofore in order to assign to the young graduate the routine tasks in the office. This has irked some office managers but it is the price that has to be paid for professionally educated rather than technically trained candidates. The Survey Commission looked into this dilemma with great care and weighed the advantages and disadvantages of the past emphasis on traditional architecture and trade school skills compared with the present understanding of the social and economic factors and comprehensive theoretical knowledge of technologies in meeting the economic and emotional needs of today's people. The Commission approved the present trend.

The practicing architect of today has to be willing to re-assume the responsibilities for initiating the young architect as did his progenitors of a century ago before there were any schools of architecture in the United States. The schools of architecture from the turn of the century until now have undertaken too great a task because the volume of information, the vast new knowhow of technology is beyond the compass of any five-year program. Just as the hospital provides internships for the medical graduate, the minor courts experience for the law graduate, the social agencies reality for the social worker, so the architects collectively through their national and local organization and individually through private office practice must replenish the architectural profession to assure meeting twentieth century needs.

Parts of this report are based almost wholly on data derived by statistical techniques ably conceived and executed by our Washington consultant, Andrew Fraser, but it includes also a good deal of material that has been derived from other sources. For instance, the Commission had a wealth of comment from the Fellows of the Institute and from the honorary foreign members.

In addition, a series of the regional conferences were held in 1951 in New York, San Francisco, Boston, Houston, Eugene (Oregon), Albany, Richmond, Chicago, Pittsburgh, and Salt Lake City. In each conference from ten to a dozen leading citizens who were not architects were invited to speak informally on three specific questions. The Commission gained a very great deal from the transcript of the conversations of this important group of individuals in preparing this, the first volume of the report. A condensation of the conferences themselves also forms an important part of the total report and is published as Volume Two under the title, "Conversations Across the Nation." This section of the report was edited by Francis R. Bellamy.

The final drafting of the report of the Commission has been a synthesis of the thoughts of some of the best minds in the land. We believe with Milton that "opinion in good men is but knowledge in the making." The Commission has not confined its recommendations to statistics of what is, or has been, nor even the extrapolation of trends susceptible of charting. The Commission has committed to writing a report that has been based on an evaluation of information and ideas from all sources. The broad experience and the keen insight of its members give every assurance that this has been well done. We were fortunate in having the services of Turpin Bannister to edit and consolidate the vast amount of material that has been developed. The clear and logical flow of text that follows is largely from his facile pen. My colleagues and I believe that a profession in a free democratic society need not be the helpless victim of circumstances or of forces outside of itself. We believe that however closely the practice of architecture is linked to its contemporary social and technological frame of reference, fundamental objectives of that practice can be shaped and can be kept under control by the members of the profession themselves.

Several other professional groups (the chemists, the civil engineers, the nurses, the pharmacists) have been looking into their professional education and status. But as far as I can determine, no study other than this one of the architectural professional has been organized or financed to encompass the fullest implications of its responsibilities both to its membership and to the society that it serves.

I want to congratulate the Institute on having had Ralph Walker as the president who launched this Survey and who had the vision and courage to implement so effectively the Houston resolution of the Chicago Chapter, on having on its professional staff in The Octagon in Washington a *deus ex machina,* Walter A. Taylor, who has borne the brunt of the administration, collation, and preliminary editorial work, and finally on having a Commission of ten busy men who gave unstintingly of their time and energy.

Truly a profession so favored is bound to flourish.

Edwin Sharp Burdell
Chairman

New York City

Acknowledgments

The American Institute of Architects wishes to acknowledge with appreciation the funds donated to it by the Carnegie Corporation to enable it to carry on this survey. The Institute is grateful also for the thoughtful guidance and aid in establishing fundamental purposes and goals for the study.

The American Institute of Architects is also deeply appreciative of the splendid efforts of our Honorary Member, Dr. Edwin S. Burdell, President of Cooper Union, who as an impartial chairman of the group of professional architects on the commission gave unstintingly of his time and rare ability to coordinate and evaluate the very divergent thoughts which of necessity arise within such a commission. That these divergencies did not develop into a matter of compromise is due largely to his leadership.

The American Institute of Architects owes a debt of gratitude and offers its appreciation to Dr. Turpin C. Bannister also, for the difficult task of authorship in compiling all the subject matter into a coherent whole, and at a great personal sacrifice.

The Institute wishes to express its appreciation to the many leaders of public opinion throughout the country who attended meetings, and who willingly and freely gave their advice as to the position in which the profession of architecture at present find itself, and the problems it is most likely to encounter in the near future. Volume Two of the report, which is called "Conversations Across the Nation," is entirely their contribution to our understanding of the world in which the architect must practice. For the editing of the summary of these conferences we are indebted to Francis R. Bellamy.

Mr. Andrew Fraser, who had previously been engaged on similar surveys for the Engineers' Joint Council and the American Chemical Society, was retained by the Commission and rendered invaluable services as Consultant; in the design of all questionnaires; in the organization and administration of the Survey, including the preparation of statistical tables from the questionnaire data; the drafting of texts of analyses; also in the preparation of the tables which appear in the report, Nos. 1 to 52, which appear at the end of the book immediately following the index. The Commission also appreciates the counsel and assistance of Miles L. Colean, F.A.I.A. in the preparation of *Table 53* and in verifying data in *Chapter I*. It likewise recognizes the cooperation of Dean Buford Pickens, secretary of A.C.S.A., in obtaining 1953 enrollment data from which *Tables 59–62* were developed.

Again, the architects of the country owe a large debt of appreciation to Walter A. Taylor, Director of the Department of Education and Research of The American Institute of Architects, who has helped in so many ways not only to organize the work of the commission but to bring about more fruitful results.

Finally, the profession owes much to the members of the commission itself, the ten men who have given their time, who have undertaken again and again to act as critics and editors of one another's thoughts and the enormous amount of data which have developed from the many questionnaires.

A Note on the Statistical Data

The analyses of responses to the 129 questions obtained by the General and War-Service Questionnaires, of those addressed to Secretaries and Members of Registration Boards, and the summarizing of responses to two questionnaires sent to AIA Chapter Secretaries, are the work of Andrew Fraser. He also was responsible for the written analyses of *Tables 1–52* for the Commission. These analyses, with required editorial changes, have been distributed among the several discussions in this report in the section on the architects' professional history, professional practice, education for practice, and registration procedures and recommendations.

Particular attention is directed to his statement, *The Statistical Bases of the Survey*, which comprises *Appendix B* of the Commission's Report, and which reveals conclusively the unusual trustworthiness of the basic data on which much of the Report is founded. The Commission believes that this result was due to Mr. Fraser's extraordinary skill and foresight. *Tables 54–62*, drawn from indicated sources, and all charts have been prepared by the Editor. All tables appear immediately following the Index starting on page 515. The Commission is responsible for the final interpretation of all data.

The Architect

At Mid-Century

EVOLUTION

AND ACHIEVEMENT

CHAPTER I

American Architecture: Achievement and Potential

1. THE RECORD AT MID-CENTURY

It is no accident that the quality of a civilization stands revealed in its architecture. Few activities intersect so many aspects of daily life. Buildings spring from the very roots of social needs, aspirations, and capabilities. They reflect inevitably the underlying conditions imposed by time and place. They disclose the purposes, preoccupations, and susceptibilities of those for whom they are built. They clearly reveal the varying degrees of technical knowledge, resources, skill, and imagination commanded by their builders. Buildings become, therefore, tangible symbols of the societies which call them into being, and architecture provides a telling measure of a people's capacity to fulfill its highest vision.

Great epochs of the past immediately call to mind their architectural triumphs. Egypt's pyramids, Athens' Parthenon, the fora of imperial Rome, the cathedrals of Gothic France, grandiloquent Versailles, and the shimmering domes of Moslem Isphahan, all epitomized the finest technical and cultural accomplishments of their times, and they still continue to reassure us that men are indeed capable of producing nobility and beauty. Nevertheless, it is at once apparent that a civilization cannot be judged solely by its most luxurious palaces or its holiest shrines. If these monuments stand hedged about by sordid tenements, tawdry bazaars, and degrading sweatshops, architecture falls far short of its duty to serve all men. Evaluation of architectural performance must, therefore, take into account all facets of the building art.

Today, at mid-century, we, the people of the United States, can well take stock of our own architectural achievement and weigh its implications with respect to our cultural progress. Blessed with a bountiful land, we have by vigorous enterprise attained an extraordinary level of material prosperity. We have evolved a social system which cultivates the integrity of individuals and the realization of their potentialities. In recent years destiny has brought us preeminent physical strength and political influence, and, because we seek only the opportunity to pursue the arts of peace, free men throughout the world, sharing this desire, look to us for leadership. Thus the quality of all aspects of American life, including its architectural setting and expression, assumes unprecedented significance. Objective assessment of our present situation, though difficult and controversial, is therefore a salutary prerequisite to the establishment of wise goals to exploit the possibilities of the next half-century.

We have demanded buildings of many kinds and in vast quantities. There are few activities of our dynamic way of life that do not require the shelter of a building. We live in more than 40 million dwelling units,[1] work in more than 240,000 factories and industrial plants,[2] shop in more than 1,700,000 retail stores,[3] struggle with our accounts at more than 14,600 banks,[4] educate our children in more than 186,000 elementary and secondary schools and 1800 institutions of higher education,[5] recoup our health in more than 6400 hospitals,[6] relax in more than 19,000 cinemas,[7] worship in more than 281,000 churches,[8] mail our letters in about 41,000 post offices,[9] and fill with elected and appointed officials the countless governmental buildings of our nation, our 48 states, our 3070 counties, and our 17,118 incorporated boroughs, cities, towns, and villages.[10] But these are only a few of the more than 270 kinds of buildings which we require for the business of living. Truly we have constructed an architecture of continental scale.

During the past generation we have built at a prodigious rate. From 1920 to 1951, despite depression and war, we have spent for new buildings more than 231.6 billion dollars (*Table 53*). If we had used all of this sum to build a continuous row of houses, one story high and two rooms deep, this row would stretch 463,000 miles, more than enough to encircle the equator 18.6 times or to reach to the moon and back again.[11] In 1950 alone, we invested almost 21 billion dollars in new buildings, a sum quite sufficient to construct a similar row of houses 28,900 miles long, equal in length to the equator plus the distance from Miami to Seattle.

Our buildings exemplify many of our most admirable traits. We boast of our towering skyscrapers, sturdy in structure, fabulously equipped, and efficient in operation. We vaunt our sleek industrial plants, so productive, spacious, and trim. We point with pride to our comfortable suburban homes. Our best schools, hospitals, and institutions equal, and perhaps surpass, the finest of any land. In many other types of buildings we have made signal progress. In all of these accomplishments can be seen something of the energy, directness, organizational skill, and enterprising individualism that typify our national character.

In attaining these results American architects, inspired in part by modern science and technology, have developed many new techniques and principles which in turn have imparted special character to contemporary buildings. New materials, new structural systems, and new erection methods have so enriched our resources that we can now build far more safely, durably, and economically than was heretofore possible. Former generalized standards of utility have been replaced by more precise principles of functional efficiency derived from the new techniques of scientific management and cost accounting. Furthermore, the very concept of efficiency has been gradually ex-

4

panded from its originally restricted physical meaning to embrace both economic and psychological factors as well. For the first time, therefore, architects have had recourse to methods by which the full utility of buildings has become relatively measurable. Even the age-old search for architectural beauty has gained new insight from experimental aesthetics, psychological studies of space and color, the empathy hypothesis, and the doctrines of functionally derived form, integrated expressivism, and the inherent appeal of natural materials. The emergence of modern democratic society has given fundamental reorientation to the social purposes of building. Architecture, once the perquisite of an aristocratic or plutocratic elite, is now "an art for all men," embracing as its proper scope the total building needs of the whole society it serves. Taken together, these new principles comprise exciting basic tools such as no other age has ever commanded. When systematically exploited, they have produced buildings worthy of the finest traditions of the art and fully compatible with the best potentialities of modern life.

On the other side of the ledger, objective observers find too large a proportion of our buildings defective, inept, discordant, and vulgar. Too many, though still used, are so far decayed as to bar rehabilitation. Too many are obsolete and beyond practical readjustment to modern needs. Too many are still built without benefit of architects' skill and knowledge, and without regard to any acceptable standard of quality.

In 1950, for example, about 4 million occupied dwelling units—9 per cent of all such units—failed to meet a very low minimal standard of livability because of deterioration or original inadequacies.[12] A third of all occupied units lacked adequate sanitation and water supply.[13] Over 2,600,000 families, packed more than $1\frac{1}{2}$ persons per room, were endangered by well known overcrowding hazards, such as markedly higher rates of fire, communicable disease, and mental maladjustment.[14] Despite long discussion and many valiant efforts, some of our slums still vie with the world's worst. But even the housing of more fortunate families is still far from ideal. Disparity between income and housing costs continues to reduce living space past the danger point, and only a few of us reside in neighborhoods planned according to approved modern standards.

In 1952 a Federal Security Agency survey indicated that 40 per cent of the elementary and secondary school buildings currently in use should be abandoned or drastically remodeled. Even an unprecedented boom in school construction leaves much to do to add the minimum 600,000 new classrooms which the U. S. Office of Education estimates as needed by 1958. Despite the completion of many new hospitals, the 1950 ratio of 9.6 beds per 1000 population has dropped 23 per cent below the 12.5 ratio of 1944.[15] By current standards, probably more than half of our retail store buildings constitute economic liabilities to the businesses they shelter. Too many of our churches, city halls, work shops, correctional institutions, and places of relaxation obstruct, both physically and psychologically, the very functions they should perform. Our downtown districts, which should promote the dignity of urban life, are too often graceless shambles of shabby outworn relics. Even our civic furniture—the signs, traffic islands, hydrants, mail boxes, lamp posts, and trash cans—forms a savage litter

5

apparently designed to produce maximum discord rather than to aid the citizen.

Surely the total picture, for all its exceptional highlights, leaves much to be desired. If American civilization is to be judged, at least in part, by the adequacy and quality of its buildings, the balance sheet thus far is in large part unacceptable. Great as architectural progress has been in the first half of the 20th century, it remains but the prelude of an architecture representative of American capacity and spirit.

2. TOWARD AN ARCHITECTURE WORTHY OF AMERICA

No gift of prophecy is required to predict for the second half of the 20th century a constantly expanding need for new buildings. This is inevitable for many reasons. First is the fact that buildings wear out, become outmoded, and must be replaced. In 1950 of all the dwellings in the United States, well over two-fifths had been built before 1920, and almost a fourth were then more than fifty years old.[16] Some, of course, deserve to be cherished because of historical associations or intrinsic beauty. Some still possess economic value, but a vast number are so obsolete and dilapidated that they constitute a national liability to health, safety, and well-being. The housing problem will be long with us. Industry and commerce find obsolete buildings to be intolerable handicaps and we can expect accelerated construction of new plants and stores designed as important aids to increased productivity and profits. Improved standards of space, equipment, and operation will prompt not only the replacement of worn-out buildings, but also the expansion of facilities which formerly were considered to be adequate. New activities will call for new kinds of buildings. Population shifts, migrations, and decentralization will continue to create a surprising volume of new construction. Restitution of destroyed buildings will remain an important source of demand. In 1948, for example, more than 388,900 building fires[17] contributed a major portion of the year's fire loss of 715 million dollars.[18] Storms, earthquakes, floods, and other "acts of God," and even the lowly termites and dry-rot fungi will add measurably to our construction bill.

But the most relentless pressure for new buildings will continue to arise from the inexorable natural growth of our population. In the decade between 1940 and 1950 the net addition of 19 million persons generated a most urgent demand for all kinds of buildings, a demand still far from being satisfied. If the current birth rate continues during the present decade, as seems clearly indicated by Census estimates since 1950, it will mean another 26 millions and a total population of about 177 millions in 1960.[19] If these new citizens are to be accommodated with building space in the same proportion to which we are now accustomed, it will be necessary, for this reason alone, to build by 1960 more than 7,500,000 new dwelling units, more than 322,000 new retail stores, new theaters sufficient to add 2,200,000 seating capacity, enough new general hospitals to add 260,000 more beds, 50,000 new churches, and a similar increase in all other types of buildings.[20] Looking beyond to 1975, the President's Materials Policy Commission foresees a growth in population of more than 25 per cent, and a level of

6

demand for new buildings and for building maintenance in the 1970's 35 per cent greater than in 1950.[21] It is obvious that we have a tremendous stake in architecture and that we will continue to be, by necessity, a nation of builders.

Nevertheless mere quantity of construction will not suffice. We must seek quality as well if we are to gain true satisfaction from our buildings. Because buildings are the most conspicuous man-made elements in our environment, they exert powerful, inescapable, and constant influences on us all for good or bad. Since most of our lives are spent in and around them, the quality of our buildings is thus of personal and intimate concern to every individual.

The contributions that buildings of high quality can make to our well-being are manifold. By providing convenient settings for our activities, they can release time, energy, and funds for other uses. The transformation of the old drudgery kitchen into the labor-saving "food center" of modern homes is but one example of the principle of physical efficiency which architects now apply to all types of buildings. Efficiency, however, must also be measured in terms of the comfort, healthfulness, safety, and happy environment which every well designed building naturally provides. The advancement and elaboration of such standards has been one of the most striking features of contemporary architecture. Today we demand as a matter of course, in even modest housing projects, amenities which yesterday were unknown to the most luxurious monarch. Buildings are thought of no longer as mere crude shelter, but have come to be regarded as devices to create optimal physiological and psychological environment. To achieve this end, architects have not only utilized the discoveries of science and technology, but have also applied their own researches in orientation, natural illumination, sound control, safety, and many other design criteria. The next half-century will no doubt expand and refine much further these important architectural trends.

The structural quality of buildings will also undergo continued improvement in order to secure the highest overall economy compatible with maximum safety and utility. Two factors will stimulate this trend. First is the paradox in which, despite a vast increase in total social wealth, resources allotted to building fall far short of the demand for additional building space. This is the result, on the one hand, of progressively rising standards of accommodation for our whole population, including an extraordinary elaboration of costly equipment installations. On the other hand it stems from the general acceptance of the idea of an economic prosperity based on mass markets supported by high labor income. It follows therefore that the conflict between increased demand and higher construction costs can be resolved, at least in part, only by maximum efficiency in the use of materials and labor. The second factor is the necessity to conserve natural resources in the face of burgeoning demand. Building is already the largest user of materials, absorbing in new buildings and building maintenance in 1950 one-third of all copper, one-sixth of iron and steel, one-fifth of both lead and zinc, and almost two-thirds of the lumber used in all industries, while almost a fourth of all fuel was consumed by the heating and air conditioning of buildings.[22] The need to discover and shift to less critical materials,

7

to improve design efficiency, and to eliminate waste, obsolete practices, and antiquated codes will become more and more urgent. To accomplish these objectives and at the same time raise the quality of building construction will require of architects consummate skill and imagination.

Of equal importance with utility and construction is the constant and cumulative influence which buildings have upon our mental and emotional health. We all react, consciously or subconsciously, but quite positively, to the environment which surrounds us, and it is manifest that the very prominence of buildings in this environment makes them powerful and insistent stimuli for better or worse. Although the malevolent effects of ugly, confused buildings have thus far resisted precise psychological measurement, their unhappy impact on our minds and spirits is nonetheless real. Beyond any doubt, experience has proved that beautiful, orderly buildings do possess a magical quality that lifts our morale, refreshes our spirit, and fortifies our determination to transform mere existence into full and humane living.

It must be recognized, moreover, that individual buildings are not isolated entities, but rather components of the whole community, which itself forms a sort of superbuilding that wields similar influences on us all. In function and appearance, therefore, our communities should conform to standards of quality comparable to those used in judging the excellence of single structures. Architecture and city planning at their best thus merge in a unified, inseparable endeavor to bring convenience, comfort, and visual order to our common life.

There are some who feel that it is too much to ask that buildings and cities be works of art, or that a virile people should concern themselves with amenities. Such persons submit overeasily to a too narrow interpretation of "practicality" and too often seem to make a cult of ugliness. Limited budgets become for them an inhibiting fetish rather than a challenge to imagination. They excuse poverty and meanness by rationalizing them as "simplicity" and "functionalism." Worst of all, they fail to realize the tragedy of opportunities defaulted or the very positive psychological penalties inflicted by ill-contrived surroundings.

Such attitudes are not new, but neither are they inherent in our time or system. Indeed, our finest traditions belie the acceptance of cheapness and ugliness as necessary corollaries of democracy. In many communities of the colonies and the young republic, a strong desire for civic attractiveness provoked vigilant supervision and control, and civic leadership in such matters was an acknowledged virtue rewarded by respect.[23] Many of these communities still reveal, by a pleasant fountain, spacious square, or institution generously housed, the wish of some local citizen to enhance his native town.

In a democracy, however, the creation of civic beauty cannot be left to accidental benefactions. It must arise from the desire of the people themselves for an architectural setting worthy of their capacities and aspirations. We must, therefore, somehow cultivate among ourselves an overwhelming sentiment for that architectural quality whence springs all civic comeliness. Some progress toward this goal can already be discerned. Mounting public sensitivity to good design in consumer goods gives hope

8

for increased appreciation of architectural excellence. Enthusiastic owners of meritorious buildings encourage others to seek similar benefits. Widening opportunity to experience at first hand the value of fine buildings stimulates discrimination and desire. Furthermore, the whole process can be accelerated by a vigorous and continuing educational campaign designed to emphasize the importance of architectural quality.

The next half-century will surely bring a more intensive exploitation of both architecture and city planning to satisfy our need for civic beauty and order. The utility and true economy of such measures are no longer controversial. The cost of attractiveness will be negligible because we will build and rebuild in any case, and because our aim will be, not ostentatious display, but order, finesse, and a nice adjustment of appropriate forms to essential functions. When such principles do gain wide approval, the exercise of crude civic manners and thoughtless bad taste will be removed from the realm of individual prerogative, not by codes and ordinances, but by the much more effective power of enlightened public opinion.

In all aspects of this development, American architects can render valuable assistance, but only the people themselves can demand and insist upon its accomplishment. The reward will be a quality of architectural and urban environment that could regenerate our common life. Through it, architecture, in its fullest sense the indispensable art for all men, can become the noblest symbol of our cooperative enterprise and the manifestation to future generations that we could create in tangible forms an harmonious and worthy expression of the democratic faith and humane destiny we so stoutly profess.

These varied trends and potentialities emphasize afresh the breadth and inclusiveness which give to architecture its manifold significance. In its fullest sense, it is at once the science, art, product, process, and profession of creating buildings which, singly and collectively, satisfy the physical and psychological needs of those who use and see them by achieving, within available resources, an optimal integration of utility, structure, and aesthetic expressiveness. It is, indeed, this power of ministering to and enriching all phases of human activity which makes of architecture the symbol *par excellence* of a society's capacity, will, and way of life. During the coming decades, the American people will write in their buildings an unequivocal record of the quality of their culture. It is not their nature to ignore so great a challenge.

3 · THE MEANS TO ARCHITECTURE

The normal process by which the need for buildings is now satisfied in the United States proceeds through five steps. First is *DEMAND*, generated and defined by the *Owner*, who is motivated by some impelling desire to undertake the building project. Second is *FINANCE*, for, since the cost of buildings normally surpasses the owner's immediate cash resources, it is usually necessary to spread payments over a manageable period by borrowing from a *Lending Agency*. Third is *PROGRAM AND DESIGN*. Because Owners rarely possess the technical knowledge and facilities to conceive fully the desired building, the programming and design functions are performed by *Architects* skilled in defining such needs, analyzing the problems involved, and developing the most feasible solution for the project. This solution is then explicitly described by the Architect in comprehensive working drawings and specifications. Fourth is *CONSTRUCTION,* in which a *General Contractor* usually undertakes to erect the building by organizing and distributing the various phases of the work among *Sub-* or *Trade Contractors,* who in turn are responsible for assembling the necessary materials, equipment, and *Labor Force* for the execution of their respective trades. Fifth is *ARCHITECTURAL SUPERVISION.* Since Owners are seldom prepared to inspect technical procedures or the quality of materials or workmanship, Architects render this service as the agent of and for the protection of the Owner, and in many other ways facilitate the progress of the construction operation.

For complex projects, the building process is often highly elaborated in personnel and organization. Thus, for a large commercial structure, the owner may be a group of many persons, a corporation, or an institution; the functions of design and supervision may require the services of a firm of architects comprising many highly specialized technicians; and construction may involve a hundred different trades, the coordination of which demands an experienced and alert general contracting company with a large staff. In such projects American building teams, composed of architects, their engineers, general and trade contractors, and skilled mechanics, have achieved extraordinary feats of construction.

Many dramatic examples of this teamwork can be cited. During World War II, American architects and builders accomplished astounding records of size and speed, such as the fabulous Pentagon, numerous military installations, and almost unbelievably vast industrial plants. An older example, however, still quickens the pulse, the Empire State Building, 1250 feet high, the tallest man-made structure in the world, and enclosing a prodigious 36 million cubic feet, equivalent to a row of one-story houses extending more than 27 miles. Its construction utilized 10 million bricks, 58,000 tons of steel, and 50 miles of piping. Sixty-six elevators and seven miles of shafts comprise its vertical highways. Yet so skillfully was it designed by its architects and their engineers, so complete and accurate were their drawings and specifications, and so efficiently was its construction organized, that it was brought to completion in the incredibly short time of thirteen and a half months. It is small wonder that European *Building Productivity Teams* which have visited the United States in recent years under the auspices of the Economic Cooperation Administration have expressed amazement and admiration for such achievements.

Smaller projects, although requiring teamwork on a proportionately simpler scale, benefit from the same high quality of technical services. On a typical small church, retail store, or dwelling, all architectural services may be thoroughly performed by one principal architect with a small staff. Nevertheless, regardless of the size of the project, the professional, analytical, creative, organizing, and supervisory functions of the architect are essentially the same, for he remains the director, leader, and coordinator of the building team.

To obtain the vast quantities of buildings erected each year in the United States requires the services of a building industry of vast proportions and of highly specialized skills. Unfortunately, estimates of the number of workers are limited to rough approximations for the whole construction industry, including maintenance and projects other than buildings. In 1950, however, it is estimated that the construction industry employed an on-site full-time equivalent labor force of 3.2 millions of

FIGURE 1: GROSS·NATIONAL·PRODUCT·&·NEW·BUILDING·CONSTRUCTION·1915-1952

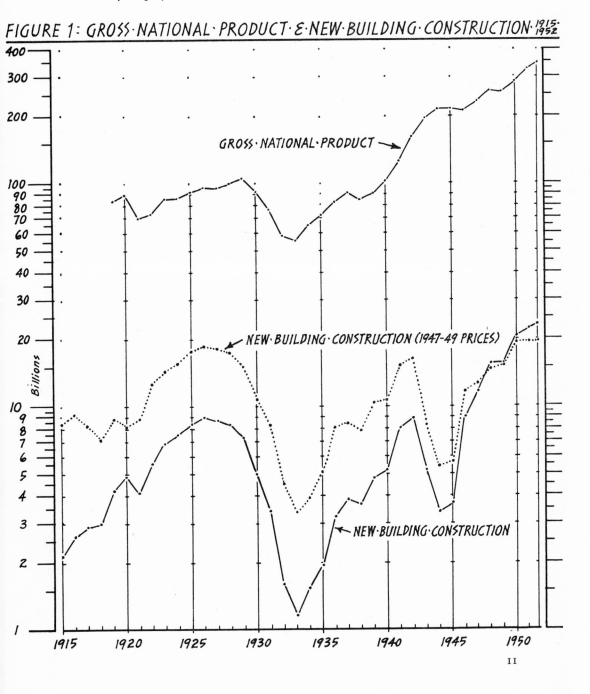

workers.[24] Supporting these direct groups were other organizations and workers who extracted the raw materials, fashioned them into usable forms, and transported and distributed them to the trades. In 1950 there were probably 3.8 millions of these indirect workers, giving a total personnel of about 7 millions for the whole industry.[25] Since building construction in 1950 represented 74 per cent of all construction, more than two-thirds of all construction workers may be assumed to have been engaged on building projects. When we recall that payrolls from building projects maintain not only wage-earners, but also their dependents, it is clear that the economic well-being of the building industry is of intimate concern to a very large segment of our total population.

The importance of the building industry in our national economy is widely recognized. *Table 53* presents estimates of annual volumes of new building construction from 1915 to 1951 inclusive, in both current and 1947–49 dollars, with corresponding estimates of *Gross National Product,* the value of all goods and services produced by the nation.[26] *Figure 1,* overleaf, graphs these data. Expenditures for buildings ranged from $1.18 billions in 1933 at the depth of the depression to $23.25 billions in 1952, with a total of $269.96 billions for the 38-year period, or an average of $7.10 billions per year. If annual volumes are translated into 1947–49 dollars, a clearer picture of volume variations is obtained. The range was from $3.35 billions in 1933 and $5.44 in 1944 to $18.85 billions in 1926 and $19.56 billions in 1950. The total expenditure from 1919 to 1952 inclusive was $435.48 billions in 1947–49 dollars, with an average of $11.46 billions per year.

Some appreciation of the magnitude of these expenditures in current dollars can be gained by comparing them with Gross National Product (*Table 53* and *Figure 2*).

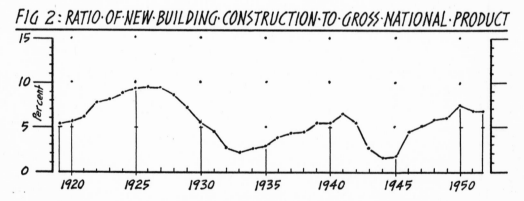

FIG 2: RATIO·OF·NEW·BUILDING·CONSTRUCTION·TO·GROSS·NATIONAL·PRODUCT

Building construction ranged from 1.6 per cent of Gross National Product in 1944 to 9.4 per cent in 1926. In 1950 building's share was 7.3 per cent; in 1952 it was 6.7 per cent. The average annual share from 1919 to 1952 was 5.5 per cent. Even these figures fail to disclose the full economic import of the industry because they omit the stimuli it injects into the related activities of procuring, manufacturing, and distributing the materials which it employs. Furthermore it is likewise closely linked to the producers of building furnishings, equipment, and maintenance supplies. Due to these wide interrelationships, it is not surprising that building construction is regarded as a most significant barometer and key to economic prosperity.

In spite of its size and achievements, the building industry operates under difficult conditions inherent in the very nature of its product. This product, the building, is of extreme complexity. A modest house may well be composed of more parts and pieces than are needed to produce a motor car. The variety of building types and the wide differences in scale and arrangement within each type usually preclude standardization, except at the level of material units or minor components. The product's large bulk and enormous weight force it to be assembled at the site, with all the costly handicaps of inclement weather, limited production equipment, and inconvenient working conditions. Operation is not only seasonal, but also sporadic due to the difficulty of scheduling projects in neat sequences. Although off-site shop fabrication of larger and larger components is increasingly used, many materials and units must still be placed by expensive hand labor. Furthermore, technological progress is obstructed by outmoded attitudes, restrictive codes, and the comparative absence of building research. Finally, the horizontal organization of the industry creates a disunity of management and control which severely penalizes effective operation.[27]

In recent years most segments of the industry have come to realize that many of these difficulties can be alleviated through collaborative programs of study, research, and education. One example is the increasing use of the principle of modular coordination of building materials, which promises important savings in material and labor and, therefore, the simultaneous attainment of improved productivity and reduced costs. During the next half-century, the building industry can be expected to devote concerted effort toward the perfection of new techniques and skills which, in turn, will provide society with higher values for building expenditures.

Because architects perform the strategic functions of *Design* and *Supervision,* the American people and the building industry look to architects for leadership in the improvement of buildings and the building process. During the past century, American architects have developed many refinements in their working methods and have raised their standards of service to a level of unprecedented completeness and effectiveness. The performance of high quality architectural services demands of the architect an unusual degree of technical competence, impartial judgment, and unquestionable integrity. For these reasons the practice of architecture is in every sense a rigorous and respected profession. Thus in each building project, as well as in the building process and the building industry, the architect, by virtue of his professional position and standards, enjoys the incentive, obligation, and opportunity to act through the profession toward the improvement of the industry and its product as an enlightened service to society itself.

NOTES: CHAPTER ONE

[1] U. S. Bureau of the Census: *1950 Census of Housing, Bulletin H-A1,* Table 1.

[2] U. S. Bureau of the Census: *1947 Census of Manufactures*, v. 1, p. 23.

[3] U. S. Bureau of the Census: *1948 Census of Business*, v. 3, p. 0.02.

[4] U. S. Treasury Department: *1951 Annual Report of the Comptroller of the Currency*, p. 18.

[5] U. S. Bureau of the Census: *Statistical Abstract of the United States: 1952*, pp. 116, 126 (Source: Federal Security Agency, Office of Education).

[6] American Medical Association, Council on Medical Education and Hospitals: *Annual Report, Hospital Service in the United States, 1951*.

[7] 1951 enumeration by Film Daily Year Book, 1951 (quoted in *World Almanac for 1952*, p. 235).

[8] National Council of the Churches of Christ in the U. S. A.: *Yearbook of American Churches, 1951*.

[9] *Annual Report of the Postmaster General* (quoted in *Statistical Abstract*, 1952, p. 475)

[10] *1950 Census of Population, Bulletin P-A1*, Tables 20, 22.

[11] The calculation assumes a house 25 feet deep and 10 feet high of brick veneer construction at annual estimated costs per cubic foot, varying from 22½ cents in 1933 to 61 cents in 1951, as given in Schedule of Unit Costs, prepared by the Detroit Real Estate Board (*Michigan Society of Architects Monthly Bulletin*, March, 1952, p. 41-42).

[12] U. S. Bureau of the Census: *1950 Census of Housing, Bulletin H-A1*, Table 7.

[13] *Ibid.*

[14] Federal Security Agency: *Environment and Health*, 1951, p. 60.

[15] American Medical Association: *op. cit.*

[16] U. S. Bureau of the Census: *1950 Census of Housing, Bulletin H-A1*, Table 6.

[17] National Board of Fire Underwriters: *Proceedings, 84th Annual Meeting*, 1950, p. 185.

[18] National Board of Fire Underwriters, *op. cit.*

[19] "Provisional Estimates of the Population of the U. S." (Bureau of the Census: *Current Population Reports, Population Estimates*, Series P-25, No 79, September 16, 1953).

[20] The rates of space accommodations were: 3.4 persons per dwelling unit (1950); 83 per retail store (1948); 12 per theater seat (see 1949 Survey by the Motion Picture Association of America, *World Almanac for 1951*, p. 585); 103.5 per hospital bed (1950, Amer. Med. Assoc., *op. cit.*); 308 per church (1950, based on a reported membership of 86.8 millions, or 58 per cent of the total population, which gives a membership increase of 15.5 millions by 1960).

[21] President's Materials Policy Commission: *Resources for Freedom*, 1952, vol. 1, p. 146. If the current birth rate continues, the total population will increase to 220.98 million in 1975—42 per cent above the 1950 ("Provisional Estimates," *loc. cit.*)

[22] President's Materials Policy Commission, *op. cit.*

[23] Laws to control the height and design of buildings facing Boston Commons were successfully pressed by Charles Bulfinch, city councilman and architect of the Massachusetts State House and the designer who completed the National Capitol.

[24] Colean, Miles L., and Newcomb, Robinson: *Stabilizing Construction: The Record and Potential*, 1952, p. 187.

[25] *Ibid.*, p. 187.

[26] Colean and Newcomb present a corresponding comparison for Total Construction and New Construction (*Ibid.*, pp. 193-194), but do not attempt to segregate Building Construction.

[27] For a detailed presentation of the problems of the building industry, see Colean, Miles L.: *American Housing, problems and prospects*, 1944, prepared for the Twentieth Century Fund.

CHAPTER II

American Architects

And Their Practice at Mid-Century

1. CONDITIONS OF PRACTICE

The role of architects in the building process consists of performing such services as will assure their clients, and through them society in general, of obtaining buildings of optimal usefulness, safety, economy, and attractiveness. Because buildings are usually complex in character, difficult to visualize, costly to construct, and expensive to modify, prudent foresighted owners safeguard the success of their building projects by enlisting those unique professional and technical skills which only architects trained by special studies and long experience can provide.

The methods by which architects perform these services are strongly influenced by the type of client to be served, the nature of the problems presented for solution, and the resources, technical, social, and economic, which are available for their use. Since these are dynamic factors, it is clear that at the mid-point of the twentieth century, American architectural practice is the product of a long and evolutionary development. Moreover, it can be foreseen that it will require continuing adjustment as new conditions arise.

The great monuments of past ages were commanded by powerful patrons—kings, nobles, priests, and magnates—who built as much for glory as for utility. To them, their architects were superior craftsmen worthy of respect and favor. To their architects, however, they were not clients, but masters to be served. Under such relationship, architects fixed design by simple drawings or models, often assembled workmen, directed and laid out the work, inspected its quality, and certified wages or quantities for payment. Since projects were normally financed from current revenues, the pace of construction was usually slow. Frequently materials had to be procured directly from forest or quarry. Primitive and capricious as such practice now seems, it pro-

15

duced, to the honor of both patron and architect, those tangible miracles to which we ourselves still yield reverent admiration.

This patron pattern dominated architectural practice until the late eighteenth century, when the emergence of a strong middle-class society so increased the demand for architectural services that a stable body of independent practitioners could thrive. With the achievement of political and economic democracy, with new wealth born of industrial and commercial enterprise, and with the rise of a progressively expanding public appetite for higher standards of living, architects entered a new and unprecedented era of opportunity. The new clients, collectively richer, but limited in individual resources, and with habits of thought derived from business, insisted on surer controls for building budgets. The appearance of the general contractor and the fixed sum contract was a direct consequence of this need, but this system itself created inevitable hazards for owners unaccustomed to building operations. To meet this situation and protect their clients' interests, architects produced more comprehensive plans and specifications, established more reliable methods of estimating and controlling costs, and developed to the full their supervisory and coordinating functions in the building process. Thus, slowly, but surely, contemporary methods of practice evolved in answer to specific needs.

The new society has satisfied its larger purposes more and more by cooperating in associations, corporations, and institutions. The building needs of such groups have become a major phenomenon in modern practice, and architects soon adjusted their methods to the special necessities of these group clients. The expanded scale of corporate projects, their investment character, and the accelerated pace of completion imposed by relentless carrying charges, have increased the scope, type, and speed of architectural services to such an extent as to foster the growth of large architectural firms and the refinement of many phases of their work. Increased construction of large projects by government, in response to expanding public demand, has created a host of new group clients comprised of boards, bureaus, and authorities, each with its own procedural problems.

Today, these direct clients are often supplemented by auxiliary quasi-clients. The necessity of long-term financial programs involves lending agencies which demand protection of their investments through close participation in planning and executing large projects. The experience of architects in such matters has frequently permitted them to give valuable financial counsel to their clients and, on many occasions, to take the initiative in promoting needed projects. Government, too, by grants-in-aid and regulatory powers, has become an important quasi-client. Some public and semi-public agencies have stifled creative solutions by excessive regulations, codes, and other circumscriptions, but when standards and principles are established by enlightened and realistic cooperation with the architectural profession, as in the case of the U. S. Public Health Service, they have contributed to real progress.

It is clear, therefore, that architectural practice has been much affected by the kind of client served. It is apparent, moreover, that the future will augment these trends. If, to some architects, this does not seem an unmixed blessing, due to the decrease in the personal relationship which individual clients permit, group clients, on the other hand, do offer such unprecedented opportunities, in both the magnitude and variety of their building projects, that architects will not fail to recognize and fulfill their challenge. Indeed, in many instances, progressive corporations have proved to be the most enthusiastic supporters of a fresh, untrammeled approach to design and practice. In mastering the technique of serving them, architects will no doubt discover new and unsuspected advantages to architecture itself.

Methods of practice are likewise conditioned by the types of problems which clients bring for solution. The pragmatic and utilitarian character of the new society has multiplied and modified these problems to an amazing degree. Although present categories of buildings may sound age-old, the past century has, in reality, so elaborated and differentiated them as to transform their very meaning. New needs, new purposes, and new modes of living have called for new thinking, new approaches, and new solutions. The tremendous and diversified advances of modern industry, commerce, transportation, communication, education, government, medicine, recreation, and many other activities have demanded parallel developments in architecture. New community patterns—neighborhoods, suburbs, satellites, and urban redevelopment—have evoked new techniques. Huge growths of population have required vast quantities of construction, and, through heightened productivity, could afford and command an unprecedented standard of architectural accommodation.

At the same time, the flowering of modern science and technology has introduced new resources in materials, structural systems, equipment, and erection methods. Buildings have become not only larger, but also infinitely more complex. Where once a shell, more or less ornamental, sufficed, today's buildings contain congeries of apparatus requisite to diverse installations of equipment. Demand for economy has encouraged off-site fabrication, standardization of materials and components, labor-saving details, and the use, wherever possible, of power tools and handling devices. The leisurely pace of former times has given way to precise scheduling and efficient management.

During the past half century, the impact of these new problems and methods upon practice has been momentous. Practice is now conceived as requiring a degree of comprehensiveness never before envisioned, and this is pointedly evidenced by heightened standards of design embodying optimal provision and integration of utility, structure, equipment, and aesthetic expression.[1] To achieve this purpose, architects have sought a more profound understanding and a more certain control of the problems to be solved by initiating more systematic investigation and analysis of their nature, social implications, and potentialities. Concentrated study of the functioning of buildings has yielded increased effectiveness in planning them, and a pragmatic approach to construction and aesthetic matters has likewise paid rich dividends. The new ideal of integration and the desire for precise control of all phases of the project, have brought not only extraordinary completeness to architects' Instruments of Service, but also have expanded and refined to an amazing degree their administrative and managerial techniques.

Since practice is affected by the type of problems posed, it is worth while to consider the range and relative frequency of the major categories of buildings in contemporary practice. *Figure 3* charts for the years 1925–1951 the proportions of new building construction devoted to eleven major categories, as measured by floor areas contracted for. It is at once obvious that the subject matter of practice closely reflects the temper and preoccupations of its time. Depression saw marked decline in industrial and residential building and the induced compensatory expansion of public building. War emergency boomed military (included in Miscellaneous Non-Residential) and industrial building at the expense of all other types. The average and range for each type over the 27-year period were:

	1925–51 AVERAGE	Range				High-Low RATIO	1949 RANK
		HIGH	YEAR	LOW	YEAR		
Residential	51.9%	64.9%	1939	27.0%	1945	2.4	1
Industrial	14.3	38.4	1945	5.5	1931	7.0	4
Commercial	12.8	20.4	1929	4.9	1943	4.2	2
Educational	7.0	13.3	1938	2.3	1942	5.8	3
Misc. Non-Residential	3.3	16.4	1942	0.1	1925	164.0	7
Hospital & Institutional	3.0	4.8	1949	1.5	1925	3.1	5
Social & Recreational	2.7	4.3	1934	1.0	1951	4.3	8
Public Buildings	2.5	10.4	1932	0.2	1946	52.0	9
Religious	1.5	2.8	1949	0.2	1943	14.0	6
Public Utility Buildings	0.8	3.3	1945	0.1	1948	33.0	10
Public Works Buildings	0.2	0.5	1944	—	1940	—	11

The relative frequency of building types in architectural practice in 1949 was studied by the *1950 Survey of the Architectural Profession*. 3377 private practitioner firms reported the first, second, and third most frequent (or most voluminous) types in their practices. *Tables 29* and *30* record the national and regional findings. *Figure 4* graphs the proportion of each type to the whole volume of practice, as determined by the total number of times each type was listed in first, second, and third place of frequency. In descending order, the national ranking was:

Commercial	23.2%	Public (incl. housing)	7.9
Residential	19.0	Hospitals	6.0
Educational	15.3	Recreational	1.3
Religious	9.3	Community Planning	1.2
Industrial	8.6	Other	7.7

In comparing the two sets of ranks, slight differences arise from the fact that the *1950 Survey* placed large-scale housing under Public Buildings, rather than under Residential, and also did not include other institutional projects with Hospitals. Since the *1950 Survey* data did not cover in this particular matter architects employed within

FIGURE 3: RELATIVE FREQUENCY OF BUILDING TYPES · 1925 · 1951

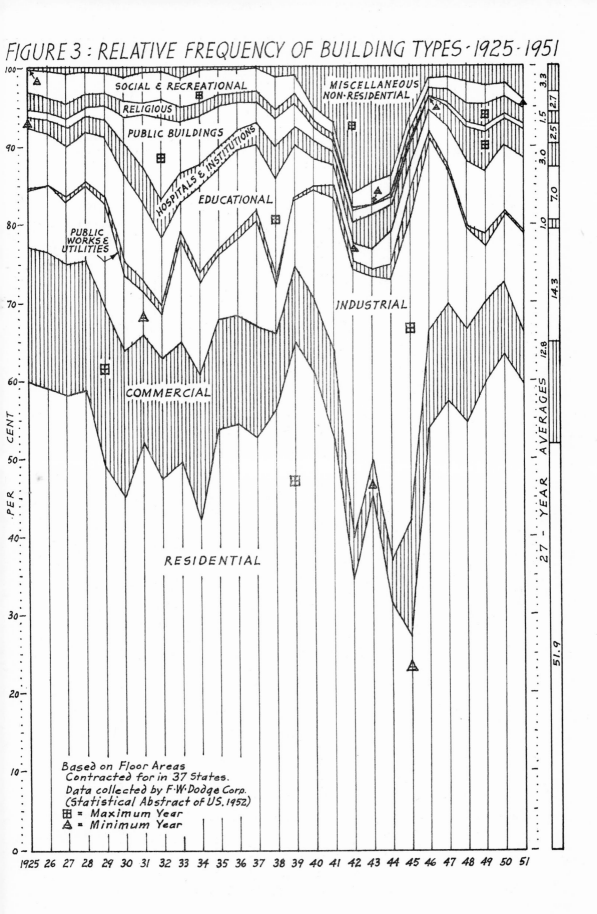

SOCIAL & RECREATIONAL

MISCELLANEOUS NON·RESIDENTIAL

RELIGIOUS

PUBLIC BUILDINGS

HOSPITALS & INSTITUTIONS

EDUCATIONAL

PUBLIC WORKS & UTILITIES

INDUSTRIAL

COMMERCIAL

RESIDENTIAL

PER CENT

27 - YEAR AVERAGES

Based on Floor Areas
Contracted for in 37 States.
Data collected by F·W·Dodge Corp.
(Statistical Abstract of US, 1952)
⊞ = Maximum Year
△ = Minimum Year

1925 26 27 28 29 30 31 32 33 34 35 36 37 38 39 40 41 42 43 44 45 46 47 48 49 50 51

FIGURE 4: FREQUENCY OF BUILDING TYPES IN PRACTICE · · 1950

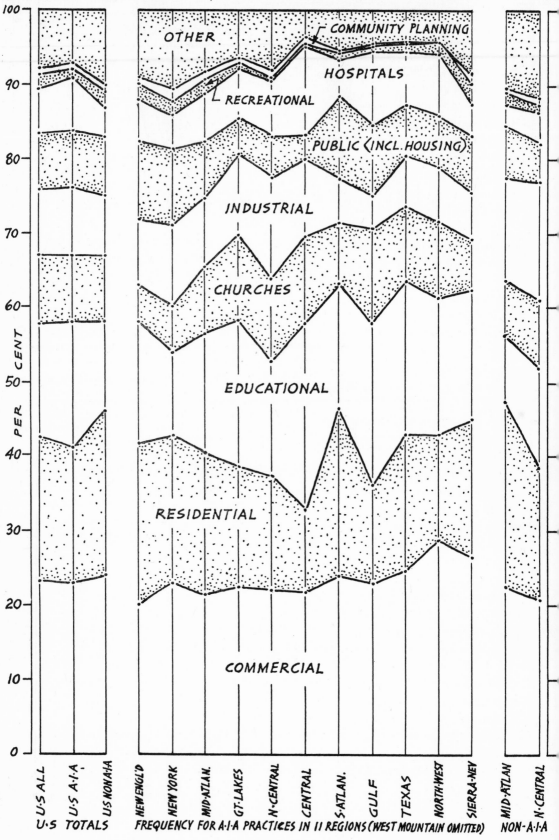

industrial corporations, its lower ranking of industrial projects must be expected. With these exceptions, the two sources yield quite comparable frequencies.

Figure 5 compares frequencies of the ten categories in eleven AIA regions. The general uniformity is striking, but variations inevitably reflect regional economic and social patterns and once again prove the intimate relation of practice to local conditions. Notable is the slightly higher proportion of commercial projects in southern and western regions. The contrast in residential practice, high along the eastern seaboard, but low in the Central and Gulf regions, is surprising. In educational projects, the high rates in the Central, Gulf, and Great Lakes regions stand out sharply against the lows of the New York and Mid-Atlantic regions. The concentration of industrial projects in the northeastern states should, no doubt, be expected, but the infrequency of public building in the midwest could hardly be anticipated. The emphasis on hospitals in the Central and Gulf areas again contrasts with lows in eastern states. Nevertheless, it is notable that commercial, residential, and educational projects form the dominant core of practice, comprising 58.1 per cent of the three most frequent types in the nation, and with no regional deviation of more than 5.6 per cent.

It is interesting to observe that frequencies of some types vary considerably with respect to whether or not the practitioner is a member of the AIA. No appreciable differences occur between AIA and Non-AIA rates for commercial, religious, industrial, public, or community planning projects. For residential, however, the Non-AIA rate of 22 per cent is 1.22 times the AIA rate of 18; for educational projects, the AIA rate is 1.41 times the Non-AIA rate; and for hospitals the AIA rate is 1.56 times the Non-AIA rate. Comparison of the AIA and Non-AIA rates for two regions, the Mid-Atlantic and North Central, reveals no significant difference from national relationships.

Finally, it should be noted that the same trends which have modified methods of practice have, in addition, increased the utilization of architectural services. Where once a self-sufficient owner might order local mechanics to build a simple shell, and thus obtain usable results, today few laymen presume to undertake similar control of complex projects. Those who might attempt it are often saved from such false economy by the insistence of lenders or regulative agencies who demand protection of their equity through competent architectural services. Though to some practitioners the converse may seem true, there has been a steady growth in public recognition and appreciation of the value of such services.

Contributory reasons are not hard to find. The increased availability of architects has been both cause and effect. Successful projects are eloquent advertisements of the value of architectural services. Public knowledge of the architect's functions has been fostered by publications of all sorts, but especially by the general and professional press. In the residential field, home magazines and women's journals have emphasized the quality of design contributed by architects. The growth of college enrollments and the provision of lay courses in architecture have raised appreciation of architectural services among an influential group. Manufacturers and distributors of building projects have stressed the place of the architect in the building process.

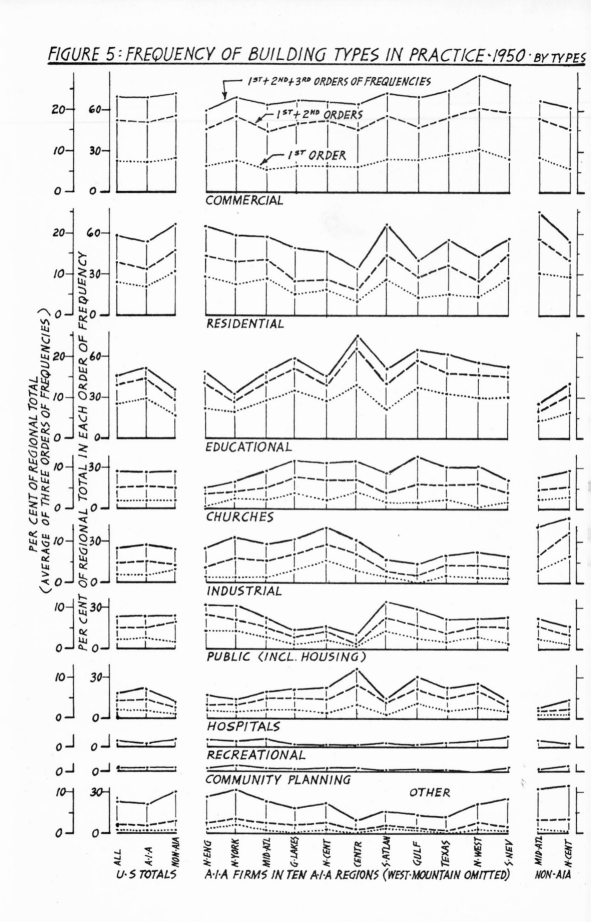

FIGURE 5: FREQUENCY OF BUILDING TYPES IN PRACTICE·1950· BY TYPES

Architectural competitions have focused public attention on the architect's creative skill. Consulting agencies for special types of buildings, such as churches, schools, and libraries, have emphasized the necessity of architectural services in attaining improved quality. Local, state, and national governments have come to require professional services for all building projects involving public funds or insured by governmental participation. And, finally, the profession itself, both through individual members and the AIA, has done much to inform all sections of society of the importance of the architect's service and work.

2. METHODS OF PRACTICE

The architect's functions in the building process have already been summarized as *Design* and *Supervision,* but fuller description is needed as a basis for more detailed consideration of current professional problems. Since the attainment of new buildings is the chief mission of the building process, it follows that architects are primarily concerned with new projects. All other services which they occasionally perform arise from their competence in this fundamental task.

In essence, the architectural process consists of five types of functions. First is the *Formulation of the Problem to be Solved,* which is expressed in the Program. Second, comes the *Creation of the Basic Design Solution.* Third is the *Preparation of the Working Documents,* the plans, specifications, and other instruments by which the proposed design can best be guided to successful realization. Fourth is *Administrative Coordination,* to promote the efficient operation of the process. And fifth is *Supervision,* by which accurate fulfillment is verified and guided.

It is manifest that these functions are neither separate isolated actions nor ends in themselves, but rather they unite to form an integrated, systematic, and time-tested method by which architects can focus their professional knowledge, skill, and judgment most effectively to serve their clients. These *Executive Services,* which form the normal method by which American architects perform their functions for new building projects at mid-century, proceed in five stages.[2]

A. Program Stage

On the basis of the needs, site, and available economic resources of the building project as presented by the owner, the architect gathers, collates, and integrates all data and conditions which determine the scope and character of the problem. After thorough investigation of these elements and their interrelationships, he organizes his findings in a definitive Program.

The purpose of the Program is to ensure initial agreement between owner and architect regarding the problems to be solved so that subsequent stages can proceed logically and promptly. Frequently, an inexperienced owner is able to conceive his needs

23

in only the vaguest terms. Others sometimes jump to unwarranted conclusions which disregard vital factors. In both cases, the architect's sagacious counsel is an invaluable safeguard. Indeed, the more experienced the owner, the more he values the fresh and independent view which an imaginative architect can contribute in his formulation of the basic Program.

For small projects architects often find informal discussions with the client quite sufficient to produce an effective Program. In recent years, however, for larger, more complex projects, and especially when group decisions are involved, many architects prepare elaborate formal Programs. Business and industry, school boards, institutions, and governmental agencies have come to depend more and more upon their architects for careful organization of data basic to their projects. Moreover, progressive architects have found such reports valuable not only in their own work, but also a dramatic means of demonstrating to clients the indispensability of the programming function. Without doubt the use of formal Programs will continue to increase.

B. Basic Design Stage

On the basis of the approved Program, the architect develops studies leading to an optimal Basic Solution acceptable to the owner.

The Basic Design Stage is the heart of the architectural process, for here is determined the actual form and character of the final building. It is here that skillful architects exhibit their superior creativeness in practical, but imaginative plans, logical structures, sensitive spatial relationships, fresh and vigorous forms, and finesse of detail.

After thorough analysis of all pertinent aspects and components of the problem in order to gain insight into its controls and potentialities, the architect synthesizes a number of tentative solutions in schematic form. In each, the necessities of site, codes, utilities, construction, equipment, operation, maintenance, attractiveness, and budget are carefully considered. All are tested for suitability, and perhaps combined or refined, until there emerges an optimal schematic solution satisfactory to both owner and architect.[3]

Once tentatively approved, this solution is further developed in greater detail until all aspects and parts join in harmonious unity. This Basic Design is then presented to the owner by means of diagrams, drawings, and models, together with a Report of Recommendations, describing salient features, specifying briefly the proposed materials, structural systems, and equipment, and providing a reliable estimate of the time and expenditures required for erection. The owner's approval at this point establishes the basis necessary for subsequent work.

C. Working Documents Stage

In this stage, the architect determines and records the means by which the basic design can best be brought to practical achievement. The delineations and descriptions

24

which fix in detail the final building and the method of its execution comprise the Working Drawings, Specifications, and General Conditions, which together form the Working Documents, or Instruments of Service.

The Working Documents supplement and complement each other to define the desired building and its construction. The Working Drawings describe, by means of plans, elevations, sections, scale details, and schedules, the kind, size, form, location, and assembly of all materials, equipment, site work, and decoration. For all but the simplest projects, the architectural drawings are supplemented by other sets showing the structural system and the mechanical, electrical, heating, ventilating, sanitary, and other special installations. The Specifications describe the types, qualities, finish, and manner of placing of all materials and components. The General Conditions set forth the rights and duties of owner, architect, and contractor.

It should be noted that many questions of design can be answered intelligently only as the Working Drawings begin to take shape. Indeed, some types of design decisions often continue to be made even during actual construction. Conversely, since methods of construction greatly influence design, they must be considered, at least in general terms, during the Basic Design Stage. Such overlapping simply emphasizes the unity of the whole architectural process.

It is manifest that the quality of the completed building depends not only on the excellence of its basic conception, but also upon the degree of skill with which it is constructed. It is axiomatic that no detail can be left to its own devices if a coordinated result is desired. Completeness, accuracy, and consistency are, therefore, utmost essentials for the Working Documents. Without these qualities, it is difficult, if not impossible, to obtain accurate estimates, secure the lowest fair market price, eliminate excessive contingency allotments in bids, or avoid embarrassing extra charges or costly delays in completing the project. With these qualities, however, the work can proceed expeditiously and with minimum friction. Since the presence of these qualities is synonymous with competence, it follows that an architect must be able and competent to stand personally responsible for the quality of service he performs.

D. Construction Contract Stage

Upon completion of the Working Documents, the architect advises and assists the owner in securing an equitable contract for the construction of the project.

This stage involves two steps: the selection of the Contractor, and the negotiation of the Construction Contract. In the first step, the architect advises the client as to the qualifications of those who are to be invited to submit bids, and the architect prepares the bid forms and notices, and issues them to those invited. Upon receipt of the proposals, the architect advises the client as to their acceptance. For public projects, this procedure is modified in some details, but the architect still performs similar important services. In the second step, after the client's acceptance of a contractor's proposal, the architect assists in the preparation of the terms, conditions, and forms of the construction contract and other accompanying instruments.

These phases of the architect's service are of great benefit to the owner because they provide guidance and protection in a highly complex technical transaction. In selecting the contractor, for example, it must be recognized that no contract can ever ensure a quality of work for which the contractor is unprepared in experience or facilities. The architect's overall knowledge of the building industry makes it possible for him to advise the client as to the most effective matching of the contractor's capabilities to the project in question. Then, too, the owner secures experienced counsel regarding his own rights and responsibilities, bonds and insurance, and the relationships of the various parties to the contract.

In certain cases, the Owner may prefer to enter into separate contracts for different parts of the construction work, and retain the architect to coordinate them. Under such arrangements the detailed knowledge of the architect with respect to the special trades is of inestimable value.

E. The Construction Stage

After the signing of the Construction Contract and during construction, the architect performs for the client eight types of services: a. Investigation and approval of Subcontractors; b. Preparation of required large-scale and full-size details; c. Approval of materials, equipment, finishes, and other matters; d. Checking of shop drawings; e. General supervision; f. Certification of requisition for payments; g. Negotiation of changes in the contract; h. Final inspection and certification of the completed project.

In certain types of projects, large details are included in the Working Drawings, but normally they are reserved for the Construction Stage. All other services during Construction are performed, however, as the client's agent, for his protection, as well as to facilitate the smooth progress and satisfactory completion of the project. Although acting as the client's agent, the architect is, at the same time, obligated to promote in every way the equitable operation of the contract.

By inspecting materials, equipment, finishes, and the like, by checking the shop drawings prepared by fabricators, and by supervising actual construction and the installation of equipment, the architect, although he cannot guarantee the contractor's work, goes far to assure the owner that it conforms to that called for by the Working Documents. If continuous inspection at the site is necessary, as is often the case on large projects, the owner can provide a *clerk-of-the-works,* who then serves under the direction of the architect. In most cases, however, if the contractor has been selected wisely and if the project is not too large or complex, the architect's supervision as needed at critical stages in the work will be sufficient. In all these services, the architect, through his technical knowledge and skill and his detailed familiarity with the specific project, contributes to the progress of the work by forestalling misunderstandings, arbitrating disputes, apprehending errors, and directing their correction.

The last three services—the Certification of Payments, Negotiation of Contract Changes, and Final Inspection—are administrative functions which help to maintain smooth operation of the contract. Proper and clear procedure in such matters, based on the impartial technical and administrative experience of the architect, protects and reassures both owner and contractor in the fullfillment of their respective obligations. In recent years, when even common materials have often been in short supply, the architect has performed an especially valuable service either by designating materials known to be available, or, when unforeseen shortages occur, by negotiating acceptable substitutes and using them so as to preserve the quality of the completed project.

The Executive Architectural Services just described are used today for practically all new projects designed by architects. The pattern of these services is the result of long development by the profession in an effort to provide the most effective and equitable method possible by which clients and society can procure maximal value in their buildings. The essential merit of the pattern lies in its insistence on a clear differentiation of functions and the maintenance of a relationship which enables the architect to perform these functions with absolute impartiality and with no other concern than the interests of client, society, and equity. It is for this reason that a reputable architect must not engage in the business of construction contracting or hold any personal interest that may tend to discredit his freedom to act impartially and independently. Thus, the absence of pecuniary profit based on construction risks or the promotion of building merchandise, and the fact that the architect's sole remuneration is his fee for service, paid by the client, form dependable safeguards that this service will be concerned only with the client's desire for quality and value.

A trend in the field of industrial building illustrates the inherent hazards of intermingling architectural and contracting functions. Some contracting organizations have also undertaken to perform architectural functions, denoting the combined result as a "package service." Through an extensive campaign of costly advertising they have claimed for this "package service" alleged advantages of simplicity and economy on the basis of unified resources and control. Such a promise has superficial appeal for some prospective owners because it seems to relieve them of all responsibility except paying the bill. These claims are based on the unwarranted promise that the design and construction of a complex building project can be reduced to the level of buying stock merchandise. This is fallacious because, while choice between competitive brands and models preserves customer control in ordinary transactions, buildings cannot be bought on such a basis.

Moreover, the purchaser of "package service" should recognize that claims of reduced cost can be fullfilled only by sacrificing design or construction or both. If the quality of design really equals that provided by normal architectural services, its cost cannot be "saved," but only hidden. "Savings" in construction are difficult, if not impossible, to demonstrate because the elimination of competitive bidding prevents any comparative check on the price of the "package." The prime danger of "package services" lies, however, in the inevitable loss of impartial design and supervision which results when remuneration becomes dependent on contract profits. Under such an

27

arrangement, the owner forfeits all protection and control. Furthermore, the system definitely limits the advantageous matching of contractors to the type and quality of work they can best perform. "Package service" is thus a vending operation devoid of professional standards and subject only to the rule of "let the buyer beware." As such, its very use of the term "service" is paradoxical and misleading. In the light of all its hazards, few owners, embarking on a major building enterprise, can afford to adopt a system which clearly involves so many shortsighted gambles.

There might be less risk to the combination of architectural and construction functions if it could be performed on the professional basis of a single professional fee for services. It is, perhaps, such a form that has led some architects to advocate an integrated "package" team, which, by pooling each member's resources and "trade secrets" and by intermingling well-differentiated functions, would supposedly surpass normal methods in exploiting the potentialities of modern technology. This claim is refuted by the excellent cross-fertilizing cooperation that has already existed over a long period between many independent architects and many contractors to the benefit of the whole industry. The truth is that, if this cooperation were to be limited to members of a single "package" team, it would automatically restrict this team's growth in architectural and construction experience to its own few projects. Such in-breeding would constitute a major calamity for the whole building process and is completely contrary to well-established lines of professional progress. It should be noted that architects have occasionally coordinated construction projects when these are let under separate contracts. This is an accepted professional service paid for by a professional fee. Nevertheless, the fact that it is not widely used, except where a suitable general contractor is not available, indicates that it has not been found particularly beneficial. Because of these facts and principles, and solely in the interest of clients and society, architects should continue to oppose the "package service" system and should reaffirm their long adherence to the normal pattern of Executive Services.

The rapidly increasing use of professional architectural services by development builders supplying the mass market for individual dwellings constitutes a revealing example of how the hazards of "package service" can be averted through enlightened cooperation. Many architects have been highly successful in serving individual residential clients of the middle and upper income groups, but this has represented only a fraction of the vast demand for housing. The development builder, on the other hand, formerly considered the architect an unnecessary luxury and obtained whatever plans he used by employing draftsmen-designers within his own organization. In recent years, however, progressive builders have discovered that architect-designed houses not only possess greater immediate sales appeal, but also incorporate new techniques leading to profitable economies in construction costs. Moreover, purchasers themselves have learned that excellence of design is a definite and positive protection for their investment. All of these factors have been publicized by the popular press, the National Association of Home Builders, and The AIA Committee on the Home Building Industry. The result has been that an increasing number of architects are providing a new type of professional service in which the development builder is at once both client and contractor. This new service has thus made high-quality architectural services available for the first time to a large segment of our people, has strengthened the status of builders by vast improvements in their product, and has afforded many architects new opportunities for service.

Just as the conditions and Instruments of Service have been modified to meet new needs, so too have contractual forms undergone continuing refinement and periodic re-codification. The AIA, in cooperation with the Western Association of Architects and the National Association of Builders, published in 1888 the first *Uniform Owner-Contractor Contract,* which gained wide use during the following 25 years. In 1907, The AIA, through its Committee on Contracts and Specifications, renewed its study, and in 1911 issued the first edition of the *Standard Forms,* including the Standard Agreement and the Conditions of the Contract. A second edition, revised in the light of initial experience and including additional forms, appeared in 1915. Since then, other new editions reflecting changes and improvements in practice have been issued periodically.

A similar evolution has characterized owner-architect agreements. In 1917, The AIA first set forth two standard forms covering service compensated by a *percentage of building cost fee* and a *fee-plus-costs.* In recent years three new types have come into common use; these are *principals' salaries-plus-costs, multiple of personnel costs* common during the war period, and the *negotiated fixed sum* used in government contracts. The problem of just fees for architectural services has likewise received close attention, usually on a state-wide or local basis. The result has been the formulation of schedules of equitable fees which take into account the type, scale, and complexity of the specific project.

As has already been mentioned, architects' skill in performing Executive Services occasionally suggests their employment in other ways. Although for the best results Executive Services should be carried through as a complete process, in certain circumstances only a portion of them may be needed. There is a growing trend, for example, for clients to employ architects to prepare special studies and surveys of a prospective building project or program. This type of service has proved especially helpful to public school boards in evaluating existing facilities and in planning new buildings on a large-scale, long-term basis. Some architects, because of their extensive experience in a particular building type, are sought out as consultants or associates. Some give continuity to protracted building programs or to large-scale building operation and maintenance by acting as supervising, or coordinating, architects. In connection with their Executive Services, architects are often called upon to design furniture, fixtures, industrial products, and other work not covered in the normal services, or they may be asked to advise clients as to furnishings, equipment, and other items designed and sold by others. Lastly, architects occasionally are called upon to act as expert witnesses, arbitrators, or appraisers in the general field of building. Taken together, however, these auxiliary services usually occupy so small a portion of architects' total effort and derive so directly from their normal functions, that they have little special influence upon practice.

It is apparent that the nature of the Executive Services emphasizes the individual project as a unique operation. The question naturally arises as to whether it is advantageous for architects to channel their efforts into specialized fields. To the layman this might seem both feasible and desirable, but it is a problem with many facets. It does not usually refer to structural or aesthetic matters. Since every individual project must be solved structurally in accord with the time, place, availability of materials and skilled labor, and its own inherent demands, it is obvious that architects must command the widest possible knowledge of all types of building construction. While some architects have acquired special experience and facility in particular types of construction, and have even developed valuable structural innovations, few, if any, have restricted themselves to the use of a single system. In the aesthetic realm, time was when some architects exploited particular stylistic predilections and were hailed primarily as "Gothic specialists," "Classicists," and even "Norman farmhouse masters." Today, such talents are rarely sought. Specialization has come to mean, therefore, emphasis upon some specific functional type.

It is difficult to determine at what point a claim to specialization is warranted. Cumulative experience in one type of building should bring increased competence in this type, but it need not prejudice competence in other types. Thus, a single firm may well be specialists in one or more specific types of buildings, but at the same time conduct a general practice. The *1950 Survey* found that 43 per cent of the firms reporting considered themselves specialists in at least one building type. Among these firms, *Table 31* shows educational and residential types, each with 23 per cent, as the most prevalent specialties, followed by commercial (14), religious (11), industrial (9), hospitals (7), and public buildings (7). Unfortunately, no indication of the degree of specialization can be gleaned from these findings. Two independent surveys indicate a lower total rate of about 15 per cent.[4] It would seem that the latter might indicate "specialized specialists," while the *1950 Survey* may have included many "general specialists."

Some degree of specialization is likewise implied when architects who possess extensive experience in a particular phase of building design are sought as associates or consultants by the primary architect of a project. The *1950 Survey* found that 40 per cent of the reporting firms had acted as associates (*Table 33*). This type of service was most frequent in the eastern and southern regions, and least frequent in the far west. The highest frequencies were in the New York and Texas regions, with 50 and 49 per cent respectively; the lowest occurred in the Western Mountain and Northwest regions, with 32 and 31 per cent. The independent surveys, previously cited, showed a higher overall rate of 61 per cent.[5]

Nevertheless, general practice remains by far the most common pattern. It is deliberately cultivated for many reasons. For a large proportion of firms, the area served needs general service and does not require most types of buildings in sufficient quantities to support local specialists. Even when unusual problems arise, the advantages of local service usually dominate. For younger architects, limited experience and opportunity normally preclude specialization, and older, well established firms often wish to avoid too exclusive dependence on the prosperity of a narrow segment of the building market. It seems, therefore, that general practice will continue to be the prevailing method of providing architectural services.

Finally, looking toward the future, it is probable that, while the pattern of Executive Services will remain much the same, architects will continue to refine and adjust their application of it as new conditions unfold. Concerted efforts to acquire new technical knowledge, through cooperative research and the organized dissemination of the results of research, will surely enhance architectural resources and skills and thus ensure buildings of increased value. Because architects are naturally alert to needs for buildings, they will no doubt assume, in the future, a more active role in the initiation of projects by bringing these needs to the attention of potential investors. Some architects, moreover, may find additional scope for their efforts by contributing counsel for the more effective operation and maintenance of completed buildings. Nevertheless, despite the beckoning temptations of such extensions of service, there will always remain as the architect's first goal, the time-honored, but always thrilling adventure which is embodied so intimately in the creation of new architecture.

3. ORGANIZATION FOR PRACTICE

Thus far, the architect has been discussed as if he himself performed unaided all the various functions and services just described. The *1950 Survey* found that one architect in ten does work in this fashion.[6] No doubt this is due in part to the genuine satisfaction which derives from personal participation in every phase of the architectural process. For many younger architects, however, a one-man office is only an evolutionary and temporary step toward wider practice.

It is obvious that, if a practitioner desires to undertake large, complex projects, or more than one project at a time, or the rapid schedule demanded by most clients, he will need to assemble a staff of trained assistants, who under his close and responsible supervision can carry out many portions of the work and thus multiply his own scope and influence. Since most practitioners do operate in this way, they are inevitably concerned with the problems of the optimal size of their staff, the most effective pattern for its organization, the best manner of ensuring high quality and quantity of production, and the maintenance of a volume of work sufficient to support its continuing existence. Thus, most practitioners must add to their normal architectural duties the administration of a considerable business enterprise.

These factors of size, volume of production, and market demand are inextricably intermixed. Their resolution requires a high degree of practical experience, logical analysis, and cultivated judgment. Indeed, the effective administration of an organization devoted to creative activities, the success of which is measurable only by the long-term quality of its work, involves so many imponderables that it becomes an art in itself.

The *1950 Survey* chose to study these problems in several ways: by volume of projects handled in the year 1949; by number and functions of personnel; and by organization patterns. Within the practicable limits at the disposal of the Commission, these constituted only the most obvious approaches, but it would be highly beneficial to all practitioners to cooperate in a much more comprehensive study of practice and office administration (*Recommendation I*).

Table 34 records the median construction contract costs of all projects handled in 1949 by 3631 firms. The median volume for private AIA practitioners was $1,082,000 and for Non-AIA firms $570,000. For architectural departments in private non-architectural organizations, those headed by AIA architects had a median of $2,345,000, and those headed by Non-AIA architects $805,000. For public architectural bureaus, those with AIA heads had a median of $2,000,000, and those with Non-AIA heads, $429,000. The medians of private practitioners in the twelve AIA regions showed surprising variation. The Gulf region was highest for both AIA and Non-AIA firms, with $1,500,000 and $962,000 respectively. For AIA firms, the North Central and Western Mountain regions were next highest, and, for Non-AIA firms, the New York and North Central regions. For AIA firms, New England's median of $852,000 was lowest, with the Sierra Nevada and South Atlantic regions only slightly higher. For Non-AIA firms, the Northwest region ranked lowest with $400,000, just under the Sierra Nevada and South Atlantic regions. Comparison with the frequency of building types (*Figure 5*, p. 22) and size of firms (*Figure 6*) shows some degree of correlation with these median volumes of practice. For example, the Gulf region had relatively high frequencies in religious, public, educational, and hospital types. It also had the lowest proportion of very small offices, and the highest of small and small medium offices. In contrast, the Northwest region had the highest proportion of very small offices and the highest frequency of commercial buildings. It would be illuminating to know the ranges of volume, the number of firms at different levels of volume, and the correlation of volume with personnel, but, due to practical limitations, these tabulations are not available.

The *1950 Survey* also studied the size of contemporary offices. *Table 26* presents the relative national and regional distributions of offices reporting one or more employees, with respect to number of employees. *Figure 6* plots the regional distributions for offices of AIA members, but for convenience combines the data in six groups of ascending size, i.e., very small offices with 1 to 4 employees, small with 5 to 9, small medium offices with 10–19, large medium with 20–39, large with 40–99, and very large with 100 or more. The national distributions for these six groups were: very small, 52.5 per cent; small, 26.1; small medium, 12.6; large medium, 5.8; large, 2.0; and very large, 0.9.[7]

Regional distributions, with only two exceptions, maintained this regular ranking with regard to their own regional totals, but there was considerable variation between the regions themselves. In general, the South Atlantic and Sierra Nevada conform closest to the national averages. The most striking deviation is exhibited by the Gulf region, which had by far the lowest proportion of very small firms, but the highest proportions of small and small-medium firms. No doubt this situation is linked to the facts previously noted, that the Gulf region enjoyed the highest median volume of work, and that, in this work, commercial, educational, religious, public, and hospital types occurred at high rates (*Figure 5,* p. 22). The Middle Atlantic region differed by preferring small-medium offices over large-medium. The New England and New York regions both show the lowest proportions of small offices, but they compensate differently, New England by large-medium, and New York by large offices. The

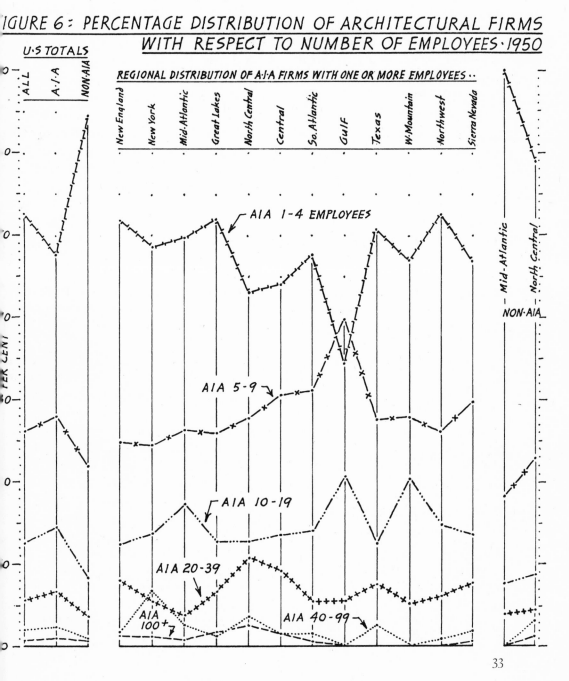

IGURE 6 : PERCENTAGE DISTRIBUTION OF ARCHITECTURAL FIRMS
WITH RESPECT TO NUMBER OF EMPLOYEES · 1950

U·S TOTALS

ALL A·J·A NON·AIA

REGIONAL DISTRIBUTION OF A·J·A FIRMS WITH ONE OR MORE EMPLOYEES ··

New England · New York · Mid·Atlantic · Great Lakes · North Central · Central · So. Atlantic · Gulf · Texas · W.Mountain · Northwest · Sierra Nevada

AIA 1-4 EMPLOYEES

AIA 5-9

AIA 10-19

AIA 20-39

AIA 100+

AIA 40-99

Mid·Atlantic North Central

NON·AIA

PER CENT

33

North Central region displays by far the highest proportions of large-medium and very large offices.

Comparison of AIA and Non-AIA offices reveals that the national proportion of Non-AIA firms with one and two employees (42.7%) is almost twice the AIA rate (22.0%). For three or more employees, AIA offices lead. The same relationships hold for the Middle Atlantic and North Central regions. This situation may arise, at least in part, from the fact that, of practitioners in the age groups under 35 and over 65, i.e., at the beginning and close of active practice when very small offices are most prevalent, only 35 per cent are AIA members (*Table 8*).

Further analysis of size-of-office data shows that for the 3377 private practitioner firms reporting employees, the *average* number of employees was 8.9. However, the *median* office had 2.9 employees. The comparable *average* for AIA firms was 10.0, and for Non-AIA firms 6.2 (*Table 24*). The AIA *median* was 3.7, the Non-AIA 1.6.[8] If calculations are confined to the 3253 firms reporting one or more employees, thus omitting one-man offices, the median was 3.8 (*Table 26*). The comparable AIA median was 4.3, and the Non-AIA median 2.6. Likewise omitting one-man offices, the highest regional median for AIA offices was 5.4 in the Gulf region, followed by the North Central and Central regions (*Figure 7*). The smallest was 3.8 for the Northwest region, with both the New England and Great Lakes regions just above with 3.9.

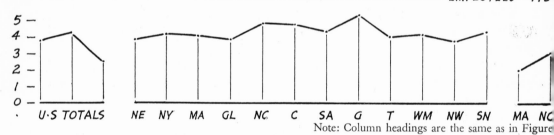

FIGURE 7: MEDIAN NUMBER OF EMPLOYEES IN A·I·A FIRMS WITH ONE OR MOR EMPLOYEES ·· 195

Note: Column headings are the same as in Figure

In contrast to private firms, departments within private non-architectural organizations averaged 34.7 employees and public bureaus averaged 37.3. (*Table 24*). Organization offices headed by AIA architects averaged 43.2 and those headed by Non-AIA architects 28.2. For bureaus, the AIA average was 22.5, and the Non-AIA 47.8.

These averages and medians have, perhaps, smaller significance than the range of size of firms and their regional distribution, because the amount and kind of service available to a community are intimately linked to local and regional demand. Although some individual practitioners with small offices have built nation-wide reputations and practices, most small firms tend primarily to serve their immediate areas where they can maintain direct and frequent contact with clients and projects. Medium-sized firms, in turn, tend to cover small or large regions, and very large firms are organized to serve on a national, and even international, basis. Far-ranging practice is not new. Town and Davis, who formed the first American architectural partnership in 1829,

34

served clients throughout the country. Richard Upjohn; H. H. Richardson; McKim, Mead and White; and Daniel Burnham carried on nation-wide practices, and maintained for their time organizations of exceptional size. Since then, the gradual increase in size and complexity of projects, together with vastly improved facilities for travel and communication, has encouraged a growing proportion of large firms whose practice extends not only throughout the nation, but often to distant lands as well. Conversely, the same facilities for communication and easy access have fostered the establishment of firms in small communities serving considerable areas in which professional skills were formerly unavailable.

It is clear, therefore, that the great variety of building projects in the country as a whole, differing so markedly in scale and type, requires and supports several kinds of architectural offices, which vary chiefly as to size, productive volume, and the degree to which certain specialized personnel are provided within the office organization.[9] For convenience of discussion, three general types can be recognized. First is the small office, conducted by one or two principals, working alone or aided by a few assistants. Usually such an office serves a limited area, and its practice for the most part deals with projects relatively small in size. Second is the medium office, headed by one or several principals, with a more numerous and diversified staff. It serves not only local needs, but often a considerable surrounding region as well. Its projects are frequently large and of specialized character. Finally, there is the large office, whose numerous principals direct a corps of highly specialized technicians of all kinds. Such an organization is equipped to undertake the largest type of projects and its range of operation extends across broad regions and the entire nation. The tendency of large corporate clients to seek a fuller and more completely integrated service has tended to stimulate the formation of large architectural firms.

Thus, each of these types has its inherent advantages and contributes to the diverse needs of a wide variety of clients. Nevertheless, the nature of the architectural process is such that the general manner of performing architectural services remains much the same. In large organizations, for example, the unit is still the individual project, so that, in many respects, such firms often seem to be a combination of many small offices, with the difference that a core of specialized personnel is immediately available to all staff units conducting the individual projects. In this connection, the tendency for very large firms to establish branches or coequal offices in various metropolitan centers and even abroad, to which the central specialized staff may be sent as needed, illustrates another method by which large-scale technical resources can be brought to bear on specific local projects.

It should be noted that, in reality, the three types of offices just described vary greatly in organization and possess considerable flexibility in their adaptation to specific projects. The association of several offices for a particular project illustrates the unusual elasticity of the architectural process. The formation of large firms to handle war emergency projects displayed this same pliancy. Furthermore, in many instances, the three types comprise evolutionary stages in the life history of a particular firm.

The *1950 Survey* studied the variety of operational functions required in the performance of architectural services and the distribution of these functions among practitioners and their employees. The following functions were noted:

1. *Functions relative to normal Executive Services*
   A. Client Relations
   B. Project Research
   C. Architectural Design
   D. Site Development
   E. Engineering Design
   F. Production of Working Drawings
   G. Production of Specifications
   H. Preparation of Estimates
   I. Counsel on Letting of Contracts
   J. Field Supervision
2. *Functions relative to Auxiliary Services*
   A. Community Planning
   B. Landscape Design
   C. Interior and Furniture Design
   D. Industrial Product Design
   E. Consulting
   F. Building Code Administration
   G. Building Operation and Maintenance
3. *Functions relative to General Operation of Office*
   A. Administration and Management
   B. Accounting
   C. Secretarial and Clerical

The *1950 Survey* requested responding firms to classify employees in nine groups:

1. *Employees primarily assisting in Executive Services*
   A. Project managers, job captains, and squad bosses
   B. Designers
   C. Research personnel
   D. Engineering personnel
   E. Draftsmen
   F. Specification writers
   G. Field inspectors
2. *Employees related to General Operation of Office*
   A. Administrators and Office Managers
   B. Secretaries, Clerks, and Accountants

Table 23 shows the relative overall proportions of these nine groups in 3377 private offices reporting one or more employees, 176 departments of private non-architectural organizations, and 98 public bureaus. It is obvious that, since 52.5 per cent of the private offices had only 1 to 4 employees, many employees perform multiple functions.

This explains the overwhelming proportion of draftsmen, 44 per cent, who often design, research, draw, inspect, and otherwise act in other diverse capacities. Next highest was the secretary-clerk-accountant group, 15 per cent, which indicates not only the vast growth of written communication, records, documents, and bookkeeping, characteristic of all phases of contemporary life, but also the tremendous expansion of government-inspired paper work relating to both projects and employees. The middle groups were engineering personnel (11 per cent), designers (8), project managers (8), and field inspectors (7). For small firms, these functions are usually performed by the principals themselves, which explains in part the lower frequency of these groups. Finally, the smallest groups were administrators (3), specification writers (2), and research personnel (2), whose specialized functions are differentiated primarily in the larger organizations.

This pattern shifts somewhat in company and bureau offices. The company office employed fewer draftsmen (36 per cent), but used more engineering personnel (18) and managers (6). The public bureau revealed its greater preoccupation with administration and inspection by higher ratios for secretaries, clerks, and accountants (22 per cent) and field inspectors (17). The bureau rate for draftsmen (20 per cent) was less than half that of private offices, but since the average size of bureaus was four times that of private firms, the actual number of draftsmen per average bureau was still almost twice that of the average private firm.

The *1950 Survey* likewise studied the average number of principals per firm and their functions. *Table 24* indicates that private firms averaged 1.7 principals, with 1.8 for AIA firms and 1.5 for Non-AIA firms.[10] Company and bureau organizations averaged 2 per office. *Table 27* shows the average activity pattern of these principals. For AIA private firms, half of the average principal's time was absorbed by "the overall activities of general practice" (20 per cent) and by architectural design (30 per cent). The remaining half was devoted equally to client relations, working drawings, specifications, field supervision, and office administration. The average principal of a Non-AIA private firm, operating a force about two-thirds of his AIA counterpart, covered exactly the same activities, but used 30 per cent of his own time for working drawings, 20 for architectural design, and 10 for "overall activities." Company and bureau architects, relieved of client relations, field supervising, and "overall practice," concentrated on fewer activities, company architects primarily on working drawings, and bureau architects on administration, working drawings, design, specifications, and building maintenance. The outstanding fact revealed by these data is that, despite a listing of 28 activities, the average pattern of company architects was limited to 4 of these, that of bureau architects to 5, and that of private practitioners to 7. The emphasis of the latter on activities relating directly to executive services may not be surprising, but it certainly was heavily underscored.

Table 28 shows the relative distribution of the total time of all architects with respect to the 28 activities surveyed. The seven core activities just noted here absorbed 80.6 per cent of the total time. Working drawings led with 17.9 per cent, followed by architectural design (15.2), "overall activities" (11.5), administration (10.7), field su-

37

pervising (9.7), client relations (9.2), and specifications (6.4). The remaining 19.4 per cent of the time was distributed thinly over the other 21 activities. The data for different types of offices show the same variations already described. The AIA and Non-AIA distributions show few differences, and these reflect chiefly the different sizes of their offices.

The performance of Executive Services involves certain functions for which it is not always feasible to provide appropriate personnel within the staff of a small, or even medium, office. This is especially true for the design of complex structural systems and the ramified assortment of mechanical, heating, electrical, sanitary, and other special installations which have expanded so rapidly in recent years. The *1950 Survey* studied current methods of handling this work and found that in 48 per cent of private firms the function of structural design was handled within the office by the practitioner (30 per cent), partner (6), or full-time employee (12) (*Table 32*). In the same way, 23 per cent of private firms cared for their mechanical problems, and 26 per cent their electrical installations. A higher proportion of company and bureau offices accomplished their own engineering work by employing appropriate full-time personnel.

The remaining firms provided this part of their services by using consulting engineers. Since, except in special cases, the architect includes such services in his total Executive Services, he assumes, in so far as the client is concerned, full responsibility for their completeness and quality. In theory, therefore, the consultant becomes a temporary assistant in the architect's office. In practice, however, certain problems arise. One of these lies in the coordination of these services so that the result is a thoroughly integrated building, which is the chief goal and final responsibility of the architect. It is one thing to design an installation satisfying perfectly its own criteria; it is an entirely different and much more difficult task to retain the same quality of operation in conjunction with other installations and the total architectural requirements of the project. To obtain an harmonious conclusion requires complete cooperation, sympathy, and understanding on the part of all concerned.[11]

Close collaboration is naturally facilitated by easy access between an architectural staff and engineering personnel. Large architectural firms enjoy this advantage by providing the necessary engineering services within their own organization. During the past decade, and especially for war projects, government insistence promoted the formation of organizations which combined architectural and engineering firms.[12] For smaller firms, however, it is more important than ever before to have readily available the cooperative services of qualified consulting engineers trained and experienced in building installations. This is most difficult for architects practicing in small and isolated communities, but, fortunately, improved transportation and communication with large centers has in part overcome this handicap and, in addition, there appears to be a growing tendency for professional engineers to practice in smaller communities. It would be helpful if the AIA and the appropriate national engineering societies would publicize the need and opportunity for engineers in this field of activity.

38

A similar situation exists with regard to landscape and interior design. The *1950 Survey* found that 33 per cent of private architectural firms handled their own landscape design (*Table 32*). Access to qualified consultants is, therefore, important for the remaining 67 per cent. For interior work, however, 90 per cent of the architectural firms were self-sufficient, and the need for consultants is less urgent. Company and bureau offices showed the same characteristics.

FIGURE 8 : ORGANIZATION OF A TYPICAL SMALL OFFICE

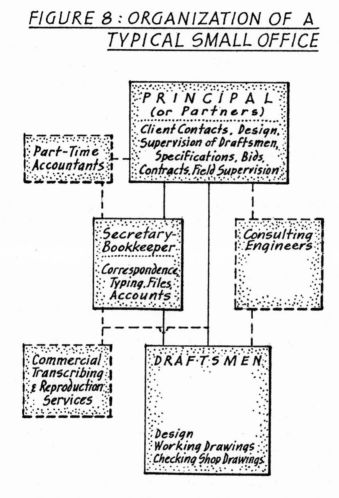

Another type of consulting service has appeared in recent years, furnished by individuals who profess special knowledge of a particular type of building, such as schools, hospitals, and churches. Normally, this kind of need has been answered by association of the primary architect with another firm possessing special experience in the type of building under consideration, and, in this arrangement, each firm undertakes well-defined responsibilities and obligations. Today, however, many of these new consultants, though not architects, exceed their legitimate counsel on matters of operational techniques and equipment, and the survey of community needs, and endeavor to usurp architectural functions which the architect cannot properly relinquish. To correct this situation, The AIA issued a statement in 1952 which recognized the usefulness of experienced consultants in providing certain types of data which can assist the Owner in making his own basic decisions regarding the project program. Beyond this, such consultants are not prepared to render competent advice.[13]

The success of an individual office in performing architectural services depends not only upon the number and type of personnel, but also upon the organizational plan by which their efforts are coordinated for maximum effectiveness. The amount of productive effort each individual can and will contribute determines directly the organization's scope and efficiency. For the maximum result, each individual should be matched with the kinds of functions to which his temperament and capacity incline him. It is manifest that these individual characteristics will lead to a variety of operational methods.

The Commission surveyed current organizational patterns and, as expected, did find considerable variation across the nation. In general, however, these coalesce around the three size types, small, medium, and large, previously noted. While the patterns which follow are typical and symbolic, rather than specific, they should clarify organizational principles, aid public understanding of the nature of practice, and help young architects to find promptly their appropriate places within the profession.

Figure 8, overleaf, shows the organization of personnel and functions in a typical small office. The principal participates directly in all phases of the work and supervises each employee. The small staff keeps overhead costs low, and, because of its economy and personal service, this type of office dominates the field of smaller buildings, especially residential and small commercial work. Moreover, each member of the limited staff must perform many functions and thus acquires a varied and well-rounded experience.

Figure 9 presents the organization of a typical medium-sized office, in which the scope and volume of practice demand more assistance. A small number of key personnel, perhaps two to four, relieves the partners of numerous operational details. One may undertake research, program, and basic design functions, always, of course, supervised by a principal. Another may oversee the production of working drawings, and a third may handle selection, specification, and approval of materials. Some medium-sized offices employ full-time engineers and other technical specialists. Many variations of this pattern occur, which permit the particular talents and capacities of the individuals involved to be used to the fullest advantage. Consequently, few principals of small or medium firms agree on a single "way to practice."

Large architectural firms are organized to offer the diverse and specialized services demanded by clients undertaking projects of the largest size. Their completeness of personnel and range of experience provide unique facilities, but also impose high overhead costs and the necessity of maintaining a continuous flow of the kind of work they are equipped to handle. Of necessity, therefore, their operations are regional, national, and even international in scope, and they tend to specialize on particular types of projects demanded by special kinds of clients. *Figure 10* diagrams the

FIGURE 9: ORGANIZATION OF A TYPICAL OFFICE OF MEDIUM SIZE

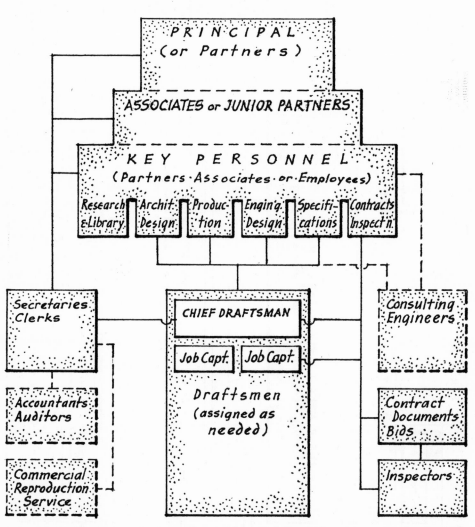

organizational pattern of a large firm with well-defined departments, each of which performs its assigned duties for each project in appropriate sequence. The result is a kind of horizontal stratification through which a project manager guides and co-ordinates the job. The advantages of this pattern rest in its standardization of each stage of the work and the rapid pace this permits. Its hazards lie in fragmentation of the architectural process and the difficulty of ensuring that continuous personal concentration which is so necessary for creative work.

Figure 11 illustrates a large firm which organizes a project team, headed by a project architect, to handle each job as a unit. In effect, the firm thus creates within itself a series of small offices and maintains pools of specialized personnel and divi-

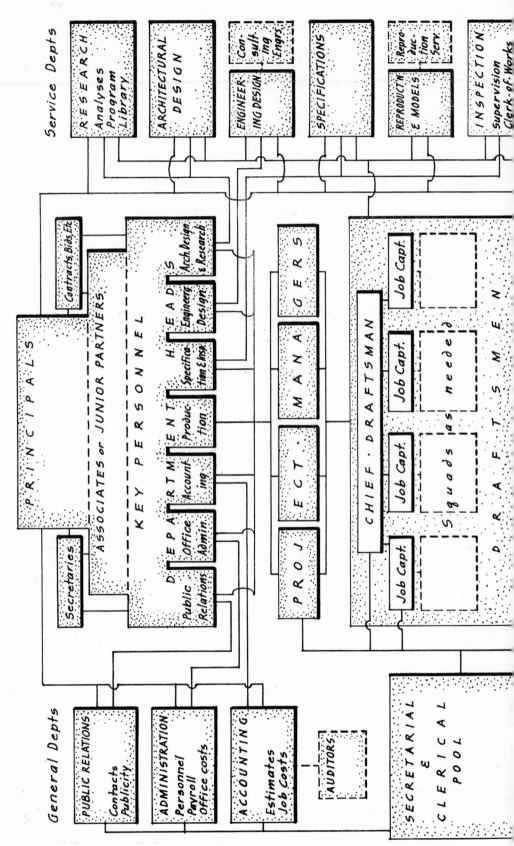

FIGURE 10 : ORGANIZATION OF A TYPICAL LARGE OFFICE WITH DEPARTMENTS

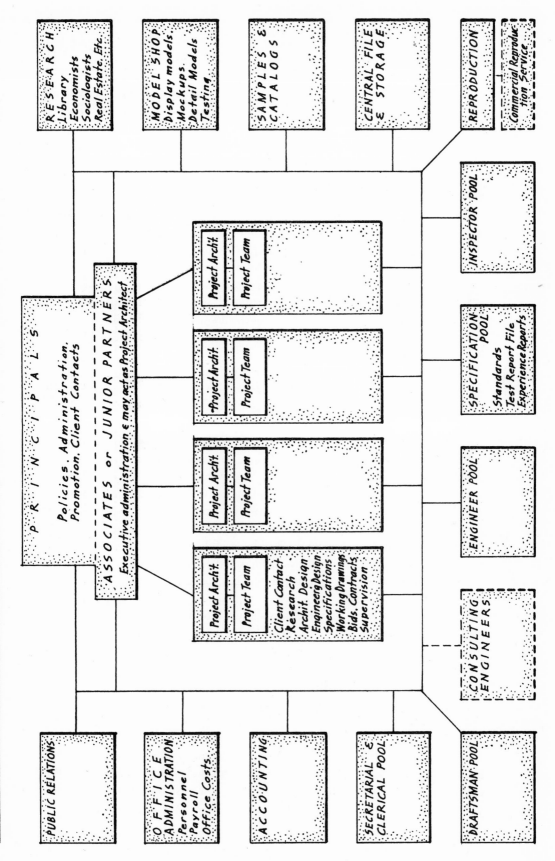

FIGURE 11: ORGANIZATION OF A TYPICAL LARGE OFFICE WITH PROJECT TEAMS

sions of special facilities from which each project unit can draw aid as needed. The advantages of this system are the continuity and close integration of personnel and project it provides. Its success obviously depends on the selection of capable project architects.[14] In actual practice, many offices have combined elements from both of these patterns.

The recent trend of forming large offices for particular projects or special kinds of work by combining smaller firms, both architectural and engineering, has already been noted. The resulting organization usually approximates the large architectural office, but the individual units remain similar to the medium office pattern.

It is apparent that the selection of an appropriate operational pattern for architectural practice is a creative opportunity and that organizational planning will become more and more a key to successful practice in the future. Time was when the test of good architectural management was a favorable year-end balance. Today, in contrast, an architect who neglects his accountant's weekly summary may be out of practice before he knows it. It is necessary, and, indeed, natural to expect that the future will bring many administrative refinements which, through improved integration of organization, will enable architects to serve their clients with still greater effectiveness.

It remains to emphasize that, regardless of organization and skilled assistants, it is the architect himself who is personally responsible for the character and quality of the services provided for the client. This concentration of responsibility is obvious in a small office where the practitioner himself does much of the actual work and closely supervises his few assistants. In larger organizations, however, the subdivision of duties is a necessary and legitimate principle, but final accountability for the quality of service and result cannot be delegated. Moreover, the conception of a project must evolve in the mind of one individual, and, unless the architect is to become a mere administrative figurehead, he cannot avoid its major decisions whether he works alone or employs an army of assistants. Even when partners share responsibilities, each individual project is usually directed by a single principal. This centralization of responsibility also conforms with the understandable and reasonable desire of most clients to deal directly with a principal who can speak with authority for the whole organization.

The architect's responsibility includes the work of any consultants he himself employs. It follows, therefore, that the architect is individually accountable for the structural soundness of the building, even in cases where its design involves novel analytical techniques normally employed only by structural specialists. Since buildings, by definition, are not simply structures, but complete architectural entities, the general responsibility of the architect for the total product cannot be subdivided. This principle is sustained by the fact that the architect selects and employs the structural and other consultants he uses.

It is this assumption of responsibility by the architect which forms the essence of his personal and professional service to his client and which confers upon him his critical importance in the building process. It is a position not to be undertaken lightly, but only after rigorous, systematic training and experience. For these reasons, professional education and licensing become paramount considerations, and professional standards and disciplines emerge as indispensable guides. Nevertheless, if responsibility is great, so are the opportunities which accompany it. Their joint challenge has been, and will continue to be, the compelling motivation of those who seek to be worthy of the ancient and respected title of *architect*.

4. PERSONNEL FOR PRACTICE

Because the practice of architecture is a personal service, the characteristics of the persons performing it hold interest and importance. When the Commission began its work, it soon discovered that few actual facts were known about these individuals, and so it pioneered a systematic study of them.

The *1950 Survey* focused its attention primarily upon the registered architects of the United States. Compilation of an unduplicated list from state registration rosters disclosed a total of 19,137, exceeding the best previous estimates. Since all states now require registration as a prerequisite to practice, this total formed the distinct group from which all practitioners had to be drawn.

The relative distribution of registered architects with regard to their employment status is presented in *Table 7*. 40 per cent were individual practitioners, 22 per cent principals, 7 per cent associates, and 1 per cent consultants, all of whom together comprised a dominant private practitioner group of 70 per cent. Architects employed on a salary or wage basis totaled 24 per cent, including 14 per cent in private architectural firms, 5 per cent in architectural departments of non-architectural organizations, and 5 per cent in public bureaus.[15] 3 per cent were teachers in schools of architecture. Only 3 per cent were retired, unemployed, or in non-architectural work. Thus, an amazing 97 per cent of all 19,137 registered architects were professionally active in 1950.

If the private practitioner group is joined with employee architects working in private architectural firms, a total of 84 per cent of all registered architects is revealed as working under conditions of private initiative. Of all architects performing direct architectural functions, i.e., omitting teachers and the miscellaneous group, those in private architectural offices comprised 89.3 per cent. The comparable proportions for architects in private non-architectural organizations and public bureaus was 5.3 per cent for each group.

This strong emphasis on private practice was even more marked among AIA architects. 81 per cent were practitioners, 11 per cent were private employees—8 per cent in architectural offices, 3 per cent in non-architectural organizations—and 3 per cent in public bureaus. In contrast, Non-AIA architects had only 56 per cent in the practitioner group, but private employees came to 29 per cent—22 per cent in architectural offices, 7 in non-architectural organizations—and 8 per cent in public bureaus. Of the totals in each group, AIA members formed 65 per cent of all practitioners, 31.5 per cent of all employees in private architectural offices, 34.4 per cent of all employees in private non-architectural organizations, and 32.4 per cent of public employees.

Considerable variation was found in the several regions (*Table 2,* and *Figure 12*). For all architects, the highest proportions of practitioners were 80 per cent in the South Atlantic region, and 76 each in New England and Texas regions. The lowest was 63 per cent in New York, which, on the other hand, had the highest proportion, 25 per cent of private employees. The South Atlantic region had the lowest proportion, 9 per cent, of private employees. For public employees, the Middle Atlantic region, including the District of Columbia, was high with 9 per cent, while five regions had the lowest rate of 4 per cent. For AIA architects, the highest region for practitioners was the Western Mountain with 89 per cent, the lowest, New York, with 75. These two exchanged places for the 17 per cent high and 5 per cent low for AIA private employees. For Non-AIA architects, the practitioner rate was highest, 69 per cent, in the South Atlantic region, low in New York with 49. The Great Lakes region had a high of 39 per cent for Non-AIA private employees, and the South Atlantic was low with 15 per cent. It is interesting to note that four regions had relatively high rates of Non-AIA public employees—the Middle Atlantic with 13 per cent, and New York, Gulf, and Sierra Nevada regions, each with 10. New England's 3 per cent was lowest in this group. In general, the highest concentration of corporate and bureau architects appears, as should be expected, in regions embracing large metropolitan and governmental centers.

The median age for all registered architects was 45.5 (*Table 8*), for AIA members 46.5, and for Non-AIA 44.5 (*Table 7*). Public employees were the oldest group with 49.9 and 49.5 for AIA and Non-AIA, practitioners midway with 46.5 and 46.0, and

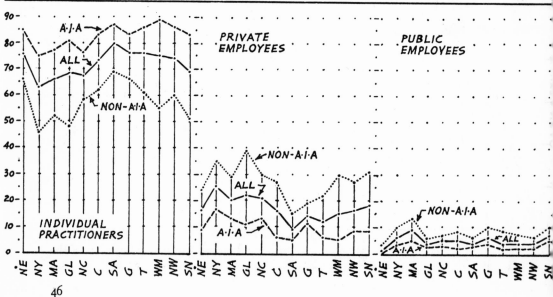

FIGURE 12: PER CENT OF ARCHITECTS IN A·I·A REGIONS IN THREE EMPLOYMENT GROUP

private employees youngest with 43.0 and 40.5 (*Table 8*). Inspection of median ages by AIA regions indicates that in the south and northwest both AIA and Non-AIA groups are slightly younger (*Table 1*).[16]

Table 8 presents the distribution of architects by eleven age-groups, and *Figure 13* plots these data. Since normal progress in education and training establishes 26 as the usual minimum age at registration, only a negligible number under 25 were reported. The distribution of all architects shows the largest proportion, 18 per cent, in 40–44 age group. Below this axis, the profile decreases in a smooth steep curve to the 20–24 age group, but above it the decline is more gradual and is interrupted by the equal percentages in the 50–54 and 55–59 groups. This distortion probably reflects discouraging depression years, the effects of which were felt especially by the 45–49 and 50–54 groups, who were then 15 to 20 years younger. For all AIA members, the distribution curve is almost identical, but for Non-AIA architects the largest group is in the 35–39

FIGURE 13: ARCHITECTS' AGE CHARACTERISTICS BY EMPLOYMENT STATUS.

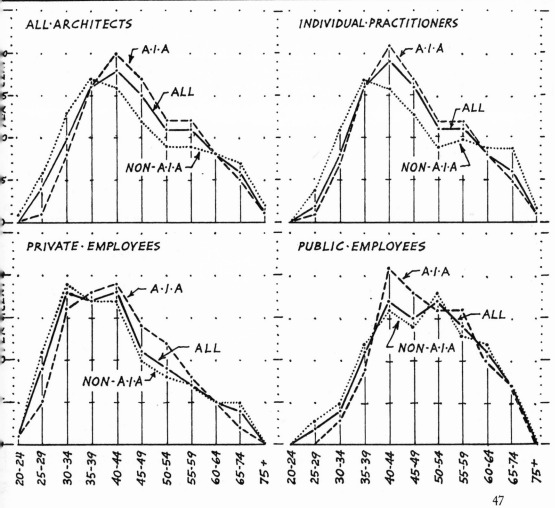

bracket, with larger younger groups and smaller older groups up to the 60–64 bracket. The distribution profiles for private practitioners do not differ significantly from the general curves. For private employee architects the largest Non-AIA group, the 30–34 bracket, is ten years younger than the AIA group. This may indicate that the Non-AIA group contained a larger proportion of the young architects working in architectural offices who had not yet been attracted to AIA membership. For public employee architects, the Non-AIA peak is in the 50–54 group, ten years older than the AIA group.

In view of the general consequences of medical progress and the specific effects of registration requirements, the proportion of architects in the older age brackets has increased markedly. Since 1870, census reports of the age distributions of architects confirm this. *Figure 14* presents these in graphic form. In 1870, only 2.4 per cent were 60 or over, whereas, in 1950, this group had increased to 15 per cent. In 1890, 22 per cent were under 20, but in 1950 this group was negligible. In 1890, 53 per cent were under 34; in 1950, the group comprised only 14 per cent. Those over 45 formed 24 per cent in 1890 and 50 per cent in 1950.

From 1870 to 1930, census reports also gave the number of foreign-born architects. In 1870, 33 per cent were foreign-born; in 1880, 29.2 per cent; in 1890, 27 per cent; in 1910, 18 per cent; in 1920, 16 per cent; and in 1930, 15.5 per cent. No data were obtained thereafter. In 1870 and 1880, the largest foreign-born groups were German and British.

The continued maintenance of a sufficient number of architects is inevitably linked to the individual's opportunity to secure an economic return commensurate with the high cost of long training and the manifold responsibilities assumed. Without the promise of adequate recompense, essential architectural services in the amount and quality needed cannot be assured. Further, the recruitment of suitable personnel for a specific vocation is directly affected by its competitive advantages and opportunities.

The *1950 Survey* studied the 1949 net incomes of architects. *Table 9* lists median incomes by age-groups and employment status. The close grouping of private and public employee architects and of Non-AIA private practitioners is striking (*Figure 15*). It is interesting to note that the maximum medians of these groups occur at different times, for Non-AIA practitioners at 55–59, and for private and public employee architects at 50–54. In contrast, AIA practitioners had medians which exceeded Non-AIA practitioners by steadily increasing proportions in each age-group. In the 20–24 group, the AIA median is 10 per cent more than the Non-AIA median; in the next three groups, the excess is 23 per cent; in the 45–49 group, it is 28 per cent; in the 50–54 and 55–59 groups, 43 per cent; and it mounts thereafter to 71, 84, and 122 per cent (*Figure 16*). The peak for AIA practitioners is in the 60–64 group.

Table 10 and *Figure 17* present the per cent of architects of each employment group in each of ten income brackets. The clustering of all groups in the lowest brackets and in the $8000–10,000 bracket is noteworthy. 52 per cent of AIA practitioners reported incomes of $10,000 or more, in contrast to 31 per cent for Non-AIA practitioners, 14 per cent for AIA private employee architects, 3 per cent for Non-AIA

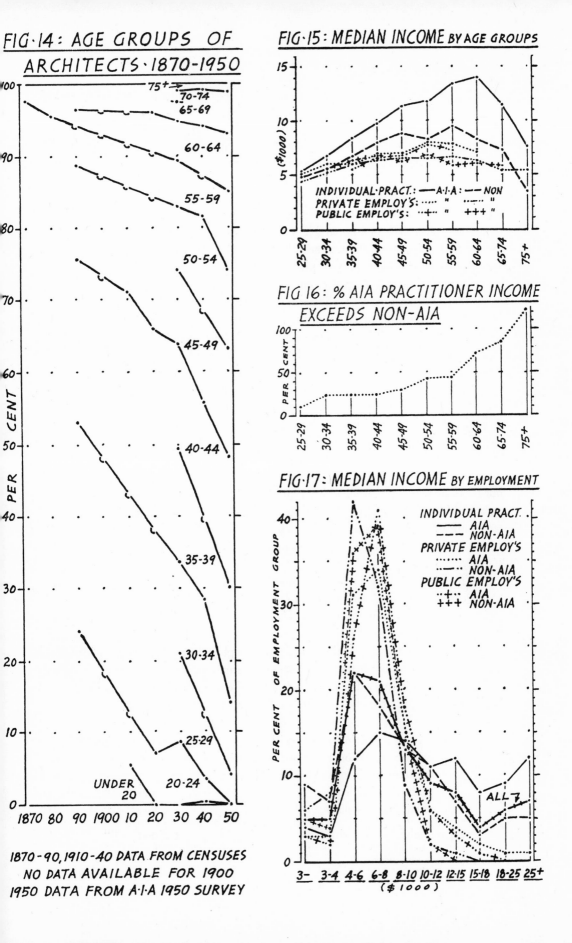

FIG·14: AGE GROUPS OF ARCHITECTS·1870-1950

75+
70-74
65-69
60-64
55-59
50-54
45-49
40-44
35-39
30-34
25-29
20-24
UNDER 20

PER CENT

1870 80 90 1900 10 20 30 40 50

1870-90, 1910-40 DATA FROM CENSUSES
NO DATA AVAILABLE FOR 1900
1950 DATA FROM A·I·A 1950 SURVEY

FIG·15: MEDIAN INCOME BY AGE GROUPS

($1000)

INDIVIDUAL PRACT.: —— A.I.A: ---- NON
PRIVATE EMPLOY'S: ······ " ─·─· "
PUBLIC EMPLOY'S: ··+·· " +++ "

25-29 30-34 35-39 40-44 45-49 50-54 55-59 60-64 65-74 75+

FIG 16: % AIA PRACTITIONER INCOME EXCEEDS NON-AIA

PER CENT

25-29 30-34 35-39 40-44 45-49 50-54 55-59 60-64 65-74 75+

FIG·17: MEDIAN INCOME BY EMPLOYMENT

PER CENT OF EMPLOYMENT GROUP

INDIVIDUAL PRACT.
—— AIA
---- NON-AIA
PRIVATE EMPLOY'S
······ AIA
─·─· NON-AIA
PUBLIC EMPLOY'S
··+·· AIA
+++ NON-AIA

ALL

3- 3-4 4-6 6-8 8-10 10-12 12-15 15-18 18-25 25+
($1000)

private employees, 10 per cent for AIA public employees, and 2 per cent for Non-AIA public employees. In the four highest brackets, the number of AIA practitioners exceeded Non-AIA practitioners by 71, 166, 80, and 150 per cent respectively. In the brackets between $3000–4000 and $8000, the employee architect groups rise to comparably high percentages, exceeding the practitioner group by about 140 per cent. Taken together, *Figures 15* and *17* make clear that the assumption of large responsibilities by practitioners is rightfully rewarded by higher recompense. They also indicate a remarkable uniformity of salaries among employee architects.

Unfortunately, lack of comparable data precludes discernment of income trends or comparison of architects' remuneration with those in other professions. As to the question of continuity and stability of practice, the *1950 Survey* found that 80 per cent of all AIA practitioners and 77 per cent of all Non-AIA practitioners had maintained continuous practices, except for interruptions due to military service (*Table 13*). The highest proportions of unbroken practices, 84 per cent for AIA and 80 for Non-AIA, both occurred in the North Central region, and the lowest in both, 74 per cent, in New York. For practices interrupted for other than military service, three-quarters were due to general economic conditions, which included the Great Depression and the suspension of civilian construction during World War II. Economic reasons were highest for AIA practitioners in the Gulf region, 90 per cent, and lowest in the South Atlantic, 72 per cent, the New York, and the Sierra Nevada regions, each 73 per cent. For Non-AIA practitioners, the highest was the South Atlantic with 87 per cent, and the lowest, the Great Lakes with 65 per cent. No significant regional deviation is found in the median ages of all architects and those who have practiced continuously, but for those whose practice had been interrupted by economic conditions the median ages of AIA members were high in the south and far west and of Non-AIA architects uniformly higher except in the Central region. While continuity of practice is not necessarily synonymous with constancy of income, the picture is one of relative stability.

The recruitment of an appropriate number of practitioners to replace retirements and to care for increased demand due to population growth is of vital concern to both society and the profession. While analysis of demand and distribution will be undertaken in Section 5 of this chapter, it is proper to point out here that new practitioners emerge primarily from the ranks of architects employed in architectural offices. This evolutionary relationship between architect and employee is perhaps more intimate in architecture than in any other profession. It is necessary, therefore, to consider in detail the employed personnel of architectural firms.

9100 private practitioner firms with	76,800 employees
1940 private practitioner one-man firms with	0 "
890 departments in private non-architectural organizations with	29,300 "
560 public bureaus with	22,800 "
12,490 establishments with	128,900 "

Precise data on the total number of employees and the number in each employee category in architectural firms, departments, and bureaus, are not available. An estimate of personnel requires first an estimate of the number of firms of each type. One such estimate, based on data from the *1950 Survey,* is indicated above.[17] By applying ratios given in *Table 23,* the size of these categories may be estimated as follows:

	Private Firms	Private Depts.	Public Bureaus	Total
Architectural personnel	56,850	19,600	13,900	90,350
Draftsmen	33,800	10,500	4,550	48,850
Designers	6,150	2,050	1,140	9,340
Project Managers	6,150	2,340	1,360	9,850
Researchers	1,530	300	900	2,730
Administrators	2,300	1,760	1,600	5,660
Specification writers	1,530	600	450	2,580
Inspectors	5,390	2,050	3,900	11,340
Engineers	8,450	5,300	3,900	17,650
Secretarial & Accounting	11,500	4,400	5,000	20,900
Total	76,800	29,300	22,800	128,900

The recruitment of these employees is a major problem for practitioners. The sources for secretarial and clerical personnel are the vocational courses of public or private schools. Accountants are obtained from the same sources and also from collegiate schools of business. Since none of these sources of training concern themselves with detailed applications to architectural practice, these applications must be acquired in the architectural office itself. The development by The AIA of uniform accounting systems for architectural firms should aid greatly in orienting new accounting personnel to the special problems posed by the practice of architecture.

Engineering personnel in architectural firms usually means specialists in building structures, mechanical equipment, plumbing, and electrical installations. Graduates of appropriate engineering curricula who have gained practical experience in the application of their knowledge to building problems are desired, but their integration into an architectural organization frequently requires considerable adjustment. Architectural graduates in structural options or graduates in architectural engineering are obvious recruits for structural design. Their success in handling this work has suggested to a number of practitioners the possibility of establishing architectural options in the other types of building engineering.

The procurement of architectural personnel, however, constitutes the architect's most pressing employment problem. Five sources are possible for the individual employer: 1. the employees of other firms; 2. unemployed workers; 3. untrained youths; 4. non-graduates of architectural schools; and 5. architectural graduates. The first group is a source of recruits to the individual employer, but from the point of view of the whole employer group it reshuffles rather than expands personnel. In recent years, intense building activity has reduced unemployed personnel almost to the vanishing point. New staff, therefore, must be obtained primarily by office training or from the professional schools.

Training raw youths within an office is a slow, inefficient, and costly process for both trainee and employer. The result is that practitioners increasingly look to the professional schools for new personnel. This, too, has had its difficulties. From the standpoint of many practitioners, recruits fresh from school still require excessive office training and supervision in practical matters. Educators, on the other hand, point out that the schools have an inescapable responsibility to provide the fundamental training for architects, rather than for draftsmen. This controversy was a primary cause for the inauguration of the present Commission. More detailed discussion of the problem will be undertaken in later chapters of this Report.

The *1950 Survey* found that, despite the reservations of employers, graduates of the professional schools formed a major portion of architectural staffs. The average number of graduates for AIA private practitioners with one or more employees was 3.2 out of 10.4, or 30.8 per cent (*Table 24*). For Non-AIA practitioners, they averaged 1.9 out of 6.6, or 28.8 per cent. For AIA non-architectural offices, they averaged 10.4 out of 43.2, 24.2 per cent; for Non-AIA, 5.5 out of 28.2, 19.5 per cent. For AIA public bureaus, 6 graduates out of 22.5 formed 26.7 per cent; for Non-AIA bureaus, 5.7 out of 47.8, 11.9 per cent.

Table 25 reveals marked regional variations in the average number of graduate employees per office. For AIA offices, the North Central region was highest with 4.5 graduates, followed by New York with 4.0 and the Central region with 3.8. The Western Mountain region was lowest with 2.1. The eight remaining regions ranged close together from 2.4 to 3.0. In Non-AIA offices, the North Central was again highest with 2.6, with Texas' 2.5 and New York's 2.4 close after. The remaining nine regions ranged from New England's 1.2 to Gulf's 2.0. *Table 25* also indicates the average number of candidates for registration in each type of office.

The effectiveness of an architectural staff is strongly influenced, not only by its technical capabilities, but also by the conditions under which it operates. Comparative security, considerate office regulations, and a sense of contributing to an end product of real quality normally engender high morale and loyalty. On the other hand, the difficulty of maintaining a steady flow of work has often led to employment for the duration of a particular project, with the consequent handicaps of insecurity and a lowered sense of responsibility.

Paralleling the expansion of labor unions during the 1930's, sporadic efforts were made to organize architectural employees. The movement made little headway. This was probably due to the preponderance of small firms, which foster close relations between employer and employee, and the independent spirit and mobility of status characteristic of these employees. There are few vocations in which creative talent and capacity to assume responsibility are so eagerly sought or so promptly recognized. Then, too, the freedom which draftsmen enjoy to become independent practitioners, tends to dissipate the clash of interests often prevalent in business and industrial organizations. In 1947, during congressional hearings on the Taft-Hartley law, representatives of The AIA, together with those of the professional engineers, while recognizing the inherent right of American citizens to organize for the purpose of collective bargaining, pled effectively for the establishment of the open-shop principle and insisted that, if so-called architectural employee unions were formed, they should be professional in character and autonomous, and not dominated by sub-professional groups. These points were incorporated in the Taft-Hartley Act, although it did not refer specifically to architects. It should be recognized that the Fair Labor Standards Act could conceivably be used by union organizers as a persuasive argument to form architectural employee unions. Careful observance of the provisions of this act, however, together with the regulations of the Wage, Hour, and Public Contracts Division of the Department of Labor, should do much to forestall such attempts.

The factor most contributory to high employee morale remains an atmosphere of genuine concern on the part of the employer for the employee's growth in professional capacity. This attitude is prevalent among architectural practitioners to an unusual degree, and its persistence is explained not only by the employer's enlightened self-interest in desiring capable assistants, but also by his recognition, whether consciously or subconsciously felt, of the uniqueness of creative talent and its essential role in the continuing evolution of the profession. To the hard-boiled entrepreneur of a "plan-factory" this attitude no doubt smacks of sentimentalism and impractical idealism detrimental to profits. In reality, for the practitioner who seeks quality in his work and who therefore must inspire his staff to maximum effort, no other approach will suffice. It is this inescapable interdependence which, if properly fostered and exploited, transforms a heterogeneous group into an integrated, effective architectural team. The extent to which this goal is realized forms a telling measure of a practitioner's own understanding of the architectural process and of managerial psychology.

5. DISTRIBUTION FOR PRACTICE

Since architectural services are essential wherever building projects are undertaken, it is patent that the availability of these services should be assured through a just and balanced distribution of firms and personnel. The *1950 Survey* investigated this problem in several ways: by geographical distribution of firms and architects by regions, states, and size of communities; by range of practice; and by the ratios of firms and architects to population served.

The distribution of the 19,137 registered architects listed by the *1950 Survey* is presented in *Table 1* by states and AIA regions and by number and percentages. As expected, New York showed the highest state concentration with 2945, or 15.4 per cent. California followed with 1922, or 10.0 per cent. Then came Illinois (7.5), Pennsylvania (6.4), New Jersey (5.4), Ohio (5.2), and Texas (5.0). Among AIA regions, the Middle Atlantic had 17.7 per cent of all architects. Next in order were New York

(15.4), North Central (10.9), Great Lakes (10.5), and the Sierra Nevada (10.3).

Range of practice was indicated by the number of states in which each architect held registration for practice. *Table 44* shows that for all architects the average number of states was 1.7, for AIA architects 1.9, and for Non-AIA architects 1.5. For private practitioners, the average was 1.8, for AIA practitioners 2.0, and for Non-AIA practitioners 1.6. It is clear, therefore, that a large proportion of architects limit their practice to their home state and one adjoining state.

Table 11 gives the distribution of architects by size of community. 46 per cent of all architects were located in cities of 500,000 or more population, 27 per cent in cities of 100,000 to 500,000, and 9 per cent in cities of 50,000 to 100,000. Thus a total of 82 per cent worked in large urban centers. Only 2 per cent were located in communities of 5000 or less, and another 2 per cent in towns of 5000 to 10,000. The remaining 14 per cent practiced in towns of 10,000 to 50,000. There was no significant difference in the median ages of architects in these various communities.

The actual number of architects in a geographical unit is less revealing than the ratio between these architects and the population they serve. Such a ratio forms a useful device to measure both the availability of services and the quantity of personnel needed by a unit of population. Since architects are seldom called upon for farm buildings, it is urban population, rather than total population, that provides the best base for calculating these ratios.[18] While the *1950 Survey* furnished for the first time the number of registered architects and revealed a ratio of 21.5 per 100,000 urban population, a more telling picture of long-term development emerges through the use of census enumerations of architects from 1850 to 1950.[19] *Table 54* gives the number of "census architects," the urban population, and the number of architects per 100,000 urban population for each AIA region for the period 1850–1950. *Figure 18* graphs the growth in number of architects and population. *Figure 19* compares the relative increase of "census architects," urban population, and Gross National Product in terms of 1890. The fact that, since 1890, the supply of architects has grown more slowly than either population or the national economy, should correct the perennial, but fallacious, opinion held by most architects that competition and overcrowding have never been so severe as at present.

Figure 20 plots the number of "census architects" per 100,000 urban population from 1850 to 1950 for the nation and for 12 AIA regions arranged in three super-regions, north, south, and west. Through the first three decades, 1850 to 1880, the national ratio remained at a low level around 20.0. In 1890 expansion and prosperity brought a sharp rise to 36.5. Depression in the late 1890's caused a slight decline to 35.2 in 1900, but renewed activity created an all-time peak of 39.7 in 1910. Thereafter the ratio dropped to 33.6 in 1920, 32.0 in 1930, and 28.2 in 1940. These declines were due in part to the disruption caused by World War I and the brief recession which followed it, to the beginning of the Great Depression in 1930, and its cumulative effects in 1940. In 1950 the national ratio was 26.5. Thus, while the number of architects increased by 2648 between 1940 and 1950, or 12.65 per cent for the decade, urban population increased 14.51 millions, or 19.49 per cent. In the failure of the profession to expand

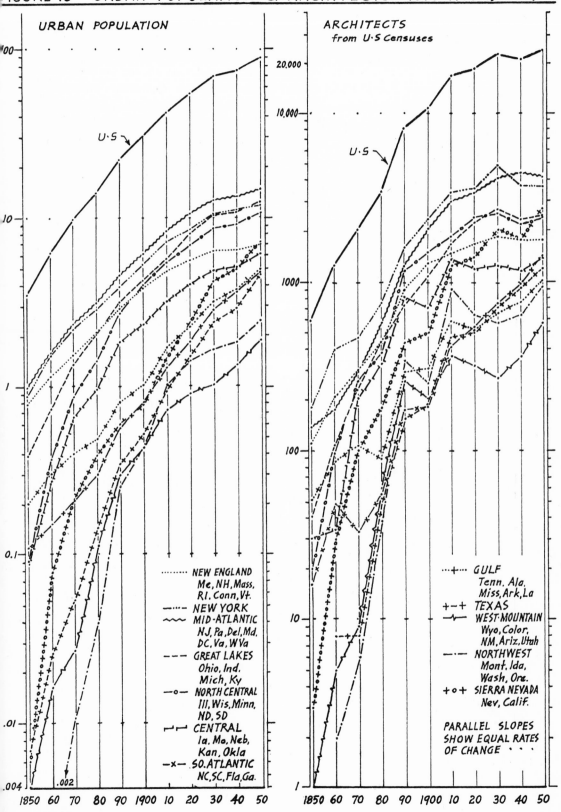

FIGURE 18 : URBAN · POPULATION · & · ARCHITECTS ~ 1850–1950 · by A·I·A Regions

URBAN POPULATION

U·S

ARCHITECTS
from U·S Censuses

U·S

NEW ENGLAND
Me, NH, Mass,
RI. Conn, Vt.
NEW YORK
MID-ATLANTIC
NJ, Pa, Del, Md,
DC, Va, WVa
GREAT LAKES
Ohio, Ind.
Mich, Ky
NORTH CENTRAL
Ill, Wis, Minn,
ND, SD
CENTRAL
Ia, Mo, Neb,
Kan, Okla
SO. ATLANTIC
NC, SC, Fla, Ga.

GULF
Tenn. Ala.
Miss, Ark, La
TEXAS
WEST-MOUNTAIN
Wyo, Color,
NM, Ariz, Utah
NORTHWEST
Mont. Ida,
Wash, Ore.
SIERRA NEVADA
Nev, Calif.

PARALLEL SLOPES
SHOW EQUAL RATES
OF CHANGE · · ·

1850 60 70 80 90 1900 10 20 30 40 50   1850 60 70 80 90 1900 10 20 30 40 50

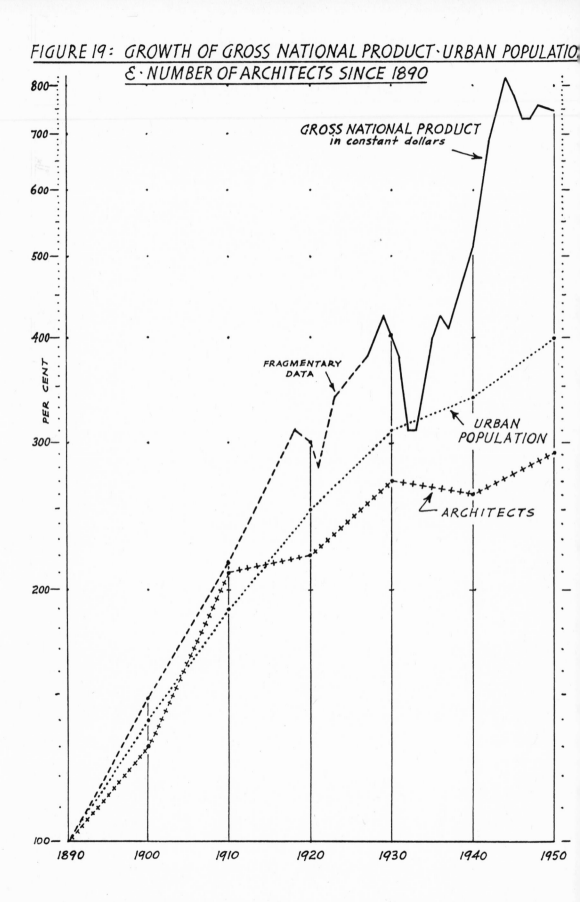

FIGURE 19: GROWTH OF GROSS NATIONAL PRODUCT·URBAN POPULATIO[N] & · NUMBER OF ARCHITECTS SINCE 1890

GROSS NATIONAL PRODUCT
in constant dollars

FRAGMENTARY
DATA

URBAN
POPULATION

ARCHITECTS

PER CENT

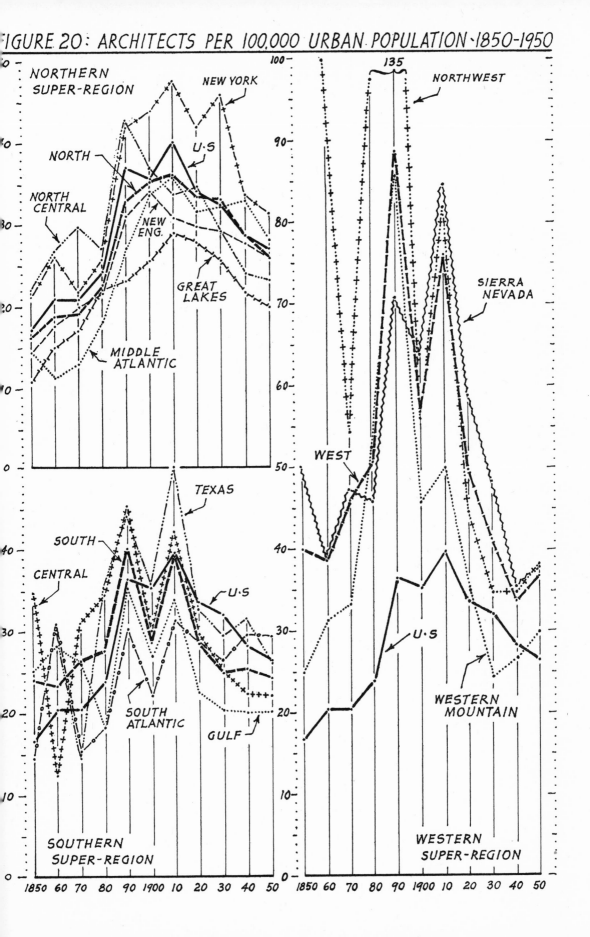

FIGURE 20: ARCHITECTS PER 100,000 URBAN POPULATION · 1850-1950

with population may be seen the effects of wartime disruptions and the increasing restriction of the use of the professional title of *architect* following more widespread adoption of registration laws.

The regional and super-regional profiles illustrate to an amazing degree the expansion of population and the profession from east to west, and they clearly reflect well known economic movements. In the south and west, the 1890 and 1910 peak ratios are very prominent due to building booms which drew an oversupply of architects. Subsequent depressions dispersed excess personnel. In recent decades, however, the south and west have gradually approached the national average. In the northern super-region more stable conditions produced smoother profiles. Thus the general homogeneity of each super-region is noteworthy, and the gradual coalescing of the regional ratios around the national ratio tends to confirm it as a valid measure of balance between demand and supply in architectural services.[20]

Because total population is a quantity susceptible of fairly accurate prediction, it is possible to forecast an urban population of 110.0 millions in 1960. If a ratio of 265 per million is applied to this population, it is reasonable to conclude that 29,160 architects will be needed in 1960. If registered architects continue to be 81.16 per cent of "census architects," the number of registered architects in 1960 will be 23,670, an increase of 4500 over 1950. The selected ratio of 265 for "census architects" assumes that a status quo will be maintained. This seems excessively conservative, especially when it is recalled that only 13 per cent of the employed personnel of private offices held registration in 1950. A higher ratio appears very desirable in order to have available a larger proportion of personnel who have attained the degree of competence represented by registration.[21]

The ratio of individual practitioner firms to urban population provides another means by which the distribution of the profession can be gauged. The *1950 Survey* obtained the data required for the calculation of ratios for that year, and, although lack of earlier information precludes the establishment of trends, the 1950 ratios, even standing alone, are of considerable interest. *Table 55* gives for each AIA region estimates of the total number of firms and the number of AIA firms by six size-groups, and the ratios of firms per 100,000 urban population.[22]

Figure 21 graphs these ratios. The ratio of all firms with one or more employees to total U. S. urban population was 10.24 per 100,000. If one-man offices are included the national ratio was 12.43. This ratio means that in 1950 each average group of 100,000 urban population used the architectural services of:

> 2.19 one-man offices
> 5.57 firms with 1–4 employees
> 2.60 "   "   5–9   "
> 1.23 "   "   10–19 "
> .56 "   "   20–39 "
> .19 "   "   40–99 "
> .09 "   "   100 or more "

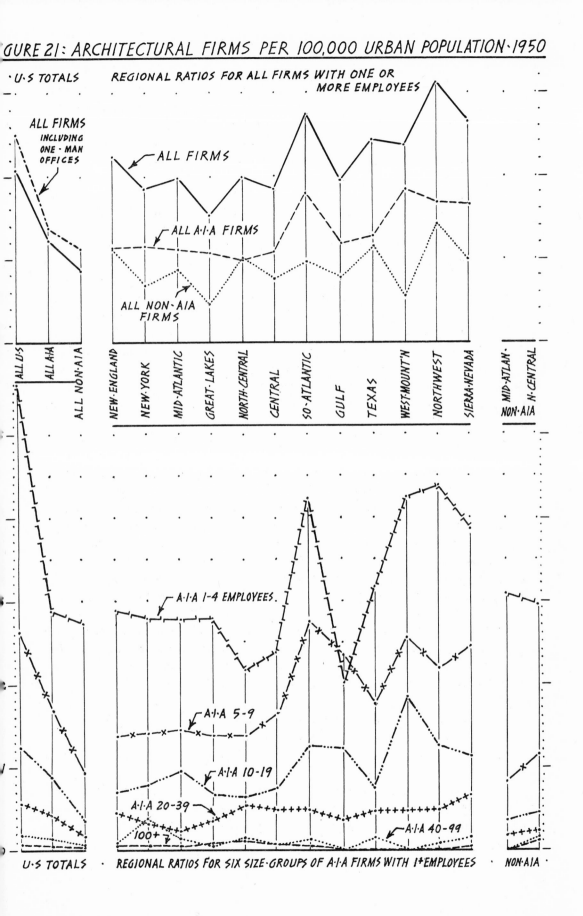

FIGURE 21: ARCHITECTURAL FIRMS PER 100,000 URBAN POPULATION·1950

U·S TOTALS — REGIONAL RATIOS FOR ALL FIRMS WITH ONE OR MORE EMPLOYEES

ALL FIRMS INCLUDING ONE·MAN OFFICES

ALL FIRMS

ALL A·I·A FIRMS

ALL NON·AIA FIRMS

ALL U·S   ALL A·IA   ALL NON-AIA

NEW·ENGLAND · NEW·YORK · MID·ATLANTIC · GREAT·LAKES · NORTH·CENTRAL · CENTRAL · SO·ATLANTIC · GULF · TEXAS · WEST·MOUNT'N · NORTHWEST · SIERRA·NEVADA

MID·ATLAN· N·CENTRAL

NON·AIA

A·I·A 1-4 EMPLOYEES

A·I·A 5-9

A·I·A 10-19

A·I·A 20-39

100+

A·I·A 40-99

U·S TOTALS · REGIONAL RATIOS FOR SIX SIZE·GROUPS OF A·I·A FIRMS WITH 1+EMPLOYEES · NON·AIA

Reciprocally these can be expressed in terms of the population served by one office:

I firm—one-man or	1–4	employees—per		12,900	urban population		
I "	with	5–9	"	"	38,500	"	"
I "	"	10–19	"	"	81,300	"	"
I "	"	20–30	"	"	178,600	"	"
I "	"	40–99	"	"	526,300	"	"
I "	"	100 or more	"	"	1,111,000	"	"

The national ratio for all AIA firms was 6.04 and for all Non-AIA firms 4.20. If one-man offices are included, the AIA ratio was 6.80 and the Non-AIA ratio 5.63.[23]

The regional profile for all firms with one or more employees shows five regions, New York, Middle Atlantic, North Central, Central, and Gulf, closely grouped around a ratio of 9.0. The highest ratio was 15.40 for the Northwest region, but the South Atlantic and Sierra Nevada regions grouped around 13.4. The New England, Texas, and Western Mountain regions lay about 11.5. The lowest ratio was 7.50 for the Great Lakes region. The profile for AIA firms shows all northern and southern regions, except the South Atlantic, with almost the same ratios. The western and South Atlantic regions were again high. For non-AIA firms the range of the variations was relatively small. While these ratios represent the totals of all large and small firms and may seem therefore to have little meaning, it should be emphasized that these totals are distributed among size-groups within the regions in a very consistent pattern (*Table 26*). They are useful, therefore, in demonstrating the general homogeneity of the national picture.

The profiles for six size-groups of AIA firms are of even greater interest since together they can be interpreted as indicating the balanced team of firms of various sizes which the region supports to serve its architectural needs. For the three largest size-groups the distribution across the country is significantly uniform. This same uniformity continues for smaller firms in the north and east, but for the south and west the ratios for these smaller firms are much higher.

It is obvious that the purchasing power of the population to be served is a major factor in determining demand for building construction, and consequently for architectural personnel. *Table 55* and *Figure 22* present the ratios of firms per billion dollars of urban purchasing power.[24] If one-man offices are included the ratio was 86.5. This means national ratios for size groups as follows:

15.2 one-man offices per $billion						} or one office per	$18 millions	
38.8 firms with	1–4	employees per $billion							
18.1 "	"	5–9	"	"	"	or "	"	"	$55 "
8.6 "	"	10–19	"	"	"	or "	"	"	$116 "
4.0 "	"	20–39	"	"	"	or "	"	"	$250 "
1.3 "	"	40–99	"	"	"	or "	"	"	$770 "
0.6 "	"	100 or more "	"	"	"	or "	"	"	$1,667 "

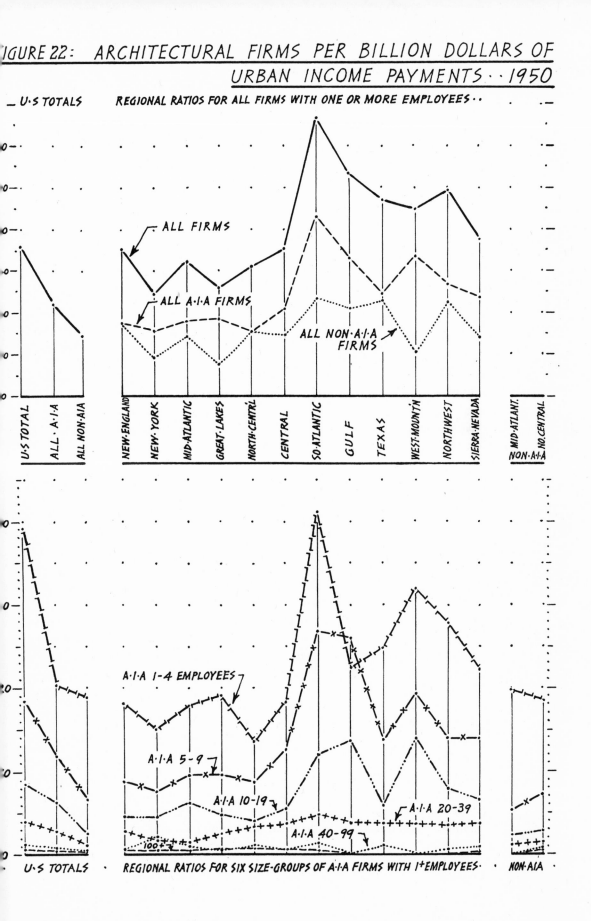

FIGURE 22: ARCHITECTURAL FIRMS PER BILLION DOLLARS OF URBAN INCOME PAYMENTS ·· 1950

U·S TOTALS   REGIONAL RATIOS FOR ALL FIRMS WITH ONE OR MORE EMPLOYEES ··

ALL FIRMS

ALL A·I·A FIRMS

ALL NON·A·I·A FIRMS

U·S TOTAL — ALL·A·I·A — ALL NON·AIA

NEW·ENGLAND · NEW·YORK · MID·ATLANTIC · GREAT·LAKES · NORTH·CENTRL · CENTRAL · SO·ATLANTIC · GULF · TEXAS · WEST·MOUNT'N · NORTHWEST · SIERRA·NEVADA

MID·ATLANT. NON·A·I·A — NO.CENTRAL

A·I·A 1-4 EMPLOYEES

A·I·A 5-9

A·I·A 10-19

A·I·A 20-39

A·I·A 40-99

100+

U·S TOTALS   ·   REGIONAL RATIOS FOR SIX SIZE·GROUPS OF A·I·A FIRMS WITH 1+EMPLOYEES·   ·   NON·AIA

Since the regional ratios are based upon the same distribution of firms used for the straight population ratios previously described, the two sets of regional profiles exhibit the same general configurations. Nevertheless, disparity of income produces marked effects. The higher income rates enjoyed by the six northeastern regions reduces the number of firms per unit of purchasing power. Conversely the lower income rates of the southern regions made their ratios the highest. This is particularly noticeable in the South Atlantic region. On the other hand high western incomes brought the high population ratios of these regions down to somewhat lower purchasing power ratios.

It must be pointed out that such studies have many defects in attempting to describe complex human activities in terms of simple proportions. The income index used, while the best available, does not reflect the higher income rates of urban, as opposed to total population, nor does it take into account important sources of construction demand, such as corporate income, except as this indirectly affects the general economy of a geographical area. Urban population likewise is an imperfect criterion of demand since it does not indicate the higher building rates of new or developing areas. Furthermore urban population fails to include temporary residents whose demand for building accommodation can support many architectural firms, as is amply demonstrated by the high ratios of the South Atlantic region which is dominated by the State of Florida. Finally no statistical method seems able to allow for interregional architectural practices. Nevertheless the ratios here given, if carefully interpreted, can be immensely useful in understanding many aspects of the profession.

It is plausible to predict the number of private practitioner firms required to serve a 1960 urban population of 110.0 millions. Assuming that 1950 ratios will be maintained, a total increase of about 2700 firms is indicated, making a grand total of around 13,700. This means a distribution among size-groups as follows:

<pre>
 464 new one-man offices for a total of 2409 offices
1174 " firms with 1–4 employees for a total of 6127 offices
 550 "   "   "   5–9   "   " " " " 2860   "
 258 "   "   "   10–19   "   " " " " 1353   "
 115 "   "   "   20–39   "   " " " "   616   "
  43 "   "   "   40–99   "   " " " "   209   "
  22 "   "   " 100 or more "   " " " "   99   "
</pre>

In conclusion it must be realized that statistical studies of architects are of recent origin and that both methods and data require prolonged investigation. Nevertheless there is increasing appreciation of the desirability of authentic information on the size, composition, character, and distribution of the profession. The *1950 Survey* constituted an important initial step in this direction, but one set of data, no matter how comprehensively or carefully compiled, remains insufficient for the discovery of trends. It is apparent therefore that if the architectural profession is to meet its problems rationally and realistically, rather than with uninformed hunches, it must undertake to collect and study such data on a continuing and systematic basis. It seems obvious that the American Institute of Architects is the logical agency to perform this neglected function (*Recommendation 2*).

NOTES: CHAPTER TWO

[1] ". . . modern architects have been unique in believing that the three demands (structural, functional, and aesthetic) are equally important, and that the best architecture is that which satisfies them equally . . . (and that) a reliable test of quality in modern architecture (is) that the less separable the expression of function, structure, and beauty in a building, the more nearly it approaches the ideal of our epoch." (Edgar Kaufman, Jr., "What is Happening to Modern Architecture," *Michigan Society of Architects Weekly Bulletin*. Vol. 23, March 1, 1949, p. 2.)

[2] Cf., AIA, Document 300, *Standards of Practice*. 1941, pp. 5–6; statements of various AIA chapters on architectural services (Cowgill, C. H. and Small, B. J.: *Architectural Practice*, 1949, revised edition, pp. 172, 180, 182, 184–185, 188); AIA: *Handbook of Architectural Practice, 1951*.

[3] These tentative studies and the Basic Design were long called "preliminary sketches." Since this latter term gives laymen an entirely erroneous impression and fails utterly to recognize the extensive and serious thought devoted to the preparation of such studies, and also seems to deny their marked importance in the development of the final building, its use should cease. The term "preliminary studies" is less frivolous, but still not sufficiently indicative of their true character. For these reasons, the term, *Basic Design,* has been adopted in this Report, following in part the term, *Basic Drawings,* used in the 1941 edition of the *Standards of Practice of the AIA* (Document 300, p. 5).

[4] Of 131 firms interviewed for *Progressive Architecture* in 1949, only 16 per cent claimed specialties, and of 100 firms interviewed in 1950, only 14 per cent. (*Progressive Architecture:* "How Building Products Get into Buildings," 1949; "Facts for Planning Building Product Sales," 1950.)

[5] 61 of 100 firms had been retained as consultants (*Progressive Architecture:* "Facts" *op. cit.*).

[6] An estimate of the number of one-man offices of individual practitioners may be calculated:
2676 AIA individual practitioner offices were reported by 3744 AIA responders (*Table 1*). This was 71.47 per cent, which applied to 8461 AIA registered architects (*Table 1*) gives 6047 offices.
1340 Non-AIA offices were reported by 2861 Non-AIA responders. This was 46.84 per cent, which applied to 10,676 Non-AIA registered architects gives 5000 offices.
Table 23 gives a total of 3377 individual practitioner offices reporting one or more employees. This total included 2377 AIA and 1000 Non-AIA offices. 2377 is 88.84 per cent of 2676 responding AIA offices. 1000 is 74.62 per cent of 1340 responding Non-AIA offices.
Applying these ratios to the estimated totals of 6047 AIA and 5000 Non-AIA offices gives 5371 AIA and 3731 Non-AIA offices with one or more employees.
Subtracting these from the totals leaves 676 AIA and 1269 Non-AIA one-man offices, or a total of 1945.

[7] In 1926 the *American Architect* conducted a survey of individual practitioner firms. (Summarized in Cowgill and Small, *op. cit.*, pp. 86–87.) The 1926 and 1950 distributions were:

	1926	1950 Survey*
Principal alone or with one employee	25.0%	26.6%
2–4 employees	43.0	33.5
5–9	20.3	22.0
10–19	9.0	10.7
20–39	2.0	4.9
40–79	0.6 }	2.4
80 and more	0.1 }	

* This distribution has been modified from that just given in the text in order to permit comparison. It is based on a total of 4016 firms and assumes 639 one-man firms (4016–3377).

It seems clear that the trend has been toward larger professional organizations. It should also be noted that, in terms of constant dollars, the volume of building construction in both 1926 and 1950 was practically the same (*Table 53*).

[8] The calculation of these medians is complicated by the fact that while 3377 firms (2377 AIA and 1000 Non-AIA) out of 4016 (2676 AIA and 1340 Non-AIA) reported one or more employees, 124 (75 AIA and 49 Non-AIA) had to be discarded for various reasons in the compilation of *Table 26*, which, therefore, gives the size of 3253 firms (2302 AIA and 951 Non-AIA) with one or more employees. The medians were consequently based on proportionately reduced totals,

$$3868 \left(= \frac{4016 \times 3253}{3377} \right) \text{ for all firms, } 2591 \left(= \frac{2676 \times 2302}{2377} \right) \text{ for AIA firms,}$$

$$\text{and } 1274 \left(= \frac{1340 \times 951}{1000} \right) \text{ for Non-AIA firms.}$$

[9] The national and regional distribution of firms and architects is discussed in Section 5 of this chapter.

[10] The average number of principals per firm agrees exactly with the number of partners per firm found by the 1950 independent survey already cited (*Progressive Architecture:* "Facts for Planning Building Product Sales," 1950).

[11] The occasional absence of these qualities has at times led to disagreements, suspicion, and even antagonism, which provoked a segment in each profession to desire the absorption of the other or to assume the other's functions. Nevertheless, these unfortunate differences should not be allowed to obscure the existence over a long period of close and beneficial collaboration between many members of both professions. In recent years, the rapidly expanding elaboration of engineering installations in buildings and a growing appreciation of the necessity of intimate cooperation to integrate these installations fully into the complete building have fostered increasing mutual understanding and respect. It is conceivable that the association and harmony of interests could be stimulated even more by organizing joint meetings, either independently or within the AIA itself, in which architecturally-minded engineers and architects with special engineering interests could participate together. Indeed, in time, consideration might be given to the provision of special AIA membership for engineers primarily concerned with building problems. In any case, the AIA should continue to strengthen understanding and cooperation at the national level by working with the American Society of Civil Engineers and the National Society of Professional Engineers. In turn, this should do much to resolve misunderstanding and frictions at state and local levels.

[12] For a case history, see John R. Fugard, "Large Offices from Small," (*Journal of the AIA*, v. 18, Oct., 1952, pp. 176–180).

[13] AIA, Document 356, *Functions of the Consultant*. March 5, 1952. This statement, the result of two years of study, should guide all architects not only in their own relations with consultants, but also in explaining to clients the proper relationship of consultants to both clients and architects.

[14] Thomas H. Creighton, "How Good is your Office Organization," (*Progressive Architecture*, Nov., 1948, pp. 77–78).

[15] Since, for the most part, these departments are maintained by large corporations with long-term construction, alteration, and maintenance programs, their employees have been referred to in several sections of this Report as *company architects*. Likewise, the comparable employees in governmental agencies have been termed *bureau architects*.

In the presentations of the characteristics of architects which follow, it should be noted that *company architects* and *architects employed by private practitioners* are classified together under the heading, "Private Employee Architects." This classification was adopted early in the Commission's study with the thought that the two groups were naturally associated. Subsequent study has indicated that it would have been preferable to keep them separate in order to obtain a clearer picture of *company architects* alone, comparable to that of *bureau architects*. It would also be desirable to know the group characteristics of *architects employed by private practitioners*.

[16] The *1940 Census* reported the median age of all "census architects" as 43, and the distribution by age-groups of 19,899 employed male "architects" as follows:

18–19	0.2%	45–54	26.1%
20–24	3.4	55–64	12.7
25–34	25.0	65–74	5.1
35–44	26.8	75–	0.7

[17] The estimates of firms and employee totals are calculated as follows:

	a. Firms responding	b. Individuals responding	Per cent	c. Total architects	d. Total firms	e. Minus 1-man firms	f. Average No. Employees	g. No. of Employees
Individual								
practitioners	4016	6605		19137	11047	9102		76,842
AIA	2676	3744	71.47	8461	6047	5371	10.0	53,710
Non-AIA	1340	2861	46.84	10676	5000	3731	6.2	23,132
Private dept.								
offices	289	6605		19137	891			29,266
AIA	124	3744	3.3	8461	276		43.2	11,923
Non-AIA	165	2861	5.8	10676	615		28.2	17,343
Public bureaus	181	6605		19137	565			22,781
AIA	74	3744	2.0	8461	167		22.5	3,757
Non-AIA	107	2861	3.7	10676	398		47.8	19,024

Sources: a. *Table 25;* b. *Table 1;* c. *Table 1;* e. *Note 7;* f. *Table 25*

Calculation: $\frac{a}{b} \times c = d$; d (or e) $\times f = g$

The total estimated number of firms is 12,503. This is roughly confirmed by an estimate of 11,000 firms made by the Social Security Administration based on those paying Old Age and Survivor Insurance contributions. Since one-man firms do not make such payments, the SSA figure is comparable when 1945 one-man firms are deducted from the 12,503 estimate, giving 10,558 firms with employees.

The calculation given above probably overestimates the number of private department offices, due to the inclusion of extra-curricular practices of architects employed by other architects. Since, however, all firms reported in the group total only 289, and since both architects and firms of departments and bureaus are approximately equal in number and proportions, the error is probably small.

[18] Urban population, as here used, conforms to the Bureau of Census' pre-1950 definition of all population residing in incorporated communities of 2500 or more. The new 1950 basis includes certain unincorporated communities lying in metropolitan areas. The earlier basis is used here in order to obtain comparable ratios for the period, 1850–1950. Although some objection might be raised as to the inclusion of villages of 2500, tests prove that no significant differences in the relative ratios are produced when the 2500 minimum is adopted.

[19] The Census enumerations, long discounted because they included all who claimed the title of "architect," have been largely vindicated by recent studies. In 1950, the total of 24,756 in this classification included landscape architects estimated at 4.76 per cent, or 1178. This leaves 23,578 "census architects," 23.2 per cent more than the *1950 Survey's* 19,137 registered architects. The 1950 Census also included under architects, occupations entitled "architectural supervisors" and "superintendents in architectural offices." On the other hand, draftsmen and architectural engineers were placed in separate classifications. Thus, while the extra 23 per cent cannot be given specific architectural titles, in number they represent only 4419 additional persons, or one for every 2.4 firms, or 4.9 per cent of the 90,350 architectural personnel estimated in Section 4 of this chapter. In view of census procedure, therefore, the totals of registered and census architects are surprisingly comparable.

The census estimate of 1178 landscape architects seems acceptable in view of the fact that in 1950 the American Society of Landscape Architects reported 457 members in the United States, or 38.9 per cent of 1178, which compares with a 36.0 per cent ratio between AIA membership and the number of "census architects."

If it is assumed that landscape architects are distributed among AIA regions in the same pattern exhibited by registered architects, the 1950 regional distribution of "census architects" may be calculated as follows:

	Census Totals	% in Region	Lands. Archts.	Census Archts.	Regis. Archts. %	Differ- ence	Cen.Ar.÷ Reg. Ar.
U. S.	24,756	100.0	1178	23,578	100.0	—	123.2
N. England	1834	7.4	87	1747	7.9	+.5	116.1
New York	3849	15.5	183	3666	15.4	−.1	124.5
M. Atlantic	4358	17.6	207	4151	17.7	+.1	122.2
Great Lakes	2581	10.4	123	2458	10.5	+.1	121.7
N. Central	2499	10.1	119	2380	10.9	+.8	114.2
Central	1418	5.7	67	1351	6.1	+.4	116.1
S. Atlantic	1476	6.0	70	1406	5.9	−.1	124.6
Gulf	1066	4.3	51	1015	4.3	0	121.8
Texas	1266	5.1	60	1206	5.0	−.1	125.1
W. Mountain	595	2.4	28	567	2.1	−.3	139.7
Northwest	990	4.0	47	943	3.8	−.2	130.4
Sierra Nev.	2824	11.4	134	2690	10.3	−1.1	136.5

The regional distribution of landscape architects could also be based on the 1950 pattern of ASLA membership, but in no case would the regional percentages be changed more than 0.2. Inspection of the regional ratios of census architects to registered architects (last column above) reveals that the three western regions taken together have a ratio of 135.5, in contrast to 120.7 for the rest of the country. This uniformly high bias in the west is an interesting phenomenon. It should also be noted that the midwestern group—North Central and Central—has a very low ratio of 114.8.

From 1910 through 1940, census enumerations grouped naval architects with architects. The Bureau of the Census estimates that naval architects formed 2 per cent of the totals. Since their regional distribution most certainly does not parallel that of architects, and since the effect of the group on the ratios and percentages is negligible, no attempt has been made to eliminate them in this study.

It would appear, therefore, that census enumerations of architects do offer valid information on the size, distribution, and evolution of the profession. Since there is no other statistical basis for such studies, the judicious use of census data seems strongly indicated.

[20] The architect-population data here presented were developed from an unpublished manuscript, *The Profession of Architecture, 1850–1950, a study of its size and opportunities,* by Turpin C. Bannister.

[21] *Table 24* shows an average of 1.4 registered architects in AIA private practitioner offices and 0.9 in Non-AIA offices. These were 13.5 and 13.6 per cent respectively of the 10.4 and 6.6 employees in these firms (*Table 24*).

[22] The estimates are confined to firms with one or more employees. The method of calculation was as follows:

1. The number of responding firms in each size-group in each region (obtained from the percentages given in *Table 20*) was adjusted to compensate for the difference between the percentage of response and the percentage of registered architects in the region (*Table 1*). The adjustment factors are given in *Table 55*.
2. The estimated national totals of 5371 AIA and 3731 Non-AIA individual practitioner firms (see *Note 17*) were distributed regionally in proportion to the adjusted regional totals.
3. The regional totals were next distributed to regional size-groups in proportions established by *Table 26*.
4. The ratio of firms to urban population was then found. See *Note 18* for definition of urban population.

Except for the national total, regional totals, and the size-groups in the Middle Atlantic and North Central regions, *Table 26* limits calculations to AIA firms.

[23] This assumes 1945 one-man offices, 676 AIA and 1269 Non-AIA (see *Note 6*). The national ratios for these were 2.19 for all, 0.76 for AIA, and 1.43 for Non-AIA.

[24] Urban purchasing power is defined as the product of urban population and Per Capita Income Payments, an index published annually for each state by the Office of Business Economics, U. S. Department of Commerce.

CHAPTER III

The Profession of Architecture

1. THE NATURE OF A PROFESSION

Because the practice of architecture has long been regarded as a profession, the meaning and implications of the term are of special concern to all architects. The nature of a profession thus deserves brief summary.

The bases of the professions rest in the fact that laymen, in meeting many problems of daily life, need recourse to special areas of learning involving knowledge, understanding, and insight far beyond their own acquaintance. For assistance in such matters, they must turn, therefore, to those who, through prolonged formal training and experience, command these disciplines and possess the skill to apply them effectively to the practical affairs of others. Thus, a profession differs from a skilled trade by requiring complex intellectual effort rather than mere mechanical dexterity, and from commerce by rendering to the client a personal service compassing a high level of objective counsel, guidance, and art.[1]

Since it is difficult for laymen to judge professional competence and procedures, they must rely primarily on the professional group to establish and maintain criteria. In other words, society has come to recognize each responsible practitioner-group as the arbiter of its own standards of practice, and, in return for the performance of this socially useful control, confers upon the group the status and privileges of a profession.

These privileges are very real. They include the sincere respect which most men willingly accord to special capacity and proven competence. The most precious privilege, however, lies in the freedom which a profession enjoys in determining, for itself and with the minimum of external interference compatible with social purpose, the means and methods of fulfilling its own highest objectives. Furthermore, since a profession is not a separate entity, but is, in fact, a group of cooperating members, these objectives, means, and methods must arise by mutual consent. This is a process which not only assures the most vital program possible, but which also, by stimulating individual members to apply their own directives to their own daily practice, promises the highest degree of accomplishment and gratification. Thus, in every sense, the opportunities and the enlightened self-interests of the group coincide with its social responsibilities.

The development and maintenance of standards of professional practice embrace three major obligations. First is the establishment of conditions of service which are conducive to optimal social benefits. As long as the relationship between individual practitioners remains at the level of ruthless unbridled competition, low quality tends to drive out high, and unsuspecting clients discover too late the penalties of cut-rate service. Inevitably the competence of all practitioners becomes suspect, and soon the whole profession forfeits the public confidence on which its very existence is premised. Therefore, in the best interest of the public they serve, as well as for their own survival, the members of a profession must create and maintain conditions which permit the most effective service. Cynics sometimes charge that this is merely a pious subterfuge to gain monopolistic advantage, but professions cannot escape their public duty to promote an atmosphere which fosters high standards of performance. On such a basis, codes of professional behavior, far from being idle pretenses, become fundamental aids to social utility.

The second obligation of a profession is to enhance the competence of its members by expanding technical knowledge and skills. In this regard, the basic concept is that there should be no private secrets, but that each member, in return for complete access to the whole body of professional knowledge, assumes the duty of sharing his own discoveries with his colleagues as promptly as possible. From their inception, professions have stimulated this course by according recognition and prestige to those who report significant findings and by providing the means of disseminating these results as widely as possible through professional meetings and publications. In many instances, professional societies have initiated for this purpose the first technical press in their respective fields. In certain professions, notably medicine and engineering, the cumulative effect of this policy has revolutionized practice by multiplying technical resources and competence a thousandfold. It is indeed questionable whether any group which fails to pursue an active program of this kind has yet earned true professional status.

The third obligation which a profession must assume is the constant renewal of its own personnel, so that the services for which it is responsible will continue to be available to society. This means not only the administration of standards of admission to membership within the profession itself, but also the recruiting and training of suitable candidates. At times, some professions have misused their power of selecting new members in order to restrict competition, but the risk of public disfavor for failure to meet social needs usually deters and corrects such shortsighted perversions. In reality, the artificial limitation of membership does not forestall competition, but only debases it by denying aspirants the guidance and discipline of the profession. It also prevents established practitioners from obtaining properly trained assistants, and this, in turn, adversely affects the scope and quality of their practice. Thus, for its own good, a profession must maintain a steady and sufficient flow of competent recruits.

Since the attainment of competence by recruits means the acquisition of the learning and skills requisite to practice, and, therefore, prolonged formal training, the professions incur the duty of promoting appropriate programs of professional education. On the one hand, this involves either actual instruction by practitioners, or general guidance and assistance for educational agencies conducting organized professional curricula. On the other hand, it also signifies a duty to initiate graduates into the practical conduct of professional services. These two duties go hand in hand and cannot be separated.

Because the professions themselves are not prepared to furnish financial support on the scale required for modern professional education, this function has perforce been delegated to institutions of higher learning. The professions have normally exerted their influence upon these institutional programs by assuming the right to accredit those conforming to approved standards. On the whole, the results have been beneficial, but in recent years the institutions, confronted by multiplying and sometimes competing accrediting groups, have resisted this external pressure as both excessive and destructive to the institution's own integrity. Fortunately, in most cases, resentment can be forestalled by tact and realism, but, if educational institutions presume to train personnel for professional careers, they cannot expect the professions to accept their graduates without question, nor can they afford to divorce themselves from reality by dispensing with professional guidance. On the other hand, unless the professions can assume the heavy burdens of independent programs, they have no other choice than to assist the institutions in every way possible. Professional education is no easy task, and the solution of its problems will require the close cooperation of all who are concerned with its success.

Because professional men are also citizens, they share, both individually and as a group, the duty of all members of society to promote general well-being and progress. Moreover, insofar as a profession merits its claim to special capacity, it must assume the responsibilities of leadership in the attainment of social goals, particularly those for which its capacity bestows special insight. Concern for such goals, far from being a burden, benefits a profession not only by the resulting achievements which its members enjoy, but also by the wholesome liaison which it establishes between practitioners and all segments of society. In turn, successful participation in community affairs promotes wider public confidence in professional competence. Thus, as so often is the case, duty to society and enlightened self-interest join in mutual support.

The concept of a profession implied by the obligations just described is the product of long evolution. For fulfillment it required the attainment of conditions permitting independent practice in sufficient volume to provide adequate economic security through professional fees, and the emergence of a consciously cohesive group whose members not only considered themselves as a profession, but also were able to win public recognition for their claim. By these standards the development of the professions has been a comparatively recent phenomenon. Antiquity produced no such groups. During the Middle Ages, the newly organized universities trained theologians, ecclesiastical lawyers, and physicians, but these practitioners, serving royal or clerical patrons, failed to coalesce into real professional groups. At a lower level of responsibility craft guilds performed some of the functions which later characterized the professions.

The first real professional groups appeared in England soon after the secularization of the universities. In 1518, the Royal College of Physicians of London became the prototype of later professional societies. In 1540, the Barber-Surgeons Company, originally a guild, attained professional status. Not until the middle of the 18th century, however, did the movement gain general headway. The Law Society in 1739, the Society of Civil Engineers in 1771, and the Veterinary College in 1791, were tentative attempts, but, with the turn of the 19th century, an increasing number of groups asserted their claims and won recognition. The first were reconstitutions, the College of Surgeons in 1800, the Institution of Civil Engineers in 1818, and the Law Society in 1827. Thereafter, new groups rapidly appeared.

In the United States, a parallel trend saw the growth first of local societies and then national organizations, such as the American Institute of Homeopathy in 1844, the American Medical Association in 1847, the American Society of Civil Engineers and the American Pharmaceutical Association, both in 1852. There followed the American Dental Association in 1859, the American Bankers Association in 1875, the American Bar Association in 1875, and a host of others in subsequent decades of the nineteenth and twentieth centuries.

The pattern of development which these professional organizations have exhibited has been remarkably uniform. In their initial stages their membership policies have tended to focus upon outstanding leaders in the larger centers to the exclusion of lesser practitioners. This is not surprising because at the beginning the adoption of any set of acceptable standards is necessarily a disruption of the status quo which has created the need for organization. Since the quality of these standards depends upon the vision which leaders have of the needs and potentialities of the profession, the professional society requires a concerted educational campaign to show that it is not a selfish device of the leaders, as some professionals may suspect, but is a body organized to improve the whole profession. In time, the new standards usually win wide support and can be progressively strengthened. Sooner or later, when the group has demonstrated its effectiveness in expanding professional knowledge and ameliorating malpractices, every practitioner comes to realize that he can no longer afford to withhold participation. Gradually, therefore, the society develops national scope and becomes the normal channel through which all individual practitioners exert their influence in ordering the conditions and standards of their service.

Some may decry the emergence of a strong and unified profession as establishing only another pressure group. This is a valid criticism if a profession forgets its social origin and purpose. When, however, it maintains these as the core of its program, the result is not self-interest but true social benefit, the only legitimate source of its recognition and the only fruitful basis for its long-term progress. Moreover, in a society as complex and as vast as our own, the individual, if he is to contribute to more than his own local sphere, must join with his fellows to secure desired action. This is the normal process of social life. Participation in one's profession is, therefore, a necessary conclusion for all practitioners who seek the enhancement of their art.

Because professions are only quasi-public institutions, membership cannot be compelled. For this reason adherence to standards of service and conduct remains on a voluntary basis. But they are nonetheless binding. No doubt there will always be a residue of selfish individuals who will continue to take parasitical advantage of the group effort, but the strength which many professions have already attained demonstrates that most practitioners wish to conduct themselves so as to retain the sanction of their colleagues and the respect of society. In such matters, the professions will find that a patient, but steady, program of education will bring surer progress than spasmodic denunciations.

The fact that a profession is an association formed of individual members cooperating voluntarily and freely, makes it a particularly appropriate instrument of democratic society. Therein lie its greatest potentialities. Its strength springs from individual recognition that cooperation is indispensable for common growth and that willing participation will not only secure tangible and intangible benefits, but that in the process a mere vocation is transformed into an exhilarating calling. It is no accident, therefore, that the term *professional* has come to connote high status and respected competence.

2. THE PROFESSION OF ARCHITECTURE

The emergence of the profession of architecture conformed to the general pattern just described. Despite the acknowledged skill of individual architects in antiquity, no professional group ever appeared. During the Middle Ages, building craftsmen associated in guilds, but architects, though they were trained in such crafts and no doubt maintained affiliation with their craft guild, never achieved a separate professional organization of their own. When architecture became a fine art in the Renaissance, architects frequently practiced as painters and sculptors as well, and thus naturally took active part in the new academies of art. Not until 1671, however, was the first solely architectural group established at Paris as the Royal Academy of Architecture. At regular weekly meetings, its members investigated and codified technical knowledge. Classes were held for members' pupils. Thus, the Academy exhibited many professional characteristics, but, since its membership was restricted to carefully selected royal appointees, it heralded, rather than fulfilled the modern concept of a profession. The academy pattern gradually spread to most European courts.

With the rise of new conditions of practice at the end of the 18th century, private practitioners began to feel the need for professional association. In England, tentative groups formed in London in 1791 and 1806, and in Paris in 1812. The first permanent national society of architects, the *Society for the Propagation of Architecture in Holland,* was founded in 1819. A similar step was taken in England with the organization in 1834 of the *Institute of British Architects.* Its members were to be

"architects of prominent position and unimpeachable character, educated for and following their profession, and free from those conflicting relations with trade which in the early part of this century did exist in some instances, and prevented that implicit confidence on the part of the public which should enable a client to regard his architect not only as his agent, but as his friend and adviser."[2]

In 1837, the Institute was chartered, and in 1866 became the *Royal Institute* so familiar today. At first the membership was composed of London architects, who formed a close-knit homogeneous group who could participate directly in its meetings, technical discussions, and committees. Conditions of practice and the problems of professional education received early attention. Stimulated by this metropolitan example, provincial societies soon appeared, at Oxford in 1837, Exeter in 1843, and thereafter many others. Gradually, however, by undertaking essential professional functions, the RIBA attained that national scope and leadership which it exercises so effectively at the present time. The example of the Institute of British Architects inspired quick emulation. In 1837, the Swiss Society of Engineers and Architects was formed, followed in 1840 by the Central Society of French Architects.

In the United States professional organization followed a similar course. The first such group may have been *The Brethren of the Workshop of Vitruvius,* which existed in New York in 1803.[3] Usually, however, architects were so few in number that they first joined forces with painters and sculptors. Thus, in 1810 Latrobe and Mills were members of the Pennsylvania Academy of Fine Arts.[4] Jefferson and Mills were active in the Columbian Society of Artists a few years later.[5] The New York Academy of Fine Arts, founded in 1802, and its outgrowth, the National Academy of Design, established in 1826 with the aid of Ithiel Town, also included a number of architects.

Increase in the number of architects and the example of the Institute of British Architects led to the formation in New York in 1836 of the American Institution of Architects, the first strictly professional group in the United States. William Strickland served as president and Thomas Ustick Walter as secretary.[6] In spite of an auspicious beginning, the society languished.

Nineteen years later, in 1857, a permanent organization, The American Institute of Architects, was finally achieved by thirteen New York practitioners led by Richard Upjohn. Meetings with technical programs were held, first in Upjohn's office, and later in quarters at New York University. Since Richard Morris Hunt was a member, since he was the first American graduate of the *Ecole des beaux-arts,* and since he was then conducting an *atelier* in his own office, it is not surprising that professional education attracted early discussion. National scope was intended from the start, and architects from Philadelphia, Providence, and Boston soon became members. Nevertheless, out-of-towners found it difficult to attend, and in 1861 a Philadelphia group formed the Pennsylvania Institute of Architects to meet local needs.

From 1862 to 1864 the Civil War forced suspension, but with the return of peace, The AIA promptly renewed its activities. The necessity for accommodating local groups was gradually recognized and, at the first convention in New York in March, 1867, a system of chapters was adopted, with the New York group becoming the first unit. In 1869, the Philadelphia and Chicago chapters were welcomed; and, in 1870, chapters were established at Boston, Baltimore, and Cincinnati. Rhode Island followed in 1875, and San Francisco in 1881.

This Institute expansion paralleled the trebling of U. S. architects between 1860 and 1880, but, during the 1880's alone, the number of architects multiplied 2.4 times. It was not surprising, therefore, that, in his presidential address to the 1886 AIA Convention, Thomas U. Walter could cite the formation of twelve new western architectural societies and envision a national confederation of architects.[7] Three more chapters were admitted in 1887, Washington, D. C., Central New York, and Michigan, but the potentialities of true national scope were embraced more vigorously by amalgamation in 1889 with the largest Non-AIA society, the Western Association of Architects. In the 1890's the addition of twelve more chapters brought the total to twenty-three.

During the first two decades of the 20th century, Institute membership increased slowly under a somewhat overconservative admission policy. By 1920, the roll stood at about 1300, and in 1930 at 3400. Depression years brought a decline to 3100 in 1940. Meanwhile, progressive leaders recognized the need to make The Institute a more inclusive professional organization and, during the early '40's, conducted an energetic unification program which resulted in the incorporation of most of the separate state associations within The Institute. By 1950, membership reached 8461, 44 per cent of all registered architects in the United States and 2.7 times the 1940 roster. In 1952, the roll totaled 9242 corporate members.

This phenomenal growth has dramatically underscored the position of The AIA as the prime professional organization of U. S. architects. For this reason the profession now enjoys a recognized and respected medium through which it can express its considered views on matters affecting its opportunities and conditions of service. In the dynamic and competitive society in which we live, the maintenance of such an agency constitutes a necessary protection for both the public at large and the profession.

A strong profession is likewise essential if its inherent responsibilities are to be met with maximum effectiveness. The winning and dissemination of new professional knowledge demand concentrated effort and resources for the promotion of architectural research in all its phases. The need for systematic investigation and refinement of the architectural process itself is clear. The adaptation of this process to new conditions of practice is a never-ending task, and the improvement of services by a heightened quality of professional education and training will always remain a fundamental problem.

The physical expansion of The Institute was undertaken because the total resources of a thoroughly unified profession were an essential prerequisite for a comprehensive program. While unification was still in progress, the operational structure of the Institute was completely reorganized. Results thus far already indicate the unlimited benefits that can be derived through the cooperation of a large, alert, and enlightened membership. The creative process by which fine architecture is won will always remain a matter of individual effort and individual genius, but even the most talented genius must depend upon the resources of the profession for the elements and principles he exploits. If these resources are meager and crude, practitioner and client suffer alike. Enhancement of resources, therefore, cannot fail to undergird both. This must be the primary motive of any professional endeavor and as such it amply justifies the most vigorous support of all who claim professional rank.

To perform the professional function of defining and administering equitable conditions of service, The AIA has developed over the years explicit policies which are given formal statement in its official document entitled *Standards of Professional Practice*.[8] The first part of this statement deals with the *Obligations of Good Practice*. Here is stressed: the necessity and meaning of competence and integrity as the indispensable bases of professional conduct; the character of high-quality services; and the duty of active support of the profession itself. The second part contains the *Mandatory Rules* which guard the quality of architectural services by outlawing practices which experience has shown to be detrimental. Thus, for example, an architect's remuneration for services must be confined to his professional compensation. The establishment and enforcement of this principle is an essential safeguard against the abuse of concealed profits from construction operations which once plagued the profession and threatened to destroy public confidence in its integrity. For this reason, an architect may not engage in building contracting or take part in or derive income in any way from the vending of building materials, equipment, or furnishings. The *Mandatory Rules* likewise prohibit unfair competitive acts which at one time seemed likely to reduce all practice to the lowest possible level. Thus, in the public interest of protecting the quality and availability of services, the rules forbid the performance of services without compensation, with the particular aim of eliminating pressure for free "sketches," the unfortunate term by which the time-consuming Basic Design drawings were formerly known to laymen. Self-protection likewise motivates the regulation that architects may participate in formal public competitions only if they comply with AIA-administered safeguards. Similarly, individual practitioners are relieved of costly promotional publicity by the restriction of advertising to improving public appreciation of the whole profession and its services.

It should be noted again that these rules of professional conduct cannot be given legal force, but rather form standards based on the profession's own collective experience and maintained by the profession's own self-discipline. Acceptance of them is integral with the assumption of Institute membership, and members who deviate from their letter and spirit are subject to serious penalties by The Institute. In a wide-flung activity, such as architecture, enmeshed as it is in complex affairs affording frequent temptations to seek short-term competitive advantages, it is not surprising that some individuals betray the very practical ideals of their profession. What is truly amazing is the extraordinary general allegiance which these ideals have won from enlightened practitioners who are actuated solely by voluntary cooperation and self-restraint. No doubt much remains to be done, but the advances of the past half-century promise that continued education, example, and leadership can bring even wider adherence to sound professional principles.

From the first organization of The Institute, professional education has occupied a prominent place in its deliberations. Early members called for the establishment of a national professional school, but with the appearance of the American collegiate system The Institute quickly bestowed full support. For many years The AIA Committee on Education served as the principal adviser and liaison to the schools. The Institute, through its Student Medals, has long fostered academic excellence, and its generous support has enabled the National Architectural Accrediting Board to perform its important functions. During the past decade, increasing attention has been given to programs of advanced studies calculated to expand the technical competence of all segments of the profession.

It is apparent, therefore, that the profession of architecture fulfills in every sense the general demands of professional status. It is also clear that The AIA, as the focal organization of the profession, has reflected in the growth and variety of its activities the progressively broadening concept of the proper scope of the professions in contemporary society. Today, this concept embraces a comprehensiveness of membership, a completeness of program, and a scale of participation that a generation ago would have seemed sheer wishful utopianism. As the second half of the century unfolds, no doubt this present concept will be modified to encompass new needs and conditions. Although prophecy is hazardous, it would seem that the greatest professional opportunity and promise lie in a conscious and concerted effort to expand architectural knowledge. This is the field which, for historic reasons, the profession has hardly begun to exploit, and which, because of its implications for competence and education, holds the greatest promise of professional advancement. The degree to which the profession and The Institute meet this challenge can well become the measure of its vitality and maturity.

3. THE QUALIFICATIONS OF AN ARCHITECT

The performance of architectural services, the conduct of practice, and participation in the profession of architecture, all imply definite traits and capabilities in the person who undertakes them. Difficult as it is to reduce these characteristics to formal expression, it is a necessary step in any serious analysis of the qualifications and education of an architect.

From the discussion of architectural services and practice presented in *Chapter II*, it is clear that an architect must excel in the following technical activities:

1. Analysis

Programming, research, evaluation, definition of fundamental conditions and elements.

2. Design

Functional, structural, equipment, aesthetic synthesis, and the integration of all aspects of a problem into an harmonious and purposeful unity.

3. Communication

Graphic: sketching, rendering, instrumental drawing, modeling.
Writing: reports, programs, specifications, contracts, directions, correspondence.
Speaking: expositions, conferences, directions.

4. Executive activities

Promotion, finance, estimates, costs, accounting, business law, supervision, administration.

Membership in the profession of architecture adds to these capabilities certain wider responsibilities to society itself. These obligations stem from the fact that, though aspirants to professional status contribute individual talent and effort, the cumulative fund of special experience which makes individual contributions productive derives from professional and social groups. In partaking of the opportunities thus afforded, the individual aspirant assumes an inescapable debt to conserve and extend the resources he has enjoyed, and to maintain and raise the standards of performance of his group. More specifically, the professional architect must accept the following responsibilities:

1. To develop himself and his profession to maximum social usefulness.
2. To improve his own competence and that of his profession by increasing and sharing architectural knowledge.
3. To ensure the future of his profession through active participation in the recruiting and training of an adequate number of high-quality candidates.

If the personal technical capabilities and the professional responsibilities just enumerated are to attain their most effective application, the architect will need to cultivate certain indispensable qualities of mind and character, which are, indeed, fundamental to excellence in any field of human endeavor. They are:

1. Knowledge

The architect must command an extensive body of facts and principles to support his activities not only as a professional man, but also as a citizen and individual. In technical affairs, he must master: the planning of many types of buildings; the kinds, potentialities, and limitations of building materials, structural systems, construction details, and equipment; and the qualities, range, and possibilities of aesthetic materials, effects, and expression. To undergird and control this technical knowledge, the architect must also seek a profound understanding of human activity in all its rich variety, ramified relationships, and subtle meanings. Only thus can he hope to approach full discernment of the complex interdependence between architecture and the society it serves.

2. *Direction*

The architect must be sensitive and responsive to the emotional and intellectual content inherent in human activities in order to attain true sympathy toward and a discriminating evaluation of the cultural forces at work in his own society. The operation of such forces can be conveniently studied in the ebb and flow of past civilizations. From this quest for mature judgment and dynamic wisdom, the architect, as both servant and member of society, must evolve a philosophy, faith, and convictions to give purposeful direction to creative action. Thus, without presuming a Messianic role, he should become an agent of the best forces working toward the realization of the noblest aspirations of his society.

3. *Abilities*

As a man of action dealing with complex technical problems, the architect must possess the capacity and habit of systematic, sustained, objective, and precise thought. He must be able to assemble full data, isolate and evaluate pertinent criteria, criticize assumptions and methods, and formulate valid conclusions. He must command a high order of creativeness which, by a just balance of imagination, flexibility, resourcefulness, intuition, and reason, will enable him to synthesize a fresh, lucid, and optimal solution for each professional problem. He must be able to communicate his thoughts, directions, and designs with precision, clarity, and persuasiveness by writing, speaking, and graphic media. He must be able to administer effectively the execution of professional services and the operation of a professional organization.

4. *Character*

Since the consummation of building projects involves many individuals, the architect must practice at all times the fundamental virtues which underlie all successful human relationships. Due to his unusual position of trust with respect to client, contractor, and community, the architect's integrity must be above suspicion. Because of his special knowledge and extraordinary opportunities, he should recognize and fulfill in letter and spirit his broad responsibility to client, profession, and society, to seek always the highest quality of achievement. He should display initiative in discovering opportunities for service and in bringing his undertakings to successful fruition. He will need perseverance and courage to surmount the obstacles concomitant to any program of action. He must be able to stimulate cooperation in order to enlist the best efforts of his co-workers. And, because of his wide experience and key position in the building industry, he must supply leadership in fostering the highest standards and progress, not only in the professional practice of architecture, but also in all phases of the building process.

If such a specification seems overidealistic and to require a paragon of all virtues, it must be remembered that, by definition, the essence of a profession is its striving for ideals. Many individuals may fall short of full compliance, but it is equally true that all will be better architects for having tried to fulfill its demands. Such a specification constitutes, therefore, a challenging goal which necessarily presents potent implications for professional life and for architectural education.

4. AMERICAN ARCHITECTS AND THEIR WAR SERVICE

Architecture is preeminently an activity fostered by conditions of peace. It is concerned with *con*struction rather than *de*struction, and it ministers to the fulfillment, rather than the frustration of human needs. Nevertheless, in modern warfare, a nation at arms requires vast quantities of buildings to house its military forces and to produce the armaments they employ. Thus, very directly, architects contribute essential professional services in times of national emergency. Moreover, in many other tasks not connected with building, architects supply valuable technical and administrative skills.

The concentration of national resources during World War II upon military activities and production reduced civilian building construction to a small fraction of its peace-time volume. In 1941–42, prodigious expansion of military camps and bases, of armament production plants, and of emergency housing for defense workers, boosted total building to twice the construction rate of the late 30's. American architects played an important part in planning and erecting these crucial facilities. The colossal bulk of Willow Run and similar structures did much to fortify morale during the grim beginning years. By 1944, however, total building construction had been curtailed to a third of the 1941 rate, a level matched only by the bleakest years of the Great Depression.

The *1950 Survey* conducted a special study of architects' activities during these difficult times. 30 per cent of all architects served in the nation's armed forces (*Table 14*). Of the 70 per cent who remained in civilian status, 82 per cent performed duties which were professional in character (*Table 19*), but only 29 per cent did so while continuing in professional practice (*Table 20*). The rest found opportunities for professional or non-professional service in other spheres. 31 per cent were formally attached as civilians to the armed forces or to governmental agencies. 38 per cent worked in industries engaged in war contracts, and 2 per cent taught in technical training programs connected with the war (*Table 20*). The record indicates how effectively the profession overcame inevitable dislocations and adapted itself to national needs.

Of those architects who entered the nation's armed forces, 41 per cent served in the Army, 40 in the Navy, 15 in the Air Force, 2 in the Marine Corps, and 2 in the Coast Guard (*Table 15*). Technical and personal qualifications drew a large number of these architects into the ranks of commissioned officers (*Table 16*). 39 per cent of the architects who served in the armed forces had already been occupied in war work, and, of these, more than four-fifths had performed duties of a professional character (*Table 19*).

Analysis of the duties performed by architects while in military service reveals that 38 per cent were assigned functions which directly used professional capabilities: 19 per cent in architecture, engineering, and public works; 15 per cent in construction, supervision, contracting, or materials; 3 per cent in maintenance, plant layout and production; and 1 per cent in housing and real estate (*Tables 21, 22*). An additional 9 per cent used their professional abilities indirectly in drafting, charting, design, and teaching, and in the military corps concerned with the preservation of historic and cultural monuments. Even of the 47 per cent who were engaged in combat, staff, or field service, half performed duties in which their professional experience could be utilized at least indirectly. Such were administration, contracts and negotiations, procurement, organization and planning, camouflage, photographic interpretation, surveying, and topographical work (*Table 22*).

It seems clear, therefore, that members of the profession of architecture contributed to the nation's war effort services which in scope and character constitute an honorable and gratifying record. There may be some question whether their capabilities were used as effectively as they might have been, but the profession itself must accept at least a portion of the responsibility for having failed to publicize these capabilities and demand that they be utilized as directly and as fully as possible. Unfortunately, war emergencies are not often conducive to logic or efficiency. Nevertheless, since the wise use of man-power becomes a vital necessity in such emergencies, all architects should constantly promote public recognition of their professional capabilities and assert their right as citizens to contribute these capabilities as directly as possible to the nation's needs.

NOTES: CHAPTER THREE

[1] F. J. Ludes and H. J. Gilbert: *Corpus Juris Secondum.* 1951. v. 72, pp. 1215–1220; A. M. Carr-Saunders and P. A. Wilson: *The Professions.* 1933; *Social Science Encyclopoedia*, art. "Professions"; *Chambers Encyclopoedia*, 1951. art. "Profession"; W. E. Wickenden, "Professional Status of the Engineer," *Civil Engineering*, v. 1, Oct., 1930, p. 23.

[2] Charles L. Eastlake, "An Historical Sketch of the Institute" (*RIBA Sessional Papers.* 1875–76, p. 260).

[3] John McComb is said to have been a member. Since New York directories for 1803 list only four architects, and only one of them claimed architecture as his sole livelihood, perhaps *The Brethren* also included builders as well. (*Architectural Review*, v. 38, August, 1915, pp. 287–288, cited in Everard M. Upjohn: *Richard Upjohn, Architect and Churchman*, 1939, p. 156).

[4] George C. Mason, "The Professional Ancestry of the Philadelphia Chapter." (*Journal, Amer. Inst. of Architects.* v. 1, Sept. 1913, p. 378).

[5] H. M. Pierce Gallagher: *Robert Mills*, 1935, pp. 26–27.

[6] Mason, *op. cit.*, p. 380.

[7] AIA, *Proceedings*, 1886, p. 4.

[8] AIA, *Document No. 330.*

CHAPTER IV

Patterns of Education
For the Practice of Architecture

1. ARCHITECTS AND EDUCATION

Professions, like societies, must undergo constant renewal if they are to survive and grow. Moreover, it is the need for conserving, transmitting, and extending accumulated experience and for ensuring its continuing and increasingly competent application to social purposes which makes intimate concern for education a fundamental obligation of every profession. It is for these reasons that architects must foster architectural knowledge and the recruitment and training of their successors.

"Education is the acquisition of the art of the utilization of knowledge."[1] It must impart, therefore, a body of meaningful facts and concepts and expound the principles which interrelate these data. It must develop those skills, insights, and value standards which will enable knowledge and principles to be applied most effectively to the problems of purposeful living. In its fullest scope, therefore, education, far from being limited to formal schooling, continues as long as experience teaches. Its ultimate goal is understanding, judgment, wisdom, foresight, and culture.

This view of education is particularly appropriate for architects. Since they must combine to as high a degree as possible the diverse functions of technician, artist, counselor, and businessman, it is obvious that the deeper their understanding, the richer their experience, and the keener their creative power, the more valuable will be their contributions to the intricate problems of their day. Because architecture is so intimately related to all phases of life, and because architects are also members of society, narrow specialization will not suffice. The objective of architectural education becomes the development of architects, who, as enlightened individuals, responsible citizens, and resourceful professional men, will serve their society in attaining a worthy architecture.

Education for the practice of architecture is thus an inclusive process embracing several complementary stages. Initially, it provides the means by which raw recruits are transformed into useful assistants. Secondly, it presides over their transition to full membership in the profession. And, finally, it aids practitioners themselves to continue their growth in professional knowledge and skill. Although administered in diverse ways and sometimes obscured by unfamiliar terms, these indispensable functions of education have always been active in professional life. This chapter will review the various systems that have been used for the education of architects and from which current methods developed. It will also include an analysis of the use which American architects, registered in 1950, have made of these systems in preparing themselves for professional practice.

2. THE DEVELOPMENT OF EDUCATION IN EUROPE

From antiquity youth gained entrance to the skilled crafts by serving as lowly assistants under mature practitioners. In 13th-century Europe, this process was formalized by the urban craft guilds as the *apprenticeship system,* in which a master undertook to instruct, house, feed, and clothe his apprentice, who repaid this maintenance and training by a long term of increasingly productive aid. In turn, apprentices became journeymen, working for masters by the day (*journée*). Eventually, the most skilled and energetic of these journeymen might themselves attain mastership, become full members of their guild, and have shops, employees, and apprentices of their own.

To head each medieval building project, the owner appointed a master-mason or master-carpenter, depending on the dominant material to be used. On small jobs, such a master not only planned and directed, but also worked in the lodge beside his journeymen. On large constructions, however, he was primarily occupied in the "tracing house," performing the functions of design and administration. In time, some won such widespread reputations for competence that they were called by kings, ecclesiastics, or private clients to undertake several different projects at the same time, and they thus came to approximate the modern general practice of architecture.[2]

Many of these masters came up through the crafts. Carpenters followed the usual guild and apprenticeship pattern, but masons, due to more shifting employment, lacked formal organization until much later, rarely used apprenticeships, and normally began as common laborers and advanced to setting, roughhewing, cutting, and carving as soon as talent, skill, and opportunity permitted.[3] Some masters, trained in this manner, learned to perform architectural services by extrapolating craft experience. In contrast, however, as the work of the "tracing house" expanded, practitioners took sons or promising workmen as apprentices and trained them directly in drawing, geometry, and other architectural skills.[4]

The apprenticeship system, whether formally or informally applied, possessed many advantages. Under it no gap existed between training and practice. Apprentices observed and helped their masters on real projects. They met live clients and had close contact with builders and workmen. They heard primary decisions being made and followed the progress of construction at first hand. The effectiveness of the system is amply attested to by the splendid monuments created by the men it produced. So strong was its practical appeal and so economical was its administration that this system of apprenticeship long remained the principal method of training prospective architects.

Nevertheless, the system also exhibited inherent weaknesses and abuses. It is a great deal to expect of busy architects that, preoccupied with the innumerable crises of daily practice, they should also have become skilled educators who could teach with equal authority and facility all the general and technical subjects essential to their apprentices' growth. Many, indeed those best qualified by wide practice, found it impossible to spare the time or energy required for systematic teaching, and were naturally reluctant to assume the cost of assigning major assistants to this task. Some otherwise competent practitioners lacked the patience, sympathy, or expository talent necessary for successful teaching. Others had little of value to offer. Some considered the system merely as a means of obtaining unpaid labor.[5] In 1847, a number of London pupils, dissatisfied with the meager training provided by their masters, organized the Architectural Association to remedy their neglect. In recent years, many practitioners, otherwise capable and willing to teach, have been faced with such mounting costs of office space and personnel that they have felt unable to afford the luxury of educating youths who rarely recognized any obligation to repay even a portion of the subsidy thus provided. What is indeed remarkable are the considerable educational contributions which many employers do continue to give, despite such circumstances.

Furthermore, the very practicality of office training was not an unmixed blessing, for the impact of its heterogeneous events upon unexperienced minds often resulted in frustrating confusion, unless by unusual penetration or sympathetic suggestion the pupil was able to resolve them into an orderly set of principles from which to gain understanding, judgment, and wisdom. Given time, pupils might indeed absorb enough skill to become useful draftsmen, but, without coordinating insight, true professional status remained out of reach. Finally, because the apprenticeship system consisted essentially of individual tutoring, its production of trained personnel was sharply limited. As demand for architectural services increased, the system became an intolerable educational bottleneck, with the result that many potential clients were forced to turn to other sources for assistance.

To overcome these difficulties, architects gradually supplemented the apprenticeship system by formal group instruction. The masons' guilds apparently taught some of their craft secrets to apprentices organized in classes.[6] About 1353, Peter Parler, court architect to Emperor Charles IV, established at Prague a "school" for his own apprentices. Toward the end of the 16th century, Bernardo Buontalenti, ducal superintendent of civil and military architecture for Tuscany, conducted a tuition school in his own house at Florence.[7]

More formal classes were undertaken when architects and artists joined to organize academies of art. First was the short-lived Academy of Design, formed in 1562 at Florence under the leadership of Giorgio Vasari. In 1593, Rome's Academy of St. Luke held classes in drawing, perspective, and architecture. From 1620 to 1631, Fabio Mengoni had charge of the architectural school of the academy at Milan. The climax of this movement came in 1648 at Paris with the founding of the Royal Academy of Painting and Sculpture.[8] Young architects shared with students of the other arts its classes in drawing, geometry, perspective, and the orders. Occasionally, however, the academicians took their teaching very lightly. In 1662, this led rebellious students to set up temporarily a cooperative class of their own, which was thus the first recorded *atelier*.[9] All such academy instruction was intended solely as a *supplementary system* to enhance the training of apprentices and relieve their masters of the responsibility of elementary instruction.

In 1671, the founding at Paris of the Royal Academy of Architecture and the inauguration of its school gave momentous impulse to technical organization and education. François Blondel, its first professor, conducted a two-year cycle of classes with semi-weekly lectures. The program included arithmetic, geometry, perspective, stereotomy, mechanics, architectural theory, gnomonics, hydraulics, military architecture, and fortifications.[10] Each academician was entitled to name one official student whom he quite naturally selected from his own apprentices, but this exclusiveness was somewhat mitigated by Blondel's privilege of appointing six more official pupils and by permitting others to attend unofficially. The supplemental character of the program was emphasized by the academicians' reservation that each would continue to instruct his own students in design in his own office.[11]

In 1694, when war so depleted the royal treasury that the Academy's subvention was temporarily suspended, the academicians continued the school at their own expense. Perhaps this emergency served to renew their interest in the school, for they soon decided to hold occasional design competitions in which exercises prepared by students in the several offices were to be judged by the whole Academy. In 1701, these competitions were placed on a monthly schedule and a jury of members awarded gold and silver medals for the best performances. In 1720, this system was extended to the selection of students to be sent at royal expense to pursue advanced studies at the French Academy at Rome.[12] This use of the *project method* soon developed into the dominant feature of architectural training. Two centuries later, the principle was again "discovered" by modern progressive educators, who proclaimed its advantages for all types of training.

The Academy's school deserves praise for its pioneering and its influence, although the quality of its teaching varied directly with the insight and industry of its personnel. It inspired similar, if fitful, efforts throughout Europe, which, however, were usually provided in academies of art.[13] As at Paris, their primary purpose was to train recruits for royal service, and this, together with their limited scope and content, prevented such institutions from satisfying fully the growing needs of the late 18th century.

In the early 18th century, youths denied admission to academy classes had three alternatives. The first, apprenticeship, was declining in favor before the second, the *pupilage system,* a modification in which architects gave office instruction in return for pupils' fees. This system dominated the English scene throughout the 19th century. The third alternative was for students to seek out isolated courses conducted by private tutors. Such classes were becoming common in the larger centers by the 1730's. Another source of supplementary instruction was provided by public lectures on architecture, such as those given by Soane from 1806 on at London's Royal Academy of Arts.

In 1742, this situation prompted Jacques-François Blondel to establish at Paris, despite the Academy's opposition, a private school of architecture which for the first time went beyond the supplementary pattern to achieve an *inclusive* system of training. Here, for those students who could afford the stiff tuition, a faculty of able teachers taught for eight hours each day a two-year curriculum which included mathematics, physics, construction, stereotomy, specifications, mensuration, ornament, modeling, *and* design.[14] Blondel's great talent as a teacher is indicated by the fact that three of his pupils later won the *Grand Prix de Rome,* and that at least nine became members of the Academy.[15] Two of these, Ledoux and Boullée, in the 1780's and 90's produced some of the most extraordinary designs of their day. Blondel's success was even more conspicuous because the Academy's school had deteriorated sharply, and because Blondel himself was called in 1762 to direct and revitalize its teaching. There is no evidence, however, that he was able to break the academicians' old monopoly of design teaching.

The remarkable expansion of science and technology in the 18th century emphasized the need for personnel trained in the new techniques. This, in turn, stimulated the inauguration under state auspices of the first schools of engineering. First came specialized schools: of mining and metallurgy at Braunschweig, 1745, Freiberg, 1765, and Clausthal, 1775; of military engineering at Mézières, 1748; and of bridges and highways at Paris, 1775.[16] When in 1770 Frederick the Great set up the Prussian Department of Public Works, its director sought in vain to revive the long-discontinued architectural classes of Berlin's Academy of Art in order to train much-needed architects for the department's staff. Not until 1790, four years after Friedrich Wilhelm II came to the throne and his minister, Heinitz, reorganized the old group as the *Academy of Art and Mechanic Sciences,* were Director David Gilly and three other members of the department authorized to begin such courses.[17]

It was Jean-Baptiste Rondelet, a Blondel alumnus and Soufflot's principal assistant and successor at the Pantheon, who, in 1789, in one of the first proposals to be laid before the French National Assembly after the fall of the Bastille, expanded the idea of a bureau of public works into an all-embracing ministry, headed by an academy of architects and staffed by a corps of administrators and workers trained in special state schools of architecture and engineering. When the old academies and their schools were suppressed in August, 1793, Rondelet was immediately commissioned to set up the *Ecole centrale des travaux publiques* with three-year curricula in architecture and civil engineering. It is interesting to note that the architectural curriculum was inclusive in character and, incidentally, that it was administered by the division of mathematics and mechanics. In 1795, after only one year of operation, scientists and engineers secured control of the school and transformed it into the *Ecole polytechnique,* the first school of general engineering.[18] Further modifications reduced its teaching to a two-year preparatory course leading to advanced state schools for the specialized branches of engineering. While the *Ecole polytechnique* continued to offer some architectural instruction and while its emphasis on science was a wholesome reaction to the Academy's teaching, the shortened schedule and the failure to set up a similar advanced school for architecture greatly reduced its usefulness in this field.

Nevertheless, these developments exerted widespread influence, especially in Central Europe. In 1797, the example of the *Ecole centrale* inspired the Prussian Department of Public Works to urge the organization of its classes into a full-fledged school of architecture and building. In 1799, this was accomplished by the establishment of the *Bau-Akademie.*[19] The 2½-year curriculum for architects included: mathematics; architectural, mechanical, topographical, perspective, and freehand drawing; the physics of construction; statics and mechanics; building construction; history of architecture; the requirements and design of both common and monumental buildings; city planning; machinery; and highway, harbor, and river works.[20] Graduates normally entered government service and obtained excellent practical experience in the Department's offices. Later, when further schooling was required for promotion. a term of office work became a prerequisite for admission to advanced courses. Thus, school and office cooperated in an integrated pattern to ensure sound preparation for official duties.

Both the *Ecole polytechnique* and the *Bau-Akademie* served as models for architectural instruction when the new polytechnic schools of central Europe were begun. First to be opened were those at Prague in 1806 and Vienna in 1815, but in their earliest years these two schools stressed general scientific training rather than specific professional curricula. The Bavarian polytechnic was created in 1823; four years later it was divided and the Munich section became a famed school of architecture. The polytechnic at Karlsruhe emerged in 1825 through the amalgamation of an older state school of construction and a private industrial school. At first both professional and vocational training were provided, but in 1833 the latter was dropped. Karlsruhe's 5-year curriculum in architecture was soon recognized as one of the strongest in Europe. Other polytechnics followed at Braunschweig, Stuttgart, Hannover, Dresden, and Darmstadt. For many years inadequate secondary education forced most of these schools to maintain preparatory divisions, but gradually the situation improved and effort was concentrated at a true professional level. In 1854, the establishment of the Swiss Federal Polytechnic at Zurich, with status equivalent to a university, and consequently with the right to confer professional diplomas, prompted the transformation of the German schools into *technischen hochschulen* during the 1870's. In more recent years these have become full technical universities.[21]

During the late 19th century, applicants for polytechnic training were required to have had at least six months of experience in an architect's office. The first two years of academic study were devoted to basic technical subjects. Then, three years of practical experience as an inspector on governmental building projects formed a prerequisite for admission to advanced professional courses. The curricula embraced an inclusive program of instruction in which design was an integral part taught within the school by teachers who usually were also able practitioners. While their teaching naturally reflected current tastes, it was also strongly flavored with a technical rationalism fostered by the scientific discipline inherent in the polytechnic system.[22] Successful completion of the program led to a state diploma, which opened the way directly to governmental appointment or private practice.[23] The most promising graduates, however, often augmented their training in design by further study in academy classes, in architects' offices, or in a *meisterklasse* conducted by an eminent practitioner. The efficacy of the system as a whole was clearly demonstrated by those outstanding architects who received all or part of their training from it, men such as Schinkel, Stüler, Persius, Adler, Raschdorff, Ende, Lucae, Martin Gropius, Wallot, Thiersch, Licht, Durm, Messel, Berlage, and Walter Gropius.

French architectural education, after its brief association with technical instruction, reverted immediately to its traditional mold. In 1795, when it became clear that the *Ecole polytechnique* would not satisfy the needs of architects, the classes of the disbanded Academy, which Leroy and Vaudoyer had continued as a private venture, were reconstituted as an *Ecole spéciale d'architecture* under the newly-founded National Institute of Science and Art. In 1797 it was joined with the Institute's other schools to form the *Ecole des beaux-arts*. This, in 1807, Napoleon made an autonomous *Ecole imperiale et spéciale des beaux-arts*. Louis XVIII returned it in 1816 to the control of the reestablished academies, and, finally, in 1864, Napoleon III placed it under direct state supervision.[24]

Because the *Ecole* became the most renowned center of architectural education of the 19th century, its organization and methods demand review. In spite of the vicissitude of the Revolution, its continuity with the Academy's school was unbroken, and, indeed, at first the staff itself was the same. Nevertheless, it soon responded to the stimuli of national prestige and support and called to its faculty a succession of able architect-educators. In 1799, for example, Rondelet himself accepted the professorship of construction. His superlative text, *The Art of Building,* published from 1802 to 1817, was in part prompted by student needs. From 1818 to 1846, Louis-Pierre Baltard applied his vast experience to the teaching of architectural theory.

Since the *Ecole* was maintained by the state, no tuition was charged, and a genuine effort was made to recruit the most talented youth. Admission was, therefore, highly competitive, and only 60 to 80 new students were chosen each year from 500 to 600 applicants. Rigid entrance examinations ensured a group already versed not only in algebra, geometry, and general history, but also in drawing, modeling, and even elementary architectural design. To secure this preparatory training, candidates were forced to depend on private tutors and studios.[25] Thus, the *Ecole* was freed of the difficult problem of elementary teaching but, at the same time, it forfeited the opportunity to develop it as an integral part of the whole curriculum.

Once admitted to the lower, or second, class, students undertook three types of instruction. One consisted of lecture courses in theoretical subjects: mathematics (trigonometry, analytic geometry, and advanced descriptive geometry), mechanics, stereotomy, surveying, perspective, architectural history, architectural theory, and building construction (including elementary applied geology, physics, and chemistry). The quality of these courses was usually high, especially in theory and construction, but, too often, they received from students less than minimum attention, since attendance was voluntary and final examinations were taken as the sole criteria of accomplishment. The second type was studio training in freehand drawing. In the *Ecole's* doctrine, all of these studies were only contributory to the third, architectural design. In Second Class design, students strove to win a prescribed minimum of points in competitive exercises devoted to meticulously rendered studies of the orders and other ornamental details and to solutions of simple buildings. Facility was also encouraged through brief solo problems. The average full-time student could complete the Second Class in about three years.

In the First Class, lectures were confined primarily to building and professional practice. Advanced drawing and modeling were also required. Design, however, became the principal study, and its problems posed the solution of more complex buildings. Originally the *Ecole* curriculum had no terminus and students could continue design until they reached their thirtieth birthday. Strong incentive to do so was given by the opportunity to compete for the *Grand Prix,* which led to four free years of advanced study at Rome and, upon return, to state appointments and commissions. In 1869, the school was empowered to confer diplomas on those who completed a prescribed amount of advanced design and passed a comprehensive examination which involved the design of a given building, and the preparation of its working drawings, details, specifications, and a partial schedule of quantities of materials. Later, a year of construction supervision under a government architect was also required.

The developed *Ecole* curriculum was remarkably comprehensive, but, at the same time, its actual operation exhibited a curious bifurcation. The *Ecole* itself conducted the lecture courses and the drawing classes. In design, however, it limited its responsibilities to issuing the programs of requirements for the problems, to presiding over students during the first few hours as they worked out their basic schemes, to administering the grading of final solutions by juries of architects, and to exhibiting the results for the edification of participants. All else—the crucial stages of preparing and guiding the student in his development of his exercise—was the province, not of the school or its faculty, but of ten to twenty independent units, the *ateliers*. These were organizations in which students voluntarily associated in order to secure for a modest fee a studio in which to work and instruction by a *patron*-practitioner. Some *ateliers* were small with only a handful of members; others had as many as 150 students, but the average was about 40.

Thus, in a very fundamental way, the new *Ecole-atelier* system preserved the split responsibilities of the earlier Academy-office partnership, but since offices could not cope with the increased number of students demanded by an expanding economy and profession, the office was supplanted by a unit inspired by the private tutoring studios of the 18th century. In theory, the *atelier* brought professional stimulus to each student through intimate contact with the *patron,* who was usually an eminent and experienced architect. Under his guidance and criticism, each essayed the role of architect for the problem at hand. Close association with like-minded students encouraged mutual assistance and mutual instruction. Rivalry within and between *ateliers* spurred ambition and effort to high pitch. All this, together with the inevitable camaraderie and gaiety of high-spirited youth, fostered a remarkable *esprit de corps* and an intense loyalty to *atelier, patron,* and fellows.

At its best, the *Ecole-atelier* system produced many accomplished architects. Duban, Labrouste, Charles Garnier, Laloux, Boileau, Dutert, de Baudot, Astruc, Cendrier, Perret, and Tony Garnier would be outstanding in any age. In addition, it gave to 19th-century France a professional corps unsurpassed in competence and spirit. In 1900, of the national total of about 5000 architects, the *Ecole* had trained approximately 1300. This, indeed, constituted a proud and enviable record.

Nevertheless, in actual practice the system developed definite shortcomings. First, and perhaps most significant, was the fact that the delegation of instruction in elementary courses and in design to private agencies made any real integration of the whole educational process impossible. It may be argued that the *Ecole* exercised tacit control through its entrance examinations and design judgments, but this could also mean a typical academic faith in the primacy of end results and disregard for the methods by which students achieved them. To some extent, this was recognized in 1864 when the *Ecole* set up three internal *ateliers,* but by the time this occurred the system was so fixed that these new units actually developed as duplicates of the independent units.

Another weakness was that the *atelier* was neither school nor office and thus lacked the disciplines of both. Moreover, in all but the smallest groups, the *patron* could not spare enough time to give personal criticism to each student. Actually, he was forced to concentrate his effort on advanced students, particularly those preparing for the *Grand Prix.* These, in turn, repaid their advanced instruction by teaching their younger fellows, but even if they had gained some practical experience in offices, they were themselves too immersed in the system to act as judicious mentors. Thus, for most students, the system's primary premise of close contact with professional realities remained for the most part an illusion. By modern standards, the *ateliers* could not supply an adequate amount of effective instruction, and it is difficult to escape the conclusion that the chief basis of its existence was its economy.

Finally, the *Ecole's* use of competition has been widely extolled as a necessary device to spur maximum performance and prepare for mature life. Even sympathetic

French critics have recognized, however, that the *Ecole* exploited this principle to harmful excess. In 1901, Eugène Muntz wrote:

"The competitive system, which is so much in vogue in French educational establishments, shines here in all its glory and keeps the young people constantly up to the mark. In order to enter the school it is necessary to pass numerous examinations of a severe nature and others take place every six months, so that while it is very difficult to become a pupil, nothing is easier than to lose that position. A mental depression lasting a few hours is sufficient to bring it about. Then there are contests from one end of the year to the other for medals, money prizes, the diploma of architect, and, finally, for the *Grand Prix de Rome*. The *Ecole* is no place for dreaming or meditating, nor even for disinterested study. Every effort has to culminate in a palpable result, in the gaining of a given number of points. One is stifled in that oppressive atmosphere, and one quits it in a state of anaemia which is not rapidly recovered from. This, in our opinion, is the school's great defect—the weak point in its armor."[26]

Paul Cret noted the same danger:

"Like all competitions, they were bound to the defects of their qualities. Invaluable in stimulating competitive ardor, they tended to place emphasis on what was most likely to please the judges. To put it another way, they tended to encourage not the best possible work, but the work most likely to win."[27]

Notwithstanding these reservations, the debt which modern architectural education owes to the *Ecole-atelier* system should not be underestimated. Although several provincial schools were established, the national status of the *Ecole* allowed it to share the extraordinary prestige of the Second Empire. The success of its graduates inspired widespread emulation of its methods. It was the product of a special heritage, and of specific conditions of time and place. In recent years it has displayed renewed vigor.[28]

Although the *Ecole des beaux-arts* constituted the predominant center of French architectural education, provincial needs led during the 19th century to the establishment of a number of state-supported regional schools. Some grew out of the classes of local academies. Others were associated with regional schools of art. Today, there are 13 such schools, located at Rennes, Rouen, Lille, Nancy, Strasbourg, Nantes, Bordeaux, Clermont-Ferrand, Lyon, Grenoble, Toulouse, Marseilles, and Algiers. Their programs of instruction are closely linked with Paris, and their students take the *Ecole's* design exercises and send their problems to its judgments. It remains to note the *Ecole spéciale d'architecture,* founded at Paris in 1865 as a private venture by Emile Trélat, architect and professor of civil construction at the *Conservatoire des Arts et Métiers.* Its three-year curriculum contained an adequate selection of theoretical courses, but for design instruction students participated in *Ecole* competitions. The diplomas of this school were recognized by the government in 1934.[29]

The development of the inclusive system in France and Germany was possible because architectural education, like technical instruction, was conceived as a public responsibility to be supported by public funds. In Britain, except for the School of Military Engineering established at Chatham in 1812, all such assistance was long resisted and private efforts, when finally applied, were confined to the trade-school level. As a result, the *pupilage system* remained the primary means of professional training throughout the 19th century. In London, pupils could supplement office training by the drawing classes which the Royal Academy of Arts had provided since its foundation in 1768. The Academy also encouraged the study of architectural design by awarding annual student medals. Nevertheless, several architects urged more comprehensive educational methods. One of the principal aims of the Architectural Society, organized in London in 1831, was "to form a British School of Architecture."[30] The Institute of British Architects, founded in 1834, interested itself in professional training, but made no attempt to initiate a school. In 1840, Alfred Bartholomew published an eloquent plea for a "Great National College of Architecture."[31]

The answer was the inauguration of academic courses designed to supplement pupilage rather than replace it. In 1840, King's College, a division of the newly chartered University of London, appointed William Hosking, an accomplished civil engineer with architectural training, to be *Professor of the Arts of Construction in connection with Civil Engineering and Architecture,* a title almost as long as his twenty-one years of able service. In 1841, University College, the non-sectarian unit of the same institution, named Thomas Leverton Donaldson as Professor of Architecture, a post he held with distinction for twenty-three years. Both programs were conducted in evening classes to enable office pupils to attend. Some years later the new College of Civil Engineers at Putney offered similar instruction.

Donaldson taught two lecture courses, each of which extended through two years. One dealt with *Architecture as a Science;* the other with *Architecture as a Fine Art.* His statement of aims was characteristically succinct. He decried the fact that

"it has hitherto been too much the practice of young men in this country . . . to neglect a systematic elementary course of education, and to rely upon the experience of actual practice to carry them through their arduous career."

He described his method:

"Commencing from first principles and masters of the elements, they proceed to the consideration of their applications. The choice of materials, their applicability and adaptation for economical purposes are brought before them; they learn the history and progressive development of invention, and the names and characters of the most illustrious men; they are also made acquainted with the value and importance of the best scientific literary works. They are thus thoroughly grounded with a fund of knowledge, which the hurry of subsequent practical life forbids their ever acquiring, and which they cannot gain in the office of the professional man. It were idle to suppose that this system can supersede the knowledge to be gained under the architect, engineer, or builder; but it completes, at all events, the practical experience acquired on the works of the master; and the education of the young man being perfected by this combination, he is enabled to follow up his pursuit as a matured and well-grounded architect, engineer, builder, or mechinist, and not with the raw inexperience of unskilled youth."[32]

Hosking's and Donaldson's supplementary courses were a forward step, but the dream of a comprehensive school persisted. In 1842, Joseph Aloysius Hansom, architect, Owenite, socialist, inventor of the Hansom cab, and initial editor of the first weekly architectural journal, the *Builder,* announced a *Builders' College for Architecture and Architectural Engineering.* The plan envisioned a combination of school, office, and workshop, and the proposed curriculum included courses in design, construction, mechanics, chemistry, decorative crafts, bookkeeping, mensuration, drawing, history, languages, and literature.[33]

Hansom's scheme was too ambitious for his slender resources, but it encouraged increasing complaints by pupils dissatisfied with office instruction. The outcome was the formation early in 1847, under the leadership of Robert Kerr and Charles Gray, of the Architectural Association as a cooperative "endeavour towards an improved system of architectural study." Weekly meetings alternated between the reading of technical papers and mutual criticisms of designs prepared from common programs. By 1851, membership stood at 166 and, except for a few temporary reverses, grew steadily.[34]

In 1855, the French movement to establish professional examinations and diplomas stimulated the Architectural Association to petition the Institute of British Architects to inaugurate a similar plan. The Institute approved the principle of voluntary examinations in 1861, and the first was held two years later.[35] To assist candidates, it also conducted at the Association a Voluntary Examination class, with lectures in mathematics, geology, physics, materials, construction, professional practice, history, and architectural literature. While the result of the voluntary examinations was disappointing, during the next fifteen years, the Association's instructional program gradually expanded in response to demand. In 1870, sympathetic practitioners began to serve as "visitors," i.e., critics for the design classes. Other important educational features were the inspections of new London buildings and the annual summer study trips both in England and on the continent.[36] The success of the Association's classes stimulated similar efforts in a number of other centers.

Meanwhile, in 1856, Sir Charles Barry, Hardwick, and Cockerell, architect members of the Royal Academy, pressed the enlargement of its educational activities. Barry urged a two-year intensive course for architects embracing composition, drawing, decoration, and design, with admission restricted to those who had completed the preliminary courses at University or King's College. Not until 1870, when it moved to Burlington House, did the Academy inaugurate a separate School of Architecture. R. Phéné Spiers served as Master from 1870 to 1906. Instruction consisted of evening classes in design criticized by "visitors," drawn from architectural members of the Academy.[37] Long afterwards, W. R. Lethaby characterized this regimen as "good fun, but anarchy."[38] It is of interest that, from 1858 to 1861, Spiers had been the first British student at the *Ecole des beaux-arts,* and that during the next fifty years the *Ecole* alumni register lists only eight British and four Scotch students who crossed the channel for their architectural training.

In 1882, the RIBA tacitly assumed direction and control of British architectural education by placing the system of professional examinations on a compulsory basis and making it a prerequisite to its associate membership. As the implications of the system became clear, the need for fully developed professional schools was emphasized. In 1890, therefore, the Architectural Association reorganized its teaching into a systematic four-year curriculum of professional calibre. In 1894, University College of Liverpool, later the University of Liverpool, established its School of Architecture, the first in Britain to conduct its program by full-time day classes. Gradually, others were formed in universities and technical schools. In 1902, the RIBA exempted graduates of the Association and Liverpool from its Intermediate Examination, and this precedent led, beginning in 1920, to complete exemption for "final" schools, except for the examination in Practice, and partial exemption for those of "intermediate" rank. In turn, this policy required the maintaining of an official list of "recognized" schools.[39] In 1920, Liverpool adopted a five-year curriculum, and this in time became a mandatory length for all "final" schools. By 1945, there were in Britain fifteen "final" and seven "intermediate" schools.

These, then, were the European sources which influenced the beginnings of architectural education in America.[40] In the first half of the 19th century, France and Germany had achieved inclusive schools through the provision of state subsidies. In France, architectural instruction had retained its early association with the fine arts, but, in effect, the *Ecole* was an independent unit, which, however, delegated major portions of its program to outside agencies. In Germany, architecture was a division of scientific and technical education, but within the polytechnics its curricula were both inclusive and integrated. By contrast, Great Britain, homeland of the Industrial Revolution, paradoxically was content to leave technical training to pupilage and the supplementary courses offered by private schools. In none of these countries before 1894 did the traditional institutions of higher education, the universities, play the slightest part.

3. THE DEVELOPMENT OF EDUCATION IN THE UNITED STATES

The buildings of the Anglo-American colonies were designed by immigrant or local craftsmen or by gifted amateurs. The necessities of isolation forced them to overcome their lack of direct professional training primarily by drawing inspiration from the numerous publications emanating from European presses. From the 1730's on, unemployed itinerant builders occasionally advertised in the larger towns "schools of architectural drawing," no doubt suggested by those which were just appearing in London and Paris.[41] It is doubtful that these ever contributed any useful result.

93

The scarcity of trained architects was all too evident when the young republic began to expand, and especially when it undertook the construction of its new federal capital. This very scarcity, moreover, made it very difficult for young aspirants to find competent masters. On the other hand, due to the independent spirit of the American scene, the use of formal apprenticeships or *pupilages* was rare, and usually the assistant received a small wage. Robert Mills, the first American definitely trained as an architect, graduated in the classical course at Charleston College and worked as a student-assistant under Hoban, Jefferson, and Latrobe. Even in Europe few architects had enjoyed such excellent preparation, and in America it was entirely exceptional.

Although office training persisted throughout the 19th century as the chief method of architectural education, more formal means were soon proposed. Private drawing classes continued to be offered, but even the best—such as those conducted by Hoban in 1790, Asher Benjamin in 1802, and John Haviland and Hugh Bridport in 1816— lacked scope and resources and were primarily means of augmenting practitioners' incomes.[42] It was Thomas Jefferson, gifted amateur architect, scholar, scientist, and statesman, who championed the necessity of education in a democracy and the need to include in the universities not only the liberal arts, but the scientific and technical disciplines as well. In 1814, he proposed the first university program in any country which specifically incorporated a professional curriculum in architecture. In this provision the influence of the *Ecole polytechnique* is clear, for, when Jefferson's project matured into his University of Virginia, budget limitations led him to place architecture in the School of Mathematics, just as the Parisian school had done. But, whereas in Paris at least three teachers of architecture were provided, in Jefferson's School of Mathematics its single professor was to teach all its courses. Despite long search, no architectural mathematician could be found, and the introduction of architectural studies in the university program was long delayed.[43]

During the next four decades, some architectural students obtained valuable supplementary training through courses offered by newly-established technical schools. The earliest was the Military Academy at West Point, opened in 1802. In 1817, under Major Sylvanus Thayer, who had spent the two preceding years in Europe studying military and technical schools, the Academy achieved the first organized technical curriculum in the country. This program was strongly influenced by the *Ecole polytechnique*.[44] The first civilian technical schools grew from the lyceum movement, in which itinerant lecturers presented in successive communities short courses in science and its applications. From 1823 to 1827, Benjamin Hale, a young Congregationalist minister, conducted at Gardiner, Maine, a Lyceum, in the form of a Pestalozzian school, which included single courses in surveying, carpentry, and civil architecture.[45] In 1825, Amos Eaton, lawyer, botanist, and veteran lyceumist, opened the Rensselaer Institute at Troy, New York, which in 1835 conferred the first American degrees in Civil Engineering.[46]

Philadelphia's Franklin Institute, founded in 1824 for the study and promotion of the mechanic arts and applied science, in the following year secured William Strickland, a Latrobe pupil who had become the city's foremost architect, to give a series of public lectures on architecture. George Strickland, his brother and pupil, conducted classes in architectural drawing.[47] Such efforts may have prompted the "School of architecture" for which in 1833 a third story was added to the "West Building" on Carpenters' Court. [48] Thomas Ustick Walter, Strickland's pupil, continued the Franklin Institute lectures after 1835. Other centers saw similar efforts. In 1830, Alexander J. Davis lectured on architecture at the National Academy of Design in New York.[49] In Washington, Robert Mills, soon after moving there in 1830, undertook a more ambitious program and set up a full school of architecture. Despite official encouragement, favorable notices, and the aid of an advisory committee of prominent architects, the school collapsed after three years of operation.[50] Disappointment likewise met the efforts of New York University when, in 1832, and possibly urged by A. J. Davis, architect of its new building, David B. Douglass was appointed Professor of Natural Philosophy (Science), Civil Engineering, and Architecture. No students registered for these courses and Douglass soon resigned.[51]

Increasing knowledge of European technical schools, and especially the new German polytechnics, stimulated a desire for American counterparts. Already in 1826, a group of Philadelphians, encouraged by the success of the Franklin Institute, proposed the formation of a polytechnic and scientific college which was to include architecture.[52] In 1836, the University of Virginia introduced courses in civil engineering and they were taught by the eminent scientist, William Barton Rogers.[53] The curriculum soon included architectural drawing and building construction. In 1837, Rogers and his brother Henry, state geologist of Pennsylvania, renewed the proposal for a polytechnic school at the Franklin Institute, and, again in 1846, expanded the idea for Boston. Both plans included curricula in architecture.[54] Harvard opened its Lawrence Scientific School in 1847. In 1849, Benjamin Franklin Greene, new director of Amos Eaton's school, extended its program to a four-year basis on European lines and transformed it into the Rensselaer Polytechnic Institute. In 1855, in a remarkable report, Greene detailed its further development with organization and buildings reflecting Jefferson's plan for Virginia. A curriculum in Civil Architecture was included, but the depression of 1857 postponed its realization.[55]

During the 1850's concern for technical education quickened and this increased opportunities for supplementary training in architecture. In 1852, Yale inaugurated a School of Engineering, with courses in descriptive geometry, shades and shadows, perspective, mechanics, construction, architectural drawing, and the *Principles of Architecture*.[56] In the same year, the University of Michigan organized its science curriculum in which perspective and architectural drawing were required.[57] In 1854, New York University set up a School of Civil Engineering and Architecture, in charge of Thomas S. Cummings, who had assisted Samuel F. B. Morse in his art classes, but once more no students materialized.[58] A number of architects benefited from such supplementary courses. William LeBaron Jenney graduated in civil engineering from the Lawrence Scientific School in 1853 and the *Ecole centrale des arts et manufactures* at Paris in 1856. George B. Post graduated in 1858 from the scientific course of City College, New York. In 1866, Charles F. McKim studied for a year at

95

the Lawrence Scientific School. John Wellborn Root earned a degree in civil engineering in 1869 at New York University. William Holabird was a West Point cadet from 1873 to 1875. Frank Lloyd Wright studied civil engineering at the University of Wisconsin from 1885 to 1887.

Nevertheless, in the 1850's, the need and desire for professional education in architecture were mounting rapidly. The decade more than doubled the number of architects, from 591 to 1263, but relatively few had had systematic training and most had had only brief office experience. A number had come to America after obtaining their technical education in Europe. But already three American students had crossed to Paris to study at the *Ecole des beaux-arts*. The first was Richard Morris Hunt, who entered the *Ecole* in 1846. Arthur Dexter and Francis Peabody from Boston enrolled in 1852.[59] On his return, Hunt opened his office in New York in 1856, and in the following year organized his office pupils in an *atelier* inspired by Paris models. One of his first students, William Robert Ware, returned to Boston in 1860, opened an office, and about 1864 set up a similar *atelier* for his own assistants.[60] It was increasingly clear, however, that such private measures could not meet the situation. At this juncture, the newly formed AIA proposed the creation of a national school of architecture, comparable to the Parisian *Ecole*.

The final solution came in the midst of the Civil War, when, in 1862, after a decade of rising sentiment, the provision of technical education was at last recognized as a necessary concern of government. In that year, Congress passed the Morrill Land-Grant Act "to promote the liberal and practical education of the industrial classes in the several pursuits and professions in life." Fortunately, the plan called for numerous schools, one in each state, rather than a centralized national unit. Real incentive was given to the states by the offer of federal aid in the form of allotments of public land. It was in three new institutions stimulated by the Morrill Act that the first American schools of architecture were inaugurated. To their presidents and the men they chose to head these schools is due the honor of having established the collegiate pattern and the inclusive character of architectural education in the United States.

First was the Massachusetts Institute of Technology, whose charter had been secured in 1860 under the leadership of its first president, William Barton Rogers. When the initial campaign for private subscriptions lagged, the receipt of land-grant support assured its realization and initial success. Rogers himself was a geologist and physicist, but throughout his long promotion of technical education, he had always included architecture. In part, this stemmed from his first-hand knowledge of the German polytechnics, for he declared his wish to develop MIT on the model of Karlsruhe. But he had also taught seventeen years at Charlottesville, where Jefferson's aims and buildings must have fostered appreciation of the need of trained architects. In 1865, he chose William Ware to head the new department. Ware's own education at Harvard, the Lawrence Scientific School, and Hunt's *atelier,* his five years of practice, and his teaching in his own *atelier,* gave him unique preparation for the task. In addition, he studied European architectural schools for almost a year before meeting his first classes in September, 1868.[61]

The second school arose in the University of Illinois where, in 1867, Regent John Milton Gregory included in his first program of instruction a "polytechnical division" with architecture as a constituent department. Gregory's interest in architecture stemmed from his student days at Union College, Schenectady, the monumental campus of which had been designed in 1813 by the gifted émigré architect, Joseph-Jacques Ramée. Gregory also knew the Germany polytechnic system and its inclusion of architecture. Moreover, his plans for training architects were warmly supported by an influential trustee, John M. Van Osdel, Chicago's first and most prominent practitioner. Instruction began in January, 1870, sixteen months after MIT, and the first teacher was James Bellangee, a graduate in science of the University of Michigan who had worked briefly in the Chicago office of Gurdon P. Randall. During the academic year, 1871–1872, the courses were in charge of Harald M. Hansen, a Swedish architect who had studied for two years at the *Bau-Akademie* in Berlin. Hansen was thus the first European teacher in an American architectural school.[62]

Cornell University, founded in 1865 and opened in 1868, was the third institution to offer a curriculum in architecture. Andrew Dickson White, its first president, was a graduate of Yale, had studied at the Sorbonne and the University of Berlin, and had served as attaché of the U. S. Legation at St. Petersburg. These experiences, together with the reading of Ruskin, stimulated a keen interest in architecture and led him to assemble one of the most extensive collections of architectural books in the country. His enthusiastic concern for his architectural school was attested by his gift to it of these volumes. Although the inclusion of architectural instruction was intended from the first, it was not until the fall of 1871 that White appointed as first head of the school, Charles Babcock, who after earning his M.A. in classics at Union College, had been successively the pupil and partner, and son-in-law as well, of Richard Upjohn, who in turn had been trained in his native country, Great Britain.[63]

Thus it was that, while the provision of architecture in the programs of MIT, Illinois, and Cornell stemmed primarily from the German polytechnics, the men in charge of these courses reflected three different backgrounds. Ware had experienced, at second hand, the French *atelier* system; Hansen was a product of the *Bau-Akademie;* and Babcock was trained by office *pupilage* under an outstanding practitioner. Nevertheless, conditions inherent in the American scene led them to develop almost identical programs and methods. In theoretical subjects, all covered much the same ground. Design was taught within each school as an integral part of the educational experience. Ware, although located in a metropolis, consciously chose this inclusive arrangement in preference to independent *ateliers* or to office-taught design. Hansen and Babcock, working in isolated villages, had no other alternative. Together, they fashioned the basic framework of the inclusive collegiate system which, while undergoing continuous refinement and elaboration, trained an ever-increasing proportion of American architects.

The year, 1873, saw each of these schools produce its first graduate. Nathan Clifford Ricker at Illinois completed the curriculum in March, 1873. Three months later, in June, Henry A. Phillips of MIT and John R. Schoonover of Cornell followed. Phillips did not continue in the profession, but he retained an active interest in the school until his death in 1926. Schoonover practiced in Brooklyn and died there in 1901. Ricker, after a European tour which included three months of study at the *Bau-Aka-demie,* returned to Illinois to replace Hansen, taught there for 43 years, was head of the Department of Architecture for 37 and Dean of the College of Engineering for 27.

During the next two decades, these three land-grant pioneers stimulated seven other institutions, six of which were privately supported, to install similar architectural programs. Syracuse University organized its curriculum in 1873 within the nation's first College of Fine Arts. Teachers were long recruited from local practitioners. In 1874, the University of Pennsylvania initiated a curriculum taught within the Department of Science by Thomas W. Richards, the university's architect.[64] In 1876, the University of Michigan began instruction by William LeBaron Jenney, but was forced to abandon the effort two years later. Columbia University obtained William Ware to start its curriculum within the School of Mines in 1881. A. D. F. Hamlin, educated at Amherst, MIT, and the *Ecole des beaux-arts,* joined the staff in the following year. In 1884, Columbian (later George Washington) University and its Corcoran Scientific School introduced courses in architecture, but a four-year professional curriculum awaited the reorganization of 1893. In 1889 Armour (now Illinois) Institute of Technology undertook a partial program, but six years later united with the school of the Art Institute of Chicago to create a full four-year professional curriculum. In 1895, Harvard established its curriculum as a department of the Lawrence Scientific School.[65]

In 1898, these nine schools together enrolled only 362 regular students. Columbia had the largest group, 78, but the average for all was only 40.[66] During their first three decades, the schools had as yet trained only a small fraction of the 10,581 architects reported by the 1900 Census. Their efforts were handicapped by inadequate secondary schools, the suspicion of many practitioners, and meager resources. Because many youths still preferred direct office training, the schools admitted them to abbreviated programs and evening courses. Despite repeated attempts to eliminate this partial and supplementary instruction, in 1898 the schools still enrolled 124 "special students."

The teaching of a creative activity such as architecture within a traditional academic framework involved many difficult adjustments. These were accentuated by the fact that enrollments were small and departments developed within other administrative divisions. Syracuse was associated with Fine Arts; Armour with both Fine Arts and engineering; all the rest were assigned to engineering on the basis of mutual interest in materials and structural theory. In most cases, the engineering point of view proved constrictive to a well-balanced program and after long struggles most architectural departments became independent units.[67]

These early schools had little contact with each other, but similar conditions produced similar four-year curricula and parallel methods. Nevertheless, each gradually acquired some special character of its own. At Illinois, strong emphasis was placed on mathematics, structures, and shop practice in the crafts. Ware at Columbia and

Warren at Harvard stressed sound scholarship in history. Syracuse, George Washington, and Armour emphasized aesthetic interests. The greatest difference, however, lay in the teaching of design. At first design exercises were reserved to the final year. At Illinois and Cornell, the aim was practical training in the preparation of working drawings, rather than in the development of creative facility. At MIT, Ware fought this tendency by appointing in 1872 as head of these courses, Eugene Létang, a former student at the *Ecole*. Although the French system underwent necessary modifications, something of the *Ecole's* breadth and spirit enriched MIT teaching. At Columbia, Ware adopted a different approach, rational, scholarly, and non-competitive. At Armour, Louis Millet, trained at the *Ecole,* applied its methods from the first.

The curricula of the early schools aimed at a just balance between the aesthetic and technical aspects of architecture. Pressed by the limitations of the four-year schedule, and by the large content required for thorough coverage of both design and structures, the result was usually a meager treatment of both. To remedy this situation and to meet a rising demand for graduates trained to handle the new complexities of steel and concrete, Ricker applied at Illinois in 1895 the principle of curricular specialization and introduced the first course leading to a degree in Architectural Engineering. This, in turn, permitted a reduction in structural content and an increase in design for students in Architecture. This solution by means of complementary options came to be adopted by many other schools.

Meanwhile, an increasing number of American students, with or without school training, followed the trail of Hunt, Dexter, and Peabody to Paris. In the 1860's, ten Americans studied at the *Ecole;* in the 70's, 26; in the 80's, 25; and in the 90's, 110.[68] A few, like Louis Sullivan, did not cherish their experience, but most—both those who had persisted through the whole program and those who had only taken design problems in an *atelier*—returned home fired with missionary zeal to recreate the whole *Ecole-atelier* system in the United States. The idea of an American alumni organization to foster this plan grew from a student meeting in Paris in 1889. Once returned and centered in New York, the group met periodically to revive old memories and discuss means and methods.[69] There, in 1893, E.-L. Masqueray established an *atelier* which reinforced the group's determination, and, in January, 1894, they incorporated the Society of Beaux-Arts Architects, with 72 members. The avowed aim was to combat current architectural "vagaries and abuses," promote the principles of taste taught at the *Ecole,* encourage American students to enter the *Ecole,* and urge the creation of a national central school of architecture modeled on the *Ecole*. The Society immediately embarked on an active educational program. Three *ateliers* were organized and the first of the quarterly student competitions was issued and judged. In the same year the Paris Prize was established. Whereas only three of the eight schools existing in 1894 had any *Ecole*-trained teachers, by 1911 all of them, plus Harvard, had one or more French or American alumni on their staffs. Despradelle succeeded Létang at MIT in 1892; Brockway and Gaggin came to Syracuse soon afterward; Pennsylvania appointed Seeler about 1893, Perkins and Nolan in 1898, and Cret in 1903; Cornell secured Van Pelt in 1896 and, later, Nash, Prevot, Hebrard, and

Mauxion. In 1905 Columbia reorganized its school and set up three internal *ateliers*.

During the next generation, American architectural education expanded rapidly. Of the nine early schools, seven were located in the populous North Atlantic region and two in the Midwest. Eleven were added by 1911, two more northeastern and three midwestern schools. The other six were distributed beyond these boundaries— four in the South, one in the Plains and Mountain States, and one on the West coast.

The next generation saw rapid expansion of population and of all branches of higher education. Architecture participated fully in this remarkable phenomenon. Thirty-three new schools were started between 1911 and 1930, bringing the total to 53, but even more dramatic was their dispersal across the nation. This shift in distribution is underscored by the following table:

Location of Architectural Schools, 1898–1930

	North-east	Mid-west	South	Plains-mountain	Pacific Coast	Total
1898	7	2				9
1911	9	5	4	1	1	20
1930	17	7	12	12	5	53

In 1930, 47 schools offered curricula in Architecture and 24, Architectural Engineering. Total enrollment had risen to 1450 in 1911, an average of 72 per school. World War I interrupted growth, but by 1930 a total of 5890 (4622 architects and 1268 architectural engineers) were in attendance.[70] It was clear that collegiate training was fast assuming a major role in the education of the profession.

Despite this increased enrollment of regular students, many schools, especially in the larger centers, still permitted office employees to supplement their practical training by registering for individual day courses or by taking evening classes. Such study often led to a certificate, but several programs, necessarily quite prolonged, made it possible to win a full professional degree while, at the same time, earning a livelihood. In 1926, New York University inaugurated a curriculum taught in mid-town quarters convenient to many offices, and working students comprised a large proportion of its enrollment. When employment plummeted during depression years, the school was abandoned. For design training, private *ateliers* served many students at all levels of skill. Finally, a large number of young employees obtained considerable assistance through the use of correspondence courses. Some of these were well organized, especially in theoretical subjects, but the teaching of design by mail presented insuperable handicaps.

Multiplication of schools was a necessary consequence to population growth and the continental extent of the country, but, while some prospered under energetic administration, others languished through inadequate vision and support, and in the process betrayed both students and the profession. Then, too, if the northeastern schools had worked in isolation, those spread at far greater distances were endangered by provincial stagnation. To mitigate these hazards, the Association of Collegiate Schools of Architecture was formed in 1912 with the purpose of stimulating interschool contacts and establishing informal educational standards through control of admission to its membership. These criteria were crystallized in 1914 as *standard minima* which specified general requirements for curriculum, admission, courses, and degree. While this quasi-self-accrediting procedure no doubt strengthened some of the weaker schools, most teachers opposed the *standard minima* as potential strait-jackets which could freeze architectural education in a rigid mold, destroy faculty initiative and responsibility, prevent wholesome variety, and discourage desirable adjustments to new needs and methods. After years of debate, the *standard minima* were abandoned in 1932 and the Association became a valuable forum for the discussion of educational problems in which all schools and teachers working in the field are welcome to participate.[71]

The Society of Beaux-Arts Architects failed to secure the establishment of a national school, but it won an even greater influence on American architectural education as the use of its student design competitions reached national scope. By 1905, 238 students were participating. In 1913, the Society enrolled 1100 students. By 1916, these educational activities had grown to such dimensions that the Society transferred their administration to a new organization, the Beaux-Arts Institute of Design. For more than another decade, the design teaching of American schools continued to be dominated by the BAID. The effects were mixed in value. At its height, with almost all schools participating, interschool competition tended to raise the standards of student performance. Isolated and metropolitan schools alike faced independent professional juries. BAID programs and judgments lightened faculty responsibilities and gave the Society's members in New York some continuing contact with the schools. Nevertheless, despite these advantages, abuses similar to those encountered at the *Ecole* soon appeared. Medals, rather than student growth, became a real, if unadmitted, goal. Decorative "salon" presentations seduced students, faculties, and juries, and subverted precision. Strong protests by heads of schools failed to prevent critics and assistants from "helping" promising *projets*. The most insidious result, however, was the schools' surrender of their inherent responsibility to determine, organize, and control their own objectives and methods of design teaching. When the fixing of subject and program was relegated to a central agency, schools lost the initiative to develop a sequence of exercises carefully integrated within itself and with parallel technical courses. Such integration could not be solved in New York by a committee of volunteers, however devoted and well-intentioned they might be. This was a task requiring prolonged and continuing study such as only a permanent faculty could undertake.

Although the basic pattern of architectural education was generally consistent throughout the country, detailed methods used showed considerable diversity. The greatest uniformity of methods was in the conduct of theoretical courses, but even here intensity and emphasis differed. Theory was sometimes a separate course, but often was delegated to design. History varied from a soothing travelogue to a systematic and thorough analysis of outstanding monuments and their relationship to their time. Construction and structures were sometimes lightly touched. In design, the problem method was universal, but organization, approach, and teaching were diversified. Some schools based their instruction exclusively on BAID programs and the grades it awarded. Others used BAID programs, more or less occasionally, but did not submit the results for New York judgment. A few schools preferred to prepare their own programs. Some schools felt compelled to segment design into term courses in order to fit the traditional academic pattern. Some overcame these bonds and introduced flexible promotion based on individual progress.

During the 1920's, three schools explored other methods. Soon after the first World War, the University of Oregon, led by Dean Ellis F. Lawrence and Professor W. R. B. Wilcox, adopted the principle that design should be taught by means of individual problems adjusted to the needs, interests, and pace of each student, who would no longer compete for grades—there were no grades at all—but be motivated solely by the challenge of personal growth. The second method, the cooperative system, was applied to architecture in 1922 at the University of Cincinnati. This system, anticipated by Scottish continuation schools of the late 80's, was first formulated in the United States in 1899 by Hermann Schneider for engineering curricula at Lehigh University, and after 1906 as Dean of the College of Engineering, he matured the idea at Cincinnati.[72] After a normal freshman year, students were divided into two groups which alternated with each other at four-week intervals between academic classes and work in the field. This field work was carefully organized as a sequence of experiences proceeding from construction jobs, through the production of materials and craft practice, to employment in architectural offices. The aim was a close integration of school and practice. The third method was initiated by Rudolph Weaver of the University of Florida in 1925. It conducted all the usual professional subjects of the three upper years entirely by means of a series of carefully integrated projects developed under tutorial guidance. These and other modifications stimulated much discussion in educational circles. Some critics have declared that organization and methodology are purely secondary considerations and that an inspiring teacher is the only essential factor. Others point out that gifted teachers are by definition those who command effective methods. The real significance of educational experimentation seems to lie in the fact that it underscores the duty and opportunity of an alert faculty to seek continuously the most effective adjustment of educational process to professional and social needs.

Thus, the American pattern of architectural education embraced an all-inclusive curriculum established with few exceptions within the framework of the American university system. In contrast to European technical institutions and to earlier American colleges, American universities, based on Jefferson's vision and stimulated by the Morrill Act, attained unique character in their comprehensive provision for the liberal arts, the fine arts, sciences, technologies, and professions. Leaders of this movement, such as Jefferson, Tappan, White, and Gregory, insisted upon professional, rather than vocational, objectives in the useful arts. Ware at MIT was especially concerned that architectural education should never be content with merely training draftsmen, but should always strive to prepare graduates who could grow to professional maturity. This objective has been vigorously maintained.

Between 1930 and 1950, depression and war created unprecedented emergencies for the profession and the schools. Four schools abandoned their programs, but fifteen others instituted new curricula, so that the net increase of eleven brought the total to 64 schools in 1950. By 1944–1945 the demands of military service had left only a handful of students in school, but in the following years returning veterans, together with the resumption of the normal flow of new students from the high schools, swelled enrollments in architecture to an all-time peak of 11,665 in 1949. By 1953 this had receded to 9427 (*Table 56*). This was an increase of 150 per cent over 1930. It should also be noted that in 1953, 25 schools offered curricula in architectural engineering in which were enrolled 1744 students.

The gradual expansion of American architectural education caused the Association of Collegiate Schools of Architecture to urge a thorough inventory of the schools as early as 1919. This culminated in 1930 in a survey and analysis by Professors Frank H. Bosworth and Roy Childs Jones and their far-seeing report, *A Study of Architectural Schools,* published two years later. The *Young-Goldsmith Report of 1939* endeavored to bring the earlier findings up to date and extend their scope. The *1950 Survey* and this present report establish the precedent of future studies at decennial intervals.

Inevitably, the growth of legal regulations governing the registration of architects emphasized the legitimate concern of both government and the profession for the quality of the educational process. Through its Committee on Education, The AIA had long striven to foster sound progress. Since the licensing acts of the several states usually granted some special consideration to graduates of approved professional schools, the various registration boards found urgent need for a uniform method of evaluation. Therefore, in 1939, The AIA, collaborating with the ACSA and the NCARB, established the National Architectural Accrediting Board. By its charter, the NAAB was directed to gather factual data from applicant schools, inspect them, evaluate the results, and publish an official annual list of approved schools. The Board was specifically denied any power to standardize the schools, and, on the contrary, was instructed to encourage each school to develop a program best suited to its special needs and situation. In 1945, after delay due to war, the Board began its operations.

Thus, in the United States, the university system has come to dominate the training of architectural students, but because of its inclusive curriculum and its self-contained organization, it has posed a difficult new problem with regard to graduates' transition to practice. In 19th-century Britain, the combination of office *pupilage* and supplementary schooling left no hiatus. The master expected to have to train his pupils to usefulness and informally encouraged their auxiliary studies. By the completion of these courses, the pupil had already acquired productive skills. In France, advanced students often interrupted schooling for office work to earn maintenance and experience. Since work was leisurely, wages low, and technical demands relatively

simple, practitioners did not find the system burdensome. In Germany, the requirement of pre-school and mid-school office work effectively bridged the gap. It should
be noted that all of these methods implied the responsibility of architects to initiate
their young employees into the conduct of practical work and thus ensure steady
growth toward professional competence. The problem in America will be examined
in detail in *Chapter VIII*.

4. EDUCATION AND
THE MODERN MOVEMENT

The ideal of an architecture in which utility and structure are integrated to produce
expressive form has been perennial among theoreticians, but, since architecture is
governed by heart as well as mind, logical principles have on occasion given way
before emotional fervor. The 19th century *par excellence* illustrated this schizophrenic
tendency. On the one hand, many of its architects met vigorously the challenge of
new materials and new needs; on the other hand, infatuated by romanticism, seduced
by a new familiarity with the past, and exchanging the patronage of an aristocratic
elite for a new middle-class clientele, many surrendered too often to misinterpreted
tradition, nervous picturesqueness, and specious ornamentation. At mid-century, the
Crystal Palace and Oxford's New Museum clearly epitomized this fundamental
cleavage.

Architectural education, being part and parcel of its time, could not by itself resolve
this bifurcation. As if the coordination of technical and aesthetic training were not a
sufficiently difficult problem, there was superimposed the premise that design vocabulary grew from the Orders, measured drawings, courses in history and ornament,
archaeological *projets,* and grand tour sketchbooks. It was a typical paradox that one
American school, the first to introduce shop practice and graphic statics, taught at the
same time "Renaissance, Gothic, and Romanesque Designing." Others taught the
same content, but usually under a more innocuous title.

By the end of the century, several methods were being used to resolve these difficulties. The followers of William Morris renounced the new techniques and rein-
voked medieval handicrafts. Others, like Richardson, Wagner, and Shaw, returned
to simple geometrical massing. Some, such as Mackintosh, Horta, Sullivan, and
Endell, invented new systems of ornament to replace historic models. Finally, there
emerged the belief—announced by Loos, Wright, and Muthesius—that valid architectural beauty could arise only from the integration of modern functions and techniques.[73] By the beginning of World War I, the first monuments of the new doctrine
had taken form.

Many of the leaders of these movements had had the normal architectural training
of their day. Morris, Shaw, Mackintosh, and Horta had been office pupils. Richardson went to the *Ecole des beaux-arts;* Sullivan for brief periods had studied at MIT
and the *Ecole;* Mackintosh also attended the architectural classes of the Glasgow

School of Art; Wagner was trained at the Vienna *Polytechnikum* and the *Kunst-akademie,* and Loos at the *Technische Hochschule* in Dresden. Wright combined academic courses in civil engineering with office training under Silsbee and Sullivan. Nevertheless, except for Sullivan's influence on Wright, it is doubtful that any of these leaders owed more than rudimentary stimulus to their educational mentors. They developed leadership by personal growth stirred by mounting emotional and intellectual impatience against the restraints and inhibitions of eclecticism.

For many years the new doctrine had little impact on the established schools of architecture. It was rather the German schools of applied arts which first endeavored to apply the new concepts. From 1897 on, many of these institutions were reorganized and received directors and teachers who supported the new approach. Since many had developed their early courses in building crafts into architectural programs of almost professional caliber, these too were reoriented. At Vienna, in 1899, Josef Hoffmann, a pupil of Wagner and a leader in the Secession group, was appointed professor of architecture of the school of the Austrian Museum of Art and Crafts. In 1902, Henri Van de Velde, painter turned architect and Belgian protagonist of the *Art nouveau,* took charge of the Grand Ducal Art School at Weimar. In 1904, Peter Behrens, trained at the Hamburg School of Applied Arts, painter, architect, and industrial designer, was called to direct the Dusseldorf School of Applied Arts. By 1907, the year in which the *Deutscher Werkbund* was founded to give designers, craftsmen, and manufacturers closer liaison, the new spirit was well-established in Central European schools of applied arts.[74]

The culminating influence for architecture came in 1914 when Walter Gropius, trained in the *technischen hochschulen* at Berlin and Munich, former pupil of Behrens, and the most thoroughgoing modernist of the group, was appointed successor of Van de Velde as director of the Weimar school. After war service, Gropius returned and reorganized the school as the *Staatliches Bauhaus.* In 1925, the school moved to Dessau and occupied the famous building group designed by Gropius. He resigned in 1928, and was succeeded by Hannes Meyer, who was, in turn, replaced by Mies van der Rohe in 1930. Two years later, the local government withdrew its support from the *Bauhaus* and after a year of private operation in Berlin the school disbanded.

The objective of the *Bauhaus* program was "a modern architectonic art, all-embracing in its scope," to be achieved by reuniting all creative crafts within a new architecture by exploiting forms and principles discovered through direct shop or field experience in modern materials and modern industrial techniques. After a six-months introductory course of laboratory experiments, students devoted three years to theoretical and practical training under a master craftsman and an artist in order to gain an intimate understanding of the nature of materials, their production and manipulation, and their aesthetic potentialities. Command of machine processes was stressed. Concurrently a limited study of sociology, history, and technical fundamentals was pursued. Upon execution of an original work, a Journeyman's Certificate was conferred. The final two years focused on architecture and construction and was conducted as an apprenticeship within the master's studio and research shop, but with great emphasis on field work.

Thus, the *Bauhaus* translated into modern industrial terms the revival of the apprenticeship system initiated by William Morris. Thanks to a brilliant faculty—pioneers like Moholy-Nagy, Kandinsky, Feininger, Klee, Breuer, and Gropius—and supported by unusually efficient publicity, *Bauhaus* influence spread rapidly and far. It was a curious paradox, however, that despite its enthusiastic embracing of contemporary building techniques, it did not attempt to provide any systematic instruction in the technical theory necessary to the exercise of those skills. It offered little, if any, training for the architectural student in mathematical analysis of the steel and concrete structures which it proclaimed so representative of the new architecture, nor was any organized instruction given in the design of mechanical or other building equipment. For such courses students were sent to the regular technical schools. In this it acknowledged its descent from a school of art.[75]

The established schools of the 1920's were, like most practitioners, immersed in eclecticism. Nevertheless, in America, the most progressive architects, teachers, and students were beginning to resist its frustrating restraints. While interest in Richardson, Sullivan, and Wright was in eclipse, their example of independent thought was still not forgotten. The work of B. G. Goodhue, Raymond Hood, Arthur Loomis Harmon, Henry Wright, and McKenzie, Voorhees, and Gmelin stirred many to seek an architectural expression more consonant with new needs, techniques, and aspirations. From Europe, not only the half-Viennese ornamental excrescences of the 1925 Paris Exposition of Decorative Arts, but, more important, the work of Ragnar Ostberg and Eliel Saarinen, encouraged a fresh view, and the arrival of Richard Neutra and William Lescaze soon furnished first-hand stimuli. By the end of the decade, the writings of LeCorbusier and the work of Mallet-Stevens had awakened considerable interest. On the other hand, Central European developments were known only from foreign journals, brief notices in the domestic press, and such American publications as Charles R. Richards' *Art in Industry* and Henry-Russell Hitchcock's *Modern Architecture,* issued in 1929. The advent of depression accelerated these tendencies. When at last, in March, 1932, New York's Museum of Modern Art opened its Exhibition of Modern Architecture, it not only accented Wright, Hood, Neutra, and Howe and Lescaze, but also focused attention upon Gropius, Mies van der Rohe, and J. J. P. Oud. The provocative ascetic spirit of this Central European "International Style" struck a responsive note attuned to the time, and seemed to promise a positive means to dethrone eclecticism and exploit the architectural potentialities of American industry. Its possession of a well developed and confident written doctrine added to its intellectual appeal.

Increasing interest soon penetrated American architectural schools. In 1936, the climax came when Harvard University replaced its French chief critic with Gropius himself, who became chairman of the department. He soon called Marcel Breuer to the faculty. Curricula and courses were reoriented, and Gropius took charge of the "master class" in graduate design. Although the *Bauhaus* point of view naturally prevailed, the result was nevertheless a new phenomenon, for it operated within the American collegiate system. This was particularly true of the graduate class in design, since a large proportion of its members were the products of other American schools. After World War II, this graduate program was in great demand.

A second American center of *Bauhaus* influence was created in 1938 when the Illinois Institute of Technology appointed Ludwig Mies van der Rohe, Gropius' successor at Dessau, to direct its School of Architecture. Mies soon reorganized its curriculum and teaching in a more drastic manner than Harvard had deemed necessary. It also was inevitable that Mies' own personal interpretation of *Bauhaus* philosophy, with his strong feeling for constructivistic classicism, has dominated the school. Great emphasis was placed on the disciplines of precise draftsmanship, absolutistic structural logic, and an aesthetic based on pristine clarity of pure geometric forms.

Bauhaus teaching and methods were also transplanted by other members of its faculty, in 1937 by Moholy-Nagy at the Institute of Design in Chicago, and in 1940 by Josef Albers at Black Mountain College in North Carolina. The latter never undertook a professional curriculum in architecture, but the Institute under Serge Chermayeff began such a program in 1947 which, however, was discontinued when it was affiliated with IIT in 1950. *Bauhaus* ideas, pure or adapted, have entered many other schools. Gyorgy Kepes introduced them at MIT in his course in visual composition. Elsewhere, elementary courses have frequently adopted exercises in the direct experiencing and expression of materials. In design courses, students have come to admire and emulate the characteristic forms and vocabulary employed by its adherents. Unfortunately, despite Gropius' assertion that the *Bauhaus* intended to establish only an attitude and method of working, much of its impact on students and practitioners has been to promulgate a new style with its own clichés. In this it has shared the fate of many previous aesthetic movements. While some critics question whether its effect on American architecture and professional education will prove to be essentially different from the preceding French influence, on the whole the *Bauhaus* has provided a valuable and thought-provoking stimulus. It entered the American scene at a moment when *Ecole* influence had already waned and it offered an appealing philosophical system to those who decried eclecticism and were restlessly seeking a basis for dimly felt new principles. As so often has been the case before, American architectural thinking has assimilated useful elements from its teaching which, in time, will constitute a worthwhile component of the synthesis which American architects and educators must ultimately formulate for themselves.

Paralleling the *Bauhaus* development and influenced greatly by it, was the trend to see the future of architecture wholly derived from science and technology. This constructivistic principle is not new. Cistercian buildings of the 12th century consciously applied it. It was also a major tenet of 18th-century rationalism. Nevertheless, with the rise of modern materials and techniques, it is not surprising that this attitude appealed strongly to purists who sought at once to fix form by direct logic and thus escape the need for intuitive creativeness in which they saw only arbitrariness and emotional irrationality. Thus this ideal paradoxically equated architecture with engi-

107

neering, and education for its practice would approximate that of the structural engineer. This notion conformed to the rising cult of engineering and its wide appeal led to the phenomenon of the "architect-engineer" firm, in which, too often, the public erroneously considers "architect" to be an adjective, rather than a coequal noun. Fortunately, since any argument which dismisses the need of architecture for creative skill is fallacious, the effect of this trend upon the schools has been, not to surrender their curricula to science, but to re-emphasize their legitimate scientific content and to alert their students to the many significant contributions which all disciplines can make to the art of architecture.

The opportunity of studying directly under an acknowledged master has long enjoyed universal appeal. Within the collegiate system, students flocked to famed critics, such as Despradelle, Cret, and Carlu. Outside this system, however, Saarinen drew to his idyllic academy at Cranbrook a select group of eager graduate students who profited greatly from his inspired humane teaching. From the mid-30's an increasing number of students also sought training under Frank Lloyd Wright, who formed his Taliesin Fellowship to receive them and built their fabulous quarters in Wisconsin and Arizona. There *pupilage* became a broad and romantic experience, going far beyond mere technical content, but it also omitted much that is usually considered essential.

The appearance of new educational systems has naturally provoked much discussion, for change always implies criticism of current methods. In a profession in which new problems and materials are constantly appearing, the evolution of the content of its educational teaching has long been accepted. With regard to the organization and methods of instruction, however, objective consideration and systematic redesign have been less frequently attempted. Nevertheless, American schools have never been static. The lack of a national directing authority has permitted healthy variety, but excessive individualism has been avoided through exchange of ideas between schools, the recruiting of faculty from many sources, and the general recognition of a core of knowledge and skills demanded by professional practice. Unfortunately, precise evaluation of the products of varying educational systems involves so many uncontrollable and non-school factors operating over so long a period that it is impossible to compute.

Frequently, the employability of graduates is asserted as an argument against radical change in education. To the extent that a young graduate must earn a livelihood, he must become productive in the work of his employer, for the novice has no just claim to philanthropic support on his own terms. Nor can he acquire effectively the additional training he seeks in the office if he is unprepared to work within its frame of reference. Another apology for maintaining the status quo is based on the demands of the state for certain types of competence in the interest of public safety and welfare. Certainly any system which neglects such necessary and logical requirements has no right to be considered professional in character.

Actually, both of these criteria deal with the content of teaching and in no wise inhibit changes in methods or philosophical approach. Indeed, continuing search for more efficient methods of instruction is widely held as one of the most important duties of a faculty. It is only when method or philosophy turn out to be so doctrinaire as to neglect vital areas of content—either knowledge or skills—that freedom to change becomes misguided license violating the fundamental principle of intellectual inquiry. Any system which restricts its teaching to a narrow set of dogmas is not education, but only propaganda. Such a system forfeits professional status by repudiating the profession which it claims to serve.

Within these reasonable limits, however, the schools have plenty of scope to pursue their necessary and legitimate objectives. They will do well to maintain the closest liaison with the profession in order to adjust content and method to the changing needs of practice. And, by the same token, the profession, too, must apply its highest wisdom, most sympathetic understanding, and most penetrating vision to the problems of education. The very term "professional education" reveals by its compound form, the necessity of enlightened and harmonious cooperation.

5. EDUCATIONAL CHARACTERISTICS OF U. S. ARCHITECTS IN 1950

The *1950 Survey* charted for the first time the educational characteristics of registered architects in the United States. Since the age range of the group extends to advanced years, there emerges from these data a composite picture of the use these individuals have made during the past six decades of the various systems of training available during this period. Although correlation of educational patterns and age groups could not be undertaken, change in dependence upon these systems is not difficult to discern, and thus it is possible to trace with some certainty the general trend of American architectural education.

The *1950 Survey* revealed that 23 per cent of all U. S. registered architects obtained their entire professional training in offices (*Table 36*). This indicates that the practical appeal and economy of the age-old apprenticeship system has persisted to a surprising degree. Indeed, veterans' "on-the-job" training, promoted after World War II, was but the most recent version, encouraged by direct federal subsidies. Nevertheless, with regard to the size of this office-trained group, two qualifying points must be considered. First, the group includes many older architects who took their professional training before collegiate education was readily accessible and who were among the 13 per cent of all architects who, having conducted practices before the adoption of the several registration acts, gained licenses under the "grandfather" provisions of these acts. It seems safe to conclude, therefore, that, after all of these acts have been in operation over a more extended time, the very long work period required by most acts for admission of office-trained candidates to the licensing examinations and the growing recognition of the limitations of office training will together discourage and reduce the exclusive use of this type of training in the future. On the other hand, since most acts do recognize such training as an acceptable method of qualifying for examination, it will no doubt continue to supply a certain number of candidates. It is, indeed, desirable to retain such provisions in order that access to professional status will not be monopolized by a single pattern of approach.

Secondly, major dependence on office training does not exclude the possibility that many within this group obtained valuable preparation, either preceding or concurrently, by means other than the professional schools. Some, for example, were probably included in the 16 per cent of all architects who won certificates in non-collegiate trade schools or technical institutes (*Table 36*). A large proportion most certainly were among the 73 per cent who reported that they had taken subsequent supplementary courses. Some, indeed, may have begun office training after having pursued liberal arts or other non-professional programs which could include subjects useful in the profession, such as mathematics and the sciences. Thus, it is clear that many of the group which reported all professional training in offices probably enjoyed educational resources obscured by the phrasing of the question. The number who followed solely the romantic and legendary route from office boy to practitioner is no doubt much smaller than might be supposed if a strict interpretation of the *1950 Survey* is imposed.

Sixty-six per cent of all registered architects prepared themselves for practice by attending at least one school of architecture, and 56 per cent attained the first professional degree. Nine per cent obtained degrees in architectural engineering (*Table 35*). Some earned degrees in both architecture and architectural engineering, but unfortunately, no computation of this overlap is possible. However, it probably does not exceed 1 or 2 per cent, so that the number of different individuals holding degrees is possibly around 62 per cent. This means that approximately 12,000 American architects have completed their formal professional training in the country's schools of architecture. When it is recalled that only nine schools were in operation in 1898, and only 20 in 1911, and that total architectural enrollment per 100,000 urban population grew from 1.27 in 1900 to 3.45 in 1910, to 6.60 in 1930, and to 12.5 in 1950 (*Table 57*), it is clear that the collegiate schools of architecture have played an expanding role in the training of professional personnel.[76]

In addition to those who obtained professional architectural degrees, the schools also provided partial training for those who for financial or other reasons stopped short of the complete course. No estimate of their number is available, for only a small portion is reflected in the difference between all attending schools and all graduating, because the *1950 Survey* reported only those few who finally won registration despite abbreviated schooling.[77] While many non-registered non-graduates probably turned to other fields, no doubt many applied their partial training by accepting secondary positions in architectural offices. In either case, this training was not lost and this contribution of the schools remains significant. A number of schools have conducted special non-degree programs, either by evening classes or individually arranged schedules of regular courses. Twenty-one per cent of all architects reported completion of such courses (*Table 35*). For some these programs constituted their only formal professional training, but for others they supplemented regular curricula.

Many architects have continued their formal studies beyond the undergraduate program; 10 per cent have earned advanced degrees (*Table 35*). Most of these have been at the Master level, for only a mere handful have obtained the doctoral diploma. Among architectural faculties, it is not surprising to find that 48 per cent hold graduate degrees. Twenty per cent of all architects have studied in a foreign country, either at undergraduate or advanced levels, or as travelers (*Table 36*). Again, teachers have a much higher rate of 38 per cent. Ten per cent of all architects and 44 per cent of all teachers have received fellowships or grants-in-aid for advanced study. Seventy-three per cent of all architects have supplemented their training with courses in varied subjects (*Table 40*). Twenty-two per cent of those reporting such studies took engineering courses, and these were followed in popularity by fine arts (14), business and economics (13), city planning (9), liberal arts (8), and social sciences (6). Landscape architecture, real estate, and law, each were selected by 5 per cent. The 83 per cent of all teachers who followed such programs chose a different order of preference, with fine arts, city planning, engineering, social science, and liberal arts as the most favored. A surprising number of architects, 4 per cent, hold full engineering degrees, other than architectural engineering, which they have used either to supplement architectural training or as the main foundation on which to build an architectural career (*Table 36*).

The advantages of general collegiate education as a broadening and enriching preparation for professional life have been gained by the 13 per cent of all architects who completed degrees in the liberal arts. An additional 20 per cent have pursued college studies in non-architectural fields for varying lengths of time as circumstances permitted (*Table 39*). Others have sought supplementary courses in them, as indicated in *Table 40*. A few architects, 4 per cent, entered architecture after earning degrees in other than liberal arts, architecture, or engineering (*Table 36*).

In addition to the types of education used by architects, the *1950 Survey* also revealed where they pursued their studies and, in turn, some indication of the quantitative impact of individual schools upon the profession during the past half-century. Ninety-seven per cent of all architects responding to the *Survey* answered the questions on education.[78] Of those, 96 per cent reported graduation from secondary schools.[79] It has already been noted that 66 per cent attended at least one professional school and that about 62 per cent obtained first degrees in architecture or architectural engineering.

Table 37 shows the distribution among 65 schools of all 4144 first degrees awarded in architecture and architectural engineering, all 661 second professional degrees, and 1323 special programs.[80] It also lists the totals of first and second attendances at each school. In comparing the records of the schools, it must be remembered that these are quantitative data summarizing more than fifty years of operation. Long operation obviously adds numbers; enrollment policies likewise affect the results; and the community served also influences the scale of activity. The table lists the 60 American schools with full curricula in the order of number of first degrees which have been awarded to registered architects. This shows that half of the schools awarded 82 per cent of these degrees; a third, 66 per cent; and a tenth, 35 per cent. Inspection of second professional degrees reveals a much higher concentration in a few schools. A third of the schools accounted for 83 per cent of these degrees, and a tenth, 52 per cent. The ten largest groups of second degrees were:[81]

MIT	12.65	Columbia	6.20	U. Illinois	4.98
Harvard	11.50	U. Calif.	5.89	Cornell	4.08
U. Penn.	10.72	Princeton	5.14	Washington U.	3.02
				Yale	2.87

Figure 25, p. 118 charts first and second degrees by schools.

It is interesting to compare the geographical distribution of high school graduations, formal professional training, and present location of these architects. The percentages for AIA regions and four "super regions" are as follows:

Super Regions & AIA Regions	High School Graduation	1st Degree School	2nd Degree School	Location in 1950
TOTAL NUMBER	6152	4144	661	19,137
PER CENT	100	100	100	100
New England	8.04	10.73	27.02	7.86
New York	13.30	13.89	13.60	15.40
Mid-Atlantic	16.50	15.52	20.65	17.73
Total North Atlantic	37.84	40.14	61.27	40.99
Great Lakes	12.25	11.94	4.93	10.53
North Central	13.79	14.86	7.09	10.90
Total Mid-West	26.04	26.80	12.02	21.43
Total Central	8.29	6.45	5.12	6.08
South Atlantic	4.53	5.38	2.57	5.89
Gulf	4.35	2.58	.75	4.36
Total Southeast	8.88	7.96	3.32	10.25
Total Texas	4.17	4.64	3.42	4.98
West Mountain	4.17	0.73	.00	2.12
Northwest	3.88	3.29	.30	3.78
Sierra Nevada	6.78	5.75	6.19	10.29
Total West	14.83	9.77	6.49	16.19
Total (Other Schools)		(4.24)	(8.31)	
DATA DERIVED FROM	TABLE 38	TABLE 37	TABLE 37	TABLE I

Figure 23 charts these data. The New England, Gulf, and Northwest regions had practically identical proportions of high school graduates and 1950 personnel. The east coast regions—New York, Mid-Atlantic, and South Atlantic—and the Texas and

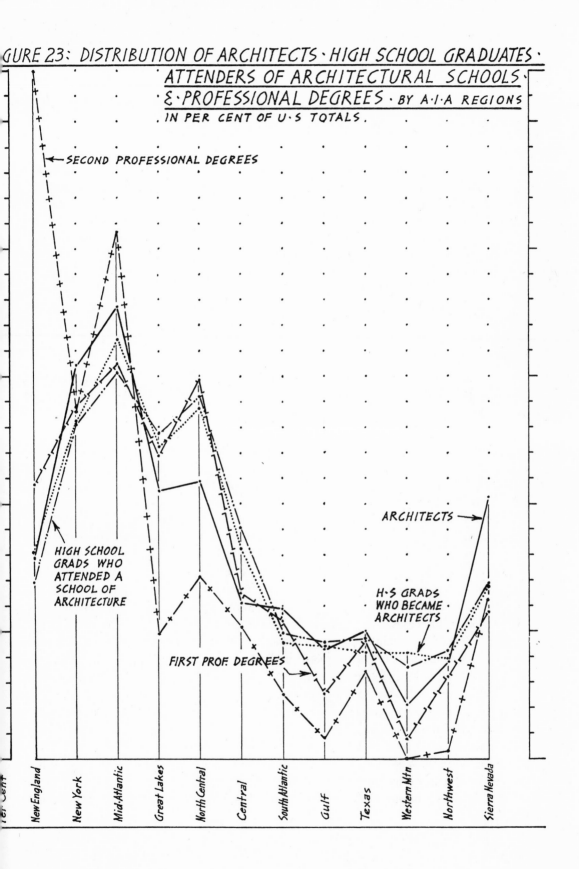

FIGURE 23: DISTRIBUTION OF ARCHITECTS · HIGH SCHOOL GRADUATES · ATTENDERS OF ARCHITECTURAL SCHOOLS · & · PROFESSIONAL DEGREES · BY A·I·A REGIONS IN PER CENT OF U·S TOTALS.

SECOND PROFESSIONAL DEGREES

ARCHITECTS

HIGH SCHOOL GRADS WHO ATTENDED A SCHOOL OF ARCHITECTURE

H·S GRADS WHO BECAME ARCHITECTS

FIRST PROF. DEGREES

Per Cent

New England · New York · Mid-Atlantic · Great Lakes · North Central · Central · South Atlantic · Gulf · Texas · Western Mtn · Northwest · Sierra Nevada

Sierra Nevada regions did not furnish enough high school graduates to supply the number of architects needed. To make good this deficit, these regions drew recruits from the Midwest—the Great Lakes, North Central, and Central regions—and from the Western Mountain region.

The geographical distribution of first degrees by the regions in which the conferring schools were located did not vary in six regions more than 1.5 per cent from the distribution of high school graduates. Marked divergence occurred in the 2.69 per cent excess of degrees over high school graduates in New England, and the deficiencies of 1.84 per cent in the Central region, 1.77 in the Gulf region, and 3.44 in the Western Mountain region. Degrees awarded were close to 1950 personnel distributions in the Central, South Atlantic, Texas, and Northwest regions. Deficiencies in degrees, as compared to 1950 locations, appeared in the New York (1.51 per cent), Mid-Atlantic (2.21), Gulf (1.78), Western Mountain (1.39), and Sierra Nevada (4.54) regions. Excess degrees occurred in the New England (2.87), Great Lakes (1.43), and North Central (3.96) regions.

The distribution of second professional degrees by regions in which the conferring schools were located reveals a high concentration in the North Atlantic regions—27.02 per cent in New England, 20.65 in Mid-Atlantic, and 13.60 in New York, a total of 61.27 per cent. A low middle group includes the North Central (7.09), Sierra Nevada (6.19), Central (5.12), Great Lakes (4.93), Texas (3.42), and South Atlantic (2.57) regions. The remaining regions—Gulf, Northwest, and Western Mountain—all together reported only 1.05 per cent. The result is that, except in the New England and Mid-Atlantic regions, the other nine showed marked deficiencies of second degrees in proportion to their roster of architects in 1950—in the Great Lakes (5.60), Sierra Nevada (4.10), North Central (3.81), Gulf (3.61), Northwest (3.48), South Atlantic (3.32), Western Mountain (2.12), and Central (0.96). Second degrees exceeded first degrees in New England (16.29 per cent) and the Mid-Atlantic (5.13), while the opposite was especially notable in the North Central (7.77) and Great Lakes (7.01) regions.

Table 38 also reveals that in 1950, 56 per cent of all architects were working in the *same* state in which they had both graduated from high school and obtained their first license to practice. Regional averages range from 84 per cent for the Sierra Nevada region, 81 for Texas, and 70 for South Atlantic, to only two with fewer than half—13 for Western Mountain and 40 for Central.[82] Thus, despite American mobility, there exists a strong urge to remain rooted in the home community. Convenient access to educational facilities fosters this tendency. In the 28 states which have had schools of architecture established long enough to affect the *1950 Survey,* 72 per cent of the high school graduates of those states who entered architectural schools, first attended schools within their home state. In these same states, 60 per cent of those architects who graduated from high school in the state, were also first registered, and were working in the *same* state in 1950. In contrast, the same ratio in states without schools was only 41 per cent.[83]

Although a breakdown of degrees awarded to in-state and out-of-state students is not available for all schools, the *1950 Survey* provides such data for individual states and, incidentally, for schools which are unique within their states. *Figure 24,* overleaf, graphs these data for 30 states, of which 17 have only one school.[84] Five states show more out-of-state than in-state degrees—Massachusetts, 62 per cent; Connecticut, 78; New Jersey, 80; Indiana, 72; and Georgia, the only state-supported school in the group, 56. Nevertheless, those states accounted for only 27 per cent of all out-of-state degrees, and Massachusetts and Connecticut together awarded 19 per cent. In all other states, in-state degrees have predominated, with eight schools having a ratio of 80 per cent or more. The percentages of all first degrees, all in-state and all out-of-state degrees, for groups of schools having various proportions of in-state students, are as follows:

Per cent of In-state Students	*Number of States*	*Number of Schools*	*Per cent of All First Degrees*	*Per cent of All In-state Degrees*	*Per cent of All Out-state Degrees*
TOTAL NUMBER 30		56	3981	2411(60.5%)	1570(39.5%)
PERCENT			100	100	100
20–49	5	6	16.10	8.78	27.43
20–29	3	3	6.46	2.45	12.67
30–39	1	2	6.98	4.37	11.00
40–49	1	1	2.66	1.96	3.76
50–79	17	32	63.04	62.08	65.66
50–59	6	16	36.96	33.00	44.00
60–69	4	7	15.96	16.85	14.71
70–79	7	9	10.12	12.23	6.95
80–100	8	18	20.58	28.70	7.12
80–89	6	16	19.70	28.04	6.99
90–100	2	2	.88	.66	.13

Thus, it is apparent that for many years there has existed a strong tendency for American architects to seek formal schooling near at hand. The 60.5 per cent national ratio does not measure the real magnitude of this custom, for it would be greatly increased if to it were added the large numbers of students who attend nearby schools in adjoining states. New Jersey, for example, sends many to New York and Pennsylvania; Indiana and Kentucky to the University of Cincinnati; and Wisconsin to the Universities of Illinois and Minnesota. There is some indication that in recent years about 80 per cent of all architectural students attend schools within their states or adjoining states.[85] Since the architects responding to the *1950 Survey* were of such ages that some received degrees as early as the 1890's, and since during this period the number of schools has grown from nine, all located in the northeastern quarter of the country, to 64 schools distributed among 35 states, it is clear that, in order to obtain an overall in-state ratio of 60.5 per cent, the proportion of in-state students must have

	No. of schools	In-State Graduates			Out-of-State Graduat
U·S	56	2411	60.5%	39 81	1570 39.
MASS	2	105	38%	278	173 62
CONN	1	35	22%	161	126 78
N·Y	7	316	55%	575	259 4
N·J	1	10	20%	50	40 8(
PENN	3	261	53%	492	231 4
D·C	2	19	54%	35	16 4
VA	3	40	62%	65	25 38
OHIO	5	171	81%	211	40 19
IND	1	13	28%	46	33 72
MICH	2	122	52%	237	115 48
ILL	2	324	64%	507	183 36
MINN	1	50	54%	92	42 46
N·DAK	1	16	100%	16	—
IOWA	1	25	71%	35	10 2
MO	1	48	70%	69	21 3
NEB	1	10	67%	15	5 3
KAN	2	77	73%	106	29 2
OKLA	2	53	88%	60	7 12
N·CAR	1	23	85%	27	4 1
S·CAR	1	32	76%	42	10 2
GA	1	47	44%	106	59 5
FLA	1	30	62%	48	18 3
ALA	1	38	75%	51	13 2
LA	1	48	86%	56	8 1
TEX	5	169	88%	192	23 12
MONT	1	17	90%	19	2
IDA	1	3	75%	4	1 2
WASH	2	71	74%	96	25 2
ORE	1	23	58%	40	17 4
CALIF	2	210	88%	238	28 12

constantly increased. This important trend was doubtless sharply accelerated during depression years, when family expenditures for education had to be reduced to a minimum. After World War II, although governmental subsidies offset the barrier of increased tuition in some schools, and although enrollment quotas forced many students to seek openings far from home, the ratio of in-state students nevertheless was again increased, due to their demand as citizens to be accommodated in local institutions on preferred status.

In 1898, only one of the nine existing schools of architecture was maintained by a tax-supported institution. By 1911, seven of 20 were such schools; by 1930, 31 of 52; and, in 1950, 35 of 62. Thus, the two decades ending in 1930 saw more than a four-fold increase in state schools. In 1898, the one state school enrolled 14.7 per cent of all U. S. students; in 1911, state schools taught 36.8 per cent; in 1930, 53.7; in 1952, 70.7; and in 1953, 69.4. The *1950 Survey* revealed that, despite the late establishment of the state schools, they had conferred 50.3 per cent of all first degrees held by American architects.[86] In the future, the ratio of degrees will no doubt approach the ratio of enrollment.

The situation with regard to second professional degrees is entirely different. Of the 44 institutions for which second degrees were reported, 21, or 48 per cent, are state-supported, but these schools have accounted for only 22 per cent of these degrees. Only four of these schools—California (5.89 per cent), Illinois (4.98), Georgia Tech (2.27), and Michigan (2.12)—have given as many as 2 per cent, while ten private schools have exceeded this figure—MIT (12.65), Harvard (11.50), Pennsylvania (10.72), Columbia (6.20), Princeton (5.14), Cornell (4.08), Washington University (3.02), Yale (2.87), Rice (2.72), and Carnegie (2.27). While it is no accident that all of these same universities have won recognition as leading centers of graduate studies in other fields, it is obvious that the principle of accessibility maintained for undergraduate curricula has not applied in the case of graduate studies.

Figure 25, overleaf, graphs the number of architects attending each school for the first time and those attending each as a second school. For most schools there was close correspondence between first attendance and first degrees, regardless of the size of en-rollment. The major variants were those schools which had high preference for second attendance. It should be noted that a shift to a second school may be due to one of several reasons, such as desire for graduate study, change of parents' residence, econ-omy, or even scholastic maladjustment. The general operation of these factors is exhibited by comparing attendance and degrees of the larger schools. At Illinois and Michigan, for example, second attendance increased first degrees primarily. At Harvard, it affected only second degrees. At MIT and Pennsylvania, it raised both first and second degrees. At Columbia, however, the number of first degrees remained the same, but despite the highest number of second attenders, second degrees did not increase as might be expected. A partial explanation may be that second attendance here includes students taking special courses or isolated graduate subjects. Two schools, Pratt and Cooper Institute, showed marked shrinkage from first attendance to first degrees, but this is due to the fact that Cooper has offered for most students

FIGURE 25: COMPARISON OF DEGREES CONFERRED & ATTENDANCE AT ARCHITECTURAL SCHOOLS   AS REPORTED BY REGISTERED ARCHITECTS IN 1950

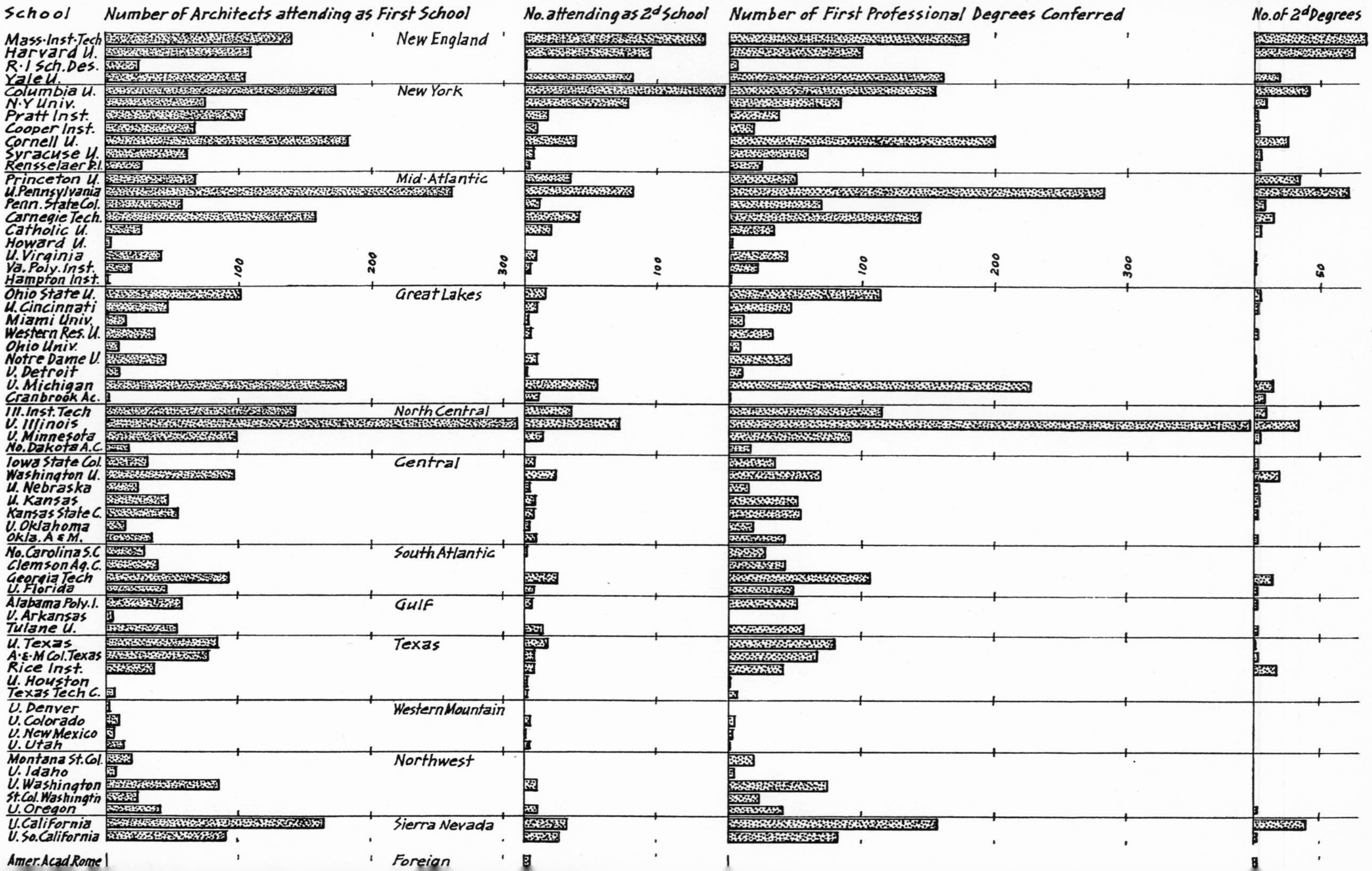

School	Number of Architects attending as First School	No. attending as 2nd School	Number of First Professional Degrees Conferred	No. of 2nd Degrees

New England
Mass. Inst. Tech.
Harvard U.
R. I. Sch. Des.
Yale U.

New York
Columbia U.
N. Y. Univ.
Pratt Inst.
Cooper Inst.
Cornell U.
Syracuse U.
Rensselaer P.I.

Mid Atlantic
Princeton U.
U. Pennsylvania
Penn. State Col.
Carnegie Tech.
Catholic U.
Howard U.
U. Virginia
Va. Poly. Inst.
Hampton Inst.

Great Lakes
Ohio State U.
U. Cincinnati
Miami Univ.
Western Res. U.
Ohio Univ.
Notre Dame U.
U. Detroit
U. Michigan
Cranbrook Ac.

North Central
Ill. Inst. Tech.
U. Illinois
U. Minnesota
No. Dakota A.C.

Central
Iowa State Col.
Washington U.
U. Nebraska
U. Kansas
Kansas State C.
U. Oklahoma
Okla. A. & M.

South Atlantic
No. Carolina S.C.
Clemson Ag. C.
Georgia Tech
U. Florida

Gulf
Alabama Poly. I.
U. Arkansas
Tulane U.

Texas
U. Texas
A. & M. Col. Texas
Rice Inst.
U. Houston
Texas Tech C.

Western Mountain
U. Denver
U. Colorado
U. New Mexico
U. Utah

Northwest
Montana St. Col.
U. Idaho
U. Washington
St. Col. Washington
U. Oregon

Sierra Nevada
U. California
U. So. California

Foreign
Amer. Acad. Rome

only a partial curriculum and Pratt operated in the same manner until the late 30's.

Table 38 lists in order of most frequent preferences the states to which those architects, who attended schools outside their home state, went for professional education.
Naturally, the main flows have been toward states whose schools have already shown
large enrollments. The highest ranking by number of listings of the 23 states mentioned ran: New York, Pennsylvania, Massachusetts, Illinois, Michigan, California,
Connecticut, New Jersey, Georgia, Missouri, and Washington, *Figure 26,* overleaf.
While this sequence does not indicate the actual magnitude of drawing power over the
past half century, necessary corrections can be observed by comparison with the number of first degrees awarded to out-of-state students. The directions of drawing power
are of interest. Three states revealed general nation-wide magnetism in number of
contributing states. New York conferred 16.50 per cent of all first degrees and drew
students primarily from 36 states; Pennsylvania, 14.7 per cent, 30 states; and Massachusetts, 11 per cent, 27 states. Eight other schools served large regions: Illinois gave
11.65 per cent of all out-of-state first degrees, and drew students chiefly from 13 states,
mostly in the Midwest and the Great Plains area, but also including New York,
Mississippi, and Texas. Connecticut had 8.02 per cent from 9 states, 5 in the North
Atlantic area; Michigan, 7.32 per cent, 12 states, 4 in the Midwest and the rest widely
scattered; Georgia, 3.76 per cent, 5 states, all in the Southeast; Minnesota, 2.68 per
cent, 4 states, 3 adjoining; New Jersey, 2.55 per cent, 8 states, 7 close at hand; and
California, 1.85 per cent, 11 states, 7 in the Far West. It should be remembered, of
course, that these are cumulative records. Present patterns are considered in *Chapter
VII.*

The incidence of special non-degree courses, pursued by architects as primary or
supplemental advanced training, either part- or full-time, has been highly concentrated in metropolitan cities. Eighteen schools, each of which gave more than one per
cent of all such courses, and which together provided 67 per cent, ranked as follows
(*Table 37*):

Columbia	11.33%	Carnegie	3.25	U. California	1.89
U. Pennsylvania	8.08	IIT	3.10	Cranbrook	1.89
MIT	6.05	Cooper Inst.	2.65	U. Illinois	1.81
New York U.	4.76	U. So. Calif.	2.65	Cornell	1.81
Harvard	4.36	Washington U.	2.19	Yale	1.21
Pratt	4.16	U. Michigan	1.96	Princeton	1.13

The first 11 of this group, accounting for 52.6 per cent of all courses, were all located in large cities. The four New York schools conducted by far the largest proportion, 22.9 per cent. The two Boston schools totaled 10.41 per cent. Philadelphia's school
followed with 8.08, Pittsburgh with 3.25, Chicago with 3.10, Los Angeles with 2.65,
and St. Louis with 2.19. Of the next three schools, Michigan and Cranbrook lie
near Detroit, and California is situated in the San Francisco region. None of these
three, however, nor the remaining four schools in relatively small communities, have
served as centers for supplementary instruction of part-time working students.

FIGURE 26: STATES PREFERRED BY OUT-OF-STATE STUDENTS FOR ARCHITECTURAL EDUCATION

Data from
Column 11
Table 38

·· PER CENT OF ALL U·S FIRST PROFESSIONAL DEGREES
CONFERRED ON OUT·OF·STATE STUDENTS

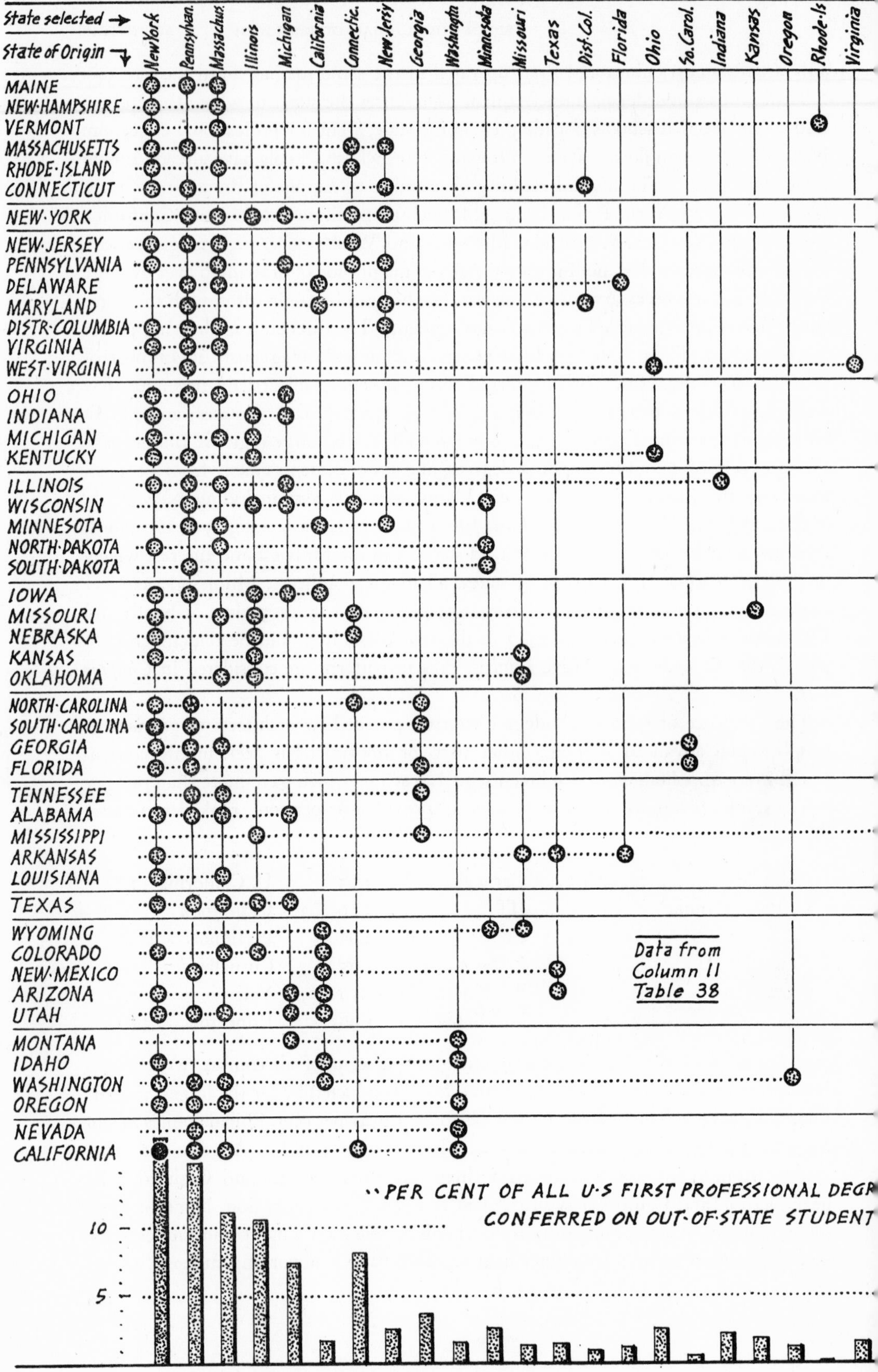

In view of the importance of European architecture and architectural education for the American scene during the 19th century, it is interesting to speculate on their more recent impact. The *1950 Survey* did not ask for place of birth and, therefore, no data are available on the number or pre-emigration training of foreign-born architects. During the third quarter of the 19th century, a large number of European architects had made signal contributions to American practice, but, with the coming of age of the profession in this country, fewer new arrivals were able to establish their own offices, although a considerable number became employees. Quota limitations after 1920 and the depression cut this source of personnel to a minimum. Nevertheless, during these two decades, some outstanding individuals transferred their talents to the United States, men such as Saarinen, Lescaze, Belluschi, Neutra, Mendelsohn, Mies van der Rohe, Breuer, and Gropius. No doubt a number of foreign professional degrees lie hidden in the classification in *Table 37* entitled "unspecified college or university."

In the reverse direction, only one European school, the *Ecole des beaux-arts,* was sought out by American students, and its direct use reached a peak in the first decade of the 20th century. A considerable number continued to enroll in the 1920's, but the grim 30's found them reduced to a handful, most of whom were sustained by fellowships. The result was that the *1950 Survey* revealed a surprisingly small number of *Ecole* alumni. Only 0.37 per cent of all American registered architects reported receiving their first "degree" at the *Ecole*.[87] Another 0.37 per cent indicated that they won a "second professional degree." One per cent stated that they had followed special courses there, most of which were doubtless participation in design exercises developed in *ateliers*. These figures witness the marked decline of the *Ecole's* direct influence on the profession in the United States. The present total of registered architects who have studied at the *Ecole* appears to be of the order of 330.

The *Ecole's* indirect inspiration, working through the Society of Beaux-Arts Architects and its Beaux-Arts Institute of Design, and the *Sociétè des Architectes diplômé par le Gouvernement Français,* was a very potent force throughout much of the period surveyed. Not only was this influence exerted through the collegiate schools, but possibly many of the "special" courses reported in both the regular schools and those "unspecified," consisted of BAID competitive exercises. Moreover, the *1950 Survey* did not list the work of numerous independent *ateliers*.

The most important foreign contribution to the education of American architects was that obtained through travel, which brought direct contact with the great monuments of other civilizations. Of the 20 per cent of all architects who reported that they had studied architecture in a foreign country, and this means approximately 3800 individuals, without doubt "foreign" meant "European" for almost all, but for a few it included the Orient and Latin America as well. The precedent of the "grand tour" as a means of architectural education is, of course, centuries old, but it has rarely been applied in such a wholesale manner. Belief in its efficacy during the early 20th century led to the endowment of many traveling fellowships. In 1930, the AIA Committee on Education found 29 were being awarded each year.[88] It may be estimated that during the period surveyed perhaps as many as 800 individuals were benefited by these sub-sidies.[89] But however generous these grants have been, the fact that perhaps 3000 more traveled at their own expense proves that the value of such first-hand experience has been very widely recognized.

The *1950 Survey* has thus furnished the first statistical inventory of the products of architectural education in the United States. The picture which emerges from this analysis is of absorbing interest, but it is far from simple to assay. The phenomenal growth of the nation called for an unprecedented volume of building. The application of science and technology required new disciplines. In the face of such demands, ap-prenticeship and *pupilage* proved completely inadequate. The unique American solu-tion was the development of a system of professional schools within a new type of comprehensive university. The operation of this system began in 1868, just 85 years ago. For three decades a handful of schools struggled to develop novel curricula with meager facilities and tiny faculties. From 1900 to World War I, substantial progress was made in enriching and extending the system, but it cannot be said to have come of age until the 1920's, when, for the first time, it actually dominated professional train-ing. It is only when the relative youth of this system is realized that the magnitude of its achievement as revealed by the *1950 Survey* can be appreciated. Only within the past generation has this system of professional architectural education gained true national scope. It was fate that made this period also one of depression and war.

Appraisal of the system's qualitative results is a different matter. No statistical method is yet available with which to identify, measure, total, and average the vary-ing degrees of genius which comprise a profession of 19,137 individuals. It is equally impossible to segregate, from a host of other cumulative experiences gathered during a lifetime, the influence of early schooling. Moreover, some critics question whether the degree of genius can be modified by any educational process whatsoever. These are moot points which must be relegated to metaphysicians.

Nevertheless, the importance of effective education to the profession cannot be gainsaid, and judgment must be rendered. Since 64 per cent of all members of the pro-fession are now graduates of the collegiate system, the quality of its instruction is a paramount issue. From this very fact, however, it becomes obvious that criticism of the system becomes self-criticism, but while humility is a virtue, the real strength and depth of the profession should not be overlooked. The truth is that the profession and its educational system are inseparably interdependent and both share alike their re-spective merits and defects. Progress will come only through shared leadership, mutual respect, and sympathetic cooperation.

Buried with the responses to the *1950 Survey* lie many additional facts which could not be processed due to limited funds. It would have been interesting, for example, to compare for different decades the salaries, size of offices, etc., of various groups of alumni, as a rough measure of the commercial value of the training they procured. Fascinating as this might be, it is highly questionable whether the groups involved would produce any statistically defensible result. Moreover, it should not be over-looked that varying costs of education and the illusive matters of prestige and sentiment act as screening elements wholly unrelated to specific programs. The paradox of too rigid evaluation of educational systems is that by the time it takes for them to be fully operative, too many factors other than education have entered the equation, and that, in any case, during intervening years the systems themselves have so changed as to frustrate valid conclusions.

Nevertheless, the *1950 Survey* did disclose one quantitative fact that bears on the professional status of school graduates. The ratio of AIA membership among all graduates was 59 per cent. On the other hand, the ratio among non-graduates was 17 per cent.[90] To the extent that participation in the affairs of The AIA has signalized competence, it is possible that some measure of credit for this extraordinary difference must be accorded the schools. The ratios for individual schools varied widely. Seven schools had alumni groups with 70 to 74 per cent in The AIA; 12 ranged from 60 to 69 per cent; 16, with 50 to 59 per cent; only 5 were below.[91] Even the lowest, with 31 per cent, was far above the non-graduate ratio of 17.

NOTES: CHAPTER FOUR

[1] Alfred North Whitehead: *The Aims of Education*, 1929. (Mentor edit., 1949, p. 16.)

[2] L. F. Salzman: *Building in England down to 1540*, 1952, pp. 14–29.

[3] *Ibid.*, p. 48; Douglas Knoop and G. P. Jones: *The Medieval Mason*, 1933, pp. 160–168.

[4] J. H. Harvey: *The Gothic World*, 1950, pp. 39–52; J. H. Harvey, "The Education of the Mediaeval Architect," (*Journal, Royal Institute of British Architects*, series 3, vol. 52, 1945, pp. 230–234).

[5] The system at its worst was caustically described by Charles Dickens in *Martin Chuzzlewit*, published in 1843.

[6] This seems indicated by guild rules contained in the late 14th-century Regius Manuscript (Knoop, Jones, and Hamer: *The Two Earliest Masonic Manuscripts*, 1938).

[7] Thieme-Becker: *Allegemienes Lexicon der bildenden Kunstler*, Art., "Buontalenti."

[8] Nikolaus Pevsner: *Academies of Art, past and present*, 1940, pp. 44–66, 70, 88–108.

[9] Reginald Blomfield: *A History of French Architecture from the death of Mazarin till the death of Louis XV*, 1921, vol. 1, p. 9.

[10] Louis Hautecoeur: *Histoire de l'architecture classique en France*, 1948, vol. 2, Part 1, pp. 465–466.

[11] This is indicated by: the theoretical character of the courses; the fact that both Blondel and La Hire, his successor, were primarily mathematicians; the employment of the students in members' offices (Hautecoeur: *op. cit.*, p. 466); and the analogous situation in the Academy of Painting and Sculpture (Pevsner: *Academies*, p. 92).

[12] E. Delaire: *Les architectes élèves de l'Ecole des Beaux-Arts, 1793–1907*, p. 92.

[13] Architectural instruction was included in the academies at Bologna (1668), Nurnberg (1674), Turin (1678), Berlin (1697), and Vienna (1705). (Pevsner: *Academies*, pp. 114–115, 118–122.)

[14] Hautecoeur, *op. cit.*, vol. 3, pp. 446–447, which, however, does not mention construction and design, but these are certainly inferred by Blondel's encyclopedic text, *Cours d'architecture*, which, after his death, his assistant, Pierre Patte, published in 1777.

[15] These nine comprised 20 per cent of the 46 members elected between 1755 and 1792. This count was checked in: Charles Bauchal: *Nouveau dictionnaire biographique et critique des architectes français*, 1887, but not all members have the details of their education given, and the number of Blondel's pupils might well be larger.

[16] F. B. Artz, "L'éducation technique en France au XVIII° siècle," (*Revue d'histoire moderne*,

vol. 13 [new series, vol. 7], Oct.–Dec., 1938, pp. 381–384). The *Ecole des ponts et chaussées* is often said to date from 1747, when Perronnet became chief of the *Corps* and immediately instituted a system of *informal* training within the Paris headquarters. Perronnet was trained as both an architect and a military engineer, and he was elected to membership in the Academy of Architecture in 1758.

[17] J. A. Eytelwein, "Kurze Darstellung der Geschichte und Verfassung des Königlichen Preussischen Ober-bau-departmente," (*Sammlung nützlicher Aufsätze und Nachrichten die Baukunst betreffend*, 5th year, 1803, vol. 1, pp. 90–112). Eytelwein, "Nachricht von der Errichtung der Königlichen Bau-akademie zu Berlin," (*ibid.*, 1799, vol. 1, p. 29).

[18] J. B. Rondelet: *Traité théorique et pratique de l'art de bâtir*, 1834 (7th edit.), vol. 5, pp. IV, XIII–XV; for the architectural curriculum of the *Ecole centrale*, see *Journal polytechnique*, vol. 1, 1795 (l'an III).

[19] Heinrich August Riedel, "Fortzetzung der allgemeinen Betrachtungen über die Baukunst," (*Sammlung*, 1797, vol. 2, pp. 3–17; 1798, vol. 1, pp. 107–116); Eytelwein, "Nachricht . . ," (*ibid.*, 1799, vol. 1, pp. 28–40).

[20] *Entstehung und Entwicklung der Königliche Technische Hochschule zu Berlin*, 1914, p. 5.

[21] William E. Wickenden: *A Comparative Study of Engineering Education in the United States and Europe*. 1929, (Bulletin 16, "Investigation of Engineering Education, Society for the Promotion of Engineering Education"), pp. 47–57.

[22] Paul Zucker, "Architectural Education in Nineteenth Century Germany," (*Journal, Society of Architectural Historians*, vol. 2, July, 1942, pp. 6–13).

[23] R. Phéné Spiers, "The French Diplôme d'Architecture and the German System of Architectural Education," (*Royal Institute of British Architects, Transactions*, 1884, pp. 123–124).

[24] Delaire, *op. cit.*, pp. 92–93; François Benoit: *L'art français sous la révolution et l'empire, les doctrines, les idées, les genres*, 1897; Paul Planat: *Encyclopédie de l'architecture et de la construction*, 1888–1893, vol. 3, pp. 224–225.

[25] The taking of entrance examinations at the *Ecole* by American students is vividly described by Louis Sullivan (*Autobiography of an Idea*, 1922, pp. 219–232) and Huger Elliott ("Examinations in Paris," *Journal, AIA*, vol. 6, nos. 5, 6, November, December, 1946, pp. 200–205, 279–284).

[26] *Architectural Record*, vol. 11, January, 1901, p. 16.

[27] Paul P. Cret: "The Ecole des Beaux-Arts and Architectural Education," (*Journal, Society of Architectural Historians*, vol. 1, April, 1941, p. 12).

[28] Julian Clarence Levi, "Beaux-Arts Training Today," (*Journal, AIA*, vol. 16, no. 2, August, 1951, pp. 79–84). The 1950 enrollment at the *Ecole* is given at about 1000. For a less flattering report, see "The Training of Architects: an Interim Survey," (*Architectural Review*, vol. 107, no. 642, June, 1950, pp. 372–373).

[29] Planat: *Encyclopédie*, art.: "Ecoles d' Architecture." Mr. Levi (see *Note 28*) gives the total enrollment of all provincial schools as about 500. The *Ecole spéciale* had about 230 (*Architectural Review, loc. cit.*).

[30] Charles L. Eastlake, "An Historical Sketch of the Institute," (*RIBA, Sessional Papers*, 1875–1876, p. 259).

[31] Alfred Bartholomew: *Specifications for practical architecture*, 1840, Sections 952–982.

[32] *Civil Engineers and Architects Journal*, vol. 9, 1846, p. 283.

[33] *Builder* (London), vol. 1, Dec. 31, 1842.

[34] John Summerson: *The Architectural Association, 1847–1947*, 1947, pp. 1–14.

[35] J. A. Gotch, edit.: *The Growth and Work of the Royal Institute of British Architects, 1834–1934*, 1934, pp. 85–87.

[36] Summerson: *op. cit.*, pp. 19–21, 23–24.

[37] Walter R. M. Lamb: *The Royal Academy*, 1951, p. 95; Reginald Blomfield: *Memoirs of an Architect*, 1932, pp. 37–43.

[38] *Journal, Royal Institute of British Architects*, ser. 3, vol. 23, Oct. 21, 1916, p. 335.

[39] Gotch, *op. cit.*, pp. 88–94.

[40] Since European influences on American architectural education derived entirely from Great Britain, France, and Germany, no attempt is made in this report to trace developments in other

countries. For an excellent description of schools at Delft, Copenhagen, Stockholm, Zurich, Madrid, and Venice, see the report of Professor Frederick M. Wells who visited them in 1951 as a Langley Fellow of The AIA (*Journal of Architectural Education,* Association of Collegiate Schools of Architecture, No. 8, Summer, 1952, pp. 21–29). A rather miscellaneous survey, accomplished by circularizing 29 schools in 14 countries, is summarized in "The Training of Architects: an Interim Survey" (*Architectural Review,* vol. 107, No. 642, June, 1950, pp. 367–373). Unfortunately, only seven American schools were covered and it is difficult to believe that their replies were correctly interpreted. The result, however, is not as misleading as the inexcusably uninformed comments on American schools published by Dr. Sigfried Giedion (*L'architecture d'aujourd'hui,* February, 1950, pp. 10, 107–108).

41 The earliest advertisement thus far noted appeared in 1735 (Louise Hall, "First Architectural School? No! But . . ," *Journal, AIA,* vol. 14, August, 1950, pp. 79–82). Theophilus Hardenbrook made a similar announcement in New York in 1758 (*The Arts and Crafts in New York, 1726–1776,* 1938, pp. 180–181).

42 Albert Simons, "Our First Architectural School?" (*Journal, AIA,* vol. 13, June, 1950, pp. 278–279); "Our First Architectural School?" (*ibid.,* vol. 13, March, 1950, pp. 139–140); Talbot Hamlin: *Greek Revival Architecture in America,* 1944, p. 68.

43 P. A. Bruce: *History of the University of Virginia, 1819–1919,* 1920, vol. 1, p. 73.

44 Wickenden, *op. cit.,* p. 62: *Dictionary of American Biography,* art., "Thayer, Sylvanus."

45 *DAB,* art. "Hale, Benjamin": U. S. Literary Gazette, August 15, 1825.

46 *DAB,* art, "Eaton, Amos": Wickenden, *op. cit.,* pp. 61–63; Palmer C. Ricketts: *History of the Rensselaer Polytechnic Institute,* 1915.

47 Agnes Addison Gilchrist: *William Strickland, Architect and Engineer, 1788–1854,* 1950, pp. 5, 137.

48 Data from Charles E. Peterson, July 7, 1953.

49 Roger Hale Newton: *Town and Davis, architects,* 1942, p. 103.

50 H. M. Pierce Gallagher: *Robert Mills,* 1935, p. 21.

51 *DAB,* art., "Douglass, David Bates."

52 Wickenden, *op. cit.,* p. 62.

53 Bruce, *op. cit.,* vol. 1, pp. 223, 323, 329–330.

54 *Life and Letters of William Barton Rogers,* 1896, vol. 1, pp. 120, 257–259, 421.

55 (B. F. Greene): *The Rensselaer Polytechnic Institute, its reorganization in 1849–50, its condition at the present time, its plans and hopes for the future,* 1855.

56 *Catalogue of Yale University,* 1852, p. 48.

57 B. A. Hinsdale: *History of the University of Michigan,* 1906, p. 78.

58 Theodore F. Jones: *New York University, 1832–1932,* 1933, p. 309.

59 Delaire, *op. cit.*

60 *DAB,* arts., "Hunt, Richard Morris," and "Ware, William Robert."

61 *Life and Letters of William Barton Rogers,* vol. 2, pp. 3, 36, 41, 77, 114, 117, 141, 200, 216, 223, 235, 288, 413, 420–427.

62 James H. Kelley: *The Alumni Record of the University of Illinois,* 1913, pp. 9–10, 33, 668, 702, 790.

63 Andrew Dickson White: *Autobiography,* 1905; *DAB,* art., "Babcock, Charles."

64 *Catalogue of the University of Pennsylvania,* 1874; Cheyney: *History of the University of Pennsylvania,* p. 263.

65 The best account of these early schools is: Arthur Clason Weatherhead: *The History of Collegiate Education in Architecture in the United States,* 1941, Chapter 2.

66 Survey of the Architectural Schools, Report of the Committee on Education, *Proceedings, 32nd Annual Convention, A.I.A.,* 1898, p. 84. (*Table I* reprinted in Weatherhead, *op. cit.,* p. 63.)

67 At MIT, Ware gradually won control of the common Freshman program which was originally dominated by the demands of the engineering curricula. Cornell became an independent college in 1896. Columbia achieved independent status in 1902. Pennsylvania was transformed into a School of Fine Arts in 1920. George Washington was shifted to Fine Arts in 1894. Although

first in engineering, the Harvard school enjoyed virtual freedom, but it became an independent unit of the Graduate College in 1906. At Illinois, architecture escaped the usual difficulties because its enrollment exceeded all engineering students and because Ricker was both head of the department and Dean of Engineering. (Weatherhead, *op. cit., passim.*)

[68] Tabulated from the biographical section of Delaire, *op. cit.*

[69] In 1907, 122 of the 176 *Ecole* alumni in the U. S. were centered in New York (*ibid.*).

[70] For the 1911 group, see Weatherhead, *op. cit.*, pp. 136–137; for the 1930 list, see F. H. Bosworth and Roy Childs Jones: *A Study of Architectural Schools*, 1932, pp. 188–189. The department at Cooper Institute, New York, is included in the table, although Bosworth and Jones omitted it because it offered only the first two years of work.

[71] Weatherhead, *op. cit.*, pp. 145–149, 199–201.

[72] Wickenden, *op. cit.*, pp. 72–73; *Encyclopaedia Britannica* (14th edit.), art., "Technical Education, Scotland;" Weatherhead, *op. cit.*, p. 195; Hermann Schneider, "New Cooperative Courses in Architecture and the Applied Fine Arts at the University of Cincinnati." (*American Architect*, January 16, 1924, p. 2).

[73] Nikolaus Pevsner: *Pioneers of Modern Design from William Morris to Walter Gropius*, 1949, Chapter 1.

[74] Pevsner: *Academies*, p. 267.

[75] *Ibid.*, pp. 276–281; Walter Gropius: *The New Architecture and the Bauhaus*, 1937, pp. 35–65.

[76] Since enrollments are available only for 1898 and 1911, these have been used for computing the ratios for 1900 and 1910. The degree of error is probably very small because neither fell within periods of substantial change.

[77] *Table 35* would seem to indicate that this group comes to 10 per cent, but it is probably less, due to the fact that the 66 per cent attending may include those with degrees in architectural engineering, having obtained them in architectural schools which also offer architectural engineering.

[78] 6418, out of 6605 responders, gave educational data (*Table 35*).

[79] 6152 graduated from high school (*Table 38*).

[80] "First degrees," here and subsequently, includes both architecture and architectural engineering, since all responders later became registered architects, regardless of the type of degree. This assumption is also necessary to avoid the exclusion of graduates of schools which, because of local stipulations, were forced to use the engineering title, although the intention and character of instruction were professional. In general, those architectural engineering curricula which were not professional have been automatically eliminated from the *Survey* because their graduates normally did not acquire registration. It should be noted that, in a few cases, respondents reported degrees from schools which do not award professional degrees, but since these represent slightly less than 1 per cent of the totals for both first and second degrees, this discrepancy has been ignored. Foreign degrees, such as are included in the "Unspecified school" category, and "degrees" obtained at the *Ecole des beaux-arts,* are retained, although the equivalency of titles might be questioned.

[81] A possibility of error occurs in the fact that three schools—California, Harvard, and Princeton —have conferred Master degrees as the first professional degree. If this confused respondents, these schools are ranked too high.

[82] These regional ratios refer to architects from a *state* living in the *same state.* Although no data are available, regional ratios of architects from a *region* who were first registered and currently working in the *same region* would probably be much higher.

[83] These states with established schools are: Massachusetts, Connecticut, New York, Pennsylvania, District of Columbia, Virginia, Ohio, Michigan, Illinois, Minnesota, North Dakota, Iowa, Missouri, Nebraska, Kansas, Oklahoma, North and South Carolina, Georgia, Florida, Alabama, Louisiana, Texas, Montana, Idaho, Washington, Oregon, and California. New Jersey and Indiana are omitted because Princeton and Notre Dame enroll few in-state students. The 28 states had 4982 high school graduates who became registered architects. 3446 attended schools of architecture, of whom 2491 entered in-state schools (72 per cent of 3446). 2992 of the 4982—60 per cent—later registered and worked in the same state. In the remaining 21 states, only 479 high school graduates later registered and worked (41 per cent of 1170).

[84] The states are the 28 listed in *Note 83*, but include New Jersey and Indiana. The six schools in Rhode Island, Arkansas, Colorado (2), New Mexico, and Utah are omitted because they have been in operation too short a time to have affected the cumulative picture.

[85] See *Chapter VII.*

[86] Out of a total of 3981 first degrees (*Table 37,* but omitting those reported as "unspecified" and *"Ecole des beaux-arts"*), state schools awarded 2002 and private schools, 1979.

[87] Since the *Ecole des beaux-arts* has never conferred "degrees," it is assumed that responders either earned the *diplôme* awarded by the French government or simply assumed their training to be the equivalent of an American academic degree.

[88] Report of C. C. Zantzinger, chairman (cited in Weatherhead, *op. cit.,* pp. 142–144).

[89] Assuming an average period of operation of 25 years, excluding war years, about 725 individuals would have used the 29 fellowships listed. To these should be added several who won at least 8 other annual fellowships for which architects were eligible to compete. Finally, it is probable that of the 10 per cent of all architects who have held fellowships or grants, it may be assumed that at least half probably were used for travel (*Table 36*).

[90] *Table 37* lists 4144 degrees in architecture and architectural engineering. This is 64.56 per cent of the 6418 responders to the education questions. This means a total of 12,354 graduates and 6783 non-graduates in the total of 19,137 architects. Of the 4144 degrees, 2449, or 59.10 per cent, were held by AIA members, or a total of 7300 graduates in The AIA. This leaves 1161 non-graduates in The AIA, or 17.11 per cent of the 8461 AIA total membership.

[91] The ratios for the individual schools were strongly influenced by the general ratios in the areas in which most of their alumni resided. Michigan, for example, had a state ratio of 72 per cent and an alumni ratio of 74. Pennsylvania, on the other hand, had a state ratio of 50, while Penn State alumni had 74 and the University of Pennsylvania 69.

CHAPTER V

Collegiate Education
For the Practice of Architecture

1. THE PROCESS OF ARCHITECTURAL EDUCATION

The objective of professional education is the transformation of raw recruits into mature practitioners. The process by which this is accomplished depends on many factors, such as, content to be taught, skills to be cultivated, students' capacity for growth, the capabilities of teachers, methods employed, and the length of time available. It is the nature of a profession, which by definition requires the continuing enhancement of competence, that education for its practice is for each member a lifelong obligation.

Since the practice of architecture is inevitably a complex activity, preparation for it is long and intricate. The student must gain expert knowledge of human behavior and institutions in order to plan useful buildings. He must master a wide range of materials and equipment and learn their scientific application. He must acquire skill in composing beautiful buildings and in expressing his ideas with both graphic and verbal precision. He must become an effective organizer. And since no other profession surpasses architecture in its intimate relationship with all phases of life, he must draw upon many spheres of knowledge to strengthen his capacities.

Education implies the existence of a systematic body of knowledge, concepts, and principles. In former times, when change was gradual, valid codifications could be formulated without excessive difficulty. In recent decades, however, the continuous addition of new architectural data and hitherto unrecognized principles has constantly modified the content of professional education. The vast extent and the accelerating rate of these changes have discouraged synthesis, and, as a result, education at all levels has been greatly handicapped. Since these changes have arisen primarily from experience gained in progressive practice, it becomes the duty of the profession periodically to reorganize, evaluate, and disseminate its evolving content. It is obvious, of course, that further growth soon makes any codification obsolete, but it is nonetheless important if new resources are to be employed intelligently. If, by default, educators are forced to essay this task, they must be accorded more intimate access to the accumulated experience of practitioners than is now enjoyed.

Education deals not only with knowledge, but also with those skills by which knowledge is used. Proficiency in communication, thinking, creativeness, judgment, and cooperation are basic qualities for effectiveness in any endeavor. But since knowledge is extensive, subject to constant change, and difficult to codify, it is tempting to concentrate attention on the development of skills. Thus, slogans frequently assert: Teach how, not what. Nevertheless, the solution is not an exclusive choice of one or the other, for, while knowledge alone remains sterile, and subject to change, it is equally true that skill cannot operate in a vacuum, but must be exercised upon substance. Education must aim, therefore, at a developing mastery of both.

The training of architects is particularly complicated by the fact that the design of buildings requires two types of skills. On the one hand there is analysis, an intellectual process of dissection and comparison; on the other hand, there is creative synthesis, which must integrate diverse parts into a unified and expressive whole. An ideal balance of two such opposed skills is a difficult goal which often seems contrary to human nature, but if either faculty is neglected, architecture forfeits either utility or expressiveness and so remains incomplete. Thus, education must strive once again to cultivate both.

The focus of the educational process is the student, both to enable him to fulfill his potentialities as an individual and to ensure society of a useful participant in its work. Capacity for growth is strongly affected by the type and quality of ability, background, and motivation which the student brings to his training. If these are adequate, he should be able to respond successfully to a skillful program of instruction.

For maximum development of the student, instruction, in turn, must be founded on a true understanding of the process of learning. Systematic method demands first the establishment of aims in order to relate the lesson to the student's total program, and thus stimulate him to wholehearted effort. Next, pertinent background should be reviewed to link the current topic to previous experience. New data, terms, and principles can then be introduced. The derivation of principles should be clearly demonstrated, and applications of these new materials should be illustrated by specific dramatic examples. Following this, the student must undertake with guidance the solution of typical problems which have been carefully posed to develop his skill and judgment in the application of old and new data and principles to a particular realistic situation. Subsequently, his performance should be objectively evaluated to correct errors and strengthen his capacity for self-appraisal. Finally, the whole experience should be welded together by a concluding summary.[1] Such a procedure emphasizes both knowledge and skill, progresses methodically from the known to the new, and presents a just combination of essential theory and essential practice.

It is obvious that such a method can benefit not only the teaching of a single topic, but also the conduct of each course, each group of courses, and the entire educational program. This is to say that, for maximum clarity, continuity, and impact, the whole educational process and all its parts should be designed to proceed in a progressive and carefully integrated manner from the most elementary through the most advanced levels. It is equally important that at each step the student should be alert to the relationship between the immediate problem and the total field. Only in this way can the dry rot of atomization and compartmentation be prevented and the exhilarating stimulus of cross-fertilization between the various parts be gained.

In addition to the acquisition of knowledge and skills, every educational experience has an inherent responsibility to nourish the student's growth in character and his discrimination of values. Knowledge, however true, when dictatorially communicated, insidiously demands unquestioning submission to authority; but knowledge won by personal effort, search, test, and synthesis cultivates not only intellect, but also the invaluable traits of perseverance, self-discipline, self-reliance, and integrity. Although such teaching proceeds slowly, its cumulative effect multiplies the student's ultimate ability to obtain and use more surely and more profoundly the data pertinent to his needs.

The construction of a systematic and wise program of education is a work of art demanding teachers of exceptional skill, insight, and industry. If to this the teacher can also add an aura of significance and zest, and can inspire confidence by his personality and personal competence, the educational process can become an exciting adventure generating within the student curiosity, momentum, and resources that will undergird his whole professional career.

Since architecture, like life itself, is dynamic, the education of architects has taken many forms. Today, in America, the normal process involves three stages: preprofessional and professional schooling, candidateship training transitional to practice, and the studies pursued by mature architects. Thus, education for the practice of architecture is conceived as an inclusive and integrated process, of which the whole and each of its parts are mutually interdependent. Each, in its turn, is responsible for encouraging the continuing personal, social, and professional growth of students. Nevertheless, their content is not mutually exclusive, for each tends to overlap and reinforce the others. General education, for example, is not the sole prerogative of pre-professional schooling, but may prove even more fruitful as the trainee approaches maturity and gains increasing ability to relate apparently irrelevant knowledge and abstract concepts to his own interests and needs. Thus, too, technical theory should not be confined to the formal classroom, but should also be expanded to advanced levels during candidateship and practice. Likewise, practical experience often begins in simple form during school days. Indeed, parallel and balanced growth in all phases of experience would, without doubt, provide the most felicitous result.

The present chapter deals with the content and organization of the curriculum of the professional school of architecture. *Chapter VII* will consider the administrative problems of these schools. Candidateship training and mature studies will occupy *Chapters VIII* and *X*.

2. PRE-PROFESSIONAL EDUCATION

The quantity of American elementary and secondary education constitutes the most inclusive program of mass teaching in history. It aims to establish the basic general knowledge and skills fundamental to individual development and group living. The quality and success of its efforts vary widely, due to many different factors, such as type of community, financial support, skill of teaching staff, and student motivation. Since the *1950 Survey* revealed that 96 per cent of American architects had completed programs of secondary education, and since all professional schools base their curricula on such programs, it is obvious that Pre-professional Education has played and will continue to play a vital role in American architecture. Unfortunately, however, few, if any, investigations have analyzed the exact interrelationships between the two stages, either as they do exist or should exist. In the absence of such studies, the comments which follow must be limited to very general observations.

The curricular offerings of secondary schools constitute a highly standardized four-year program. For those for whom secondary education is terminal, the need is chiefly vocational. Since this is the largest group, its program usually dominates the school. Thus, the "college preparatory" curriculum no longer occupies its former dominant position. Some critics discern in the increasing growth of vocational courses and extra-curricular activities, a tragic capitulation to a positive "anti-intellectualism," reflecting all-too-prevalent attitudes within the community itself. Such an atmosphere discourages concentration on former basic disciplines. The result is that the subject-matter areas available for those who will pursue advanced academic training are relatively restricted in amount and variety, and it is claimed that the limited demand for them does not justify further elaboration.

The typical program of potential college students consists of 15 or 16 units of courses distributed between English, mathematics, a classical or living foreign language, elementary science, history, and social studies. Limited participation in art and music is sometimes possible. Schools of architecture, in greater or lesser degree, usually specify a core of secondary courses as prerequisites for admission. Of 60 schools responding to the *1950 School Survey,* 59 called for mathematics, 37 for English, 26 for science, 13 for foreign language, 11 for history, 5 for social studies, and only 2 for an unspecified type of drawing. Four schools which require pre-professional college training should not, of course, be considered. The relatively low specific requirements of the schools must not be interpreted as laxity or indifference. Many depend upon the general admission requirements of their parent institutions. Moreover, the secondary schools, on their own initiative, normally demand as large a variety of courses as their facilities will afford. The universal requirement of mathematics by architectural schools is, however, significant, especially since the amount demanded usually exceeds the normal amount offered by secondary schools. A median of 3 units was stipulated by 24 schools. Although these were unspecified, the limited subjects offered in this field would mean that beginning and intermediate algebra and plane and solid geometry must be taken. Seventeen schools named algebra as a specific requirement, 10 plane geometry, and 6 solid geometry. Most interesting was the demand of 5 schools that applicants must have completed trigonometry. This saves college time, but, since relatively few secondary schools offer it, any wide enforcement of this stipulation would mean considerable individual hardship to obtain private tutoring or the disruption of the beginning college schedule by non-credit remedial classes.

The particularization of subject matter for secondary courses does not guarantee the quality of the teaching, or the total achievement of the program. The best secondary schools sometimes surpass college instruction in the same subjects, but many outspoken critics claim that too much secondary teaching is soft, undisciplined, and slipshod. They cite as evidence the numerous college freshmen who lack facility in the use of language, are inaccurate in simple arithmetic, and display a blithe disregard for precise knowledge or thought of any kind. These critics often discover progressive deterioration in standards of secondary education. Defenders of the schools deny these charges and claim marked improvement in standards and performance. They point out that the tremendous expansion of enrollments has brought to secondary schools a host of hitherto neglected youths for whom the former exclusive emphasis on verbal academic training cannot be valid. It is not the province of this report to decide such controversies, but it is well to underscore heavily the crucial responsibility of secondary education to lay a sound foundation upon which the professional schools can build a secure superstructure. The question as to whether this objective could be attained in less than the present four-year schedule will be discussed in Section 2 of *Chapter VII*.

Within this context of secondary preparation, students usually fix their ultimate choice of vocation. Since entrance to architecture today normally requires collegiate training, candidates must come from among the graduates of secondary schools. Such restriction eliminates more than half of each age group. Moreover, since architectural personnel includes very few women, the available candidates are reduced again by half, or to about a quarter of the age group. Further limitations arise from the fact that only one out of every three high school graduates proceeds to advanced training. It is from this small restricted group that all the professions of the country must compete for personnel. Among these professions, that of architecture is numerically small and not widely understood. The problem of attracting youth of outstanding talent and promise to the profession is thus a very real and vital matter. It is of such essential importance as to command comprehensive analysis and a concerted program of action.

No statistical survey has listed the critical reasons why or how architects came to choose their profession. Casual queries reveal that a large number of architectural students make their initial contact through high school courses in architectural or mechanical drawing. Many are inspired by close relatives working in architecture or building. Others choose it as the most practical outlet for artistic talents and some through intellectual interest stirred by reading, observation, and travel, or even perhaps attendance in a well-designed school building. If the decision is valid, motivation is stronger for it having been a personal choice. The neophyte may not realize the difficult task he has assumed, but it is perhaps merciful that he does not comprehend all his problems at once. Growth in capacity is often stimulated by unfolding challenge.

Nevertheless, such choices are often based on only the most superficial knowledge of the qualifications required for a successful career in architecture. Moreover, this method of recruitment is highly accidental and misses many youths who would be promising candidates. It would seem desirable, therefore, for the profession to explore the possibilities of a positive program of guidance to advise the first group and to discover the second.

The function of modern vocational guidance is to assist young people in matching their talents, interests, and preparation with the qualifications required by the various occupations. Many secondary schools and most colleges and universities maintain guidance counsellors. Public and private guidance bureaus are also available. The usual procedure is to explore talents, interests, aptitudes, and scholastic attainments by batteries of tests which have been more or less validated by long experience. The use of achievement, placement, and general interests tests by schools, as a part of admission procedure, will be discussed in *Chapter VII*. Unfortunately, aptitude tests are not definitive with regard to specific vocations. They reveal areas of capacity, rather than precise directions. Despite some attempts, no trustworthy tests for aptitude in architecture have come to the attention of this Commission, and, due to the complex nature of the profession, many doubt that a satisfactory test can be designed for it. While a student can learn whether he is sufficiently prepared to undertake college work in English, mathematics, and other specific subjects which are pertinent to architecture, there are no valid tests to discover whether he has the capacity for artistic creativeness. Many such tests have been proposed. Those which claim objectivity usually require selection on the basis of aesthetic preference of one of several drawings, and these answers are graded by comparison with the preferences of assumed experts. Unfortunately, this measures, not artistic promise, but only familiarity with fashionable taste. When different tests have been given to the same group, the correlation turns out to be so low as to undermine completely any confidence in the results.[2] It would seem, thus far, that the solution lies, not in attempting to compose an absolute measure of taste or creativeness, but in endeavoring to isolate those factors which correlate with actual performance in the professional curriculum and later in practice. These factors may well prove to be very obscure and oblique, but certain studies now under way seem to indicate progress, and, therefore, hope of ultimate solution. Therefore, the Commission urges that The Institute investigate the development of an aptitude test for prospective architects (*Recommendation 3*).

The quality of vocational guidance depends, however, upon the quality and resources of the counsellors who must interpret tests and suggest possibilities. In many schools, the number of students to be advised precludes thorough study of each individual, and excessive reliance is placed on school grades, teacher opinions, and general tests. While the counsellor may be familiar with the detailed requirements of common occupations, too often he does not know and does not have access to the qualifications needed by highly specialized professions such as architecture. Despite the best of intentions, opinions rendered under such circumstances are often fallible. A few guidance manuals for architecture have been published to assist counsellors and students. That issued in the series prepared by the U. S. Office of Education is perhaps the most notable.[3] In 1945, The AIA, through its Committee on Education, published an excellent pamphlet, *Architecture, a Profession, a Career*. The Commission believes that The AIA should review this problem and prepare and circulate an up-to-date manual written for counsellors and students (*Recommendation 4*).

Other channels for recruitment and guidance should be developed. The faculties of schools of architecture frequently have opportunities to perform such functions, although they are usually not strategically located for such service and, in most instances, contacts are limited to those who have already applied for admission. Occasionally, they join guidance teams sent by colleges to secondary schools. A more available source of guidance is the individual architect, especially since the recent trend toward wider distribution of practitioners has provided most communities of any size with such personnel. Many architects have been accustomed to give informal counsel to youths who seek them out. In some communities high schools have enlisted local leaders in many vocations to cooperate in a formal advising program. Occasionally, service clubs set up guidance clinics. It would appear, therefore, that AIA chapters could provide an important public service for their local areas by organizing and publicizing a well-considered system of advising. In addition, it would be helpful if the student could gain a closer view of an architect's work, either by visiting an office or by obtaining vacation employment in it. Even the most menial position at the most nominal wage, if any, would give him invaluable insight for his future course (*Recommendation 5*). Unfortunately, the tendency to postpone the choice of vocation until high school graduation or later would rule out many from such trial experiences, but for the rest it would be most worth while.

It should be emphasized, however, that such counselling is a serious responsibility, for on its issue hangs one of the most important decisions that the recipient must make. The counsellor must be motivated, not by ulterior motives, but solely by the best interests of the advisee. Furthermore, encouragement should not be restricted to only the few who already exhibit the full range of talents required for complete development. The adviser should remember that the practice of architecture needs many varied talents, and that some deficiencies can be overcome by the challenging of latent abilities or by the conscious correction of shortcomings. Finally, if full professional status seems too high an ambition, the adviser may suggest other opportunities in the building industry.

Any discussion of Pre-professional Education is incomplete if the influence of home and family is omitted. Standards and patterns of behavior, outlook, and morality are established and nurtured more surely here than by any other agency. If these are lacking, formal education faces a precarious task. In seeking these qualities in its recruits, the profession is at the mercy of private and social forces beyond its control.

One variation of Pre-professional Education remains to be noted, i.e., the inclusion of a full or partial collegiate program in liberal arts before undertaking professional studies. The expansion of the junior colleges has lent emphasis to this type of preparation. The cultural and personal benefits of such a program are obvious. The student gains contact with major areas of knowledge, grows in understanding of the fundamental principles, values, and ideas underlying civilizations, and expands his capacity for logical thinking and facility in expression. Such experience not only enriches his personal outlook, but also contributes an invaluable background for later professional studies. Moreover, such a program means that the student is older, and presumably more mature, when he is ready to begin his technical curriculum.

Since architectural curricula require certain basic general subjects, such as rhetoric, mathematics, science, etc., which are usually included in liberal arts curricula, the student who takes advantage of a preliminary liberal arts program can reduce proportionately the length of his professional curriculum, limited only by certain irreducible sequences of technical courses. To this extent, a full liberal arts curriculum need not add four full years, although to the extent of overlap the benefits likewise are curtailed. In any case, the additional time greatly increases the cost of education and for this reason such programs have remained, for the most part, on a purely voluntary basis. Instances of mandatory programs will be discussed under professional curricula.

Nevertheless, the lengthening of the total educational program is not an unmixed blessing for professional men. Counterbalancing, in some degree, the advantages of longer academic training, is the fact that this general education is concentrated at the beginning, whereas if distributed more uniformly the student, being more mature, would be better prepared to derive full benefit from it. Likewise, a student who postpones entrance into professional courses loses the advantage of a longer, slower, and probably surer assimilation of technical skills. Moreover, he misses the immediate stimulus of strong professional motivation. Some educators believe that a large proportion of general studies might well be reserved for adult education, when it would probably be more thoroughly appreciated and absorbed and, at the same time, serve as a welcome avocation amid advanced technical studies. In addition, delayed entrance into actual practice due to prolongation of formal education, and also to enforced military service, exaggerates personal problems, such as the establishment of a family and the transition into practice. This problem will be examined further in the sections on professional curricula and on students.

Because of the importance of Pre-professional Education in the training of architects, some idealists have suggested that a broad, but specific, secondary program should be required for admission to architectural schools. Some have even proposed special treatment of prospective architects on elementary levels. In reality, however, there does not appear to be any method by which such students could be wisely chosen at such an early age, and, indeed, even if this were possible, it might do more harm than good by isolating these pupils from the socially unifying experiences of a common program. Likewise, since the profession needs enrichment by many types of personalities, it seems wiser to avoid too early specialization and to allow more scope for the development of a normal diversity of backgrounds.

It is possible, of course, that the common program should include, for all students, types of training that incidentally would be of special value to those who do choose careers in architecture. For example, an expansion and intensification of training in art and drawing would benefit all students, and particularly future architects. Not only would art help to counterbalance the present overweighted emphasis on verbalized learning, but it would also help to instill a heightened sensitivity to artistic values, and, thus, encourage a more widespread and alert interest in architecture itself. Another possibility is that of centering a series of instructional units in several fields around a local architectural theme. One experiment of this type was conducted with considerable success for a sixth grade class at the Lincoln School sponsored by the Teachers College of Columbia University.[4] Such projects would be more frequently used if stimulating "work books" were available. Since many industries and businesses already provide such materials as a means of gaining understanding and good will, it would seem to be an excellent type of public service that might well be rendered by The AIA (*Recommendation 6*).

3. THE CURRICULUM
OF THE COLLEGIATE SCHOOL OF ARCHITECTURE

Objectives: Definition of the proper objectives of the school's professional curriculum within the total framework of architectural education is an essential task. Coming between the end of the Pre-professional Stage and the beginning of candidateship, its function consists of guiding students in the acquisition of such general and technical knowledge, skills, and judgment as will stimulate a rich and sound personal, social, and professional growth in school, candidacy, and mature practice.

Quantity and effectiveness of accomplishment depend upon efficiency of method, the skill of the teacher, the capacity and effort of the student, and the time available. Assuming an academic year of 32 weeks and a work week of 50 hours, the minimum curriculum of five years provides a rough limit of 8000 usable hours, during which the student must transform himself from a layman into a candidate. Students' rate of sound growth is a finite quantity. While this rate does vary somewhat, the nature of architecture suggests that superior students need challenge, not by larger quantity, but by encouragement to higher quality of performance. Therefore, establishment of curricular limits seems both proper and feasible.

The question becomes one of fixing a just and attainable threshold for student accomplishment at the time of entering candidacy. Many architects, apparently impatient of human limitations, seem to expect a standard which to educators is highly unrealistic. Too often, this attitude arises in an unreasonable expectation that the candidate should have acquired a level of maturity which the practitioner himself has achieved only after years of experience. Others, however, remember their own development sufficiently to accept a more modest level of attainment. A second fallacy is the tendency of some architects and more than a few students to think of education merely as a means of cramming for a licensing examination. Finally, another source of conflict lies between the employer, who demands immediately usable vocational skills, and the profession, which must make certain that its recruits are adequately prepared to rise beyond mere vocation to real professional status. These two attitudes are not entirely antagonistic, but the compromise must be wisely adjusted. Such a compromise must fix a healthy balance between the general and the technical, between essential theory and practice, and between the fundamental and the esoteric. Finally, any threshold must provide some measure of flexibility in range to reconcile it with students' special talents and interests.

In the light of the qualifications of an architect presented in Section 3, *Chapter III,* the threshold of accomplishment at the beginning of candidacy may be defined as embodying the following knowledge, skills, traits, and experiences:

1. Technical knowledge of facts, concepts, and principles relating to:
   a. Building planning: typical use centers, rooms, room clusters, services; minimal and optimal sizes; optimal space conditions; types and characteristics of building traffic, design criteria for circulation elements; acoustics; typical organizational patterns in buildings; orientation; safety in buildings; building groups; site development; sources of information; methods of evaluating functional efficiency.
   b. Building construction: thorough knowledge of typical materials, their production, forms, properties, use, maintenance, performance in combination, specification, and cost; some familiarity with new materials under current development; thorough knowledge of typical structural components and systems, including design principles, methods, and criteria of selection; effects of loading, impact, temperature, distortion, stress redistribution; codes; safety from fire; construction of typical details, openings, stairs, finish; shelter comfort; some familiarity with current structural research developments; general survey of costs; general understanding of erection procedures and equipment.
   c. Building equipment: general understanding of water supply, sanitation, heating, air conditioning, electrical, illumination, fire fighting, etc.
   d. Architectural aesthetics: space and surface elements, types, effects in combination; psychology of vision; decorative materials, physical qualities, production, effects; color; ornament, function, types, content, pattern, effects; principles of aesthetic organization, types, emotional and intellectual reactions; character, types, principles of selection; style, scope, bases, types.
   e. Related fields: general understanding of city planning, landscape design, furniture, painting, sculpture.
   f. Architectural administration: general knowledge of building promotion, building finance, building law, techniques of performing architectural services, office management.

2. Technical skills:
   a. Considerable facility in sketching, delineation, and instrumental drawing.
   b. Considerable facility in programming and analyzing building projects of intermediate complexity.
   c. Considerable facility in systematic selection of building materials and structural systems, and in the design of common structural elements.
   d. Moderate facility in the design of simple installations of typical building equipment.
   e. Considerable facility and discrimination in aesthetic design.
   f. Considerable facility in the appropriate solution of typical building problems of intermediate complexity with optimal integration of functional, structural, equipment, and aesthetic factors.
   g. Moderate facility in preparing accurate, legible working drawings, and simple specifications.
   h. Some experience in collaboration and executive direction in the design development of simple building projects.
3. General knowledge and skills:[5]
   a. Considerable facility in writing and speaking for precise, lucid, and forceful communication.
   b. Considerable facility in: precise, logical, and concise thinking; making valid assumptions; assembling and verifying data; deriving principles; using abstract concepts; recognizing significant factors; and drawing just conclusions.
   c. Sufficient facility in mathematics to support technical analyses and calculations.
   d. Moderate knowledge of physical and natural sciences, with emphasis on physics, chemistry, and geology, and a general understanding of scientific method.
   e. Basic knowledge of the social sciences, especially history, sociology, economics, and government.
   f. Basic knowledge of the humanities, especially philosophy, ethics, and the history of ideas.

Such a specific definition of the goal of collegiate professional education runs the risk of appearing as a mere pious hope. Nevertheless, it is only by attempting the ideal that progressively closer approximations of it can be obtained. Certainly no examining board and no practitioner could ask for a better standard for prospective employees, although the goal leaves many areas of professional education for later acquisition. Only after experiment can educators determine whether the goal is realistic or overambitious.

Content

Definition of a legitimate general goal leads directly to determination of the specific content of the curriculum. It is here that both practitioners and educators hazard disagreement between each other and among themselves. It may be argued that considerable flexibility should be allowed, but unless the goal is to be vitiated at the very beginning, some measure of general consensus on definite limits seems desirable.

It is obvious that five academic years is an all too brief period in which to implement such a goal. The problem of curriculum length will be discussed later. If it is undesirable to expand it further, the only hope of approaching the goal lies in adopting the most efficient organization and methods, in order to ensure that as many courses as possible perform several functions at the same time, and to secure through ingenious integration a total educational experience which will transcend the mere sum of its parts.

In fixing curricular content, it is of the utmost importance to adjust quantity at a level which will permit utilization of the full learning process described in Section 1. Unless this is done, instruction is reduced to simple factual description and the student fails to master principles through exercises in their application. Descriptive courses are allowable only for those topics in which application is most effectively illustrated during candidacy and mature experience.

In endeavoring to attain courses performing multiple functions and closely integrated into the whole curriculum, it is tempting to establish special sections of general courses restricted to architectural students alone. This raises certain difficulties. It isolates architectural students from stimulating contact and competition with other students in the institution and thereby surrenders a useful comparative check on the academic performance of architectural students, which is all the more desirable because architectural students are so largely occupied by their own professional courses. It also restricts flexibility in preparing student schedules. These difficulties are offset in some degree by the increased motivation given architectural students through appeal to their special interests.

Within these general boundaries, the goal of collegiate professional education suggests minimum and optimum limits for the various groups of courses in the curriculum. These groups are usually formed as follows (accompanying each are the different areas of knowledge and skills which they normally provide; they are also keyed to the preceding list defining the goals of the curriculum:

1. Graphics. 2a, part of 1e. (Projections, Shades and Shadows, Perspective, Freehand Drawing, Water Color, Painting, Modeling, Rendering.)
2. Construction. 1b, 2c, 2g. (Materials and Methods, Mechanics of Materials, Resistances of Materials, Structural Theory and Design, Working Drawings, Specifications, Estimating, Erection Methods.)
3. Equipment. 1c, 2d. (Heating, Air Conditioning, Water Supply, Sanitation, Electrical Equipment, Illumination.)
4. Theory of Architecture. 1a, 1d, 2e. (Theory, Planning, Composition, lectures in Design, Philosophy of Architecture.)
5. History of Architecture. 3b, 3e, 3f, and to provide an understanding of the growth of architecture and architectural ideas leading up to the consideration of contemporary architecture. (Survey course, detailed courses in special periods, history of related fields.)

140

6. Architectural Design. 1a, 1d, 2b, 2c, 2e, 2f, 2h. (Basic Design; Elementary, Intermediate, and Advanced Architectural Design.)
7. City Planning. 1e, 2b, 2f. (Urban Sociology, City Planning.)
8. Practice. Part of 1b, 1f. (Office Practice, Architectural Administration, Finance, Building Law.)
9. Language. 3a. (Rhetoric, Report Writing, Business Correspondence, Public Speaking, Foreign Language, written exercises in other courses.)
10. Mathematics. 3c. (Trigonometry, College Algebra, Analytic Geometry, Calculus.)
11. Physical Sciences. 1b, 1c, 2c, 3d, 3e. (Physics, Chemistry, Geology.)
12. Social sciences. 3e. (General History, Sociology, Economics, Government.)
13. Humanities. 3b, 3f. (Philosophy, Ethics, Logic, Fine Arts, Literature.)

Some measure of the relative importance of the various courses of the architectural curriculum is provided by the *1950 Survey*. Architects were asked to rate these courses as either "Important," "Desirable," or "Of Minor Importance" (*Table 41*). If these are valued at 2, 1, —1 respectively, the resulting composite ranking on a scale in which 200 is the highest possible score, was as follows:

1	Architectural Design	198
2	Building Materials & Methods	194
3	Mathematics	174
4	Structural Design	173
5	Theory of Architecture	172
6	Working Drawings	167
7	Specifications	164
8	English	163
9	Fine Arts	147
10	Graphics (Des. Geom., Persp., Presentation)	145
11	Equipment	142
12	Freehand Drawing	139
13	Professional Relations	135
14	Physics	127
15	History of Architecture	116
16	Bldg. Codes, Law, Real Estate	114
17	Psychology & Human Relations	110
18	Site Design	107
19	Applied Sciences (light, color, sound)	103
20	Office Administration	102
21	Interior Design & Furniture	100
22	City Planning	93
23	Landscape Design	62
24	Economics & Sociology	58
25	Chemistry	22
26	Foreign Language	11

A similar ranking by teachers of architecture, but only those who were licensed to practice, revealed much the same order:

			Practitioners' rankings	Points more than practitioners
1	Architectural Design	199	1	1
2	Building Materials & Methods	189	2	−5
3	Structural Design	188	4	15
4	English	188	8	25
5	Theory of Architecture	178	5	6
6	Mathematics	176	3	2
7	Graphics	168	10	23
8	Equipment	159	11	17
9	Working Drawings	156	6	−12
10	Freehand Drawing	153	12	14
11	Physics	149	14	22
12	Fine Arts	148	9	1
13	History of Architecture	148	15	32
14	Specifications	144	7	−20
15	Professional Relations	138	13	3
16	City Planning	137	22	44
17	Applied Sciences	129	19	26
18	Economics & Sociology	127	24	69
19	Bldg. Codes, Law, Real Estate	121	16	7
20	Psychology & Human Relations	118	17	8
21	Site Design	99	18	−8
22	Interior Design & Furniture	97	21	−3
23	Office Administration	94	20	−8
24	Landscape Design	79	23	17
25	Foreign Language	27	26	16
26	Chemistry	21	25	−1

Comparison discloses marked agreement as to most and least important courses. The higher scores awarded by teachers seem to indicate a natural bias toward a more comprehensive curriculum. The chief points of difference were the greater emphasis placed by teachers on History, City Planning, Social Sciences, Applied Sciences, English, Graphics, and Physics. Practitioners, on the other hand, placed more stress on Specifications and Working Drawings. Nevertheless, the overall correspondence of the rankings is indeed noteworthy.

Even closer agreement is revealed when the relative emphasis on groups of subjects is compared:

	Practitioners' emphasis % OF ALL POINTS	Teachers' emphasis	
		% OF ALL TEACHERS' POINTS	% OF ALL PRACT. POINTS
Drawing	8.8%	9.1%	9.9%
Math and Construction	27.0	24.2	26.4
History of Architecture	3.7	4.2	4.6
Architectural Design	11.4	10.7	11.6
Other technical Subjects	29.6	29.9	32.6
General Subjects	19.7	22.0	24.0

It is obvious that these rankings must not be viewed as bases for the distribution of actual time in curricula. No one could maintain, for example, that design should be allocated so small a portion of the total effort. Nevertheless, comparison of the percentages given the several groups by practitioners and teachers displays a surprising unanimity of opinion.

Once the relative desirability of courses is established, the practical problem of allocating available time for the several groups raises the question of the inevitable compromise imposed by the restricted length of the curriculum. As a general indication of the major trends in relative emphasis over the past half-century, it is instructive to compare the average allocation of hours in eight schools in 1898 with the Standard Minima of 1924 and with the average of 25 schools in 1948.

	1898 (4 yrs.)				1924 (4 yrs.)		1948 (5-yr. Curriculum)					
	MIN.	MAX.	AVG.	%	HRS.	%	MIN.	MAX.	AVG.	%	% (INCR. TO 5 YR.)
Drawing	30	69	55	13.9	16	14.6	240	990	601	12.6	15.7
Math & Constr.	52	127	75	18.9	20	18.2	570	1320	1008	21.0	26.2
History of Arch.	26	53	32	8.1	8	7.3	90	315	168	3.5	4.4
Arch. Design	125	215	174	43.9	30	27.3	1080	3015	2147	44.9	56.2
Other Technical					16	14.6			331	6.9	8.7
General	24	127	61	15.4	20	18.2			531	11.1	13.8
Total	380*	414*	397	100%	110	100%	3675*	5645*	4786	100%	125%

* These totals are not the sums of the columns above them, but ranges in different schools.

Note that 1898 units are an unspecified type of hours; 1924 units are semester hours; and 1948 units are in contact hours of instruction. It is possible, therefore, to compare only the percentages of the total programs. Since the 1898 and 1924 allocations are within a four-year curriculum, the actual quantity of time scheduled in the five-year curricula of 1948 can be compared to 1898 and 1924 only by increasing the relative quantity by 25 per cent.

Thus this comparison indicates that in 1948 design has been expanded by 28 per cent over 1898 and by 106 per cent over 1924, and now occupies nearly half of the student's time. Likewise, the time devoted to construction has increased more than 38 per cent over 1898. The emphasis on drawing has remained practically constant. Miscellaneous technical courses, absent in 1898, now absorb 6.9 per cent of the schedule. These increases have all been made at the expense of the general courses which have declined by 39 per cent since 1924 and of history which has been reduced by almost 46 per cent since 1898. The trends reflect the expanded demands and prestige of modern technology and an increased concentration on training in the solution of design exercises.

The wide variation in time allocated to the several groups of subjects underscores the fact that each school has insisted upon meeting the problems of professional training in its own way. Although some allowance must be made for the difficulties of compiling curricular statistics from the obscure descriptions contained in college catalogs, nevertheless, variations of 200 to 300 per cent in the 1948 allotments of actual hours do seem excessive. In the light of present institutional individualism, it is easy to understand the vociferous revolt which was provoked by the Standard Minima of 1924. Part of the variation is due no doubt to the habit of teaching combinations of topics in a single course. Thus design often incorporates part of the training in instrumental drawing, the work in theory, and in some schools even structural theory and history.

Some critics would resolve such variations by a new promulgation of uniform standards by an authoritative central agency. Theoretically objective study of a specific educational problem should provide a definitive instructional program which all schools could adopt and practice. Some have suggested that The AIA, ACSA, NCARB, or the NAAB could singly or in concert perform this function. Such a solution, however, would have many hazards. It presumes, for example, too much faith in the omniscience of any central agency which would be charged with fixing the scope, character, and details of a system which would have to be administered by many separate faculties. It would open the way for a rigid pattern which would stifle the initiative of individual faculties, and make common-sense adjustments, valuable experiments, and necessary changes very difficult, if not practically impossible, to accomplish. The educational process, like life, is dynamic in nature and should not be subjected to a straitjacket. Moreover, such regulation could define only minimum standards, with the danger of ultimately leveling all institutions to a sterile and mediocre compromise. Finally, since primary responsibility for American architectural education has been delegated to collegiate institutions for more than eighty years, and since such institutions have an inalienable duty to their own constituents to administer their programs according to their own best judgment, no super-agency is in a position to impose a uniform policy. It can only render advice and seek co-operation. This system of check and balance affirms a basic principle of American social action.

In any case, a curriculum is only one aspect of an educational program. It provides a useful framework by which to organize the several parts of the program, and give general definition to scope and content. If it is not brought to life by high quality instruction, it is of little avail.

Nevertheless, despite these limitations, it is instructive to review three typical allocations of time within the functional divisions of the professional curriculum, and within the five-year, 8000-hour length. The time assigned therefore includes lectures, class discussions, laboratory and drawing work, and also outside preparation. It should be noted that the inclusion of preparation time forbids a direct comparison with the previous analysis of curricula in 1898, 1924, and 1948.

Basic & General Subjects	*School A*		*School B*		*School C*	
	HRS.	%	HRS.	%	HRS.	%
Phys. Educ., Hyg., & Mil. Sci.	480	6.0	180	2.5	no credit?	
Rhetoric	288	3.6	240	3.3	270	4.2
Mathematics	432	5.4	255	3.5	540	8.4
Physical Sciences	480	6.0	810	11.2	390	6.1
Humanities & Social Sciences	912	11.5	810	11.2	420	6.6
Total Basic & General	2592	32.5	2295	31.8	1620	25.5
Technical Subjects						
Graphics	864	10.8	420	5.8	630	9.9
Construction	480	6.0	420	5.8	360	5.6
Structural Theory	864	10.8	495	6.9	420	6.6
Equipment	432	5.4	615	8.5	180	2.8
Theory of Architecture	96	1.2	210	2.9	—	—
History of Architecture	528	6.6	270	3.7	360	5.6
Architectural Design	1872	23.5	2055	28.4	2340	36.8
City Planning	144	1.8	180	2.5	90	1.4
Architectural Practice	96	1.2	—	—	90	1.4
Other	—	—	180	2.5	270	4.2
Total Technical	5376	67.5	4935	68.2	4740	74.5
Total Curriculum	7968	100.0	7230	100.0	6360	100.0

The schools listed above were selected because their graduates are generally recognized as having relatively superior training and because their curricula illustrate normal variations of approach to the educational problem. It should be noted that in total number of hours of work scheduled, *A* exceeds *C* by 25 per cent. Nevertheless, the actual hours of student effort are probably much the same in most good schools. It is characteristic of architectural education that design courses and courses requiring involved exercises, such as structural theory, absorb whatever extra time the student is willing to work. The high percentage of hours devoted to design at school *C* is believed to be due in part to the incorporation of theory and other topics in the design courses. The general comparison does reveal fundamental variations in time assigned to the humanities and social sciences, to graphics, construction and structural theory, and history.

While it is probably impossible to obtain complete agreement among educators or, for that matter, among architects, as to the details of curricular content, except by arbitrary and dictatorial fiat, such uniformity even if attained would not mean that graduates would become identical products. For human nature being what it is, there is normally as much variation between graduates of the same school as there is between average graduates of different schools. The evaluation of a school cannot be based upon curriculum alone, but must take into account all the other factors, tangible and intangible, and particularly the faculties, which implement the educational process. Good composition of the curriculum is important only to the degree that it provides an effective, balanced framework for the general guidance of the process.

Because student talents and interests vary, and because the scope of architecture is so broad that it needs many kinds of special personnel, many schools deem it proper to encourage such special talents by offering alternative options. Such options usually diverge from the basic course only in the last year or two, and they are normally close enough to the basic course to ensure all graduates of true professional status. The rise of such options has encouraged the renaming of the type of curriculum already described, as a General, or Design, Option. The newer options occasionally deal with special types of buildings, such as industrial plants, but the most common is the Structural Option, which usually replaces fifth-year advanced design with a year of advanced structural theory. In many schools Structural Options evolved from curricula in Architectural Engineering, the development of which will be discussed in *Chapter VII* in the section on related curricula. The Structural Option of school *A* alters the group percentages by increasing mathematics from 5.4% to 9.0% and structural theory from 10.8% to 20.5% while decreasing design from 23.5% to 15.0%, Graphics from 10.8% to 9.6%, the humanities from 11.5% to 9.6%, and eliminating the course in City Planning.

Finally, the amount of general education, or non-professional cultural courses, needs consideration. The NAAB recommends that General Background Courses should comprise from 20 to 30 per cent of the curriculum, but the term includes the mathematics, physics, and rhetoric directly necessary for later technical subjects. The Engineers' Council for Professional Development, the accrediting agency for engineering curricula, recommends that in such curricula 20 per cent of all credit hours be assigned to "humanistic-social" courses. In practice, however, this term is so liberally interpreted, by including report writing, public speaking, business law, engineering economics, and other semi-professional subjects, that actual cultural content is much reduced.

In academic terminology, general education means courses outside the student's field of concentration which are intended to broaden his horizons and deepen his understanding. Too often this is conceived as providing a superficial veneer to be used to win contacts and influence clients, but at its best general education leads the student to an awareness and appreciation of the vast range and implications of human experience. For an architect, however, few areas can be unrelated to his purpose. Philosophy defines optimal conditions of living. Music can clarify architectural aesthetics, and astronomy contributes to the control of natural lighting. Nevertheless, contact with great minds, works, and ideas, embracing the amazing heritage of mankind's intellectual, emotional, and spiritual development, can stretch the narrow mind, entice it to curiosity, and plant a desire for humane wisdom. More than most men, architects need such adventures.

The architecture curriculum, therefore, despite the press of technical needs, should offer opportunity for general cultural education. Some schools prescribe specific subjects; others provide electives restricted to the humanities and social sciences. Perhaps 10 per cent might be arbitrarily set as a just proportion for this purpose. This would offer the possibility of several general courses of standard length. The location of such general courses has already been discussed, but here should be noted an additional argument for an even distribution of them throughout the curriculum. By such means a student can be encouraged to follow up with additional courses some field which has aroused his interest and thus penetrate beyond the usual introductory survey. If properly guided by sympathetic advisers, few students will squander such an opportunity on sinecures.

Although the proportion just suggested may seem small, it should be remembered that courses in architectural history may well be counted among cultural studies. The inclusion of such courses would raise the cultural content of the curriculum to more than 15 per cent, and this proportion compares very favorably with the non-major part of most college curricula today.

Organization of the Curriculum

If an architectural curriculum is to lead students through their collegiate training in a lucid, logical, and integrated manner, it must schedule the sequences of its component courses very carefully. In conformity with the general educational methods cited in Section 1, the grand curricular plan should proceed smoothly from known to new experiences. Ideas broached in one course should be reinforced wherever possible by applications in concurrent and later courses. Architectural curricula are unusually susceptible to this principle because each design problem can serve to focus on its solution all the knowledge and skills which the student has thus far gained. No other collegiate curriculum provides such opportunities for unification, reiteration, and motivation.

There are a number of considerations which complicate the preparation of an ideal schedule. The temptation is to impose a fixed pattern which must be followed

without deviation. Such patterns become ends in themselves and provide no amelioration for essential adjustments to variation in students or to their vicissitudes. It seems
unnecessarily severe to penalize a student, who fails in a single course because of
illness, slowness, or circumstances beyond his control, by interrupting his progress
until the next full sequence is offered. Transfer students likewise suffer, and an excessively rigid system might actually work to discourage a pre-professional year or
two of liberal arts. Superior students are likewise deterred from undertaking additional work. Therefore, it seems desirable to give the curricular pattern some degree
of flexibility.

Curricular organization is also made more intricate due to the desire for an
integrated relationship between courses. There are at least four long course sequences
which should be completed as soon as possible if they are to contribute with maximum effort to design; they are graphics, construction, structural theory, and history.
The result is that the second year, when all of these sequences should be under
way, becomes a difficult bottleneck. For this reason some schools prefer to postpone
to later terms as many of the general education courses as possible. This conforms
to the view already expressed that the more mature student will benefit more by
taking these courses at a later time.

A number of schools relieve this pressure somewhat by requiring for admission
certain elementary courses. Thus, college algebra, trigonometry, and physics are
occasionally demanded. This problem will be discussed in the section on the selection
of students in *Chapter VII*.

The curricular organization thus far analyzed is characterized by the fact that the
whole program is planned and administered by the professional school as a single
unit. Originally this pattern derived from the traditional four-year curricula, as practiced for liberal arts, the ministry, and law. By the beginning of this century, however,
the stronger schools had become increasingly aware that the general and technical
aims of architectural education could not be adequately fulfilled within four years.
In 1906, Columbia and Harvard both raised their entrance requirements to include
pre-professional general collegiate training. Columbia set this prerequisite as a minimum of two years, which made a minimum total time of six years to obtain the
professional degree. Harvard, on the other hand, went even further in requiring a
general four-year undergraduate degree for admission, while the professional curriculum became a three-year unit with graduate status. Thus, at Harvard, the
minimum time to obtain the professional degree rose to seven years.

Harvard remains the only American school working entirely at graduate level.
Nevertheless, the student entering from Harvard College can now elect to anticipate
professional work by following an undergraduate major in architectural sciences.
Analysis of this major reveals that it, together with the basic general prerequisites
of mathematics, physics, and statics, absorbs 67.5 per cent of the whole undergraduate
curriculum. This is equivalent to two and a half of the four undergraduate years.
Only 37.5 per cent, or six courses, is left for the humanities and social sciences. Thus,
in actual practice, the liberal content of the complete Harvard program is not as far-

reaching as might be assumed at first glance. Moreover, the seven-year length of the total program makes it available to relatively few students.

Columbia's six-year program also greatly restricted its enrollment. During the 1920's, to meet this situation, a combined general and professional program was set up which, by counting elementary professional courses as an undergraduate major, awarded a liberal arts degree at the end of four years and the professional degree at the end of six. Under pressure of depleted enrollments during depression years, Columbia reduced the admission requirement to one year of college work and awarded the professional degree at the end of five years. After World War II, however, although the one year of college work remained the minimum requirement, the huge increase in number of applicants permitted restriction of admission to those who had completed undergraduate degrees.

In 1915, the University of California reorganized its instruction to provide a four-year undergraduate professional curriculum leading to a non-professional degree, followed with a two-year graduate curriculum leading to the professional degree. Later, the professional master degree was awarded at the end of the fifth year. In practical effect, California's experience was closely comparable to the Columbia program. In 1929, the graduate curriculum enrolled only 29 students. In 1920, a similar four-plus-two curriculum was established at Princeton.

It seems significant that, in spite of the long operation of three of these four schools, the four together had trained by 1950 only 7.2 per cent of all present U. S. architects (*Table 37*), in comparison with the total effort of all schools, measured by the fact that 64.5 per cent of all architects in 1950 held first professional degrees either in architecture or architectural engineering. In contrast, four other schools, the Universities of Illinois, Pennsylvania, Michigan, and Cornell, have trained 17.1 per cent of all architects, or 26.5 per cent of all holders of first professional degrees. It can be presumed that the additional training provided by high entrance requirements of the former group has had beneficial results both for the recipients and the profession. Unfortunately, however, the impact of these extended programs has had only limited influence in creating the contemporary profession of the United States. The record seems to prove that this kind of remedy is too stringent to effect a general cure.

It should be noted, of course, that general academic training has not been confined to graduates of these extended programs. *Table 39* reveals that 33 per cent of all architects have pursued non-architectural studies at the collegiate level over varying lengths of time. If graduates of the four schools which require liberal arts training as a prerequisite are subtracted from the total, 26 per cent (33 − 7) of all architects are thus shown to have taken such training voluntarily as circumstances permitted. The proportion of voluntary liberal arts degrees is also high. The three schools requiring such degrees—Harvard, California, and Princeton—together total 4.75 per cent of all graduates, which means that more than 8 per cent (13 − 4.75) of all architects have completed liberal arts degrees on their own volition. From this, it seems reasonable to conclude that those who are able to afford the time and cost of additional training will do so without compulsion.

A more influential solution to the need for an expansion of general and professional content was the adoption of the five-year curriculum. In 1911, Cornell offered such a program as an option. In 1920 ACSA urged general consideration of the idea. In 1922 Cornell was the first school to offer only a five-year curriculum. By 1935, twenty-four schools had adopted the plan, and in 1949 NAAB set five years as the mandatory minimum for accreditation. This move stimulated some opposition based on the fear of some high-tuition schools that enrollments might be drastically reduced and on the sincere belief that earlier entrance into the offices constituted a greater benefit than additional academic courses. Thus far these hazards have not materialized. The new problem of integrating the academic program with enforced military service may reopen the question. This is discussed in the section on students in *Chapter VII*.

The *1950 Survey* studied the lengths of curricula and found, as expected, that at least 47 used the five-year plan. Four others reported up to 6 years. Harvard gave 3 to 4 years for the first professional degree, but this did not include the 4-year liberal arts degree prerequisite to admission. Six other schools offered only 4-year programs, all unaccredited and some actually in architectural engineering. It should be noted that there is some variation in actual amount of teaching time per academic year. Thus, in two schools a year with two semesters totaled 30 weeks, while in one this came to 40. For five-year curricula, this gives a range from 150 to 200 weeks, or a difference of 33 per cent. However, 38 schools on the semester plan had from 32 to 36 weeks. For 16 schools with quarter terms, the year covered from 30 to 36 weeks. The yearly averages were 33.8 weeks with semesters and 33.6 with quarters. In five-year curricula this totals 169 and 168 weeks for actual instruction. An interesting variation was furnished by the cooperative plan of the University of Cincinnati which, in a 6-year schedule of 7-week periods alternating between school and on-the-job experience totals 126 weeks of each. The job work is accepted by NAAB as equivalent laboratory credit in amount sufficient to raise the academic total to normal levels.

During the past fifteen years, university educators have reacted strongly to the prevailing atomization, compartmentation, and specialization of higher education, and have set up in many institutions core curricula to regain a broader and more coherent base for intellectual unity among citizens. The usual mechanism is to require a series of fundamental courses which synthesize large areas of knowledge, such as philosophy, the social sciences, the natural sciences, world literature, the arts, etc. At their best, as in Columbia's Contemporary Civilization course, they provide a most stimulating and profitable educational experience; too often they subside into superficial surveys which lack point or substance. Since core courses were usually scheduled in the first two years of college, there has appeared a corresponding administrative separation of lower and upper divisions. Within the liberal arts program, students proceed from general studies in the lower division to specialized studies in the upper division. The general studies thus act not only to give a more comprehensive view, but also to suggest possible fields for subsequent concentration. Since concentration is limited to only two years, its scope can rarely extend beyond a short sequence of courses.

Because specialized engineering curricula are founded on common mathematical and scientific courses, engineering colleges have often rationalized this necessity by adopting a "common Freshman year."

When the principle of the "core curriculum" or the "common Freshman year" is imposed on the architectural curriculum by excessive administrative rationalizing, certain embarrassing difficulties arise. If all professional courses are delayed until the third year, or even the second, the scheduling bottleneck previously noted becomes greatly exaggerated. Moreover, the advantages of the five-year curriculum, with its opportunity for slower, but longer development of skills, and for close integration through applications in design problems, are largely vitiated. Consequently, in almost all instances, such cores and common years have been modified to provide architectural students with introductory training in at least graphics and basic design. The result approximates the unitary organization, but is arbitrarily divided to appease administrative theory. The lower division type of organization is used by some schools as a screening device by which to select students who in the limited elementary skill courses of the lower division have displayed promise of success in the upper professional subjects. In practice, it seems immaterial whether screening is done by this device or whether students screen themselves in the normal unitary curriculum.

Again, it must be noted that if the organizational pattern permits a lucid, logical, and integrated flow, albeit with some flexibility, its administrative subdivisions are purely a matter of taste. On the basis of logic and experience, it seems quite satisfactory to leave such matters to the preference of the individual institution.

The First Professional Degree

Despite general similarity of architectural curricula in organization and content, the titles of first professional degrees have varied widely. Since technical curricula in the second half of the 19th century were closely associated with the introduction of scientific studies into collegiate institutions, such programs were awarded a *Bachelor of Science* degree to distinguish them from the traditional classical course. As technical curricula multiplied, there was a strong trend to qualify the *B.S.* degree with an appropriate designation. Seven of the first nine American schools of architecture thus used the form, *B.S. in Architecture.* In contrast, the other two schools—Cornell and Syracuse—followed the ancient medieval custom of named professional degrees in medicine, law, and theology, by choosing the title, *Bachelor of Architecture.*

Of the 20 schools operating in 1911, 12 used *B.S. in Arch.* and 6 *B. Arch.* The first professional degree at Harvard was then *Master of Architecture,* and at California, *Graduate in Architecture.* By 1935, this balance was reversed, largely because the growing number of five-year curricula tended to select *B. Arch.* Of 45 schools, 27 used this designation and 13 still retained *B.S. in Arch.* Michigan used both, *B.S. in Arch.* for its regular four-year program, and *B. Arch.* for its five-year option. Nebraska selected *Bachelor of Arts in Architecture,* and Yale chose *Bachelor of Fine Arts.* Princeton's first professional degree was *Master of Fine Arts in Architecture,* and California continued its *Graduate in Architecture*. In 1953, of the 45 accredited schools, 36—80 per cent—use *B. Arch.,* and 6 retain *B.S. in Arch*. The three remaining schools all use *master* titles—California *M.A. in Arch.,* Virginia Polytechnic Institute *M.S. in Arch.,* and Princeton *M.F.A. in Arch.,* and it should be noted that each awards a non-professional bachelor degree at the end of the first four years of their curricula.

Some critics feel that the use of the master degree for professional curricula is highly desirable for all schools and point to the fact that graduates of mandatory five-year curricula rewarded only by a bachelor degree carry an unfair handicap when professional graduates in other fields obtain their master degree in exactly the same amount of time, and when the rank and salary of appointments in government, the armed forces, industry, and even professional circles depend more and more on degree status of the candidate. While the truth of this point must be recognized, others maintain the obvious fact that it is the training and not the name that counts, and that any appointive agency which neglects such inspection can be appropriately dealt with. There are, however, three additional important objections to the five-year master degree in architecture. First, it would lead to considerable public confusion for professional schools to award non-professional degrees, as would be the case if the degree, *B. Architecture,* were to be conferred at the end of four years. No doubt some non-professional graduates might use this ambiguity to mislead the public and to seek special treatment by registration boards. Second, such an arrangement might tend to discourage a number of students from completing their full five-year training. In 1952, Dean William Wurster reported that out of 55 graduates of the most recent class completing the non-Professional *A.B.* curriculum at the University of California, only 26 returned for the fifth year to take their professional *M. Arch*. degree.[6] Third, and perhaps most important of all, it would without doubt tend to reduce the number who would be inclined to continue on for an additional year of graduate study. Although doctoral degrees in architecture will be discussed and recommended in *Chapter X,* such programs normally require a more extended program and are commonly reserved for training in research, rather than advanced subject matter courses or design. It would be very unfortunate, therefore, to deprive a shorter program of graduate study of whatever incentive the master degree affords.

To purists the diversity of names of first professional degrees remains a disturbing conflict, unhappy evidence of that institutional independence usually regarded as desirable. In some cases, divergence is caused by charter stipulations. However, the marked voluntary trend during the past decade toward concentration on the *B. Arch*. degree gives considerable hope that continued progress will be made in this direction.

4. INTERRELATION OF SCHOOL AND PRACTICE

Throughout preceding sections, the importance to architectural students of thorough-going contacts with actual buildings, construction, and practice has been stressed. Certain aspects of this school-practice interrelation now need further consideration.

For some architects and educators, the gap between school and practice seems too wide to bridge. Professor Gropius, for example, wrote in 1950:

"Should architectural education then be separated from its present academic framework? Many architects would agree with a decisive turn towards greater emphasis on practical experience. I, personally, have grave doubts as to whether the present bookish climate of universities can offer at all a healthy breeding ground for architects. The impact of industrialization on our profession has been so decisive that the young generation should be trained in close touch with the building industries and with their laboratories."[7]

This seems to mean that the American collegiate system is only to be tolerated as a regrettable and transitional compromise.

Nevertheless, for numerous reasons cited in *Chapter IV,* a major role in education for the practice of architecture has been assigned to the collegiate schools. They share with all professional schools the duty to create "environments in which mental discipline and growth may rightfully be expected to develop faster than if left to the casual chances of everyday experience, unplanned, unguided, and untested."[8] The problem, therefore, is not to surrender before difficulties, but to discover and implement the most effective means by which school and practice can reinforce each other. This is a perennial question, and, although American schools have in the past employed many methods to meet it, it demands constant attention.

It should be noted at the outset that the necessity for student contact with practice is inherent in the learning process and its fundamental need of demonstration and illustration. In the study of architecture, these are indispensable because the complex nature of its processes and the predominantly visual character of its large-scale elements are otherwise impossible to grasp. The essential qualities of a building cannot be directly experienced except at first-hand by walking around and through it. Construction projects hold similar lessons for the sharp observer. If a student is to gain command of these arts, he must first perceive them in reality. Not even stereoscopic color motion pictures superbly composed would in any way reduce the need for direct contact.

The chief difficulty lies in the fact that no one community—however large—can offer a convenient full-size museum of all the pertinent examples the student needs. Even in a metropolis, he must search them out at a considerable cost of time and effort. Furthermore, projects under construction are not located or timed to cater to teaching needs, and unique experimental works are even more difficult to visit.

In spite of these inherent problems, most schools have long made strenuous efforts to overcome them. Columbia has for two decades exploited its metropolitan location by conducting a freshman course which methodically surveys Manhattan buildings. More isolated schools have for years organized field trips to neighboring centers. Rensselaer students, to cite a typical example, though making full use of examples in the Capitol District, enjoyed semi-annual three-day trips to New York, Boston, Philadelphia, and the Connecticut valley. Each trip included recently completed buildings of outstanding quality with owners, managers, or architects as guides, construction projects, historic monuments, city planning agencies, material manufacturers, and craft shops. Blueprinted guides with pertinent plans and data prepared students for their visit. In many cases, students of isolated schools with a well-organized program of this kind actually see more examples of more varied character than those of metropolitan schools which depend solely upon student initiative.

For trips farther afield, the individual school can rarely spare sufficient time, but no doubt some students range widely in their search for significant work. It would seem, however, that much could be done to increase such activities and make them more beneficial. The high cost of travel naturally discourages most students from attempting such excursions. This barrier might be overcome in part by developing in major centers a system of summer field trips organized through the cooperation of local AIA chapters and the local student chapters. Lodging of the hostel type might be found, and the program could include all the features listed above, and also evening discussions with local architects. If such trips were scheduled for about two weeks in a center and others in sequence, a student could participate in as many as he could afford. During four vacations, and even later during candidacy, he could obtain guided access to a large number of centers and thus enjoy a profound educational experience, both professionally and personally, at minimum cost. The Commission urges that such a plan be studied (*Recommendation 7*).

Many schools administer endowed fellowships to provide travel and study in Europe, and thus perpetuate the principle of the grand tour in subsidized form. While these fellowships provide extraordinarily valuable experiences, they affect relatively few graduates. Recently, additional opportunities have been provided under the Fulbright Act, but the conditions of tenure, drawn up primarily for academic scholars, restrict use to a single country and consequently do not fit the need of architectural students for wider travel. The Commission believes that The AIA should press for modification of these rules in order to permit architects to participate in the important benefits to be derived from these funds (*Recommendation 8*).

In addition to field trips, most students of architecture seek practical experience in offices during vacation periods. Many also obtain vacation employment on buildings under construction. In either form, such work constitutes a revealing check on the student's choice of vocation, a source of tremendous professional stimulus, and an invaluable introduction to the problems and methods of office and site operations. A few schools require such work as prerequisite to graduation. Some offer informal aid in finding suitable openings. Most, however, stress the advantages to be gained, but leave actual arrangements to individual initiative. The most highly organized and integrated scheme is the cooperative plan used at the University of Cincinnati, where academic studies alternate with carefully controlled periods of site and office work.

While all educators emphasize the importance of such experience, a number of factors influence its operation. First, it depends on the volume of construction. Prosperity and personnel shortages create openings; depression bars such opportunities. Second, it needs and usually receives the generous support of architects and builders who can rarely hope for any real productivity from the beginner, whose wage, even when nominal, is, for the most part, a donation. Third, since such work is not organized as training programs comparable to those in industry, the student himself must take the responsibility of alert and questioning attention. And fourth, many self-supporting students must seek more remunerative non-professional work in order to continue schooling. Despite these problems, it is indeed remarkable how many students do procure a considerable degree of experience before graduation. In general, students who have enjoyed such experience gain much more from their school training. In many states, registration boards count pre-graduation office work toward the time required for candidacy. The Commission believes that a formal statement by the boards, indicating a liberal policy in such matters and permitting the inclusion of site work up to about 20 per cent of the total, would greatly increase the incentive to seek such work without jeopardizing in the least the intent and effectiveness of the candidate training program (*Recommendation 9*).

It should be noted that occasionally students gain office experience by working for teachers who maintain part-time practices or, in some instances, the university architect furnishes some employment opportunities. In American schools, such work is on an informal and individual basis. Apparently, the only systematic program of this kind has been the "clinic" organized in the late 1930's by C. C. Briggs at Pratt Institute. In it, students guided by members of the faculty undertook the performance of architectural services for small projects and alterations brought to the school by various owners. Competition with local architects was avoided by assuring them that any project which they wished to procure would be immediately transferred to them. The system had the advantage of introducing advanced students to professional problems more or less in miniature, but nonetheless real. It required, however, a metropolitan location to provide sufficient projects to make it operate. Some foreign schools have gone a step further. About 1925, Otto Bartning conducted his practice in his school at Weimar and used students as assistants. In 1950, the University of Melbourne in Australia, under Professor Brian Lewis, introduced a system of a school "office" staffed by students to which private architects could assign commissions.[9] If such a system is carried to its logical conclusion, it is difficult to understand how it could escape the hazards already noted in connection with apprenticeship and pupilage.

In addition to first-hand contacts with actual buildings and construction, there are many ways in which the quality of academic instruction could be improved through the practical demonstration of the principles of architecture. It is generally recognized that the greatest strength of American technical education lies in its development of ingenious demonstration apparatus and the provision of teaching laboratories in which students are led by carefully controlled projects to intimate knowledge of materials and their manipulation. By and large, however, American schools of architecture have woefully neglected this primary educational method. In recent years, many schools have assembled more or less limited exhibits of building materials. A few have acquired equipment to demonstrate sun angles and orientation. Several maintain well-equipped workshops for making models of buildings. But this is

155

about all. Most teachers depend primarily on slides and texts to illustrate their points.

This situation seems to stem from lack of precedent, lack of imagination, and lack of courage to demand for schools of architecture instructional facilities comparable to those provided for schools of medicine, engineering, natural science, and agriculture. *Chapter VI* will suggest a number of courses which could benefit from special apparatus and laboratories. For those in materials and methods of construction, it would be useful in connection with the teaching of standards of workmanship and supervision to have demonstrations of craft techniques performed by building mechanics. No doubt the cooperation of local unions could be enlisted, or personnel could be borrowed from the institution's maintenance crew. Model-making shops could easily be used to build mock-ups and models of construction details, as Howard Fisher has ably shown. A few schools have used a project in which students assist in the planning and actual construction of a house, but for various reasons such schemes have not continued. It might be possible for schools of architecture to cooperate with high school vocational classes in such ventures. For courses in structural theory, limited apparatus for demonstrating the strength tests of materials should be obtained if not otherwise available on the campus. The effects of stress upon members and systems should be shown by photo-elastic and other methods. Scale models of structural systems and details should be on display. Advanced students in structures should have access to computing machines.

Courses in design and theory can likewise benefit from the demonstration of principles. The school's exhibit of materials should certainly include a full complement of finish and decorative samples, with examples of different methods of treatment, and including wood, textiles, metals, etc. Instructors could draw upon football crowds to illustrate the flow of people through a gateway orifice. The effects of color lend themselves to dramatic experiments. Finally, every school of architecture needs facilities for the easy erection of full-size mock-ups of rooms to illustrate the definitive quality resulting from varying shapes, scales, proportions, colors, and lighting.

These few examples are intended only to suggest the infinite possibilities which could result from an imaginative and thorough application to architectural education of the principle of demonstration and laboratory teaching. No doubt, in the light of past budgets, such proposals will seem fantastic, but, if they are deemed educationally desirable, there is no legitimate reason why, in comparison with other technical fields, schools of architecture should continue to be relegated to the status of poor relations.

Finally, it should be noted that intensified use of demonstration and laboratory teaching does not necessarily mean that architectural students must use it as an exclusive method of training. In embracing the immediate and physical, the ability to absorb ideas and data from verbal sources should not be neglected. The fact that such methods have been overemphasized in the past should not lead to the opposite extreme. Rather, the two are complementary and must parallel each other. The gradual mastery of visual and tactile values experienced in direct demonstration can develop a disciplined imagination which can then interpret and check the printed text. Without this capacity, the great storehouse of accumulated experience would remain inaccessible, and each individual would be limited to his own restricted observations. Thus, in all phases of professional growth, all methods must be used in order to secure a well-balanced and comprehensive preparation for practice.

NOTES: CHAPTER FIVE

[1] Adapted from Ogan, R. W.: A College Looks at its Program, 1937. (Cited in Cole: *Background for College Teaching.*)

[2] Phillip P. Fehl, "Tests of Taste." (*College Art Journal*, vol. 12, no. 3, Spring, 1953, pp. 232–248.)

[3] Another is: William Thorpe: *Opportunities in Architecture*, 1951. (Grosset and Dunlap's Vocational Guidance Manuals.)

[4] Emily A. Barnes and Bess M. Young: *Children and Architecture*, 1932.

[5] For a similar analysis of skills desired for the practice of engineering, see Frank Kerekes, "Limitations on what Engineering Colleges can produce to meet the Requirements of the Practical Applications subsequent to Graduation." (*Report of the Committee on Engineering Education, American Society of Civil Engineers*, 1951, pp. 5–14.) The functional skills listed are: analyzing, investigating, designing, planning, developing, organizing, operating, producing, promoting, selling, communicating, and teaching.

[6] *Journal of Architectural Education*, no. 8, Summer, 1952, p. 46. Dean Wurster reported in December, 1953, that the University of California recently decided to abandon the four-year non-professional degree.

[7] Walter Gropius, "Blueprint for an architect's training." (*L'architecture d'aujourd'hui*, February, 1950, p. 72.)

[8] Kerekes, *op. cit.*

[9] "The Training of Architects: an Interim Report." (*Architectural Review*, vol. 107, no. 642, June, 1950, p. 372.)

CHAPTER VI

Courses for the

Architectural Curriculum

1. GENERAL CONSIDERATIONS

The designing of the component courses comprising the architectural curriculum is an intricate process. Each course must be clearly envisioned as to optimal scope, objectives, content, skills, methods, standards, relationship with all other courses, teaching materials and facilities, and staff capabilities. Unfortunately, in one sense, despite eighty years of development of American architectural education, there are no easy formulae by which to solve such highly complex equations. The evolution of architectural courses has been accomplished by the day-to-day experiments and refinements of devoted teachers. The problem of recruiting and training capable new teaching personnel to succeed them will be dealt with in the section on Faculty, in *Chapter VII.*

The scope of component courses varies from highly compartmented treatments to broad, wide-ranging amalgamations. Compartmentation offers the obvious advantage of a clear, sharp focus on a limited sequence of closely related topics. It emphasizes the logical relationships and the common attitude and skills required to deal with them. An able and alert teacher can overcome to a large degree the atmosphere of isolation by introducing at every opportunity allusions to interconnections with other subjects. In larger schools having a numerous faculty, compartmented courses allow teachers to concentrate their effort on a few subjects which can thus be brought to a higher state of refinement. Naturally, such teachers must continually guard against subsiding into narrowness. Some faculties have assumed that narrowness can be controverted by periodic reassignment, but, since this squanders accumulated experience and insight, the cure thus seems more severe than the malady. A teacher's mastery of subject matter and methods cannot be won either easily or overnight;

it is rather the accumulated result of prolonged and searching thought and experience.

When smaller faculties must be accepted, compartmentation often dissipates teachers among many courses. The resulting fractionating of effort is frequently surmounted by combining related subjects into a single integrated course. Thus materials and methods of construction and structural theory are sometimes linked together, or construction and intermediate design, or construction and equipment, or theory and history, or even graphics and design. While such combinations can form a very stimulating experience under able teachers, the danger is that the teacher's special interests and talents may prevent uniform treatment of all the necessary parts and may even cause neglect of some topics. It is obvious that whatever the scope adopted, the crucial factor is an able and conscientious faculty.

Perhaps the most thoroughgoing instance of an integrated method is that developed at the University of Florida by the late Rudolph Weaver. As already noted, all professional work in the three-year upper division is encompassed in seventeen carefully composed projects. Each project is fundamentally concerned with the design of a building, but accompanying each are closely linked reports and exercises which carry the student along in drawing, history, theory, construction, structural theory, equipment, and office practice. Although these associated exercises are not accompanied by formal classes and depend a great deal on extensive readings in assigned texts, in actual practice two faculty members, one in design, the other in construction, preside over each group of students and act not only as critics in design but also as tutors for the theoretical exercises. In recent years, seminars have been introduced to allow much of this tutoring to be carried out in groups. The project system has the advantage of permitting each student to work at his own pace and is, therefore, highly flexible and adjustable.

A fundamental difficulty in such a project system is that the student is forced to depend for most of his facts, interpretation, and principles upon the general literature of the field. In construction and structural theory, adequate texts are procurable, but in subjects such as history, no satisfactory general texts exist. At the present time, unfortunately, a true understanding of historic monuments and their meaning can only be gained from a competent architectural historian. This fact suggests that the application of any specific organizational pattern should be adjusted to conditions and facilities within the particular field of study.

In planning individual courses and their supplementary exercises, the result should, whenever possible, simulate conditions and methods typical of contemporary practice. This does not mean, of course, that the school should duplicate the office. Although office situations are highly instructive, they cannot be neatly organized for efficient teaching. Academic projects are first and foremost teaching devices intended to give maximum educational results in a minimum of time. Nevertheless, it is possible and profitable to design each project to give the student an illusion of reality and thus motivate and prepare him so that later entrance into real situations will be smooth and natural and without abrupt adjustments.

2. COURSES IN GRAPHICS

The primary aim of courses in Graphics is to develop students' facility in graphical representation. Since architecture deals with three-dimensional material, ability in drawing is therefore a basic tool for studying and communicating architectural ideas and designs. There have been excellent architects who never mastered skill in drawing, and mediocre practitioners who were superlative draftsmen, but the former triumphed over serious handicap and the latter fell victim to shallow talent rather than to excessive craftsmanship.

The architect has need of many types of representation. He must command a high competence in instrumental drawing, its theory and techniques. Such skill presumes acquisition of good habits in the use of equipment, thorough mastery of at least the intermediate principles of descriptive geometry in its application in deriving the conventionalized shades and shadows necessary to indicate common architectural forms, and in the preparation of accurate and revealing geometrical perspectives. Specific courses in these skills need not be overelaborated if the skills are regularly exercised in other courses such as basic and architectural design, and construction. Instrumental drawing is a valuable discipline cultivating precision, orderliness, and legibility.

Parallel skill in freehand drawing is likewise indispensable in order to create facility in rapid sketching for recording and studying architectural ideas, as well as in more finished drawings of whole buildings, interiors, details, and decorative features. Not only are such drawings useful in communicating visual ideas to clients and craftsmen, but they are also essential aids to the architect himself in fixing his own intentions. While the student should eventually explore many media and styles of techniques, it is best that he confine himself at first to acquiring facility in a few, such as pencil, pen, and monochrome and colored wash, which will prepare him immediately for exercises in elementary design. Later, others can be essayed.

A secondary, but highly important contribution of freehand drawing is its use to develop increasing discrimination of form, color, and composition, and for free experimentation in personal aesthetic expression. Development in such matters stimulates perception, imagination, and creativeness, and thus has immediate influence on all phases of the student's training, especially in design. Even exercises in purely representational drawing can cultivate good taste if the objects drawn are carefully selected. Part of the unfavorable reaction to classical ornament was no doubt due to the dilapidated and revolting plaster casts which gave their delineators not the slightest hint of authentic quality. The day of Chianti-bottle still-lifes is also definitely passed. If drawing classes are to fulfill their potentialities, what is drawn is almost as important as how it is done. It is appropriate to note that instrumental exercises can be similarly planned. At least one course in perspective has taken subjects displaying modern architectural forms. Even descriptive geometry plates are regarded at the Illinois Institute of Technology as excellent devices for inculcating aesthetic quality.

One architectural school, Carnegie, has experimented in its freehand teaching by concentrating on the drawing of vegetation. Here the study of free foliate forms of trees, shrubs, and landscapes serves triple duty in emphasizing organic structure, the indication of silhouette, mass, and texture, and the building of a vocabulary always useful in building studies.

The hazard of modern freehand courses lies in the fact that its teachers are recruited chiefly among artists who are impatient with precise representational discipline. These teachers are often extremely effective in the experimental and creative aspects of their subjects, but they tend to neglect the primary need of architectural students for clean-cut, accurate graphic skill. These teachers must bear most of the blame for the definite decay in draftsmanship that plagues most schools today.

Another difficulty lies in the difference of scale at which architects and artists work. The large-scale technique used by painters of landscapes and still-lifes is far removed from the smaller scale of the vigorous, but quiet technique required for the delineation of buildings. It is sometimes argued that techniques of architectural indication should be taught as a part of design, but, if so, instruction should actually be performed and not be left to chance. Some schools solve the problem by offering a definite course in rendering, conducted by a teacher who has had professional experience in such work. The success of such a plan at Columbia seems to indicate its wisdom. It is axiomatic that no system will succeed unless the other courses of the curriculum demand and premiate high quality draftsmanship.

Finally, it remains to consider the courses in sculpture, or relief modeling. The older function of these courses, to train architects in the handling of plastic ornament, has been largely superseded by direct exercises in the creative manipulation of free form and the exploitation of the inherent qualities of the material employed. Such an aim is therefore akin to craft courses. Both can be of value in stimulating an understanding and appreciation of fine craftsmanship and materials.

3. COURSES IN CONSTRUCTION

The fundamental importance of courses relating to materials and methods of building construction needs no argument. It is one of the most thoroughly accepted principles of modern architectural education. Fortunately, too, these courses deal with the most tangible and logical aspect of architecture and are, therefore, the most teachable. This fact is verified by the unusual seriousness with which present-day students accept its discipline.

The aim of these courses is to establish a thorough knowledge of: typical materials of construction and finish, their production, forms, properties, appropriate use, performance in combination, specification, maintenance, and cost; the principles of stability, shelter, durability, economy, and safety; the currently common systems of construction; the principles, factors, and codes governing the selection of an appropriate system; the construction details of typical special features, such as openings, stairs, trim, etc.; and the principles and practice of preparing working drawings and specifications. Some attention should be given to the organization, operation, and equipment of building erection, and to new materials and systems under development.

The usual component courses deal with light wood frame construction, ordinary construction, semi-fire resistant construction, incombustible construction, and fire resistant construction, working drawings, specifications, estimating, and occasionally separate courses in acoustics and construction methods. Presentation is usually by text, illustrated lectures, field trips, and supplementary exercises. Teaching aids normally include a more or less extensive display of material samples, and a collection of slides and motion pictures. Through the efforts of ACSA and the Producers' Council these aids are being rapidly improved. Sets of slides of the production and use of typical materials, prepared under the editorship of Professor Kenneth Sargent of Syracuse University and supplied free of charge by the Producers' Council, have proved extremely useful. Recently, Techniques and Materials, of New York, has circulated excellent semi-monthly traveling exhibits of important materials which create much student interest. Motion picture films seem at first thought an ideal and universal aid, but in practice they appear to serve best as introductory or review devices. Their action is too rapid to permit full absorption or sufficient explanation.

The text situation in construction is better than for most other courses. Professor W. C. Huntington's *Building Construction* makes available an unusual wealth of data, and although modest in size, is tersely accurate and systematic. The *Technical Series,* edited by Professor Walter Voss, promises seven volumes on construction, and therefore is on a scope more commensurate with the needs of architectural schools. Nevertheless, it would be useful to have a completely revised edition of Hool and Johnson's two-volume treatise, which in completeness and tone long ago set an enviable record in this field.

The supplementary exercises that normally accompany construction courses vary considerably in character and method. Some schools assign them solely as supervised laboratory work, others as outside problems. Occasionally this work consists of copying or assembling standard details even when the student himself owns the handbook from which they are taken. Elsewhere the problem calls for a small set of working drawings integrating various details treated in class. At the University of Illinois, however, supplementary exercises have been developed by Professor William S. Kinne, Jr., which lead the student to apply his knowledge more creatively by solving typical contemporary design situations by alternate methods, such as standard vs. modular, and then evaluating the results by comparing quantities of materials used, cost estimates at given unit prices, etc. The results have been very gratifying and seem to give the students a clearer understanding and a surer command of the principles involved.

A number of schools accelerate the impact of courses in construction by assigning teachers of construction for occasional construction criticism of problems in the courses in architectural design. While this is a useful stimulus to the student in linking the two areas, and to the construction teacher in keeping in touch with student needs, it seems to imply that criticism of the construction aspects of design is a function beyond the responsibility of the design staff. Effort toward integration is futile if such an attitude exists. In most instances of this practice, however, design teachers welcome reinforcement of their own emphasis on buildable designs.

Instruction in working drawings may be given in a separate course, as a special project in design, or it may be assigned as a part of a final comprehensive thesis problem. The difficulty is to stress principles without absorbing excessive time. It is foolish to expect results comparable in scope to actual office projects, or to absorb an undue amount of instruction time in a slow and often repetitious task. One safeguard lies in limiting stringently the size of the project; sometimes only a small part of a building suffices to illustrate the desired techniques. It is beneficial to the student, however, if he is forced to carry one of his own intermediate design exercises into the working drawing stage. If the work is still unmanageable, the working drawings may be assigned to a team of two to four men and thus further simulate office conditions. An active file of working drawings from competent offices is essential to show quality of draftsmanship, the organization of work, and variations in techniques.

It is important that courses in construction, while stressing standard practices, illustrate applications with up-to-date cases typical of contemporary design. Too many texts and handbooks give the impression that the development of construction stopped a generation ago. In this connection, too, occasional discussions, either in or out of class, should be planned to introduce current research and thus establish in the students' minds the fact that building construction today is a dynamic, evolving field. Modular coordination, prefabrication, reinforced brick masonry, prestressed masonry, and network frames can be used to expand horizons. The use of outside lecturers is an obviously important resource.

The criticism is often made that drawing exercises seldom develop a direct feel for the nature of materials or their use in assemblies, qualities universally recognized as having paramount influence, not only on construction, but also on design itself. Many schools have attempted to overcome this difficulty. Some have required experience on actual construction projects as a condition for graduation. Usually the arrangement is left to student initiative, but the cooperative plan at the University of Cincinnati attempts a more methodical experience. Some schools have considered enlisting the aid of the craft unions in demonstrating good craft practice. Others have undertaken the actual erection of a building, usually a house, on which students perform as much of the work as their schedule permits. A recent development, explored under the leadership of Howard T. Fisher, of Chicago, employs full-size mock-ups of typical assemblies which are made and modified as the design itself progresses.

The importance of student contact with real materials and operations is unarguable, but unless skillfully administered it runs serious hazards. The subtlest is the tendency to reduce the solution to the level of the student's meagre knowledge of techniques which forfeits many ingenious methods familiar to mature mechanics. In other words, the student oversimplifies in the belief that he thereby attains maximum practicality and economy. If the student can be exposed long enough under capable craftsmen, and if he is made aware of the best, as well as the simplest, techniques, he will, of course, gain invaluable insight. This is an objective far beyond the limited time and resources of schooling, and must, therefore, be sought throughout the student's whole professional career. Although most such pedagogical experiments have been focused on handicraft operations, there is no reason why the same method cannot also be directed toward industrial processes.

One aspect of the use of materials is rarely emphasized, the maintenance of finishes under prolonged use. This important factor could easily be demonstrated by drawing upon the direct experience of the university's own maintenance force and similar organizations in the local community. The selection of materials for minimal maintenance and the determination of the best methods of cleaning and renovation is, indeed, often neglected or misjudged by architects themselves.

Instruction in the organization and preparation of specifications varies greatly in method. Some schools provide a separate course. That taught by Professor Goldwin Goldsmith at the University of Texas is regarded with awe by alumni long after graduation for the rigor of its discipline in precise knowledge and writing. Some teachers, on the other hand, note that while a senior course in specifications serves as a useful review and summary of previous construction courses, most exercises in preparing actual sections of specifications inevitably, and perhaps inescapably, degenerate into routine copying of trade literature or sample sets filed in the library. In this, students are not more culpable than many practitioners. Some teachers, therefore, prefer to incorporate instruction in specifications in their courses in materials and methods of construction, presenting their discussions of materials and methods in specification terms and requiring periodic exercises in outline specification form. A final summary exercise can be assigned in the senior year as a portion of the thesis problem. If this is done, the preparation of the specification section must be done under careful guidance.

A few schools provide short courses in estimating. These function not to provide detailed cost figures, which soon become obsolete, but rather to present methods of calculating quantities and preparing estimates. Some schools also offer a brief survey of the methods and equipment used by contractors during the erection of buildings. Most schools, however, incorporate such data in the courses in materials and methods of construction or omit them entirely in the belief that this knowledge is most effectively gained from office experience.

Only a small number of schools require courses in shop practice, such as carpentry, machine, sheet metal, and welding. Because these courses are usually offered primarily for engineers and thus do not apply directly to building crafts, they may be of limited value for students of architecture.

4 · COURSES IN STRUCTURAL THEORY AND DESIGN

The quantity of structural theory required by contemporary architectural practice is one of the most controversial questions of educational policy. Some architects maintain that the employment of structural engineers, either within the office or as consultants, precludes the practitioner's need of all but the most elementary understanding of structural theory. Others assert that, while architects can more profitably delegate such work, it is still necessary that architects have general competence in order to coordinate and control this phase. Still others declare that architects must themselves perform such work if they are to regain a dominant position in architecture. Such incompatible points of view no doubt arise from differences of interest, talent, and capacity.

The *1950 Survey* revealed that only half of the architects reporting used consultants for structural engineering (*Table 32*). Of those who did their own structural engineering, 80 per cent stated that they themselves or their partner did the actual work. No doubt most of this work presented few structural complexities or novelties. It is apparent, therefore, that many architects are equipped to handle all but the most unusual structural problems, find it rewarding both financially and because it permits close coordination with other phases of the work, and consequently have benefited from sound preparation in structural theory. Furthermore, licensing examinations establish need for at least a minimum of structural knowledge as a fundamental public safeguard.

While the inclusion of structural courses in architectural curricula is essential for reasons of direct utility, it is likewise important because they exhibit those revolutionary principles which lifted one phase of architectural design above rules of thumb. It is unfortunately true that to some individuals structural theory still means formulae instead of principles, and that many empirical assumptions still adulterate its pretensions to scientific method. Nevertheless, it constitutes a system of thought that has contributed to modern architecture much of its basic character, and it therefore forms a significant part of the professional birthright of all architects today. The emphasis accorded structural studies by practitioners in the *Survey's* evaluation of importance of various parts of the curriculum indicates general acceptance of its essential place in architectural education.

The question, therefore, is not whether the curriculum should include structural theory, but rather how much. Quantitative definition involves two levels, one for the general option, the other for the structural option.

In the general option, the objective of the structural sequence is to achieve sound command of fundamental principles relating to the analysis and design in steel, timber, and concrete of common structural elements, such as simple floor systems, columns, foundations, and statically determinate frameworks, plate girders, and trusses, together with their usual combinations and details in typical contemporary buildings. This program begins with the study of mechanics, covering algebraic and graphic analyses of force systems and the determination of resultants and reactions. Mechanics is often undertaken without benefit of calculus. Next, the physical properties and behavior of structural materials under stress and building conditions must be mastered. Then follows an analysis of building loads due to occupancy, dead weight, snow, wind, impact, etc. These principles are then applied to the design of structural elements, their details, and connections. For foundations, basic concepts of soil mechanics should be introduced. For steel and timber construction, beams, girders (including built-up plate girders), columns, and trusses, together with bolted, riveted, welded, and ring-connected joints, should be included. In reinforced concrete, slabs, joists, T-beams, footings, and axially-loaded columns should be mastered. Both moment area and moment distribution methods of analysis should be considered. Some attention can be devoted to influence lines and moving loads. Arches and retaining walls in plain concrete and masonry should be covered. Finally, a study of the criteria and principles by which entire structural systems are selected for specific situations can provide a valuable climax and summary.

The structural option sequence normally uses the general option sequence as a preparation for advanced work. If the preparatory requirement of the structural option differs from the general option, it is usually in the inclusion and use of the calculus. This difficulty will be considered in connection with the courses in mathematics. The objective of the structural option sequence is to lead the student to a more thorough mastery of simple structures, a sound working knowledge of advanced structures, such as are met in tall, or wide-span buildings, and an introduction to new structural principles and techniques currently under development. Emphasis is laid on the theory of elasticity, partial and moving loads, deflections, continuity, secondary stresses, rigid frames, the analysis of statically indeterminate structures, multiple bents, continuous frames, two-hinged and fixed arches, and wind bracing. Reinforced concrete theory is extended to complex T-beams, double reinforced beams, slab and joist patterns, flat slab construction, eccentrically loaded columns, plastic flow, caissons, spread and combined footings. With such knowledge the graduate of the structural option should be well equipped to undertake the design of major structures or to proceed to graduate study and research.

Throughout all structural courses care should be taken to stress precise understanding of the principles underlying theory, design, and practice. Students must be guarded against surrendering to memorized formulae or type problems, but after fundamental techniques are mastered, time-saving summary methods should be considered. Above all, the spirit of the structural courses should be creative in tone to emphasize the fact, too often submerged in a welter of detail, that structural theory to fulfill its promise in a dynamic contemporary architecture must likewise be used imaginatively. The study of structures must not be permitted to erect dogmatic barriers to freeze past practice or inhibit exploration, but it should comprise a liberating, stimulating technical and disciplinary tool promoting evolutionary progress. Contemporary buildings have already received from structural advances some of their most poignant characteristics, such as clarity, lightness, and boldness. The aesthetic impact of future buildings may well gain new heights by a more purposeful and freer exploitation of logical structural principles.

The teaching of structural courses is variously assigned. In many schools all courses are provided by the department of civil engineering. While this arrangement is often due to the original establishment of architectural curricula in engineering divisions, it is also frequently prompted by economies realized by combining engineers and architects in the same classes on the plausible argument that useless duplication of effort is thus avoided. Most experience has shown that while the basic principles are the same, their applications differ markedly for engineers and architects. Occasionally, such courses seem barely to tolerate architectural students as an unwelcome intrusion and make no effort to satisfy architectural needs. Even if the course is compromised, both groups are to that extent penalized. In other cases, the engineering department provides special courses designed especially for architectural students, but, although this seems an adequate solution, it encounters two hazards. First, even with the best-intentioned instructor, it is extremely difficult to integrate the course with the rest of the architectural curriculum. Second, since the instructor usually teaches other courses to engineers and since his professional interests and ambitions lie within his own department, the service courses for architects are too often accounted a thankless chore to be assigned to teachers who are not deemed essential to the engineering program. If these hazards are overcome and if the outside instructor is competent and experienced in actual building, the service course solution can be quite satisfactory.

Many architectural schools find it better to provide their own courses in structures taught by members of their own faculties. The problem of discovering suitable teachers for these courses is a difficulty which will be discussed under the section on faculty in *Chapter VII*. Nevertheless, such courses can be designed for the specific needs of architectural students and they are more apt to be integrated with other courses to the mutual advantage of all. Integration can take the form of structural criticism of architectural design problems, similar to that by construction teachers, already noted. It can also be fostered by requiring typical structural calculations as a part of the design thesis. In schools offering both general and structural options, structural option seniors may occasionally be assigned as consultants to general option seniors, thus initiating both groups to a collaborative situation normal in practice.

The action of force systems and of material under stress can be dramatically demonstrated by standard apparatus and techniques, but little use has been made of such aids in normal structural courses for architects. The abnormal receptivity of visual stimuli by architectural students suggests that such demonstrations would clarify principles and induce a more secure feeling for structural reactions. The structural laboratories of the departments of architecture at Rensselaer Polytechnic Institute and Iowa State College have already proved the value of such aids. In a number of schools demonstration tests and even material testing laboratory courses are used to show the resistance and behavior of structural materials under loads. Such demonstrations

168

give students better insight into basic facts and assumptions. These and other visual aids should be more thoroughly and imaginatively exploited by structural teachers.

5. COURSES IN BUILDING EQUIPMENT

Modern technology has vastly increased architects' resources to attain the long-cherished ideal of architectural space as an optimal environment for the activities housed. The refinement of apparatus furnishing pure water, safe waste disposal, filtered air, proper humidity, healthful temperature, easy communication, ever-watchful safeguards against fire and intrusion, effortless movement of occupants and goods, and appropriate illumination, as well as many other features and the automatic control of all of them is one of the most amazing innovations of contemporary architecture. Today, in many building projects this plethora of equipment absorbs a major portion of both space and budget.

Present-day architects, if they are to maintain their proper function of overall control of design in its full sense, must, therefore, command a sound knowledge of building equipment. But mastery of all the diverse techniques necessary to the actual design and development of such equipment would occupy many lifetimes of specialized study and experience. The ramifications of modern technologies demand whole corps of specialists; not even a single engineer can win proficiency in more than a few of these numerous techniques. For conscientious architects, this paradox is one of the most perplexing questions of the day.

The inevitable result in practice is that architectural firms employ competent equipment designers either as consultants or on their own staffs. The *1950 Survey* found that approximately three-fourths of all architectural firms draw upon consultants for such work. Large firms, on the other hand, maintain design engineers as permanent employees. For simple, normal installations, however, small offices usually perform this function without special assistance.

In attempting a curricular solution, it is obvious that, despite the importance of equipment design, other urgent phases of training do not leave enough time to include the extensive prerequisites in basic sciences and applied engineering essential to gain design competence in these fields. Students in mechanical engineering, for example, are required to take a long sequence of courses in engineering physics, thermodynamics, and heat engineering, before beginning the study of air conditioning. Consequently, the normal architectural curriculum only provides courses in which the scope is primarily descriptive and in which design is limited to the simplest applications. The aim of such courses is necessarily restricted to a moderate understanding of the basic criteria and systems of mechanical, electrical, and sanitary equipment, together with the implications of these systems with regard to the layout of the building itself.

Occasionally, these courses are conducted by a member of the school's own faculty, but it is more usual to assign them to the appropriate engineering departments.

Either choice presents difficulties. If the school teaches its own equipment courses, it must, of course, provide instructors experienced in these various techniques, but since the total teaching load usually justifies only a single position, and in many schools only part of one teacher's time, the teacher must either command more techniques and experience than is fair to expect, or he must treat one or several with distressing superficiality. He does have the advantage, however, of having opportunity to adopt an architectural approach and to integrate his instruction with other courses, such as design, especially, as is frequently done, by requiring some attention to equipment aspects of the undergraduate design thesis. If, one the other hand, equipment courses are allocated to engineering departments, the architectural school must make sure that teachers assigned are competent, sympathetic, and experienced in actual building installations. Too often, such service courses, like those in structural theory, are regarded as routine chores, blocking professional advancement and unworthy of special effort. Too often a narrow engineering approach frustrates the architectural objectives of the courses. Moreover, engineering faculties are not immune to technical obsolescence. Thus, the solution of the problem must depend upon careful analysis of local conditions.

The difference between the architectural and engineering approaches is well illustrated in the study of illumination. The application of normal engineering criteria may ensure adequate, and even excessive lighting for specific tasks, but it rarely concerns itself with the total architectural effect. Probably such a consideration must be assigned to some spot within the architectural school, possibly to theory of architecture or design.

The limited scope of equipment courses within the professional curriculum emphasizes the great need of special studies in this field during candidacy and practice. This problem will be discussed in *Chapters VIII* and *IX*. Such advanced studies, combined with experience on actual building projects, should provide the prospective architect with adequate insight into the establishment of appropriate criteria for space conditions and the basic principles underlying the selection of equipment systems and elements. Thus, the architect can acquire a general foundation for judgment by which to check and coordinate the proposals of his assistants and consultants.

6. COURSES IN THE THEORY OF ARCHITECTURE

No other aspect of architectural education means so many things to so many architects and educators as the theory of architecture. The pragmatic bias of the American character renders any study of theory suspect, and, together with the complex nature of architecture, has both discouraged systematic analysis and fostered the use of empirical rules. Especially among those architects who rely primarily upon intuition, theory seems a superfluous foible, a search for formulae, an enthronement of dogma, and a frustration of personal freedom. Such fears indicate misunderstanding of the proper purpose, scope, and content of theory.

The theory of architecture may be defined as embracing the comprehensive and consistent organization of its facts and principles. In this sense any architectural activity whatever necessarily implies the use of theory. If the theory used is sound, thought and action will be more certain of success. Thus, every building design and every architectural curriculum presupposes an adequate theory and, in turn, inevitably reveals the quality of the theory on which it is based. Without command of theory, the practitioner and educator fall easy victims to dogmas and specious generalizations.

Organization means clear perception of constituent facts, their orderly classification, and their logical interrelations. With such understanding the processes by which they are manipulated can be more surely controlled and exploited. Theory, therefore, becomes a most useful tool to the architect, liberating him for the freer exercise of his creative faculties.

Theory of architecture deals with the elements and principles of function, structure, and aesthetic effect, and their optimal integration. Thus the substance of the curriculum itself consists of theory and its demonstrable applications. Each course elucidates some segment of theory and each exercise in design forms a test case of the student's personal command of theory. Too often, however, such integration proceeds practically unguided and the student ends in frustrating mental confusion. Some educators deem an atmosphere of chaos to be the environment most conducive to the attainment of ultimate order, and believe that a clash of ideas, even if expressed with equivocal and mystic vagueness, will automatically force young minds to achieve lucid maturity. This attitude seems to propose that education owes no duty to present objectively its fundamental beliefs and the alternatives to them. It is as if a novice to become wise need only undergo a barrage of promiscuous, academic potshots. Such a view defaults one of the primary responsibilities of education.

There is need, therefore, for a carefully devised, progressive presentation of architectural theory throughout the curriculum. Various methods are currently employed. One common plan is to assign it as an informal accompaniment of design. Another formalizes it by class discussions and lectures supplementing design. Other means are separate courses on architectural philosophy, the literature of architecture, architectural thought, etc. In many schools theory is conceived as the responsibility and the principal *raison d'être* of courses in the history of architecture, but although history must deal with significant theories of the past, theory evolves with changing conditions and it seems unwise to divert history from its proper and essential contributions by charging it with instruction in or the justification of contemporary theory.

Systematic organization of instruction in theory should begin with a brief orientation during the first semester of the curriculum. This may include a survey of the building industry, the building process, and the place of architecture and the architect within the whole. It could establish by cursory review the highlights of architectural evolution. It can encourage immediately the habit of observation by outlining the basic intentions and character of contemporary design. If, at the same time, a series of guided field trips is included, as in Columbia's freshman course, *The Architect in Society,* the impact can be further heightened. Orientation should likewise present an analysis of the educational process and the functioning of the curriculum. Thus, this beginning course becomes a preview in miniature of the profession and of architectural education, and students are better prepared to relate immediately each forthcoming experience to their whole program.

About the midpoint of the curriculum, it is helpful to schedule a small course which presents and discusses architectural theory as a unified subject. By that time many elementary facts and principles will already have been established and demonstrated in other courses, and many students will welcome opportunity to organize them into a more orderly pattern. If the process is delayed until later years, its impact on advanced work will be reduced.

Such a course can weld together the principles and methods of functional planning. It should not, however, degenerate into mere exposition of the requirements of many building types; this is a responsibility of courses in design. It is rather the *principles* of planning that should here occupy attention. The course should also synthesize the principles leading to optimal structural solutions, thus bringing construction and structural courses into close relationship to the whole. Nevertheless, the primary concern and opportunity of the course will probably lie in encouraging the student to think through for himself the basic problems of architectural aesthetics and expression. Such matters may have been touched on lightly in earlier years, but by the third year the student's experience has been sufficiently enlarged to permit serious consideration of such matters. Here should be explored the way in which eyes see and minds perceive architectural forms. Here, physiological optics, psychology, and experimental aesthetics can contribute to understanding. Here, too, the aims, vocabulary, and organizing grammar of aesthetic expression can be investigated. The intellectual and emotional overtones and meaning of aesthetic elements and compositions can be explored. The question of appropriate character and the optimal integration of functional, structural, and aesthetic solution into a unified whole demand attention. These and many other problems can furnish stimulating analyses and discussion.

Either at the end of the undergraduate curriculum or at graduate level, it would be profitable to explore theory further by examining the writings of critics and architects and by comparing the latter with the authors' actual performances. Such literature is not particularly suited for use in the earlier theory course, due to the mystical and transcendental spirit of many authors, but they supply heady sustenance for advanced students. The graduate course, *The Literature of Architectural Theory,* developed by Professor Talbot Hamlin at Columbia, is a notable example of this type of instruction.

From improved instruction in theory not only the student, but the profession as well, should benefit. The development of a consistent terminology would certainly reduce the present semantic confusion of tongues and make possible a more mature evolution of architecture itself. It could encourage research in hitherto neglected questions. And it might give surcease from frantic rushes to embrace each new ism and cliché. What is here envisioned is not an absolute and permanent formulation of final truth. It is the inescapable right and pain of each new generation that it must answer for itself the fundamental questions. Today, however, after one of the most profound revolutions in the history of architecture, it is the duty of architects to formulate these questions once again and think them through within the limits and possibilities of our own time. This does not mean that logic and formulae can ever replace the creative act, but, unless all intellectual effort is futile, creativeness can surely profit by clear thinking.

7. COURSES IN THE HISTORY OF ARCHITECTURE

Eclectic architects studied history to obtain an immediately usable vocabulary for design. When eclecticism died, history as vocabulary became obsolete. Today, however, most architects and educators agree that the study of history has far greater importance than ever before and that its contributions to architectural education are inescapable and invaluable.

The function of architectural history is now five-fold. First, it serves the architect as the only available laboratory in which he can observe full-size demonstrations of the effects of space and mass, the psychology of planning, and the efficacy of diverse structural systems. Through study of outstanding buildings of the past, he can come to appreciate and discriminate architectural quality which will, in turn, lift his own standards of performance. Second, by tracing the growth of fundamental techniques, history can reinforce dramatically lessons which are usually confined to other classrooms, such as the age-old struggle to overcome destruction by fire. Third, history stimulates insight and understanding of contemporary problems by confronting the student with philosophies other than his own, broadening his frame of reference and impelling him to a more objective evaluation of current dogmas and methods. Fourth, through contact with master architects of all ages, history emphasizes the rich legacy of intricate techniques bequeathed by them. Thus it aligns the student with the great traditions of his profession, endows him with a powerful professional momentum, and challenges him to make whatever contributions his own circumstance permits. Finally, architectural history serves as an inviting gateway to cultural enrichment arising from awareness and understanding of the complex life and thought of past civilizations. Since great buildings form the most tangible symbols of the skills and aspirations of the societies which called them forth, architectural history is, for the architectural student, the surest path to general cultural appreciation.

The approach and content of history courses differ considerably in the several schools. Since architectural students have little opportunity to take general history courses, architectural history is usually organized as a broad methodical survey from antiquity to the present day. Some courses proceed with strict attention to chronology and develop carefully the transitions linking periods of culmination. Others pass lightly over such problems and stress only major climaxes. Some concentrate on a

173

few building types; others essay a more complete picture. Some are content with plodding description and superficial anecdote; others utilize all available disciplines to select key examples, reveal their original form, and interpret their true meaning. Some are satisfied to portray only the ebb and flow of styles; others present architecture as a dynamic, integrated solution of functional need, structural capacity, and aesthetic insight. Some subside into a mere parade of dusty ruins; others conduct exciting excursions into vibrant, illuminating civilizations.

Instruction in history is usually given by illustrated lectures. One might suppose that of all the components of the curriculum it should enjoy the most satisfactory teaching aids. Unfortunately, this is not true. Slide collections are often obsolete, black-and-white, and of uninspiring quality. The use of colored slides is slowly expanding, but stereoscopic color illustration, though a decade old, has been used in only a few schools. Even with a skillful lecturer, oral communication remains much less certain than visual. Some schools furnish lists of examples and even syllabi and require supplementary library readings. Nevertheless, there is great need for up-to-date texts written for professional students. Such texts would expound the necessary factual data, facilitate preparation and review, relieve the instructor of the necessity of communicating facts verbally, and allow him to do what a skillful teacher can do best, i.e., provide fresh interpretations, personal reactions, cross comparisons, and provoke stimulating discussions.

No adequate up-to-date texts are now available. Old stand-bys, such as A. D. F. Hamlin, Kimball and Edgell, Simpson, and Banister Fletcher, are completely obsolete in point of view and content. Recent works, such as Talbot Hamlin's *Architecture through the Ages* and Nikolaus Pevsner's *Outline of European Architecture,* though excellent in their own way, were expressly intended for laymen on the run. Monographs, such as Baldwin Smith's *Egyptian Architecture,* or William B. Dinsmoor's *Architecture of Ancient Greece,* are superior in quality, but too restricted in scope. Perhaps the architectural volumes of the promised *Pelican Art Histories* will collate a body of material which can be distilled into suitable texts.

Some schools have experimented with other types of instruction in history. Yale, for example, after a freshman survey of the history of art and architecture, has employed a series of courses which develop the historical evolution of those building types which are current subjects in design. Florida's teaching of history by the project method has already been noted. In some schools history seems to be synonymous with theory. Elsewhere, a curtailed general survey is supplemented by one or two advanced courses in which a particular period receives detailed exposition.

Since the decline of *analytiques* and archaeological *projets* in design, equivalent exercises have occasionally been assigned in history. While romantic *archaeos* may be of doubtful value, a carefully rendered presentation of an historic monument displaying its authentic form, as found by measurement or from texts, can give excellent training not only in historical techniques but in precise delineation as well. Sometimes such exercises have been posed as original designs within a given historic style. At Harvard, Professor Kenneth Conant has assigned exercises in the form of models and has assembled over the past decade a veritable museum which, in turn, serves as useful teaching material. Written and illustrated term papers encourage the exploration of library resources or local monuments. The University of Illinois' Ricker Prize Competition is a notable example of the exploitation of this device.

In the past, when history provided ornamental vocabularies for immediate application in design, it was common to initiate its study in the freshman year. In recent years, with the assignment of new functions, many schools have delayed their history courses until later terms. Some use it as a final summary of architectural philosophy for seniors. Most schools, however, schedule these courses in the middle of the curriculum in the belief that, while beginners are yet unprepared to reap its benefits, its lessons and impact should be experienced soon enough to contribute to the thinking of advanced students.

One further use of history remains. In recent years public interest in historic buildings and their preservation has shown marked increase. As new projects arise, it becomes important for architects, if they are to participate in such work, to master the essential historical knowledge, research methods, and preservation techniques. While detailed study in this field may well be restricted to the graduate level, such study must be based on thorough undergraduate training.

8. COURSES IN CITY PLANNING

Because building activity is for the most part centered in communities, large and small, architecture and city planning are inseparably interrelated. The location of buildings, their siting, access, servicing, and long-term values depend directly upon stable community patterns of land use, transportation, and utilities. Conversely, the appearance of the community is strongly influenced by the buildings which form its major physical manifestation. It is obvious that architects, if they are to attain high quality in their individual projects, must learn how to foster and cooperate with the forces leading to high quality communities.

The influence of architects on the development of planning in the United States has been of considerable duration, but not always enlightened. The era of "the City Beautiful," promoted by architects in the first decade of this century, mistook the pretensions of grand façades for the key to civic order. In reaction, planners concentrated attention primarily on analytical techniques which were necessary prerequisites to planning, but too seldom were followed with creative results. Gradually it has become clear that planning must enlist the collaboration of many professions and agencies and that architecture is one of the most essential of these for success. Architects, in general, are slowly but surely recognizing this opportunity and responsibility, although few perform primary planning service.

The *1950 Survey* found that city and site planning absorbed only 1.3 per cent of architects' time, and that such planning constituted only one per cent of architectural practice. Since city planning demands the mastery of special skills, the small quantity of planning by architects is not surprising. Nevertheless, 9 per cent of all architects reported that they had undertaken special supplemental courses in planning. Some of these courses were no doubt of comprehensive character and provided sufficient training to support a competent practice in planning. It is a fact, however, that the major influence of architects on planning today is through participation in promoting planning and in serving on planning boards within their local communities. A 1951 survey of planning in 54 small cities and the participation of local architects, conducted by A. Whitney Murphy as an AIA Langley Fellow, revealed that while architects generally expressed interest in planning and had shown interest in 60 per cent of the cities, in only two cities had they taken a leading role in promoting such activities, and they furnished only 7 per cent of the membership of all of the planning boards studied.

The place of city planning in architectural education reflects this evolutionary trend. Time was when architectural design courses culminated in vast grand plans of pompous plazas bordered with structures whose chief purpose was to create enclosing façades. Today, many design problems demand more fundamental knowledge of zoning, parking, market surveys, and other basic factors. This change of approach is reflected in the *1950 Survey* by the differing ranks accorded city planning in the curriculum by architects who scored it in 22nd place, and architectural teachers who gave it 15th place. The greater emphasis by teachers is due in part to the fact that 16 per cent of them have taken supplementary training in planning, as contrasted with the 9 per cent of practitioners previously noted.

The aim of planning courses for architectural students is not to train them to become city planners. That is the function of special curricula in planning. Not infrequently, architectural graduates do complete graduate degrees in planning and thus may become professional planners, but this is not the problem at hand. The aim of such courses in architectural curricula is rather to provide prospective architects with an awareness and understanding of the basic facts and techniques of contemporary planning so that they will be able to relate their building projects intelligently to their specific communities and to assist in promoting enlightened planning in their own communities. Thus better architecture and better citizenship can be fostered at the same time.

In a survey of 25 curricula in 1948, ten schools did not offer any instruction in planning. Two schools devoted 270 and 300 class hours to such courses, and for the 15 schools requiring planning courses, the average was 110 class hours. Within this brief scope, most courses offered a descriptive survey of urban conditions, analytical techniques, and master planning. This cursory provision probably approximates the maximum available within curricular limits.

The impact of a short planning course can be increased in several ways. Inclusion of such courses as urban sociology, economics, or political science as required or elective subjects can give valuable preparation for it. History of architecture courses must present significant examples of past patterns of communal organization if balanced understanding of former civilizations is intended. This is particularly true in studying the 19th century when rapidly increasing urbanization provoked many utopian and some practical, but partial solutions for relief. Such considerations can also help to set the stage for more effective response to the planning course itself.

The most potent and most widely used device, however, is the thoroughgoing and continuous employment of planning concepts in the teaching of architectural design. In many schools, each design exercise, from the beginning, includes careful attention to planning factors during preliminary discussions, programming, and development, as basic to sound architectural analysis. The cumulative effect of this policy not only can be tremendous in itself, but because of it the short planning course can function as an organizing summary of familiar ideas and be freed to include more advanced material than would otherwise be possible. Some schools, notably the University of Michigan, have grouped all concurrent design exercises around a central town planning project, real or hypothetical, based upon planning solutions previously prepared by planning students. Such a program goes far to create an atmosphere of unity and stimulus throughout the entire student body.

Thus by ingenious integration city planning instruction can far transcend the limits of a single short course. Taken as a whole, therefore, the planning content of the curriculum cannot be measured by the course alone. Under such conditions, the graduate architect should gain ample understanding of this essential field and be prepared to harmonize his future activity with the best planning practice, or in minimum time to gain by advanced studies professional competence in planning itself.

9. COURSES IN ARCHITECTURAL PRACTICE

Courses in architectural practice usually discuss such topics as the nature and composition of the profession, professional cooperation and ethics, the techniques of performing architectural services, and the administration of architectural offices. Occasionally, they also include building promotion, financing, investment, as well as other subjects, such as specifications, estimating, etc., which have already been discussed in connection with courses in Construction.

While such matters seem among those most suited to detailed study during candidacy, when immediate applications are experienced almost daily, brief consideration just before graduation can smooth transition to candidacy and establish an orderly outline and sound point of view to guide later development. Most courses in practice conform to this aim and scope.

It is especially important in discussing architectural practice to go beyond mere description and stress the fundamental principles that must guard the integrity of both the individual architect and the profession. Rules and regulations dare infraction, but just principles can inspire loyalty.

Usually scheduled in the final term, the course in practice can integrate the whole curriculum by relating its diverse parts to the ultimate goal, the performance of architectural service. More specifically, it can correlate its supplementary exercises by preparing contract and other documents for the terminal project in design. If time permits, it can bridge the transition from school to candidacy by using practitioners as visiting lecturers on pertinent problems in practice. Indeed, if feasible, the whole course may very logically be conducted by a visiting architect.

10. OTHER TECHNICAL COURSES

A study of the curricula of architectural schools reveals the inclusion of a number of courses which particularize or supplement the course groups hitherto noted. Some schools offer a separate course in interior design, although others assign such material to architectural design. Some schedule special courses in furniture. Where this implies the historical development of furniture, other schools include it in architectural history and use it to give a more realistic picture of historic rooms. If furniture design is meant, others deal with it in architectural design. A few schools require courses in the crafts, or their modern counterpart, industrial design. Courses in historic ornament, so prevalent in the past, have been for the most part absorbed by architectural history. Some schools provide architectural students with a survey of landscape architecture.

Another type of special course presents certain aspects of science applied to architecture. Representative of these are the excellent courses in architectural acoustics at MIT and Rensselaer. Many schools require brief courses in elementary surveying.

In general, while many of these courses open valuable vistas and utilize unique facilities or personnel, they are made possible by drastic reduction of general education in the humanities and social sciences. When this occurs, the value of these special courses seems to be bought at excessive cost.

11. GENERAL ACADEMIC COURSES

Since architects are not only technicians, but also professional men and citizens, their education must transcend narrow vocational limits. Indeed, the claim of architectural curricula to collegiate status rests on the premise that they are built upon a firm foundation of general collegiate training. This training is of two kinds which are not, however, mutually exclusive. The first provides certain basic skills, such as facility in communication and reasoning; the second establishes fundamental concepts needed for the development of subsequent technical studies.

The benefits of general education for architects have been stressed in *Chapter V*. The contributions which the humanities and social sciences make to personal enrichment, appreciation, and discrimination are incalculable, and it is worth repeating that they also add in many unexpected ways to technical competence as well. Electives in general education are not academic luxuries, but perform an indispensable function in professional training. It is unfortunate that the normal architectural curriculum provides so few opportunities to gain these advantages. Here, however, discussion must be focused on those non-architectural courses which render direct service to professional development.

Courses in Rhetoric

To judge from current widespread criticisms, no non-architectural course exceeds in importance those in rhetoric which seek to cultivate forceful speech and writing. This work usually runs throughout the freshman year and, building upon similar high school courses, emphasizes the methods and mechanics of verbal communication through appropriate exercises and themes. The results, evidenced in later courses and afterwards, have been the subject of bitter complaints against allegedly declining standards of both secondary and collegiate instruction in this field. In this connection, the similar censure of British students expressed by the Special Committee on Architectural Education of the RIBA indicates that the problem is not confined to America.[1] It should be recognized, of course, that verbal talents, like others, are distributed by nature in uneven portions, and that the expansion of college training, once the preserve of literary-minded students, has added many whose chief abilities lie in other directions. Those who are most facile with words tend to gravitate to fields such as journalism.

Explanations of causes, however, do not reduce the great importance to architects of a command of verbal expression, and, if architectural students are recruited on the basis of other criteria, they must nevertheless exert themselves to remedy their deficiency in this area. This need could be amply and dramatically demonstrated by citing specific examples of costly lawsuits arising from ambiguous specifications and contracts, or the positive appeal to clients of lucid reports, or the irrevocable damage which an ill-conceived and poorly-expressed presentation can inflict upon a campaign for an important commission. The interest of the professional student can also be stimulated by the use of exercise topics directly related to his architectural development. Once enthusiasm and motivation are stirred, the solution of the problem is well advanced.

The systematic use of such measures suggests that architectural students should be grouped in their own sections. Otherwise, the instructor of a mixed class will find it difficult to challenge individual students. The disadvantages of isolating professional students from their already meager cross-campus contacts have previously been noted, but these seem to be outweighed by the benefits that should accrue to special sections in rhetoric.

No limited period of the study of rhetoric can accomplish the desired goal unless it is actively supported and followed up by a continuing demand for competent verbal expression in each exercise of every course in the curriculum. It may be said that students will live *down* to any standard which a faculty will accept, and *up* to that which it will firmly enforce. Holding to a high level of expression is not easy.

Exercises must be carefully planned for variety, content, and timing. They should include occasional spoken presentations. Oral defenses of design projects are particularly useful, because here the student has usually mastered enough content to overcome hesitation.

Perhaps the greatest barrier to such a program is the architectural faculty itself. It will consume much additional time and effort, and it will sometimes seem unjust to penalize a student who commands content but expresses it unskillfully. Moreover, the faculty itself may need refreshing on the principles of verbal composition, but this might be a blessing in disguise for the improvement of their own class work.

Carnegie Tech has initiated a very thorough system to emphasize competent expression. A member of the department of English is permanently assigned to the school of architecture, and this teacher not only conducts the courses in rhetoric, but also criticizes and grades all written exercises given in the school. In effect, instruction in rhetoric thus continues throughout the curriculum. Substantial improvement has been noted in student performance.

Courses in Mathematics

Practitioners ranked mathematics highest in importance among all non-professional studies and third highest among all subjects. This prestige derives from the geometric character of building forms and the need for quantitative techniques by which structural security can be predicted. No doubt another major factor was the widespread belief that mathematics disciplines the mind in precise and abstract thinking and thus provides fundamental preparation for life in a world preoccupied with science and technology. In any event, the necessity for mathematics as a professional tool will at the same time instill whatever cultural values it can contribute.

The student of architecture needs facility in the handling of three-dimensional masses and volumes. Geometry, plane and solid, have therefore been considered for centuries the key to professional capacity, and high school courses in both are normal requirements for admission to schools of architecture. The professional curriculum extends this training by courses in descriptive geometry, which, however, have tended in recent years to be reduced to the barest essentials needed for applications in simple shades and shadows and perspective. Indeed, in many schools, all three of these subjects are combined in one package. To some degree, the study of analytic plane geometry reinforces general knowledge of geometry.

The second group of mathematical courses provides the operative skills needed for later work in structural theory. These are usually based on high school courses in elementary and intermediate algebra, although in the larger high schools college algebra and trigonometry are sometimes available. The professional curriculum, therefore, must usually begin its mathematics with college algebra, but the upper limit has been the subject of considerable controversy. Some schools are content with college algebra and trigonometry. Most prescribe analytical geometry, and a few include brief or complete courses in the calculus. Occasionally, the calculus is required in the structural option, but is omitted in the general, or design, option. In general, the argument for the inclusion of the calculus is two-fold. First, it is claimed to be indispensable for a true grasp of certain fundamental concepts in structural theory, and, second, it is held a prerequisite for any advanced studies in this field. Opponents question the first claim by pointing to graduates of numerous curricula who, without benefit of calculus, have nevertheless obtained sufficient command of structural calculations to satisfy the demands of both licensing examinations and practice. They likewise reject the second plea by pointing out the small number who undertake advanced work in structures.

The desirability of calculus can be accepted, but there are many other disciplines of which the same is true. The question becomes, therefore, whether the time absorbed by calculus pays greater dividends than an equal period devoted to other fields. For the structural option, the answer is surely affirmative, but for general students of architecture this is not so certain. To require it of them means a 66 per cent increase in time devoted to mathematics and the loss of two courses in the humanities and social sciences, in order to gain a somewhat improved grasp of a few structural concepts. This seems an excessive price to pay. Several schools have met this situation by raising admission requirements. Most frequently, trigonometry must be completed before entrance, or be taken as an extra non-credit course after admission. Another solution is to introduce into analytic geometry enough basic concepts of differential calculus to serve the minimum needs of structural theory. Occasionally, the resulting combination course is actually called "calculus." By such devices, an acceptable compromise may be found without a drastic increase in time.

Since the regular courses in mathematics are developed around a more or less arbitrary selection of specific topics, it is legitimate to expect the cooperation of the department of mathematics in the formulation of an outline tailored to the needs of architectural students. This implies, of course, that these students will be handled in special sections, and that special problems couched in terms of building situations will be provided. The benefits of such treatment seem large enough to counterbalance the disadvantages of isolated sections.

As with rhetoric, mathematical skills, once acquired, should be exercised frequently in appropriate professional courses. In general, there has been an unfortunate tendency for subsequent discussions and exercises to be oversimplified. Neglect makes rusty weapons and if they are indeed unnecessary the effort absorbed in their acquisition should be directed to more pertinent disciplines. There would seem to be a need for a general study to obtain a concensus of opinion on the amount of structural theory to be included in architectural curricula, and this, in turn, would permit rational determination of the extent of mathematics to be included.

Courses in the Physical Sciences

Sir Ben Lockspieser has pointed out that "the architect who wants little to do with science is living in the wrong century."[2] The impact of modern science has led to a broadening of the scope of architecture to include the total sensory impact of the environment thus created. The objective thus embraces an optimal sense of well-being, or "euphoria," and in order to attain it the architect must command all of the pertinent resources of the physical and social sciences.

Present curricula fall far short of this concept. Most include the study of physics, to supply basic principles for later courses in construction, structural theory, and equipment. A few require the study of chemistry, hoping that it will enhance understanding of materials and their interactions when used in combination. Some schools rely upon requiring high school courses in one or both of these subjects.

Unfortunately, the results obtained from these courses are usually of very limited value, especially in comparison with the amount of time and effort absorbed. In part, this arises from the fact that the available time permits only introductory courses to be scheduled. Institutional policies of economy foster overcrowded classes which prevent any attempt to stimulate the interest of special groups of students through the posing of applications relevant to their particular needs. Here, particularly, the design of courses primarily to please the ego of the instructor or to cater to the needs of students intending to major in the field seems at its worst. Unfortunately, the typical physicist appears to consider that anything less than nuclear reactions is beneath his consideration and should be supplied elsewhere when needed. In short, in the age of science, the scientist seems to feel little obligation to those who must apply his hard-won principles. The effect is to overemphasize science as a cultural phenomenon and to frustrate the essential contribution it should be making to architectural competence. That this is not special pleading for indolent architects is amply proven by similar complaints in other fields as well. Professional students are quick to sense this indifference to their interests, and it is impossible in such circumstances for the architectural faculty to overcome their students' natural disaffection. The situation demands prompt and sympathetic attention from those responsible for the general administration of the universities.

If the situation cannot be corrected, two alternatives are possible and, indeed, might in any case prove preferable. The first is to allot the time and responsibility for the development of principles now scheduled for science to those courses in which applications must be made. The interactions of forces would then be studied in structural classes, heat phenomena in heating and air conditioning, and electricity and light in illumination. This solution would exploit the sound principle that integration is best achieved through immediate demonstration and application. The second alternative would be to introduce a special course, perhaps entitled *Science for Architecture*, to be administered and taught by the school of architecture. This is the solution now being explored in British schools.[3] The advantages of such a course are the concentration of responsibility and objectives, and the provision of special demonstration apparatus. Moreover, it should be possible by the judicious selection of topics to free enough time to consider other sciences not now included, such as meteorology, geology, and acoustics. The immediate criticism will be that the result will have a superficial descriptive character unworthy of the name of science. The example of survey courses will be cited. Nevertheless, such an outcome need not be inevitable. The course would require an unusual teacher, but no doubt this difficulty can be surmounted. Laboratory exercises should do much to overcome superficiality, although the provision of equipment will pose a new problem. If such a course proves effective, it could well be that the faculty would be willing to expand its scope to gain the benefits of other disciplines.

Whatever the solution, the need for exploring the architectural implications of all the sciences is incontrovertible. Most of this effort will require pioneering research before it can enter undergraduate teaching. Discussion of such research will be reserved for *Chapter X,* but its effects for architecture and architectural education could be incalculably great. Sooner or later, the schools must face these issues.

Courses in the Social Sciences and the Humanities

Whereas physics and sometimes chemistry are included in architectural curricula as prerequisites to subsequent professional courses, the social sciences are incorporated less frequently and less systematically. To a considerable degree, of course, the history of architecture stresses political, economic, and social phenomena and principles. The 1930's provoked a flurry of interest in economics, and the expansion of urban housing and planning stimulated the same concern for sociology, but hardly ever did this mean more than scheduling a brief introductory course in these subjects. In a few schools, general survey courses have aimed at a more integrated and broader coverage.

For the most part, the inclusion of such courses has been more often concerned with fostering general education, but here it is their direct application which must be considered. This has occurred most frequently in connection with courses in design, in which the technique of the economic and sociological survey has been used in formulating the requirements of programs. Rarely, however, does the total impact of such devices produce any orderly understanding of the contributory fields themselves.

Just as with the physical sciences, the problem consists of desiring the fruits of these disciplines without devoting the whole curriculum to their pursuit. If all the disciplines desirable for the architect were followed to the point of diminishing returns, the architectural curriculum would require many times its present five-year schedule. This is a dilemma typical of our day when the sum of knowledge has far outdistanced the absorptive capacity of single individuals. Again, it must be emphasized that the best remedy does not consist of crowding the curriculum with a plethora of introductory surveys, but rather to present the problem to the student, stir his appetite, and encourage his continuing intellectual growth throughout his professional life.

The situation is similar with regard to the humanities—literature, philosophy, the fine arts—and languages. Except for the history of painting and sculpture, specific subjects are now rarely specified in the curriculum. The tendency is to provide more or less time for electives in these areas, and the objective has again been more that

183

of general education and a broader outlook than direct support of professional subjects.

The solution in both fields would appear to be the provision of as generous an opportunity as possible to choose under guidance specific fields to which the individual student is personally attracted. Moreover, the student should be urged to go beyond the introductory phase in as many fields as possible. Tool courses, such as business law, finance, letter writing, etc., are not acceptable for this purpose, however useful they might be. This solution may appear to be the result of indecision, but, in the face of so many choices equal in merit, it has positive advantages. It exploits personal inclinations; it permits students to seek out the most stimulating teachers; and it encourages students to mutual discussion of their chosen electives and thus serves, even if indirectly, to open wider vistas to all.

The application of these elected disciplines to professional training need not, therefore, be rigidly organized, but will depend on the ability of each student to contribute the special criteria he has explored. Wisely directed, the composite result for the whole group could be of wider scope and more stimulating character than could be furnished by prescribed courses, and more profound than studies limited to introductory surveys. Successful coordination with architectural topics will nevertheless require an unusually knowledgeable and ingenious architectural faculty who can bridge the gaps, suggest correlations, and explore parallels. The result could be a real broadening of the base for architectural education within the temporal limits of present curricula.

From the discussion just given, it is evident that the professional school needs and has a legitimate demand for the close cooperation of all divisions of the university which serve its students. If the ideal of integrated professional courses is worth while, there can be no valid reason for excepting basic non-architectural subjects. Indeed, if the objective of these other divisions is the stimulation of student growth, and not mass instruction for the sake of low cost and administrative convenience, then special treatment for special groups is the only defensible policy. Where the need is demonstrable, the professional school should be able to depend upon the support of the general university administration in implementing this policy. In many institutions, this is accepted practice and there is no barrier to interdepartmental collaboration. In some, however, the divisions serving professional students pretend omniscience in what these students should be taught. In such cases, direct appeal for relief should be made to higher authority.

It has been suggested that in rhetoric, mathematics, and the physical sciences, the adjustment of content and even method would increase their utility to architects. It should be stressed that the purpose of this proposal is emphatically not to lower the standards of such courses, but, quite to the contrary, to increase their effectiveness and meaning. No conscientious architectural faculty will seek easy courses for its students, for every teacher in the professional schools sees all too well the need for better, not worse, instruction.

It may be objected that the segregation of architectural students in special classes will reduce contacts, competition, and comparison with students from other parts of the campus. The essential value of this might be questioned, but, if it is important, the recommended electives in the social sciences and humanities can perform these functions. Actually, extra-curricular activities can be trusted to supply adequate contacts. The educational stimulus to be derived from instruction pointed more directly to specific student needs would appear to be well worth these hypothetical hazards.

Even if cooperation is undertaken by the departments serving the professional school, difficulty is apt to arise in staff assignments due to the fact that many instructors dislike to teach service courses because they fear that these courses will prove to be dead-ends within their own departments and professions. Too often the outcome is that the service course gets short shrift in the assignment of permanent staff, and if it forms only part of the teacher's load, the courses taught for his own department tend to receive his major effort. Too often the service course is relegated to an inexperienced graduate assistant who teaches on a temporary basis in order to pursue graduate studies, and who thus has no real stake in building a program integrated to the needs of professional students.

If these handicaps are to be remedied, the professional school must find some way to challenge the teachers assigned to its service courses and to create a close liaison which will build morale and create interest in its problems. If these teachers can be made to feel an intimate, if unofficial, part of the school faculty, and if they can see the results of their efforts in the improved capacity of their students, a major hurdle will be cleared. If they can be stimulated to the point of enthusiasm and imagination in their approach, the benefits should prove startling.

12. COURSES IN ARCHITECTURAL DESIGN

To the architect the term *design* means many things. In its traditional sense, by its association with painting and sculpture, design was either the pictorial symbol representing the conception of an architectural composition or the creative process by which the conception was accomplished. It was perhaps inevitable that the excitement and uniqueness of the creative act should loom large in the minds of the creator and his audience. The age of Romanticism glorified uninhibited creativeness into the ultimate test of merit, but with a marked tendency to confuse the physical symbol, the conception, and the thing conceived.

In its broadest and truest sense, design in architecture can only refer to the complete process and its final product, the completed building. Since the purpose of architecture is to create buildings—purposefully controlled environments within three-dimensional volumes—the concept and its pictorial symbol are merely means to that end. Any aesthetic or other merits which this symbol, process, or concept can possess are distinctively fortuitous and non-architectural in character. It is no accident that architects reserve their most castigating criticism for "paper architecture."

The full process of architectural design, as practiced by skilled practitioners, encompasses, therefore, all the stages by which the final form of a building is determined. Thus design operates continuously, starting with preliminary investigations, analyses, and programming, through tentative studies to the approved basic solution, is explicitly defined in working drawings and specifications, and undergoes further refinements as numerous final decisions are rendered during supervision up to the moment of completion. All of these stages are properly termed creative. Such a view does not reduce the importance, skill, or quality of the creative synthesis demanded by the fixing of the basic solution, but it focuses more clearly the proper relationship between the two. Indeed, a higher skill is required to achieve a basic solution which is capable of effective development throughout the full process. · · · · · · ·

Quantitative verification of the relationship between basic and full design is offered by the *1950 Survey*. AIA practitioners reported that 50.9 per cent of their total productive effort was devoted directly to the full design process. Of this, however, only 15.2 per cent of their total effort, or 30.5 per cent of full design effort, was absorbed by basic design (*Table 28*). If the total efforts of employees were also included, basic design would represent an even smaller proportion.

Architectural design, as a comprehensive process and product, must be supported in high degree by all the technical knowledge, principles, and skills relating to the various aspects it seeks to harmonize. To these must be joined a high quality of creative synthesis. It is obvious that competence in design can be developed only by active participation in real projects. The complexity of the design process and of design situations cannot be acquired at second hand.

Nevertheless, training in design is a necessary task of architectural education. The apprenticeship system theoretically provided an ideal method through gradually increasing participation in buildings under way, but in actual working it revealed major handicaps. Its failure to teach supporting techniques has already been cited. A more subtle difficulty was the fact that while the pupil would probably devote a large proportion of his effort to time-consuming working drawings, the master seldom relinquished the exciting function of basic design. If the pupil acquired such experience it would be obtained after hours on voluntary personal exercises developed with or without criticism.

The haphazard results of this kind of situation no doubt were the reason that the Royal Academy of Architecture in Paris inaugurated around 1700 occasional design competitions on a given subject. The students, already competing informally in their supplementary courses in the Academy's school, in this instance may actually have pushed their masters into applying the competitive method to design. In any case, the masters' prestige became involved and gave positive incentive for better teaching. Thus individual exercises were transmuted into the *problem method* which grew to dominate design teaching. At first, problem subjects aimed exclusively at facility in current styles, but during the latter part of the 18th century, increasing interest in construction among architects and better instruction gave somewhat greater breadth to student designs. With the establishment of the *Ecole des beaux-arts* and its design competitions, and the organization of the *atelier* system, students were no longer under office discipline and the problem method began to acquire a very special character of its own.

The problem method as developed by the *Ecole* consisted of a series of exercises progressing in content and difficulty from analytiques and simple buildings in the Second Class, to complex buildings in the First Class. In both classes, two-month major and 12-hour sketch problems were posed. Programs, prepared by the professor of theory, established the type of building to be studied, the areas of required rooms, and the site. The student was then required to solve these conditions schematically in an *esquisse* in 12 hours of strictly individual effort. In preparation for the *esquisse,* the title of the program was usually announced in advance, but no systematic discussion was provided to orient the student as to approach or fundamental data. It was assumed that the student, by attending the lecture courses in theory of architecture, by personal observation of notable Parisian buildings, and by searching in architectural publications, could through his own effort gain sufficient command of facts and principles to enable him to arrive at a definitive scheme. The necessity to do so was heightened by the strict prohibition of significant deviation from the *esquisse* during subsequent development of the problem. Under such circumstances it was not surprising that most students promptly took refuge in *esquisses* which were masterpieces of obfuscation and ambiguity.

Through the device of the *esquisse* the better students became very facile in rapid, direct organizing of the major elements of the problem, but too often the organization pattern, the *parti,* rather than growing out of the inherent functioning of these elements, fitted them into some standard pattern formula which had won success in preceding competitions. At a time when the concept of function was still very generalized, when efficiency was not yet measurable, and when modern building types were just beginning to be differentiated, the abstract *parti* was perhaps a useful device. And for students who worked under extreme pressure without adequate functional criteria and analytical method, the abstract *parti* comprised almost the sole avenue of approach. Facility was dearly bought at the expense of synthesis based on careful analysis. Moreover, in a system which claimed to emulate the methods of actual practice, the principle and working of the *esquisse* completely violated that practice by substituting impetuous superficiality for calm and thoughtful deliberation.

Not only were students effectively inhibited in functional analysis, but the use of programs specifying fixed areas completely blocked any training in the method of determining program requirements. This serious omission is all the more surprising because the *Ecole's* professors of theory in the 19th century, Baltard, Blouet, Guillaume, and Guadet, were very able and progressive men directly concerned with the development of functional programs for several new types of buildings. Perhaps they themselves were helpless under a competitive system which demanded that all must solve identical requirements and therefore could permit no individual variation or discretion. Perhaps, too, they felt that immature students should be relieved of this additional responsibility in order to concentrate on other matters. Whatever their reasons, and despite the penetrating lucidity and method for which French thought

187

is so famed, the French system contributed little to the evolution of modern principles of functional planning.

Problem development was probably the strongest feature of the *Ecole* design system. The process was often handicapped by the demand that the *esquisse* be followed without change, a requirement completely absent in actual practice. Nevertheless, the endless succession of studies, progressing from small to final scale and from basic elements to intricate details, at its best set a standard of craftsmanship and thoroughness never before attained. Much of this care, however, was sacrificed to externals, the mosaics and entourage which made plans more readable, but which often led to a tapestry of abstract pattern that became an end in itself. Nor did the system discourage that weakness of human nature, the procrastinating trait, which transferred disproportionate effort to a final grand *charette*.

The final presentation of *Ecole* problems evolved during the 19th century from early straightforward crispness toward a lavish pictorial bravura calculated to seduce the most dispassionate jury. At its best, presentation and technique combined to reinforce the inherent character of the solution, but at its worst, presentation was a device to camouflage design defects. Seldom were perspective drawings required and three-dimensional models were wholly forgotten. Emphasis on plan frequently left elevations neglected and sections rudimentary. The specification of drawing requirements gave no scope for individual initiative in planning presentation for maximum benefit to clients.

Finally, the *Ecole's* juries evaluated the resulting problems wholly on pictorial evidence, on the theory that the final product alone was significant and the quality of the accompanying process and method, so emphasized as its chief goal, had no importance. Thus the industrious, steady plodder received no consideration for his plodding and was easily outranked by a brilliant but erratic talent. The jury system was never opened to verbal exposition or defense by students, nor were written reports or explanations accepted. In spite of limited judgment time, it was assumed that the experienced practitioner-juryman could infallibly fathom the detailed intent and reasoning of more than a hundred students solely from graphic data.

Perhaps the most revealing pedagogical question prompted by the *Ecole's* problem system lies in its boast of adjustment to the varying rates of development of individual students. Promotion to First Class design was based on the accumulation of six values. Two values were obtainable if the student passed the required two *analytiques*. One or two could be earned by each Second Class *projet*, devoted to simple buildings. One was awarded for each successful 12-hour *esquisse-esquisse*, or sketch problem. Thus a superior student could complete Second Class design with a minimum of one building problem. Since originally the *Ecole* offered no terminal certification, a student continued First Class design as long as he was able. For the best students up to the age of 30, opportunity to train and compete for the coveted *Grand Prix* supplied adequate incentive to persist. Some are recorded as having won as many as sixteen first medals in the process. In 1864, however, the *Ecole* inaugurated a *diplôme*, among the qualifications for which were nine values in First Class design. Major

188

problems commanded 1, 2, or 3 values, according to quality, and sketches 2 or ½. Thus, the nine required values could be amassed with good fortune by a minimum of two major and two sketch problems, or by three major problems. In actual practice, these minima were possible for only the most gifted and industrious students, but it is of interest to note, however, that it was possible for such youths to complete their training with a total of only four or five exercises in the design of a building. In theory, this would be desirable, since such a superior student should pass into an office as promptly as possible. Nevertheless, it raises the fundamental question whether adequate preparation in design consists only of a few problem experiences and a facility in the problem-taking process, or whether design should present a wider range of experiences and communicate a modicum of knowledge as well. The *Ecole* system seemed to assume that any problem is equal to any other in teaching function and that it is the inculcation of the design process that is important. It was impatient with the formulation or transmission of a systematic body of design knowledge.

This analysis of the *Ecole's* use of the problem method in design need not obscure its many positive objectives and accomplishments. The *Ecole* inherited the somewhat casual system of the Academy and transformed its philosophy and machinery into the best teaching program of its day. The analysis implies, however, that as time and circumstances have changed and as contemporary architecture and practice evolved, the teaching of design must undergo continual reevaluation, refinement, and modification. In recent years, the *Ecole* itself has responded to such changes.

The inauguration of collegiate architectural education in America coincided with the culmination of the French Second Empire. France radiated tremendous architectural influence throughout the world, and the *Ecole des beaux-arts,* as its educational agent and as the most highly organized system of professional instruction of the day, inevitably shared this prestige. The result for America has already been described in Section 3 of *Chapter IV*. Hunt in his New York *atelier,* Ware and Létang at MIT, Ware and Hamlin at Columbia acclimated the French system to the American scene. This temperate attitude was supplanted by more unquestioning acceptance when, in the 1890's, the return of a growing number of American *Ecole* alumni led to the formation of the Society of Beaux-Arts Architects for the express purpose of promoting *Ecole* methods. It has already been noted that by 1915, 15 of the 20 American schools were participating in the competitive student problems of the Society, that nine schools had procured French critics, and that 13 schools had *Ecole*-trained American critics on their faculties. In 1928–1929, 31 of the 48 schools were affiliated with the Beaux-Arts Institute of Design and they and 32 independent *ateliers* registered for BAID problems 2146 students who submitted 8151 drawings for judgment.[4]

This widespread adoption of the *Ecole* system of design training disseminated many desirable benefits. It raised current standards of student effort and skill in presentation. It encouraged breadth of conception. It promoted French architectural fashions which at the time were accounted the acme of high taste. It emphasized in theory a generalized expression of generalized function and generalized structure.

And it also permitted some degree of public comparison of hitherto isolated schools.

Nevertheless, it transmitted its inherent abuses as well, and since it was imposed upon an alien situation, these abuses tended to become further aggravated. Competition, so beneficial on the level of the individual students, soon came to include teams of students, corps of assistants to render sure-fire winners, teachers, the schools, and even jury members. Programs were rarely satisfied to deal with non-monumental subjects, but stressed "imaginative" and "inspiring" types escaping into fanciful situations far removed from the life, comprehension, and expectations of the student. The rigid *esquisse* required of the student a synthesis no serious practitioner would attempt in a few hours or without considerable preparation. Explicit function and explicit construction were of less importance than the illusion of each. Plans and exteriors suffered from the limitations of two-dimensional paper studies, and aesthetic eclecticism discouraged a valid creative approach. It is possible that those abuses which sprang from human failures might have been corrected through steadfast control based on strong convictions, but their persistence despite repeated denunciations leads to the suspicion that the system itself demanded stringent alteration.

Beyond such perversions, however, there were inherent shortcomings that could not be overcome except by basic functional changes. The stimuli of local sites, conditions, needs, and clients were forsworn. Integration of design with other courses could operate on only a fortuitous basis. The teacher could not adjust problems to the needs of his individual students. Nor could the faculty, using programs prepared at a distant center, be certain that every student would experience a systematic, progressive cultivation of knowledge, skill, and creative power. Thus, design teachers, products of the system and relieved by it of their responsibility for determining and controlling their own courses and methods, too frequently came to prize the system for its own sake and for their own convenience.

It has already been noted that in 1928, a typical year, 31 of the 48 schools were affiliated with the BAID. These 31 schools enrolled 3150 students. Therefore, the BAID program affected almost 70 per cent of all architectural students in the U. S. These schools included 15 of 17 in the Northeast, 6 of 10 in the Midwest, 4 of 10 in the South, 3 of 5 in the Plains states, and 3 of 6 in the Far West. Thus there were almost as many BAID schools in the northeastern states as in all other regions. In 1928 all of the 11 schools founded before 1900 were affiliated; 3 of the 8 founded in the 1900's; 11 of 19 founded in the 1910's; and 6 of 10 founded in the 1920's.

Bosworth and Jones noted in 1930 that the affiliated schools used BAID problems in varying degrees. Columbia, Pennsylvania, Carnegie, Illinois, Georgia Tech, New York University, Catholic University, and the University of Washington, based their whole design teaching on BAID programs and judgments. Others used such programs only occasionally. Of the 17 unaffiliated schools, several, like Washington University, employed BAID programs but did not participate in central judgments. All but two adopted a competitive problem method closely akin to the *Ecole* system, and two of these schools had French critics on their faculties. Thus, local adaptations spread the *Ecole* influence far beyond BAID membership.[5]

As has already been noted, reaction against BAID domination appeared as early as 1920 in the non-competitive, individual problem method developed by Professors Ellis Lawrence and W. R. B. Wilcox at the University of Oregon. In 1925, Professor Rudolph Weaver introduced his integrated project method at the University of Florida. After 1929, depression reoriented architecture and architects from eclectic monuments to less pretentious, but more socially significant types. The schools soon felt this shift of emphasis. Gradually, even BAID problems responded to it, but during the '30's an increasing number of schools withdrew affiliation and issued locally written programs. This trend was reinforced as the influence of the *Bauhaus* grew. After World War II, the use of BAID competitions steadily declined.

Nevertheless, the actual changes in most schools were more in subject matter, style, and philosophy than in teaching method. Problems became more realistic and "practical" and were studied with greater attention to functional operation, structural directness, and aesthetic freedom. At best, the results attained vitality and freshness, but, too often, students merely exchanged new clichés for old. The qualities of creative logic, breadth, harmonious and refined detail, orderly organization, and warm humaneness proved as difficult of conquest in the new regime as in the old. Former disciplines relaxed, but transitional experimentalism did not immediately achieve new disciplines to replace them. Students were not alone in these quandaries, for practitioners likewise exhibited them in their striving for a new synthesis.

The resolution of this perplexing situation demands careful analysis of the nature of architecture and the process by which it is attained. Architecture was defined in *Chapter I* as the art of creating buildings which singly and collectively satisfy men's physical and psychological needs by achieving within available resources an optimal integration of utility, structure, and aesthetic expressiveness. Thus, architecture embodies physical, intellectual, and emotional qualities the harmonious fusion of which implies inevitable compromise. As already noted, the process of design by which the final tangible product is gained begins with the definition of the problem by preliminary investigations, analyses, and programming, and proceeds through tentative solutions to the fixing of an optimal basic synthesis, which, in turn, is progressively refined during the working drawing and supervision stages.

The expansion of the scope of design teaching may be shown by the following chart:

Stages	Former responsibility	Present responsibility
1. Statement of need	Instructor	Instructor, but students
2. Analysis	Little attention	often participate
3. Program	Instructor	Student, with guidance
4. Design solution	Student	of instructor
5. Working documents	Some attention in construction courses but no integration	Some integration in design, chiefly in final thesis
6. Bids and contracts		
7. Inspection and supervision	Not included	Some attention in construction and practice courses

The objective of instruction in architectural design is, therefore, to cultivate in the student understanding, resourcefulness, judgment, and facility in the operation of the whole process. In this sense, the whole curriculum focuses upon and nourishes design by supplying the varied knowledge and skills essential to it, but the courses in design must bring together these partial phases, complete the inevitable gaps, integrate the whole, and provide the crucial exercises in application, manipulation, and synthesis. It is this unifying function which gives design courses their dominion over the whole architectural curriculum, and which makes the architectural curriculum unique in the academic world.

The problem method has come to overshadow all other aspects of design training. Originally preoccupied exclusively with aesthetic form and composition, its purview has gradually come to include functional and structural considerations as well. The aggrandizement has proceeded so far that practitioners sometimes appear to think that design problems should duplicate the realities of practice. Since, as already noted, the full process of design can be experienced only by active participation in real building projects which often extend over several years, it is obvious that school exercises must be confined to lesser scope. On the other hand, the *Ecole* system and its derivatives equated the design problem solely to the stage in which the basic synthesis was achieved for conditions already stated in the given program. Here, the scope of training was excessively narrow. Between these two extremes, therefore, each problem must be conceived as a teaching device to: instill new facts and principles; organize and apply all knowledge and principles thus far gained; and establish a modicum of reality to prepare for smooth transition into office practice.

Unfortunately, the achievement of these goals is hampered by an apparent belief that the mere taking of any problem suffices to attain these ends. Consequently, it cannot be too strongly emphasized that each problem is an exercise in the application of certain definite facts, principles, and skills, in other words, the content which the problem is intended to illustrate. It is here that so much design teaching is remiss in its failure to satisfy the basic demands of the learning process. In organizing its content, demonstrating its principles, and controlling the learning process, design teaching is perhaps the most backward phase of architectural education. The reasons for this are easy to ascertain. The fear of formulae, the difficulty of discussing emotional criteria, the fallaciousness and special pleading of past theories, the glorification of intuition, and an unfortunate aversion against study and research of such problems on the part of both teachers and practitioners, have left the theory of design and design teaching poorly defined and only partially understood. The results are the easy slogans that "one learns to design by designing," and that "designers are born, not made." If these are true, it is futile to attempt any analysis, control, or refinement of design teaching, but this is a position neither architects nor educators can afford to accept.

Design teaching, therefore, must exploit the full learning process. Each step must perform a definite educational function within the total program. It must lead logically from previous experience, introduce and demonstrate new facts, terminology, and principles, and illustrate their occurrence by dramatic examples selected from the best contemporary practice. Only thus can students be methodically prepared to undertake their own experimental exercises, and only in the light of these criteria can their progress be equitably judged.

Problems, thus conceived, are no longer isolated entities, but taken together form a closely interrelated and progressive series carefully calculated to produce the desired final result. Such a sequence would be composed of projects systematically arranged as to: difficulty, the principles involved, types of use, the design phase to be emphasized, the method of solution, the organization of design personnel, and manner of presentation. The total impact of such an integrated series will not only be heightened because each part is better defined and organized, but, by ensuring a well-balanced total training and by mutual reinforcement of design exercises and their coordination with other courses, the effect can be multiplied many fold. Moreover, as pressure mounts to increase both technical and cultural content of curricula, the effectiveness of design teaching can be raised without requiring a proportionate addition of design time.

Twenty years ago, in 1931, Bosworth and Jones noted this opportunity, and the difficulty of attaining it:

"The writing of a good programme is not an easy matter. The writing of a series of correlated programmes for a given class of students for a whole year is still less simple. When such a task is extended to include the four or five years of design work, properly graded and related, one year to another, it requires thinking in terms of a definite educational policy, not only as to design, but also as to design in relation to other coordinate parts of the curriculum. The Beaux Arts, however good its intentions in this respect, works under the handicap of having to depend on the more or less casual and hurried efforts of busy practitioners. In the schools, too many of our critics in this country have shirked this work. They take the Beaux-Arts programmes *in toto* not from the conviction that they best fit an educational scheme, for which no one could criticize them, but because they don't think in broad enough terms to write their own."[6]

The benefits of a skillfully integrated sequence of design problems seem obvious. This need not presume a single, universal pattern since, in any case, each architectural faculty must accept final responsibility for determining and controlling its own program. It is conceivable, nevertheless, that a measure of general agreement might emerge from mutual discussion and experience. Such congruity must be the result of a common approach to similar conditions. It should never be the consequence of inertia or dictatorial fiat.

A well-balanced sequence can incorporate many problem types. The general building problem, which poses the full determination of functional arrangement, structural system, and aesthetic form for a single building, presented in scope and manner comparable to the Basic Design of a practicing architect, will no doubt dominate the series. Even here, however, wide variation of emphasis can be obtained either by requiring fuller development of some particular element or by relating it to a subsequent problem of another type. Special types include: the Elevation Problem, the Interior Problem, the Decorative Problem, the Structural Problem, the Specification Problem, the Site Plan Problem, the Group Plan Problem, and the undergraduate Thesis. The Thesis, inspired by the *Ecole's* examination for the *diplôme,* has long been used by American schools in varying degrees of completeness as a summary of the whole curriculum. For it the student under faculty guidance selects his project, prepares the program, develops the solution which comprises basic drawings, working drawings whole or partial, and a written report containing his analysis, justification of the solution, typical structural calculations, an outline specification, and a preliminary cost estimate. These results are presented graphically, verbally, and in writing before a jury of faculty and visitors.

The amount of time devoted to design training in American schools varies widely. In 1948, the survey of 25 curricula already noted disclosed a range from 1080 to 3015 scheduled class hours. No comparison of number of design exercises is available, but marked differences are known to exist with the smallest requirement being two or three and the BAID affiliated school normally using about four major and four sketch problems per year, or a four-year total of about 32 exercises. In some schools, the number is closer to 40 exercises. At the *Ecole* it has been noted that a superior student could gain eligibility to the *diplôme* thesis after two *analytiques,* four or five major problems, and one or two sketch problems, a total of about eight or nine exercises. Unfortunately, no objective study has ever attempted to determine the optimal number of design exercises in undergraduate design courses.

The length of individual problems has varied in the past from short sketches lasting a few hours to term-long theses, but general building problems have usually been allotted four, five, or six weeks. Too often, the achievement of a basic solution absorbs all the scheduled time, and refinement, general or detailed, must be neglected. In a skillfully arranged integrated sequence it should be possible to adapt the length of problems to their educational function, and thus benefit by frequent shifts of pace which would relieve the usual monotonous cycle of major problems.

The number and length of problems too often absorb the full time allotted to design and leave little or no space for systematic presentation and development of concurrent design facts, principles, and ideas. It would seem profitable to explore a reduction in number of problems and the establishment of a series of carefully coordinated supplementary class readings, lectures, and discussions calculated to reinforce the remaining exercises with a sound body of orderly knowledge and clearly understood principles. It might well prove true that the problem method has overreached itself and by its excessive consumption of student time and effort has prejudiced both its own real benefits and the acquisition of fundamental knowledge and habits of thinking.

While the number and character of design exercises must be determined from carefully controlled experiments, it is possible that there is a point of diminishing return. It might be argued, for example, that eight or ten major problems with more

194

thorough study and development could produce sounder results than 14 or 18 such exercises. Even with the addition of classwork, enough time could be left to permit more extended refinement of the remaining major problems. Sufficient exercises must be kept to ensure that each student gains a high degree of facility, ability to work under pressure, and a reasonable familiarity with common building types, but, on the other hand, facileness can inhibit depth, quickness does not ensure quality, and familiarity may mean only superficial acquaintance. It is difficult to escape the feeling that design teaching has glorified quantity at the expense of quality and multiplied problems in belief that benefits accumulate in direct proportion to the number of exercises.

The hesitation of faculties and practitioners to question established teaching practice is understandable. The hallowed prestige and magic of the "problem method" tends to categorize any questioning of the *status quo* as heresy. Lacking a tradition of systematic general knowledge and particularized principles, the initiation of such material seems overformidable and to individuals trained under prevailing conditions wholly unnecessary and even impossible. The immense difficulty of describing the non-verbal content of a formal, visual activity discourages those who have acquired skill by action, rather than by facility in explanation. They fear that formulae might replace spontaneity, imagination, and intuition. They distrust any rationalizing as akin to dogma, as well they may. Nevertheless, such attitudes must be overcome, for without such philosophic rationale educational method is reduced to mere osmosis.

It must be emphasized that reason alone can never dominate any creative activity. The mysterious process by which the complex factors of a problem are resolved into a moving, dynamic synthesis has thus far defied psychological investigation. In certain arts, such as painting, it can be argued plausibly that creativeness, unfettered by any control other than its own nature, has value in itself. In architecture, however, by definition concerned to a large extent with practical criteria susceptible to intellectual methods, creativeness for its own sake is inadmissible. Thus, it is essential that the logical organization of the rational criteria of architecture must support and reinforce the final intuitive act of the designer. The aim is not to deprive architecture of its legitimate emotional content, but by perfecting the designer's command and control of its rational elements to enable him to win a surer and more satisfying synthesis. Only incorrigible romanticists can forego such assistance.

The conduct of a general building problem within the framework thus proposed implies the establishment of its aims, not only in the curriculum, but also in the life of the community. A basis analysis should follow, including the sociological function of the building type, a general description of the various classes of the building type, the functional elements and patterns usually involved, the derivation and demonstration of principles associated with the type, the formulation of design criteria, the analysis of significant contemporary examples, a discussion of site selection and conditions, and consideration of auxiliary materials common to design in general, and especially emphasized in the problem under way. The assembly, organization, and effective presentation of such material is an arduous task, but without such background the preparation of the student for creative work remains defective. To accomplish this basic analysis as efficiently as possible, the teacher should have adequate teaching aids such as texts, syllabi, bibliographies, supplementary readings, and fully published reports of the best examples. In selecting the specific subject of the exercise, account should be taken as to the availability of such teaching aids. Lectures, discussions, class committee reports, and field trips are normal techniques to communicate and interpret such data. Visiting lecturers can be used with profit. Far from discouraging students from seeking other resources from library, campus, or community, a skillful teacher can stimulate them to more enthusiastic and rewarding effort in their use. A summary report should be required of each student to ensure assimilation and organization. This report should be graded on thoroughness, understanding, format, and effective presentation, both written and graphic. It is obvious that by graduation the full series of these reports could form a valuable reference document which, though much would become obsolete, would present a useful framework for organizing additional data as these appear.

After the Basic Analysis, the Program can be posed. If this is given first, students tend to concentrate attention on only those phases of the general discussion which seem pertinent to the specific program, and thus miss the broad implications of the analysis. The Program should establish only the most fundamental assumptions of the problem, equivalent to the general statements normally furnished by clients. It should include: the type and scope of the proposed building; the general character desired; the economic limitations, such as resources, financing, and the assumed economic life of the project; the site, its size, shape, location, topography, orientation, access, utilities, soil conditions, existing vegetation, legal restrictions, surroundings, and relation to the community.

Utilizing the Basic Program and the Basic Analysis, the student should then develop the detailed requirements of the project. Thus, he can gain experience and insight into the creative influence of the whole preliminary programming phase of design. Through class discussions, individual aberrations can be easily controlled and, if desired, a final approved list of requirements can be issued as the basis for subsequent problem development.

This preliminary study will vary somewhat with the growing ability of the student. At the beginning, when the chief concern is to establish good procedures of study and elementary principles, requirements and site must be kept relatively simple, and guidance must be firm. Nevertheless, even at this stage the illusion of student responsibility and participation is essential. In more advanced work, this responsibility can be real and invaluable.

The selection and general determination of such Basic Programs in an integrated series should be the function of a Program Committee of the design faculty. Under its supervision, individual instructors can survey the literature, field, and profession, and prepare the actual draft. On occasion, practicing architects are usually pleased to cooperate in contributing basic materials, situations, or even complete programs written to fit specific program needs. Sometimes the programs of general architectural competitions might be suitable. The use of BAID student programs presents the difficulty of fixed requirements, and, since the details are purposely released only a brief time before issue, it is usually too late to fit them into an integrated series. It could be argued with justice that the organization and preparation of an integrated series of 40 to 60 programs per year is of such vital importance to vivid and stimulating design teaching as to warrant the employment of special personnel for this work. An analogous situation exists in Harvard's Graduate School of Business Administration, where instruction is almost entirely by the Case Method. An annual budget of $80,000 is devoted solely to the preparation of cases and a file of 20,000 cases is available to the teaching staff. Although in architectural schools the number of problems is much smaller, their scope is much broader. Nevertheless, if at all possible the design staff should undertake this work since they should maintain constant check on the operation and direction of the courses. The possibility of syllabi on specific building types prepared by a central agency will be discussed later.

Problem development follows completion of a detailed program. The first step is a Preliminary Study, which, like the old *esquisse,* serves to bring the student's thought to immediate focus and to lead him to developmental studies without delay. With the background of basic analysis and program preparation, the fallacy of the *esquisse de novo* is eliminated. Moreover, if the Preliminary Study is allotted two or three days and if access to the instructor for general discussion is provided, the Preliminary Study, though carefully restricted to the student's own work, should be immensely improved in quality. It should be presented in a simple, direct, clear, and precise manner, and should be graded on the basis of solution and presentation. Such Preliminary Studies can provide training similar to, but sounder than former sketch problems, and it can also serve as preparation for registration examinations in design. Since the retention of the preliminary solution would not be required during subsequent development, there would no longer be any motive for vagueness and ambiguity.

From the Preliminary Study, the problem is developed and refined through successive small- and medium-scale drawings, diagrams, sketches, perspectives, models, and color studies. The purpose is two-fold: to achieve a solution having a maximum of professional quality, and to train the student in systematic habits of work, facility in expression, ambition for high standards, and taste, judgment, and self-criticism, which will lead him progressively to capacity for independent action. Many schools require periodic intermediate studies to ensure a continuous and steady rate of development and to guard against frantic *charettes.* Such studies have a tendency, however, to become minor *charettes* in themselves and by demanding additional presentation absorb time needed for development. If the development schedule is sufficiently long, such studies provide useful checks and interim summaries.

During the development stage, the student should be urged to plan an efficient schedule of work. This is difficult to check because daily criticism is not always feasible or desirable. It is also hard for the student to carry out until he acquires some power and confidence in his own judgment. Some schools have attempted to meet the problem in the earlier years by breaking down problem development into a series of small stages with definite material to be handed in and graded at the end of each class period. The resulting rate of progress has been unusually rapid. While such methods seem overly rigid and adolescent, they have at least proved that regularity and concentration of work can eliminate much of the procrastination that ends in *charettes*.

A steady rate of progress is likewise necessary if the development is to be well rounded. Many students enjoy the more tangible phases, such as the accommodation of use requirements, and devote so much time to them that structural and aesthetic matters receive brief, if any, attention. Today, when materialism is such an all-pervading force, it is especially important to insist that design must deal equally with all aspects of the problem. If courses in construction, theory, and composition are fully integrated with design, this problem becomes measurably easier.

Instruction during development is primarily on an individual basis, but, on occasion, group discussions form time-saving adjuncts. In general, all teaching should stress the application of principles enunciated during the Basic Analysis or in other courses. Due to the intimate character of criticism in design, the critic has a unique opportunity and obligation to stimulate the student's imagination, taste, judgment, resourcefulness, and desire for professional quality in his work. With beginning students, the instructor should feel free to demonstrate his precepts by actual sketches, but, as quickly as possible, criticism should be confined to discussion of principles, evaluation of the student's success in applying them, additional data and factors for which the need has been revealed by development studies, and the means of testing the quality of scheme and work. A skillful critic can make ingenious use of the Socratic device of answering questions by asking counter-questions that will lead the student to arrive at his own answer. The close personal relationship between teacher and student provides an ideal opportunity to challenge every student to his best effort, urge gifted students to additional accomplishment, prod the sluggard, and repair the deficiencies of others. For such results, a critic must keep his students long enough to learn their needs. One term would seem the minimum time before reassignment, but even an academic year might prove more propitious. The amount of criticism per student per week varies with the stage of student development. For beginners, frequent short periods are necessary, but later, two crits per week each from 15 to 30 minutes are usually sufficient. For all these reasons, the number of students per critic should not exceed about 15, and in advanced courses this, together with grading, jury, and program preparation, should constitute a full teaching load.

While the regular design critic must assume the supplying of the major part of instruction and the coordination of the course, the use of architects and specialists is occasionally beneficial. Such personnel provides students with contact with the profession, special knowledge, and a change of pace and outlook. It is difficult to procure such visitors for the whole duration of one problem, and even if this is possible, it is hard for them in this limited time to adjust themselves to an educational program.

Thus, in order to preserve the continuity of the program, it seems advisable to restrict their use to one problem per student. To overcome this difficulty, some schools bring visitors to serve, not as full critics for the entire problem, but as "consulting critics" for a short period, one or two weeks, during which by scheduled conferences with a single student or a group, the consultant can discuss the problem and work of each student. Such an arrangement has proved very profitable to students and a more effective use of the visitor's time. Many schools assign non-design teachers, especially those in construction, as occasional critics of special aspects of design problems. This practice not only reinforces the quality of design work, but also serves to integrate the other courses with the needs of students. Finally, auxiliary criticism of younger students by advanced students, can add stimulus to both groups. It is obvious that such a revival of the *atelier* system should not be depended upon as a substitute for the mature instruction of a regular teacher, but in limited amount it can improve group morale.

Some schools encourage students to seek criticism from several sources on the principle that the inevitable differences of approach, interpretation, and opinion will create a welter of healthy chaos from which the student will be forced to distill his own answers. If such conflict is kept on the high level of principle, and is safeguarded from personalities, and if the contenders seek truth and not just verbal victory, this method can be tremendously stimulating. Since architecture must by its nature remain an art, and since many of its factual phases are still controversial, enlightened debate parallels the Socratic questioning already recommended. Perhaps this method, as has been suggested, is more beneficial for advanced students, but even for beginners a limited use of it might prove profitable. Nevertheless, debate cannot substitute for sustained thought. Each teacher owes the student a definite statement of his own working principles, not as a mandatory system to be accepted blindly by the student, but as a point of departure for his own thinking.

The function of the next stage, Presentation, is to communicate the final product of the development stage so that it will be clearly and effectively understood by a lay client. Since such skill is a great asset to a practitioner, all students should be trained to plan their own presentation for maximum exploitation of their particular problem. Careful presentation also assists the designer in fixing the final form and materials of his project. Such an aim discourages the older salon type of presentation which was intended primarily to shout down its neighbors in a judgment and to seduce susceptible jurors. While salon presentations provided some training in abstract composition, they became means of camouflaging, rather than of communication. In reaction, some schools have so deemphasized presentation that it is questionable whether their students actually realize the appearance of their own designs.

Presentation should include plans, sections, elevations, and diagrams, at a scale sufficiently large to permit revealing indication of use, construction, and finish materials. Furnishings and equipment should be shown in order to ensure that they are properly provided. The general style should approximate that used by progressive offices in preparing Basic Drawings for the consideration of clients. Drawing and lettering should be of a high order of craftsmanship, but as economical as possible. The result should be straightforward and restrained. Various media and techniques may be explored, but the need for effective reproduction in newspapers, publicity campaigns, and other outlets should be stressed. At least one realistic, carefully-rendered perspective, frequently in color, and approximating those used in practice, should be required. This should show a normal, truthful view, and reveal form, decoration, and materials. Forced, distorted, and faked views should be scrupulously avoided. Occasionally, a second exterior perspective from the opposite direction, and an interior perspective showing decoration and furnishings, should be included. Additional sketch perspectives should be encouraged.

The use of three-dimensional models, both exterior and interior, is highly profitable. Rough study models are almost universally urged during the development of the problem, but the high cost of finished presentation models in both time and materials usually restricts them to one or two problems in the whole course. If the school provides a model workshop, students need no compulsion to use it. Indeed, model making is such a prevalent hobby and such a fascinating pastime that the temptation to overindulge often requires strict control.

An interesting variation in presentation has been developed at Carnegie, in which the student submits a portfolio of all intermediate studies and final drawings. The whole group is reviewed to ascertain a complete estimate of progress, product, and ability.

Finally, presentation can include non-graphic elements. Reports, written explanations, and auxiliary features can stimulate forceful writing. Some schools also require verbal expositions and defenses in order to give the student some experience in speaking before a group. If this part of the exercise is carefully prepared and coached, it can accomplish much more than the usual undergraduate course in public speaking because the student is on familiar ground and is well motivated. Both written and verbal presentations form valuable preparation for professional practice. That they are very time-consuming limits the frequency of their use, but several schools have found them well worth the effort.

The evaluation of student work in design has positive teaching functions. It forms a valuable check as to whether the student has mastered sufficient skill to proceed to the next stage of his training. It implements the age-old stimulus of hope of reward and fear of penalty which is so potent in all phases of life. It can serve as a valuable summary of the whole project experience. And it can, by comparison of different solutions, point the various possibilities inherent in the same conditions, illustrate again the standards by which they can be judged, and display the opportunities and pitfalls arising from the exercise of imagination and experiments.

All this implies the desirability of some degree of competition, but competition used legitimately and within strict control. The dangers arising from the abuse of the competitive spirit have already been cited in considerable detail, but most practitioners testify that competition is an inescapable characteristic of professional life. Theoretically, a student should set his own pace and absolute standards and thus compete against himself. Practically, this asks of the student a quality of will power, purpose, and self-discipline which only occasionally develops even in maturity. This problem should not be confused with the merits or defects of architectural competitions which are another matter. Non-competitive systems, where they have been tried, by apprentices or schools, sometimes create an atmosphere of romantic preciosity, a lack of pace, and an introspective attitude that fails to provide the disciplines normally considered as desirable training for life itself. Excessive prolongation of problems can cause the student to become stale or exhaust the value to be derived from them. Wholesome competition, on the other hand, can not only raise the horizon of ambition, but it can also enlist the aid of a constituent force in human nature and introduce verve and good-natured rivalry into an arduous regimen.

The mechanics of maintaining competition among design students demand the fixing of a definite termination for each exercise. No doubt this handicaps a slow student and prevents an energetic student from making additional refinements, but life is full of dead-lines, and the ability to meet them has essential value. Moreover, unless the curriculum is itself left indeterminate in length, definite time limits permit a steady flow of class work and, therefore, ensure broader training.

The establishment of standards of performance is difficult in any educational area, but this is especially so in a creative field like design. Under former conditions, when individual problems had no special functions, and when the final evidence was solely the paper indication of a design, the demonstration of orderly organization and skill in presentation was the basis of evaluation. While final over-all quality must still be considered, the advantage of an integrated series in which each problem emphasizes particular teaching functions gives a surer set of criteria for grading. Moreover, preliminary and intermediate studies may be considered in gauging the total effort of the student. Without such definite criteria, it is tempting to be over-lenient, since a poor solution covers the same area of paper as a good performance, and thus tends to claim recognition due to its very existence. In setting the passing threshold, the crucial questions are whether the result is a fair sample of ability and effort, and whether the ability displayed is adequate to enable the student to undertake subsequent work with profit. It is no kindness to a student to sidestep such a difficult decision and permit him to attempt a level of work for which he is unprepared. At the highest level, a valuable criterion is whether any better performance could be reasonably expected at that stage of development. A review of the best work of recent years aids materially in this determination. It is important to premiate excellent performances and not make the highest grade unobtainable. Once these extremes are fixed, it is fairly easy to set the intermediate levels.

The agency by which design problems are evaluated has long been the jury, composed of visiting architects and experts, or faculty, or both. Practitioners bring to the judgment a wealth of practical experience which is of great value to both student and school. Jury service is an important means of securing the continued interest of the profession in the school, of acquainting the profession with educational trends, and of discussing future possibilities. Nevertheless, it is often difficult for visiting jurymen to grasp within the short time available the import of the problem. It is important, therefore, that such visitors be thoroughly briefed as to the purpose, content, and interpretation of the program. Care must likewise be exercised that the jury is not dominated by a single person or idea, so that it runs amuck and wrecks the teaching value of the problem. Despite such reservations, the use of visiting jurymen can be proper and successful. The integrated problem offers explicit guides for equitable judgments.

Teacher jurymen have the advantage of close familiarity with the general educational objectives of the full design program, and probably of the problem being judged. While they are usually considered as commanding less practicality than practitioners, the difference is perhaps immaterial in judging student designs because these solutions cannot encompass professional completeness, and because, in any case, they have been developed already under the limitations of the teachers' criticism. It is unfair to expect too much of the student or to underrate real, though necessarily limited, accomplishments. Therefore, student performance must be judged primarily within its own frame of reference. Thus a combination of architect and teacher jurymen can best balance the educational and practical aspects of the judgment.

Judgments in the past have usually been secret. Increasingly, however, it has been realized that the discussion of problems by jurors could become an important instructional device. Consequently, many schools have reversed this tradition and have opened the judgment to all students. In some schools where physical facilities preclude admission of all students, classes elect a small group of representatives to report the proceedings. In some instances, students are welcomed during discussions of problems, but withdraw when grading begins. The benefits of the open discussion are not obtained when students attend the judging of only their own problem. Another human hazard is the danger toward the end of a long session when weary jurors may forget the strict seriousness of students and indulge in tactless comments not calculated to inspire confidence or understanding. If such difficulties can be overcome, the open jury system can hold positive educational values.

It has long been a fetish of architectural schools to deny a teacher any voice in evaluating a problem he has criticized. No doubt this policy was inherited from the *Ecole,* where patrons were assumed to owe their allegiance to their *atelier,* rather than to the educational institution itself. In American collegiate schools, the adoption of this rule was tantamount to denying any teacher, whatever his subject, the responsibility of checking the success of his own instruction. It is true that in courses with multiple sections a common examination is frequently administered, but such exams are prepared and graded by all participating instructors. In no other area than design is the teacher excluded on the grounds of possible bias or suspicion of defective standards. If either is true, he should be summarily dismissed. Actually, acquiescence to such a stricture by design teachers seems to have been based in part upon willingness to transfer responsibility to the jury group and thus escape inevitable student queries. Whatever the reason, the effect is to premiate a final result and disregard the process by which it was attained.

Some teachers have experimented with juries composed of the students themselves. While such practice is not generally defensible, it is amusing to note that the students' standards of grading are frequently harsher than those set by the faculty.

Regardless of the membership of the jury, it is most important that sufficient time be taken to discover the real quality of each problem. Superficial judgments are not only opportunities lost, but they can also quickly destroy hard-won morale and bring to naught the best-laid educational plan. A conscientious student cannot be convinced that the product of several weeks of thought and effort can be understood at a glance. This feeling was well put in a student complaint posted in 1950 at the *Ecole des beaux-arts*, which read, in part:

"How is an architectural competition judged? Forty gentlemen, in two committees, parade for an afternoon along a narrow labyrinth lined with drawings which have cost some four hundred students each two months of work. At most, the juries can devote one minute to each design."[7]

Even when more committees are used, the press of time is severe. Some measure of the issue can be gained by noting that at a normal BAID judgment on December 11, 1951, 388 problems—48 Class A, 135 Class B, 72 Class C, 92 Class B sketches, and 35 Class C sketches—were evaluated by 24 jurors, each of whom served on an average of 1.7 sub-juries, which reviewed major problems at least twice and the best a third time. If each major problem was given at least 5 minutes, and no doubt many took longer, it would have taken $4\frac{1}{2}$ hours for the 8 assigned jurors to judge the 48 Class A problems. Five of these 8 then served on sub-juries for the Class B and C major problems they handled. While such large judgments are now exceptional, they serve to emphasize the point that any jury duty is a demanding task if real justice is to be attained.

In the light of the foregoing discussion, it seems obvious that the evaluation of the student's design performance should appraise a number of facets. His final presentation reveals his ultimate solution and this may include both written and verbal exposition. It is appropriate that a major portion of the award should be made on this tangible product by some sort of group judgment. Some measure of the student's progress can be added by consideration of preliminary and intermediate studies. This may be the duty of the critic, with or without the assistance of a jury. And, finally, some authority should be delegated the critic to assess effort, attitude, and realization of potential. In securing an overall evaluation, these components must be appropriately weighted. Few faculties delude themselves that any system can determine a precise hierarchical order between few or many students. It is well, therefore, to avoid too fine distinctions. High and low are usually self-evident; between these, the boundaries usually are blurred.

Thus, it is clear that the older simple system of evaluation was too often deficient in both equity and sound pedagogy. It follows that if a more just and beneficial system is to be practiced, the local faculty must assume responsibility. Most American schools have zealously guarded their right to determine their own standards. This is an inescapable obligation. This, therefore, underscores the fact that any system of central judgments can at best be only auxiliary in nature. Since such central evaluation must be limited in scope, it is highly controversial whether it can serve any useful purpose, assuming that the tendency toward abuses might be avoided. Whatever its contributions of former days, it now seems inadmissible if present progressive educational methods are to be maintained in a consistent manner.

Moreover, the principle of central judgments is inextricably linked to centrally prepared programs, which implies at the same time a centrally determined educational philosophy and policy in design teaching. After almost sixty years of operation, the only central agency thus far attempted, the BAID, has never found it possible or feasible to formulate such a policy. Fortunately, it is inherent in the collegiate educational system that no such central agency can impose such a mandatory policy, even if it wished to do so. The authoritarian academy does not fit the American scene. Every attempt to promulgate one has been successfully opposed. While American architectural schools have not always exploited the advantages that their diverse situations and independence provided, they have at least maintained the possibility of doing so.

The final stage of each design exercise is to interpret to the student the meaning of the evaluation of his problem and summarize the whole design exercise. Without this provision, the value of the judgment is lost.

Although the preceding discussion has centered on the general building problem, the possibilities and advantages of other types have already been suggested. Some exercises might follow the same procedure through the Preliminary Study or to the equivalent of an Intermediate Study. Thus the function of the sketch problem could be realized, but by carefully preserving the Basic Analysis stage, the danger of superficiality can be eliminated. Even despite this danger it would be worth while in later years to pose an unfamiliar situation, a variant of some earlier exercise, or a combination of two or more, to force the student to apply his general knowledge under conditions similar to office pressure. Again, special phases of a general problem may be posed, such as the elevation problem, interior problem, etc.

The generally serious conception of design exercises here described stresses precision, soundness, and methodical procedure, perhaps in reaction to former casualness. Laudable as these qualities may be, they must not submerge the other essentials of imagination, spontaneity, emotional warmth, richness, humor, and fantasy. These are the saving graces which keep life bearable. Even in a materialistic and economy-minded generation, play, escape, and spectacle are still all-pervading necessities. In the attempt to gain acceptance as more than long-haired artists, architects have come perilously close to losing one of their most significant functions. Students too often reflect this view and resent any exercise calculated to give facility in such matters. Since there are many indications of a desire for a "new monumentalism" and a new humaneness in architecture, design instruction must not neglect its duty to explore the use of decorative materials, effects, and composition, the vocabulary and functions of ornament, and the range and determination of aesthetic character. Since contemporary students are usually innocent of these techniques, careful preparation is all the more a necessary accompaniment to exercises devoted to them.

Frequently the inculcation of a vocabulary of forms and patterns is begun in a freshman introductory course. When the drafting of classical orders and the rendering of analytiques became outmoded, many schools substituted small building problems of the simplest type, on the theory that the quicker a direct plunge is taken into design, the better for all concerned. Vocabulary and study techniques were absorbed as the need for them arose. As might be expected, the results were often undisciplined and derivative.

Later, under the influence of the *Bauhaus,* many schools adopted a sequence of exercises in "Basic Design," intended to give direct experience in the nature of materials, their manipulation, and combination in expressive form. Ingenious exploratory experiments were devised to demonstrate visual and tactile qualities, and abstract compositions were discussed in terms of abstract principles. From such experience the student was to attain a "new language of vision," which he could then apply to architecture through similar exploitation of its constituent materials and criteria.

The evaluation of such an approach is still being studied. It is always difficult to untangle permanent validity from excitement due to novelty. On the one hand, it stirs the student's imagination and discourages unthinking acceptance of the familiar and commonplace. On the other hand, it would seem that exercises more directly pertinent to architecture would be more profitable than paper cutting, collages, and plaster squeezing. It is likewise tempting to wonder whether the involved dialectic usually accompanying such experiments, and primarily derived from the painter-theoreticians of the early 1920's, would not be more effective if stated in direct and lucid architectural terms. Perhaps the most reasonable solution is an introductory course in which similar architectural exercises would be combined with the elementary theory and survey of the building industry previously suggested. Further, it is certain that the analysis of aesthetic materials and principles should not be confined to the introductory course, when the student is least prepared to absorb them, but should be continuously developed throughout all design instruction.

The character of present-day students also suggests that introductory exercises may well begin with tangible phases, such as planning, adding structural considerations as supporting background is acquired. Some purists maintain that no design exercise can be essayed until all subsidiary techniques are mastered. Under this theory, however, the study of design would be possible only at the end of the curriculum. This view seems much too narrow and it does not recognize the necessity of the gradual evolution of design facility which it recognizes for other subjects. It is not to be expected that beginning problems will be mature performances, and it must be remembered that all exercises are devices incident to prolonged training.

On the other hand, many advanced undergraduate exercises undertake much too complex subjects, and forfeit the possibility of thorough study and refinement. It is probable that senior problems should not exceed in complexity a level represented by the design of a medium-sized school. More complicated types may well be reserved for graduate problems. The reduction in total number of major problems, already advocated, combined with a reduction in problem complexity, will permit a more systematic and well-balanced design experience from every standpoint.

While an integrated sequence of problems affords opportunity for regular observation and control of student progress, some schools also test their students' ability in self-criticism by requiring occasional solo exercises done entirely without criticism. Solo problems are thus similar to short problems ending with the Preliminary or Intermediate Study, but the former are sometimes thought of as comprising a kind of prerequisite examination to promotion. However, it is doubtful that any faculty would be willing to deny promotion on the sole basis of failure to pass a single brief exercise. Nevertheless, the solo problem is a useful supplementary gauge of capacity. The undergraduate thesis type of problem often serves as a final comprehensive examination in design, and this view is plausibly asserted. The University of Florida employs a definite final comprehensive examination conducted over several days and embracing all subjects, including design. It is conceived as to scope and method in much the same terms as a typical registration board examination, and, indeed, serves as a useful preparation for it.

Much has been said already as to possibilities of integrating design with other courses. It remains to note here a number of experiments in which all levels of design itself have been integrated. In the early 1940's, at Yale, all design classes took problems dealing with the same building type. Over a series of semesters a cycle of different types was scheduled and later repeated itself. Thus each student could be assured of some methodical contact with a given number of types. The faculty could prepare and develop appropriate analytical material. Visiting experts could benefit all students. Inter-class discussions were encouraged. Even history could contribute by tracing the evolution of the type being studied. At Michigan, since 1948, all design work has been oriented around a hypothetical or adapted community designed by city planning students. Groups of design students explore the community's needs for various categories of buildings, prepare their programs, and develop suitable solutions. At the University of Cincinnati a similar broad project undertook with great success the redevelopment of a large local slum area. Recently, the University of Illinois has integrated its three upper years of design by posing sets of problems which all focus on the development of one site, such as Pere Marquette State Park. While in certain respects such integrations may seem over-contrived, they have resulted in an enhancement of student interest and morale which has proved well worth while.

Another type of integration varies with the group to which the problem is assigned. Individual problems for individual students are usually confined to the undergraduate thesis. The most usual type of assignment and the easiest to administer is by year class. However, if used to the exclusion of other groupings, it tends to impose a monotonous repetition of the problem cycle. It is possible to vary it by a number of devices. One very successful means is to pose a problem with several contrasting sites, on each of which two or more members of the class base their solutions. The effect of diverse topography, vistas, access, and orientation on the several solutions forms a dramatic demonstration of the operation of these basic criteria. Another method assigns parts of the same problem to separate groups. This is particularly useful during the

Basic Analysis stage, but it could be applied in later stages as well. Again it is stimulating to give the same program to two or more classes, as sketch problems to advanced students, and as major problems in lower grades. Thus the advanced results can serve as valuable challenges for younger students. Finally, certain problems can be assigned to teams of students, either of the same class, or with one or two younger men working under a senior, who then functions as chief designer or job-captain. This is, of course, but a modernized version of the ancient *atelier* system. It is especially adapted to the last stages of the undergraduate thesis, when it not only assists the senior in an arduous schedule, but also prepares the assistants for their own future theses. In some schools, teams enlisting students from other departments—landscape architecture, city planning, agriculture, home economics, sociology, economics, law, and education—have proved stimulating. The possibilities of such groupings are limited only by the ingenuity of the teacher.

The marked decline in the participation of American architectural schools in the educational program of the Beaux-Arts Institute of Design amply proves that the criticisms of its theory and practice, heretofore mentioned, are almost universally recognized as valid. The centrally issued programs are incompatible with the principles of an integrated sequence of exercises and of the incontrovertible responsibility of each faculty to determine and perfect its own curriculum and courses. The central judgment has long been considered as only supplementary to local evaluation.

Nevertheless, the BAID has been the only agency which could provide, at least in theory, a means of permitting the individual schools to see what others were doing in design. Actually, comparison has been possible only by attending judgments or by the limited illustrations in the *BAID Bulletin*. A few groups of schools have accomplished this function by organizing among themselves inter-school competitions, each, in effect, a sort of miniature BAID. At various times, ACSA has been asked to consider the administration of circulating exhibits of student design work, but the cost and voluntary basis of the project have prevented its consummation. The need is apparent, but, since at present the BAID offers the only mechanism for its accomplishment, most schools have considered such participation as a prohibitive prerequisite.

At the 1951 Annual Meeting, the ACSA adopted a resolution to investigate a proposed solution to this and associated problems. The proposal provided for four functions, each of which had long been discussed, but not hitherto coordinated into a unified and feasible program.

1. Preparation of Study-Texts for Building Types.

The need for adequate, up-to-date study texts has been emphasized in discussion of the Basic Analysis stage. These texts are conceived as written by the best minds and experts in the profession, gauged for student needs, edited by a permanent staff, and issued to students on a subscription basis. In scope they could approach a small volume. Such material would put into the students' hands in efficient form, the basic background of data, principles, and examples underlying the type discussed. A critical bibliography would stimulate additional study and more effective use of library and professional literature. Several such texts would be issued each year. By graduation, the texts would comprise a valuable file of data, which, though gradually growing outdated, would serve as a nucleus for orienting newly acquired data. With such material both teacher and class would save time now absorbed by undirected search and apply their effort to profitable additional study. No individual school has sufficient staff or funds to perform such work alone. The cost of such texts would require a sizable budget, but the proposal included a plan of financing which is described below.

2. *Coordinated Design Problems.*

Given the regular publication of worthwhile study-texts on various building types, it can be assumed that many individual schools would wish to plan their design sequence to make use of them in approximately the same order in which they are issued. Since any sequence of problems used by individual schools will normally use the same building types employed by other schools, the only imposed restriction would be in the sequence of use, but no doubt a satisfactory agreement could be reached on this point through group discussion. The central organization would then announce a problem dealing with the current building type, and stating in the most general terms its scope and character. The problem would then be taken in such manner, with such a site, and such a detailed program as the student and his local critic would determine. Length of problem could vary from sketch to thesis scale. The method of instruction, approach, philosophy, and presentation would be controlled by the local critic and school. Local conditions, sites, clients, and other controls could be freely exploited.[8]

3. *Circulating Exhibits of Problems.*

After the local judgment, the individual school would send to the central agency a small number of its best or most interesting problems. The central agency would *not* judge, grade, or rank the problems of the combined group, but only form several sets of perhaps ten to twenty problems in each, so distributed as to display various approaches, analyses, and solutions. The aim of these sets would be to present high-quality problems showing many different kinds of merit, to stimulate discussion, and to acquaint all concerned with the quality of student work done throughout the country, but at the same time to recognize each problem in the light of its own assumptions. The honor of being selected for the traveling exhibit would be incentive enough to stimulate the best efforts of student and school. Each set would circulate among a regional group of schools. Upon arrival the school would hold a meeting of students, faculty, and local practitioners to discuss the solutions and quality of work displayed. Since the discussion would not directly affect student grades, attention would be directed to objective consideration of ideas and principles. It would, therefore, constitute a magnificent teaching device. At the end students, teachers, and practitioners might rank the problems independently and compare their results. Comments of the central panel, either written or recorded, could be introduced. When the several sets are returned to the central office, a composite vote might be compiled and announced. The entire exhibit, or the winners from the various problems of the year, could form a stimulating exhibition at the Annual AIA Convention, and a Student Honor Award might be presented. At the end of each problem, the results of the whole exercise would be issued to students and schools in a final illustrated report which, joined to the original study-text, would form a comprehensive record of the student's experience with one phase of architectural design.

4. Financing.

The BAID annual student fee for programs and judgments has in the past been set at $10. Since collegiate institutions consider such a fee as extra-curricular, no school can force any student to obtain such registration. If, however, a similar fee were charged as payment for necessary texts or class materials, it could be made mandatory, and, if such materials proved to be important professional resources, few students would need urging to acquire them. If only half of the schools participated in the plan, their 5000 students would pay at $10 each a total of $50,000. If all schools participated, an annual income of more than $90,000 would be available.

It is worth serious consideration as to whether the schools could by any other means increase their teaching efficiency in design so easily, so widely, and so quickly. The proposal as a whole could accomplish important functions, often requested, which the individual schools cannot achieve in isolation. It would preserve complete local responsibility for teaching methods and control. It would supply invaluable teaching aids not otherwise procurable, and it would implement without sacrifice or hazard the common review of current education in design. All of these advantages could be supported by sound and feasible financing.

It is apparent that, by creative manipulation of functional analysis, methodology, and subject matter, the progressive evolution of education in architectural design is not restricted to traditional patterns, but can be revitalized and brought into consonance with present professional and social needs. Long as this discussion has been, it remains far from definitive. Critical though these comments may appear, it must be stressed that whatever imperfections traditional methods now exhibit, they were the cradle from which arose in large measure whatever value resides in present practice. Nevertheless, it must always be remembered that method, past or future, is but a convenient framework within which dynamic, dedicated, and enlightened teachers operate by sure intuition and overflowing inspiration to fire the understanding, imagination, confidence, and ambition of eternal youth. If past method was defective, it was the human personalities that breached the gap. Future methods likewise can only be implemented by dedicated teachers.

NOTES: CHAPTER SIX

[1] *Report of the Special Committee on Architectural Education.* 1945. p. 11.
[2] Address before the Building Research Congress, London, 1951.

3 Such a course was advocated in 1941 by the First Report of the Education Committee of the Architectural Science Group of the RIBA Research Board. (*Journal, RIBA,* ser. 3, v. 48, June, 1941, pp. 133–144). During the first three years of the five-year program, science and its applications to building problems would be treated as: 1. A special, integrated course in Building Science; or 2. Two courses, one in Physics, and one in Chemistry, each of which, however, would be focused on topics pertinent to building construction. Mathematics, through the calculus, was to be required. The course in Building Science would present, in each year, progressive topics in Materials, Structural Theory, and Equipment, with pertinent scientific principles introduced as needed. During the final two years, the course would complete more advanced phases of structures, equipment, and acoustics. The full program, including mathematics, was estimated to need from 1200 to 1740 hours, the equivalent of from 80 to 116 semester credit hours in American curricula, or 3600 to 5220 hours as used in the three typical curricula in Section 3. For the largest of these three curricula, this building science program would absorb, therefore, from 45 to 66 per cent of the total available time, in contrast to the 33.6, 35.9, and 29.5 per cent for the three typical American curricula. Fortunately for the Committee, they were dealing with only one portion of the curriculum and, therefore, did not have to recommend the manner in which all the remaining necessary studies would be reduced or crowded into the 55 to 34 per cent of the total time which would be left for them. Nevertheless, the sample syllabus for the course is of great interest for its inclusiveness and organization. The Committee rightly stressed the need for integration with other parts of the curriculum and the fact that study of advanced topics in building science should be continued throughout practice.

4 Bosworth and Jones: *A Study of Architectural Schools.* p. 8.

5 *Ibid.,* pp. 37–38.

6 *Ibid.,* pp. 48–49.

7 "The Training of Architects: an Interim Report" (*Architectural Review,* vol. 107, no. 642, June, 1950, p. 373).

8 It is interesting to note that the Beaux-Arts Institute of Design conducted a student competition in 1953 for which each student selected a local site.

CHAPTER VII

Facilities, Personnel, and Administration
For Architectural Education

1. FACILITIES FOR COLLEGIATE INSTRUCTION

A. Building Space: Since buildings exert strong influences for good or bad upon those who use them, it is obvious that students of architecture can be either directly benefited or handicapped by the quality of the space provided for their work. The importance to them of direct contact with outstanding examples of architecture has already been stressed. For this reason alone, they have a legitimate claim to quarters which exemplify to the utmost degree the scientific and aesthetic precepts which they must master. It is axiomatic that a school of architecture should occupy a building which in itself comprises an integral part of the education of its occupants and becomes a teaching device in the educational program.

Such is the rare exception. In practice, most schools of architecture have been forced to inhabit dilapidated cast-off academic slums. The *1950 Survey* did not inquire specifically into the age or appropriateness of the schools' quarters, but a rough check of the 63 schools shows that at least 22—more than a third—occupy old space, which though occasionally refurbished can in no sense be considered as assisting the teaching program, except in the very negative way of pointing out what should be avoided. Five schools enjoy new space which, however, was not planned for their specific use. Only 18 schools have ever secured new buildings designed specifically for their needs, but of these only 8 are recent enough to have been influenced by new teaching methods. One of these is commodious, but distinctly uninspired; another functions satisfactorily, but the school catalog pointedly omits any exterior views. Only three, Alabama Polytechnic, the University of Arkansas, and Georgia Tech, have built quarters since World War II. Each goes far in serving as a good teaching example for the schools' students.

Just after World War II, a flood of returning veterans clamored for admission. Enrollments rose to 2.6 times those of 1939 and the shortage of instructional space formed a major crisis. Some schools escaped this emergency by firmly restricting admissions to not much more than pre-war capacities. This policy passed the pressure on to other schools which struggled to meet the situation. Temporary quarters of every description—war surplus barracks, Quonsets, lofts, and sheds—were pressed into service. But, despite the ebb of veterans, the drop in enrollments has been small, due to the continuing stimulus of population growth and high rates of construction. It is expected that this downward trend will soon reverse itself for statisticians warn that an unprecedented expansion of college enrollments will occur in the late 60's. Many universities are already initiating steps which will enable them to care for this new wave of students.

Not only are the facilities of most schools deplorable in amount and quality, but also, as measured against the potentialities of the new and intensified instruction methods suggested in *Chapter V,* even those which at first might seem adequate today form a discouraging barrier to further progress. There is negative comfort, of course, in the fact that new buildings can now be planned to accommodate improved educational methods. The Commission is convinced that faculties should carefully investigate the space implications of these suggestions whenever new quarters are contemplated. The Commission also desires to stress emphatically that, in the light of past neglect, most schools of architecture should conduct the strongest possible campaigns to obtain high priorities in the construction programs of their institutions. To this purpose, it likewise urges all members of the profession to support before the appropriate authorities the seriousness and importance of this need and to emphasize the many social and technical benefits to be derived from its satisfaction.

It must be stressed that architects and architectural educators have in the past been much too meek in pressing their claims for adequate support for their educational needs. The result has been that in expenditures per student, particularly for facilities, architecture is probably the cheapest professional curriculum on the campus. Compared with the unquestioned demands of medicine, dentistry, pharmacy, engineering, physics, chemistry, the biological sciences, agriculture, and even physical education, it has asked for and received almost nothing. In the competition for academic funds, architects will obtain little unless they demand their due with vigor and constancy.

The Commission has not attempted to investigate or formulate optimum space standards for instruction in architecture. NAAB, however, has compiled ample statistical proof of existing deficiences. Specific solutions will, of course, depend on local methods and organization, but these may be checked against NAAB findings. Nevertheless the Commission desires to emphasize certain obvious, though often neglected, principles which it considers to be fundamental to efficient and effective teaching.

Every architectural student, for example, should be assigned exclusive use of an adequate drafting desk including or adjoining ample locker storage, and these must be freely accessible for both day and evening work. Although this principle is generally accepted and applied, wherever possible, it is frequently resisted by non-architectural administrators who seek maximum, rather than optimal, use of space. Actually, multiple use can be attained if graphics and working drawing courses are held in the design studios. NAAB reported that only six of the accredited schools, with from 60 to 70 square feet of drafting space per student, could be considered better than merely adequate. Nine other schools reported from 50 to 60 square feet and were rated "acceptable." Sixteen of the remaining schools provided 41 or less square feet per student and were warned that this was grossly insufficient. When it is recalled that these areas include necessary access aisles, it is difficult to see how the very undesirable multiple use of desks can be escaped.

Some schools have found that large open drafting rooms are subject to excessive distractions due to unavoidable noise and movement. Many prefer smaller and quieter units which may perhaps be less easily supervised and lacking in wholesale cameraderie, but are definitely more conducive to concentration. Adjacent to each set of studios, but insulated against disrupting sound, a small model-making shop should be provided to encourage and facilitate the habit of quick three-dimensional sketches for studying optical effects and construction details as design exercises progress. Each studio should have ample tack boards to encourage group discussions of studies, and additional display space should be centrally arranged for each group of studios. If studios are not sufficiently isolated to allow uninterrupted talks and discussions, a small class or seminar room should be available nearby and reserved for the exclusive use of the design groups. These criteria apply to all levels of instruction.

The number, size, and equipment of classrooms depend on specific operations, but it is important that it should be possible to assign permanent and exclusive use of a unit to each primary group of courses. By this means, equipment, displays, and exhibits can be conveniently used and stored. Particular attention must be paid to securing optimal sight lines, lighting, ventilation, and acoustics, since poor scholarship can frequently be traced to neglect of these factors. Special study needs to be given to the perennial problem of note-taking when slides are used. For classes employing elaborate demonstrations, a trend emphasized in *Chapter V,* adequate preparation and storage space for apparatus should adjoin. It is especially desirable that the construction and structural classrooms, laboratories, and the materials display room be as close together as possible. Several seminar rooms are mandatory for small classes and meetings.

If the use of demonstration laboratories assumes its rightful place, the exact criteria for their design will need close study. Small material testing shops can be based on similar engineering units. The experience of Rensselaer and Iowa State will be helpful for structural laboratories, of the University of Kansas for heliometric rooms, and of Princeton for one kind of aesthetics shop. The structural computing lab is a simple, straightforward problem. Syracuse and no doubt others can give guidance for effective material displays and model shops. A shed and yard for demonstrations by building craftsmen is needed. The only precedent for a space design laboratory would seem to be the stage lofts of little theaters, but the arranging and equipping of this unit will need much thought. Darkrooms for printing drawings and for photography are valuable adjuncts. Studios for drawing, modeling, and industrial design are important units which need no elaboration.

Other familiar general facilities need only brief mention. Each school should have ample exhibition space for its exclusive use and in addition to any similar space controlled outside the school itself. Only in this way can a well-coordinated program of traveling exhibits, exchange exhibits from other schools, and materials pertinent to its own program be possible. Service space for handling, shipping, and storage should be directly accessible both to the exhibition room and to the service dock. A separate judgment room is a necessity and it must be large enough not only to accommodate the drawings but also to permit jurymen to circulate freely and the classes involved to attend as spectators. Storage for reserved drawings and models, and for miscellaneous drawings and sets of plans should adjoin. Each school has definite need for an auditorium capable of seating its entire student body so that lectures and convocations can be easily scheduled. An additional aid in fostering school morale is a lounge for meetings of student organizations and for encouraging those informal discussions between students and teachers which often result in some of the most effective education a school can offer.

No teaching facility of a school of architecture is more important than its library. Immediate access to technical journals and books is indispensable for all courses, but particularly for those in design. This definitely means that the professional literature must be located as near as possible to the design studios. The head librarians of the parent institutions often oppose the formation of separate departmental libraries distributed over the campus because supervision is more difficult, staffing for full service is more costly, and, if generally applied, access for other than departmental students is reduced. Nevertheless, whatever justice lies in such a view as a matter of general policy, the inherent needs of architectural instruction are solved only by a departmental unit. While, at certain times in the development of design exercises, architectural students can use the library in the same occasional, but concentrated manner as students in liberal arts and sciences, during most of their work architectural students must refer to the literature for innumerable small points as they crop up. If on each occasion such consultation necessitates a long trek to a central library, the cost in time becomes an intolerable waste and, as a tragic consequence, the temptation to forego extensive interruptions is often too strong to resist. A statistical check at one school revealed that proximity of the departmental library to the design studios raised the architectural ratio of borrowings per student to 7 times the ratio for other students at the central library. There is no question among architectural schools as to the importance of having a departmental library. A survey of 67 American and Canadian schools conducted in 1951 by Professor John A. Russell, Director of the School of Architecture of the University of Manitoba, found that 55 schools—82 per cent—possess departmental libraries. Of the other 12 schools, 8 had been operating a relatively short time and 5 had small enrollments, but only 2 questioned the value of separate facilities. Such unanimity of opinion cannot be controverted. Provision of adequate school library space and materials must be regarded as an absolute essential.

Unfortunately, recent increases in enrollments have not been paralleled by expansion of space assigned to departmental libraries, so that the past decade has seen a 50 per cent decline in the number of square feet of library space per student. NAAB rated as "acceptable" or better only 17 schools with more than 10 square feet per student. The highest had 32. At the other end of the scale, 15 schools with 5 square feet or less per student were considered as wholly inadequate.

Finally it remains to consider the facilities accorded the teachers themselves. Discussion of faculty responsibilities and activities is reserved for a later section, but the type and size of offices provided are intimately connected with the results demanded. If teachers are to accomplish efficiently the duties expected of them outside of their formal classes, it is only fair to furnish space conducive to their work. Such provision is all too rare. NAAB requires a minimum of 150 square feet per teacher for an "acceptable" rating, but this seems overconservative in view of the fact that many teachers must have large work tables upon which to review large drawings submitted in their classes. Several factors have contributed to deficiencies in office space. The most prevalent has been the recent general expansion of faculties which has not often been matched by proportional increases in amount of office space. Overcrowding has greatly reduced faculty productivity. It is paradoxical to employ a highly trained and expensive staff and then make it virtually impossible for it to accomplish its tasks. No industry or business could long afford to tolerate such conditions. Educational institutions often appear to take sadistic delight in devising such handicaps. The Commission believes that every institution has a duty to provide individual, or at least double, offices for the teaching staff. Each office should offer adequate privacy so that study, preparation, grading, and consultation with students need not be uselessly interrupted. Each teacher should also have his own drafting space. Institutions differ as to whether teachers should be permitted to use school facilities for the execution of private commissions, but, since such work is universally recognized as necessary for professional status and growth, some equitable adjustment might well be developed so that those who do not need complete private offices could share them at the school. The saving of travel time to distant private offices or in increased efficiency over makeshift operations at home could be devoted to teaching duties with benefits to the school as well as to the teacher.

In conclusion, it is perhaps gratuitous to add that space provided for schools of architecture should not only be adequate in amount, but also of high quality. Architectural students and teachers, despite their supercritical tendencies, are unusually responsive to attractive surroundings. This does not mean luxury, but rather an inspired application of the principles they profess. To all of these ends the Commission lends its urgent and vigorous demand (*Recommendation 10*).

B. Teaching Aids

In the past the demands of schools of architecture for teaching equipment have been very modest, and confined largely to the collection of library materials and stereopticon slides. It is obviously difficult to state what the optimal needs of a typical school might be for such materials. Columbia's Avery Library, handsomely endowed in 1890, now constitutes with its 60,000 volumes one of the greatest architectural collections in the world. It is, of course, a reference center, but Columbia also maintains an excellent working unit, the Ware Library, immediately adjacent to the school's design studios. The architectural holdings at Harvard are likewise formidable when the separate collections in Robinson Hall, the Fogg Museum, and the superlative Widener Library are considered together. Illinois' Ricker Library and those of Yale and Princeton are also outstanding. All of these, however, are exceptional. The median number of volumes in all schools was 4800 and the smallest collection reported had 1500. NAAB rates 2000 books and 500 bound volumes of periodicals as the lowest "acceptable" collection.

It is, of course, obvious that usefulness, rather than quantity and rarity measures the adequacy of an undergraduate working library. Where once the library was primarily a source for eclectic details, the new emphasis upon investigation and analysis in all courses greatly extends the types of materials it must furnish. Moreover, the undergraduate library must serve not only students, but the faculty as well. It is here especially that holdings beyond elementary levels pay rich dividends because college teachers in architecture do not have neat textbooks on which they can base their instruction. They cannot develop vital courses unless they share reports drawn from a wide community of scholars and practitioners. Penurious administrators would no doubt like to limit the library to a grudging minimum, but it is well to note that, despite interlibrary loans and microfilms, it is difficult for students and teachers to use a book which is not easily available in their library. Thus, the best minimum for the budget of the school's library is the maximum that can be obtained. The anomaly of the situation is that, once a publication is passed by, it is increasingly difficult and more costly to procure it later on. This is particularly true of periodicals.

The assembling of even an adequate library is not an easy task, but rather one which requires prolonged and sustained effort over many years. It cannot be left entirely to library staff even though its members have the best of training, judgment, and intentions. On the contrary, it is a project in which the enthusiastic cooperation of the entire faculty must be enlisted in order to spread the search for appropriate accessions and to ensure the acquisition of materials beneficial to the teaching program. This runs the occasional risk of some teachers who lack discrimination, but a balanced policy can usually be secured through a coordinating committee drawn from both the faculty and library staff. The practice of reserving all approvals to the head of the school discourages faculty interest and may well bias the development of the collection.

Although few schools can afford extensive purchasing of rare volumes, there is no reason why every school should not be able to procure at almost nominal cost microfilm copies of representative historic examples of the literature of architecture or indeed of any useful work which has passed beyond the control of copyright restrictions. Some years ago the Society of Architectural Historians broached a cooperative project by which microfilms of selected historic architectural texts could be made available to any school desiring them. The Avery librarian offered enthusiastic assistance. The war emergency discouraged the proposal at the time, but the idea was sound and should be revived. Although such resources might be used for scholarly study in only a few schools, they would be valuable auxiliary enrichments for all.

The proliferation of publications in recent decades makes it more and more difficult to focus readily upon the most pertinent materials for the topic at hand. For this reason the school's library must be served by experienced personnel who can not only guide students and faculty to desired materials, but who also will train them—often in spite of themselves—in the use of bibliographical tools and methods. The library catalog should include ample cross references. The periodical indices—the Industrial Arts Index, the Art Index, and the Engineering Index—form basic tools which, however, demand some degree of ingenuity for maximum results. Most of the larger architectural libraries also keep lists of references on special topics. The annotated bibliographies on technical subjects, published in the *Bulletin of the AIA,* render valuable assistance and should be expanded as rapidly as possible. These and other aids must be mastered if students and teachers are to profit from the resources which their library affords.

Although such tools have long existed, architectural teachers have in large part failed to exploit them. Because architectural education formerly neglected well-documented analysis, teachers were seldom trained in the effective use of professional literature, and today, even while acknowledging the increased importance of such resources, many leave to their students and the librarian the whole responsibility of discovering appropriate materials. At worst, this amounts to daring a student to find what he needs on the excuse that time-consuming search is good for the student's soul. While it is true that students need experience in using library facilities and that in the process they will become more familiar with the general content of the collection, it is also true that by more efficient direction to available sources, students would be less likely to miss pertinent materials and could devote the time saved to more rewarding browsing through the whole field. It seems obvious that teachers cannot escape the duty of attaining an intimate command of the literature of their field.

The general use of illustrated lectures in the schools—particularly in history, construction, and theory, and in lesser degree in design—has usually led to extensive collections of stereopticon slides. NAAB reported that one school possessed 46,000, while the smallest holding was only 1900. The smallest "acceptable" rating is 5000. As with books, usefulness is the criterion of excellence, and many collections are numerically large only because none are discarded. Even if needed, many slides are often of miserable quality, faded, weak in contrast, cracked, and poorly adapted as illustrations of specific points.

The procurement of slides of high quality and usefulness has always been a problem. When the process first became available, sets of general views were marketed by photographic agencies. Specific architectural material, however, had to be reproduced at second hand from printed sources by the instructor or a local photographer. Occasionally other schools could procure duplicates from the same negatives. Rarely, if ever, were these aids planned directly for the use of architectural educators. As time passed, however, some improvement was attained. The Stoedtner slides, for example, were printed from top quality negatives taken from the original monuments. In time, the larger schools secured more competent services from institutional visual aids departments. Finally, as noted already, the quality and coverage of construction slides has been vastly improved through the effort of the Visual Aids Committee of the ACSA, which not only has issued a comprehensive list of available materials, but also, with Professor Kenneth Sargent of Syracuse as editor and with the close cooperation of the Producers Council, has obtained free distribution to all schools of sets of 2 x 2 inch slides illustrating typical building materials, equipment, and processes of application. By May, 1952, each school had received 420 slides comprising 17 sets. Each slide is mounted on a 3 x 5 inch card which also carries descriptive comments to assist the instructor in preparing his class presentation. This program is being continued as fast as possible, although lack of assistance imposes an unfair burden on the editor.

It should be emphasized that, while this type of project has been welcomed in the non-controversial field of materials and construction, profitable extension to other subjects would seem to require more agreement among the schools than now exists with regard to desirable course content. Nevertheless it might develop that, if initiative were taken, many schools would use the material offered, even though they might not agree entirely in detail. The Microfilm Slide Project, sponsored by the College Art Association and achieved through the efforts of Professor Elizabeth R. Sunderland of Duke University, is an example of what can be done by cooperation. In 1947 the project issued 35mm black-and-white film strips containing 4000 slides of the history of painting from Giotto to the present day. Although purchasers had to perform the labor of mounting these 2 x 2 inch slides, all mounting materials—masks, cover glass, binding tape, and printed labels—were included in the price of 10 cents per slide. The cost of preparing the master negative was subsidized by the American Council of Learned Societies. The quality of copy was superlative, and each set of prints was matched in intensity to the purchaser's projection equipment.[1] A comparable plan was started by ACSA several years ago, in which the schools were to exchange color slides of outstanding contemporary buildings in their areas. Unfortunately, as often happens, initial enthusiasm subsided in the face of the enormous amount of volunteer effort involved.

The rise of color photography has greatly enriched all visual aids for architectural study. The presentation of stone, marble, brick, wood, and other materials of the architect's palette by this means has made it possible to emphasize and interpret the use of color too long hidden from the student by black-and-white printing processes. Procurement of suitable color slides has not been easy. While every faculty no doubt includes several devotees of photography, one teacher or even several unfortunately cannot cover much ground, especially if funds for reimbursing travel costs are lacking. From time to time, duplicates can be obtained from other individuals, who, however, as amateurs in photography or architecture or both, usually end up with random snapshots poorly adapted to teaching needs. Some schools have benefited by commissioning their European traveling fellows to bring back specific views, but usually these too fall far short of professional quality. The situation seems to call for organized effort supported by a large number of schools. Nevertheless, there remain several difficulties. The conflict between 35mm, 2 x 2 inch, and 3¼ x 4 inch sizes would have to be resolved. The 35mm size, now most widely marketed, has the advantage of being grainless and therefore capable of almost limitless magnification for projection, but its exaggerated color balance has been standardized on the basis of popular appeal. The larger color slides differ in several important respects; they have some grain, but in the opinion of many the color is better balanced. But both sizes, when duplicated, run the risk of further color distortion. Nevertheless either makes present monochrome collections obsolete. Recently the development of stereoscopic color slides has attracted wide discussion and many believe that, if an organized project is attempted, it should adopt this technique. The question needs close study since the nature of stereoscopic perspective gives greater advantage for nearby objects than for distant ones such as buildings. Despite this handicap, ingenious handling could bring startling realism to the classroom.

Motion pictures have been increasingly used in education, but despite much discussion their application to architectural training has been very limited. This has been due, in part, to an enforced dependence on either amateur production on the one hand or, on the other, on high-pressure promotional films which extoll industrial products, rather than teach sound principles. Since the market for architectural educational films is relatively small, it can hardly be expected that such works will be undertaken by commercial agencies even though some have operated effectively in the large market of visual aids for public schools. Although the interest of architectural teachers might shift if suitable films become available, there is, on the part of many, a feeling that the use of such films would normally be very limited because the speed and broad treatment characteristic of the media lends itself to general and supplemental, rather than primary use. In other words, a number of teachers who have experimented with them seem to prefer to use them as quick reviews or highlights. For this reason and because of cost, slides have remained the dominant visual aid in this field. However, given sufficient funds and talent, it is not difficult to imagine the exciting contributions that might result from well-conceived motion pictures in three dimensions and color.

Notwithstanding these difficulties, the Commission believes that through organized cooperation between ACSA and The AIA much could be done to improve the scope and quality of visual aids available to schools of architecture. The AIA might well discover that at least part of the materials thus secured might also appeal to chapters and regions as bases for seminar discussions, thereby justifying substantial support. Some of the sequences of training films, if carefully planned, might also be used for showings before the general public. Suggestion has been made that a central clearing and deposit office for slide negatives, loan sets of slides, slide films, and motion pictures would be a useful service which the Institute's staff could well perform. With respect to slides alone, investigation should be made of the slide negative pool, organized by *Taurgo, Inc.*, of New York, to which the collections of Vassar, Wellesley, New York University (Washington Square College), Oberlin, and the Metropolitan Museum of Art, have been sent on indefinite loan.[2]

The need and popularity of materials displays and model-making shops have already been sufficiently emphasized. Nor is it necessary to elaborate further upon equipment for demonstrations. Here, however, it would be helpful to publish detailed descriptions as such apparatuses are developed in order that all schools can add to and benefit by the common effort. For types which prove particularly successful, several schools could place joint orders to secure substantial savings.

Finally, the problem of textbooks must be considered. The function of a text is often misinterpreted by being viewed as forming a sort of definitive manual for its subject which must be memorized and regurgitated for quizzes and examinations. Such teaching by rote has long been obsolete. Nevertheless, the communication of basic data and operational methods must somehow be effectively projected. If major dependence is placed on lectures, course content is too often restricted to routine, elementary levels; the teacher is apt to discover that what the student has received is only a partial and garbled version of what was said; and the student has no second chance to review other than from what he has been able to commit to his notebook under the most adverse circumstances. One look at such records can fill any lecturer with dismay.

A suitable text can render valuable aid in overcoming this situation. If properly organized, it can impart fundamental facts and concepts by eye, rather than by ear; it can be reread as often as necessary for the student to absorb its information; and it can thus relieve class time for what only a skillful teacher can accomplish, that is, personal interpretation, correlation with other fields, and extension to more advanced aspects of the subject. Moreover, with adequate preparation before class, the student could then profit from class discussions, one of the most difficult but at the same time one of the most effective methods of learning. From this point of view, therefore, it is difficult to foresee any major intensification of architectural education unless appropriate texts are procurable.

Despite this obvious need, architectural education is handicapped more than any other area by the lack of suitable texts. In previous discussion of specific courses, the most obvious gaps have been noted. Reasons for this situation were explored at a joint meeting of representatives of the Commission, The AIA, and technical publishers. The two major factors which cause this deficiency were found to be: a market of such limited scale that it automatically discourages commercial ventures; and a tradition among the schools of not using texts which derives in large measure not only from the lack of texts, but also from wide diversity in course organization, teaching methods, and philosophical approach. It was noted, however, that in 1947 an ACSA survey of 39 schools revealed that 25 schools were dissatisfied with the text they were using for architectural history. A similar inquiry in 1948 regarding texts for structural theory courses seemed to disclose indifference to a plan for concerted action. The problem of enlisting cooperation between schools was again dramatized in 1952 when members of ACSA rejected a plan to prepare syllabi on building types for use in design classes.[3] Nevertheless the joint meeting also noted that the reluctance of publishers to accept architectural texts naturally discouraged potential authors from preparing manuscripts and this, in turn, eliminated the healthful competition which has been so productive in other fields.

The meeting discussed several means by which the market for such texts might be increased in order to make them economically feasible. First, some general consensus of scope, content, and method might be fostered if those who are responsible for each type of course in the several schools might meet together in committees, teaching institutes, or workshops. Second, publications might be gauged to appeal not only to students, but also to candidates and practitioners. Third, in some subjects, such as history, construction, structural theory, and interior design, texts might be planned to include the needs of students in other curricula, such as engineering, home economics, art, etc. And fourth, if such compromises would destroy their usefulness for architectural students, custom-designed texts could be produced by the aid of subsidies. The Commission is convinced that the procurement of adequate texts is a matter of vital importance to the progress of architectural education and, therefore, it urges The AIA to cooperate with ACSA in the closest possible manner in exploring these and other means of remedying a situation too long neglected (*Recommendation 11*).

In the meantime a number of teachers have reduced this deficiency to some extent by issuing syllabi for their courses. These range from the barest outlines and lists to relatively complete treatments approaching the scale of texts. Some are mimeographed; others are printed in photo-offset; almost none include pictorial illustrations. An inventory and comparison of currently used syllabi might serve as a starting point for the teacher workshops mentioned above and it might be found that the areas of general agreement are larger than now realized. Moreover it should be stressed that a syllabus benefits not only the students, but also the teacher who prepares it. The discipline of designing and writing it often leads to a fresh and skeptical inspection of hitherto unquestioned practices. Frequently the results are improved organization and the refinement of aims and methods.

2. THE STUDENT

The effectiveness of the educational process is influenced by many factors operating outside, as well as inside, the classroom. Thus it is the duty of the school to create a total educational situation in which the student can best fulfill his potentialities. This does not mean that the school can or should assume paternalistic responsibility for the success of each student, for each is ultimately accountable for his own acts. Nevertheless, the school owes to every student such counsel as will encourage and release his best energies to the accomplishment of his purpose.

The first impact of such an attitude comes at admission. By one means or another the applicant has elected to embark upon a career in architecture. The question arises, therefore, as to whether the school has a right or duty to impede this decision. Since, for most schools, enrollment capacities have been fixed by resources, policy, or fiat, it seems plausible that they should admit only those who, in their best judgment, they believe can benefit from their programs. In such cases the right to select is well established. This immediately raises the problem of the criteria by which selection is determined.

The *1950 School Survey* found that a number of methods are in use, either singly or in combination. First, is the use of the applicant's scholastic record in secondary school. Two schools ask only that applicants be graduates of approved high schools. Only four schools, however, depended on numerical grade averages—two set 75, and two set *C* as their minimum requirement. Because numerical grading standards vary considerably and are impossible to correlate, 15 schools used the applicant's rank in his graduating class. Two schools demanded standing in the upper two-thirds, seven in the upper half, and three in the upper third. In most cases these were requirements established by the parent institutions, and thus had little connection with specific promise in architecture. Several schools base admission to the professional curriculum on college grades received during a common freshman year or upon two years of work in a lower division of the university. In these cases the inclusion of an elementary architectural course may give some clue as to the applicant's professional promise. As previously noted, this shifts the responsibility for screening from the school to the lower division, but in actual practice results seem to parallel closely those of the unitary five-year curricula. Those schools which demand full or partial liberal arts training naturally depend on the applicant's college record which may or may not reveal fitness for professional studies.

A second method is to administer various entrance tests. Today, with most secondary schools accredited as to general quality, these tests rarely re-examine the student's mastery of his secondary subjects. Rather they sample his achievement in fundamental knowledge or his command of reasoning or his range of interests. Thus, eight schools use the College Aptitude Test, and two the American Council of Education Psychological Examination. These likewise deal with general matters which bear only obliquely on professional promise. Four schools reported use of an architectural aptitude test for applicants from secondary schools. Subsequent communications from three of these schools indicate that the tests explore general, rather than architectural aptitudes. The fourth school, Cooper Union, requires all applicants, including non-architects, to take a battery of tests, part of which consists of three 40-minute design problems—one in architecture, one in sculpture, and one in drawing. The problems are then judged by members of the faculty on the basis of design and content, but without regard to technique of presentation. For students in architecture and art, correlations between the whole testing program and later academic work have over a fifteen year period been relatively low—0.26 to 0.48, as against 0.60's and 0.70's in the same institution's School of Engineering—and this fact has been interpreted as evidence of the influence of other non-academic factors upon success in school. No segregation of architectural students, as distinct from art students, was available. It seems clear that the problem of testing architectural aptitude should receive detailed investigation.

The third method is by direct first hand appraisal. Two schools require letters of recommendation; two others specify recommendation from the applicant's secondary school, presumably the principal. Two report that applicants are interviewed by the school. The first two mentioned above ask that samples of art work or other drawings accompany the letters.

Thirteen schools used various combinations of these methods.

In summary, it is clear that, while most schools decline to admit applicants who do not seem prepared for any training at the college level, prior judgment of fitness for a professional career in architecture is another matter. In almost all cases, there is little else to go on except the applicant's own decision, and too often this has been reached with only the most superficial idea of the nature and qualifications needed for the vocation selected. Under these circumstances, the schools must continue to use present shot-gun methods. At best these assume that applicants who have done well in secondary schools will excel in a collegiate curriculum in architecture, regardless of the difference in character between general and professional courses. While this often seems true, there is a tendency to forget those with good secondary records who do not succeed in architectural studies. Moreover it is worth noting that the two schools of architecture which have worked most assiduously to screen their students recently reported no significant improvement in their subsequent ratios of withdrawals and failures. At worst, present selection methods lose to the profession not only those students who do not respond to the over-verbalized instruction common to most secondary and collegiate education, but also those who mature slowly. It is a temptation to discount such applicants, but many valuable and successful practitioners are visually and constructively, rather than verbally, minded, and every educator can cite numerous students who have found themselves only after discouraging delays. Cynics have wondered whether this or that famous architect of the past could today obtain a license to practice; they might also wonder whether they could gain admission to a school of architecture.

Three recommendations, discussed in Section 2, *Chapter V* in connection with guidance during pre-professional education, would likewise greatly improve current admission methods. Trial experience in an architect's office, access to a suitable guidance manual, and opportunities to discuss the choice of a career with a sympathetic practitioner could furnish the school with more specific evidence of interest, motivation, and perhaps promise. Most important, however, would be the development of a thoroughly validated aptitude test gauged to discover traits and capabilities of proven correlation to professional competence. Such a test would be of service to both school and applicant. Although much speculation has been directed to this end, no systematic research has been attempted. Until this is accomplished, the selection of students will remain primarily a process of self-selection by trial and error with all of its accompanying frustrations, waste, and embitterment.

While the primary objective of professional education must always be the training of true professionals, it must be repeated that too narrow an interpretation of this aim may well endanger its attainment. The field of architecture requires many diverse capabilities. The difficulty of predicting precise results for any educational process should likewise encourage caution. Furthermore those who do not attain full professional status are yet able to perform valuable service in secondary or auxiliary capacities. Unless such alternatives exist, the implication is that all products of the schools who do not become practitioners have worked in vain. This is certainly contrary to experience and logic.

Once admitted to the school, the student faces many perplexities, both personal and professional. He must make as rapidly as possible a whole series of adjustments: living away from home; disciplining his own time and efforts; new relationships with fellow students; more exacting standards of instruction; the opportunities and distractions of a modern organized campus; and the profession he has chosen. The decisions, attitudes, and habits he acquires in his college years can be of great importance not only for his professional education, but also for all later growth. For help in solving most of these problems, he will turn to the example of his classmates and the advice of his teachers. It is for this reason that the quality of the morale of the professional school, for both teachers and students, takes on such importance. New students are quick to sense indifference, ineptness, and ill will, but there will be few who, under the spell of wholesome, friendly challenge, will not be delighted to expand their first naïve eagerness into that mature enthusiasm which springs from confidence in a well-understood purpose and program.

The role of the faculties in stimulating high morale within the schools is obvious, but there is also much of unique importance that the profession and its members can do to reinforce and extend their efforts. It will be of little avail for teachers to stress the professional spirit if to students the profession and its members remain aloof and unapproachable. The establishment of cooperative liaison, however, must be predicated on an atmosphere of mutual understanding, regard, and good will between teachers and practitioners. Fortunately the contacts fostered by chapters of The AIA can provide a firm basis for such cooperation.

The contributions of architects to students can take many forms. Visits to the schools will indicate interest, lead to increased understanding of the educational program, and offer occasions for informal discussions with teachers and students. These, in turn, will no doubt bring more formal opportunities to discuss the problems of practice and to report actual projects and their lessons. Students would likewise appreciate invitations to inspect construction operations when these are accessible. Such contributions would not constitute a hardship on architects because they would require a minimum of preparation and would carry the strong appeal of direct experience. They would, moreover, constitute a positive educational approach, in contrast to the negative effect sometimes conveyed by dwelling upon the deficiencies of youth and the infallibility of experience.

Practitioners can also perform a valuable service to professional students by serving as informal advisers. This relationship can grow naturally out of guidance rendered before entering school or during summer employment, and it can easily lead to continued counsel when the student passes to candidacy. Few architects realize the degree to which sympathetic human interest inspires the recipient to strive to merit it. It would be highly advantageous for both students and the profession if the formation of such relationships is not left to chance, but instead is encouraged and assured by systematic cultivation. The Commission urges that The AIA stimulate its chapters to work towards this end (*Recommendation 12*).

The most direct stimulus which The AIA can exert for the enhancement of professional morale among students is by emphasizing and encouraging its student chapters. The idea of such units, stimulated by the success of similar groups maintained by several engineering societies, was first broached for architectural students in the late 30's. A student chapter was installed at Kansas State College through action of the local Institute chapter. In 1938, after some hesitation, The AIA authorized its chapters to accept student associate members and to sponsor student branches in schools within their jurisdiction. Soon a number of branches were installed, but during war years such activities were largely suspended. After 1946, however, The AIA encouraged the direct formation of student chapters. By 1953, 41 such units had been established.

The purpose of the student chapter is to foster within architectural students understanding of and adherence to those attitudes and standards which must characterize a professional architect. The most effective and appropriate means of achieving this goal is conceived to be through the guidance of and close affiliation with the profession's primary society, The AIA. Contact with The Institute is provided at four levels; national, regional, the local AIA Chapter, and through teacher-members. Thus, during school years, a natural pattern is established by which the student, upon entering candidacy, can proceed immediately to more direct association with his professional society.

Professional morale can be cultivated by the student chapter in many ways. The very act of voluntary association of like-minded students stimulates more active awareness of and interest in professional matters. Participation in student chapter work, as officers and as members of committees, provides students with excellent training in responsibility, cooperation, planning, and leadership. Such experiences have life-long value. Enlightened administration of the chapter's activities can stress the opportunities of self-planned education beyond the regimen of the formal classroom, an attitude of fundamental importance as the scope of professional studies expands. Such realization can also instill a wholesome interest in the welfare and development of the school itself.

The range of worth-while chapter activities is very large. Formal lectures on professional topics—technical subjects, the procedure of practice, the nature and work of the profession and The Institute—by local or visiting speakers can reinforce and supplement the schools' courses. Students themselves should present occasional programs —talks, reports, panel discussions, and debates—thereby gaining valuable training in public speaking. Films, displays, and technical demonstrations likewise provide ex-

225

cellent program media. The chapter can also sponsor and organize other useful events, such as field trips, interschool exhibits, a school calendar and news sheet, a yearbook, an annual school banquet, and even occasional social gatherings.

Through the student chapter, students can gain beneficial contacts with practitioners, either by inviting them to participate in programs or meetings, or by themselves attending the sessions of the sponsoring AIA chapter, regional conferences, and the Annual Convention of The AIA at which special student sessions have been organized in recent years. It is likewise feasible to hold regional student meetings.

The successful operation of a student chapter depends on many factors. The over-organization of most campuses creates such a barrage of competitive demands that students too often either dissipate their time and effort among worthy but extraneous activities, or become indifferent to all opportunities. In such a situation, vigorous emphasis is needed to acquaint students with the importance of cultivating professional contacts. As in any organization, the maintenance of a core of enthusiastic members, willing and able to devote the time and energy to its work, is a fundamental condition. The natural turnover of school enrollments, variations in students' personalities, and the accidents of elections inevitably affect the chapter's strength. It is here, however, that the perennial services of a wise and tactful faculty adviser are most valuable as a stabilizing force. While students themselves should take primary responsibility, they usually need and welcome the active support and aid of respected teachers. Since a strong student chapter program can contribute outstanding benefits not only to the individual student, but to the entire school as well, its encouragement deserves, and usually receives, active faculty emphasis.

The Institute has come to realize the importance of its student chapter program and has made considerable progress in assisting in its development. It issues a *Student Chapter Handbook* which gives sound advice on organization and activities. It distributes an annual review of chapter reports. It furnishes modest subsidies to enable student representatives from nearby schools to attend its conventions. It has been helpful in arranging lectures by leading architects. The Institute might well spearhead the organization of summer field trips suggested in *Section 4, Chapter V*. Thus far, however, it has been difficult to infuse a spirit of solidarity among the widely dispersed units due to the absence of suitable channels of communication. Since The Institute's existing journals have not performed this mission, in 1951 a considerable group urged the publication of a periodical by and for students. The Institute granted financial aid, but thus far the plan has not matured. The accomplishment of such a goal by voluntary and inexperienced personnel is a formidable undertaking. Nevertheless, since it would serve a most important function in enhancing student morale, suitable arrangements should be made to achieve it.

The Commission believes that the development of the student chapter program has been a signal advance and that its further expansion constitutes an opportunity which will return major dividends to the profession and The Institute. It should be pointed out that these benefits will accrue not only to students and the schools, but that contact with youth can also bring a rewarding stimulus to sponsoring AIA Chapters and their members. Therefore the Commission urges continued and close study of means by which the program can be refined and intensified (*Recommendation 13*).

In stressing the development of student chapters, the Commission at the same time recognizes the functions and contributions which previously existing national architectural fraternities and honor societies, such as Alpha Rho Chi, Scarab, Gargoyle, and others, have performed for their members and the schools in which they are active. By recognizing excellence in academic studies, the honor societies reinforce the objectives of the schools, and in their activity programs they offer the added stimulus which can spring from the association of superior students. Nevertheless, there is need for an overall unifying organization open to all qualified students, and operating within the framework of the profession and The Institute. Thus, though the rosters of chapter, fraternity, and society may overlap in part, there is no conflict in their goals all of which emphasize professional growth. Many purely local groups have served as a logical nucleus for the establishment of student chapters.

Incentive for academic excellence can also be stimulated through awards and prizes. For many years, The Institute has annually conferred its School Medal on the leading scholar of each school's graduating class. Many schools have received gifts with which to award prizes—in the form of fellowships, cash, or books—for outstanding scholastic achievement in the whole program or in particular subjects. Some educators feel that such awards tend to become ends in themselves and thus distract students from realizing their individual responsibilities to fulfill their highest potentialities. They point out the similar danger of overemphasizing grades at the expense of motivation based on sincere desire for personal growth. They recall the abuses of competition which have already been noted as plaguing the *Ecole des beaux-arts*. The problem, however, is not "either-or," but the retention of a just balance. If the goal of personal growth is stressed, and if awards take cognizance, at least in part, of this basic aim, recognition of success in this endeavor can be safely and profitably accorded. In view of the tremendous pressure exerted by the welter of non-scholarly activities which crowd present-day campuses, awards for academic success can stress the fundamental purpose of the school. For this reason, the source of the award often connotes more prestige than the instrinsic cost of the prize. This is especially true if the donor is a part of the profession because this fact underscores the value which the donor and the profession attach to students' success in gaining professional education.

Morale is also one of the basic factors influencing the continuation of students in school. Student mortality is also affected by change of goals after initial experience, inability to meet minimum scholastic standards, financial difficulties, and problems arising in personal affairs, such as health, marriage, and domestic problems. Furthermore, the mortality records of the schools are also related to their admission requirements. For example, a school which admits only those who have survived pre-professional college training will automatically show fewer losses than a school which admits applicants direct from secondary schools. As already noted with regard to admission tests, a pre-professional college record can reveal ability to pursue regular academic studies, but it gives little, if any, specific indication of professional aptitude.

Since the applicant with previous college study is also older and presumably has exercised more mature judgment in selecting his vocation, he may be better motivated and adjusted and thus more liable to complete the professional curriculum. Nevertheless, to the extent that the verbal bias of normal academic instruction screens out those whose major talent lies in creative visual arts, the effect is to prevent them from attempting architectural studies.

The *1950 School Survey* obtained only limited statistical data on student mortality; 28 schools reported recent studies. For 25 of them, an average of 76 per cent of all entering students continued into the second year of the curriculum. The highest ratios were 90 per cent at three schools and 88 in another. Two of these four schools require pre-professional collegiate training. Two schools reported the smallest ratio, 50 per cent. For 26 schools, the average per cent of new students continuing until graduation was 48. The highest was 85 per cent, and the lowest three reported 10, 13, and 24 per cent.

Another approach to student mortality utilizes the annual enrollment reports issued by ACSA. Analysis of 47 schools for the academic year 1952–1953 reveals 2652 new students, who comprised 29.4 per cent of a total enrollment of 9015. In a five-year curriculum, such a ratio is entirely plausible. Of these schools, the 29 public institutions, with 67.5 per cent of all students, had a ratio of 30.3 per cent, and the 18 private schools, with 32.5 per cent of all students, had a ratio of 27.6 per cent. This difference is negligible. The range of the ratios was large:

Per cent	Schools	Per cent	Schools
17.8–19	4	35–39	4
20–24	8	40–44	3
25–29	14	45–49	2
30–34	10	Max. 51.4	1

The highest and four lowest ratios all occurred in private institutions. At first thought, it is difficult to explain why, in a five-year program, ratios could drop below 29 per cent, but this situation is probably the result of a period of gradual decline in the size of entering classes. Indeed, in 1952 this lowered the relative proportions of freshmen and sophomores in almost all schools. In a period of stable enrollments, an over-all ratio of 31 per cent would probably represent a more balanced entering class. The higher ratios, above an arbitrary 40 per cent, seem to indicate excessive mortalities in an eighth of the schools.

ACSA also reports the number of first professional degrees awarded, and this may be assumed as equivalent to the number of fifth-year senior students. In 1952–1953 in the same 47 schools, a total of 1416 seniors comprised 15.7 per cent of the total enrollment. In public schools, the ratio was 14.7 per cent and in private schools, 17.8 per cent. The lowest was 4.0 per cent and the highest was 37.8. 17 schools had ratios between 10 and 14 per cent, and 15 schools between 15 and 19 per cent. Since in 1952 the senior class of five-year curricula would have begun their studies in 1948, during peak conditions, it is probable that in a more stable situation 15 per cent would constitute a more normal proportion of seniors. This would seem to indicate a survival of 48 per cent of the 31 per cent which formed the entering class.

While this survival ratio would seem to affirm the average reported to the *1950 School Survey,* in actuality it does not take into account those seniors who entered as transfers with advanced standing. In certain schools, transfers constitute a considerable, and even predominant portion of total entries. Furthermore, since previous collegiate study has already screened such transfers automatically, their survival ratio in professional schools can be expected to surpass that of students entering directly from secondary schools.

Although no post-war studies of the survival of architectural students are available, the operation of this process can be ascertained from a detailed record of mortality compiled for a large state school for the years 1931–1941. Of 1160 entries over the ten year period, 631—54.4 per cent—came directly from secondary schools and 529—45.6 per cent—were transfers; 52 per cent of these transfers had had one year or less of previous college work; 31 per cent had had one to two years; and 17 per cent had had more than two years; 478—41 per cent—of all entries graduated; 189 of these had entered directly from secondary schools, giving a survival ratio of 30 per cent; and 289 had entered as transfers, a survival of 55 per cent; 49 per cent of those transfers who had had one year or less of previous collegiate work obtained professional degrees; 59 per cent of those with one to two years; and 66 per cent of those with more than two years. Thus the screening effect of earlier studies is obvious. It should be noted, however, that of those entering from secondary schools, 405—64 per cent—continued into the second year of the professional curriculum. The 189 graduates furnished by this group comprised 47 per cent of these survivors of the freshman year. This ratio was thus practically the same as that for transfers who had had one year or less of previous college training. The study also showed that 72 per cent of the students entering from secondary schools survived 4 semesters of professional study, while 78 per cent of the transfers survived 2 such semesters. This close correspondence indicates that the effects of the two avenues of study gave practically the same survival result. It is interesting to note that of the 682 students who did not complete their studies 63 per cent had a scholastic average under *C* at the time of withdrawal; 37 per cent, therefore, withdrew for other than scholastic reasons. During the period studied, financial difficulties probably were the predominant cause.

While these indications of mortality may seem high, they are closely paralleled in engineering. A study conducted by ETS in 1952 surveyed the survival of 13,000 non-veteran freshman admitted to four-year curricula in 101 engineering colleges in September, 1948; 44 per cent survived to graduate. Of the 56 per cent loss, 57 per cent had withdrawn by the end of the first year, 28 per cent at the end of the second year, 10 per cent at the end of the third year, and 4 per cent during the fourth year; 46.9 per cent of withdrawals were due to scholastic deficiencies, 41 per cent were due to military service, change of schools, academic discipline, etc., 6 per cent were due to changes to other fields, and 7 per cent were due to personal and family problems.[4] A four-year school experiencing such withdrawals would have an enrollment distribution, omitting transfers, of 37.6 per cent freshmen, 25.5 per cent sophomores, 19.5 per cent juniors, and 17.4 per cent seniors. Year to year survivals would be 67.7, 76.5, and 89.2 per cents. If these ratios are applied to a five-year curriculum and a survival of 95 per cent is assumed at the end of the fourth year, the enrollment distribution by the five classes would be: 32.3, 21.8, 16.8, 14.9, and 14.2 per cents. These are remarkably close to the averages already observed in architectural enrollments. The slightly higher survival to graduation in architecture and the small decline in architectural enrollments during the period studied fully account for the differences in class proportions.

Although the depression of 1930–1940 subsided, the cost of education has remained a formidable problem for both students and the schools. Post-war inflation has increased not only students' cost of living, but likewise the cost of institutional operation. The *1950 School Survey* reported tuitions charged by 60 schools. Two privately endowed schools charge no tuition whatsoever. Three state schools charge no tuition for residents of their respective states. For the other 55 schools, the maximum tuition was $800 per year. For in-state students the minimum tuition was $30. The average tuition for these 55 schools, using resident rates where offered, was $287 and the median was $165. Thirty-two schools, mostly in state-supported institutions, set a higher tuition for out-of-state students. This differential ranged from $30 to $350 per year, with an average of $177 and a median of $160. For out-of-state students the lowest total tuition was $100, and for the 58 schools operating on this basis, the average was $373 and the median $315. The highest total tuition charged by a school which used an out-of-state differential was $507. It should be noted that this was exceeded by 13 private schools whose tuitions ranged from $512 to $660, with an average of $588. Thus, for a five-year curriculum, the total tuition cost for a student who maintains the normal schedule can vary from nothing to $4000, with an average of $1316. The average total cost for a student who cannot or does not choose to exercise residence privileges was $1804. In some schools which charge low tuition, this is offset by other required fees, but the *1950 School Survey* did not investigate these disguised charges. Neither did the *1950 School Survey* attempt to discover the costs of subsistence, texts, or supplies. No doubt these vary so much with particular circumstances that any generalization would be futile. It is certain, however, that the total cost of academic training in architecture represents a considerable financial investment ranging from $5000 to $10,000.

Such an expenditure probably bars many talented students from selecting an architectural career. Nevertheless, almost all institutions offer some financial aid in the form of scholarships; 45 schools of architecture reported possession of funds for scholarships and prizes. The total amount available per year was $79,975, and the average per school was $1775. The maximum reported for one school was $9000, the minimum $25, and the median $650. Most institutions also maintain revolving loan funds for worthy students, but requests for loans have steadily declined. With the general expansion of free scholarship funds, it is not surprising that those in need are reluctant to assume the obligation of repayment, especially if this must be met during the first years after graduation. Given the choice, most students apparently prefer to obtain part-time or occasional employment rather than accept student loans. At present such employment on or off campuses has been relatively easy to find. Its greatest drawback is its distraction of students' time, energy, and attention from primary academic duties and worth-while extracurricular activities.

From time to time various proposals have been made to alleviate unequal opportunities for higher education which arise from economic causes. Thus far the most comprehensive plan suggested is that formulated in 1948 by the President's Commission on Higher Education. National expansion, the Commission noted, will demand a very sharp increase in advanced education and it called for an undergraduate enrollment in 1960 of 4 million students. In order to eliminate economic status as a basis of participation in higher education, the Commission proposed the abolition of fees for the first two years and reduction of fees for later years. In addition, it urged the establishment of an extensive system of federal scholarships in number equal to a fifth of all college and university enrollments, and with stipends adjusted to need, but with a maximum allowance to any individual of $800 for an academic year.[5] Congress rejected the plan and, in view of its current temper, there seems little likelihood of its revival in the immediate future. Nevertheless, as its proponents have pointed out, it would merely extend to collegiate levels the principle of public responsibility long ago accepted for secondary schools and it is entirely conceivable that future shortages in trained manpower will require its ultimate application to higher education as well.

For the student who undertakes professional training, not only its cost, but also its length creates many problems. In architecture the mandatory increase of curricula from four to five years has accentuated this situation. Moreover it must be recognized that the standard five-year length can easily be prolonged through accidents of health, scholastic difficulty, and even of scheduling the required courses. While the *1950 School Survey* did not investigate actual vs. scheduled completion of the five-year program, the detailed study of student mortality, previously cited, indicated that for a four-year curriculum over the ten-year period 1931–1941, 47.6 per cent of the graduates who had entered directly from high school received their degree at the end of eight semesters; 16.9 per cent continued for an extra semester; 27.6 per cent required two extra semesters; and 7.9 per cent took from three to five extra semesters. The survey of engineering enrollments, previously cited, found that only 75 pr cent of those graduating did so within four years; 21 per cent of these graduates had to repeat one or more courses; 12 per cent had been on probation during their course; and 11 per cent had attended summer sessions, in most cases presumably in order to continue on schedule. Some students deliberately choose to extend their program in order to enjoy a more leisurely pace or to devote more time to certain courses. For example, in the foregoing architectural study more than one-seventh of all graduates who added one or two semesters had an overall grade average of *B* or better, and one-quarter had an average midway between *B* and *C*.

A student who follows a regular schedule enters elementary school at the age of 6, secondary school at 14, college at 18, and receives his diploma in architecture at 23.

231

Candidate training absorbs another one to five years, with an average of three, which brings registration at the age of 26. The recent addition of two years of military service delays this to age 28. Any deviation from standard schedule can easily postpone it to 29 or 30. Pursuit of graduate studies can add one or two years more. Thus almost a fifth of adulthood must be passed in preparation. The personal and social consequences of this long regimen are very real. Productive maturity and economic self-support are deferred. The natural urge for marriage, home, and family must usually be suppressed. Moreover the beginning of participation in the life of the community is long delayed.

This lengthening of professional training—a trend seen in medicine and law as well as in architecture—has been motivated by the laudable aim of raising the competence of practitioners, and the need is for more, rather than less, emphasis upon this goal. It is also true that the addition of a few years can add measurably to the maturity of candidates. Nevertheless there is grave danger that in the process of achieving such ends, the social and personal costs will be so multiplied that the total result will be less, rather than more, efficiency. Unfortunately the educational program in architecture has over the years grown by a process of accretion and with little overall evaluation or integration. Any attack on the problem should aim not only at increased competence, but on reduction of length and cost as well. Agreement on a specific solution is made more difficult because certain concepts and requirements have been long accepted, have acquired the odor of sanctity, and are now defended by vested interests. Certain elements of the program, such as the length of military service, are fixed by agencies uncontrolled by professional aims. Reduction in overall length and cost must come, therefore, from greater efficiency throughout the educational process.

Some critics would shorten time spent in education by adopting permanently the accelerated schedule used during World War II. Under such a system, a secondary curriculum could be reduced from four to three calendar years, and a professional curriculum from five to four. A total of two full years could thus be eliminated. Nevertheless, educators agree that, under such a tempo, the quality of student work declines sharply. The war period itself was so fraught with complicating factors that objective evaluation of acceleration is impossible. During the early post-war years, however, the effects of acceleration were clearly evident. Many veterans wished to complete their training as rapidly as possible, but, despite this strong motivation, most found that continuous course work beyond a certain point yields diminishing returns. Many, realizing that they had gone stale, that their power of absorption had fagged, and that their work, especially in design, was falling far short of their real capabilities, dropped out for a term and upon return reassumed their studies with refreshed energy. Continuous attendance also prevents students from gaining vacation experience in offices, from earning funds for further schooling, or from beneficial visits to significant buildings. Even the ablest and most conscientious teachers found that acceleration drained their energies and greatly reduced their effectiveness. Without any doubt the whole experiment proved that acceleration defeats its own objectives.

The problem of length still remains, and a number of solutions have been suggested. One has proposed a "middle school" to include grades 7 to 10. Those who do not intend to follow advanced or professional studies would proceed to a terminal two-year junior college program of general or vocation character. Those who show aptitude for advanced studies, research, or the professions, would undertake a rigorous two-year intensive curriculum in the physical and social sciences and the humanities in a collegiate school similar to a German *gymnasium* or a French *lycée*. After two years of required military service, the student would then proceed to professional studies at a university. Because previous college studies would take care of the general and basic courses which now absorb much of professional curricula, the latter could probably be completed in four years. With a three year candidateship, the total length would still bring age at registration to 27.[6]

A variation of this proposal suggests the admission to the professional schools of certain students who have completed three years of secondary schooling, who have mastered certain prescribed subjects, and who by their superior scholastic record and by appropriate tests show promise of success in advanced studies. While such a plan would not bar those who need full secondary training or who do not choose careers until later, it could still save an entire year for a considerable number of more mature, industrious, and foresighted students. From the standpoint of the university, the architectural graduate would have the same eight-year total schooling—three secondary and five professional—as the normal four plus four provides. Moreover the university's entrance requirements can be easily satisfied by a temporary certificate from the secondary school which could be exchanged for a regular secondary school diploma upon successful completion of the first year's work in the architectural school. The basic principle is thus applicable to existing school systems and is, moreover, identical to that already used in a more extreme form by the University of Chicago.

It is obvious that such a plan would be pointless if it simply transfers to the professional curriculum subjects now delegated to the secondary program. It seems quite feasible to expect, however, that the twelve major courses which normally comprise three years of work in the secondary program can include all the subjects now usually prescribed for entrance to architectural schools. The twelve courses can thus include three units of mathematics ($1\frac{1}{2}$ in algebra and $1\frac{1}{2}$ in geometry), three of rhetoric and literature, two of language, one of science, one of history, and two electives. The fourth year of rhetoric usually demanded could be safely replaced by the universally required college freshman course, especially in view of the fact that only superior students would be permitted to participate in the shortened program and that current language mechanics placement tests can be used.

Another feature of the proposal would be the scheduling of military service between the second and third years of the professional curriculum when the normal student is 19–20 years of age. The first two years of professional studies could thus serve as a probationary period during which actual experience in several technical courses can permit both student and school to judge his future potentialities for a professional career. Upon return, those who have displayed sufficient promise can com-

233

plete the three remaining years of academic preparation, while those who have shown a lack of aptitude for advanced academic work, or who for other reasons cannot complete the program, can be given a one-year terminal course designed to fit them for drafting or other positions in architectural offices, or for work in other phases of building. To a degree present programs already operate in this manner, but the purpose of the terminal course here proposed is to round out the vocational training of as many of these students as possible and thus make them more useful and available for the profession. The completion of this terminal course could be rewarded by the granting of an appropriate certificate. It should be recognized, moreover, that the election of such a course need not bar these students from further professional growth, since they could still become eligible in time for admission to registration examinations and their academic years would count in full toward the longer requirement for office experience. Students who mature at a slower pace would be thus saved the frustration and stigma of apparent inability. On the other hand, those who would continue into advanced studies could concentrate on intensive professional training.

Finally the possibility of intensifying the studies of the remaining students suggests that this, together with a more orderly and purposeful candidate training program—which will be discussed in *Chapter VIII*—might well permit the duration of candidacy to be reduced from three to two years. The total length of training, including military service, would thus be cut by two years and the normal age at registration would become 26. It must be noted, of course, that such a reduction would affect only those who could be accepted after three years of secondary schooling. The establishment of the exact threshold of performance would require careful experimentation, but it is entirely possible that one-third to one-half of present architectural students could participate in such a system without adversely affecting current standards of quality. The over-all effect of the system might well prove to raise these standards, and the promise of increased overall productivity suggests that it should be seriously investigated by The Institute, NAAB, ACSA, and NCARB (*Recommendation 14*).

3. THE FACULTY

The faculties of the schools of architecture play a crucial role in organizing and administering the basic educational process whose purpose is optimal student preparation for candidacy. It is the teacher who furnishes the student's first close contact with the profession, who cultivates his motivation, and who contrives the learning situations in which he can best discover for himself a gradually expanding mastery of knowledge, skill, and judgment. It is patent that the quality of academic education is thus in direct proportion to the effectiveness of its faculties. It is also clear that the availability of a sufficient number of able teachers is of primary importance to the profession.

The 1950 statistical report of the ACSA disclosed that the 63 U. S. schools used 1454 teachers in conducting technical instruction;[7] 993 of this total were members of faculties of the architectural schools, and of these 651 held full-time appointments and 342 on part-time status performed service equivalent to 183 full-time teachers. The remaining 461 taught technical subjects for architectural students, but were members of other faculties in their institutions. The report does not indicate the full-time equivalent of these teachers, nor does it include the large number of instructors who taught non-technical courses used in the architectural curricula. Since the total undergraduate enrollment of these schools was 13,491 in 1950 (*Table 56*), there were 16.18 architectural students for each of the 834 full-time teachers (651 + 183) on the architectural faculties. The actual student-teacher ratio, however, was considerably higher because the same architectural faculties also provided some instruction for 6829 non-professional students. Calculation of a realistic ratio is also obstructed by the fact that some schools teach all technical courses while others delegate a varying number to other faculties.

Comparison of schools of architecture with regard to the number of teachers provided relative to the teaching load is furnished by NAAB which calculates for each school inspected a "Faculty-Task Ratio." This index indicates the total adjusted student credits per teacher. NAAB assigns arbitrary evaluations to these ratios, as follows: 1200 and under, Very High; 1200-1500, High; 1500-1800, Acceptable; 1800-2100, Low; more than 2100, Very Low. During the period 1949-1953, NAAB conducted 43 inspections of 39 schools. Omitting earlier duplicate inspections, the Faculty-Task Ratios observed were rated as follows:

	All Schools	Private Schools	Public Schools
Very High	15	8	7
High	13	5	8
Acceptable	6	1	5
Low	3	1	2
Very Low	2	1	1

The most favorable ratio reported was 777 and the least was 2690. It must be emphasized that the evaluations currently used by NAAB do not constitute absolute standards based on a definitive analysis of the most desirable ratios of staff to load, but rather they compare current conditions in the schools. If NAAB were to be delegated definite powers to improve these conditions, it would then be possible to upgrade its standards and insist that the schools meet them.

The Commission investigated architectural faculties by means of two questionnaires, the first directed to heads of the 63 schools and the second to all teachers in these schools. Only 3 schools failed to reply;[8] 455 teachers responded; this was 45.8 per cent of the total of 993 listed by the ACSA report, and it is well to note that this exceeds the 34.5 per cent response of all the registered architects to the *Survey's* General Questionnaire by 32.7 per cent. Heads of the 60 responding schools reported a total of 922 teachers. Assuming ACSA figures for the 3 non-responders, their 39 additional teachers brings the total to 961. The difference of 32 between the ACSA and the *Survey* totals may perhaps be due to the fact that they were compiled in different terms of the academic year. Additional data were secured by the *1950 Survey's* General Questionnaire which included those teachers who are also registered architects. The resulting data provide the first comprehensive statistical inventory of the faculties which serve the basic educational needs of the profession.

The activities of architectural teachers may be grouped in five general categories: instruction, school, institution, profession, and community. It will be well to review these duties in some detail in order to establish a frame of reference by which the accomplishments and problems of these faculties can be objectively appraised.

The most obvious function which the teacher performs is the conduct of formal instruction so designed as to exploit all the potentialities of the learning process, create the most effective situation conducive to its application, and stimulate the student to the fullest realization of his opportunities and possibilities. It must be emphasized, of course, that personal growth—the mastery of knowledge and skills and the attainment of judgment and wisdom—remains the ultimate responsibility of the student. Education is not the filling of a passive vessel nor the cultivation of a hothouse plant; it is rather the dynamic self-disciplining of body, mind, and spirit in the pursuit of understanding, capacity, and fulfillment. In such a process the teacher becomes a mentor and collaborator who can facilitate its operation by suggesting methods, organizing and interpreting content, clarifying obscurities, illustrating techniques, and guiding experimental application. Under such conditions, authoritorian didacticism is obsolete, but the role of the able teacher expands greatly in scope and importance.

Although this basic concept of instruction is pertinent to all architectural education, the diversity of its many phases requires great ingenuity in adapting it to specific subjects. In some subjects the lecture method must still be used due to the absence of other means of communicating information. The difficulties of oral presentation have already been noted in *Chapter VI,* but it often remains the only feasible method. As soon as students have acquired sufficient grasp of content, the lecture can be supplemented by student participation in discussions of its meaning and applications. In both instances, the teacher must strive to overcome methodological and personal pitfalls if he is to produce satisfactory results. The architectural curriculum contains numerous studio and laboratory courses in which teachers lead students primarily to the acquisition of skills or to facility in solving illustrative exercises. In these subjects student participation is immediate and direct, but here too teachers must take care to employ the full learning process in order to ensure that the student obtains equal command of both theory and application.

The organization and practice of every phase of architectural instruction demands far more than mere presence in the classroom or studio. Each step of each course must be carefully planned if it is to make its maximum contribution to the whole course and the entire curriculum. The design of a specific course thus requires of its teacher the closest liaison with the whole faculty and its general objectives. Moreover, if the course is to maintain a vital relationship to its field, its content must be selected on the basis of the fullest knowledge of that field and it must be periodically reviewed and revised. All of this means that the building of an effective course is a dynamic, cumulative operation requiring thoughtful and continuous preparation. It is difficult for laymen to appreciate this fact, but every conscientious teacher knows its truth. The school which fails to allow its teachers adequate time for such preparation soon defeats its own ends.

Finally, instruction, if it is to fulfill the complete learning process, must evaluate student achievement in such a manner as to train him in self-appraisal. Thus, the correction and grading of quizzes, reports, problems, and examinations is not the awarding of prizes, but an integral function of the learning process. This means that each test and exercise must be designed to promote definite educational objectives and that each student must be advised in detail as to the quality of his performance. It is obvious, therefore, that preparation and grading form a major responsibility for each teacher and large consumers of his time and effort. Too often this task is viewed as a routine chore to be rushed through in the shortest possible time; the effective teacher, however, realizes its value not only to the student, but also as a means of checking the success of his own teaching.

If the school of architecture is to become more than an aggregation of courses, the faculty must devote continuous thought and effort to general and auxiliary activities. The restriction of such matters to a chief executive not only narrows the program in scope and ideas, but also evades the fundamental responsibility of the faculty as a whole, vitiates essential liaison, and destroys group morale. The *1950 Faculty Survey* found that the most frequent general school activities involved service on committees dealing with curricula, admissions, related courses, equipment needs, library, exhibitions, etc. The counseling of students was the next most frequent duty, and this was followed by the administration of course groups, particularly those in design. Every teacher knows that such duties, if conscientiously performed, absorb much time.

Similar duties are imposed by the parent institution, and, to the degree that the institution's faculty participates in the formation and execution of policy, the responsibilities of such service can comprise a major demand upon its energies. In addition to such general duties, the architectural teacher is frequently asked to supply professional services for the institution's buildings. This may mean anything from informal advice to complete practice. The *1950 Faculty Survey* found that 13.2 per cent of all architectural teachers rendered professional services to their institutions which consumed from $\frac{1}{2}$ to 100 per cent—with an average of 32.5—of their time. The 4.4 per cent who spent half or more of their effort in such work might well be considered as only part-time teachers. Without considering the general question of institutional architectural bureaus, it is clear that the teaching program of the school must be zealously protected from diversion of its personnel to other duties.

Beyond his primary obligations to school and institution, the architectural teacher must maintain active contact with the profession of which he is an integral member and from which the content of his teaching must be drawn. Three channels offer this contact. First is participation in professional societies. Both the *1950 Survey* and *Faculty Survey* agreed exactly that 71.2 per cent of all teachers were members of The AIA; 55.2 per cent were Corporate Members and 31 per cent had served as chapter officers. Similarly 65 per cent of those reporting held memberships in many other professional societies related to special aspects of architecture or education. Thus, teachers as a group have sought ready access to whatever benefits such associations provide.

A second and even more important channel is continued experience in the actual performance of architectural services either as principals or employees. Since the teacher of architecture is expected to prepare his students to carry on such duties, it is axiomatic that he cannot do so with assurance unless he is himself competent in such work. Many teachers have acquired such competence before accepting academic positions, but, although such experience is invaluable, the dynamic character of architecture and practice requires that each teacher must constantly refresh and extend his practical abilities. Other teachers, who for valid reasons have assumed their duties without sufficient field experience, have a similar problem in correcting their deficiencies. The situation thus presents a very real dilemma: how within the limits of time and energy can one individual excel both as a teacher and as a participant in the work of the profession? Furthermore, whatever specific solution is adopted, the interests of the employing institution must be protected from abuse. Detailed consideration of this knotty problem will be undertaken later in this section.

The third channel offering professional contact for the teacher lies in advanced study and research. If such activities are undertaken in an enlightened manner, they lead to fundamental questions arising directly from practice, and any theoretical answers to them must, in turn, be referred to practice for test. Valuable as such studies and research would be for the individual and the profession, they have rarely been exploited. In the *1950 Faculty Survey* only 11 per cent of all teachers claimed to have authored research papers. Many of these, however, were theses for master's degrees and hence were probably not comparable in rigor, depth, or originality to research work in other disciplines. The problem of graduate study and research will be discussed in detail in *Chapter X*.

The *1950 Survey* revealed relatively little professional activity by teachers outside of the performance of architectural services. Only 19 per cent had authored published articles, only 6 per cent had produced books, and less than 6 per cent had prepared pamphlets, handbooks, catalogs, or indices; 1.7 per cent reported that they had developed a new technique or an invention. The meagerness of these results does not constitute a special indictment of teachers, but proves only that they, like practitioners themselves, have yet to exploit the reportorial duty of professional men by which knowledge is disseminated to all colleagues.

Finally, because teachers are also citizens, they share with all members of their communities the obligation of general participation in social enterprises. The *1950 Faculty Survey* disclosed that teachers of architecture fulfill this responsibility as well as, or better than, the typical educated citizen or professional man. Many teachers contribute their special knowledge to important civic agencies, such as planning boards, traffic councils, housing boards, commissions for the preparation and administration of building codes, school development councils, and art and other cultural programs. The amount and quality of such services constitute an excellent record of community service.

The range and intensity of teachers' activities and duties are thus of formidable scope. Together they suggest an ideal specification which only the most exceptional individual could satisfy completely. What is indeed remarkable is not that some fall far short of the ideal, but that so many strive and succeed in approaching it. As with every large group, the general average of performance needs lifting through individual and group effort. This is a goal to which every member of the group will heartily subscribe and to which the profession as a whole should give sympathetic and intelligent assistance.

The Commission investigated in some detail the personal characteristics and the professional preparation of architectural teachers. The *1950 Survey* included teachers who were also registered architects. *Table 8* reveals that AIA teacher-architects ranged from 25 to 75 years of age, with 58 per cent between the ages 35 and 50. Only 11 per cent were under 35, but 31 per cent were 50 or older. The median age was 45.5. It is interesting to note that the age distribution of this group follows closely that of AIA practitioners shown in *Figure 13*. The axis of the largest groups—at age 40 to 44— coincides, although the teacher axis dips between equal adjoining maxima. This may be due to greater recruitment among the 35–39 group when large veteran enrollments forced rapid expansion of faculties. The teachers' distribution shows the same plateau at the age bracket 50–59 as exhibited by practitioners, due no doubt to the same depression factor which depleted both practice and enrollments. The large group of teachers of age 60–64 is unique and may be due to either or both the continuance of more teachers in education during depression years and a greater susceptibility of this older group to post-war recruitment. In any case, the distribution of this teacher-architect group is weighted toward older groups by the use of the registration criterion. Unfortunately the age characteristics contained in the *1950 Faculty Survey* were not tabulated.

The *1950 Survey* disclosed many details regarding the resources of professional education and experience which teachers brought to their tasks. The markedly higher proportions of teacher-architects who have won professional and other degrees is not surprising due to the natural tendency of educational institutions to select for faculty appointments those who have been trained in the academic system. The *1950 Survey* permits comparison of the educational preparation of teacher-architects and all other registered architects, as tabulated on the following page (*Tables 35 and 36*).

The *1950 Survey* also revealed the length of time that teacher-architects had devoted to collegiate education. Despite the fact that in proportion half again as many teacher-architects gained liberal arts degrees as did all other registered architects, the teachers' group averaged only 2.7 years of general education as against 3.0 years for all others (*Table 39*). On the other hand, 46 per cent of the teachers reported general studies in

239

	Teacher- architects	All other registered architects
Hold first degree in architecture	86%	54.7%
Hold second degree in architecture	14	9.5
Hold degree in architectural engineering	12	8.1
Attended one architectural school	87	65.6
Attended two architectural schools	45	21.6
Hold degree in engineering	2	4.2
Hold degree in liberal arts	20	13.5
Hold degree in other than architecture or liberal arts	11	4.0
Hold certificate from a trade school	13	15.9
Completed a special course in architecture	19	20.8
Have studied architecture in a foreign country	38	19.5
Have received a fellowship or grant	44	8.4
Hold no degrees in architecture	14	45.2
Entire training in architectural offices	6	23.0

comparison to 33 per cent for all others. In technical studies, however, 92 per cent of the teacher-architects averaged 6.5 years, while 82 per cent of all others averaged 5.1. The *1950 Faculty Survey,* since it included all teachers, gave slightly shorter lengths; 74.4 per cent of those reporting general education averaged 2.4 years, and 80 per cent averaged 4.3 years in technical studies. Unfortunately the manner in which the two questionnaires asked their questions differed slightly and this may explain the shorter length of technical training given for all teachers.[9]

The *1950 Faculty Survey* showed that teachers had obtained their undergraduate and graduate technical education in a total of 140 institutions of which 100 were located in the United States and 40 were located in 20 foreign countries. Of the domestic institutions, 53 were schools of architecture which were accredited by NAAB or which were members of ACSA. No foreign country or school was represented by more than a very few teachers. The *Ecole des beaux-arts* was the most frequently cited, but was reported by only 1.5 per cent of the group. France and Germany were each named by 2 per cent, and Britain by 1.1 per cent. The total impact of formal foreign training was thus very small whether measured by the number of trained emigrant teachers or by Americans who have attended foreign schools.

As already noted, teacher-architects have extended their training through supplementary studies to practically the same degree as have all other architects, but they have selected their subjects in differing proportions. *Table 40* shows that 17 per cent sought further training in fine arts as against 14 per cent of the practitioners; 16 per cent took city planning in contrast to 9 per cent for others; 11 per cent social sciences against 6; 7 per cent landscape architecture instead of 5. On the other hand, teachers showed less interest than practitioners in courses in engineering, business and economics, law, and real estate. Each group, therefore, directed its attention to areas pertinent to its particular needs, but it should be noted that neither neglected entirely any of the areas of study.

American architectural teachers have been keenly aware of the value of travel as a means of studying important buildings at first hand; 23.5 per cent of all teachers reported domestic travel for the serious study of architecture for an average total length of 6.5 months; 30.6 per cent had spent an average of 10.5 months in domestic travel, but without the intent of serious study; 7.9 per cent had traveled within the country for an average of 10.7 months in connection with professional practice; 33.5 per cent had pursued foreign travel, averaging 14.5 months, for serious study; 32.1 per cent, averaging 13 months, had traveled abroad without serious study; and 5.5 per cent had spent an average of 16.8 months abroad in professional work. It seems clear that the group record in this aspect of education stands very high.

Of major significance in the preparation of teachers of architecture is the extent and depth of their direct experience in the performance of architectural services as either employees or principals. It is here, more than any other aspect of professional education, that the average practitioner looks for the root of all faculty deficiencies and shortcomings. Although he may be too polite to say so directly, too often he suspects that the popular jibe "only the incompetent teach" may be true. For the first time the *1950 Faculty Survey* reveals the actual situation, as follows:

Length of Teachers' Experience in Practical Professional Work

| Number of Years | Architectural Duties | | Engineering Duties | |
	FULL TIME	PART TIME	FULL TIME	PART TIME
NUMBER RESPONDING % OF 455	252 100%	184 100%	60 100%	23 100%
TOTAL	55.5	40.5	13.2	5.0
Over 20 years	18 7.1%	15 8.1%	5 8.3%	2 —
10 to 20 "	36 14.3	24 13.1	4 6.7	2 —
5 to 10 "	57 22.6	26 14.1	6 10.0	2 —
2 to 5 "	69 27.4	49 26.7	15 25.0	4 —
Under 2 years	72 28.6	70 38.0	30 50.0	13 —
AVERAGE TIME	6.75 yrs.	6.22 yrs.	5.66 yrs.	6.12 yrs.
MEDIAN TIME	4.35 yrs.	3.35 yrs.	2.00 yrs.	1.77 yrs.

It should be noted that a particular teacher may have participated at different times in both full- and part-time work. A few may have undertaken both architectural and engineering duties. It appears, therefore, that the schools as a whole possess faculties which base their teaching on a considerable amount of direct practical experience.

The *1950 Faculty Survey* also asked each teacher to describe his most important professional work and indicate the degree of responsibility which he had assumed for it. The result is tabulated on the following page.

Teachers' Responsibility for Their Most Important Professional Projects

Type of Project	Total Reported			Full Respons.		Partial Respons.		Not Given	
	NO.	PER CENT OF ALL	PER CENT OF TYPE	NO.	PER CENT OF TYPE	NO.	PER CENT OF TYPE	NO.	PER CENT OF TYPE
TOTALS	403	100	100	255	63.3	105	26.0	43	10.7
Residential	116	29.8	100	90	77.6	18	15.5	8	6.9
Educational	81	20.0	100	42	51.9	32	39.5	7	8.6
Commercial	70	17.3	100	47	67.1	14	20.0	9	12.9
Institutional	58	14.4	100	42	72.4	11	19.0	5	8.6
Industrial	32	7.9	100	19	59.4	10	31.2	3	9.4
Civic & Recreational	29	7.2	100	12	41.4	10	34.4	7	24.2
Military	11	2.7	100	—	—	8	72.8	3	27.2
Utilities	6	1.5	100	3	50.0	2	33.3	1	16.7

The distribution of types of projects upon which teachers have worked are thus seen to correspond very closely with the distribution found in normal practice (*Table 29*). Furthermore, the degree of responsibility assumed by teacher-architects in all types of projects was surprisingly complete. Since only the "most important projects" were asked for, the tabulation represents only a portion of the full professional experience of the group.

The *1950 Faculty Survey* also revealed that 47.5 per cent of all teachers were licensed architects. *Table 43* shows that 51 per cent of both the teacher and practitioner groups passed written examinations in obtaining their first license. Moreover, the average teacher was registered in 1.75 states, and this equalled exactly the average for all architects (*Table 44*).[10] 9.2 per cent of all teachers hold NCARB certificates.[11] The *1950 Survey* showed that the corresponding percentage for all architects was 15. In view of the limited scope of teachers' practices, their use of NCARB seems relatively high.

Thus, from the standpoint of length and type of professional experience and the attainment of legal status as architects, it is fair to conclude that teachers as a group compare very favorably with the profession as a whole. The idea that architectural teachers barricade themselves within ivy-clad ivory towers is therefore proved contrary to fact. It would seem incontrovertible that the group brings to its teaching an amount of direct practical experience which is fully adequate to ensure its relevance to the needs of undergraduate professional education.

In addition to the performance of architectural services, the *1950 Faculty Survey* disclosed that many teachers had acquired valuable experience in other ways; 3.5 per cent reported that their most important professional work consisted of consultation, and 0.5 per cent cited projects of architectural research. Many responders brought to their teaching a considerable body of experience in fields more or less related to architecture; 16.3 per cent of all teachers had worked full time in these related fields for an average of 4.68 years, and 9.4 per cent had worked part time for an average of 4.75 years. The largest group—about one-fourth—had worked in closely related areas, such as city, site, or regional planning, landscape architecture, interior design, building construction and contracting, and acoustics. Others reported activity in fine, graphic, or commercial art, and industrial design. Some had been employed in engineering fields—industrial, military, and naval. A few had taught courses related to architecture.

It must be recognized, of course, that the quantity of practical experience of various kinds reported by all teachers as a group was necessarily distributed in differing amounts among individuals according to whether they taught on full- or part-time appointments. Teachers who entered teaching from practice had naturally enjoyed concentrated field experience, but those who then devoted full time to academic duties could not continue to participate to the same extent as did part-time appointees. Thus the total experience record of the whole group is somewhat overweighted by the activities of part-time teachers. Nevertheless since part-time teachers constituted only 18.9 per cent of the whole group, and since all teachers reported only their "most important professional work," the record as given above presents a trustworthy general picture of faculty experience.

A more serious reservation lies in the question as to whether the total group experience is equitably distributed among the faculties of the individual schools. The ability of a school to attract and retain highly qualified teachers varies with its academic standards and its financial resources. Unfortunately the *1950 Survey* data did not furnish statistical analysis of this point. It is logical to assume, however, that the total practical experience of individual faculties varies greatly in amount and quality.

The importance of practical experience for teachers of architecture is universally emphasized by practitioners and educators alike, but paradoxically the significance of experience in teaching is too often overlooked or discounted. Nevertheless the effective organization of subject matter, the refinement of methods, and the ability to stimulate student development are skills that can grow through continuous and conscientious effort. Architectural education would be much less mature today if it had been denied the accumulated know-how of able teachers.

The *1950 Faculty Survey* revealed data with respect to the length of teachers' academic experience. This is shown on the following page.

In interpreting these data, it is to be expected that teachers on full-time appointments should stand higher in length of teaching experience than those who had taught only part time. Nevertheless it is surprising to find that the average full-time teacher with 8.18 years of teaching has 5.8 times the 1.40 years of academic experience held by the average part-time teacher, and that the total years of teaching by all full-time teachers is 11 times the full-time equivalent experience of all part-time teachers. It is also interesting to note that, of the total of 396.2 full-time equivalent teachers, 70 per cent had 2 or more years of teaching experience, 37.7 per cent had 5 or more years, and 22.4 per cent had 10 or more years. For the 327 full-time teachers, these ratios

Length of Teachers' Experience in College Teaching as of 1950

Number of years of teaching	Total*		Full-Time		Total Part-Time		3/4 Time		1/2 Time		1/4 Time	
	FULL-TIME EQUIVALENT TEACHERS	PER CENT	NUMBER REPORTING	PER CENT	F.-T. EQUIV. TEACHERS	PER CENT	NUMBER REPORTING	F.-T. EQUIV. TEACHERS	NUMBER REPORTING	F.-T. EQUIV. TEACHERS	NUMBER REPORTING	F.-T. EQUIV. TEACHERS
TOTAL REPORTING	396.2	100	327	100	69.2	100	12	9.0	80	40.0	81	20.2
10 yrs. plus	38.0	9.6	37	11.3	1.0	1.4	—	—	—	—	4	1.0
10 to 20 yrs.	50.7	12.8	46	14.8	4.7	6.8	2	1.5	4	2.0	5	1.2
5 to 10 yrs.	60.7	15.3	58	17.7	2.7	3.9	—	—	5	2.5	1	0.2
2 to 5 yrs.	128.0	32.3	109	33.3	19.0	27.5	3	2.2	21	10.5	25	6.2
Under 2 yrs.	118.7	30.0	77	23.5	41.7	60.3	7	5.2	50	25.0	46	11.5
TOTAL YEARS REPORTED	3306.5	100%	2673.5	80.8%	633	19.2%	50	1.5%	240	7.3%	343	10.4%
TOTAL FULL-TIME YEARS	2916.7	100%	2673.5	91.6%	243.2	8.4%	37.5	1.3%	120	4.1%	85.7	3.0%
Average Yrs. per Teacher	8.18		8.18		3.66		4.16		3.00		4.24	
Aver. F.-T. Equiv. Yrs. p. T.	8.18		8.18		1.40		3.12		1.50		1.06	

*The Total number of records reported were 500. Since the total number of responses received was only 455, this means that some teachers had served under two or more types of appointments.

were 76.5, 43.2, and 26.1 per cent respectively, and for the 69.2 full-time equivalent teachers on part-time appointments 39.7, 12.2, and 8.2 per cent in the same order. The fact that 30 per cent of current faculties had less than 2 years of teaching experience reflects the expansion which the sudden upsurge of post-war enrollments imposed on the schools. In normal times the ratio would presumably be much lower. Nevertheless, for teachers as a group it is clear that there was a large core whose total teaching experience formed a sound pedagogical control for the schools' instruction.

No tabulation of the *1950 Survey* was made of the total amount of teachers' combined academic and practical experience, but comparison of the foregoing tables reveals that a considerable overlap must exist and that most teachers have acquired both types in varying degrees. It is important to note that full-time academic appointments do not preclude continuing practical work. Most schools permit full-time teachers to carry out occasional practical work, and many encourage it on a continuous, though necessarily limited, basis. All teachers are free to undertake practical duties during vacation periods. Thus, in reality the "full-time teacher," in terms of total effort, often approximates part-time status.

The range and complexity of faculty duties—instructional, school, institutional, professional, and community, as previously described—are so encompassing that the question of a full- vs. a part-time staff becomes a perplexing problem of policy. On the one hand, the school has a legitimate right to demand of those who accept its full-time appointments their whole-hearted application to its entire program. On the other hand, although continuing professional experience is manifestly in the interest of both individual and institution, its tendency to absorb an excessive proportion of teacher effort frequently prejudices other duties which are essential to a vital, well-rounded educational program. A further dilemma lies in the inevitable clash of economic interests. The teacher should receive standard fees for the competent performance of professional services, but, if he succeeds in maintaining a steady volume of commissions, the temptation to give this work priority usually grows to almost irresistible proportions. Thus the full-time teacher who becomes involved in practice is, even with the best intentions, likely to approximate only part-time performance with the result that a bare minimum of effort remains available for teaching and the development of the school.

These hazards have prompted some schools to prefer a staff composed primarily of part-time teachers. The *1950 Faculty Survey* revealed that 19 per cent of all teachers held fractional appointments in the following amounts:

Per cent Time	Per cent Teachers	Per cent Time	Per cent Teachers	Per cent Time	Per cent Teachers
80	0.8	40	0.6	15	0.6
75	1.1	33	0.8	10	1.7
67	0.6	30	0.8	5	0.3
60	0.3	25	3.4	.02	0.3
50	5.1	20	2.3	0	0.3

Appointments for 15 or less per cent of time were undoubtedly special cases and, in in part, may have been carried on teaching budgets for special administrative reasons. The surprising fact is that all part-time teachers together, although comprising one-fifth of all teachers, held only 7.9 per cent of the full-time equivalent appointments.[12] Thus, the schools on the whole depend relatively little on part-time teachers. The situation with respect to individual schools is another matter. The *1950 School Survey* disclosed that 19 responding schools—32 per cent—used only full-time teachers. The remaining 40 responding schools, however, used part-time teachers in widely varying extent, as follows:

Teachers on Part-Time (%)	Schools No.	%	Teachers on Part-Time (%)	Schools No.	%
80–71	3	(5.1)	40–31	7	(11.9)
70–61	2	(3.4)	30–21	2	(3.4)
60–51	4	(6.8)	20–11	8	(13.6)
50–41	6	(10.2)	10– 1	8	(13.6)
			0	19	(32.0)

The average for all schools was 24.9 per cent and the median 15 per cent. Furthermore it is interesting to note that of the 22 schools which had 40 or more per cent of their faculty on part-time status, all but one were located in large cities where it was easy to secure such personnel.

There have of course been notable part-time teachers who have made signal contributions to academic instruction. Paul P. Cret was an outstanding example of the successful combining of practice and teaching. Many architects, however, have preferred to relinquish practice upon assuming teaching responsibilities. Frank W. Chandler, when he became head of the school at MIT in 1888, voiced the classic decision "not to attempt to ride two horses" at once.[13]

The chief problem thus focuses upon the school's policy with respect to practice by full-time members of its faculty. In general, universities encourage all teachers to exercise their creative talents. Indeed unproductive teachers are often viewed with suspicion and penalized by the withholding of promotions. Research and publication by scholars in the humanities and the sciences are recognized as enhancing the prestige of the institution. Teachers of engineering are more highly regarded if they are sought as consultants. Teachers of music are expected to concertize. Teachers of art are urged to practice their craft. Exhibitions of their work are often sponsored by their institutions and frequently lead to sales. Moreover, while such activities are lauded for their scientific and cultural values, it is no secret that many teachers pursue them also as means of obtaining additional income. Some universities are thus able to attract teachers who would otherwise be quite beyond slender budgets. The dangers to sound instruction are self-evident, and a few universities have adopted the policy of returning all financial gain therefrom to the institution itself. In general, however, the view is widely held that the resulting benefits of scholarly and creative

246

activities outweigh the risks, and that abuses can be avoided through firm administration. One common safeguard is the requirement that research and consultation can only be undertaken if they promise positive contributions to the teaching competence of the division involved.

Teachers of architecture, no less than other faculties, need continuing access to professional experience. The importance of this matter was declared in 1950 by ACSA which adopted at its Washington convention a resolution endorsing the following statement of the Committee on Education of The AIA:

"A teacher should show evidence of professional productivity and promise of continued professional development through practice, research, publication, or other scholarly means. It follows that an educational institution, if it is to remain alive to current practice, must foster an intellectual atmosphere that will encourage the professional development of its architectural faculty. If the teacher is denied or avoids the intellectual stimulation of practice or research, his teaching must lose the exuberance of dealing with real problems and become only scholarly and academic."

The application to full-time teachers of architecture of the usual university policies described above is handled in many diverse and conflicting ways. Some institutions rule that teachers may undertake professional work only during vacation periods. Since it is difficult to schedule clients' demands and even more difficult to complete all but the smallest projects within such time limits, the teacher is thereby restricted for the most part to salaried employment or to commissions for small residences. Other schools permit their faculty to accept during the academic year occasional commissions of limited scope. In either case the teacher must perform his work as isolated ventures without the resource of an organized and continuing office. Since most institutions do not allow their facilities to be used for private work, the architectural teacher is thus usually forced to perform his work at home in an atmosphere which is rarely conducive to efficient production. The effect is to discourage and frustrate the fundamental objective of the system.

At the other extreme some schools insist that all members of their faculties continue at least some degree of active practice. A few enforce this policy by using as many part-time teachers as possible. Others, in effect, define full-time schedules in such a way as to leave substantial blocks of time, even whole days, vacant for office work. In one case a group of teachers have formed an office whose practice consists of the institution's own building projects. In other instances the faculty contributes to their institution's building needs on an intermittent basis. The *1950 Faculty Survey* disclosed that 13.2 per cent of all teachers rendered their institutions some form of

Per cent Time	Per cent Teachers	Per cent Time	Per cent Teachers
½–9	3.3	40–69	2.4
10–19	2.2	70–89	0.7
20–39	3.1	90–100	1.5

architectural service—from advice to complete executive services. The extent of these services is indicated in the above tabulation.

The average teacher of this group devoted 32.5 per cent of his time to these duties. Two-thirds of those who performed such services reported that they did not receive extra compensation for it beyond their normal salaries as teachers, but 27 per cent of this group said that a fraction of their salaries, usually equal to the time spent, was designated for such work. A fourth of the whole group were compensated by additional payments outside the teaching budget. In most cases the supplement was in direct proportion to time, but one received only 20 per cent for 50 per cent of his time, while another got 80 per cent for 25 per cent of his time. It would seem that some institutions tend to maintain an architectural office via the architectural teaching budget. Most, however, recognize the value of the services received by awarding equitable compensation.

The search for an appropriate framework of practice by full-time teachers must be guided by certain basic principles. First, continuing contact with professional practice is a necessity for a vital program of architectural education, and the schools should foster such contacts by their faculties. Second, teachers must not allow nor the schools permit such contacts to deter the maximum development of their full educational program. Third, the total practical experience thus gained should be controlled so as to ensure the school of as wide a variety of experience as possible. From this it follows that the supplementing of faculty income must be kept a secondary consideration.

Within these limits certain solutions suggest themselves. For experience with small projects, especially in the residential field, all teachers should be free to establish small offices if they so desire. Such projects provide excellent training in client contacts and the operation of complete professional services. Since the size of office needed for such work can be very modest, its overhead is low, and may be further reduced by sharing space with fellow teachers. Moreover such projects can usually be scheduled with minimum conflict with teaching and other duties. Nevertheless teachers also need experience in larger building types beyond the capacity of individual performance. If the teacher attempts to maintain an office sufficiently large to handle large projects, he soon becomes involved in increased overhead charges; meeting them soon demands more time to maintain a steady flow of commissions. Under such conditions his academic duties tend to suffer. Therefore for this kind of experience, employment, association, or partnership in an established firm would seem more feasible solutions. Often, no doubt, special arrangements can be devised so that attendance at the office can mesh conveniently with the school's schedule. In some cases a considerable part of the work might be performed outside of the office in accord with individual convenience. This type of solution also combines well with full-time summer employment. The *1950 Faculty Survey* found that 78 per cent of all teachers favored the development of an organized plan which would facilitate the placement of teachers in progressive offices for limited periods of time.

A variant of this latter plan might be a cooperative faculty office in which a number of teachers could enjoy facilities for individual small projects and when opportunity arises they could join forces to undertake large commissions. In the latter case, however, it would probably be wise to procure at least one non-academic person to relieve the teachers when work conflicts with school duties. Whatever the specific solution, it should be attained with the full collaboration of the university, the school, and the entire faculty. In addition, for the protection of the individual participating teacher, as well as the school, he should report regularly to the school any extra-curricular projects undertaken and in special cases he should confer in advance with the responsible administrator of the school as to whether these outside demands will jeopardize his teaching obligations. It is obvious that any solution requires mutual good will and confidence to prevent abuse, but, if the full-time teacher accepts such privileges, he automatically assumes particular responsibility to safeguard the school's interest.

Unfortunately there have been occasions, especially when general building activity has been slow, when some practitioners have resented practice by teachers. This opposition has usually been based on grounds of unfair competition with the implication that teachers have enjoyed low overhead through the free use of institutional facilities and that this has permitted them to obtain commissions because of low fees. Since teachers who practice are architects and must therefore conform to the same legal requirements that control all practitioners, and since a higher proportion of teachers are members of The AIA than are practitioners, it is axiomatic that they must be bound by the same standards of professional competence that regulate all architects. As teachers, they should and must support the highest professional ideals, and, if infractions occur, they should be charged and disciplined no less than others. The fact is, however, that few, if any, institutions permit the use of their facilities for private work, and, as already noted, teachers, far from working under favorable conditions, usually are forced to practice in circumstances which render efficiency and low production costs very difficult to attain. It is probable that a more fundamental, but unexpressed, basis for opposition, at least during depression years, lay in the fact that teachers enjoyed steady, if modest, salaries and that any commissions they obtained reduced the already low income of private architects. During prosperous years, such criticisms are rare. It is, therefore, important for the profession as a whole to declare the general principle of faculty participation in architectural practice as a valid and essential foundation for the sound development of its educational program (*Recommendation 15*).

Independent private institutions can resist such pressures, but public institutions are more sensitive to complaints. If, however, the principle of teacher practice is necessary and just, the profession itself must insist on its application for all schools, private as well as public.

An interesting method of ensuring the acquisition of practical experience by young instructors has been used by some West Coast schools, notably the University of Oregon. Graduates who indicate interest in and aptitude for teaching are employed as instructors for a one-year period. Those who continue to show promise are then given informal leaves, usually for two years, in order to obtain field experience. They are then encouraged to secure teaching appointments at another school to broaden their points of view with regard to educational systems and methods. After a further period of office work, the trainee then returns to his alma mater as a more or less permanent member of the architectural faculty. It is obvious that the success of this system depends on careful selection of the trainee, on his will to pursue it, and to some degree on interschool cooperation. If these can be attained, it has considerable merit as a long-term plan for the building of a faculty.

In emphasizing teachers' participation in practice, there is danger that other important opportunities for professional contact may be forgotten. It has already been noted that teachers of architecture usually work in institutions in which many divisions pursue research in both its basic and applied phases. Though the profession and the schools have in the past been slow to share in this activity, there is increasing realization that systematic investigation has become a prerequisite to the extension of architectural knowledge. While detailed discussion of architectural research will be presented in *Chapter X,* it should be stressed here that faculties of architecture, no less than those in other disciplines, have the obligation of adding to professional knowledge. This need not await the establishment of elaborate organization or facilities, important as these are. The capacity of able teachers for methodical thought and orderly presentation can be profitably applied in systematizing data already available. In the process of research, the teacher of architecture should soon acquire a fund of valuable knowledge which could lead, as in other fields, to demands for his special skill by means of consultation. In this way, not only would the profession benefit directly and promptly, but the teacher himself could gain contact with a wider range of architectural practice than is usually supplied by a few private commissions. The fact that consulting services are not widely used at the present time does not mean that they would not be used if they were available and of high quality.

Although the exigencies of academic operations have led the schools to depend for the most part on full-time teachers, the contributions of part-time teachers or of visiting practitioners can be of considerable value. As already noted in *Chapter VI,* part-time teachers can be particularly useful in those courses, such as Professional Practice, which require the exposition of office procedures. It is obvious that a practitioner should not be selected for academic work simply because he practices, but rather because he also possesses the ability to organize his knowledge and present it effectively to students. Furthermore he must take sufficient time to accomplish this end. In other words, the part-time teacher must meet the same standards of teaching performance as the regular full-time staff.

The use of practitioners as occasional visiting lecturers has already been mentioned in connection with student organizations. It would be profitable, however, to develop such participation in a more systematic way. A lecture series, scheduled on a regular basis, perhaps as a non-credit course, might reach the whole student body more effectively than intermittent meetings, and form, by its methodical coverage of current developments, an important means of stimulating closer contact with professional activities. Such a series might be worked out in collaboration with nearby AIA chapters. Similarly, practitioners can serve as consulting critics, students counsellors, and as advisers to the faculty.

In recent years there has been an increasing trend on the part of the schools to invite practitioners to serve in these or similar capacities, but the question of expense is always a limiting factor. Few schools can afford to compensate visiting architects at a rate comparable to regular earning power. This handicap could be easily overcome by adopting the device used so successfully by schools of medicine to whose faculties outstanding practitioners are given formal appointments entailing limited service without pay. The professional prestige accruing to the appointee is considered ample recompense for his occasional attendance. In most cases, however, such practitioners are drawn from areas near the schools and they thus incur little, if any, out-of-pocket expense. It would seem only fair of course for schools of architecture whose locations are less accessible to reimburse travel expenditures and maintenance while at the school. On such a basis almost all schools should be able at minimum cost to extend their contacts with the profession, receive up-to-the-minute reports of field developments, and provide continuing stimuli for both students and faculty.

The building, training, and maintenance of an able faculty is a paramount and constant problem in the conduct of all schools of architecture. It is easy to draw up a specification of an ideal teacher. He should possess wide professional experience and competence. He should be a specialist in the subjects to which he is assigned. He he should be a gifted teacher, an inspiring leader of youth, able and willing to cooperate with his colleagues in developing the whole educational program of his school, and an example of all the professional and personal virtues. Since these are the same qualities which are most conducive to high success in the professional practice of architecture, and since all professional education is rightly aimed to stimulate in students a strong desire to practice, it is understandable that the recruitment and holding of able teachers is a major task and that the ideal specification is difficult to realize.

The source from which teachers must be recruited is of course the profession itself: from practitioners, teachers at other schools, unemployed teachers, and recent graduates. The recruitment of teachers from other schools is a natural method of securing personnel who presumably have already acquired teaching skills. Moreover, for the individual teacher, the opportunity to transfer to other schools serves as a stimulus to build a sound reputation beyond his own campus. Nevertheless this transfer does not enlarge the corps of available personnel, but only shifts its members from school to school. Major dependence for new teachers must therefore rest elsewhere.

The meager listings in the employment bulletins of ACSA issued in recent years prove that there have been very few qualified teachers seeking appointments. Many applicants have just graduated. Others were trained in related fields, such as painting and sculpture, and have sought positions in these subjects. A number were European architects whose background and experience would need augmentation if they were to train American youth in American methods. All in all, these sources have not been sufficient to have much impact on the problem.

The recruitment of teachers from the ranks of practitioners is a logical solution when it can be accomplished. In times of inactivity, architects are eager enough to accept the comparative security of academic salaries, but in prosperous periods the type of individual who would make an ideal teacher usually commands an income far beyond the reach of the schools' resources. Occasionally other considerations offset this handicap. While the amount and intensity of academic work is, for a conscientious teacher, not appreciably less than that demanded by average office duties, it proceeds at a more even pace and thus has for some individuals a very definite appeal. Others are attracted to teaching by a desire for opportunities for advanced study or for the enjoyable stimulus of working with effervescent youth. Most mature architects, however, find it impossible to forego the higher compensation and the admitted excitement furnished by successful practice.

Younger practitioners are often amenable to part-time teaching as a temporary sustainment until their practices are firmly established. Such individuals are usually energetic and enthusiastic, but they do not solve the problem of permanent staff. It is natural that teaching should remain for them a secondary consideration.

Another source of teachers is the higher echelon of office employees. While these individuals may not command the full experience of mature practitioners, they are often quite competent in the techniques and skills of production which form so large a portion of the professional curriculum. If, however, they are to be attracted by faculty appointments, their office income is usually such that it requires the offer of an academic rank and salary formerly reserved for long experience and tested teaching ability. If these are given there is serious danger of resentment on the part of some members of the existing faculty.

Finally it is sometimes possible to enlist recent graduates to accept teaching appointments. This violates the criterion of experience which has been so strongly emphasized in this discussion. Indeed, a conscientious administrator knows that premature teaching is often as prejudicial to the recruit as it is to the school. Nevertheless, unless a school is so fortunately situated that it can maintain a faculty whose members all enjoy high academic ranks, it is necessary to use younger men in order to secure a staff wisely balanced in age and position. When recent graduates are appointed, it becomes especially important to assist the young teacher in planning and following a program to ensure growth in professional experience through vacation employment.

The selection of an effective teacher involves much more than judging an individual's technical knowledge and competence. Even when these are obviously of high quality, the candidate may be incapable as a teacher, as a cooperating member of a faculty team, or as a person to guide youth. These are imponderable factors which often impose an element of chance upon the process of selection. For candidates drawn from other schools, fair indication of teaching performance can usually be gained. In large measure, however, the final choice demands keen insight into character, bearing, and potential. Since judge and judged are both subject to human limitations, the result is not always ideal.

The difficulty of recruiting professionally qualified teachers has caused many schools in recent years to appoint individuals trained in other related fields. Artists have become drawing teachers. Art historians have taught the history of architecture. Civil engineers have served as teachers of structures. And in a few emergencies painters have criticized architectural design classes. Willing and well-intentioned as such teachers may be, it is well nigh impossible for them to provide the essential impact which their subjects should contribute to the professional training of architects. For example, art historians are unprepared to interpret the real actions of or the reasons for structural systems, or to expound the functional and aesthetic criteria pertinent to architects' procedures.

One very strong appeal which each school normally enjoys in the recruitment of teachers is the sentimental affection of its graduates. This, combined with the faculty's long observation of a superior student during his school career, fosters a tendency on the part of the faculty to turn to its own graduates when new teachers are needed. The fact that recent graduates are familiar with and predisposed to fit in well with the school's existing program and methods also weighs in their favor. Certainly a faculty should regard its products with a measure of confidence, but, if too large a proportion of a faculty is thus chosen, its combined experience becomes narrowly circumscribed and the hazards of inbreeding arise.

It must be emphasized that an architectural faculty is a continuing group of individual teachers cooperating in the development and operation of a complex work of art, its educational program. All members bring to this task their particular talents and experiences which form a rich composite resource for the school. In building and maintaining a faculty, therefore, the aim should be not only to select individuals capable of performing effectively the manifold duties already enumerated, but also to achieve a balanced team whose diverse members can complement each other in the total picture. Thus while the group must join in reaching some measure of agreement regarding general objectives and methods, their differing private personalities, insights, and approaches protect the school from lapsing into an atmosphere of monolithic dogmatism. Confronted with such nuances, students can be led to the rewarding endeavor of fashioning their own points of view.

A balanced faculty includes men of differing backgrounds, experience, personalities, and ages. An appropriate distribution of ages can do much to ensure the preparation of candidates for key positions as older teachers relinquish their duties. Diversity in other qualities, coupled with mutual respect, fosters healthy inquiry and exchange of ideas. Under such circumstances, the overall result can far transcend the sum of the component individuals. The opportunity to participate in such a stimulating environment is itself sometimes a major factor in attracting new teachers.

The recruitment and development of an able faculty and the attainment of high morale within the group are inseparably linked to the conditions controlling their service. Devotion to duty is for teachers an essential motivation, but, since, they are also confronted with the problems of daily living, personal responsibilities, and professional ambition, they cannot do their best work when such matters are a continual source of anxiety. In times of general building prosperity, it cannot be expected that teachers will resist the generous rewards of active field work unless they can enjoy conditions which ensure them and their families a reasonable degree of comfort, stability, and dignity.

Conditions of academic service include: duties, opportunities, rank, compensation, tenure, advancement, leaves, retirement, participation in the development of the school's program, and the opportunity to earn professional recognition and respect.

The general range of a teacher's duties has been cited. The question here turns to the amount of these duties. It must be assumed that each teacher desires to perform such duties in a thorough manner, satisfactory to both the school and himself. This cannot be accomplished, however, if the time allotted precludes competent execution. Thus there emerges the need for a realistic determination of a reasonable schedule covering the total expectation of course, school, and institutional work. Public acceptance of a forty-hour total work week has tended to influence academic circles as well. While conscientious and ambitious teachers rarely gauge their effort by the clock, some reasonable limit must be established for formal duties if other activities— professional, community, and personal—are to be realized. On this basis it would seem fair to accept 40 hours as a proper weekly maximum for full-time formal teaching duties.

Distribution of the work week among teaching duties varies with the type and number of courses taught, the methods employed, the size of classes, and the efficiency of the teacher. While each individual and each situation differs, the following may be taken as reasonable standards for three types of courses: lecture or seminar, lecture and laboratory, and studio.[14]

	Lecture	Lecture & Laboratory	Studio
Number of sections taught	2	2	1
Students per section	25	25	15
Credit hours per section	3	3	5–6
Total hours per week	40	40	40
Class contact hours	6	10	15
Preparation hours	12	8	4
Hours of grading	9	10	8
Student consultation	3	2	3
School & Institution service	5	5	5
Self-development *	5	5	5

* It is obvious that any ambitious teacher will consider additional time devoted to self-development as a wise investment in his own future.

The teaching loads here assumed are somewhat lower than frequently occur, but they prevail in a number of outstanding schools. With the time given for preparation, an excellent quality of instructional content and presentation can be attained and required. Adequate provision for the grading of quizzes, exercises, and design problems means not only a regular check on student performance, but also time to transform such devices into positive educational aids.

The most important lesson to be derived from these distributions is that if a teacher is assigned a larger number of courses, or if he must cope with larger sections, the time required to do so can only be found by extending the work week or by reducing the time available for other teaching and auxiliary activities. In such cases preparation is curtailed to the detriment of content and presentation, grading becomes perfunctory and merely a hasty means of fixing marks, students are denied additional tutoring and advice, and school and teacher stagnate for want of thoughtful development. The quality of an educational program is thus clearly linked to the establishment of reasonable teaching loads and this in turn is an important factor in maintaining high faculty morale.

One of the most curious paradoxes of academic life is the fact that institutions employ at considerable expense a highly trained faculty and then provide them with less than meager assistance. This does not refer, of course, to such grinding, but essential chores as grading, for, unless sections are so large as to make grading assistance inescapable, the teacher owes it to both the student and himself to do his own grading. The point is rather that an energetic teacher should have access to secretarial and clerical assistance to facilitate the activities required by his position. Nevertheless, the *1950 Faculty Survey* disclosed that 41 per cent of all teachers received no such assistance whatsoever. The 59 per cent who did have assistance ranged from one to 78 hours per week with an average of 8.14 hours. Except for a fortunate few, institutions seem to take a perverse delight in denying their teachers help that any commercial organization would deem it highly improvident to withhold.

It is obvious that rank and compensation are very important factors in attracting and holding qualified teachers. The hierarchy of instructor, assistant professor, associate professor, and professor usually indicates the degree of responsibility conferred and thus becomes a mark denoting recognition and prestige. In most institutions rank is closely correlated with increasing salary brackets, which in turn are normally kept fairly comparable for the same rank throughout each campus. Institutional policy in the past often insisted on a graduated distribution of ranks within a department or school. In some schools, usually those with small faculties, only the head of the school held a full professorship. In larger schools senior teachers in charge of major course sequences were likewise designated. In recent years, however, many institutions have liberalized such practices under the necessity of providing higher salaries to secure and hold qualified teachers. In some measure, therefore, the proportion of a faculty holding upper ranks reflects the recognition and status accorded to the field by the parent institution.

In 1948 a survey conducted for the American Society for Engineering Education disclosed the distribution of ranks among faculties of architecture, engineering, business, law, and dentistry.[15] The results were:

Distribution of Teaching Staff by Academic Ranks in Five Types of Professional Schools, 1948–49

Field	No. of Schools Reported	Positions Reported		Professors includ. Dept. Heads	Assoc. Profs.	Asst. Profs.	Instr.
		NO.	PER CENT	PER CENT	PER CENT	PER CENT	PER CENT
Law	93	871	100	59.5	14.6	20.0	5.9
Dentistry	26	501	100	44.8	15.6	15.0	24.4
Business	54	2444	100	32.4	16.0	19.9	31.7
Engineering	123	9375	100	27.9	16.4	20.4	35.4
Architecture	43	554	100	27.3	21.3	26.0	25.4

From these data it is obvious that as to the ratio of full professorships to total faculty architecture was the lowest of the five professions surveyed. The high ratios enjoyed by law and dentistry can be explained, at least in part, by the fact that these faculties do not conduct the pre-professional courses which are often assigned to teachers in lower ranks. Nevertheless, the ratio in architecture seems low when it is remembered that its curriculum extends over five years which means that a fifth of its instruction is equivalent to graduate courses in other disciplines. In addition, the high ratio in law is probably abetted by the use of large lecture classes which permits higher salaries without increasing the cost of instruction per student. In any case it is clear that schools of architecture should work to secure for their faculties a larger proportion of the upper academic ranks.

Salary scales vary directly with institutional resources. The improvement of such scales has always constituted the most acute problem facing institutions of higher education because there is a close relationship between such scales and the quality of instruction. Income from endowments has steadily declined in the face of increasing inflation and private institutions have consequently suffered severely. Public institutions, on the other hand, long restricted by inadequate support, have in recent years received substantial increases in appropriations due to expanding public demand for education and to unprecedented veteran enrollments. These appropriations are always subject, however, to epidemics of economy and retrenchment. Then, too, the range of salary scales has differed markedly in the several geographical regions, but progress in adjusting these differences has been made as regional economic levels have risen.

The *1950 School Survey* investigated the average salaries of teachers in 1950, calculated on the basis of full-time equivalence.[16] The average for all schools was $4762; the median school had an average of $4550. The highest school averaged $6842; the lowest, $2734. It is interesting to note that both of these schools were located in metropolises and were the second and third highest in proportion of part-time teachers. The averages for all schools in twelve AIA regions and in three super-regions are tabulated on the next page.

Average Salaries of Full-time Equivalent Teachers, in 58 Schools, 1950[17]
(by AIA regions and 3 Super-regions)

	All Schools				Private Schools				Public Schools			
	NO. SCHOOLS	NO. F.T. EQ. TEACHERS	TEACHING BUDGET ($1000's)	AVERAGE SALARY	NO. SCHOOLS	NO. F.T. EQ. TEACHERS	TEACHING BUDGET ($1000's)	AVERAGE SALARY	NO. SCHOOLS	NO. F.T. EQ. TEACHERS	TEACHING BUDGET ($1000's)	AVERAGE SALARY
N. Eng.	3	45.2	$296	$6540	3	45.2	$296	$6540	—	—	$—	$—
N. York	5	73.7	307	4170	5	73.7	307	4170	—	—	—	—
M. Atlan.	9	86.3	407	4720	5	48.0	230	4800	4	38.2	176	4620
G. Lakes	8	82.5	400	4850	4	19.0	91	4790	4	63.5	309	4870
N. Centr.	4	88.9	452	5080	1	14.0	58	4160	3	74.9	394	5250
N. East	29	376.6	1862	4950	18	200.0	983	4910	11	176.6	879	4980
Centr.	7	92.5	$408	$4420	1	18.0	$76	$4230	6	74.5	$332	$4450
S. Atlan.	3	64.2	321	5000	—	—	—	—	3	64.2	321	5000
Gulf	3	27.5	118	4290	1	9.0	36	4050	2	18.5	81	4400
Texas	5	55.4	228	4110	2	20.2	83	4130	3	35.2	144	4100
S. & Centr.	18	239.6	1075	4500	4	47.2	196	4150	14	192.4	879	4560
W. Mtn.	4	22.3	$93	$4160	1	5.5	$23	$4280	3	16.8	$69	$4130
N. W.	4	58.6	267	4560	—	—	—	—	4	58.6	267	4560
Si. Nev.	3	38.6	207	5370	2	16.4	87	5320	1	22.2	120	5410
West	11	119.5	567	4750	3	21.9	110	5060	8	97.6	456	4680
U. S.	58	735.7	$3504	$4762	25	269.1	$1289	$4800	33	466.7	$2215	$4740
					25	295.6	$1415	$4800	33	440.1	$2089	$4740
					CITY SCHOOLS				NON-CITY SCHOOLS			

Thus, for all schools, regional averages ranged from the New England high of $6540 to the lows of $4110 in Texas, $4160 in the Western Mountain region, and $4170 in New York. The super-regional averages rose in even stages from $4500 in South-and-Central, to $4750 in the West and $4950 in the Northeast.

For 25 schools in private institutions, regional averages varied from $6540 in New England to $4050 in the Gulf region. The super-regional averages were highest in the West ($5060), lowest in South-and-Central ($4150), and intermediate in the Northeast ($4910). For 33 public institutions, the Sierra Nevada region was the highest with $5410; Texas with $4100 and the Western Mountain region with $4130 were lowest. The Northeast super-region led with $4980, followed by the West with $4680 and the South-and-Central with $4560. In eight regions with both public and private schools, average salaries in the former exceeded the latter in five regions. It is also interesting to note that the average salary in 25 schools located in large cities—$4800—surpassed that of 33 non-city schools by only $60.

The data also disclose, for the whole group of schools, the per cent of teachers affected by these averages:

Per cent of Teachers in Six Brackets of Regional Averages of Salaries

Regional Salary AVERAGES	All Teachers		Teachers in Private Schools		Teachers in Public Schools	
	NUMBER	PER CENT	NUMBER	PER CENT	NUMBER	PER CENT
$6500 & above	45.2	6.1	45.2	16.8	—	—
6000–6499	—	—	—	—	—	—
5500–5999	—	—	—	—	—	—
5000–5499	191.7	26.1	16.4	6.1	161.3	34.6
4500–4999	227.4	30.9	67.0	24.9	160.3	34.3
4000–4499	271.4	36.9	140.4	52.2	145.0	31.1
Totals	735.8	100.0	269.1	100.0	466.7	100.0

This tabulation makes clear that as a group teachers do not receive compensation commensurate with their training or experience. It also reveals that more than half of all teachers in private schools are included in the lowest salary bracket, a situation which underscores the decline of endowed income.

In 1929 Bosworth and Jones found that the average salary for teachers of architecture was $2611.[18] The 1950 average of $4762 represents, therefore, a dollar increase of 82.4 per cent during the 20-year period. At the same time the cost of living has increased 40.7 per cent, and indices for food have risen 54.3 per cent and clothing 62.8 per cent.[19] When increased taxes and deductions are subtracted, it is clear that teachers as a group have obtained little if any improvement in their economic position since 1929.

Unfortunately the 1950 Survey did not itself procure data on the distribution and extent of salary ranges by individuals. It seems obvious that periodic studies of these

258

Maximum, Minimum, and Median Salaries for the 10-Month Academic Year, 1948–1949, in 43 Schools of Architecture, by Number of Schools in Each Rank and Bracket.[20]

Salary Brackets DOLLARS	Department Heads			Professors			Associate Professors			Assistant Professors			Instructors		
	MAX.	MIN.	MED.	MAX.	MIN.	MED.	MAX.	MIN.	MED.	MAX.	MIN.	MED.	MAX.	MIN.	MED.
12000+	1														
11500+															
11000+				1		1									
10500+															
10000+			1	1		1									
9500+						1									
9000+	2	2	2	2	1										
8500+		3	3	1	1	2									
8000+	3	2	2	2	1		1								
7500+	2			2					1						
7000+	4	4	4	4	1	3		1							
6500+	3*	3	4*	3*	3	5	3								
6000+	5	5*	4	4	4	3	5								
5500+	4	5	5	4	2	3	2	5	4	2					
5000+	5	5	5	6	13*	12*	4	8	6	2		1			
4500+	4	3	3	9	9	10	8*	16*	7*	8	4	8	3		
4000+		1		1	3		13	6	15	12*	8	7	15		
3500+					1				3	10	13*	14*	13*	5	
3000+					1					3	10	8	5	11	5
2500+											3			14*	19*
2000+														6	12
NO. OF SCHOOLS	33			41			36			38			36		
NO. OF POSITIONS	38			113			118			144			141		
NO. OF POSITIONS REDUCED FROM 12-MO. BASIS	22			21			10			22			10		
% OF ALL IN THE RANK	58			19			8			15			7		
% OF ALL 554 POSITIONS	4			4			2			4			2		

*The media of maxima, media of minima, and the media of media lie within the brackets indicated.

matters are mandatory in order to ensure a just appraisal of teachers' economic status and the schools' ability to recruit qualified instructors. The Commission believes that this is a function which should be performed by ACSA (*Recommendation 16*). In this connection, however, two surveys by other agencies help to complete the picture of salary ranges.

First was the study, already noted, carried out in 1948 by the American Society for Engineering Education. It compared the salaries of faculties in engineering, architecture, business, dentistry, and law. The data disclosed by this study is tabulated on the preceeding page.

With due allowance for subsequent cost-of-living increases, it is clear that on the whole the normal academic incomes of teachers of architecture do not correspond in any reasonable way with the qualifications which are usually prescribed for such positions of responsibility, influence, and trust.

The ASEE study also provided a comparison of architectural salaries with four other disciplines:

Maximum, Minimum, and Median Salaries of all Teachers in Responding Schools in Five Professional Fields, by Ranks, for the 10-Month Academic Year, 1948–1949.[21]

Field	Professors (*incl. heads of Departments*)			Associate Professors		
	MAX.	MIN.	MED.	MAX.	MIN.	MED.
Law	$15000	$3500	$7100	$8000	$3600	$5000
Business	14000	3800	6500	9500	3500	5000
Architecture	12000	3000	5800	8000	3600	4600
Engineering	12000	3400	5800	9500	3200	4400
Dentistry	10800	3000	6600	7300	3800	5300

Field	Assistant Professors			Instructors		
	MAX.	MIN.	MED.	MAX.	MIN.	MED.
Law	$ 7000	$2500	$4200	$7500	$2400	$3600
Business	7000	3000	4000	5400	1900	3100
Architecture	8000	2800	3800	4000	2000	3200
Engineering	6800	3100	3800	4700	2500	3000
Dentistry	6300	2500	4300	5400	1000	3100

This table indicates that, as in the distribution of ranks, median architectural salaries closely parallel those in engineering and are surpassed by 22, 9, 13, and 12 per cent by the highest median salary in each rank. There does not seem to be any logical excuse for such a situation.

A second study compiled in 1952 showed for eight schools of architecture and allied arts in public universities the distribution of ranks and salaries for 150 full-time teachers on the basis of an academic year of 9 months. Material from this study is tabulated on the next page.

Distribution of 150 Full-time Teachers of Architecture and Allied Arts in 8 Public Institutions, by Ranks and Salary Brackets, 1951–1952.[22]

Salary Bracket	Professors		Associate Professors		Assistant Professors		Instructors		Total	
DOLLARS	NUM-BER	PER CENT	NUM-BER	PER CENT	NUM-BER	PER CENT	NUM-BER	PER CENT	NUM-BER	PER CENT
14–15,000	1								1	
13–14,000	—								—	
12–13,000	—	14.3							—	4.0
11–12,000	1								1	
10–11,000	4								4	
9500–9999	1	7.1							1	2.0
9000–9499	2								2	
8500–8999	3	16.6							3	4.3
8000–8499	4								4	
7500–7999	6	33.4							6	9.7
7000–7499	8								8	
6500–6999	6	14.3	2	35.9					8	13.7
6000–6499	—		12						12	
5500–5999	4	14.3	10	41.0	1	43.6			15	26.0
5000–5499	2		6		16				24	
4500–4999	—		8	23.1	13	46.1	2	43.3	23	26.3
4000–4499	—		1		5		11		17	
3500–3999	—		—		4	10.3	10	56.7	14	14.0
3000–3499	—		—				7		7	
Total: No.	42	100	39	100	39	100	30	100	150	100
%	28.0		26.0		26.0		20.0		100	
Average	$7870		$5521		$4743		$3800		$5832	
Median	7500		5600		4850		3900		5160	

It should be noted that the average of all salaries was $5832 which is $1070 above that found by the *1950 School Survey*. This is accounted for by the fact that the *School Survey* included all schools, whereas the 8 institutions of the 1952 study were selected for their progressive salary policies. The difference is also due in part to the exclusion of all part-time teachers from the 1952 study.

Many full-time teachers augment their academic salaries by working during summer vacations, or on an occasional and concurrent basis, or by teaching in summer terms or serving their institutions on a 12-month basis. The ASEE study mentioned above affords some data on these points; 85 architectural teachers—15.4 per cent— served on 12-month appointments; 22 heads of departments—58 per cent of all such officers—held such contracts. If heads of departments are omitted, 63 teachers on 12-month appointments constituted 12 per cent of all 516 remaining staff members. This may be compared with 9 per cent in business, 11 per cent in law, 19 per cent in engineering, and 74 per cent in dentistry.[23] It may be assumed that some of the summer service of heads of departments and most of that of the remaining staff formed a permanent nucleus for summer term instruction. Normally few architectural schools offer summer terms, but in 1948, during the post-war period of peak veteran enrollments, about three-quarters of the schools did do so. In addition to the 12-month staff already noted, this summer load required 172 other teachers—34 per cent of the whole group. Furthermore, 12 teachers—2.3 per cent—undertook sponsored research for their institutions during the summer. Another 29 augmented their academic incomes by carrying overloads during the year, 18 by extra teaching and 11 by sponsored research projects.[24] Therefore, of all 554 staff members, including heads of departments, a total of 53.8 per cent received from their institutions during 1948 about 20 per cent more income than their basic salary rates indicate. This would mean additions ranging from $350 for the lowest-paid instructor to $2000 for the highest-salaried head of a department.

Many teachers prefer to use their summers not only to earn additional income, but also at the same time to gain further field experience. While no data were forthcoming on the extent and remuneration of this type of summer activity, it is probably substantial and, since it gives change of scene and pace, it usually results in greater benefits to the individual teacher than comparable summer work within an institution. Indeed this was amply demonstrated during the post-war years when year-round teaching and the lack of compensating refreshment in the field seriously reduced staff effectiveness and even endangered health.

The *1950 Survey* included responses from a number of teachers who also were registered architects. *Table 10* shows that 33 per cent of these teacher-architects had incomes from salaries and fees of from $4000 to $6000; 11 per cent fell below $4000; 27 per cent earned from $6000 to $8000, and 17 per cent from $8000 to $10,000; 12 per cent received $10,000 or more, including 1 per cent with $25,000 or more. Of the total productive effort of all teachers responding to the *1950 Survey,* 43.4 per cent was devoted to activities other than teaching (*Table 28*). It is clear, therefore, that the *1950 Survey* included many part-time teachers and that the incomes which they reported were in no small part derived from other than academic salaries.

Although these salary studies leave much to be desired, it is possible to conclude that, except in a few favored institutions and in a few exceptional cases, teachers of architecture are not adequately compensated for the quality and extent of experience and skill brought to their tasks. It is true that, despite public demand for education of high quality, support for adequate teaching budgets is difficult to secure at all levels and for all disciplines. Few areas of education, however, are faced with such competition for qualified personnel as are the professional fields, and in none is this situation more severe than in architecture. Under such circumstances, it is not surprising that many schools feel it necessary to permit, and even to encourage, their full-time teachers to seek supplementary incomes to a degree which has prejudiced other essential phases of their educational programs. Too often schools have condoned excessive outside work and consequent neglect of other academic duties under guise of maintaining professional contacts. It is well to repeat the principle, already stated, that for the full-time teacher the privilege of professional work must be based on the enhancement of the school's total resources of experience, and not for the purpose of obtaining additional income. Without such a reservation a school soon loses control of the situation and its program inevitably suffers. Academic salaries must be raised to a point that will enable the schools to enforce such a policy.

Because of diverse local conditions, the Commission believes it unfeasible to recommend specific salary scales. Nevertheless it maintains emphatically that compensation should reflect the quality of training, experience, responsibilities, talent, and industry which the teacher applies to his work. It follows that both the schools and the profession must insist that an effective teacher should be accorded a salary not less than similar qualifications would bring in comparable positions in practice itself. Only thus will superior individuals be able to undertake academic duties without incurring personal sacrifice, a demand that no profession which values its own future has a right to ask. Such an attitude would soon strengthen the morale of present faculties and would do much to overcome current problems of recruitment.

There are a number of other conditions of academic service which directly affect faculty morale. Opportunities for advancement with regard to responsibility, personal growth, rank, and compensation appeal to teachers' legitimate desire for a sense of accomplishment and recognition. In order to gain the maximum effectiveness of such motivation, its operation must be administered with fairness and objectivity. Some institutions have clearly stated their policies for advancement and promotion. In general these use as criteria the success with which the teacher performs the duties already described.[25] The problem lies in their application and evaluation by those responsible for making formal recommendations. While such decisions are usually the function of the head of the school, it is often difficult for him to obtain all the pertinent evidence and it would seem appropriate and conducive to good morale for him to consult with senior members of his staff on such matters. In recent years some outstanding institutions have required that all appointments to full professorships be made on the basis of recommendations of independent committees composed of members drawn from successful practitioners and outstanding teachers from other institutions. In this way it is hoped to eliminate the possibility that extraneous non-professional factors might inadvertently influence such decisions.

To the individual teacher, advancement always seems slow, and indeed this may be true for the younger members of the staff when institutional policy limits the number of higher positions. Then, too, there is always the question whether long service alone—of acceptable but perhaps not outstanding quality—should constitute sufficient qualification for advancement. The promotion of younger over older teachers, regardless of merit, can create disunity. If however advancement is too often made synonymous with durability, the school and institution suffer. Some universities have sought protection from such eventualities by adopting an "up-or-out" rule, under which a teacher must, after a stated period in a lower rank, be promoted or released.[26] The advantages of such a system are that all appointments in the lower ranks are periodically reviewed, appointees are stimulated to plan and carry through an acceptable program of self-development, and the institution is able to release unpromising appointees with minimum friction. However, unless this policy is accompanied by an unrestricted number of positions of high rank, its practical effect is excessive turnover of younger teachers and the loss of a considerable amount of accumulated teaching experience.

Most institutions accord tenure to the ranks of associate and full professorships as a safeguard against administrative change and whim. Such appointments can be terminated only by formal conviction for gross negligence or misconduct. Promotion or recruitment to these ranks should therefore be subject to severe scrutiny. On the other hand, tenure is an essential factor in building faculty morale, and it constitutes a valuable attraction in drawing outstanding personnel to a faculty.

Other privileges, normally provided for university teachers, include illness and retirement benefits and sabbatical and other leaves. Measures to alleviate the hazards of sickness and old age have won such wide public acceptance that argument in their favor is unnecessary. The degree of protection afforded most teachers is often very meager and an increase of such benefits is highly desirable. The function of sabbatical leaves is less widely understood. This device affirms the belief that periodic relief from academic duties for the purpose of refreshment and the extension of experience increase teachers' professional and personal growth and thus raise their usefulness to the institution they serve. Laymen are apt to consider such leaves as glorified vacations, but securing them is not a casual or automatic matter. To be eligible, the teacher must have served effectively for six years. He must propose a plan which the institution can accept as beneficial to itself and the individual concerned. Sabbatical leaves do not permit the recipient to undertake remunerative employment. Usually the institution participates to a maximum of six months' salary, but permits a half or full year absence. If the latter case, the recipient loses half his salary, but he can recoup part of this loss if he is fortunate enough to receive a grant from other sources. On his return he is expected to submit a formal report on his work. Institutional approval is also usually contingent on the school's ability to absorb the teacher's normal teaching duties and it is at least tacitly agreed that the teacher will resume his duties at the end of his leave. All in all, sabbatical leaves are acknowledged as highly desirable, but, surprising as it may seem, many teachers of architecture are reluctant to apply for them because of family responsibilities, loss of income, or other reasons. It is often necessary to encourage the architectural faculty to participate in the program. Most schools also cooperate when leaves without pay are requested. The increasing availability of foundation and Fulbright grants has multiplied such possibilities.

A faculty of architecture, like any group, can fulfill its maximum potential only if its members can join wholeheartedly as a cooperating team to develop and operate the school's educational program. Under such an atmosphere the diverse talents, experiences, and insights possessed by individuals can combine to stimulate a vitality and breadth far surpassing the sum of individual contributions. Obvious as this is, it is sometimes barred by authoritarian administrators and academic prima donnas who seem to think that their personal decisions on every question of policy and detail, large and small, are final and infallible. In this case teachers become only routine assistants carrying out orders, are denied opportunity for initiative, and are excluded from any real participation. The paradox is that, since no single person can know or solve all the plethora of problems arising in all phases and classes of a complex curriculum, he is dependent on others but refuses to draw upon their experience.

This does not mean that there is no place on architectural faculties for strong personalities with mature convictions. Otherwise, the profession would have been deprived of some of its most effective educators. If such teachers can also act as members of the faculty team, they can furnish a powerful stimulus toward the growth of their colleagues. The pitfall of the "great man" system arises when dictation supplants collaboration.

Finally, faculty morale flourishes when each member feels confident that he and the group are participating effectively in a sound, progressive program based on mutually acceptable principles. No one should expect or desire to achieve monolithic, uniform agreement among a group trained in individual creativeness, but, nevertheless, good will, tolerance, and devotion should permit the growth of a healthy and reasonable consensus on objectives, content, and methods.

Since architectural teachers have usually had considerable direct experience in professional practice, the objectives and content of the school's program are understood with some degree of assurance. Few, however, have undertaken any systematic analysis or investigation of the mechanics of the art of effective teaching. In this they share the shortcoming of most college and university faculties, who are selected almost wholly for their knowledge of subject matter and for their personal skill in its application. Illogically, such accomplishments are assumed to imbue them automatically with pedagogical prescience. Such criticism need not provoke dispute as to the priority of content or method. Teachers of architecture must command both. It follows that recruits and many who are already teaching could increase their effectiveness by studying the nature, operation, and exploitation of the process by which students of architecture learn. It is also evident that the schools, individually and as a group, have a direct responsibility in encouraging and facilitating the improvement of teaching methods employed by their staffs.

There are a number of ways in which better teaching can be fostered.[27] Some schools encourage young teachers to seek regular guidance from the ablest senior members of the faculty who may at times attend their protégés' classes and afterwards offer friendly suggestions. Groups of young teachers can conduct sample classes and criticize each other's presentations for organization of materials, clear delivery, annoying mannerisms, etc. Teachers could benefit from consultation with their institutions' speech clinics. Tape recordings of lectures and even of design criticisms would be revealing. Instructors in psychology and education could be enlisted to discuss at faculty meetings what is known of the learning process at the college level, its stimulation, and its measurement. These constitute only a few of the many possible means available to any school of architecture which enjoys imaginative leadership.

On a wider scale, more formal measures suggest themselves as an appropriate field of endeavor for all schools through their participation in the ACSA. In recent years ACSA has, through its annual conventions and regional meetings, encouraged discussions of teaching methods used in various subject fields. The publication of its proceedings makes its convention papers available to all teachers. Nevertheless, the brevity and turmoil of conventions and regional meetings is hardly conducive to serious interchange. Usually, the time is too short for a teacher to overcome his first and natural reaction to defend and rationalize his own particular methods and go on to a free give-and-take discussion of principles. Moreover, for national meetings the cost of travel too often restricts attendance to heads of schools. Valuable and enjoyable as such meetings are, they do not begin to meet the real need of teachers to exchange ideas with those in similar courses.

One means of strengthening instructional methods would be to organize institutes, clinics, or workshop courses for teachers of comparable subjects. These could be scheduled during the summer vacation and extend from a week to a full term. In the latter case, they could be organized as regular academic courses affording graduate credit. In combination with other courses presenting advanced subject matter, a reasonable study load could be arranged. Teacher institutes are well established in other fields. Those conducted for many years by the American Society of Engineering Education have been particularly successful. The only instance of the actual operation of such a plan in the field of architecture is afforded by those teachers of architectural history who during the summers from 1937 to 1942 attended at Harvard the graduate courses in this field conducted by Dr. Kenneth J. Conant. Discussion of teaching methods, while on an informal basis, was nevertheless lively. The group received such stimulus that it founded in 1940 the Society of Architectural Historians which by 1953 had grown to a membership of more than 700. The Society's quarterly *Journal* has attained international recognition. Its well attended annual meetings produce papers of excellent quality and local groups are active in Boston, New York, and New Orleans. The Society confers an annual Book Award to recognize superior publications by American architectural historians. These activities and the stimulus they have engendered have contributed notably to the improvement of history teaching in the schools of architecture. This example suggests that similar benefits would also accrue to programs in other phases of architectural education.

The *1950 Faculty Survey* found that 92 per cent of all teachers favored the organization of teaching institutes in their special fields. The largest group voiced a strong preference for a duration of one week; a group half as large called for two weeks; and a group one-fifth as large were willing to devote four weeks to such study. Inquiry as to the financing of participation revealed that most teachers would expect their schools to pay a substantial part of the cost. The average response asked the school to reimburse 74 per cent of the expense. One teacher stipulated 150 per cent! And 37 per cent said that they wanted 100 per cent of their expenses paid. This reaction to a new proposal was no doubt due to lack of appreciation of benefits to be gained, failure to realize that teachers themselves have an obligation to improve the quality of their own academic competence, and reluctance to forego income expected from vacation employment. These attitudes might well be reversed when institutes attain firm footing. If eventually participation should become a factor in promotion, many teachers would certainly recognize that personal expenditures for such purposes would constitute a wise investment for their own future. In initiating such a plan, however, assistance by the schools would no doubt be an essential prerequisite.

Regardless of the difficulty of arranging such details, the Commission is convinced that improvement of teaching methods is a necessary and promising function to which teachers, the schools, and ACSA should address themselves with vigor. The Commission, therefore, urges the development of a positive plan looking toward the organization of teaching institutes as one means to this end (*Recommendation 17*).

The interchange and comparison of ideas on the improvement of teaching would be greatly aided by the establishment of a special journal for this purpose. ACSA attempted such a venture in 1947. One issue of the *Journal of Architectural Education* appeared and was devoted to the subject of research. The mimeographed format was adequate and inexpensive. Subsequent numbers have presented the proceedings of the Association's annual conventions, including the papers read, but no further general issues have been forthcoming. Nevertheless, the need for a medium of exchange remains and it should not prove too difficult to revive the original purpose of the *Journal*.

Another means of stimulating interest in educational methods is afforded by teachers' visits to other schools. The *1950 Faculty Survey* disclosed that, omitting deans and heads of schools, 82.4 per cent of the responding teachers had paid such visits. The percentages of all responding teachers by number of visits were as follows:

No. of Schools Visited	Per cent of Teachers	No. of Schools Visited	Per cent of Teachers	No. of Schools Visited	Per cent of Teachers
0	17.6	6	4.8	12	1.1
1	8.8	7	2.8	13	.3
2	16.5	8	2.3	15	.6
3	19.9	9	1.4	17	.3
4	9.9	10	2.6	18	.3
5	9.1	11	1.1	TOTAL 352	100%

The average number of schools visited per teacher was 3.38. While this seems relatively low, it must be remembered that in many parts of the country the distance between schools and the cost of travel has limited contacts between schools. Of those reporting visits, 72.4 per cent met the full cost themselves; 20.7 per cent were reimbursed in part by their own school; and 6.9 per cent received full subsidy. Those who paid their own expenses made 66.2 per cent of all visits and averaged 3.75 visits. Those who were partially reimbursed accounted for 26.4 per cent of all visits and averaged 5.23 visits. Those fully subsidized made 7.3 per cent of the visits and averaged 4.35 visits. The fact that school assistance did not materially increase these averages must be balanced by the probability that subsidized visits may well have involved longer travel, as well as professional meetings and official business en route. The value of such visits varies with their length. No doubt many were superficial calls which gave no insight into methods of instruction. Others were perceptive inspections which influenced not only the visitor, but also, through subsequent reports, his own school. Institutions would do well to encourage and aid this latter type of visit to the full extent that funds allow.

A final form of stimulating contact between schools is that which provides for the temporary exchange of teachers for a term or year. While this has been done occasionally in the past, it might be profitable to extend its use to include a larger number of schools. The effect for each school would be similar to the use of visiting professors, brought for periods of varying durations to perform general or special duties. The *1950 Faculty Survey* revealed that 87.4 per cent of all teachers favored an organized program of exchange and visiting teachers.

This discussion of the problem of improving instruction in schools of architecture has suggested many ways by which the profession can support and assist in attaining this goal. Notwithstanding there remains one method which could surpass all others in direct effectiveness and which has thus far been almost wholly neglected. It is none other than formal and official appreciation of the contributions which teachers as a group have made to the profession in whose progress they yield to none a greater concern.

This is not special pleading. Teachers know well the long record of interest which architects have shown for professional education as such. On the other hand, though quick to criticize shortcomings, architects have been singularly lax in recognizing able teaching. The accolade of Fellowship in The Institute has been reserved almost entirely for administrators of schools, and has seldom been awarded for excellence in teaching. Indeed, in some instances, practitioners have apparently considered teachers as a fringe element unworthy of inclusion within professional circles. As recently as 1946 one chapter of The AIA decreed that only the head of their local school—and no other member of its faculty—was eligible for full membership in the chapter! This by-law was promptly declared void by the directors of The Institute, but the attempt was certainly not calculated to foster the professional morale of faculties.

If the profession desires better teaching, it could take positive action by recognizing outstanding teachers. Recipients of chapter and regional awards could become nominees for annual national citations selected by an Institute jury on the basis of evidence submitted by sponsors. Such citations would not only constitute rewards for effective services, but would also demonstrate to prospective teachers that the profession regards education as an important avenue to high prestige within its circle. National awards might be designed to carry automatic elevation to Fellowship within The

Institute. The Commission urges the establishment of a suitable system to recognize excellence in teaching (*Recommendation 18*).

Finally, the delicate problem of leadership in education must be considered. The functions, status, and qualifications of a dean, director, or head of a school of architecture vary with time and place. When faculties and budgets were small, responsibility and authority in each discipline were concentrated in a single professor who directed his few assistants with an iron hand. Some institutions still retain this "great man" system in the belief that only thus can a unified program and approach be attained. The obvious dangers of such a system are that it assumes continuing omniscience, invites petty despotism, and discourages the growth and participation of other members of the faculty. In reaction to this traditional pattern, some institutions have come to entrust all decisions to departmental faculties. This system is based on the concept that the formulation and operation of educational programs should be determined by majority vote of all teachers who are involved in them. At best, such a democratic arrangement encourages each teacher to maximum cooperation; at worst, it reduces action to the lowest common denominator of agreement. Between these extremes lie various compromises. The most frequent is the formal or informal sharing of leadership between the administrator and the senior members of his faculty.

It is patent that the success of any organizational system depends directly upon the qualities of mind and personality of those who must make it function. If a faculty is of mediocre quality, it can hardly see beyond its limited horizon; but if it is composed of enlightened and competent individuals, it will be satisfied only with a progressive and dynamic program. It is for this reason that the recruitment of teachers of outstanding stature looms so important. If this is neglected, the result will be stagnation which can only be overcome by painful correctives applied through the ultimate authority of the institution's trustees.

Within this framework the function of leadership has a very different character from that of the "great man" system. While a dean or director may well have and should have definite convictions, their realization can rarely be instituted by decree. He must lead, if he can, only by convincing his colleagues of the eminent desirability of his proposals and by influencing within reasonable bounds the selection of new faculty. This process will be facilitated to the degree that he can gain the respect and confidence of the group. If this is denied, justly or unjustly, his position becomes untenable.

The character and circumscriptions of this concept of leadership have little in common with the authority wielded by a private practitioner in his own office. It mitigates against rapid change and it demands unusual patience and constancy of purpose. Nevertheless its opportunities for securing progressive action are still considerable and once accepted produce more certain results. Thus exercised, leadership challenges a faculty to grow in its capacity to fulfill its responsibilities and potentialities. Such a condition is the only sound basis for the conduct of a vital educational program.

It is clear that the discovery and recruitment of leaders who can work effectively within such a framework is a problem of the first order. Professional competence is a most necessary asset, but to it must be added a penetrating understanding of the goals, principles, and methods of education, and an ability to establish and maintain rapport with a diverse faculty. Such a combination will always be difficult to secure.

4. RELATED CURRICULA AND COURSES

In addition to curricula in architecture, many schools administer other programs in related fields. The *1950 School Survey* revealed 19 curricula in Architectural Engineering, 5 in Building Construction, 5 in Planning, 4 in Landscape Architecture, and one in General Design. All of these programs usually have certain courses in common with professional curricula in architecture and their association within a school of architecture is therefore logical and mutually advantageous.

The first curriculum in architectural engineering was established at the University of Illinois soon after 1890 at the urging of Dankmar Adler who had found it difficult to secure personnel competent to handle the new structural techniques then being introduced in Chicago skyscrapers. At first the program of studies eliminated all training in design in favor of additional courses in mathematics and advanced structural theory. The first degrees were conferred in 1894. By 1913 there were 112 graduates; 25 of them became structural engineers; 49 worked in construction and the production of materials; 10 were architectural draftsmen; and 14 became practicing architects.

By 1912, 11 of the 20 existing schools had instituted programs in architectural engineering. Seven were conducted as separate curricula and four as options in one or two years of the architectural curriculum. By 1930, 24 of the 52 schools offered such curricula. In that year the distributions of curricula and students in 11 areas were as follows:[28]

Area*	Curricula	% of Total Enrollment	Area	Curricula	% of Total Enrollment
New England	1	5.5	Southeast	1	2.4
North Atlan.	1	7.6	Southwest	5	15.9
Midwest	4	28.0	Mountain	—	—
North Plains	2	6.9	Northwest	2	6.7
Central Plains	5	18.8	California	—	—
Central Atl.	3	8.3	Total U.S.	24	100 (1268)

* For composition of these "areas," as distinct from AIA regions, see Note 45.

Thus the concentration in three midwestern regions of 11 curricula and 53.7 per cent of all students is noteworthy. In 1950, 24 schools, but not all the same ones as in 1930, maintained architectural engineering curricula and enrolled a total of 1748 students in them.[29] The *1950 Survey* reported that 13.6 per cent of all degrees held by registered architects were in architectural engineering.

The objectives, content, and products of these curricula have varied greatly. Some schools, due to legal stipulations, used the title of architectural engineering to describe programs which were in reality professional curricula in architecture. Others adhered to the original structural emphasis. Some were intended to train only building contractors and construction personnel. The term, architectural engineering, itself was ambivalent. Its earliest use by Hansom in 1842 has already been noted. During the second half of the 19th century, when structural design was carried to new heights, architects, despite their contributions to this development, so stressed their preoccupation with styles that, for the public, architecture lost its traditional structural connotation. Thus, to many, architectural engineering came to mean "practical" vs. "decorative" architecture, and, although architectural engineers were handicapped by incomplete training, they were often called upon to furnish complete professional services. Confusion increased when a number of state registration boards came to accept degrees in architectural engineering as equivalent to those in architecture. The situation reached an absurd extreme when during the early stages of World War II the armed forces adopted the popular bias for any title incorporating "engineering" and utilized directly the skills of architectural engineers, but, for many months, failed to investigate or recognize the valuable technical contributions which architects themselves could make.

During the past 30 years an increasing number of schools have sought to resolve this problem by clearly differentiating between curricula intended to train for the professional practice of architecture and those which concentrate on the structural design of buildings to the virtual exclusion of all other considerations. These schools have recognized the desirability of providing opportunity within the professional curriculum for some degree of specialization and thus have instituted optional programs. The most common are those which provide for advanced studies in either architectural or structural design. With the establishment of five-year curricula, students in the structural option not only can be given as much structural training as was contained in architectural engineering programs, but, in addition, can complete a solid core of architectural studies, including design, which amply justifies the conferring of a professional degree in architecture. The Commission believes this to be a wise and proper solution (*Recommendation 19*).

According to this view, curricula which continue to employ the designation of architectural engineering assume the function of training structural personnel for the building field. Such a program thus approaches very closely the structural options offered in many civil engineering curricula, with the important difference that applications are drawn from building, rather than from heavy construction, such as bridges, dams, highways, etc. There is clearly a need for this type of personnel and such curricula in architectural engineering have a useful and honorable purpose to perform. While their graduates cannot properly seek professional careers in architecture, they can attain in many states appropriate registration and status as professional structural engineers. Nevertheless, continued use of the name, architectural engineer, leads to public confusion and encourages graduates to aspire for registration as architects. One

271

school has adopted the title "building engineering" in order to clarify its objectives.

A second type of related curriculum is that intended more explicitly to train technical and administrative personnel for the building construction industry. In the past, construction firms have recruited their personnel from the ranks or, when advanced skills were needed, from graduates in civil, mechanical, or architectural engineering. Since none of the latter provided direct training for such work, all graduates were forced to acquire as best they could the special knowledge required. The result was that both large and small construction firms worked under difficult handicaps. About 1940 the Johns-Manville Company initiated a movement to establish curricula in "light building construction" focused primarily on the home-building industry. At first few schools of architecture accepted the challenge, and the programs were located in such diverse departments as civil engineering, business, and forestry. At the close of World War II, however, several schools of architecture instituted such curricula and expanded their scope to include large as well as small operations. By 1950 six schools of architecture offered such programs.

The content of such a program may be illustrated by the 4-year curriculum conducted at the Alabama Polytechnic Institute. Students take the same courses provided for architects in building construction, working drawings, structural theory, and architectural history. In place of design, however, they pursue a sequence of courses in accounting, cost analysis, purchasing, real estate, labor relations, and erection methods and administration. The undergraduate thesis consists of the preparation of estimates and bids for an actual project based on plans obtained from architects. Graduates receive the degree *B.S. in Building Construction* and proceed to positions as assistant estimators or superintendents. By 1950 enrollment had reached approximately 200. The close association of architectural and construction students in school promises a high degree of mutual respect and wholesome cooperation as both groups take their places in their respective vocations.

The small number of curricula in interior design, industrial design, landscape architecture, and planning which were reported by schools of architecture indicates only that such programs are commonly administered by other departments or divisions. Each, however, is linked to architecture not only by complementary objectives, but also by sharing a similar creative approach. Where such programs have been conducted in close physical proximity, students of each have benefited greatly by the inevitable interchange of ideas. The Commission believes that schools of architecture should seek to establish intimate connections with such curricula.

As integral units of their parent institutions, schools of architecture should not only draw upon other divisions for relevant instruction, but also offer opportunities for other students to gain appreciation and understanding of the character and value of architecture. In some instances, students of other curricula, such as illumination engineering or home economics, can attend certain professional courses, particularly if such courses develop aesthetic understanding and are required in their regular undergraduate programs. However, since most such students lack sufficient preparation in both knowledge and skills, specially designed service courses are usually a more effective arrangement. Beyond such needs, however, lies the schools' obligation to reach as large a portion as possible of the whole student body in order to emphasize to future citizens and clients those essential contributions to good living which only an architecture of high quality can provide. In the past, courses in the history of architecture have been used by some non-architectural students for this purpose or to enrich their grasp of historic cultures. Nevertheless, it would seem more to the point to organize for lay students a general survey of current architectural problems which cut across the manifold needs of contemporary society. For example, such a course could sketch the principles of home design, the planning of neighborhoods, new developments in schools, other primary building types, and finally the concepts basic to attractive and healthful communities. Such a missionary effort might do much to predispose its recipients to use and value the services of the profession in years to come. The Commission urges the schools to explore the possibilities of such an offering (*Recommendation 20*).

The success with which the school at Pennsylvania State College presented in the late 40's in many communities throughout the state an off-campus extension course for laymen on the problems of home building suggests that this and other topics could serve large audiences. Likewise, every school is frequently petitioned by laymen for correspondence courses on architectural subjects. It is obvious that there exists a considerable need for well-conceived adult education in this field. To satisfy such needs would require definite assignments of staff and this, in turn, would demand budget support. Many institutions, however, already operate such extension courses in other fields, and therefore should not deny to their schools of architecture participation in such programs.

5. FINANCING ARCHITECTURAL EDUCATION

The formulation and realization of a sound, progressive, and vigorous program of architectural education depends upon the provision of faculty and facilities of high quality and adequate quantity. Thus, as in all complex activities, the problem of finance assumes central importance. This is true not only in attaining a minimum acceptable standard of support for each school, but also in permitting each to refine and extend its teaching to reach the optimum fulfillment of the educational process and its own potentialities. Although thus far attention has been concentrated only on undergraduate curricula, the need—to be discussed in *Chapter X*—of sufficient resources for graduate studies and research is increasingly recognized as having vital significance for the advancement of the profession. It is obvious, therefore, that the profession must concern itself in the most intimate way with obtaining adequate funds for the conduct of its schools.

In the United States, the delegation of formal architectural education to the universities was a direct consequence of the fact that its adequate financial support was far beyond the means of the profession itself or of individual architects who had from time to time attempted to establish proprietary courses of instruction. Nevertheless although general and professional education at the university level is easily demonstrated to produce large returns both for individuals and society as a whole, it is a paradox that the cost of higher education has never been, nor can it ever be, self-supporting on the basis of fees collected from its students. Indeed the social gains accruing from higher education are so self-evident that the principle of social support, either by philanthropic or public contributions, is taken for granted. Thus, academic budgets are indeed balanced, but only when the picture is viewed in its entirety.

For generations the chief support of American higher education derived from the liberality of private benefactors who for humanitarian, intellectual, or personal motives gave vast sums for facilities, operation, and endowments. Originally such gifts were general contributions; later they were usually designated for specific programs in which the donor was interested. Only two American schools of architecture—Columbia and Harvard—have been the recipients of large gifts of this type, and both were given as memorials to deceased students. The effect of lowered returns from endowments and of the marked restriction of private fortunes through increased tax rates on income and inheritances has been to reduce greatly the number and size of benefactions to education. The prestige accorded to such fields as medicine has tended to channel remaining gifts to their development. Except as schools of architecture participate in the increased general funds of their parent institutions, they have seldom attracted significant support from private sources.

The development of tax-supported public institutions of higher education in the United States has depended upon public demand for educational opportunities and the degree to which the public was willing to underwrite the cost. In the beginning such institutions were usually starved by the barest minimum of appropriations, and thus rarely could challenge the supremacy of private universities with regard to quality of instruction. The establishment of land-grant universities for the provision of technical training stimulated the interest of special groups, such as agriculture and engineering, which in turn could focus strong pressures for increased funds. The profession of architecture has, unfortunately, never been sufficiently large to make its needs felt in this way. In recent years, although public universities have indeed received increased appropriations which have enabled them to widen their offerings and meet higher standards of instruction, they have also been called upon to provide training for vastly increased numbers of students. This was evidenced particularly when the post-World War II deluge of veteran students made it imperative on political grounds for legislatures to vote increased funds. Nevertheless, requests for appropriations invite cries for economy and organized resistance to new tax levies. This is a stumbling block not only for the whole institution, but especially so for a division, such as a school of architecture, which does not enjoy the support of a large, well-organized following.

Thus, in all phases of both private and public higher education, the funds available have been limited. The situation is further complicated by the extraordinary scope of the total program. The number of curricula has become legion, and each program must compete strenuously for any support it obtains. Within the limited total budgets available, it is obvious that few programs can receive support commensurate with their needs and potential benefits. The inevitable result is that administration becomes an agent for compromising rival claims and pressures. Few programs, therefore, can fulfill their best potentialities and most must struggle along at a mere subsistence level. The difference between the desirable and the possible is usually so great that frustration has almost become a normal state of mind for educational administrators.

The *1950 School Survey* obtained data on the budgets provided for schools of architecture. The total for the 59 responding schools was $4,191,001.31. Of this, $3,672,420.78 was devoted to the teaching budget and $518,580.53 to administration. These figures have little meaning, however, unless they are related to the types and quantities of educational services which they provide. The *Survey* data does not permit such analysis. The proportion of courses taught within the school varies in each case and makes impossible the calculation of ratios of cost per student or per course credit unit.

Fortunately, as a part of its accrediting procedure, NAAB computes a Budget-Task Ratio, which reveals for each school the funds provided for the adjusted teaching load in technical subjects. Currently NAAB rates $6.00 or more per adjusted credit unit as Very High; $4-$6 as High; $3-$4 as Acceptable; $2-$3 as Low; and under $2 as Very Low. During the period 1949-1953, NAAB conducted 42 inspections of 39 schools. Omitting the first ratios of the reinspected schools, the distribution of the 39 schools by Budget-Task Ratios were:

	All Schools	*Private Schools*	*Public Schools*
Very High	7	5	2
High	15	5	10
Acceptable	15	8	7
Low	2	1	1
Very Low	—	—	-
Total	39	19	20

These distributions must not be taken as indicating a satisfactory condition. NAAB comparisons are made, not on the basis of desirable standards, but rather in relation to the existing range of observed ratios. In order to promote a higher quality of instruction, for which more highly qualified teachers, smaller teaching loads, and better facilities would be prime requisites, NAAB might well inaugurate a progressive upgrading of standards.

Unfortunately the Commission was unable to discover any systematic comparison of the unit costs of various curricula in universities. Such studies are greatly complicated by the difficulties of segregating the costs of non-professional courses attributable to professional students, and the distribution of general operational and plant charges. A committee of the Association of American Universities is currently studying the accounting practices of Big-Ten universities and the University of California in an effort to establish uniform procedures by which such unit costs can be computed. In general, however, it is probable that the cost of architectural curricula is approximately the same as those in the liberal arts, but much lower than those in engineering, the sciences, and medicine which demand expensive laboratory instruction and facilities.

Any program of improvement of staff and facilities which involves increased costs and therefore a reorientation of balance in existing budget patterns is bound to meet resistance from competing curricula, conservative administrators, and the sources of funds. If schools of architecture are to obtain appropriate sums for their legitimate needs, they must, singly and collectively, aggressively work to secure direct access to the higher administration of their institutions and organize strong support among all who can be interested in architectural progress through the development of education.

The *1950 School Survey* studied the administrative relationships between the units conducting architectural instruction and the chief executives of the parent institutions. In 12 institutions the head of the architectural curriculum reported directly to the chief executive. In 46 he reported to the head of an administrative division and thus was twice removed from the chief executive.[30] In 2 small schools he was thrice removed. Of the 46 units reporting to divisions, 9 of the divisions carried "architecture" as a part of their titles, and, since the administrative heads of these divisions were in most cases architects and in some cases doubled as heads of the architectural units, these 9 units, to all intents and purposes, enjoyed direct access to the chief executive of the institution; 13 other units were incorporated in divisions of fine or applied arts, and in many instances these too were headed by architects. They thus approached direct access, although the possibility of appointing non-architects as division heads made this access less secure; 21 other units reported through divisions of engineering whose heads naturally have almost never been architects.

These administrative patterns reflect the origins of architectural curricula within the collegiate framework. Of the 64 teaching units studied by the *1950 School Survey,* 41—64 per cent—were started within engineering divisions; 16 began as units of divisions of fine or applied arts. Three were set up within divisions of liberal arts. Only 6 were independent divisions from their inception. The initial assignment of architectural curricula to divisions devoted primarily to other fields of instruction was due to small enrollments which made independent status unfeasible. Their association with engineering sprang from the polytechnic system and their inclusion of courses in construction and structures. In some instances, such arrangements have operated effectively when the architectural unit has been given virtual autonomy or when the engineering executive has recognized the special character of architectural instruction. In general, however, experience has revealed inherent incompatibilities due to lack of understanding, sympathy, or interest on the part of division officers. The result has been a marked trend to overcome these handicaps by transfer to other divisions or by attaining status as an independent division.

During the period of maximum influence of the *Ecole des beaux-arts,* many institutions adopted its organizational pattern by establishing divisions of fine and applied arts in which architecture at first served as the nucleus, either by transfer from engineering or by first assignment. Unfortunately such association has tended to spread the impression, particularly in recent years, that architecture is closely linked to the spirit of bohemian individualism which pervades so much contemporary art. It was no accident that the high point of this type of organization coincided with a less rigorous attitude toward courses in construction and structures. It has been commonly held that students of architecture receive considerable benefits through close contacts with those in the arts. In large measure, however, this is not the result of sharing administrative officers. The problems, faculties, and facilities required by curricula in art, music, and drama have little or nothing in common with architecture and the combination of these departments becomes largely an artificial convenience for the institution's general administration. Any benefits which may accrue to students of architecture from such contacts are due rather to the sharing of a few courses or extracurricular events—exhibitions, lectures, or collaborative projects—which is not dependent on administrative connection.

In recent decades architecture has won increasing recognition as a primary discipline which, though linked in some aspects to both engineering and art, nevertheless possesses its own unique qualities and conditions. This realization has produced a definite trend to transform architectural teaching units into independent administrative divisions of the parent institutions. The school of architecture thus becomes a homogeneous entity able to formulate appropriate policies which it can submit directly to the institution's chief executive for approval and implementation. Such an arrangement removes the hazard of presenting the needs of architectural education through an intermediary who may not be capable or willing to press them effectively and who in any case regards architecture as only one competing unit of the whole group for which he is responsible. Independent status likewise places architecture on an equal footing with other professional schools, such as law, medicine, veterinary medicine, and engineering, which have long been accorded full divisional privileges. It also forces the higher administration of the institution to interest itself directly with the development of architectural education. For all of these reasons the Commission believes emphatically that all schools of architecture should work toward full divisional status (*Recommendation 21*).

While direct access to an institution's chief administrator can provide opportunity for effective presentation of the needs and objectives of architectural education, it obviously does not guarantee the securing of adequate funds. It only ensures that these needs will be considered at the top level of decision. A chief executive is the focus of all the various demands within the institution. This fact sometimes raises an objection against independent status for the architectural division in the belief that it cannot alone exert enough pressure to secure satisfactory support. It is at this point that the profession and all its members must unite vigorously in reinforcing the schools' demands for adequate support. Unfortunately in the past practitioners with few exceptions have tended to assume that occasional visits, jury service, and infrequent talks amply fulfill their duty to professional education and that the effort to obtain reasonable financial backing is the concern solely of schoolmen. Under such circumstances architectural educators may be excused if they sometimes feel that architects are overcomplacent and even indifferent to the needs of their schools.

Procurement of adequate support for improvement and expansion of architectural education inevitably means the obtaining of new funds. Past modesty has won for architecture a relatively small share in institutional income and no important readjustment of present resources can be expected. Unless additional support is secured for architecture, the profession will have to be content with its limited traditional methods of education and most of the developments envisioned by this Report will remain only idle dreams. Furthermore, it is axiomatic that any solution to this problem must provide for increased support for schools in both private and public institutions.

The great difficulty lies in the fact that architects as a group are neither numerous enough to exert strong pressure nor wealthy enough to provide the requisite funds. In this, they are at a marked disadvantage in contrast to agriculture, the combined engineering groups, medicine, and law. Nevertheless architects have failed to exploit their very real strength as leaders of the building industry and it is here that a possible solution could be found.

Basic to this idea is the expansion of the schools' scope to embrace the training of professional personnel not only for architecture, but also for other aspects of building. Some schools have already moved in this direction by inaugurating curricula in building construction, housing, and interior design. The full program of such studies and its potentialities has been well described by Tyler S. Rogers, past president of the Producers Council.[31] He envisions an integrated school for the design professions, the contractor-builder group, the manufacturers and suppliers of building materials, and building management. Although it is not explicitly stated, he would no doubt include in the design professions the closely related fields of community planning, landscape architecture, and interior design. Mr. Rogers foresees the clear possibility that participation in harmonious educational objectives might well be a rallying point from which to achieve more widespread understanding, coordination, efficiency, and mutual support among all branches of the presently disjointed building industry.

An alliance embracing all the design professions, the builders and contractors, building labor, and material suppliers could indeed organize unprecedented support for a comprehensive educational program at the collegiate level. Not only would architecture itself share in additional funds, but it would also receive a profound stimulus from association with truly related fields of endeavor. Such an alliance could not be denied when it sought increased appropriations for tax-supported schools of architecture, building, and planning, and it would greatly strengthen appeals for specific endowment of schools maintained by private institutions. The implications of this proposal for the financing of graduate programs and building research will be treated in *Chapter X*.

No doubt some members of the profession will object that such a plan would be at once undignified, special pleading, and an invitation to domination by non-architects.

It must be emphasized that the problem is not one of raising of a few thousand dollars; the realization of the proposals for architecture alone indicate increases on the order of 100 per cent of current budgets—approximately 4 million dollars per year—and for the development of an industry-wide program, an additional national total on the same scale would be needed. The architectural profession alone could not possibly secure such sums. If it is to achieve better training for its own recruits, it must join forces with all the allies it can find. If more capable faculties and improved facilities should be made available for such training, if systematic training should be extended to all phases of the industry, and if improved quality of American buildings is in reality important to the American people, then, far from it being undignified or self-interest for the profession to take such steps, it is a public duty to do so. In such a movement, architects need fear outside domination only if they fail to make good their perennial claim to leadership of the building industry.

Ambitious as such a plan appears to be, the Commission believes that it offers promising bases for rational administrative organization and for securing adequate financing for professional education. Therefore the Commission urges that The Institute and the schools explore further the feasibility of expanding their activities to serve the educational needs of the whole building industry (*Recommendation* 22).

6. PARTIAL AND NON-PROFESSIONAL INSTRUCTION IN ARCHITECTURE

In recent years collegiate schools of architecture have encountered two types of situations which directly affect their objectives and operation. The first has stemmed from the rapid multiplication of junior colleges which grew in number from 46 in 1918 to almost 500 in 1950 and in enrollment from 4504 to 217,572.[32] These junior colleges found a useful function by providing two years of collegiate training easily accessible to local students. For many students this abbreviated course is terminal, but for many others it serves as an economical and convenient transition to advanced studies at regular colleges and universities. For the most part, instruction is confined to general and basic subjects.

The transfer of junior college students to professional curricula in architecture does not in itself involve difficulty since the schools frequently admit students from other curricula in their own or an equivalent institution. Such transfers are subject to all normal tests for the evaluation of amount and quality of credits. If these are satisfactory, transfers proceed without prejudice except that their schedules are usually irregular and in some degree longer, because of irreducible sequences of professional courses in design and structures.

Difficulties and friction have arisen, however, when some junior colleges have attempted to offer the equivalent of elementary professional courses and thus have led their students to believe that they could transfer to full professional curricula without penalty. When this proves to be impossible, as it frequently does, students are natu-

rally distressed and are apt to blame unfairly the professional school. In order to minimize such disappointments, a number of architectural schools have voluntarily advised
the junior colleges in their areas of these difficulties and of the requirements that such
students must meet to be fully acceptable. Such counseling thus amounts to a sort of
informal quasi-accrediting of the junior college courses, especially with regard to
teachers, facilities, and standards. In some instances, the junior colleges themselves
have taken the initiative in consulting nearby professional schools. If a junior college
can provide effective instruction for these courses, there does not seem to be any valid
objection to their work in this area. Indeed, by offering such opportunities at the local
level, they assist the profession by bringing to the attention of talented students the
possibility of careers in architecture which would otherwise go unrecognized. Moreover, if the junior college teachers of architecture have a sufficient grasp of the professional character of architecture, they can perform a useful selective function by
encouraging talented aspirants and discouraging unlikely candidates. Junior colleges
would therefore be well advised to use local architects as part-time teachers or as coun-
selors.

Due to the growth of the junior college movement, especially in certain areas, it has
been suggested that more formal recognition and control of the offerings in architecture should be instituted by the profession.[33] The feasibility of such action may be
questioned. The variation of curricula and curricular schedules in the professional
schools makes it preferable that junior colleges relate their programs to nearby schools.

The second situation confronting the professional schools is more perplexing, and
involves their relationship to technical institutes. The purpose of such technical institutes is to prepare personnel for subordinate positions in technical fields, especially
those in industry. These programs go beyond the artisanship aims and "rules of practice" approach of vocational training, require the use of mathematical and scientific
principles and rational processes beyond the high school level, but limit the length and
intensity of their instruction below that of professional curricula. Such programs are
administered in many ways: as full- or part-time institutes which are endowed, public supported, or operated on a proprietary basis; as terminal courses in junior colleges
or in extension or evening divisions of universities; as training schools of individual
industries; or as correspondence courses. While such programs are not new, their organized development has been greatly intensified in recent years, as for example in the
group of technical institutes created by state initiative in New York.[34]

Technical institutes were at first intended primarily to serve industry and their
greatest success has been in training engineering aides for industry. Many, however,
have extended their work to include partial training in phases of architecture and
building. The avowed objectives are to prepare students to become draftsmen in the
offices of architects, contractors, or builders, or to serve as inspectors, estimators, sales-
men, or similar employees. Curricula extend through one or two years and usually
emphasize drafting, construction materials and methods, and, in some cases, elementary design. Teachers are often graduates of professional schools, and instruction,
though limited in scope, is frequently of good quality.

Although the products of such training may find useful subordinate positions in building and material organizations, the suitability of the program for architectural personnel is less well established. For example, those students of the professional schools who are unable to complete their full curricula are usually better prepared to enter architectural offices than students who have received the abbreviated non-professional training provided by technical institutes. The proposal in *Section 2* of this chapter for the professional schools to provide a terminal third year would seem to solve this problem in a more satisfactory manner. Another difficulty arises in the fact that, despite the limited aims of the technical institutes, a significant portion of their students will apply for transfer to professional curricula and will exert increasing pressure to have their courses accepted at full value. Certainly no professional school would wish to penalize those applicants whose promise transcends the restricted objectives of the technical institutes, but unless they are carefully placed and guided these students could pose serious problems for both themselves and the school. In this regard it should be remembered that the *1950 Survey* disclosed that 16 per cent of all registered architects held certificates from trade schools or technical institutes. Without disparaging this past contribution, it is probable that this type of preparation will diminish in importance. Perhaps the gravest danger is that the creation of a body of partially trained men will lead some to demand partial professional status. In 1946 in Alabama, for example, strong political pressure was exerted on the legislature to recognize the products of such courses as "junior architects" empowered to design any residence or "one story building!" Only prompt and vigorous protest by the profession defeated this paradoxical pretension.

As with junior colleges, it has been urged that the architectural programs of technical institutes be accredited, presumably by NAAB. The Engineers' Council for Professional Development has accepted such responsibility for engineering courses, because of the dominant place such courses have in the technical institute program. The Commission, however, has found no data on the number of technical institutes which offer architectural training or their enrollments. The *1950 School Survey* revealed, however, that the number of transfers received from them by 46 responding professional schools was only 255. Twenty of the schools reported no such transfers. The largest number in one school was 41, but the average for the 26 schools reporting such transfers was only 9.8. Two schools of architecture reported that they exercised formal control of architectural courses offered by technical institutes in their states. Twelve schools provided informal advice on such courses. The Commission believes that at the present time national accrediting of these programs is premature and that schools receiving a significant number of such transfers should evaluate for themselves the programs in their areas.

Some indication of the number and distribution of junior colleges and technical institutes which offer partial training in architecture and related fields is furnished by a recent survey (1954) conducted by The Institute's Department of Education and Research. The table that follows shows the result of this survey by areas.

The concentration in California of 22 of these programs—38 per cent—affirms the

	Total	Archi- tecture	Arch. Engr.	Arch. Drawng.	Bldg. Constr.	Gen'l Engr.	Indust. Arts
New England	2	1	1	—	—	—	—
North Atlantic	2	—	—	—	2	—	—
Midwest	6	4	—	1	1	—	—
North Plains	0	—	—	—	—	—	—
Central Plains	5	—	—	1	—	4	—
Central Atlantic	3	1	—	1	—	1	—
Southeast	4	—	—	—	—	4	—
Southwest	8	1	1	2	1	3	—
Mountain	3	—	1	—	—	2	—
Northwest	3	1	—	—	—	2	—
California	22	4	—	12	—	4	2
Total U. S.	58	12	3	17	4	20	2

general picture obtained by the *1950 School Survey*. The wide dispersion and small number in other areas do not seem as yet to constitute a national problem.

Nevertheless the Commission recognizes that the profession has a legitimate interest in and a potential duty to these courses. It suggests therefore that The AIA should follow these developments with careful attention, offer assistance to the National Council of Technical Schools and the American Association of Junior Colleges in fixing appropriate objectives and standards for such instruction, and urge its chapters to observe and report any programs in their territories (*Recommendation 23*). Furthermore it recognizes that any considerable future expansion of these programs might well require The Institute—no doubt through NAAB—to undertake an accrediting function in this area.

7. THE ACCREDITING OF ARCHITECTURAL SCHOOLS

It was inevitable that American architectural schools, developing as they did in autonomous institutions and under specific local circumstances, would come to exhibit differences in objective and teaching effectiveness. Some enjoyed adequate support and progressive leadership and thus were able to keep abreast of expanding professional demands. Others, however, despite fine intentions, were denied sufficient funds and consequently failed to attain an acceptable quality of instruction. In time architectural education varied widely in aim, content, and rigor. It became clear that, just as the profession itself was striving to establish a uniform meaning for the terms "architecture" and "architect," educators must in some way achieve a workable consensus as to the legitimate purposes and operation of their programs.

The first attempt to evaluate schools of architecture arose as part of a general movement in American higher education. The U. S. Bureau of Education, from its establishment in 1867, had issued a list of "colleges," but political expediency forced the inclusion of any institution which reported students and granted degrees. In 1911 a tentative classified list rating colleges by their students' records in graduate studies provoked such a storm that accrediting by any federal agency was thenceforth abandoned. In 1908–1909 both the National Association of State Universities and the Association of American Universities had urged the adoption of minimum standards for higher institutions. It was however the North Central Association of Colleges and Secondary Schools, which had from 1904 issued annual lists of accredited secondary schools, that undertook in 1909 and published in 1913 the first list of accredited higher institutions. Other regional associations soon followed suit. In 1914 the Association of American Universities finally accepted responsibility for a national accrediting system. Evaluation was based on quantitative criteria.[35]

Meanwhile the professions had interested themselves more and more in their several curricula. The AIA from its earliest years had discussed architectural education; its Committee on Education presented periodic reports on school operations; architectural educators gathered informally at its conventions and frequently addressed the delegates. Other professions exhibited similar tendencies. The American Bar Association established its Section on Legal Education in 1893; the American Medical Association, its Council on Medical Education in 1904; the pharmacists' Syllabus Committee was formed in 1906, and the Dental Education Council in 1909. A parallel trend was the forming of associations of professional schools, such as those of the medical colleges in 1890, and in 1900 the schools of law and pharmacy. Still another type was the Society for the Promotion of Engineering Education, founded in 1893, with a membership of individual teachers drawn from all schools and curricula.[36] Finally in 1910 Abraham Flexner's monumental study, *Medical Education in the United States and Canada,* financed by the Carnegie Foundation for the Advancement of Teaching, not only led to drastic elimination of weak schools in that field, but also suggested the need of scrutinizing and strengthening other professional education.

These trends and the startling increase in the number of architectural schools from 9 in 1895 to 20 in 1911 formed the context which prompted the representatives of eight schools to establish in December, 1912, at the AIA convention in Washington, the Association of Collegiate Schools of Architecture. Membership and voting power were confined to schools, although all except executive sessions were open to teachers from all schools alike. Ten schools—exactly half, enrolling 75 per cent of all students—became charter members. The question of the basis for admitting new member schools immediately arose. It was determined in 1914 after a detailed survey of the 25 then existing schools, conducted by Clarence A. Martin, that applicants must conform to a set of "Standard Minima," which stipulated collegiate status, entrance requirements, length of schooling, course content and credits, and the degree to be awarded. Evaluation was based on an applicant's report since the cost of first-hand inspection was deemed prohibitive. It is interesting to note that this quantitative approach conformed exactly to that adopted by the AAU. By 1923 seven additional schools had qualified for membership, and by 1928 another eight brought the roster to 25.[37]

The objective of ACSA was the improvement of architectural education, and the

Standard Minima proved at once to be a valuable goal and a lever in aiding new or weak schools to secure adequate support from their parent institutions. Membership was indeed the only source of national approval that a school could then attain, and in professional and educational, as well as public, circles, it came to be accepted as quasi-accreditation. Especially as the number of state registration acts grew—there were 28 by 1925—and to the degree that these acts recognized training obtained in approved schools, and because most boards came to use the ACSA roster as their official list of approved schools, a school's membership in the Association took on increasing importance. Thus, to its original educational goal was added a legal and public function which it had not intended and which it was reluctant and unprepared to exercise.

The impact of Flexner's report stirred other professions to undertake similar investigations with the aid of Carnegie grants. In 1918 C. R. Mann published *A Study of Engineering Education;* surveys of legal education appeared in 1921 and 1922; a second engineering inquiry, begun in 1923, led to William E. Wickenden's *A Comparative Study of Engineering Education in the United States and Europe,* published in 1929. W. J. Gies' *Dental Education in the United States and Canada* was issued in 1926, followed in 1928 by A. Z. Reed's *Present-Day Law Schools in the United States and Canada.* Martin's 1913 survey of architectural schools had necessarily been cursory and it was soon apparent that a more thorough investigation was needed. In 1919 ACSA sought Carnegie aid, but not until 1929 was a grant secured. Frank H. Bosworth, Jr., and Roy Childs Jones were appointed to carry out the project and, during the academic year 1930–1931, visited 49 schools in the United States and Canada. Their succinct and penetrating report, *A Study of Architectural Schools,* appeared in 1932.

Meanwhile, during the 20's, educators reacted strongly against accrediting based primarily on arbitrary quantitative criteria which, literally imposed, neglected many other factors of consequence, threatened standardization, and discouraged wholesome individuality and experimentation.[38] In schools of architecture, which were so concerned with the development of creative skills, such restrictions proved to be unbearable, the more so because they ran counter to mounting impatience with prevailing eclectic taste. The onslaught of the Great Depression accentuated this feeling. When Bosworth and Jones took great care to analyze the schools from the standpoint of quality of teaching principles, methods, results, and potential, and reported much of value and promise in exceptional non-standard schools, ACSA immediately abolished the Standard Minima and adopted a much more liberal qualitative basis for membership based upon first-hand inspection of applicants. Nevertheless, in lieu of any other criteria, many registration boards continued to use the Association's roster as equivalent to an accrediting list.

Concurrently in 1932 The AIA sponsored the formation of an Advisory Committee on Preparation for the Practice of Architecture, with representatives from The Institute, ACSA, NCARB, and BAID. The purpose of the group was the correlation of professional education both in school and during candidacy. The first outcome was the setting up in 1934 of the Mentor plan for the guidance of candidates, which will be discussed in *Chapter VIII.* The problem of accrediting the schools continued to grow as new schools were established and as new registration laws were enacted. Despite the fear of definite standards, the adequacy of individual schools had to be determined. ACSA lacked both funds and authority to undertake the task, and a growing number of educators came to believe that a national system of accrediting should be the responsibility of the profession itself. This view gained reinforcement when the five major engineering societies, the SPEE (now the American Society of Engineering Education), and the National Council of State Boards of Engineering Examiners joined in 1932 to establish the Engineers' Council for Professional Development which in 1936 began national accrediting of engineering curricula. In 1937–1938 ACSA delegated George Young, Jr., and Goldwin Goldsmith to conduct an exhaustive factual survey for the accrediting of the schools, but lack of funds prevented the intended first-hand visitations to schools with apparent weaknesses. This experience clearly demonstrated the urgent need for a fresh approach to the problem.[39]

The solution came in 1938 when ACSA proposed to The AIA and NCARB that accrediting should be co-sponsored by the three organizations. The Advisory Committee likewise agreed to this decision. This led in 1940 to the creation of the National Architectural Accrediting Board, composed of six members, two from each of the three groups. Edwin Bergstrom, president of The Institute, was elected first president of the Board. The NAAB charter charged it to publish annually an official list of accredited schools. Furthermore it was directed to judge applying schools by gathering factual data and by conducting first-hand inspections. Nevertheless NAAB was expressly required "not to create conditions or have conditions created that will tend toward standardization of educational philosophies or practices." The charter reiterated this point by stating, "the list of accredited schools shall be issued as a list only and no standards shall be set up or published concerning the manner in which or concerning the basis on which accrediting has been or will be made."[40] The formulation of procedures absorbed considerable thought and time, and the advent of war also postponed the beginning of operations. The first inspections were carried out early in 1945 and the first list was issued in the same year. After initial approval, all schools are reinspected at five-year intervals.

The determination of minimum adequacy was one of the first and most difficult problems which confronted the Board. Although the Board studiously observed the charter's prohibition of rigid "standards," the obligation to judge nevertheless required bases for decisions and these have been euphemistically denoted as "significant criteria." After long analysis and experience, these criteria were fixed in accordance with conditions and practices of those schools which were generally recognized as conducting superior programs. Some 50 of these criteria are provided by the applicant's Factual Report, and these include:

Parent institution: type, support, enrollment, accreditation, officers, tuition and fees, term length, credit units.
School: administrative relationship, divisional association, professional and other curricula, options, degrees, objectives.

Budget: teaching, administrative, fee income, endowment income, funds for prizes, scholarships, and student aid.

Facilities, Quarters: instructional, staff, library, exhibition, judgment.

Library: staff, books, periodicals, slides, purchase funds.

Students: enrollment, geographical origin.

Curriculum: entrance requirements, curricular length and credits, curricular content, outside contacts.

Faculty: number, rank, full-time equivalents, assigned courses, courses for non-professional students, outside staff used, general and technical education, travel, teaching and field experience, registration, professional societies, creative activities, academic and professional distinctions.

Most of these data are then rated by numerical scales based on ranges observed among all schools and classified in five grades from Very High to Very Low. Some are combined to provide certain informative ratios, such as the Faculty-Task Ratio and the Budget-Task Ratio described earlier in this chapter. Finally the results are presented graphically by means of a Factual Map which clearly reveals for each item the position of the school in relation to the range of existing conditions in all schools.[41] This device has proved very useful not only to the Board, but also to the schools themselves. While the data thus collected are primarily factual and quantitative in character, they constitute only part of each investigation and, far from being ends in themselves, they are regarded simply as indicative of conditions which facilitate or retard the achievement of quality. They are not used as automatic evaluators, but rather to aid the Board in arriving at its final over-all judgment. For some schools which labor under excessive handicaps, perhaps unrealized, this first factual stage permits self-appraisal and delay in further investigation until corrective measures can be taken.

The second stage in the accrediting process entails on-the-spot inspection of the applying school by a team of visitors representing the Board. Such a visitation usually extends over two or three days and allows observation and appraisal of the more intangible aspects of the school's operation. Conferences with institutional executives can give insight into existing liaison and opportunities for future support. Direct contact with the school's faculty and students is invaluable in assessing spirit and rapport. Attendance at various classes tells quickly the quality of the instructional climate. Direct sampling can ensure review of not only superior, but also average student work. From such first hand experience, the visiting team can with considerable confidence report formally to the Board on the 25 qualitative items which the inspection questionnaire contains.

In the selection of its three-man inspection teams, NAAB has always attempted to include representative points of view by choosing one educator, one practitioner, and one member of a registration board. Often, of course, individual members have had experience in all of these fields. Frequently members of NAAB have served as visitors, but the magnitude of the program has necessarily required the recruitment of others. Between 1944 and 1952 the Board conducted 95 inspections of 43 different schools. To accomplish this, it enlisted about sixty practitioners and teachers. This was not only a service to the profession, but it also provided an excellent means of acquainting practitioners with the current problems, objectives, and operation of the schools.

Fortified with the school's Factual Report and the Inspectors' Report, the Board itself determines the applicant's acceptability. This step is performed at the annual meeting. In many instances there is little question of the outcome. Other decisions, however, involve scrupulous weighing of ponderable and imponderable factors, for, while the fundamental public responsibility is clear, NAAB must strive to administer it in a way that will aid each school in attaining acceptable status. The AIA Commission believes that NAAB has produced in its first nine years of operation a sound record of accomplishment. By 1953, 45 schools—80 per cent of the 56 which are considered to have strictly professional curricula—have been accredited. In 1953 these 45 schools enrolled 89 per cent of all architectural students. That the Board has successfully carried out its initial mandate to avoid any rigid standardization is amply proved by the diverse characters of the schools which it has accredited. It has implemented the general consensus that five years is the desirable minimum length of architectural curricula and, beginning in 1949, all accredited schools have had to conform to this requirement. It has also reduced the former diversity in the amount of technical studies in curricula from a range of $2\frac{1}{3}$ to $4\frac{1}{2}$ years to a range of $3\frac{1}{2}$ to 4 years. A number of schools have been aided in correcting obvious weaknesses. Excessive ratios of students to faculty and budgets have been eased. Perhaps the strongest possible evidence of the success of NAAB was given by the *1950 School Survey* which polled 41 inspected schools as to their reactions to visitation procedures; 88 per cent considered that the Pattern Map gave a helpful appraisal of their situations; 98 per cent believed that members of the inspection team were adequately qualified for the task; 95 to 88 per cent felt that the teams displayed proper interest and understanding as to curricular and course organization, faculty qualifications, student problems, and administrative questions. Most important of all, 56 per cent reported that their accrediting inspection had given valuable aid in ameliorating local difficulties. Another indication of the success of accrediting has been the almost universal use of the Board's lists by state registration boards. In 1952 New York was the only state which still compiled its own list.[42]

The development of accrediting has raised many knotty problems. One of the most portentous is the upward modification of the level of minimum adequacy. In this connection it is well to recognize that, since the basic purpose of accrediting is defined as the preparation of an official list of approved schools for the use of registration boards, accrediting acts only as a safeguard against the weakest programs. It does not certify—as many laymen and some architects seem to suppose—anything beyond minimum acceptability. The envisioning of and striving for superior and optimal effectiveness remains the responsibility of individual faculties and the profession. Nevertheless it is unthinkable that any current minimum can ever be permitted to become a permanent and static barrier to social progress. While high quality cannot be legislated, it is legitimate for society and the profession to expect and demand a gradual and continuing upgrading of the threshold of minimum adequacy which, by stimulating the improvement of weak programs, can progressively lift the average of the whole group. Such changes can succeed only if they represent a general consensus of opinion. NAAB has already moved in this direction by raising, in 1952, the acceptable minima of its Faculty- and Budget-Task Ratios. The Commission believes that its own appointment arose from such a point of view and that this Report presents many proposals which after full discussion can in time effect new definitions of adequacy. It holds that it is the continuing duty of The Institute, ACSA, and NAAB to consider accrediting as a dynamic process and to use it judiciously for the improvement of professional education. Thus, while accrediting is primarily a legal function, the modern conception of law as an implement of social purpose amply justifies the interpretation and use of accrediting to achieve the fundamental purposes of society, the profession, and the schools.

Another particularly vexing problem has concerned the status of curricula in architectural engineering. In this matter, NAAB has from the outset felt compelled by the terms of its charter to limit its jurisdiction to curricula intended to prepare for the professional practice of architecture. The wide variation in the character and content of curricula in architectural engineering has already been noted in *Section 4*. When such curricula were devoted primarily to the training of structural, equipment, or building erection personnel, or when they failed to provide an irreducible minimum of professional training in architecture itself, NAAB took the logical stand that they could not be considered for architectural accrediting. On the other hand, it maintained that, if the real intent was architecture and if sufficient training in architecture was indeed provided, such training should be designated as a structural or construction option in architecture in order to avoid confusion and ambiguity.[43]

This position at first provoked heated opposition by some schools which regarded the action as excluding graduates in architectural engineering from the profession of architecture. The situation was further complicated by the fact that many registration boards had for many years made little, if any, distinction between degrees in architecture and architectural engineering, particularly when schools in their own state offered the latter course. Confusion and inequity would be further compounded if graduates of a four-year curriculum in architectural engineering were to be given equal recognition with those of a five-year program in architecture. NAAB, however, had pointed out from the beginning that its purpose was not to bar from the profession those who have special interests in structures, but to make it possible for them to resume their proper place in it. Only thus, so NAAB reasoned, could the profession overcome the distressing misconception inherited from the late 19th century under which architecture had been deprived of its inseparable structural content. Whatever the cause that produced this unhappy effect, the intent of NAAB's action was to reestablish the historic integrated meaning of architecture which had already reasserted itself as a primary tenet of contemporary architectural thinking. Although opposition arose in part from sentiment developed from half a century of use, the proponents of the term, architectural engineering, were thus placed in the untenable position of

288

championing the independence of the discipline for which they had so long claimed prime importance in architecture itself. For curricula in which structural content was conceived as integrated into the broad field of architecture, NAAB has always accorded full recognition on their individual merits, with the sole proviso that they were designated as architecture and not as engineering. Only one school, the State College of Washington, has thus far found itself barred from the new terminology by the wording of its legal charter. The net effect of NAAB's stand has been to accelerate the transformation of architectural engineering curricula into options of the curricula in architecture.

Nevertheless NAAB also recognized that in its narrower, non-professional sense architectural engineering, or better, building engineering, could apply useful specialized personnel. Many architectural engineering curricula had indeed chosen this engineering objective and the accrediting of them remained a problem, the scale of which was indicated by the fact that in 1950 there were in 26 schools about 1700 students in architectural engineering, about one-seventh of the number in architecture. For this type of curriculum, NAAB considered itself not to be the appropriate accrediting agency. Early in its development NAAB had conferred with the Engineers Council for Professional Development which was then studying requests to accredit the engineering content of architectural engineering curricula because so many of these programs were administered in engineering colleges. One proposal for dual jurisdiction by which ECPD would accredit the engineering portion and NAAB the architectural portion of architectural engineering was rejected as fallacious in principle and unworkable in practice. The outcome was that NAAB accepted jurisdiction for curricula intended to train students for the practice of architecture and ECPD for curricula intended to train engineers in certain specialized structural and mechanical phases of building. By 1952 ECPD had accredited 18 curricula enrolling about half of the students of architectural engineering.

The validity of NAAB's decision in this matter has gained general recognition. In 1948 The Institute adopted a resolution submitted by its Committee on Education and endorsed by NAAB confirming the principles on which it was based. Moreover, the extension of the effects of registration acts makes it increasingly desirable to attain uniform terminology. The Commission, after close review of the present situation concurs that the sole official designation of architectural curricula should be the name *architecture.* It further urges that the name *building engineering,* or similar descriptive title, be substituted for *architectural engineering* to designate engineering curricula devoted primarily to building problems (*Recommendation 24*).

The increasing number of architectural courses offered by junior colleges and technical institutes and the applications of their students for admission with advanced standing to professional curricula has encouraged the demand that NAAB should undertake the accrediting of them. The fact that ECPD has become the accrediting agency for technical institutes seems to reinforce this request. It is obvious, however, that the multiplicity of semi-professional courses in engineering produces a volume which permits ECPD to operate with reasonable economy in this field. The *1950*

School Survey found, as already noted in Section 6, that the total number of architectural transfers from technical and vocational institutes was only 254 for the whole country. The largest group in any one school numbered 41 at the University of Texas. The concentration of these programs for the most part within a few areas and the scattered distribution of the rest would present considerable difficulties if NAAB were to attempt accrediting on a national basis. For the time being, it would seem best to accomplish these ends on a local or regional basis through the cooperation of the technical institutes, the schools of architecture, and local representatives of The AIA. In the meantime, the Commission recommends that The Institute and NAAB should keep in close touch with this situation so that, if developments warrant it, appropriate measures may be taken (*Recommendation 25*).

It has also been suggested that NAAB should undertake the accrediting of graduate curricula in architecture. Detailed consideration of this question will be reserved for *Chapter X*.

Another problem which has confronted NAAB concerned the mechanics of the accrediting process. In addition to the formulation of a consistent body of principles the Board has found that their application to specific cases and to the whole group of schools has involved a prodigious amount of detail. This was especially true during the initial period when both theory and practice had to be developed and refined simultaneously, but the operation of the permanent program which entails the publication of the annual list and the reinspection and re-evaluation of each school every five years, or about ten schools per year, will also comprise a formidable task. This work falls upon the six members of the Board and the members of the profession whom they enlist for inspection teams. Since their decisions are of far-reaching importance to the reputation and character of individual schools, to legally constituted registration boards, and to the welfare and quality of the profession itself, responsibility for the effectiveness and justice of the process becomes a taxing and serious business.

The accomplishments of NAAB thus far have been achieved despite very slender financial resources. Members of the Board and inspectors serve without pay, but travel costs for meetings and visitations have formed a major expense. In the formative years, 1941 through 1944, before inspections began, total expenses came to about $5500, of which The AIA contributed 90 per cent, ACSA 7 per cent, and NCARB 3 per cent. In 1945 when visitations were first undertaken, fees from 35 applying schools totaled $3500, but the balance of expenditures was provided by contributions of $1500 from The Institute, $300 from ACSA, and $100 from NCARB. In 1947 an annual school fee of $50 replaced the $100 fee for inspection, so that during the five-year period between reexaminations the schools would contribute a larger portion of the cost of their inspections.

These budgetary limitations have made it necessary to restrict NAAB operations to one annual meeting per year, to select visiting teams with an eye to minimum travel, to forego all but the most rudimentary clerical assistance, to transact much business by correspondence, and to impose upon the voluntary service of its officers an excessive amount of routine executive detail. Such conditions plague many worthy causes, but the Commission believes that the accrediting process in function and importance has passed well beyond its initial altruistic stage and should be accorded firm support commensurate with a broader concept of its proper duties. At its present scope of operations, the Board estimates that an annual budget of $9000 is required. A plan to increase the annual school fee to $75 is under discussion. On the basis of 45 currently accredited schools, this would yield $3375. For the balance of $6000, the Commission believes that, while The Institute is vitally concerned in the program and may be disposed to contribute half of the necessary subsidy, it is unfair to expect it to underwrite entirely a service which has developed for and is utilized in such large measure by state agencies, i.e., the registration boards. For this reason the Commission strongly urges that the state boards, or their association, the NCARB, recognize the benefits which they derive from the work of NAAB by contributing fees or subsidy in the amount of at least half of the required balance (*Recommendation 26*).

Several aspects of the mechanics of the accrediting process might be restudied with profit. It has been suggested, for example, that the membership of NAAB should be increased from six to twelve in order that one member could be drawn from each AIA region and thus permit the Board to maintain closer touch with the schools, the registration process, and the profession's views on education in each region. The enlarged Board would allow greater participation of members on inspection teams and thus give the group a more direct insight with regard to school problems. Such an increase, however, would double the cost of the Board's meetings and therefore cannot be considered apart from the question of additional financial support. Nevertheless the Commission believes that The Institute, ACSA, NCARB, and NAAB should study the proposal of an enlarged NAAB and give careful consideration to its implications (*Recommendation 27*).

Another criticism has arisen from the considerable interval which often occurs between actual inspection and the annual meeting of the Board when it approves or rejects applicants for annual listing. For example, cases have been noted when notification of deficiencies was so delayed that schools operating on the basis of biennial budgets have been deprived of the strong support which the NAAB report could have given to their request for corrective funds. While the diverse schedules of budget preparation of the institutions involved no doubt prohibit complete coordination, it is possible that most would benefit by the publication of the accredited list sometime in the late fall rather than during the summer. It is difficult to say whether this change would be of major concern to the schools, but it would be easy for NAAB to conduct a poll of school administrators to ascertain their views. A second alternative would be to hold an additional midwinter meeting of the Board to act upon those schools which have been inspected during the preceding fall. These schools could then be notified of the results without delay, even though the official list could still be issued on an annual basis. The holding of this additional meeting would depend, however, upon securing additional funds. While the Commission does not wish to suggest any specific changes in these mechanical details, it believes that NAAB should review its own procedures at regular intervals and refine and adjust them promptly in order not only to achieve its own purposes, but also to permit maximum cooperation by the schools (*Recommendation 28*).

The basic principle of accrediting is the rendering of judgment as to the minimum adequacy of the educational program of the applying schools. NAAB's charter, however, contained in addition the phrase "with the general objective that a well integrated and coordinated program of architectural education be developed which will be national in scope. . . ." This might be interpreted as implying that NAAB should formulate an over-all master plan for architectural education in the United States and modify its judgments of individual schools according to their presumed validity in this general plan. Since, however, NAAB's charter expressly forbade it to establish or impose any standardized pattern upon the schools, it has remained in a somewhat ambiguous position with regard to national criteria. Indeed, except for occasional consultations regarding probable demand for a school within a specific area, it has wisely limited itself to raising questions in its annual reports as to the minimum size of a school for effective instruction and the desirability of strengthening existing schools rather than the establishment of more schools. While members of NAAB are in a favorable position to formulate opinions on these questions, the Commission believes that official advice regarding the establishment of new schools is more properly the province of The AIA. This question will be considered in detail in *Section 8*.

The growth of accrediting in American higher education has produced undoubted benefits. It has enabled many institutions and divisions of institutions to secure more adequate support and to measure themselves against their neighbors. Nevertheless it would have been surprising had this method of supervision and control escaped abuse. In recent years, indeed, accrediting agencies have proliferated to such an extent that universities and colleges have found themselves forced to deal with scores of outside, self-appointed, and often arbitrary, agencies, and in a number of fields even with rival agencies. The cost to institutions has often become a burden. One Midwestern university reportedly pays $27,000 per year in accrediting fees. Moreover some agencies and some inspectors have been cited as attempting to control matters outside the province of any proper definition of accrediting. Even when accrediting is confined to legitimate ends, institutional officials tend to resent the implication that they cannot be trusted to order their own affairs but must be subjected to outside pressures to ensure the proper development of their constituent divisions.

As a means of self-protection, some associations of universities have maintained committees to accredit accreditors. ACSA, and later its successor, NAAB, were thus recognized as the official agency in the field of architecture by the Joint Committee on Accrediting, representing the AAU, the National Association of State Universities, the Association of Land-Grant Colleges and Universities, and the Association of Urban Universities. In 1951, however, a National Commission on Accrediting was organized by a group of institutions with the intent of suppressing independent accrediting agencies and substituting for them a number of regional accrediting associations sponsored by regional groups of universities and colleges. In 1952 this National

Commission requested all professional agencies, including NAAB and ECPD, to suspend their activities pending organization of these regional associations. The outcome was a direct refusal by NAAB and ECPD on the basis that their accrediting operations had semi-public status in ensuring public bodies, the registration boards, of the minimum adequacy of the schools' instruction.

This review is pertinent here because, while strongly criticizing accrediting agencies in general, officers of the National Commission were forced to recognize that NAAB had conducted its operations in an unusually enlightened manner. It is clear that the profession can take legitimate pride in the way in which NAAB has fulfilled a difficult assignment during a period characterized by tumult and emergency. While no doubt future developments will suggest adjustment and refinement of its procedures, NAAB has already created a constructive means by which the profession can implement at least a part of its obligation to architectural education.

8. THE DEMAND FOR ARCHITECTURAL EDUCATION

The quality of architectural education is of transcendent importance, but the conception of architecture as "an art for all men" means that the schools must also train enough personnel to meet the needs of an expanding profession which serves a growing and maturing society. Therefore the quantity of architectural education and the number, size, and location of schools of architecture become significant problems of policy alike for the public, the profession, and educational institutions.

Table 56 presents the enrollments of U. S. architectural schools for the years 1898, 1911, 1930, and 1933–1953.[44] It also groups these schools in 11 geographical areas.[45] *Figure 27A* charts the area and national totals of students in curricula in architecture. While favorable conditions multiplied total enrollment fourfold between 1898 and 1911 and again threefold between 1911 and 1930, the incompleteness of the record does not reveal the marked expansion about 1910, the declines due to World War I and the subsequent adjustment, and the renewed expansion in the late 20's. These variations can be seen in the enrollment record of a specific school plotted in *Figure 28*. *Figure 27A* does show in dramatic form the effects of depression and World War II. Between 1930 and 1935 the number of architectural students dropped 32 per cent. By 1940 two-thirds of this loss had been regained, but the total of 4131 was still 11 per cent under 1930. In 1943 the war emergency had cut total enrollment to 1382, a loss of 66 per cent in three years. With the ending of hostilities and the realization of building shortages created by depression and war, a deluge of students—veterans and civilians—flocked to the schools. At the peak in 1949, enrollment reached 11,665, an increase of 844 per cent over 1943 and 252 per cent over the previous record in 1930. In 1953 the passing of the emergency brought a decline in enrollment to 9427, 19 per cent below 1949.

Figure 27B shows the percentage distribution of these enrollments by areas. In 1898, 80.1 per cent of all students were concentrated in the New England, North At-

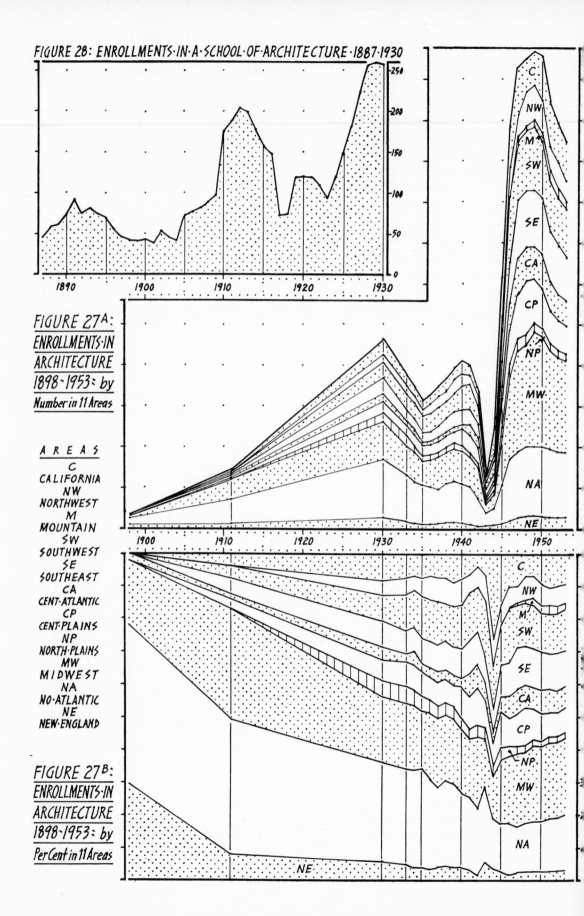

FIGURE 28: ENROLLMENTS·IN·A·SCHOOL·OF·ARCHITECTURE·1887-1930

1890   1900   1910   1920   1930

FIGURE 27ᴬ:
ENROLLMENTS·IN
ARCHITECTURE
1898~1953: by
Number in 11 Areas

AREAS
C
CALIFORNIA
NW
NORTHWEST
M
MOUNTAIN
SW
SOUTHWEST
SE
SOUTHEAST
CA
CENT·ATLANTIC
CP
CENT·PLAINS
NP
NORTH·PLAINS
MW
MIDWEST
NA
NO·ATLANTIC
NE
NEW·ENGLAND

FIGURE 27ᴮ:
ENROLLMENTS·IN
ARCHITECTURE
1898~1953: by
Per Cent in 11 Areas

lantic, and Central Atlantic areas. In 1911 these areas enrolled 50.7 per cent; in 1930, 40.1 per cent; and in 1950, 24.9 per cent. Although the actual number of students in these areas grew tenfold from 290 in 1898 to 2881 in 1950, it is noteworthy that in 1950, despite peak demand, enrollment in these areas was only 155 per cent of 1930, whereas the remaining areas took care of 314 per cent of their 1930 enrollments. The relative decline of these Eastern areas emphasizes the marked development of architectural education in other sections of the country. For example, the North Atlantic area accommodated the largest number of students—from 20 to 30 per cent during the 30's, but with the closing of the curriculum at New York University, and especially after 1945, it declined to 14 to 16 per cent and relinquished first place to the Midwest area which grew from 18 to 20 per cent in the 30's to slightly more than 23 per cent in the 50's. The other areas have expanded in similar fashion.

A comparison of area enrollments and the schools attended by architects also emphasizes these shifts (*Table 37*). *Figure 30* (p. 302) plots the data. Since the attendances reported in the *1950 Survey* occurred over several decades, the large proportion concentrated in the Northeastern areas is not surprising. For the decade, 1934-1943, the greater Northeast still led, but all other areas, except the Central Atlantic and Mountain, show higher shares of the national total. In particular the Southwest received enrollments twice the proportion accorded the attendances reported by architects. During the following decade, 1944-1953, with the enormous increase of enrollments due to veterans, the Midwest area held its former percentage, but the North Atlantic—despite acceptance of approximately twice their previous enrollments, declined by 38 per cent. This loss reappeared as substantial gains in the Central Atlantic, Southeastern, and California areas.

Since all but one of the schools of the New England and North Atlantic areas are maintained by private institutions, and since those elsewhere are preponderantly in public institutions, the expansion of architectural education outside the Northeastern superarea has increased greatly the proportion of the total enrollment cared for by public schools. In 1898 there was only one tax-supported school of architecture and it enrolled only 14.7 per cent of all architectural students. By 1911 public schools accounted for 36.8 per cent; in 1930 this had grown to 53.7 per cent; and by 1940 they enrolled 66.2 per cent of all students. In 1950, 70.7 per cent were thus enrolled; but in 1953 this had declined slightly to 69.4 per cent. Comparison of the relative changes of the private and public groups is instructive:

	School Enrollments			*Per cent of 1930*			*Per cent of Change*		
YEAR	TOTAL	PRIVATE	PUBLIC	TOTAL	PRIVATE	PUBLIC	TOTAL	PRIVATE	PUBLIC
1930	4622	2140	2482	100	100	100	—	—	—
1935	3151	1238	1913	68	58	77	−32	−42	−23
1940	4131	1392	2739	89	65	110	+131	+112	+143
1943	1382	549	833	30	26	34	−66	−61	−69
1949	11665	3447	8218	251	161	331	+844	+628	+990
1953	9427	2893	6534	202	135	263	−19	−15	−21

Thus, the public institutions suffered only half as much from the depression and were able to recover more completely and more promptly from it due to the appeal of low tuitions and convenient locations. They were also able to expand more rapidly to care for the pressure of veteran applicants due to their access to public funds to meet the added costs not covered by student fees. Private schools, on the other hand, have since 1949 declined less. This is probably due to the decline of the public schools from their higher degree of expansion. The net result in 1953, however, was that during the preceding 23 years the enrollment of the public schools had increased twice as much as that of the private institutions.

The foregoing discussion has dealt only with students enrolled in curricula in architecture. It has been observed in *Chapter IV,* however, that a considerable number of registered architects are graduates in architectural engineering. Since some of these curricula are intended as preparation for the practice of architecture, it would be desirable to review enrollments of the whole group. Unfortunately the records are very fragmentary.[46] *Table 56* presents data for 1930 and 1950–1953.[47] In 1930 the 1268 architectural engineering students reported had a relationship of 27.4 per cent to the 4622 students in architecture. In the early 50's this ratio had declined to about 16 per cent, due no doubt to the conversion of many of these programs to structural options in architecture.[48] In 1930 and 1953 the number of schools offering such curricula and their enrollments by areas were as follows:

| | Number of Schools* | | Students in Architectural Engineering | | | | PER CENT OF |
| | | | NUMBER | | PER CENT | | |
	1930	1953	1930	1953	1930	1953	1930
New England	1		69	—	5.5	—	0
North Atlantic	1	2	96	74	7.6	4.7	81
Midwest	4	2(1)	355	243	28.0	15.3	69
North Plains	2	1	88	29	6.9	1.8	33
Central Plains	5	5	238	192	18.8	12.0	81
Central Atlantic	3(2)	3	105	106	8.3	6.7	101
Southeast	1	2(1)	31	215	2.4	13.5	695
Southwest	5(1)	6(1)	201	411	15.9	25.8	490
Mountain	—	1	—	45	—	2.8	—
Northwest	2(1)	2(1)	85	117	6.7	7.3	138
California	—	1(1)	—	160	—	10.1	—
Total	24(4)	25(5)	1268	1592	100	100	125

* Figures in parentheses indicate schools offering solely the curriculum in architectural engineering.

The marked drop of enrollments in the Northeastern areas of the country and the shift of concentration from the Midwest and Central Plains to the Southeast and Southwest are noteworthy. The average enrollment in 1930 was 52.8 and in 1953, 63.7.

In the latter year however, five schools totaled 819 students, 51.5 per cent of all. The average enrollment of the remaining 20 schools was 38.6. The largest enrollment was 219 and the smallest 14.

The relation of architectural enrollments to the profession, to urban population, and to the college age group provides three ratios which over a period of years indicate recognizable trends. *Table 57* lists these data for architecture, engineering, and law, over the period 1900–1950.[49] *Figure 29,* overleaf, compares the results. The ratios of members of these three professions to urban population contrast the 50-year 43 per cent decline of lawyers from 356.3 to 203.8 per 100,000 and the 24 per cent decline of architects from 35.1 to 26.5 with the marked expansion of engineers from 175.4 to 449.8, an increase of 155 per cent. The size relationship between these ratios should be noted. In 1900 lawyers stood highest; the engineers' ratio was 49.3 per cent of the lawyers'; and the architects' 9.9 per cent of the lawyers' and 20 per cent of the engineers'. Since 1920 the engineers' ratio has been highest and in 1950 the lawyers' was 45.3 per cent of it. In 1950 the architects' ratio stood at 13.0 per cent of the lawyers' and only 5.9 per cent of the engineers'. Thus during the past half century architects had gained 32 per cent relative to lawyers and dropped 70.5 per cent relative to engineers.

In considering all ratios involving students in architecture, two points must be kept in mind. First, all enrollments in 1950 were much larger than normal due to veterans who constituted 37.7 per cent of the men enrolled in universities, colleges, and professional schools. Moreover 51.6 per cent of all men in these schools were 23 years of age or older.[50] Thus, all 1950 ratios reflect the presence of those groups—both veteran and non-veteran—whose education had been delayed by the war emergency. Therefore estimates of non-veteran student ratios have been attempted.[51] The second point is that none of the decennial years under consideration can be termed *normal. Figure 28* reveals this clearly. The 1898 architectural enrollment came just after a sharp decline of almost 50 per cent due to economic depression. The 1910 figure occurs just after the beginning of a remarkable expansion of enrollments—both general and architectural. In 1930, though depression had set in, enrollments still reflected the peak of the previous year; 1940 totals were obviously low. Nevertheless if these limitations are kept in mind the ratios retain considerable interest.

The ratios of students per 100,000 urban population, shown in *Figure 29,* all display upward trends. For all architectural students, the 1950 ratio is 9.7 times that for 1898. For non-veteran students, however, the growth is 6.1 times. For all engineering students the 1950 ratio is 4.5 times that for 1900, and for non-veterans 2.8. For all law students the 50-year period shows a rise of only 1.5 times, and for non-veterans, there is a drop of 4.5 per cent. The relative small change in law ratios is to be explained, however, by the fact that during the 20's and 30's admission to most law schools came to require at least two years of pre-law college training.[51a] Unfortunately no statistics are available on the number of pre-law students. If the mortality of such students approximates that in other curricula, it would require about 3 admissions to pre-law training to produce one admission in law school. This also means that law school enrollments would represent only 46 per cent of the whole group. This implies a total of 122,580 pre-law and law students which would give a 1950 ratio of 3.3 times the 1900 ratio. This would correspond roughly with the 4.5 growth in engineering. On the same basis, the 1950 ratio for non-veteran pre-law and law students would be

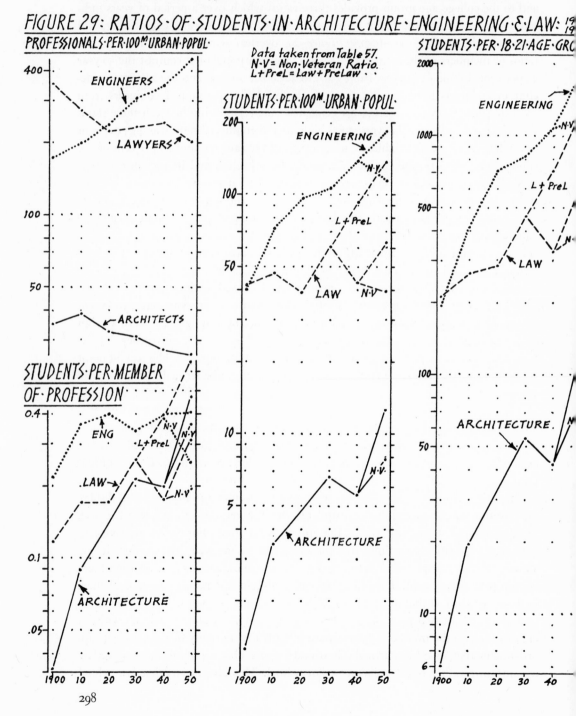

FIGURE 29: RATIOS·OF·STUDENTS·IN·ARCHITECTURE·ENGINEERING·&·LAW: 19/19

2 times 1900. It is quite clear therefore that all of these expanding ratios reveal the rapid transfer of professional education from practitioners' offices to college class-rooms. Since this has been especially true in architecture, the fact that the growth of its ratio was 2.1 times engineering and 2.9 times law need not cause alarm. It should also be emphasized that all architectural ratios show a much lower relative level than either engineering or law.

If the ratio of students to urban population can be interpreted as response to de-mand, that of students to the size of the college age group reveals the portion of available youths who are attracted to professional curricula. Again, the 50-year trend has been expansion. The 1950 ratio of architectural students per 100,000 of the 18–21 age group was 20.8 times the 1898 figure; or 12.9 times for non-veterans. Comparable proportions in engineering were 9.5 and 6.0, and in law 3.0 and 1.9, or, including pre-law, 6.1 and 4.1. All of these increases parallel the 13-fold upsurge of college at-tendance in the past half century and also show the increasing tendency of youth to secure collegiate training for professional careers.

The third ratio, that of students to members of the profession, reflects both per-sonnel demands and opportunities and has often been interpreted as an indication of prospective competition within a profession. In contrast to other ratios based on population, this set shows individual characteristics derived from the developmental patterns of the professions themselves. In 1898 the ratio of architectural students per architect was 0.0342, and it mounted steadily, except in 1940, to 0.472 per "census archi-tect" and 0.582 per registered architect in 1950. The first was 13.8 and second was 17 times the 1898 ratio. The comparable ratios for non-veteran students was 8.6 and 10.6 times. On the other hand, the ratios in engineering, after doubling by 1920, have re-mained surprisingly constant at about 0.4. If veterans are subtracted in 1950, the ratio shows an alarming drop to 0.252. The explanation of this situation lies in the extraor-dinary increase—53 per cent—in the number of engineers during the preceding decade, as against 14.9 per cent for architects and 0.4 per cent for lawyers. For law, the 1910, 1920, and 1940 ratios were identical, but in 1950 it mounted to 0.311, or to 0.678 if pre-law students are included. Although architecture had the highest ratio—17 per cent above engineering, it stands 30 per cent below the ratio for pre-law and law students.

The 0.582 ratio of all architectural students per registered architect may be expressed as 1 student per 1.72 architects. An Appendix to the *1951 Annual Report of NAAB* compared this ratio unfavorably with a ratio given as 1 medical student per 8.6 medi-cal practitioners, calculated on a 1951 medical school enrollment of 23,400 and a roster of 201,300 doctors. Since this comparison has received widespread circulation, it seems necessary to point out here that this ratio likewise does not take into account the large number of students enrolled in pre-medical curricula. Considering the minimum 3-year length of such pre-professional programs, the high scholastic average required, and the acceptance by the medical schools of only about half of all applicants, it may be calculated that it required an enrollment of 128,863 pre-medical students to provide the 1951 medical school enrollment.[52] When these are added, the ratio becomes 0.772

students per doctor, or 1 student per 1.3 doctors. The correspondence of this ratio with that for pre-law and law students is quite close, but it is 33 per cent higher than that of architectural students per registered architect.

ACSA also reports each year the number of first professional degrees conferred by schools of architecture. *Table 58* lists these data by schools and areas. During the 20-year period, 1934–1953, a total of 15,949 first degrees were reported. Unfortunately, however, of 41 professional schools operating in 1930, ACSA data, up to the end of World War II, cover only its own members, about three-quarters of the group. Reported degrees, however, were 13.3 per cent of the total annual enrollments of the schools reporting them, and, if this ratio is applied to the total enrollments of the two decades, a total of 17,270 first degrees is indicated. A comparison of these data by decades and areas is tabulated on the following page. *Figures 31* and *32* (p. 302) graph this material. The 13.3 per cent ratio means that it required 7.5 annual enrollments to produce one first professional degree. It should be noted that in the more recent decade this has increased from 6.6 to 7.9. No doubt most of this increase stems from the shifts from 4- to 5-year curricula, but another factor was that while the number of students carried over to graduate at the beginning of the second decade was small, the large enrollments at the end included a much larger proportion who would graduate after 1953. During the first decade, however, both sets of quantities were smaller and were in better balance in these respects. For a 5-year program, 7.9 constitutes a 60 per cent addition and this may seem excessive at first glance. It can be demonstrated, however, that observed student mortality rates make it entirely reasonable. The New England ratio of 21.8 per cent—4.6 enrollments per degree—is materially lowered because the first professional degree at Harvard is based on a 3-year graduate curriculum.

The number of graduates produced in a year has ranged from the wartime low of 139 to the 1949 record of 2012. During the decade 1934–44, the average of about 500 rose 140 per cent to 1199 in the succeeding period. *Figure 33* (p. 302) compares the area distributions of enrollments and degrees during the second decade with the distribution of registered architects in 1950 and the location of the schools from which they graduated. The result discloses the same shifts already observed between attendances and enrollments (*Figure 30*, p. 302).

Since the foregoing ratios have exhibited compatible trends for more than half a century, they suggest application of their current values as a means of estimating future enrollments. Unfortunately since factors, such as the increasing use of academic facilities, the drastic effects of depressions and wars, and variations in birth rates, have made observed ratios unique, it is extremely difficult to select ratio values which can be accepted as "normal" or as applicable to future situations. Moreover any realistic view of the future must acknowledge the fact that society and architecture are dynamic, developing, and interacting entities subject to human will. Nevertheless keeping these conditions in mind it will be helpful to explore the consequences of certain reasonable assumptions.

The most certain basis for quantitative estimates of future social activities is growth in population. Assuming the maintenance of current annual birth rates of about 25 per

300

Degrees and Total Enrollments reported by ACSA for 1934–43 and 1944–53

AREA	1934–1943			1944–1953			1934–1953		
	ENROLL.	DEGREES	PER CENT	ENROLL.	DEGREES	PER CENT	ENROLL.	DEGREES	PER CENT
New England	1125	236	21.0	2520	550	21.8	3645	786	21.6
No. Atlantic	8182	1436	17.5	14364	2282	15.9	22546	3718	16.5
Midwest	6606	1079	16.3	20216	2812	13.9	26822	3891	14.5
No. Plains	1027	182	17.7	2065	290	14.0	3092	472	15.3
Cent. Plains	1979	296	14.9	8362	1183	14.2	10341	1479	14.3
Cent. Atlantic	331	54	16.6	6030	783	13.0	6361	837	13.1
Southeast	1837	242	13.2	10511	1122	10.7	12348	1364	11.0
Southwest	2594	252	9.7	12042	1165	9.7	14636	1417	9.7
Mountain	—	—	—	1437	74	(†)	1437	74	(†)
Northwest	1774	140	7.9	5293	670	12.6	7067	810	11.4
California	2435	324	13.3	9313	777	8.4	11748	1101	9.4
Total	27890	4241*	15.2	92153	11708	12.7	120043	15949	13.3
Total Enroll. (Table 56)	33985			94381			128366		
Total Degrees (Est.)		5170			11986			17156	

* 22 omitted from total in Table 58 due to incomplete enrollment data.
† Schools recently established. Ratio not comparable.

301

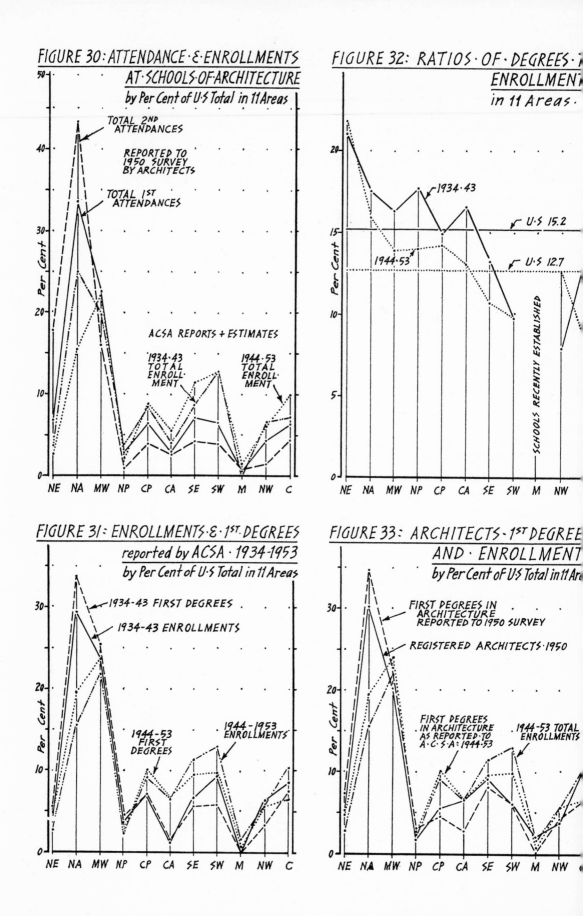

FIGURE 30: ATTENDANCE·&·ENROLLMENTS AT·SCHOOLS·OF·ARCHITECTURE
by Per Cent of U·S Total in 11 Areas

TOTAL 2ND ATTENDANCES

REPORTED TO 1950 SURVEY BY ARCHITECTS

TOTAL 1ST ATTENDANCES

ACSA REPORTS + ESTIMATES

1934·43 TOTAL ENROLLMENT

1944·53 TOTAL ENROLLMENT

Per Cent

NE NA MW NP CP CA SE SW M NW C

FIGURE 32: RATIOS·OF·DEGREES· ENROLLMEN in 11 Areas·

1934·43

U·S 15.2

1944·53

U·S 12.7

SCHOOLS RECENTLY ESTABLISHED

Per Cent

NE NA MW NP CP CA SE SW M NW

FIGURE 31: ENROLLMENTS·&·1ST·DEGREES
reported by ACSA·1934-1953
by Per Cent of U·S Total in 11 Areas

1934-43 FIRST DEGREES

1934-43 ENROLLMENTS

1944-53 FIRST DEGREES

1944-1953 ENROLLMENTS

Per Cent

NE NA MW NP CP CA SE SW M NW C

FIGURE 33: ARCHITECTS·1ST·DEGREE AND·ENROLLMENT
by Per Cent of U·S Total in 11 Are

FIRST DEGREES IN ARCHITECTURE REPORTED TO 1950 SURVEY

REGISTERED ARCHITECTS·1950

FIRST DEGREES IN ARCHITECTURE AS REPORTED TO A·C·S·A·1944·53

1944-53 TOTAL ENROLLMENTS

Per Cent

NE NA MW NP CP CA SE SW M NW

1000, total population in 1960 will reach about 177.4 millions and in 1970 204.2 millions.[53] In 1950 urban population was 59.0 per cent of total population, the slight upward trend of the recent past may be assumed to reach 62 per cent in 1960 and 65 per cent in 1970.[54] These give an urban population of 110 million in 1960 and 132.74 millions in 1970. The size of the college age group, 18–21 years, in 1960 and 1970 has been calculated to be 9,273,000 and 13,609,831 on the basis of survivals from actual births occurring through 1952.[55] It is instructive to compare the ratios of urban population and the college age group in 1930, 1950, and 1970 to the quantities of 20 years earlier. To these may be added the 1930 and 1950 ratios of architects and architectural students.

	1930 PER CENT OF 1910	*1950* PER CENT OF 1930	*1970 Estimate* PER CENT OF 1950
Urban population	164.2	129.0	149.3
18–21 yr. Age group	123.1 (census)	97.5 (census)	154.6 (Thompson)
Architects	132.4	109.3	
Architectural Students	314.0	244.6	
Non-veterans		152.4	

It is interesting to note that in 1930 the rate of increase in architects was 81 per cent of rate of increase in urban population and in 1950 91.5 per cent. Since depression and the war emergency operated very actively in restricting the expansion of the profession, the assumption of a roughly equivalent relationship between population and professional growth during the next two decades seems to be warranted if the same intensity of the use of professional services prevails. As already noted in *Chapter II,* this indicates that the number of registered architects needed in 1960 will be 23,670. The same ratio would require 28,570 in 1970. If the use of architects increases the 1950 ratio by 10 per cent, which would still be 7 per cent below the comparable 1930 ratio, it would expand these needs to 26,000 and 31,400. In 1950 the estimated total of 90,350 architectural personnel in offices found in *Chapter II* gave a ratio of 101.6 per 100,000 urban population. This would suggest for 1960 a total of 111,760.

For the moment, without accepting the continuance of current student per architect ratios, it is of interest to observe what enrollment they would produce in 1960. The results are as follows:

	Students per Registered Architect		*1960* *Enrollment*
1950	All students	0.582	13,775
	Non-veterans	0.362	8,568
1953	All students to		
	1953 archts.*	0.435	10,296

* 1950 Architects plus 3-year increase at rate to produce 1960 estimate.

The same procedure may be used with age-group ratios:

		Students per 100,000 of 18–21 Age Group	1960 Enrollment
1950	All students	132.18	12,257
	Non-veterans	82.35	7,636
1953	All students	111.42	10,332
	Non-veterans	99.39	9,217

The general magnitude of these diverse results can be tested by approximations of additions and replacements required to attain 23,670 registered architects in 1960. The estimate may be made as follows:

Additional architects required by growth in population (23,670–19,137)	4533
Replacement of architects aged 55 or more in 1950 (26%, *Table 8*) less 7% of 1960 architects remaining active after reaching 65 (4975–1656)	3319
Replacement of withdrawals from 25–54 year group due to death and other causes (8% + 5%)	1841
Total new architects needed................	9693

Although the *1950 Survey* showed that only 56 per cent of all architects held first degrees in architecture, it may be assumed, in view of increasing use of the schools, that the schools will be responsible during the current decade for training 80 per cent of the new personnel. On the other hand, it is probable that, even with increased opportunities, only 70 per cent of all graduates will continue in direct professional work.[56] Thus by 1960 it may be estimated that the schools should have produced about 7760 graduates to maintain the status quo. If, however, a 10 per cent increase in the use of architects develops, this would require an additional 1864 graduates.

Furthermore the *1950 Survey* revealed that 26 per cent of the architectural employees in offices held first degrees in architecture. In 1960 this group would number 29,000, an increase of 5570 over 1950. *Table 24* shows that slightly less than half of the employed graduates were candidates for registration. Thus, the maintenance of this school-trained employee group would require about 2800 graduates during the decade. If the degree of training represented by this group is a valuable asset, it would seem desirable to increase its proportion to 50 per cent. This would demand another 2550 graduates to supply the needed employees.

Estimates of the average annual enrollments required to produce these graduates by 1960 can be made on the assumption that 70 per cent will continue in architecture and that it will require 7.9 annual enrollments per graduate. Moreover the 6638 graduates who completed their work in the first four years of the decade must be subtracted. The results are as follows:

	A. Registered Architects (1950 ratio)	B. Graduate Employees (1950 ratio)	C. Additional Graduate Employees	D. Additional Registered Architects
Graduates needed by 1960	7,760	2,800	2,550	1,864
Graduates to be produced ($\frac{1}{70} = 1.43$x)	11,085	4,000	3,643	2,663

	A	A + B	A+B+C	A+B+C+D
Graduates to be produced, 1950–59	11,085	15,085	18,728	21,391
Graduates, 1950–53	6,638	6,638	6,638	6,638
Graduates needed, 1954–59	4,447	8,447	12,090	14,753
Total enrollments, 1954–59 (7.9x)	35,130	66,731	95,511	116,448
Average yearly enrollment, 1954–59	5,855	11,122	15,918	19,408
Per cent of 1953 (8916)	65.7	124.7	178.5	217.7
Students per 18–21 yr. age group, 1960	63.1	120.1	171.9	209.3
Students per 100,000 urban popul., 1960	5.32	10.11	14.47	17.64
Students per architect, 1960	0.25	0.47	0.67	0.82

Thus it is apparent that the 1953 total enrollment is about 20 per cent too low to maintain in 1960 the 1950 ratios of registered architects and graduate employees.[57] The general correspondence between 1953 ratios and those estimated in *Column B* for 1960 is noteworthy. Likewise, the students per architect ratio in *Column C* would be approximately the same as the ratio of pre-medical and medical students to doctors in 1951.

The enrollment indicated in *Column B* is practically the same as the record load of 1949 which had to be accommodated on an emergency basis. A similar calculation for the decade, 1960–1970, suggests that an average total enrollment of the order of 17,500 will be needed to preserve current ratios of architects and graduate employees. *Figure 34* presents a graphical comparison of these estimates and the bases upon which they rest. Furthermore, it is clear that if additional architects and graduate employees are to be provided, enrollments must be greatly increased. In this case, however, the limiting factor will not be the demand for personnel, but rather the capacities of the schools' facilities and the portion of the college age group which can be recruited to the profession. The latter restriction is currently the most critical block to such expansion and promises to remain so until about 1968. While these estimates are necessarily general in character, they nevertheless imply that under stable economic conditions there need be no fear of expanding architectural education, but that, on the contrary, the chief danger lies in overconservative attitudes on the part of both the schools and the profession.

In addition to the national picture, it is highly desirable to learn the location of demand and of the use of existing facilities. The *1950 School Survey* requested each school to list all of its students by state of their legal residences. Unfortunately many totals thus reported could not be reconciled with those given in the 1950 ACSA annual report. A second attempt in 1951 presented the same difficulty. Finally in 1953 ACSA cooperated by securing geographical distributions of students at the same time it collected enrollment data from the 62 schools which reported to it. Although curricula in architectural engineering were omitted in the discussions immediately preceding, the ACSA data includes four such schools. Their combined enrollments totaled 494—4.9 per cent of all 9983 students reported. They have been retained in the following study because the professional function of these particular schools seems to be locally recognized. Their omission would materially alter ratios for only one state, Michigan.

The 62 schools enrolled 559 students—5.9 per cent—coming from U. S. territories and foreign countries. This leaves a total of 9424 students from the continental U. S. For the first time, an accurate picture takes form of the number of students originating in each state. *Table 59* presents the data for states and areas, and further shows the number contributed by each state to the nation's 11 educational areas. It is instructive to compare the percentages of areas of origin, areas of attendance, and students attending within their home area.

	Area of Origin Per cent	Area of Attend. Per cent	Per cent of Area Students Attend. in Home Area		Area of Origin Per cent	Area of Attend. Per cent	Per cent of Area Students Attend. in Home Area
New Eng.	2.0	2.6	50.3	Southeast	10.5	10.1	82.3
No. Atlan.	19.1	16.1	70.4	Southwest	11.2	12.4	94.1
Midwest	24.5	24.9	87.5	Mountain	2.3	2.0	69.7
No. Plains	1.9	1.7	77.5	Northwest	5.5	6.2	90.7
Cent. Plains	7.1	7.2	83.9	California	10.4	10.4	90.3
Cent. Atlan.	5.6	6.4	77.7	Total U. S.	100	100	82.7

Thus, five areas trained a larger proportion of students than they furnished. This interchange of students between the 11 areas is summarized in *Table 60*. Although these areas were designed to be as homogeneous as possible, the final gains and losses are revealing. The Southwest received the largest net gain of 112 students, followed by the Central Atlantic with 86 and the Northwest with 67. By far the largest net loss—279 students—was that of the North Atlantic area. This area sent to the Midwest the largest single block of 214 students. The Midwest received the largest group, 333, from

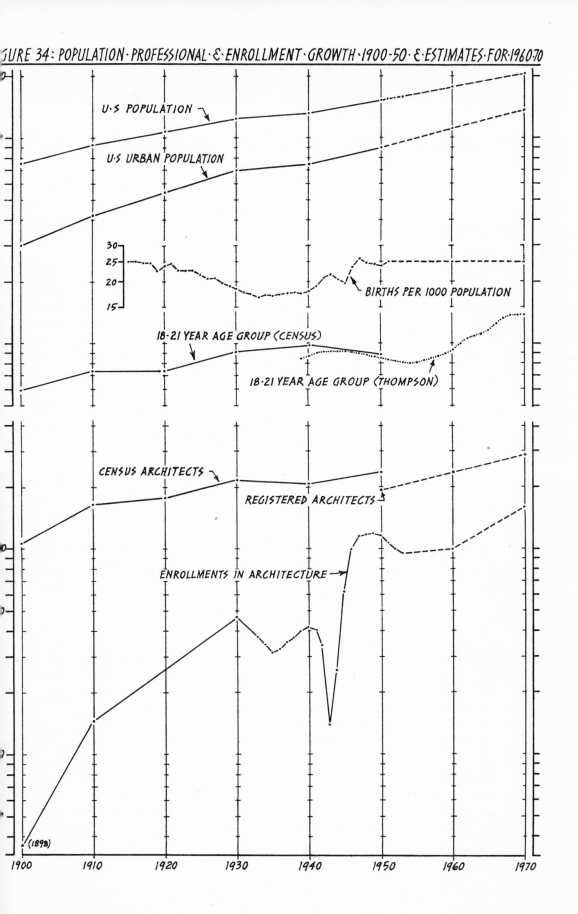

FIGURE 34: POPULATION · PROFESSIONAL · & · ENROLLMENT · GROWTH · 1900-50 · & · ESTIMATES · FOR · 1960-70

other areas, but exported 290, and ended with a net gain of 43. Nevertheless these inter-area migrations involved only 17.3 per cent of all students.

Table 61 organizes the data to reveal attendance of the students of each state by four zones: in the same state, in adjoining states, in the next adjoining states, and elsewhere; 70.3 per cent of all students remained within their home state for professional schooling. In 1949–1950 a study of 2,486,396 students enrolled in all higher institutions disclosed that 80 per cent remained in their home states.[58] Since 14 states had no schools of architecture, the close correspondence of the two ratios is striking. Moreover these proportions bear a close correspondence to the 74.4 per cent of the whole population which in 1950 resided in the same state where they had been born. 15.2 per cent of the students in architecture went to schools in adjoining states. It is surprising, however, that when the remaining 1365 chose their schools, only a third went to next adjoining states, but two-thirds traveled beyond that circle. This seems to prove that once determination to move is made, selection of a school is fixed by factors other than location.

By grouping states with corresponding educational situations, the effects of absence or presence of private or public schools of architecture emerge (*Figure 35*, p. 309). States with schools in tax-supported institutions obviously attract very high proportions of in-state students. States with privately supported schools alone serve about half of their states' students. In states without schools, 61 per cent attend in an adjoining state. The data confirm the obvious attractions of economical tuition, travel savings, familiarity, and convenience. *Table 61* also indicates the selection of private and public schools by in-state and out-of-state students. The dominance of private institutions in the east and of public institutions in the south and west largely influences this choice.

Table 59 lists for each state and area the ratios of students per registered architects (as of 1950), urban population (as of 1950), and the college age group (as of 1953).[59] *Figure 36* graphs the ratios, *Figure 37* (pp. 310–311) plots the area ratios in per cent of the national ratios. The general conformity of the ratios to architects and urban population are indeed remarkable. The chief deviations are the higher ratios to architects in the Midwest and North Plains areas, and the converse relationship in the Central Atlantic, Southwest, and Northwest areas. While the ratios of architectural students to the 18–21 year age group follow the same general pattern of Eastern lows and Western highs, they are much more exaggerated, especially in the North Plains area where the smallest proportion in the U. S. is attracted to architecture, and in the Northwest and California areas where the ratios mount to 261 and 336 per cent of the national ratio. These marked divergencies might seem suspicious if the ratios of all students in higher institutions to the college age group did not follow a very similar profile. In the New England, North Atlantic, North Plains, and Mountain areas, architecture attracted a decidedly smaller relative share of the college age group than did all higher institutions. In the Southwest, Northwest, and California area, the reverse was true in a most emphatic manner. In the North Plains area, the architectural ratio was only 34 per cent of the general institutional ratio, and in New England, 45 per cent, but in California, it climbed to 125 per cent, and in the Mountain and Northwest

areas to 138 and 139 per cent, four times the lowest. This striking contrast underscores the psychological impact on youth of living in expanding areas in a period of a
rapidly developing economy.

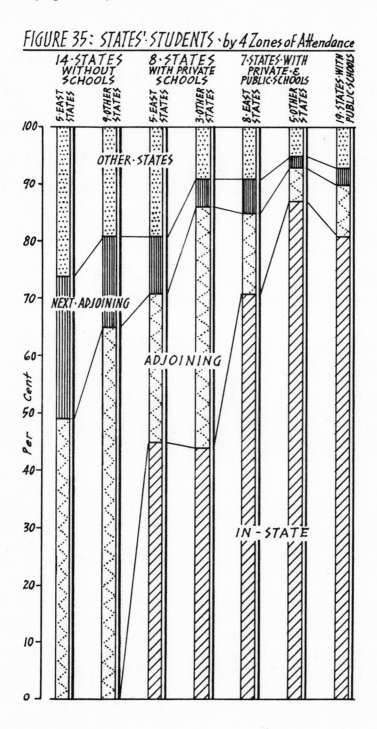

FIGURE 35: STATES' STUDENTS · by 4 Zones of Attendance

FIGURE 36: RATIOS·OF·ARCHITECTURAL·STUDENTS·FROM·AREAS·&·STATES·TO·ARCHITECTS·POPULATION·&·AGE·GROUP

The geographical distribution data permit the analysis of the enrollments of individual schools. *Table 62* lists for 62 schools the number of students by four zones of legal residence and thus gives a picture of the existing types of attraction patterns.

FIGURE 37: RATIOS·OF·ARCHITECTURAL·STUDENTS·IN·11·AREAS
by Per Cent of corresponding U·S Ratios

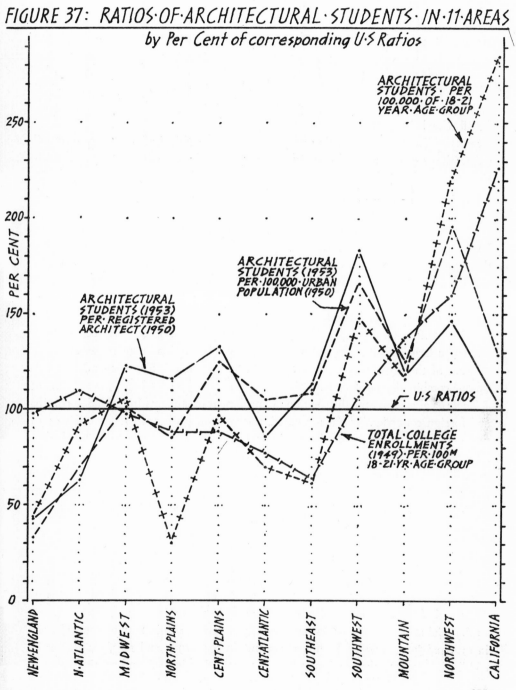

Figure 38 (p. 313) graphs these enrollments by number and percentages for each school and area. Comparison of the 11 areas shows that schools of the New England, North and Central Atlantic areas enroll the lowest proportions of in-state students, 31, 59, and 56 per cent respectively, while California's 90 per cent is by far the highest. The Southwest, Mountain, and North Plains areas form the next highest group, with 81, 79, and 80 per cent. The larger areas of the western states, the appeal of the low in-state tuitions of their public institutions, and the converse situation in the east account in large part for these differences. *Figure 38* also emphasizes the fact that for many large schools actual numbers of out-of-state students, although constituting a small portion of its enrollment, may exceed those of a small school where they form a high percentage. *Figure 39* (p. 314) compares the composite distribution by zones of origin for all schools in each area.

Study of *Table 62* suggests that groups of schools exhibit similar patterns of enrollment. *Figure 40* (p. 314) plots the distribution for all schools in descending order of the percentage of in-state students enrolled. The location, size of enrollment, size of community and type of support of each school are indicated. Nevertheless, only the most general relationships emerge. Schools with the highest proportion of out-of-state students tend to be small in size, in private institutions, and located in eastern cities. Notre-Dame and Cincinnati are notable exceptions. All large schools, i.e., with more than 250 students, except Cincinnati, have very high proportions of in-state students. Cincinnati, located close to two adjoining states and offering a unique cooperative curriculum, attracts 55 per cent of its students from adjoining and next adjoining states. Another notable group includes 13 schools clustered around the national average of 70 per cent of in-state students. All are located in the central or southern sections; only one has a large enrollment; and 10 are in public institutions. Otherwise, the inter-mixture of the remaining schools suggests that enrollment patterns tend to reflect unique combinations of factors.

Table 62 also shows the distribution of enrollment of students from U. S. territories and foreign countries. As already noted, the total of 559 bears a relationship of 5.9 per cent to the students from the continental U. S., or 5.6 per cent to the total of all students. The North Atlantic schools attracted the largest number, 17.9 per cent, but the Midwest, California, and Southwest areas attracted 15.4, 14.5, and 14.3 per cent respectively. Individual schools reporting the largest number of these students were the University of California, 9.1 per cent of the U. S. total, the University of Florida with 5.4 per cent, and the University of Washington with 5.0 per cent. Nine other schools, well distributed throughout the country, each reported more than 3.0 per cent.

One aspect of school enrollments, though of considerable importance, is very controversial. This is the question of the size of enrollments, particularly in relation to economy of operation and optimum educational effectiveness of individual schools. The trend of enrollment magnitudes can be seen in the record tabulated on page 315. In 1898 Columbia had the largest enrollment; in 1911 the University of Pennsylvania; in 1930 and 1935, New York University; and, in 1940, 1950, and 1953, the University of Illinois.[60] In 1953 the maximum was 11.2 times that in 1898 and 2.7 times that of

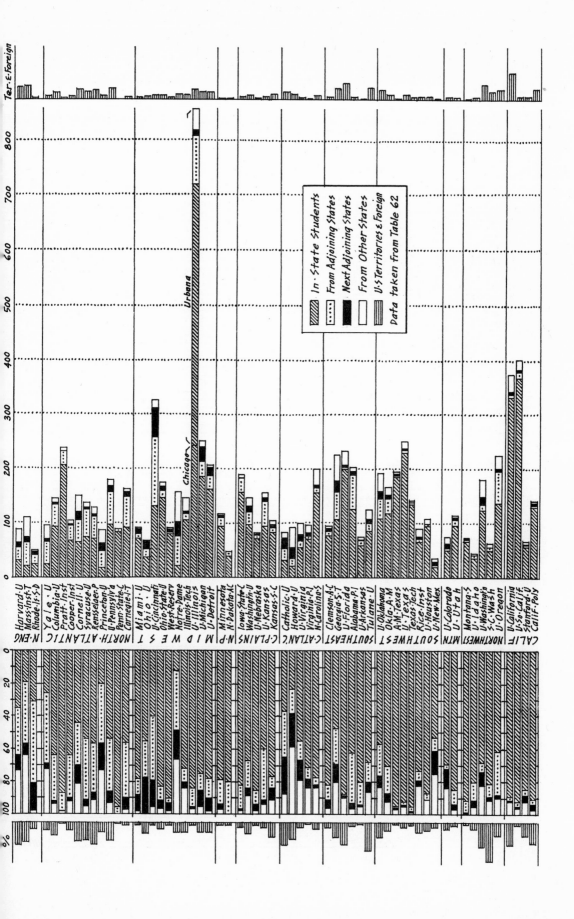

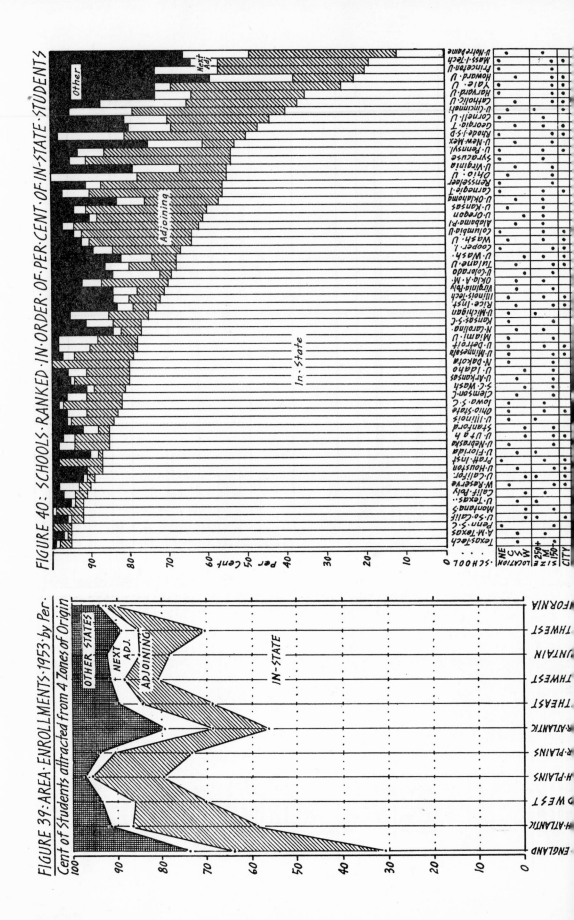

FIGURE·40: SCHOOLS·RANKED·IN·ORDER·OF·PER·CENT·OF·IN·STATE·STUDENTS

FIGURE 39: AREA·ENROLLMENTS·1953·by·Per·Cent of Students attracted from 4 Zones of Origin

Schools by Size of Enrollment, 1898–1953

Number of Students	1898	1911	1930	1935	1940	1950	1953
500 or more	—	—	—	—	—	2	1
400–499	—	—	—	—	—	2	2
300–399	—	—	1	1	1	6	1
250–299	—	—	1	—	1	1	3
200–249	—	2	1	1	—	8	7
TOTAL 200 OR MORE	—	2	3	2	2	19	14
175–199	—	—	6	—	—	7	5
150–174	—	—	1	1	5	6	8
TOTAL 150–199	—	—	7	1	5	13	13
125–149	—	—	3	2	2	8	3
100–124	—	3	4	5	4	9	10
TOTAL 100–149	—	3	7	7	6	17	13
75–99	1	3	5	4	8	4	11
50–74	2	3	16	12	16	4	3
25–49	3	5	5	13	9	2	3
UNDER 25	3	4	4	6	3	—	1
TOTAL UNDER 100	9	15	30	35	36	10	18
NUMBER OF SCHOOLS	9	20	47	45	49	59	58
AVERAGE ENROLLMENT	40.2	72.5	98.3	70.0	84.3	196.2	162.5
LARGEST	78	216	320	314	318	955	874
3RD QUARTILE	53	98	129	95	114	215	199
MEDIAN	41	51	69	55	65	158	143
1ST QUARTILE	11	25	54	34	48	116	93
SMALLEST	8	9	15	12	20	31	10

Per cent of Students in Schools within Quartiles

	1898	1911	1930	1935	1940	1950	1953
4TH QUARTILE	41.2	53.7	51.3	50.6	48.2	48.3	48.4
3RD QUARTILE	32.6	26.5	23.2	26.4	25.1	24.6	24.4
2ND QUARTILE	1.0	14.5	16.4	14.8	17.0	16.4	17.3
1ST QUARTILE	5.2	5.3	9.1	8.2	9.7	10.7	9.9

1930. The 1953 3rd quartile was 3.8 times that of 1898; the median was 3.5 times as large, and the 1st quartile was 8.5 times. Thus, the half century produced general enlargement in all size groups. The almost constant distribution of students among the quartiles is an interesting phenomenon.

In 1953, of 58 schools, 24 per cent of the total were large; 45 per cent were of medium size; and 31 per cent enrolled fewer than 100 students. The tabulation of the enrollment size groups in the 11 areas and by private and public institutions is shown on the following page.

Number of Students	Total	New England	N. Atlantic	Midwest	North Plains	Cent. Plains	Cent. Atlantic	Southeast	Southwest	Mountain	Northwest	California	Private	Public
200 OR MORE	14	—	1	3	—	—	1	3	2	—	2	2	2	12
150–199	13	—	5	3	—	3	—	—	2	—	—	—	8	5
100–149	13	2	3	—	1	1	2	1	2	1	—	—	7	6
UNDER 100	18	1	2	3	1	1	3	2	1	1	2	1	7	11
LARGEST		124	237	874	119	193	206	260	256	115	241	423	404	874
MEDIAN			152	164		155	101	176	176				134	150
AVERAGE		91	147	245	83	141	102	171	169	96	133	299	137	181
SMALLEST		50	90	72	47	84	10	75	95	77	34	72	10	34

The occurrence of a specific size of enrollment in a particular school is an amalgam of many interacting factors. Demand for its service is basic, but this in turn is closely related to the social and economic milieu and the standing of the profession in the area in which it is located. A vigorous school, on the other hand, can and should influence this milieu, and, in short, stimulate demand. Then, too, reputation for effective and progressive instruction adds powerful momentum to demand. Convenient accessibility to large concentrations of population can likewise foster the growth of a school. These are positive influences which need no demonstration.

From the standpoint of educational policy, there are other important considerations. First is the availability of financial support and physical facilities. Where these are limited and without prospect of significant expansion, the fact that tuition covers only a fraction of the cost of instruction means that size of enrollment is determined, not by demand or social need, but by budget and space limitations. The decline of returns from endowments and the drying up of the sources of potential additions thereto have created a major crisis for all privately supported institutions. It is tempting to attribute to this situation a large part of the fact that, while architectural enrollments in public institutions grew 2.81 times between 1930 and 1950, private schools expanded only 1.54 times.

A second point of educational policy limits enrollment in the belief that the number of qualified applicants is distinctly limited and that only in a relatively small student group can the educational process maintain a humane, personal character. If this view is based on an objective comparison of the results of large and small programs, it demands serious consideration. If it only rationalizes existing budgetary restrictions, it requires none. The fact that it is popular with many practitioners is understandable when it is recalled that the educational experience of a large proportion of them has been acquired in small schools.

The difficulties of evaluating the efficacy of an educational process have already been noted in *Chapter IV*. It would have been pertinent, but no doubt indiscreet, had the Commission requested tabulation of the *Survey* data to compare the present responsibilities and earnings of alumni of different schools. Unfortunately no method, other than human judgment, can weigh the professional quality, creativeness, or leadership of a person or a school.

Nevertheless, the question of optimum enrollments does have tangible aspects susceptible of analysis. It is possible to investigate, for example, the relationship of size of enrollment to the scope, flexibility, and economical operation of an educational program. Such a study was made by the Commission.[61] On the basis of a specific curriculum and with exactly the same standards of class sizes and teaching loads, enrollments of 75, 100, 150, 200, 400, and 800 were distributed in exactly the same year-groups and scheduled in all courses—general and technical—semester by semester.[62] From the resulting teaching loads, the number of teachers needed to staff each school was easily calculated. Assuming an average annual salary of $5000 for each full-time teacher, the general, technical, and total teaching budgets emerged. A supplemental teaching budget of $5 per student was assumed for lectures, exhibitions, etc., and similarly $234 per student was used for the institution's fixed charges and maintenance for building space.[63] The administrative budget of the architectural school was assumed to be 10 per cent of the total salaries of the technical staff.

For the schools with 75 and 100 students, it was assumed that the curriculum offered one standard program without options, that each course was given only once each year, and that no new students were to be admitted at midyear. For schools with 150, 200, 400, and 800 students, the curriculum had two options with a division of students of 60 and 40 per cent. For each of these sizes, courses were to be given once each year and no midyear students were to be admitted. Finally, for the school with 400 students, an alternate plan was estimated in which the courses for students of the larger option would be repeated each semester to give greater flexibility for making up failures and to accommodate a small off-phase class entering at midyear. For the school with 800 students, the alternative included the repetition of all courses in both options and a midyear class in each. In each case the midyear class was estimated to be one-sixth of all new students.

Upon these premises the results in the following table were obtained. On page 319 *Figure 41* compares these costs graphically. For single-phase operation, the cost per student declines sharply from enrollments of 75, 100, and 150, but at 200 reaches a stable level. The reason for this lies in the fact that with the larger enrollments course sections more regularly reach full capacity. This is revealed by the rise of over-all average number of students per teacher from 6.3 for an enrollment of 75 to the 8.6 for 200 or more students. It should be noted that the 150 enrollment shows a 9.8 per cent saving in the teaching and administrative cost per student over the 100 enrollment—as against 11.8 per cent for 100 over 75 enrollment—despite the provision of two options.[64] It may be concluded that, under the assumed conditions of single-phase operation, there is no significant advantage in enrollments of more than about 200, but that if economy is desirable 200 is about the minimum enrollment needed.

Double-phase operation presents definite advantages of flexibility in that it permits the accommodation of irregular students and those who for valid reasons should be

Estimated Cost per Student in Schools with Enrollments of 75 to 800

No. of Students	75	100	150	200	400	400	800	800
Options	1	1	2	2	2	2	2	2
Phases	1	1	1	1	1	1.5	1	2
All Teachers	11.9	14.0	18.9	23.2	46.5	49.8	93.1	96.4
Technical	9.1	10.8	14.4	17.2	33.0	37.6	68.1	70.2
General	2.8	3.2	4.5	6.0	13.5	12.2	25.0	26.4
Students per Teacher	6.3	7.2	7.9	8.6	8.6	8.0	8.6	8.3
Total Budget ($1000's)	$82.0	$99.3	$138.0	$172.8	$344.4	$363.7	$690.6	$708.5
Total Cost per Student	$1094	$993	$919	$863	$860	$909	$863	$886
Tech. Teach.	606	542	480	431	412	470	425	439
Genl. Teach.	189	158	152	150	168	153	156	164
Special Educ.	5	5	5	5	5	5	5	5
Administration	60	54	48	43	41	47	43	44
F. C.-Maint.	234	234	234	234	234	234	234	234
Total Cost (%)	100	100	100	100	100	100	100	100
Tech. Teach.	55.4	54.5	52.2	49.9	47.9	51.8	49.3	49.6
Genl. Teach.	17.2	16.0	16.6	17.4	19.5	16.8	18.1	18.5
Special Educ.	.5	.5	.6	.6	.6	.5	.6	.6
Administration	5.5	5.4	5.2	5.0	4.8	5.2	4.9	4.9
F. C.-Maint.	21.4	23.6	25.4	27.1	27.2	25.7	27.1	26.4
Cost (% of 150)	119.1	108.0	100	93.9	93.6	98.9	93.9	96.4

given prompt opportunity to repeat occasional courses. In single-phase schools, such students are often delayed a full year and are therefore unjustly penalized. Some single-phase schools have mitigated this difficulty by conducting summer terms, but this practice is not felicitous for either students or faculty. Therefore, when conditions permit, double-phase operation is an excellent solution. For a school of 400 students, it was found, however, that the off-phase group in the second option would yield only 6 or 7 students. Since, by the final year, few, if any, students would need to repeat the special advanced courses in this option, these classes would be only a third or a quarter of the normal section size. Consequently for the school of 400 only the first option was considered to be on the double-phase system. For the school of 800, both options were scheduled at double-phase, but even here the second option off-phase group totaled only 12 or 13 students, and thus their classes would operate at half capacity.

The cost per student of the more flexible double-phase system was found to be 7.9 per cent greater in teaching and administrative costs on the basis of 400 students, and 3.7 per cent for 800 students. This does not seem to be excessive, especially in view of

318

the saving to students in time and living costs. In addition to the added advantage of full double-phase scheduling, the school of 800 showed a saving of 3.4 per cent of the cost per student over the school of 400 with its partial double-phase operation.

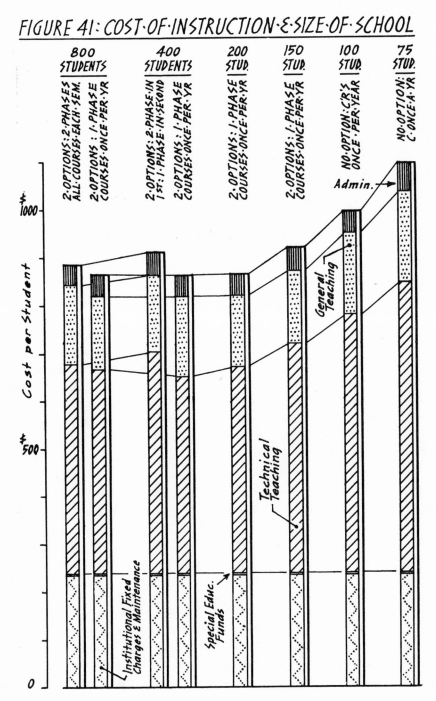

FIGURE 41: COST·OF·INSTRUCTION·&·SIZE·OF·SCHOOL

The magnitude of these savings can be illustrated by comparing the cost of educating all U. S. students of architecture in 1953—roughly 9000—if all attended schools with the same enrollments.[65]

Individual Enrollment	Number of Schools	Cost per Student	Total Cost
SINGLE PHASE			
75	120	$1094	$9,846,000
100	90	993	8,937,000
150	60	919	8,271,000
200	45	863	7,767,000
409	22	860	7,740,000
818	11	863	7,767,000
DOUBLE PHASE			
409	22	909	8,181,000
818	11	886	7,974,000

While any such uniformity is distinctly hypothetical, it seems safe to conclude that one of the most fruitful methods of approach to the increasingly difficult problem of financing high quality architectural education would be to foster larger enrollment units.

This view is reinforced by two considerations which these cost estimates do not reveal. First is the problem of providing in a small faculty a sufficient quantity and variety of talent, training, and experience to ensure that the development of all phases of instruction will be of maximum quality. In a small school, although the ratio of students to teachers may be very low, assuring a high degree of personal attention, at the same time the range of the content of architectural education remains constant and faculty effort is often so dispersed that even the most conscientious and industrious teacher cannot encompass the diverse courses assigned to him. While the curriculum of a small school may employ combined courses to simplify some of the overlapping administrative detail, the range of content is not reduced. This problem is well illustrated by the foregoing case of the school with 75 students and a technical staff of 9.1. Assuming that semester loads could be balanced, the staff loads would be:

Design	3.25	History	0.92	Freehand	1.17
Construction	1.17	Theory	0.17	Mechanics	0.50
Structures	1.00	Graphics	0.33	Equipment	0.58

One alternative is to combine assignments. Another possibility is to assign some courses, such as mechanics, to other departments. A third is to secure, if available, part-time teachers for fractional loads. The hazards involved in all of these methods have already been noted. It is clear that such problems are much easier to solve when a larger number of positions are available. To the degree that concentrated attention to the development of a few specific courses is acknowledged beneficial to instruction, the opportunity in a large staff to match need and capacity must be considered highly desirable.

The second advantage to be derived from large enrollment is the provision of special facilities. The estimated costs per student in the six enrollments studied assumed an unvarying area of 130 sq. ft. of instructional space per student, an average which comes from many campus surveys. While this was used as a constant quantity, it must be recognized that the sizes of some facilities are not directly controlled by the number of students served. Thus, for larger schools either the space standard could be reduced somewhat, giving lower fixed charges and maintenance costs and increasing thereby the differences of total costs in favor of larger enrollments, or, better, additional space can be made available for a greater variety of uses. In view of the new facilities suggested as desirable in Section 1 of this chapter, the utility of large enrollments is further emphasized as a means of obtaining them without proportionately increased costs per student. Moreover, the same reasoning applies to such facilities as the architectural library. Even though two schools may have library purchase budgets based on identical ratios to enrollments, the larger school does not buy multiple copies of a specific publication, but rather expands its holdings by diversified accessions. Collections of slides, building materials, and much other equipment follow the same principle.

On the other side, it must be admitted that a portion of the savings to be derived from greater concentration of enrollments in fewer schools would be offset by increased travel costs for many students. It might also be claimed that certain schools regardless of size are justified by their fulfillment of special objectives, though those reported to the *1950 School Survey* almost without exception should in reality be fundamental aims in any well-considered professional curriculum in architecture. No doubt the strongest reservations against larger schools stem from psychological preferences on the part of some teachers, students, and alumni for a personalized academic environment which they believe can only be provided by small enrollments. In this regard it should be noted that the foregoing cost study assumed identical maximum section sizes and that the differences in the ratios of students per teacher were negligible. Thus, in each case, liaison between student and teacher is a function of the quality of their personal attitudes rather than of size of enrollment. While it is true that a student in a large school would study under a larger number of teachers and be subject to the stimulus of contacts with more classmates, there is no inherent reason why the depth and character of his personal relationships with them should not be wholly as satisfying as in any other situation.

Thus, the Commission concludes that there are important advantages to be gained for both students and the profession from a conscious fostering of larger enrollments. It recognizes, however, that movement in this direction involves many problems. It appreciates fully the signal contributions which many small schools have made to the profession despite their limited resources. It understands the delicacy of urging upon autonomous institutions any curtailment of their programs. Nevertheless, it believes that, if the development and strengthening of architectural education envisioned in this report are to become realities, the profession and the schools themselves must seek conditions which will make them attainable.

Fortunately, a reasonable course of action can be suggested. First, it has been shown that the demand for architectural education will increase steadily in response to an expanding population and profession. The estimate for 1960 indicates that a minimum average annual enrollment of 11,100 will be needed to maintain current ratios of architects and graduate employees. By 1970, to accomplish the same end will require 17,500 students, 96 per cent above 1953. Any expansion in the demand for architectural services will in turn cause increased enrollments. Thus the time does not appear to be far off when demand will attain such levels that, if the present number of schools remains relatively constant, average enrollments of much more practical size can be secured.

This approach suggests that the profession should adopt immediately a positive policy to discourage the establishment of additional schools, except in such locations and under such conditions where demand can be demonstrated to be of extreme urgency and where resources sufficient for a vigorous, progressive, and high quality program are definitely assured. The Commission believes that responsibility for executing this policy should rest with The AIA in order to bring the full weight, influence, and prestige of the profession to bear upon its realization. The Commission suggests that The Institute should formulate a definite procedure for considering such cases and that it could appropriately assign the execution of this policy to its Committee on Education, to which would be added The Institute's Director of Education and Research and the member of the Board of Directors representing the region in which the proposed school is to be located. In its consideration of such questions, the Committee on Education should consult freely with the officers of NAAB and ACSA (*Recommendation 29*).

If such a point of view is not to be interpreted as underwriting the status quo, two corollaries must accompany such a policy. First, The Institute should actively foster means by which localities in which demand and resources are insufficient to develop a strong school can still have economical access to excellent educational programs. The most promising answer to this problem appears to be the principle of formal inter-state agreements by which a state without facilities in a particular field joins with another possessing them by contributing to their development in return for preferential treatment of its students. The first such agreement was signed by West Virginia and Virginia in 1944 in order to provide medical training for West Virginia students. In 1947 twelve Southern states initiated a study of regional facilities for professional education which, two years later, led to the establishment of the Board of Control for Southern Regional Education which administers the resulting inter-state agreements. Medicine, dentistry, and veterinary medicine were the first fields placed under this system.[66] In 1953 the Board began a study of the South's facilities for architectural education. It is apparent that the pattern thus established seems eminently suited for other areas as well.

The second corollary is that society and the profession have every right to demand that the quality of architectural education must be subject to continuing reappraisal and improvement. It would be tragic if an Institute policy of discouraging the formation of new schools were to become a protective cloak condoning the ineffectiveness of existing weak units. Thus, it is the profession's duty to lead the way in a gradual but relentless upgrading of minimum standards of instruction and facilities. It also must be assumed that such a course would demand the intimate cooperation of NAAB and the schools as represented by ACSA. The long, but effective, fight to obtain the five-year curriculum illustrates what can be done. Through collaboration, other equally beneficial developments could be secured. It may well be that in the process some schools may fail to respond to such demands, but unless the principle of the survival of the fit is abrogated such schools have no just claim to the support of a dynamic profession.

In summary, it is clear that intelligent thought, policies, and effort can win many desiderata which at first glance seem utopian. Viewed eighty years ago, as the first schools struggled to evolve a new educational pattern, the schools of today would have seemed just as millenial. During coming decades the measure of the vision and determination of the profession and of faculties will stand fully revealed by the schools they will create.

NOTES: CHAPTER SEVEN

[1] Elizabeth R. Sunderland, "Microfilm Slide Project" (*College Art Journal,* vol. 6, no. 2, Winter, 1946, pp. 147–148).

[2] *College Art Journal,* vol. 11, no. 1, Fall, 1951, pp. 35–37.

[3] *Journal of Architectural Education,* No. 8, Summer, 1952, pp. 14–20, 76–82.

[4] Henry H. Armsby, "Graduation and Withdrawal Ratios for Engineering Studies" (*Higher Education,* vol. 10, no. 3, Nov. 1953, pp. 45–46).

[5] President's Commission on Higher Education: *Higher Education for American Democracy,* 1948, vol. 2, pp. 51–57.

[6] Edwin S. Burdell, "For a Faster Schooling." (*Atlantic Monthly,* April, 1952, pp. 63–65.) Since Dr. Burdell wrote at the time Universal Military Training seemed imminent, and since its duration was then envisioned as six months, he ended with an architect's age of $25\frac{1}{2}$ at registration. However, the continuation of selective service calling for two years of active duty increases this to 27 at registration. Thus, for architects the proposal would eliminate one year from the present 17 years of schooling. Dr. Burdell's plan might well possess positive advantages in the regrouping of school years, and in the provision of a separate terminal vocational program for those who do not need advanced training. Although the introduction of these special programs would no doubt produce more effective long-term results, they would require basic changes in public education which would be very difficult to accomplish. Moreover, the added cost would tend to restrict their availability to large school systems which in turn would discourage recruitment of architectural students from smaller communities.

[7] The 1950 ACSA report included actual data on 59 schools. For the other four—Clemson, MIT, Denver, and Hampton—the figures had to be estimated from the preceding year.

[8] No response was obtained from Clemson, Rensselaer, or the University of Idaho. No estimates have been attempted.

[9] The *Faculty Questionnaire* stipulated that only three years of a four-year professional curriculum, or four of a five- or six-year curriculum, should be counted as Technical Education. The remaining undergraduate time plus any additional general studies were counted as General Education. Graduate professional studies were added to technical years. The *General Questionnaire,*

on the other hand, did not call for such a separation of undergraduate professional curricula, and it is highly improbable that any responders made such a distinction voluntarily. The difference of a full year between the two results is thus readily accounted for, although to some slight degree it might be expected that the greater inclusiveness of the *Faculty Questionnaire* would show a somewhat shorter length. This might also be due to the inclusion of non-architect teachers, such as drawing instructors, but this may be counteracted by the fact that the average age of all teachers is younger than that for all teacher-architects. The latter are more likely, therefore, to have enrolled in four-year curricula, and the former in five-year programs.

[10] The *1950 Survey*, on the basis of 191 responders, found that the average AIA teacher-architect was licensed in 1.5 states and the corresponding non-AIA man in 1.1 states (*Table 44*). The *1950 Faculty Survey* produced 455 responders and was therefore a better sample.

[11] The *1950 Survey* reported that 14.6 per cent of the 191 responding teacher-architects held NCARB certificates, a ratio that corresponded almost exactly with the 15 per cent of all architects (*Table 46*).

[12] The 67 part-time teachers reporting held 24.6 full-time equivalent appointments. This was 7.9 per cent of the total of 312.6 full-time equivalent appointments (24.6 + 288 full-time appointments).

[13] Arthur Clason Weatherhead: *The History of Collegiate Education in Architecture in the United States,* 1941, p. 30.

[14] The following were assumed: the lecture course involved bi-weekly quizzes which required 15 minutes per student for grading and a term paper which would absorb an average of one hour for reviewing the outline, trial draft, and final version; the lecture-laboratory course consisted of two lectures and one 3-hour laboratory per week with 12 minutes per week per student for grading short quizzes and exercises; the studio course provided a total of one-hour per week per student for individual criticism in class and an average of 32 minutes per week per student for the grading of intermediate studies and final presentations. In large schools where a teacher could handle two sections of the same course, preparation time might be halved and the hours saved could be added to grading, student consultation, and school service.

[15] American Society for Engineering Education, Engineering College Administrative Council, Committee on Faculty Salaries: *A Survey of Teachers' Salaries in Engineering Schools . . .* June, 1949, p. 66, Table V. This table does not include the heads of departments in the columns labeled "Total Teachers Reported" and "Professors," despite the words "including Department Heads" in the latter. Since most department heads do give instruction and, in any case, perform necessary services for the organization of instruction, the table given in the text of this report has been recalculated to include them.

[16] The Regular Teaching Budget (i.e., excluding administrative funds and funds for bringing visiting teachers) was divided by the sum of the number of full-time teachers and the number of part-time teachers reduced to the equivalent number of full-time teachers.

[17] Four schools had to be omitted. Rensselaer, Clemson, and Idaho did not respond. The data for Rhode Island was for some reason confused.

[18] Bosworth and Jones: *A Study of Architectural Schools,* p. 140.

[19] Indices issued by the Bureau of Labor Statistics, U. S. Department of Labor: cost of living: 1929, 122.5; 1950, 171.9; food: 1929, 132.5; 1950, 204.5; clothing: 1929, 115.3; 1950, 187.7.

[20] ASEE, *op. cit.,* pp. 37–40, 67.

[21] *Ibid,* p. 65, Table III. The minimum salary of dentistry instructors has been changed from $800 to $1000 in accord with the tabulation given on page 52.

[22] The survey was conducted by Dean William T. Arnett, University of Florida. The data obtained were for the academic year, 1951–1952.

[23] ASEE, *op. cit.,* pp. 37–41, 67.

[24] *Ibid,* p. 41.

[25] E. Kent Springer, "Criteria for Advancement and Promotion of the Teaching Staff" (*Higher Education,* vol. 7, no. 10, January 15, 1951, pp. 117–118).

[26] *Ibid.*

[27] For similar efforts, see "Improvement in Engineering Teaching: Report of the Committee on Improvement of Teaching of the American Society of Engineering Education." (*Journal of Engineering Education,* vol. 43, no. 1, September, 1952.)

[28] Bosworth and Jones: *op. cit.,* pp. 188–189.

[29] *ACSA Enrollment Report,* 1950–1951. For 1952 the U. S. Office of Education reported 18 Architectural Engineering curricula enrolling 1908 students (Circular No. 364, *Engineering Enrollments and Degrees,* 1952. January 21, 1953).

[30] The nomenclature of teaching units, divisions, and even institutions varied widely; 36 teaching units reported as "departments," 21 as "schools," 2 as "colleges," and one as a "graduate school." Divisions were usually termed "schools" or "colleges." It is obvious, therefore, that the title of a teaching unit cannot be taken as a safe indication of the unit's relationship to the chief executive of the institution. Furthermore, insitutions themselves are termed "universities," "colleges," "institutes," and "schools." The reason for this variety appears to lie in part in functional description—institutions devoted more or less exclusively to technical curricula often prefer "institute" or "school"—and in part to historical accident.

[31] Tyler S. Rogers, "Education for an integrated building industry" (*Architectural Forum,* September, 1952, pp. 141, 164, 168).

[32] *Statistical Abstract of the U. S.*

[33] The general problem was discussed in a joint meeting, held April 21 and 22, 1950, of the California Conference of Junior Colleges and the schools of architecture located in that state.

[34] H. P. Hammond, "Accrediting Technical Institutes" (*Journal of Engineering Education,* vol. 38, no. 9, May, 1948, pp. 616–621).

[35] George F. Zook and M. E. Haggerty: *The Evaluation of Higher Institutions: I. Principles of Accrediting Higher Institutions,* 1936, pp. 18–38.

[36] Lester W. Bartlett and Mildred B. Neel: *Compensation in the Professions.* 1933, p. 15.

[37] Weatherhead, *op. cit.,* pp. 145–149.

[38] Zook and Haggerty, *op. cit.,* Chapter 4.

[39] These events are summarized from the official reports in Weatherhead, *op. cit.,* pp. 200–203.

[40] *Agreement Establishing a National Architectural Accrediting Board.* January 20, 1940, p. 2.

[41] The NAAB Pattern Map was developed from a similar chart used by the North Central Association of Colleges and Secondary Schools (Zook and Haggerty, *op. cit.,* Fig. 2, and pp. 98–105).

[42] 1952 Report of NAAB (*Journal of Architectural Education.* No. 8, 1952. Proceedings of 38th Annual Convention, ACSA, p. 70).

[43] *1945 Report of NAAB.*

[44] The sources of *Table 56* are: 1898, for 9 schools, Report of the Committee on Education, *Proceedings of the 32nd Annual Convention of The AIA* (reproduced in Weatherhead, *op. cit.,* p. 63); 1911, for 21 schools, compiled by Weatherhead from school bulletins and records (*ibid.,* pp. 136–137); 1930, for 52 schools, compiled by Bosworth and Jones (*op. cit.,* pp. 188–189, in which the total is incorrect); 1933–1953, Annual Enrollment Reports, ACSA. From 1933 through 1944 the latter covered only member schools, for example, 31 out of 47 existing units in 1935. Enrollments for non-member schools in 1934 were obtained independently by Weatherhead (*op. cit.,* pp. 236–237). For the remaining years, enrollments for these non-member schools have been estimated so as to be consistent with 1934 and the year of their first official report, and with the trend of enrollment in nearby schools. In seven instances, ACSA reports for specific schools appeared inconsistent and have been adjusted to harmonize with earlier and later years. These inconsistencies have occurred no doubt from the fact that some school administrators have misinterpreted the terminology of the ACSA report forms. Moreover, in some cases curricular organization makes it difficult to relate local enrollments to the national picture. For example, schools with a common Freshman year often have no means of identifying students who intend to elect architecture. Another source of confusion has been the ACSA request to schools to include in their report not only the actual number of students enrolled in the fall term, but also an estimate of the additional students expected to enter at mid-year. In practice, however, many schools have disregarded this estimate. Although before 1950 ACSA restricted its coverage to curricula in architecture and excluded those in architectural engineering, some schools seem not to have differentiated these classes. It is clear, therefore, that, as in the gathering of all vital statistics, these enrollment reports have varying degrees of accuracy, but, in lieu of more rigorous sources, *Table 56* may be accepted as giving a reasonably correct indication of magnitude and trends. The Commission believes that ACSA could well review its statistical practices and seek in the future a more uniform and complete coverage of the field. *Table 56* includes 68 schools. Five are

no longer in operation. Of the remaining schools, NAAB has stated that probably only 56 are now or potentially of full professional character. This leaves seven schools, four of which have only curricula in architectural engineering. The rest have special objectives: Cooper Union provides a three-year program from which students transfer to regular schools; Ohio University offers a non-professional four-year curriculum; and Hampton Institute confers a non-professional degree. All architectural engineering students are tabulated separately, although it is suspected that some have been inadvertently included among regular architectural students. All students of the special programs have been included in the totals for architecture, since they must be considered as preparatory students for regular curricula.

[45] All geographical distributions presented in this section employ the following areas, which include the following states:

1. *New England Area:* Maine, New Hampshire, Massachusetts, Rhode Island.
2. *North Atlantic Area:* Vermont, Connecticut, New York, New Jersey, Pennsylvania, Delaware.
3. *Midwest Area:* Ohio, Indiana, Illinois, Michigan, Wisconsin, West Virginia, Kentucky.
4. *Northern Plains Area:* Minnesota, North Dakota, South Dakota.
5. *Central Plains Area:* Iowa, Missouri, Nebraska, Kansas.
6. *Central Atlantic Area:* Maryland, District of Columbia, Virginia, North Carolina.
7. *Southeastern Area:* South Carolina, Georgia, Florida, Tennessee, Alabama, Mississippi, Arkansas, Louisiana.
8. *Southwestern Area:* Oklahoma, Texas, New Mexico.
9. *Mountain Area:* Wyoming, Colorado, Utah, Nevada, Arizona.
10. *Northwestern Area:* Montana, Idaho, Washington, Oregon.
11. *California Area.*

These areas include groups of states related by the natural lines of student migration. There were only four exceptions to this rule: Maine sent more students to the North Atlantic, South Dakota to the Central Plains, and Arizona and Nevada to California, than to the areas in which they were assigned because of geographic and other similarities. While it would have been desirable to employ census or AIA regions for these data, either of these systems would have been foreign to the nature of the material. A third system, used by Bosworth and Jones in 1932, subdivided states without schools and distributed these portions to nearby states with schools. This method does not reflect satisfactorily the student migration patterns, here tabulated for the first time, and, furthermore, does not permit the determination of relevant state ratios.

[46] The annual reports of engineering enrollments issued by the U. S. Office of Education include a classification on "Architecture" (the first report in 1950 was issued as Circular No. 266 and covered 1949 enrollments) but must be used with caution because data given for many of the schools apparently confuse architecture and architectural engineering.

[47] Bosworth and Jones (*op. cit.,* pp. 188–189) is the source for 1930, in which the total is incorrectly added. Beginning in 1950 ACSA has issued enrollments for 25 schools offering architectural engineering as a supplement to its regular report. The U. S. Office of Education, however, lists 12 other schools as having such curricula and accords them a total of 713 students. Two schools, the Chicago Technical College with 260, and the Lawrence Institute with 193, account for 64 per cent of this total.

[48] This effect may be roughly demonstrated as follows: if, in 1950, architectural and architectural engineering students had enrolled in the same proportions as in 1930, there would have been 2901 in architectural engineering; since the actual count was 1918, a shift of 983 students to structural options is indicated; this group would be 7.3 per cent of all 13,491 students enrolled in 1950, or 34 per cent of 2901 students. The order of magnitude of such a shift seems entirely plausible.

[49] The sources of data in *Table 57* are:

1. Students from U. S. Territories and foreign countries: 1950 and 1951, the Commission's *School Surveys;* 1953, geographical origins of students gathered for the Commission by ACSA.

2. Percentages of veteran students: 1950–1952, from reports of fall enrollments in all institutions of higher education, published in *Higher Education.* These give total and male enrollments for all institutions and total enrollments for a group limited to universities, colleges, and professional schools. The numbers of male veterans in all institutions and of all veterans in universities, colleges, and professional schools are also given. The percentage of veterans in male enrollments of universities, colleges, and professional schools was calculated as follows:

$$\frac{\% \text{ Vets in Univ. Male Enroll.}}{} = \frac{\text{Total Enroll. x All male vets x Univ. male vets}}{\text{All vets x Total male enroll. x Univ. enroll.}}$$

The 37.7 per cent used for 1950 may be somewhat low. If percentages observed in engineering schools in 1949 are translated to 1950, application to architecture suggests 46.4 per cent. On the basis of the latter ratio, there would have been 5968 non-veteran and 5167 veteran students in architecture. For 1953, total enrollment was issued in *Higher Education,* but veteran data was no longer included. The total number of veterans was reported by Walters (*School and Society,* December 12, 1953) and the direct percentage was used.

3. Estimates for total population from 1951 to 1953 are taken from "Provisional Estimates of the Population of the U. S." (Bureau of the Census: *Current Population Reports, Population Estimates,* series P-25, No. 79, September 16, 1953).

4. The 18–21 year age group data is taken from Ronald B. Thompson: *Estimating College Age Population Trends, 1940–1970.* (Report to the American Association of Collegiate Registrars and Admission Officers.) August, 1953. The sizes of the 18–21 year groups was determined by survivals from actual recorded births. Since the recording of births has in some states been comprehensive only in recent years, the totals for 1940 and 1950 are somewhat less than census enumerations.

5. The number of engineers from 1910 to 1940 is from *Employment Outlook for Engineers* (U. S. Dept. of Labor, Bureau of Labor Statistics, Occupational Outlook Series, Bulletin 968). 1949, p. 98, Table D–1. The 1900 figure is from David L. Fiske: "Are the Professions Crowded" (*Civil Engineering,* vol. 4, no. 1, January, 1934, p. 16). Enrollments in engineering curricula are from Henry H. Armsby: "Engineering Education in the U. S." (*Higher Education,* vol. 9, no. 7, December 1, 1952, p. 78). Armsby also estimates the number of engineers in 1950 as 400,000. This latter is considerably below the 534,424 enumerated by the 1950 Census, which has been questioned as including a large number who claimed the title without having professional training or status. This constitutes an overenumeration of 31 per cent if the estimate of 400,000 is used, and this may be compared with the 23 per cent by which "census architects" exceeded registered architects in 1950.

6. The number of lawyers and the enrollments of law schools are from Joseph A. McClain, Jr.: "Legal Education in the U. S." (*Higher Education,* vol. 9, no. 14, March 15, 1953, pp. 162, 166).

50 *1950 Census,* vol. 2, pt. 1, p. 210.

51 While the estimates of veteran enrollments for 1950–1953 have been calculated on the same basis (see note 49, section 2), a difficulty presents itself in that the non-veteran enrollment in architecture increases at curiously irregular annual rates of 3 per cent for 1951, 11 per cent for 1952, and 1 per cent for 1953.

51a In 1952, the American Bar Association increased required pre-professional college work from two to three years.

52 The calculation assumed the following survival ratios: Pre-medic Sophomores, 50%; Juniors, 60%; to end of Junior year and submission of application, 70%; Medical Sophomores, 90%; Juniors, 92%; Seniors, 97%. The pre-medic ratios were set lower than similar ratios of 67.7%, 76.5%, and 89.2% observed from 1948 to 1952 for non-veteran students in engineering curricula (Henry H. Armsby, "Graduation and Withdrawal Ratios for Engineering Studies," *Higher Education,* vol. 10, no. 3, November, 1953, pp. 45–46) because of the high scholastic records demanded for admission to medical schools. The medical school ratios are assumed so that they produce the observed 80 per cent survival from admission to graduation (Milton Friedman and Simon Kuznets: *Income from Independent Professional Practice,* 1945, p. 16, note 23a, part 2). A ratio of 50 per cent for admissions to applications was assumed (*ibid,* p. 16, note 23). Thus the distribution of the resulting 7 classes by per cent of total enrollment would be 46.1, 23.0, 13.8, 4.8, 4.4, 4.0, and 3.9. Pre-medical enrollment is therefore estimated to be 4.86 times the medical school enrollment of 26,515, which gives 128,863 pre-medical students. This added to 26,515 gives a total of 155,378, and divided by 201,300 practitioners gives a ratio of 0.7719. The discrepancy in the NAAB ratio was originally pointed out by Professor Stanley A. Smith and he also provided the correct figure for the 1951 medical enrollment.

53 "Illustrative Projections of the Population of the U. S., by Age and Sex, 1955 to 1975" (U. S. Bureau of the Census: *Current Population Reports: Population Estimates,* series P-25, no. 78, August 21, 1953). For 1970, four sets of projections are furnished based on different assumed birth rates. *Set A,* based on the continuation of current rates, was used because the assumption of declining rates seemed arbitrary.

54 "*Urban population*" here follows the Old Definition employed by the Bureau of the Census prior to 1950.

55 Thompson, *op. cit.*

56 No studies of this point have come to light. In 1950 a rough check of architectural and architectural engineering alumni of one large school graduated since 1928 disclosed that 40 per cent

had become architects or architectural employees and that another 40 per cent were employed in the building industry. Since this survey included the lean years of depression and war, and since the current high demand for architectural graduates promises to continue, the assumption of 70 per cent survival of graduates in professional work seems warranted. If this is regarded as too high, a lower figure will increase proportionately the number of graduates needed.

57 It is possible to contend that the difference would be partially satisfied by the addition of graduates of those curricula in architectural engineering which claim to train their students for the professional practice of architecture. Although in the past many such graduates have obtained registrations in sympathetic states, it has been assumed in this analysis that, as NAAB official listing is accorded increasing importance, the number of architectural engineers admitted to registration as architects will decrease sharply. *Table 57* reveals that their inclusion for the past 20 years would create little change in the ratios studied.

58 *Higher Education,* vol. 7, no. 11, February 1, 1951, p. 125.

59 These bases consequently differ slightly from those used in calculating the national ratios previously stated. Here the number of students is restricted to those resident in the continental U. S. instead of all students. Likewise the use of 1950 state data on registered architects and urban population without adjustments for 3 years of growth makes these ratios exhibit slightly higher values than 1953 bases would give. The age-group ratios, however, are produced entirely with 1953 data. If the architectural engineering students of the University of Detroit, the State College of Washington, and the California State Polytechnic College are eliminated, the ratios of their states, their areas, and the U. S. become:

| | No. Stud. | | S/RA | | S/UP | | S/AG | |
	ALL	ARCH. ONLY	ALL	ARCH. ONLY	ALL	ARCH. ONLY	ALL	ARCH. ONLY
Michigan	422	260	.67	.41	10.3	6.3	133	82
Washington	217	166	.51	.39	17.0	13.0	264	202
California	977	848	.51	.44	13.7	11.9	336	291
Midwest area	2307	2145	.60	.56	10.7	9.9	124	116
N. W. area	517	466	.72	.65	20.8	18.7	261	235
U. S.	9424	9082	.49	.47	10.6	10.2	118	113

These changes do not alter the general configuration of *Figure 36.*

60 Since 1946 the University of Illinois has reported a total enrollment which includes two separate departments, that long established at Urbana, and a department which offers the first two years of the architectural curriculum in Chicago. In 1949 the university enrolled an unduplicated total of 1132 students in architecture, and in 1950 this was 1037. The 1950 and 1953 enrollments used in the text table are for the first semester. In each case, 72 per cent were students on the Urbana campus. The maximum number at Urbana at one time, i.e., in the first semester, was 704 in 1949, 667 in 1950, and 625 in 1953. The marked increase in these enrollments since the war is due in part to the inclusion of students in the engineering option, who previously were omitted in ACSA reports because they were then following the curriculum in architectural engineering.

61 The method of approach was developed by Professor Clinton H. Cowgill.

62 The section sizes assumed in all cases were: design, freehand drawing, graphics, 15 students, with an absolute maximum of 18; lecture-recitation classes in construction, history, theory, etc., 30–40; lecture-problems classes in structures, mechanics, sociology, etc., 20–30, and advanced structures, 20–25; rhetoric and mathematics, 18–22; all general elective courses, 25. In scheduling all general courses, fractional loads were used on the assumption that architectural students would join with others to compose normal sections. No attempt was made to adjust class enrollments to include repeating, irregular, or special students. The last two are subject to close control, but some definite provision must be made for the first. However, the total load resulting from repeated courses could amount to from 3 to 5 per cent of each section. While the sections and loads here assumed conform to the best current practice, the level at which they were set is, for the purpose of the study, less important than that they be kept constant throughout.

63 The fixed charges come to $78 per student, which is 3 per cent of 130 sq. ft. per student at $20. per sq. ft. Annual maintenance is estimated at $1.20 per square foot. The cost of general institutional facilities—general library, recreational, etc.—is omitted because it varies widely and is not directly related to architectural enrollments.

64 It was determined that the restriction of the school of 150 students to a single option would

make no change in the cost per student, due to the fact that although one structural teacher would be eliminated, one in advanced design would have to be added. In either case, undersize sections resulted.

65 All of these estimates are considerably greater than the total of $4,191,000 reported for all schools in Section 5 of this chapter. It should be noted that the previous total did not include any expenditures for technical or general instruction given by other departments of the institutions, nor for any fixed charges or maintenance. It is interesting that, if it is assumed that in 1950 architectural divisions taught 75 per cent of all technical courses, and if costs per student for technical staff, special education, and division administration are assumed at the estimated rates of schools with 200 students—i.e., the case nearest the 1950 national average, the total cost for the 11,573 students enrolled in 1950 would come to $4,175,000, a sum very close to the reported total. Since it is difficult to believe that all schools maintained average section sizes and staff loads as favorable as those from which the assumed costs per students were derived, it is likely that the proportion of technical courses taught was somewhat higher than 75 per cent. At the average rates of tuitions reported by the *1950 School Survey* students enrolled in 1950 would have paid tuition totaling $3,465,000, which is 44.5 per cent of the $7,767,000 estimated as the total cost of their instruction. Since the loads assumed for this estimate were low, in reality tuition probably represented a somewhat higher ratio.

66 John I. Ivey, Jr., and William J. McGlothlin, "The South's Evolving Pattern of Regional Planning in Higher Education (*Higher Education,* vol. 6, no. 9, January 1, 1950, pp. 100–103). The system operates as follows: a state without facilities contracts with the Board for a quota of students and agrees to pay a fixed sum per student ($1500 per year in medicine; $1000 in veterinary medicine). The student pays tuition at in-state rates and obtains admission, whereas previously he rarely gained entrance in out-of-state schools. The admitting school is thus assured of regular quotas and the payments received enable it to expand its facilities proportionately. The state making the payments secures access to facilities at a fraction of the cost of maintaining an independent school.

CHAPTER VIII

Candidate Training
For the Practice of Architecture

1. THE ARCHITECTURAL OFFICE AS WORKSHOP AND TRAINING CENTER

For nine out of ten practitioners the practice of architecture involves the assembly and maintenance of a staff of assistants to aid him in producing the professional services desired by the community he serves. The continuing operation of an architectural office depends, therefore, upon the productivity of the principal and his team. Under such circumstances it is understandable that a practitioner should seek to employ personnel of proven competence born of wide experience in their assigned tasks.

In reality, however, the recruitment of pre-trained employees is made difficult by the fact that demand exceeds supply. Moreover, every office develops special methods of production and special technical preferences in which new employees must be indoctrinated. Then, too, personal and other factors create a natural attrition of staff and impose the need of replacement. Even if experienced employees can be procured, few will possess such finished competence that further development is unnecessary. Therefore, as in all enterprises which utilize the cooperative effort of many individuals, the act of employing is inevitably linked in large degree with the provision of in-service training, and the architect, if he is a realistic administrator, must also assume to a considerable extent the role of teacher.

With respect to in-service training, two types of personnel may be discerned. On the one hand, there are those who display limited ambition, preparation, or talent and are content to remain permanently in an employee status. For them, training means the acquisition as rapidly as possible of useful, though restricted, vocational skills, capable of providing each with a stable, if modest, livelihood. On the other hand, more aggressive individuals value employment primarily for the opportunity it gives for continuing professional growth. These look forward to the eventual attainment of full professional status and the establishment of their own offices. At first glance, an architect-employer might prefer to concentrate his effort on the former group with the hope of building up a staff of perennial assistants and thus in time minimize the need for instruction. On second thought, however, the benefits of including within an organization a large proportion of those who seek more responsible careers become apparent. These advantages accrue to both office and the whole profession through the enhancement of capabilities. While the demands upon the employer are wider and more continuing, he serves through his teaching not only his own interest, but the goals of his profession as well.

Thus the enlightened architect cannot conduct his office—even if he wished—solely for personal convenience or profit. Indeed, if, as an employer, he neglects to cultivate a concern for his employees' growth in competence, he loses the most potent possible appeal for their maximum effort, loyalty, and personal interest in his own work. Without such motivation the best-intentioned staff suffers low morale and rarely achieves the quality of performance for which the employer himself should strive.

2. THE CANDIDATE

Candidacy may be defined as that period of training in which a candidate seeks to acquire the advanced practical knowledge, skills, and judgment which are the prerequisites to full professional status.[1] In its narrow sense the goal of candidacy is the attainment of professional registration and legal certification of minimum competence. But from the standpoint of the profession this limited objective is not enough. Any serious training program must also emphasize the goal of maximum competence and the complete fulfillment of the candidate's potentialities. While this is a long-term, indeed a lifetime, endeavor extending well beyond any realistic interpretation of the word *candidacy,* it is equally true that any program which falls short of this wider vision also betrays true professional needs. Consequently, in the present discussion candidacy is assumed to embrace both goals.

Since the candidate program is by definition concerned with advanced practical training, it follows that candidates must have already secured a command of elementary knowledge and skills. This elementary training can be obtained in two ways. First is the method of office training, descended from the traditional apprenticeship and *pupilage* systems. The decline of these systems has been described in *Chapter IV*. The modern equivalent of apprentice and pupil is the youth who enters an office as a novice—often as an office boy—and absorbs as best he can the rudiments of drafting and practical knowledge. Up to a generation ago this process was facilitated by the custom of duplicating drawings by laborious tracing, which could be delegated to novice draftsmen whose wages were so nominal that their tracings were cheaper than other methods of reproduction. In recent years, however, tracing has been abandoned and this opportunity for this type of elementary training lost.

The training of novices in the offices is usually haphazard, because the organization of a systematic course of instruction demands much time and thought which most practitioners are unable to devote to the task and to which they are reluctant to assign highly paid members from their staffs. In many cases, employers advise novices to seek supplementary training in evening classes or through correspondence courses, and on occasion they have assisted promising youths with loans or gifts to finance attendance at regular professional schools. In doing this, they acknowledge the strong tendency of office training to develop specific vocational skills at the expense of a systematic, integrated understanding of both theory and practice. Nevertheless, there will no doubt continue to be a number of candidates who will enter candidacy via office training.

The second source of candidates are, of course, the professional schools of architecture. While to laymen and some practitioners it may seem that much of the training here assigned to candidacy should have already been covered in professional curricula, it is evident from foregoing chapters that school training is subject to inherent limitations of time and approach. It is universally recognized, therefore, that the school-trained candidate must supplement his academic training by the discipline which only practical office experience can provide in the application of theory to specific situations, the expansion of knowledge to more comprehensive scope, and the development of mature judgment and wisdom. Thus, school and office training must complement each other in the attainment of professionally competent personnel.

Graduates of professional curricula thus comprise the primary source and the best prepared group for candidate training. Nevertheless, midway between these graduate candidates and office-trained non-graduate candidates stands a third group, those who have completed a portion of the school curriculum and have then entered architectural offices. While these candidates have obtained systematic coverage of beginning subjects, they have unfortunately missed the advanced courses which the final years of the curricula provide.

From the point of view of the candidate, his training program should have well defined objectives, progress in methodical steps, and enjoy the active guidance of a responsible leader and instructor. This is to say that the candidate would prefer a program organized as an educational process for the special purpose of achieving the goal he seeks. Unfortunately several factors obstruct such a solution. One of the most difficult to resolve is the fact that by definition the candidate's goal is experience in the actual performance of professional services which rarely arrange themselves in a neat educational pattern. It was this characteristic of practical affairs which long ago led to the decline of the apprenticeship and *pupilage* systems and the delegation of basic instruction to the schools.

While it is no doubt unreasonable to expect that offices can ever satisfy educational criteria completely, several approaches to the problem do promise improvement. First is the general recognition by the profession that it must strive for heightened competence among its members and that in the long run this will require unification and integration of all professional training, whether in school, candidacy, or practice.

333

Second, this in turn has led individual practitioners to realize more fully their responsibilities for the training of candidates, to think more often in terms of educational patterns, and whenever possible to adjust office procedures to educational needs. Third, the schools have made considerable progress in incorporating a more realistic and practical point of view in their instruction and their future graduates should have less difficulty in adjusting themselves to office work. And, fourth, candidates themselves are coming to understand that, although the educational methods of school and office necessarily differ, office experience can yield excellent instruction if candidates exercise initiative and industry in seeking and organizing the lessons contained therein. Nevertheless, the Commission firmly believes that much remains to be done in ordering candidate training to secure more effective use of the efforts of trainees and practitioners. Indeed, the Commission considers this problem to be one of the most urgent confronting the profession today.

3. THE CANDIDATE TRAINING PROGRAM

The relationship of architects and candidates is not a new problem. In small firms—and these were the rule in earlier periods—candidates have long had easy and informal access to employers. Moreover, most employers seemed to enjoy their role of adviser to promising youths. While direct instruction was often on a very casual and occasional basis, it was usually stimulated by warm personal concern. A generation ago this attitude existed even in many large offices where employers often acted as patrons and critics to groups of draftsmen who organized themselves as an *atelier* for the study of design problems issued by the BAID. The decline of such groups has not prompted the development of any compensating device.

In 1933 The AIA, ACSA, and NCARB cooperated in developing the Mentor plan which was intended to provide each architectural candidate with the guidance of an experienced practicing architect during the period of preparation for the registration examination. The administration of the plan was assigned to NCARB. Under it the candidate was directed to nominate a Mentor, and could, if he wished, call upon the Committee on Education of the local AIA chapter or the NCARB itself for counsel in this choice. It was pointed out that the candidate need not select his employer as a Mentor. The architect so nominated was expected to record with NCARB his willingness to serve as a Mentor, but, when this was accomplished and the candidate registered at a nominal fee with NCARB, active prosecution of the plan devolved upon the Mentor and his protégé. As originally conceived, the goal was the successful passage of the NCARB Junior Examination, and it was intended that the NCARB would not admit the candidate to this test until the Mentor certified that he was properly prepared to attempt it.[2]

Unfortunately, despite the high hopes of the plan's proposers, the ready support of schoolmen, and considerable interest on the part of many practitioners, the Mentor system never matured. A number of factors contributed to this disappointment. No

334

doubt the disturbed conditions due to economic depression and later to war prevented many potential candidates from obtaining any experience whatever, much less a coordinated planned program. The same factors disrupted many offices whose principals would otherwise have been glad to activate the system. Another probable cause was the fact that no real guidance was provided the Mentors, with the result that each had to develop his own *modus operandi* on the basis of an extremely brief and generalized paragraph contained in a one-page NCARB circular. Then, too, the link with NCARB was somewhat tenuous since in most cases candidates aimed their attention, not toward the NCARB, but toward the registration board of their own state whose examinations often stressed questions related to academic studies rather than knowledge derived from practical participation in office work. Whatever the reasons, the Mentor system never became an accepted, vigorous solution to the problem of candidate training.

Any attempt to reconsider the candidate program must start with an explicit definition of objectives. The desired end product is an individual fulfilling those qualifications described in Section 3, *Chapter III,* and capable of successfully performing the professional services enumerated in Section 2, *Chapter II.* On the other hand, the raw material of the process, the individual entering upon candidacy, should bring to the program a degree of basic knowledge and skill approximating that listed in Section 3, *Chapter V.* The function of candidacy is, therefore, to bridge the gap between these two sets of qualifications.

It is apparent, of course, that both sets of standards are ideals and that specific individuals will conform to them in varying degrees. Thus, if the employing architect is prone to find the candidate imperfectly prepared at the start, he should, in all fairness, measure himself against the ideal standards of his own profession. Moreover, he should remember that during the first adjustment to unfamiliar office procedures the candidate may well feel at a serious disadvantage and give an erroneous impression of less preparation than he actually possesses. Further, the architect should recognize—what every successful teacher knows—that refreshment of knowledge forgotten or the filling in of gaps is more surely stimulated by sympathetic encouragement than by indignant denunciation.

In general, the function of the training program is to build upon the candidate's preparation by expanding his knowledge and skills and by illustrating their application in the actual performance of professional services. This is most directly accomplished if the candidate can experience a series of complete project cycles by following the evolution of several projects from inception to completion. Since many offices have found it advantageous to organize project teams to handle each specific commission, it is more and more feasible to assign a candidate as a minor assistant in such a team. In this way he should be able to observe preliminary discussions with clients, the accumulation of basic data, the formulation of the program and the basic design, the preparation of working drawings and specifications, the refinement of details, the selection of materials, the checking of shop drawings, the writing of contract documents, the choice of general and trade contractors, and the inspection of

335

construction. If, as these steps progress, his teammates and his employer can provide informal commentary on the reasons for decisions, the candidate will begin to absorb professional and practical modes of thought. Moreover, he can also begin to review the facts and principles obtained in his earlier studies and relate them to the problems at hand. If he is alert, industrious, and intelligent, it will not require many repetitions of this cycle to give him real value as a member of a team. If subsequent projects differ in character and scope, additional growth can be stimulated.

The suggestion that the most effective candidate experience is to be gained through participation in a project team raises the question of the candidate's selection of an office for his training. When all offices were small, their limited volume of work and restricted personnel gave candidates easy contact with all stages of practice, not only those to which they were personally assigned, but also those on which officemates were engaged. From this situation has arisen the common belief that small offices provide the best initial experience. It must be noted, however, that small offices do not usually afford experience in large, complex projects. With the development of large offices, a phenomenon described in *Chapter II,* a decided trend appeared toward the assignment of personnel to specialized tasks in order to reduce the cost of preparing working documents. The extreme result was the departmentalized office (*Figure 10,* p. 42). In such firms a candidate has little opportunity to observe a complete project cycle and if his experience is derived entirely from such a situation, it will be very difficult for him to gain any broad understanding of the field. As previously noted, some large offices set up project teams to handle specific jobs (*Figure 11,* p. 43), and thus provide excellent experience in large projects. The candidate who desires a full range of training might well seek experience in offices of various sizes. It must be realized, however, that size is only one factor influencing the selection of offices for training. Quality of work, morale of personnel, and the integrity of the principals are certainly of equal importance.

It must be emphasized, however, that as absorbing and valuable as such experiences are, they do not satisfy the candidate's entire need. While each project raises many questions for decision, introduces new situations, conditions, and data, and involves new materials, techniques, and procedures, the pressure of production rarely permits systematic organization of the lessons to be derived from these experiences. In this, the candidate is not alone, since too often both employer and employees labor under the same handicap. For this reason it is time most profitably spent if periodic reviews can be scheduled for all projects.

Furthermore, such experiences can suggest to an alert candidate subjects for special study and investigation, by means of which he can acquire advanced knowledge and enhanced competence. While it is tempting, in the hurry of daily affairs, to relax the habit of concentrated study, the regular exercise and extension of theoretical thinking is as indispensable to sound professional growth as the accumulation of practical observations. This is to say, for example, that the graduate candidate should not regard his completion of a prescribed curriculum as satisfying all his future needs for systematic study. Due to limitations of time and students' limited powers of absorption and insight, many phases of the undergraduate program can at best form mere introductions to important topics. No candidate will be able to benefit fully from his office experience if he is content to continue to base his thinking on the limited fund of knowledge which he has gleaned from undergraduate courses. Indeed, both school and office fall short of their mission if they fail to arouse the candidate's curiosity sufficiently to prompt him to further systematic studies. The provision of means for advanced study will be discussed in detail in *Chapter X*.

Finally the candidate should be constantly reminded that he must aim for a goal far beyond mere technicalism. Most schools endeavor to quicken their students' awareness and desire for general cultural development, but, here too, unless a candidate is encouraged to expand this elementary experience, the excitement of his new technical activities is apt to restrict excessively his overall growth as a whole person. If this happens, both he and the profession suffer. It is surprising what influence an enlightened employer and adviser can exert on the young candidate by example and concern in such matters.

The full program here described is conceived as a well-rounded educational process which continues, complements, and extends the candidate's earlier preparation and which in turn should lead him naturally to that technical and personal maturity on which alone true professional life can flourish. Candidacy, thus envisioned, transcends the limited goal of registration and minimum competence and looks rather to each candidate's realization of his fullest potentialities. If such a view seems to spring from an incurably romantic ideal, it may be observed that without idealism the very idea of a profession is meaningless. Moreover, it should be remembered that youth itself needs the stimulus of the ideal to awaken maximum response.

The optimum duration of such a program is naturally indeterminable, because it depends upon the talent, industry, and insight of the individual candidate and the effectiveness and opportunities of the experience afforded him. Nevertheless, it is convenient to separate the more tangible aspects of the program in order to establish a definite period in which preparation for the limited goal of registration can be accomplished. Although many foresighted candidates will no doubt desire to continue candidacy for a longer period in order to acquire a more comprehensive range of experience, an immediate objective, such as registration, is useful as a device to measure normal progress, emphasize certain characteristic phases of the program, discourage overlong delay in attaining legal status, and prevent suspicion that full status is restricted for ulterior motives.

The *1950 Survey* investigated the profession's opinions as to the desirable length of this limited concept of candidacy. *Table 47* reveals surprising unanimity for 3.6 years of practical experience for graduate candidates. Teachers, however, favored an average of 3.1 years. Another source of opinion is expressed in the NCARB requirement of 3 years of office experience as a prerequisite for admission to a recognized registration examination. This NCARB regulation derived from and in turn influenced similar stipulations in the registration acts of 23 states, but this length is by no means universally accepted. Three states require one year; four specify two years;

two demand four years; and one—Delaware—asks five years. Five states do not require any period of experience. For non-graduate candidates, most acts demand a longer term of candidate training. In view of these widely divergent regulations, it is clear that the determination of the minimum legal length of candidacy has been an arbitrary process which should be reviewed and re-evaluated. It is highly probable that much of the opinion gathered by the *1950 Survey* was not based on any objective study or any definite program of training.

One approach to the problem is to fix a minimum period which will permit the candidate to participate in a suitable number of the project cycles previously described. Too short a term—one year, for example—cannot ensure observation of even a single cycle, much less different types of cycles. While four or five years may indeed be profitable if a varied and deepened experience is obtained, a mandatory period of such length seems excessive and motivated by reasons other than the acquisition of a reasonable standard of minimum competence. Within a period of two or three years, however, a candidate who is fortunate in the selection of his employer and the time of his employment can participate in several projects, some of which he will be able to follow from inception to completion. Moreover, if he develops properly, he will be able to assume increasing responsibilities in successive projects. From a minor assistant in a project team, he might be able toward the end of his candidacy to rise to the level of job captain on a project of limited scope. It should be recognized, of course, that such responsibility cannot be entrusted to him merely on the basis of a standard time schedule, and this simply means that for some candidates the length of candidacy must be prolonged. Indeed, for diverse reasons, some will never achieve their original goal. If registration examinations can be gauged to reveal an appropriate capacity for responsibility rather than merely to display a knowledge of fact or formula, the adjustment of a fixed term of candidacy to human variations can be easily and equitably controlled. Within these conditions the Commission believes that three years is a reasonable minimum period in which to expect an alert candidate to acquire the minimum experience compatible with registration.

It must be emphasized, however, that this belief does not exclude the desirability of eliminating one year of the present three-year term if the reorganization of academic instruction, as proposed in Section 2, *Chapter VII,* can be accepted and implemented. The intensification of professional and technical studies for a selected group of students could raise, at least for this group, the level of achievement upon entry into candidacy to such a point that a two-year office experience might well prove entirely feasible from professional and technical, as well as from personal and social, points of view. The end result, not the number of years, is the primary consideration.

Up to the present time the organization of the candidate program has been left to the initiative of the candidate and his adviser. If by chance a candidate has gained some insight into the meaning and demands of professional status, if by good fortune he has been foresighted and aggressive enough to formulate and pursue a systematic course, or if he has enjoyed the guidance of an enlightened and sympathetic employer, this informal approach has at times yielded satisfactory results. Too often, however, even well-intentioned candidates and employers have failed to give the problem adequate attention and thus effort is dissipated for want of direction and method. In other cases, candidate training has been left entirely to accident and whim.

The *1950 Survey* substantiated this appraisal. *Table 49* reveals that while 94 per cent of all registered architects considered their pre-registration experience in working drawings and detailing to be adequate, and 87 per cent had the same opinion with regard to general design, those who had had inadequate or no training in equipment installations totaled 63 per cent; in site planning and administration, 60 per cent; in client relations, 55 per cent; in specifications, 51 per cent; in supervision, 42 per cent; and in structural design, 40 per cent. It is probable that in large measure the high proportion of failures in licensing examinations may be ascribed to the lack of systematic experience in these aspects of practice.

Because of this situation and because wide-scale achievement of desired results demands efficient methods, dissatisfaction with the status quo has mounted in recent years. Calls for a planned program of training have risen with increasing frequency. The Commission believes that professional and social needs for improved competence make continuance of a laissez-faire attitude insupportable and it has therefore given much thought to the development of an appropriate formal organization for candidate training.[3]

The plan proposed by the Commission assumes the scope of training already described. Therefore, the formal schedule for candidacy should provide a progressive experience in each stage of the performance of Executive Services, as follows:

1. Project research, analysis, and programming
2. The determination of the Basic Design Solution
3. The preparation of the Working Documents
4. The negotiation of Construction Contracts
5. The performance of services accompanying construction operations.

Within these broad categories, however, there are many special phases in which beginning candidates usually lack any sound training. Consequently, experience in the following areas should be especially stressed:

1. Client Relations
2. Site Planning
3. Structural Design, both in calculations by the candidate and in collaboration with engineering personnel
4. Building Equipment, in determinations by both the candidate and engineering personnel
5. Working drawings
6. Detailing, from the standpoint of both design and construction
7. Selection of materials
8. Writing of specifications
9. Checking of shop drawings
10. Supervision

339

Finally, there are certain general phases of practice about which candidates must gain understanding and skill:

1. Office and administrative procedures
2. The economics of practice
3. Contacts with personnel associated with building: code officials; lending agencies; construction contractors and mechanics
4. Professional relations

It is obvious that these categories add up to a comprehensive initiation into professional practice.[4] If such a program seems over-ambitious, particularly for a three-year period of candidacy, it should be recalled that it is intended to emphasize both long- and short-term goals.

The Commission recognizes that the time required to provide adequate experience in each specific area cannot be fixed as a definite number of months, because the character of an experience varies from project to project and each candidate responds to a given situation in a different manner. The Commission believes that a much more certain check of the adequacy of a candidate's experience in each area could be furnished by the employing practitioner acting in the capacity of the candidate's personal adviser. At the same time the Commission proposes a double safeguard to promote careful advisement and systematic progress—which the Mentor plan did not provide—through the use of a *Candidate's Logbook of Experience* and through periodic interviews of candidates by appropriate committees of local AIA chapters.

The Commission conceives the candidate's logbook as a continuous detailed record of the projects on which a candidate has worked and the specific duties and experiences he has gained thereby. In format, this record should be so arranged that regular memoranda of such data can be entered by the candidate. It should also include a chart on which monthly summaries of experience can be checked showing the types of duties performed. This chart would help to impress upon both candidate and employer the types and ranges of experience that comprehensive training demands, and at the same time it would reveal instantaneously an up-to-date picture of the candidate's cumulative coverage of experience. In order to ensure the accuracy of the candidate's entries and the employer's faithful review of the program, the employer should check, initial, and seal the logbook at regular intervals, perhaps bimonthly. The logbook should also record any supplementary studies which the candidate has completed. Chapter seminars for candidates, evening or correspondence courses, conferences and short-courses, and even any systematic, self-directed studies would form appropriate entries. In addition, the logbook might well include a transcript of the candidate's academic record.

The second provision—that of interviews with a chapter committee—is intended to provide an objective inspection of the candidate's progress by a group of practitioners outside the employee-employer relationship. Such counsel would give additional emphasis to well-rounded training, and, according to the character of the record, furnish an excellent opportunity to encourage good progress or warn an un-suspecting candidate of deficiencies. In the latter case, it would be beyond the province of the committee to suggest change of employer, but certainly the com-mittee's reaction could lead an alert candidate to evaluate his current opportunities and, if necessary, to seek a more auspicious situation.

Other agencies of external review have been suggested. One such proposal would delegate this function to schools of architecture. The Commission believes that this solution is unfeasible because of the wide dispersal of graduates. Another scheme would assign the responsibility to the registration boards. While this idea has some merit, it seems preferable to link this duty with the profession itself through its local representative, the AIA chapter. In the first place such service would emphasize in the minds of the members of both the committee and the chapter the scope and problems of candidate training, and, second, it would associate the candidate more intimately with his professional group and encourage him to seek participation in it. Moreover, it would stress the importance of true professional attitudes by assuring him of the positive concern of the profession for his progress. It is obvious that the success of such a program will involve a considerable volume of voluntary service on the part of committee members, but certainly no other phase of chapter work would be more worthwhile or more satisfying.

Committee-candidate interviews should be scheduled at fixed intervals, perhaps on a semi-annual basis. It may be objected that candidates' access to such committees may not always be convenient. The rapidly expanding chapter roster seems to over-come this criticism, but in any case the advantages to the candidate are so marked that most will surely regard two visits per year as well worth the effort.

Since the program and administration thus described presume adequate prior preparation, some method of formal admission should be provided. It is proposed that The AIA itself undertake this function by receiving applications, enrolling candidates, and issuing official logbooks. Although one suggestion urges a formal qualifying examination for candidacy administered by The AIA, the setting up of the necessary apparatus, the duplication of school examinations, and the implied lack of confidence in the ability of the profession's accredited schools to ensure a minimum standard of training, all seem to make such an examination superfluous. Conse-quently, it is here assumed that applications from graduates of accredited schools would be automatically accepted. It might also prove to be advantageous to encourage students in good standing to apply as early as the third year of the curriculum in order to prevent delay and possible confusion after graduation and to enable them to enter summer vacation experience in their records. Pre-graduation status could be labeled *Probationer,* which upon confirmation of graduation would become full candidacy. When the logbook is issued, a list of Institute chapters and the names and addresses of chairmen of chapter candidate committees should accompany it to encourage each graduate to establish prompt contact with the committees. For non-school applicants, admission to candidacy could be based upon joint recommenda-tions of an employer and the chapter committee certifying adequate basic preparation for candidacy. It should not be overlooked that the issuing of logbooks by The AIA will allow, for the first time, the compilation of national statistics of the number of candidates, their distribution, and type of preparation. Such data would also indicate to AIA chapters the candidates under their jurisdiction. It will, moreover, show the proportion of graduates continuing toward professional careers, and this, in addition, would assist the schools themselves to learn a great deal about the progress of their own alumni.

It should be noted that the candidate's logbook is not intended to replace data required by registration boards directly from schools and employers. The Commission believes that the keeping of his own records will be a considerable stimulus to a candidate to give serious thought to his own development. Moreover, the record thus compiled can be of assistance in his proper placement if for some reason he changes offices or chapters. Since the record in the logbook would not include any comment on quality of performance, it cannot become a disguised means of influencing a candidate's future position. Employer recommendation—either to other employers or to registration boards—should be kept entirely apart. Nevertheless, it is conceivable that the logbook could also become a valuable aid by which registration boards could advise an applicant for examination as to the general adequacy of his professional experience. The Commission believes that the state boards should give serious consideration to a uniform policy in this matter.

Thus, the proposed plan of candidate training enlists the cooperation of candidate, his employer-adviser, and the profession, as represented by The AIA and its chapters. The adoption of definite objectives and the assignment of specific functions to each, which should be stated in a special guidance manual, will permit each to make special contributions to its successful operation, provide a useful check and balance, and escape that vagueness of responsibility and intention which discouraged the development of the Mentor system. For these reasons, the Commission urges adoption of its new plan (*Recommendation 30*).

It is often suggested that some portion of candidacy should be spent on actual construction operations in order to gain at least an elementary understanding of erection techniques and conditions. The *1950 Survey* found that 63 per cent of all registered architects were of the opinion that such construction experience should be recognized as equivalent to office experience (*Table 48*). It may be significant that this group corresponds closely with the 60 per cent who considered their direct experience on construction jobs before registration as adequate (*Table 49*). On the other hand, 31 per cent reported inadequate experience, and 9 per cent had no such experience whatever. Furthermore, it is interesting to note that, whereas 61 per cent of all private practitioners favored the equating of construction and office experience, 77 per cent of all teacher-architects registered approval (*Table 48*). Unfortunately, the *Survey* did not explore the reasoning behind these responses.

The question naturally arises as to how candidates can fit into such work and what type of benefit they can expect to receive. Some candidates may have turned to architecture because of earlier experience on such jobs, and a few may have become skilled mechanics. Most, however, know only the theory of construction and are innocent of craft techniques or erection methods. Ideally, architects should command encyclopaedic knowledge in such matters, and indeed, after considerable experience in professional practice, many do approach this state. Nevertheless, the immediate need of the candidate is to gain appreciation, not of the details of production, important as these are, but rather of the "feel" of the construction process, in other words, the design implications arising from the assembly of materials at the site. In discussing courses in construction (Section 3, *Chapter VI*), it was suggested that a systematic program of inspection trips of buildings under erection would do much to provide such training, that the making of construction models can reveal the interrelation of elements in assembly, and that craft demonstrations could convey an understanding of quality workmanship. Furthermore, such experiences could also be obtained by candidate field and shop trips organized by AIA chapters. Then, too, architects should constantly encourage candidates in their offices to visit all available construction jobs at regular intervals. Finally, definite provision in the candidate's program for experience in supervision—even perhaps as a clerk-of-the-works—can furnish similar opportunities. If a concerted effort can be made in all these directions, a candidate should be able to gain quite adequate experience without the necessity of actual employment in a construction firm. Former slighting of these devices explains sufficiently the current belief of a considerable proportion of the profession that the only solution is such employment. In any case, it is well to repeat the warning that a little knowledge may lead the candidate to oversimplification and the neglect of advanced craft techniques. Whatever means the candidate employs to gain such knowledge, he should not consider it as a substitute for direct office experience.

It remains to note that much discussion has been devoted to the problem of an appropriate title for candidates which will recognize the considerable training that admission to candidacy implies, which will dignify their status both professionally and publicly, and which will enhance their own morale by emphasizing the goal of full membership in the profession. The current situation in architecture is in direct contrast to medical usage which accords internes the respected title of *doctor*. Due to former usurpation of the title, *architect,* those who have won official designation have come to demand its restriction and this belief has been firmly imbedded in law. Nevertheless, the need for a definite title persists. The Commission has learned of only one official move in this direction. The Minnesota registration board for architects and engineers has adopted the titles, *Engineer-in-Training* and *Architect-in-Training* to designate candidates. The only other proposal that has come to the attention of the Commission is *Junior Architect*. Since the latter seems to imply permission for limited practice, it is not acceptable at the present time. Other possibilities are *Probationary Architect, Trainee-Architect,* or *Candidate-Architect*. Since none of the titles is entirely satisfactory, possibly because all are unfamiliar, the Commission inclines to *Architect-in-Training,* which, though somewhat cumbersome, does express the candidate's actual status with clarity and dignity. Moreover, its acceptance by the Minnesota board and its conformity with the analogous engineering

343

title give it additional appeal. The Commission favors its adoption (*Recommendation 31*).

4. FINANCING CANDIDATE TRAINING

The conduct of candidacy training is greatly complicated by the desire of candidates to be self-supporting. Because graduate candidates are rarely under 23 years of age, and are frequently older, custom and personal considerations usually require that they must assume responsibility for their own maintenance. Since it can be assumed that in most cases non-graduate candidates have chosen to approach candidacy via office training because of insufficient means to attend school, they too are compelled to earn their own way. In addition, both graduate and non-graduate candidates are of the age when family responsibilities begin to demand consideration. Thus, almost all candidates desire to combine further training with earning power.

The difficulty is that, in contrast to those who are content to exploit for immediate income those skills which are rapidly acquired, but of limited range, candidates wish to extend their skills by moving to a new assignment as soon as they master one phase of training. This prevents their employer from obtaining promptly any reasonable benefit or profit from his investment in their previous training. It is this perplexing paradox which has for so long plagued the development of an adequate candidate program.

Under the apprenticeship system the apprentice was required by legal contract to reimburse his master for his maintenance and instruction by a long period of increasingly competent assistance. The *pupilage* system required the pupil or his guardian to pay stated fees for the training received. When administered by capable conscientious masters, the *quid pro quo* relationship of these arrangements was eminently fair. During the 19th century, however, and especially in the United States, the custom arose by which an architect paid at least a token wage even to the lowliest office boy. There were many chores which such employees could perform and thus earn their minuscule wages. Some of these tasks, like the tracings already mentioned, were at once useful to the employer and instructive to the learner. In time the novice gained positive skills, received more responsible assignments, and increased his earnings. Such an arrangement was satisfactory for both novice and employer.

In recent decades new conditions have greatly altered this idyllic picture. Where once practice was on a leisurely basis, the problem of production costs was still unknown, and overhead charges had not yet become a major anxiety, today the pace and economics of office operation require continuous control. At the same time, the scope and technical complexity of architectural services have greatly expanded, wage scales have inflated, and office rentals have soared. The result has been that a practitioner in accepting responsibility for an inexperienced trainee no longer simply admits him to an opportunity to observe, but he also undertakes to contribute the cost of his own or his employees' efforts for such training, the uneconomic minimum wage decreed by law, and a considerable and continuing expense for the tools, supplies, and space which the trainee absorbs. No doubt if the full cost of such contributions were known, probably few practitioners would feel able to afford the luxury of satisfying generous impulses. What is truly remarkable is that so many youths still do enter upon architectural careers by the route of office training.

The desire for heightened competence for prospective architects, created by these new conditions and emphasized by increasing legal regulation of the profession, has caused the demand for an improved preparation of candidates conducted as an organized educational process. For office-trained candidates, this means the attainment of broader and more systematic training, but since they have already acquired productive skills, they can usually pursue their program with a minimum reduction in earnings.

In contrast, however, the rise of the professional schools and the appearance of graduate candidates have introduced a new factor into the equation. On the one hand, the schools have relieved practitioners of a large proportion of the instruction which once had to be provided in the offices. It is not difficult to envision the consternation that would now arise if the 9427 students currently enrolled in the schools had instead to be trained from raw innocence by architects in their offices. Nevertheless, for self-evident reasons, the initiation of graduates into the practical performance of professional services has had to remain the responsibility of practicing architects.

Thus, the problem of candidacy—for graduates as well as non-graduates—though of recent origin, is of paramount importance to the profession not only because it involves the recruitment of necessary assistants and the training of future practitioners, but also because of the demands it makes upon individual architects for positive investments of time, thought, and support. From the standpoint of the employer, the problem consists primarily of securing an equitable adjustment between the out-of-pocket costs of supplying the desired training on the one hand, and the employee's immediate contribution to office productivity on the other. For the candidate, it is the reconciliation between desire for training and the necessity of immediate self-support.

For the graduate candidate, the crucial point is his first entry into an office. Unless he has obtained an earlier introduction to office procedures through vacation employment, he needs at least a short period of orientation. Unfortunately, it is during this initial phase that some employers are apt to be most critical. Some seem to expect that the candidate should have acquired already the degree of facility and knowledge which they themselves have won only by long experience. Just after World War II this type of criticism was especially common because, with the scarcity of experienced personnel due to the cumulative effect of depression and military service, employers were often forced to assign candidates responsibilities for which they were unprepared with often dismaying results. In normal circumstances, however, most practitioners are more tolerant.

The question resolves itself into what is a reasonable level of employability to ask of the graduate when he embarks upon candidacy. The answer involves a number of factors. First, of course, is the nature and quality of the candidate's academic training. It is perfectly possible for the schools to conduct curricula which would produce highly efficient draftsmen. To accomplish this would mean the introduction of a long series of purely vocational courses and the deletion of most courses which provide the theoretical and cultural bases for future professional growth. Unless opportunity to acquire such fundamental education would be provided in some manner during candidacy, the next generation of American architects would no doubt subside into a narrow technicalism which would reduce, rather than expand, the opportunity to enhance that general leadership which the profession has always claimed. Immediate employability bought at such a price would be a disastrous bargain.

Fortunately, professional curricula in their present form can provide a considerable amount of immediately usable knowledge and skills, and such training is legitimately given as illustrative applications to reinforce the meaning and use of essential theory. It is to be expected, of course, that some schools emphasize such applications more than others. A few schools have indeed tended to neglect the teaching of standard practice and focused their applications on novel techniques which they presume will become future standards. It is no accident that it has been their graduates which have aroused the strongest complaints of employers. Nevertheless, these schools are exceptions. In recent years most schools have increased considerably the practical aspects of their programs, and in some instances it might be plausibly argued that this tendency has even gone too far. In general, therefore, while no school aims at immediate employability as an end in itself, there is no inherent reason why graduates should not acquire a modicum of useful knowledge and skills, or why they should not soon become reasonably useful employees.

A second factor in employability is the candidate himself. It is obvious that the award of a professional diploma does not guarantee more than that the recipient has satisfied the minimum requirements for the degree. While these minima may be perfectly adequate, there is still room for considerable variation in candidates as to quality of personality, accomplishment, industry, attitude, and insight. The best candidates not only are better equipped in training, but are also better prepared to profit by the opportunities afforded by their employers. Some graduates, however, seem to approach employment and candidacy without realization of their own responsibilities. Some seem to regard themselves as missionaries charged with the conversion of their employers to new dispensations. Others bask in release from academic pressures and fail to appreciate that candidacy demands its own special kind of effort. These, too, are exceptions. Most candidates are eager to apply themselves in the acquisition of practical experience.

Finally, a third factor is the employer himself. Given the fact and necessity of the candidate system, it can only succeed if the practitioners who must implement it do so with understanding, sympathy, and positive effort. Too often, little serious thought is given to the most effective means of integrating the candidate into the office team, of orienting him efficiently not only in the how, but also the why of office procedures, and of releasing his best energies and talents to take advantage of his opportunities.

346

It would be well for the over-critical employer to reconsider his own approach to in-service training before venturing condemnation of all candidates and schools. If candidates fail to contribute useful service, to some degree the office itself may well be responsible.

Nevertheless, it is doubtful that the pursuit of the educational goals of candidacy will ever allow the candidate to attain the productivity of a permanent employee. For this reason, the problem of financing candidacy remains. A number of suggestions have been broached to remedy the situation. Some architects who have won renown and therefore have attracted numerous applications from graduates have accepted only those who can maintain themselves without pay. A few have even charged a fee for permitting candidates to work in their offices. While this is an excellent means of self-defense in the face of excessive requests, it not only can be subject to abuse, but any general application would also bar many talented and worthy trainees who lack sufficient resources. By thus drastically limiting the number of candidates, it would reduce the roster of professional personnel far below social needs.

Other suggestions seek to provide candidates with at least minimum subsistence. One proposes that grants-in-aid be given. One firm has awarded an office scholarship by which one or two graduates of a particular school have been supported during their first year in the office. It should not be overlooked that the firm itself benefited by attracting outstanding graduates to its staff. Although a program of subsidized office scholarships would not only relieve financial problems but also provide an excellent device by which to encourage and select the most promising graduates, it is quite unlikely that sufficient funds could be secured to affect the large number of candidates which must be trained.

A more plausible proposal would revive the essence of the apprenticeship system in modern financial dress. Under it, during the early months of training, that part of a candidate's subsistence salary in excess of his actual productivity would be paid as a salary loan. Subsequently, as the candidate's productivity increased, he would repay the loan with interest by means of salary deductions. If the candidate makes reasonable progress and elects to accept a full wage commensurate with his productivity, the debt could probably be repaid by the middle of the second year.[5] If, however, he wished to be free to devote more time to new phases of his training program, the rate of amortization could easily be extended into the third year of candidacy. It may be noted that the objective of this proposal could also be attained through an agreement by which the candidate undertakes to remain in the office at a fixed wage for a certain length of time, determined by an estimate of the period required to balance early subsistence against later productivity.

There are advantages in such arrangements for both candidate and employer. It would emphasize for the candidate the economic facts of his office training and encourage him to strive for maximum progress. If the candidate enters into formal agreement with an employer on such a basis, it would also give him a positive right to expect that a definite program of training will be provided. For the employer, the

347

advantage lies in the fact that he is not called upon to finance the whole cost of the candidate's practical education.

Despite these aspects, there are serious hazards in the plan. Since the minimum length of such an agreement would appear to be not less than 18 months, and since it is extremely difficult to gauge a strange candidate's capacity for development, his ability to fit into the staff, or his sense of responsibility for carrying out his part of the bargain, many employers will prefer to reserve their own freedom of action even though they may thus risk their initial investment. The candidate, too, upon reflection, may also wish to be free to change positions, especially if the promised training does not materialize. Nevertheless, it is conceivable that those firms which would develop and conduct a very worthwhile candidate program would in time gain such a reputation in this activity that they would attract a large number of applicants from which they could select superior candidates willing and able to cooperate under such a system. If such a development does occur, it might well be that other firms would be forced to follow suit in order to recruit high quality talent for their own staffs. Furthermore, the general adoption of the candidate training program described in Section 3 will no doubt require candidates to devote attention to the educational aspects of their programs, and this may necessitate a more formal relationship between work and study.

The acceptance of such an arrangement on the part of graduates will demand early indoctrination by the schools, for it runs counter to expectations fostered by the practice of industrial and business concerns which, in competing for a limited supply of graduates, have come to offer liberal beginners' salaries despite lengthy in-service training. It is difficult for architectural graduates to appreciate the difference in scale and operation between vast corporate operations and the limited resources of individual enterprise. While the prospect of a prolonged shortage of personnel continues, they will no doubt continue to try to obtain at once both income and experience on the theory that the cost of in-service training is a legitimate charge on professional operations. Such a view can be modified to more worthy professional objectives only if candidates can be convinced that they will secure—through well-conceived and conscientiously administered educational programs—personal and professional benefits, which will counter-balance lower rates of initial compensation.

NOTES: CHAPTER EIGHT

[1] The Commission, after considerable discussion, adopted the terms, *candidate* and *candidacy,* as used in the NCARB *Circular of Advice, No. 15: The Mentor, Concerning His Duties.* The Commission considered and rejected a number of alternatives. *Apprentice* was felt to connote a relationship which no longer exists in its traditional meaning. *Interne,* while denoting a comparable status in medicine, connotes formal residency which is not practiced in architecture. Terms such as *neophyte* and *tyro* were likewise excluded.

[2] *Ibid.*

[3] The general elements of the Commission's plan were foreshadowed by a statement on *Apprentice Architects* issued in 1950 by the AIA Committee on Education.

4 The Commission benefited greatly by a study of a *Proposed Schedule of Experience Training for Architects* prepared by the Committee on Education and Registration of the Pennsylvania Society of Architects of The AIA. This *Schedule* recommended a similar list of categories and, in addition, proportional allotments of time to be devoted to each during a three-year candidacy. The topics and months were: *A. Design:* (a) research, analysis, and programming, 2 months; (b) preparation of preliminary designs of several diversified projects, 12 months; *B. Site Planning,* 2 months; *C. Application of Structural Design,* 3 months; *D. Application of Mechanical Design,* 3 months; *E. Specifications,* 4 months; *F. Administration,* 2 months; *G. Professional Relations,* 2 months; *H. Field Supervision,* 6 months. The Committee did not envision that these experiences need be obtained in the chronological order in which they are listed.

5 This proposal was developed by Professor Sherley Morgan. Its operation can be illustrated as follows: assume that the candidate requires a minimum of $200 per month for living expenses; assume that he can produce $100 worth of service per month during the first three months, $150 during the second three, $200 during the third three, $250 during the fourth three, $300 during the second year; at 5 per cent interest per year the total loan and interest at the end of 9 months would be $463.30; if all excess earnings were applied to amortization, the debt would be cleared during the sixteenth month of candidacy. After that the candidate could enjoy his full earnings, or apply part of his time to educational aspects of his program.

CHAPTER IX

Registration

For the Practice of Architecture

1. THE FUNCTION OF PROFESSIONAL REGISTRATION

An individual who adopts the title of *architect* and who offers to perform architectural services thereby claims to possess special knowledge, skills, and judgment in such matters, and the capacity to apply these abilities effectively to the affairs of his clients. The truth of these claims is of the utmost importance not only to the client, who entrusts to him the planning and direction of costly, complex projects, but also to all subsequent users of the resulting buildings who thus commit—often unwittingly—their personal safety and well-being to their care.

In theory the title, *architect,* should denote membership in a profession which restricts its roster to those of proven competence. It has been pointed out in *Chapter III,* however, that, while professions are recognized by society as essential institutions which perform highly useful services, they operate in actuality through voluntary associations, the professional societies. Although such societies may accept only those whose qualifications meet their standards, nevertheless they do not possess the legal power which is necessary to prevent unqualified persons from fraudulently usurping a title which implies professional status.

It might appear that an individual's possession of a sound professional reputation, signifying previous success in the performance of technical services, could constitute an adequate safeguard for both private and public interests. While indeed good reputation is an excellent criterion of merit, it is exceedingly difficult for laymen to investigate and judge the quality and relevance of the factors which compose it. For clients who are wholly unfamiliar with building operations, the use of a professional title is naturally taken as presumptive evidence of competence and reputation. If such a title can be made to signify possession of requisite competence, laymen can

351

then with confidence select their architects on the basis of other important factors, such as reputation, experience with special types of services, completeness of organization, and compatibility of outlook.

Unfortunately, it is universal experience that meritorious status, like all products of high quality, inevitably inspires counterfeits, one characteristic of which is that discovery always comes too late. Whether the act results from ignorant pretense or conscious fraud makes little difference after the damage is done. Fatalities from structural collapse, destruction by fire, and unheeded hazards to safety are but the most obvious and extreme consequences which can often be laid, at least in part, to technical incompetence. Wasted expenditures, inefficiency, and ugliness in buildings can likewise produce tragic consequences from public, as well as private, points of view. Furthermore, if services of subminimal quality and quantity are tolerated, they soon compete on the basis of cut-rate fees, which thus inevitably make it extremely difficult and even impossible to maintain in quality or amount those technical services which society must have to accomplish its purposes.

Thus, despite individual dislike of public regulation, social need has prompted social control of the use of professional titles and the offering of professional services. The result has been the formulation of the legal principle which abandons the laissez-faire custom of individual freedom to assume professional prerogatives and substitutes the policy of selective admission to a profession on the basis of proof of some reasonable minimum standard of professional competence. The attainment of these controls, now so universally accepted, was a process which developed over a long period of time. It required the efforts of strong professional groups and of numerous individual practitioners who envisioned the social benefits to be derived from enhanced competence and improved conditions of service. In working toward such ends, professional men have, of course, been open to the charge of self-interest, expressed not only by those whose activities were thus curbed, but also by laymen who have not understood the problem. It is true that sometimes and in some places unworthy motives have indeed obstructed the proper operation of such laws, but public regulation cannot legitimately be used for private gain, nor in the long run will society permit such a perversion. In reality, however, the interests of both society and a profession coincide, for the availability of quality services demands equitable conditions from which alone a strong profession can grow. Furthermore, since need for improved services is a requisite to social progress, the principle of controlled admission to professional status becomes an essential device in advancing both minimal and optimal standards of competence.

2. THE DEVELOPMENT OF REGULATIONS
FOR ARCHITECTURAL PRACTICE

The principle of controlling professional practice is age-old. The licensing of physicians has had the longest history. Under the Chou dynasty (first millennium, B.C.), admission to medical practice was by annual state examinations.[1] Roman laws of the first century, A.D., restricted practice to graduates of the medical schools founded by Vespasian.[2] In the tenth century, Islamic physicians, druggists, and barber-surgeons were required to hold a state certificate obtainable only by examination.[3] In medieval Europe, Roger II of Sicily decreed similar regulations in 1140, and in 1224 Frederick II added the stipulation that the medical examination must be that administered by the University of Salerno, which required eight years of study and one of apprenticeship.[4] An English law of 1422 demanded that practitioners of "physic" must hold a Bachelor of Science degree. In 1511, under Henry VIII, admission was by examinations conducted by a committee of physicians or the applicant's bishop. With the chartering of the Royal College of Physicians in 1518, state licensure became a function of professional societies, thus establishing a pattern of control which lasted for more than 300 years.[5]

The application of such regulations to architects came much later. While, during the Middle Ages, they usually came up through the craft guilds and so were subject to practical tests, no real professional organization evolved. Even with the founding of the royal academies in the seventeenth and eighteenth centuries, membership in them was determined, not by official examinations, but by royal appointment of established practitioners. About the midpoint of the eighteenth century, however, a new arrangement appeared in Spain when Ferdinand VI (1746–59) decreed that the title of *architect* and the privilege of professional practice would henceforth be restricted to members of the Royal Academy of San Fernando and those who held its diploma. To secure this diploma, a candidate was required to:

A. Submit a certificate from an academician that the candidate had worked under his direction and was conversant with building practices.
B. Submit a building design, with working details, specifications, and an explanation of its construction.
C. Demonstrate skill in architectural drawing.
D. Pass a 2–3 hour public examination in practical geometry and the theory and practice of architecture.

Holders of the diploma received the right to practice in Spain and all its dominions. Only academicians could be employed by the crown, but, while private persons were not required to use architects affiliated with the Academy, they forfeited, if they did not do so, any redress of grievances arising from the practitioner's incompetence or negligence.[6]

During the first half of the nineteenth century, Prussia, under the influence of its *Bau-Akademie* and the Royal Department of Public Works, developed an elaborate system to establish officially the competence of architects, surveyors (supervisors of building projects), and builders. Qualification as an architect required:[7]

A. Graduation from an approved *gymnasium* (secondary school).
B. Attainment of Surveyor status, which required:
    a. Completion of one year of practical experience in an architectural office.
    b. Completion of a two-year professional curriculum.

353

    c. Submission of satisfactory drawings in surveying, sketching, perspective, and ornament.

    d. Passing of written and oral examinations in scientific and technical subjects.

C. Completion of two additional years in architectural offices.

D. Completion of a one-year advanced professional curriculum.

E. Certification of experience in Land Surveying.

F. Passing of examinations in architectural subjects, conducted by the Department of Public Works.

Surveyors were authorized to direct construction projects under the supervision of an architect, and their independent statements as to quantities of materials were accepted as evidence in court. Only architects, however, were permitted to design and direct building projects on their own responsibility, and only they were eligible for governmental appointments. Indeed, the system served primarily as a means of screening applicants for governmental posts.

In France the report issued in 1840 by Charles-Pierre Goulier advanced the idea of an official examination to be administered by the *Ecole des beaux-arts* to establish the competence of prospective architects. The *Société Centrale des Architectes,* founded in 1843, began two years later to work toward this goal.[8] After interminable discussions, approval was finally secured and the first diploma examination was given by the *Ecole* in 1862. Admission to the examination demanded previous completion of 9 values in the *Ecole's* work in First Class Design, composition, and ornament, and one value in the history of architecture. The examination itself consisted of the design of a building and the preparation of its working drawings, details, specifications, and a schedule of quantities for one trade. Subsequently the candidate was questioned orally on materials, construction, history, building physics, building chemistry, building law, and accounting. After a slow start and the interruption of the Franco-Prussian war, the system gradually developed and, by 1883, 94 candidates had won their diplomas.[9] Later, a year of practical experience under a government architect was added to the requirements. It should be noted that, while a diploma certified the professional training of its recipient, the French system did not include any legal provision to prevent unqualified persons from usurping the title of *architect.*

In Great Britain control by professional society was extended to architecture. In 1855, as already noted, the Architectural Association undertook to conduct formal classes, but lacked a charter to confer degrees. Stimulated by Adolphe Lance's book, *Du diplôme d'architecte,* just published in Paris, the Association petitioned the Institute of British Architects to organize examinations and confer diplomas. In 1860 the Institute set up the system on a voluntary basis, two years later held its first tests, and, to aid candidates in preparing for them, conducted lectures in mathematics, physics, geology, materials, construction, the history and literature of architecture, and professional practice. Despite these efforts, the voluntary system drew an average of only three candidates per year. The receipt of a royal charter in 1866 transformed the Institute into the RIBA and gave it semi-public and national status. Finally, these events led in 1882 to the adoption of compulsory examinations for admission

354

to Associate membership in the Institute. However, while membership indicated professional attainment, there were no means to control use of the title of *architect*.[10]

The British medical profession had faced the same problem 30 years earlier and had secured a logical remedy by the Medical Act of 1858 which created a state system of registration of practitioners—physicians, surgeons, and apothecaries—who had won licenses from their several professional organizations.[11] In 1884 a similar solution was suggested by the Society of Architects, but it was bitterly opposed by an influential group of leading architects who decried the interjection of governmental regulation. The resulting controversy split the RIBA during the next two decades.[12]

Professional licensure in the American colonies naturally followed English precedents. Virginia in 1639, Massachusetts in 1649, and New York in 1684 made tentative attempts to regulate the practice of medicine. In 1772 a New Jersey law assigned medical licensing to two Supreme Court judges, with such assistants as they desired. The rise of professional organizations offered more appropriate agencies. In 1781 the medical societies of Massachusetts and New Hampshire received state charters which included the right to examine candidates and confer "letters testimonial." It should be noted that the country's new Constitution continued to leave such regulation to the states. In some, societies performed this function, but in others the new medical schools were empowered to license immediately their own graduates.[13] In some districts licenses had to be registered with the county clerk. From 1830 on, however, the failure of the societies to maintain any real educational standards, together with the rising pretensions of medical cults, brought the repeal of all but four state acts and once more threw the field wide open to all comers.[14]

The British Medical Act of 1858 suggested a solution for this dilemma. In 1859 North Carolina created a State Board of Medical Examiners to both license and register physicians.[15] In 1861 Alabama applied the same principle to the regulation of pharmacists.[16] Other states did likewise, but again cult opposition soon led to repeal. Nevertheless by the close of the Civil War it was increasingly apparent that the protection of public health from quackery demanded regulation. Beginning in 1873 with the establishment of the Texas board, by about 1895 all states had enacted controls for medical practice.[17] The Illinois State Board of Health, created in 1877, clearly demonstrated during the next two decades the benefits of such regulation by securing particularly notable improvements in the standards of qualifications for medical practitioners and schools.[18] It should also be noted that the enforcement of these laws has resulted with regard to the medical field alone in more than 500 decisions by the Supreme Court which repeatedly upheld their constitutionality.[19]

These events soon stirred the interest of American architects. Between 1880 and 1890 national expansion and the resulting demand for buildings had multiplied the number of architects 2.4 times, from 3375 to 8070 (*Table 54*). Such an increase meant the influx of many persons with little, if any, preparation to support their claims to professional status. Competent practitioners viewed this degradation of their profession with mounting alarm. Nowhere was this danger felt as keenly as in the greater Midwest area. During the same decade, for example, the number of Illinois architects

355

more than tripled, and, concurrently, the rapid introduction of new structural techniques emphasized all the more the necessity of sound training. The result was the formation of new professional societies dedicated to the improvement of conditions of service. In 1882 the Architects Association of Minnesota, the first of its type, pointed the way toward professional cooperation. In November, 1884, the establishment of the Western Association of Architects immediately stimulated other state groups as integral units of its organization. Iowa, Illinois, and Missouri associations were formed early in 1885.

At its initial meeting WAA appointed a Committee on Statutory Revisions, with Dankmar Adler of Chicago as chairman. Although the work of this committee was first envisioned as concerned with the codification and refinement of laws pertaining to construction, the idea of requiring qualifications as a legal prerequisite to practice soon emerged.[20] The Minnesota association attacked the problem immediately. In January, 1885, the group prepared a licensing and registration bill, and in February obtained its introduction before the legislature. Its tabling there foretold the long and arduous struggle which would be required to secure such novel legislation.[21] Apparently the fundamental importance of such a step preoccupied Adler more and more, for, when WAA gathered at St. Louis for its first convention in November, the committee's report, primarily the product of Adler's own thought and authorship, proposed a fully developed act which, with insignificant changes, became the model for all subsequent legislation. The convention accepted the report enthusiastically and urged all associations to secure equivalent laws in their respective states.[22] With Adler as the new WAA president to promote the movement, within a few months, Illinois, Missouri, and Iowa were planning their campaigns, and new groups in Ohio, Texas, and Kansas were formed, in part for this purpose.[23]

Eleven more years of steady effort were required to attain the passage of the first act, that of Illinois. Adler continued to press the attack despite discouragements and the setbacks of the mid-90's depression. The successful conclusion on June 3, 1897 was in part due also to the efforts of Nathan Clifford Ricker, Head of the Department of Architecture and Dean of the College of Engineering of the University of Illinois, who enjoyed considerable prestige and influence with the state legislature. Although Adler and Ricker were aware of European regulations, Adler's final instrument was chiefly inspired by the state's existing regulatory systems in medicine and law.

As a pioneering achievement, the Illinois Act and its early administration by the Board of Examiners deserve study. Adler served from 1897 to late 1898 as its first president. Ricker, a charter member, succeeded Adler as president and held this office for 18 years. By February, 1898, after only 6 months of operation, the Board had received more than 800 applications, had approved 714 under "grandfather" provisions, and, in the same month, had given its first 3-day examination to 19 applicants.[24] It is interesting to note that in 1902 the Board adopted Rule 9 which provided that any graduate of an approved 4-year curriculum in architecture or architectural engineering could be accepted, at the Board's discretion, as having obtained a competent knowledge of construction, sanitation, and the strength of materials, providing that the applicant could show acquisition of ability to apply such data to design, construction, and supervision.[25] A ruling in 1903 recognized the diplomas of MIT and the universities of Illinois, Cornell, Columbia, Pennsylvania, and Harvard as satisfying this requirement. In December, 1906, after its first nine years of operation, the Board reported that 704 licenses were in force, 501 granted to "grandfather" applicants and 203 won by examination.[26]

The pattern thus established in Illinois gradually spread to other states, but not until 1951 did it become universal. The record of this expansion is shown by the following table:[27]

AIA Regions	1897–1909	1910–1919	1920–1929	1930–1939	1940–1951
NEW ENGLAND:				'33 Conn.	'41 Mass.
				'36 R. I.	'45 Me.
					'48 N. H.
					'51 Vt.
NEW YORK:		'15 N. Y.			
MID-ATLANTIC:	'02 N. J.	'19 Pa.	'20 Va.		
			'21 W. Va.	'33 Del.	
			'24 D. C.	'35 Md.	
GREAT LAKES:		'15 Mich.	'29 Ind.	'30 Ky.	
				'31 Ohio	
N. CENTRAL:	'97 Ill.	'17 N. D.	'21 Minn.		
		'17 Wis.	'25 S. D.		
CENTRAL:			'25 Okla.	'37 Neb.	'41 Mo.
			'27 Ia.		'49 Kan.
S. ATLANTIC:		'13 N. C.			
		'15 Fla.			
		'17 S. C.			
		'19 Ga.			
GULF:	'01 Ark.	'10 La.	'21 Tenn.	'31 Ala.	
			'28 Miss.		
TEXAS:				'37 Tex.	
W. MOUNTAIN:	'09 Colo.	'11 Utah	'21 Ariz.	'32 N. Mex.	'51 Wyo.
NORTHWEST:		'17 Idaho			
		'17 Mont.			
		'19 Ore.			
		'19 Wash.			
SIERRA NEV.:	'01 Calif.				'49 Nev.
U. S. TERRIT.:			'23 Hawaii	'38 Alaska	? P. Rico
TOTAL:	5	15	12	11	9

Conditions of the American scene thus led to the solution of professional regulation by means of law, but, while this method used the authority of the state to restrict the practice of architecture to properly qualified persons and to deny the use of the title of *architect* to others not so qualified, the same conditions required that this authority had to be distributed among the several states. Therefore, the American solution could not be unified into one central system of regulation, and an architect who practices beyond the boundaries of his state of residence has had to satisfy the regulations of each state in which he obtains a commission.

The logical conclusion to regulatory problems on a national scale was achieved in Great Britain and France only in recent years. In Great Britain the Architects (Registration) Bill became the controlling law in 1932, under which the state accepted responsibility for the examination of applicants, albeit with those standards and methods which had been carefully developed by the RIBA. The bill also denied to unqualified persons the use of the professional title. The French law, enacted in 1940, accomplished the same objectives, but, except for a few minor and temporary exceptions, it accepts for official registration only those who hold diplomas from either of two schools, the *Ecole nationale superieure des beaux-arts* and its 13 associated regional schools, or the *Ecole spéciale d'architecture* in Paris. In addition it should be noted that the diplomas of these schools are regarded as sufficient proof of qualification for registration and that no further examination is required of the graduate.

The principle of registration is now almost universally recognized as necessary and just. Nevertheless, since man-made law and enforcement are inevitably subject to shortcomings, it is not surprising that complaints of inequities and ineffectiveness have arisen. Such questionings were in part a factor leading to the inception of this Commission. To some degree, the final achievement of nation-wide coverage has in itself made its impact felt everywhere. Post-war restlessness, a flood of applications from returning veterans, and the stimulus of record levels of construction all tended to reveal whatever latent weaknesses there might be in operational procedures. Nevertheless explanations do not cure; it is obvious that registration practices must always be subject to impartial review, clear-minded judgment, and enlightened improvement. Such study and the conduct of the registration process require the cooperation of the wisest members of the profession.

3. THE LEGAL BASIS FOR THE REGULATION OF ARCHITECTURAL PRACTICE

The regulation of architectural practice in the United States is an application of the principle of the police power, under which a state has the right to legislate for the general welfare, health, safety, morals, and good order of the community.[28] The right of society to control the actions of individuals and groups affecting such interests is supported by centuries of precedent. Although the Federal Constitution delegated to the nation responsibility for some areas of welfare and order, the exercise of police power with respect to the actions of individuals was reserved almost wholly to the several states. No doubt this provision reflected a legitimate fear that a remote and over-centralized government might seek to dominate and dictate the daily activities of citizens. At first, the independent, individualistic temper of public opinion permitted only sparing use of police power, primarily in the realm of public safety; but, as new conditions and activities made further controls imperative, its scope was gradually extended to include matters of general welfare as well. The extent of this evolution has been and will be limited only by public desire for such measures and by judicial demands that objectives must be definite and desirable social goals and that the specific means of achieving these ends must be direct and reasonable. While reasonableness is not subject to precise definition, its empirical meaning in this connection implies that middle point at which public reluctance to enforce restraints is overcome by social need for positive action.

The validity of the specific application of a state's police power for the regulation of architectural practice springs from a general realization that the quality of a community's buildings is of major concern not only to their owners, but to the public as well. This is true because almost all buildings, even those intended for the most private use, are continually frequented by others than their owners—by the public generally, and by employees, guests, tradesmen, repairmen, etc.,—and thus acquire, in greater or lesser extent, public character. Even when direct public use is at a minimum, a building, because it is seldom completely isolated, can create dangerous hazards for its neighbors. In many less obvious, but very positive ways, buildings also affect the general welfare, comfort, and convenience of communities, and their character and the proficiency of those who design them have, therefore, become subjects of social concern and control. Thus, while an individual must suffer the consequences of his own poor judgment in the conduct of his personal affairs, society has every right to protect itself when the results of private actions create social dangers.

Society has long sought to minimize building hazards by enacting laws and codes prescribing the use of good construction practices and by exacting penalties from those who neglect proper precautions. Controls of this kind have for centuries attempted to prevent structural failures and conflagrations, and in recent times have done much to conserve life and property by establishing fire zones, by regulating occupancies, and by specifying fire-resistant construction, safe exits, and other safeguards. Some have sought to protect health by requiring adequate lighting, ventilation, and sanitation. Others have controlled land use and coverage and even the aesthetic character of buildings. It might be argued that the enforcement of adequate codes would give ample public protection and eliminate any need to regulate architectural personnel. The fallacy of this point of view lies in the fact that it is the nature of a code that it cannot be formulated to foresee all the eventualities arising from the changing needs, resources, and capabilities of a dynamic society. Even when progressive codes emphasize performance standards, the application of these precepts to each unique project demands the exercise of extensive knowledge, skill, and judgment in order to fulfill their spirit as well as their letter. This is to say that design is always an art and can never become an automatic process. Moreover, since all codes are the product of human effort and must be interpreted, applied, and enforced by all too human officials, the protection of the public solely by such means would demand that they bring superhuman omniscience, wisdom, and vigilance to the task of preventing infractions. Even if these qualities could be secured, the result would be a negative process whose chief aim and control would be the censoring of error. Although codes will continue to provide useful safeguards, their inherent limitations do not permit exclusive reliance on them for the purpose at hand.

It is also frequently suggested that the protection of client and public is adequately assured by their opportunity to seek through civil or criminal court actions redress for injuries arising from incompetence or negligence. This view presumes that incompetent practitioners would soon be bankrupted or jailed and that in any event the resulting publicity would end their predatory careers. It should be noted that such recourses have always been and will always remain available. Nevertheless, since building projects are inevitably complex operations and since many factors and agencies cooperate to achieve the final result, responsibility and negligence are always difficult to determine precisely. In any case this approach is likewise negative, the equivalent of locking the barn after the horse has vanished. It is well to remember that no court action, however just the verdict, can possibly force a defendant to perform professional services which are beyond his real capacity.

It is evident, therefore, that the quality of buildings can never rise above the quality of the architects who design them. It follows that, if a community desires high quality in its buildings, it must concern itself with measures to secure qualified architects. While the details of administration and enforcement of such measures can be solved in different ways, the essential functions to be provided are: 1. the granting of officially recognized professional status to those who satisfy and maintain an established standard of competence; and 2. the denial of such status to those who do not or cannot qualify. It must be noted that, while the state thus applies its authority and power for the achievement of a desirable social goal, the requirement of reasonableness which controls the exercise of police power means that it cannot be used to impose desirable, but extraordinary, standards of optimal competence. Such objectives are the responsibility of professional groups which, due to their voluntary and private character, are free to adopt any standard on which their members can agree. On the other hand, while public policies in such matters must proceed more slowly and conservatively, such policies are the result of consensus of opinion and in time, as need and support develops, public standards also can be raised. Thus, although public and professional objectives must operate at different levels, they are intimately interrelated and can reinforce each other in the long-term search for a continuing improvement of competence.

While the primary objective of professional controls is the insurance of public protection, they also work to safeguard individuals who use professional services. When practice is restricted to those judged to possess such competency as will secure the safety and welfare of the community, individual clients may infer that practitioners so recognized likewise possess reasonable professional capacity. It is on this basis that the extension of legal qualifications for professional status to include general aspects of competency has been accepted as necessary and legitimate. To a considerable degree, therefore, such controls over professional qualifications tend to strengthen restraints on fraud and deceit.

The social obligation of a professional group to seek actively the enhancement of its competence and the fact that laymen are rarely prepared to appreciate the need of or the problems involved in professional regulation inevitably place the responsibility for leadership in such matters upon professional men themselves who are thus laid open to the charge that they act primarily in their own self-interest. It is true that, under the guise of serving social goals, some individuals and some groups have at times supported registration as a device to restrict the number of practitioners, reduce competition, and increase personal profits. The administration of a registration law for such ends is illegal, an abuse of public trust, and a perversion of social needs. Any official who becomes a party to such misuse of registration betrays the spirit and letter of his appointment. The *1950 Survey of Board Members* revealed that 102 of 104 responders believed that architectural registration had not unduly restricted the number entering practice in their states.[29] It is patent that all professions must scrupulously avoid any dalliance with such motives.

Nevertheless, the attainment of equitable conditions which foster the continuing availability of good services is of interest not only to the profession, but to the public as well. Past experience clearly reveals—as witnessed by the opinions of the older Fellows of The AIA—that incompetent men have always been willing to sell their inferior wares at fees far below the actual cost of competent services. Under such circumstances, it was not surprising that the utilization of competent services was greatly reduced. The anomaly was that, while incompetent services cost less, the resulting buildings were of such low quality that the eventual waste far exceeded the promised savings. In recent decades the protection afforded by registration acts, imperfect as it has been, has done much to improve the conditions under which the profession performs its services, but, far from benefiting practitioners alone, the community too has profited immeasurably. Thus, once again, the health of the profession is seen to be linked closely and legitimately with public good.

Since the proper performance of professional services demands for the protection of clients and society that architects fulfill the highest standards of trustworthiness and integrity, it is in the interest of society that the registration process should operate positively to foster these qualities. While virtue cannot be ensured by legislation, it seems both valid and necessary that professional privileges should not be granted to those whose past deeds clearly indicate lack of will to strive for and maintain such standards. The equitable administration of such an extension of police power is always difficult, but it is nonetheless important. It is on this basis that registration authorities have a specific right and duty to restrict the practice of architecture to persons of "good moral character."

361

4. THE ELEMENTS AND METHODS
OF ARCHITECTURAL REGISTRATION

Architectural practice in the United States is now regulated by 52 individual acts—48 state laws and those of the District of Columbia, Hawaii, Puerto Rico, and Alaska. Since these regulations were enacted over a period of 54 years, prepared under the influence of local conditions, frequently modified by amendments, and are administered by local boards, it is to be expected that their provisions, procedures, and effectiveness should differ greatly. A detailed analysis of the content and administrative methods of these acts would be very useful in many ways. In 1950 the Commission attempted to do this for some aspects of the problem by means of questionnaires directed to the secretaries and all members of the 47 boards then operating in the continental United States. Unfortunately 14 of the 47 secretaries and 137 of the 242 board members did not respond.[30] No replies at all were forthcoming from four states. While the data obtained were thus regrettably incomplete, they have nevertheless been incorporated into the following discussion in order to give some indication of prevailing conditions.

Although existing acts for the regulation of architectural practice exhibit considerable variety in organization and clarity of statement, most of them include the following provisions.

A. The Constitutional Basis of the Act

Protection of public safety, health, and property is the legal justification on which such acts are based. Of 33 responding secretaries, 23 reported that their acts expressly limited the application of regulation to such purposes. As the question was phrased, it may be assumed that the remaining ten acts either invoked additional grounds or simply implied such a basis as being generally understood. In seven acts the basis of *general welfare* was cited and this may be taken as recognizing public interest in such matters as aesthetic quality and other amenities. It is desirable to include both bases.

B. The Activities to Be Controlled

Most acts restrict the legal *practice* of architecture to certain qualified persons. Practice is usually defined as the responsible *performance* of or the *offering to perform* such professional services as are required in the development, design, direction, and supervision of buildings, their enlargement, or alteration, which services involve the application of the art and science of construction based on mathematical, scientific, and aesthetic principles. In some acts, professional services are described in greater detail. Twenty-seven of the acts reported included control of *practice*.

A corollary to the restriction of practice is the reservation of the title of *architect* to those persons who are licensed to practice. Protection of the public by this means was reported by 19 states. In 5 states the practice of architecture by unlicensed persons is permitted if they do not use the title of *architect*. *Designer* is the usual substitute title in such states.

It should be noted that not all acts control both practice and title. Three acts restricted the use of the title, but not practice. Eleven governed practice, but did not restrain the use of the title. Two secretaries reported that their acts did neither.

The enactment of architectural registration is frequently opposed by special groups who have demanded exemptions as the price of adoption. Agricultural interests have been especially vocal in this regard and 13 acts exempt all farm buildings. Merchant builders, building material dealers, and realtors likewise have often required freedom to construct small houses without architectural services. Ten acts thus exempt all single-family dwellings, and 8 exempt two-family houses. In such cases, small projects are often defined by limits of size (12 acts) or cost (18 acts). Fluctuations in the cost of construction have made the latter basis of limitation unacceptable. Some acts also exempt buildings erected for the designer's own occupancy. Buildings built by the Federal Government do not come within the control of state acts.

Perhaps the greatest conflict has arisen over claims of exemption for structures designed by engineers. These claims have usually been asserted on the grounds that engineering projects often involve buildings incidental to industrial, transport, power, and other enterprises for which engineers can supply all necessary services. Whatever the justice of such claims may be, many acts have been forced to exclude such incidental structures from their jurisdiction or to permit design by either profession.

C. The Registration of Qualified Persons Permitted to Practice Architecture

All acts provide for the establishment of certain qualifications to be required for practice and the determination of whether a specific applicant satisfies these criteria. Discussion of these problems will be reserved for a later section of this chapter.

Once this satisfaction is determined, the acts then provide that the applicant shall be licensed to practice, enrolled on the public register of qualified practitioners, and issued an official certificate which during the period of its validity publicly identifies the registrant and witnesses his right to practice.[31] Identification of the registrant is also strengthened by the requirement that all drawings or sets of drawings be marked with a seal bearing his name and the title *registered architect*. The use of such a seal certifies that the practitioner possesses a valid certificate of registration and that the plans so sealed have been prepared by himself or under his personal direction and supervision. In some jurisdictions it also certifies that the plans so sealed comply with all applicable building laws. Many acts direct that an official roster of registrants shall be published at regular intervals. Provisions for the renewal of certificates are also included. Fees for examination, registration, and renewals are usually stipulated. In most cases these are paid to a designated officer of the registration board, but some acts require that all funds be handled by regular state offices.

It should be noted that the registration process applies only to individuals and thus follows the long-established principle that professional service must be based on personal responsibility which cannot be delegated or subdivided. All acts, however, recognize the formation of partnerships or associations for the conduct of professional practice, either between two or more architects or between architects and professional engineers. Moreover, such firms are usually permitted to use the combined title, *architect (s) and engineer (s)*, provided that each member is a registered architect or a registered engineer and are so designated specifically in all public listings of the firm. Some acts permit under certain conditions the continuation of a firm name incorporating the names of retired or deceased principals. The import of these provisions is that licenses to practice architecture cannot be granted to corporations, and most acts explicitly state this restriction. In recent years much discussion has been devoted to this regulation. Many advantages, particularly in tax and estate matters, have been cited by the proponents of incorporation, but thus far it has gained little favor with most practitioners. Since this provision affects associations in all professions, and since the supposed advantages of incorporation stem from inequities applying to associations as such, the best solution would seem to be the rallying of all professional groups for the removal of these inequities, rather than modifying the traditional pattern of professional responsibility.

Because the registration process concerns only those licensed for responsible practice, most acts clearly state the right of registrants to employ assistants who, though they may perform many of the services involved in practice do so only under the personal direction and supervision of their employer. The work of such assistants does not comprise practice, and they need not be registered.

D. The Revocation of Registration

Registration acts usually include detailed provisions for the receipt of charges, the collection and hearing of evidence, and the suspension or revocation of certificates held by those judged guilty of fraud or deceit in obtaining registration, of gross negligence, incompetency, or misconduct in the course of practice, of violation of any provision of the act, or of aiding or abetting any violation or evasion of the act by others, such as affixing his seal, or permitting it to be affixed, to any documents not prepared by the registrant or under his personal direction or supervision. Means of appeal and reinstatement are often specified.

E. The Restraint of Unregistered Persons from Violating the Act

Most acts provide means of restraining unregistered persons from violating or evading their provisions. It is clear that no act can accomplish its purpose if it can be flouted with impunity. The most effective way to accomplish enforcement is to place responsibility upon the board itself and give it means to carry it out. Infractions are usually designated as misdemeanors and specific penalties named. Many acts state methods of procedure, such as the instituting of criminal proceedings or by injunction which the board may invoke to halt such violations. Some assign prosecution to certain officials, often the state's attorney-general. Where prosecution must depend on local authorities—county or municipal—it is sometimes difficult to obtain prompt action or to secure convictions. The difficulties of collecting evidence and of obtaining convictions in such cases are well known, but in flagrant violations every effort must be made to prevent the act from becoming a dead letter. Such enforcement requires the active cooperation of the whole profession. Architects cannot limit such assistance to mere complaints; they must also stand ready to help in gathering evidence and offering testimony.

In recent decades, with the gradual expansion of governmental agencies concerned with building—local building inspectors, state bureaus for factories, schools, hospitals, housing, and hotels—many registration acts have been greatly strengthened by expressly stating that all departments and subdivisions of the state, together with their staffs, must conform to and support the provisions of the acts. At the state agency level, considerable progress has been attained in preventing approval of plans prepared by unregistered persons. Much work remains to be done, however, to obtain enforcement at the local level. Only 12 board secretaries reported that plans submitted for city building permits were required to bear the seal of a registered architect, but 17 were of the opinion that permits were being issued on unauthorized plans regardless of stated policies.[32] Only a few secretaries reported that architects are required to certify that their plans conform to appropriate building codes, although about a third of them stated that such is demanded by registration acts, the codes themselves, or because of judicial orders. In some states, AIA chapters have undertaken, with excellent results, active educational campaigns to remind building officials of the provisions of the law and their responsibilities in its enforcement. Concerted effort in such an approach seems the most promising means of making registration acts more effective. It is obvious that if registration boards and the profession expect to obtain cooperation of such officials, these officials must have in their hands an up-to-date official list of registrants. It is an important reason why every board is under obligation to publish such data promptly and accurately.

F. The Establishment of an Administrative Agency and Its Procedures

All acts must assign the execution of its provisions to some administrative agency. The usual solution has been to create a special registration board for architects. Twenty-five of the secretaries responding indicated such an arrangement. All members of such boards, being architects, are directly cognizant of professional problems and therefore may be presumed to be sympathetic to fulfilling the purposes of the act, both in spirit and letter.

Seven states reported the use of joint boards which register not only architects, but also engineers and land surveyors. All but one of these states are located in the central part of the country.[33] The reason for such association seems to be a legislative desire to reduce the number of separate boards. While such joint boards promote an understanding of common problems among the associating professions, the participation of one profession in the regulation of another seems to be a questionable procedure. Moreover, since the size of joint boards tends to expand in order to ensure appropriate representation, they may lose in flexibility what is theoretically gained in the grouping of similar functions.[34] Another motive for such an arrangement could be that the combined fees might support paid clerical or enforcement assistance, but the *1950 Survey* did not reveal actual conditions with regard to this point.

A few states have created state bureaus to administer all professional and occupational licensing. In most of these states architectural registration acts usually establish boards of architects which decide matters of policy, but in some cases the boards are reduced to acting merely as advisors or examiners for the bureaus. While the latter arrangement might be thought to protect the regulatory process from domination by special interests, it can also mean that policy decisions intimately affecting vital professional matters can be made by bureau officials who as political appointees are rarely equipped to perform this function and may themselves be subject to special pressures. The advantages of centralized administration and enforcement are often cited as justifying such bureaus, but these should be secured without sacrificing board initiative and control. Loss of control by some boards has on occasion led to very unfortunate situations.

Of the 33 responding board secretaries, 22 reported boards with 5 members, 5 with 3, 1 with 6, 3 with 7, and 1 with 9. In most states members are appointed by the governor. In Illinois, members are appointed by the Director of the State Department of Registration and Education; in New York, by the Regents of the University of the State of New York, which is equivalent to a state department of education; and in Wisconsin, by the state's Industrial Commission. In 21 states gubernatorial appointments are made without mandatory consultation with the profession; in 8 states, recommendations are submitted by the registration board; and in 13 states, recommendations are offered by professional organizations. As to qualifications for board membership, 27 states require experience in professional practice ranging from 2 to 15 years, with 23 states demanding 10 years. Some acts declare that members must hold registration in the state. In 10 states, minimum age is stipulated ranging from 21 to 36. Twenty-one states stipulate that members be residents and 18 require periods of residence of from 1 to 10 years. In 2 states, Illinois and South Carolina, teachers of architecture serve on registration boards by express provision of law.[35] Five other states reported that teachers have served as board members. Only 2 secretaries reported opposition to teacher-members by their boards and only 3 by the profession within the state.

Only 2 states, Illinois and Washington, reported that board memberships are not limited to fixed terms. In 29 states the terms of office range from 3 to 7 years, with 13 states using 5 years, 5 using 4 years, and 4 each using 6 and 3 years. Reappointments are limited only in two states, one with a maximum of 2 terms, and the other with a maximum age of 70 years. Many acts establish an official procedure for the accrediting of appointees by issuance of a certificate of appointment and by requiring the filing of the appointee's written oath or affirmation for the faithful discharge of his duties. Many likewise state the conditions and means by which a member may be removed from the board for cause.

The *1950 Survey of Board Members* investigated their actual length of service and their opinion as to an optimum length of service. The results were:

Years of Service	Actual Service		Optimum Service	
	NO.	%	NO.	%
UNDER 2	24	23	1	1
2–5	35	34	19	23
5–10	19	19	42	52
10–15	13	13	8	10
OVER 15	11	11	11	14
TOTAL	102	100	81	100
NO RESPONSE	+3		+24	

Criticism has been frequent—especially among younger members of the profession —that boards tend to be dominated by architects of advanced years, conservative tastes, and pedestrian practicality. It is, perhaps, inevitable that, as long as proven responsibility and solid reputation are criteria for board appointments, there will be few youthful members. While the Commission did not investigate the ages, training, or progressiveness of board members, it has been impressed with the seriousness of purpose, readiness to question, and eagerness to act on the highest principles, which have been exhibited by all those known to it. If, on the one hand, at least one board erred in requiring candidates to solve a design examination in a style now widely repudiated, on the other hand, almost all boards recognize that the examination of taste is beyond their purview. If, however, a candidate shows evidence of blind, uncritical dogmatism, it seems entirely legitimate for a board to probe his ability to reason and his power of judgment.

Nineteen acts provide that members of the board shall receive a per diem fee for their services; 5 stipulate a set fee for each meeting; 2 place remuneration on an annual basis; and in 13 states members serve without any recompense.

The organization of the boards is usually relatively simple. Thirty elect their own chairmen. In 2 states the chairman is designated by gubernatorial appointment. The business of the boards involves a considerable volume of correspondence, record-keeping, and detail, but, since board funds are usually limited, secretaries normally serve on a part-time basis. Only two boards—Missouri and Montana—reported full-time secretaries. In 24 states all application, renewal, and other fees are paid to the secretaries; 7 name other state officials. Fees for original applications and examination range from $5 to $52.50. Some such fees are contingent upon grant of registration. Renewal fees vary from $1 to $21, and in 4 states renewals are on a 2- or 3-year basis. Eighteen boards control the disposition of fees collected; in 16 states all fees become part of the states' general funds; and in 6 states all or part of surplus funds go to the state. The boards' annual reports are presented to state officials, in most cases to members of the boards, and in 15 states to all architects registered in the state.

A registration act must convey to the board the specific powers necessary to administer its provision. These powers include: adoption and amendment of reasonable and necessary bylaws and rules of procedure; the evaluation of applicants' qualifications; the hearing of charges and testimony, the subpoenaing of witnesses, the requiring of the production of records, and the adjudicating of all cases involving the revocation of licenses. Acts vary to a considerable degree, however, as to the details of qualifications to be required for registration and as to the conduct and grading of examinations. In 12 states, boards were reported to have authority to modify qualifications for admission to examinations, while in 20 states such a change would require legislative action. On the other hand, almost all boards are able to determine for themselves the character of their examinations and the basis of grading them. Such discretionary power is highly desirable in order to encourage systematic improvement in the examining process. Flexibility is even more necessary in the details governing fees, applications, examinations, official reports, publication of lists of registrants, etc., and it is preferable to regulate these matters by bylaws and rules which can be easily and promptly adjusted to meet new conditions.

G. The Enactment and Legal Protection of the Act

Most acts include a formal clause of enactment. Similarly, it is necessary to provide for the repeal of laws or parts of laws which may be in conflict with the act. Finally, most acts protect themselves against attack for unconstitutionality by declaring that the invalidation of any part or parts of the act shall not serve to invalidate those parts which remain.

In the development of architectural registration over the past half-century, it was inevitable that experience would gradually reveal provisions which needed improvement. Unfortunately, because of inexperience or ineptness in their preparation, some acts proved ineffective. It is not surprising, therefore, that 23 of 33 responding board secretaries stated that their acts had from time to time been modified by amendments. Indeed, in some cases, whole acts have had to be replaced. It is common knowledge that requests for such legislative changes invite an upsurge of opposition by the same interests which resisted the original enactment. Secretaries reported such opposition on the part of small builders and contractors, material dealers, stock plan groups, and some business organizations. 14 secretaries reported unsuccessful attempts to secure amendments. In almost all cases where amendments were secured, secretaries stated that they improved the operation of registration.

Some acts have proved to be ineffective because they claim too much jurisdiction;

others have been found equally defective because they claim too little. Those which protect the title of *architect*, but fail to control practice rule out only false pretensions; where the converse is true, conditions of professional service soon deteriorate. Some laws have come to naught because of failure to convey any effective power for enforcement. It is easy to be supercritical of existing laws and it is very difficult to secure the passage of a thoroughly satisfactory and trouble-free act. Sometimes acts admittedly inadequate have been accepted as temporary expedients and as stepping stones leading to later improvements. Occasionally sources of future friction can be avoided by conferring with interested groups and with legislative committees before initiating action. Whatever the legal solution, two points are crystal clear: first, enforcement must be pressed vigorously and continuously, not only by the registration board, but also through the aid of all registered architects; and, second, when it becomes apparent that the act can and will be enforced, potential violators soon realize that the penalty of illegal practice far outweighs possible gains.

The *1950 Survey* asked board members whether architects in their state were satisfied with the provisions and operation of their registration laws. As to content, 63 of 96 responding members were of the opinion that a majority were satisfied; 16 thought about half were satisfied; and 17 thought few were satisfied. As to operation, 60 thought a majority were satisfied; 24 thought half; and 12 thought few. The *Survey* asked what improvements seemed desirable and the suggestions advanced called in general for a minimum of 3 years of office experience, elimination of veterans' exemptions, rewording for maximum clarity and consistency, especially in relation to registered engineers, and increased power for boards to facilitate enforcement. The *Survey* also asked members about weaknesses in the acts of neighboring states with much the same results.

The Commission queried board members as to whether the preparation of a "model law" would be of service when revisions of existing laws were undertaken. Of 100 members responding, 78 approved the suggestion, 12 gave qualified acquiescence, and 11 did not feel it to be worth while, primarily because local problems would make practical application very difficult. For this reason the Commission modified its approach and prepared a *Statement of Elements for an Architectural Registration Act* (*Appendix C*).

5. NATIONAL ASPECTS OF REGISTRATION

Since positive public and professional benefits have been secured through the operation of a multiplicity of state regulations, despite their varied requirements and provisions, it seems obvious that uniform controls on a nation-wide basis would produce even greater gains. There are two avenues of approach to this problem. First is the use of a national registration act similar to those now in force in Great Britain, France, and many other countries. Second is the attainment of approximate uniformity through modification of existing state acts. It is interesting to note that the latter goal formed the first part of the resolution proposed by the Chicago Chapter and adopted by The AIA at its Houston Convention in 1949:

"Resolved, That The Institute investigate the status of architectural registration laws in the various states of the country toward the end of achieving uniformity concerning the requirements of registration: . . ."

It was this resolution which precipitated the establishment of the Commission for the Survey of Architectural Education and Registration.

The logic, convenience, and practical savings in time, effort, and fees obtainable by a system of national registration can be easily appreciated by all who must now maintain numerous state licenses. The advantages of consistent standards of competence, uniform examinations, and homogeneous enforcement by federal agencies and courts likewise have strong appeal. Nevertheless, such a system would have its own inherent handicaps. National administration could hardly escape bureaucratization, and centralization would inevitably reduce the participation and support of local professional groups. Even if such hazards could be eliminated, the problem of attaining such a change seems insuperable. The Federal Constitution does not contain any provision which can be interpreted as empowering the transfer of professional regulation to national jurisdiction. To accomplish such a goal would require a constitutional amendment which, because it would affect all professions alike and have many other implications of centralization, would involve a fundamental reorientation of the existing balance between state and federal powers. It is conceivable that such a campaign might be conducted jointly by a large number of professions, but the necessity of obtaining concerted action by such diverse groups multiplies the difficulties many times. Such an effort could consume decades, and the overcoming of other opposition, certain to be widespread and bitter, would greatly prolong the process. There seems to be little likelihood that such an approach would have any chance of success.

Nevertheless, Americans have long since learned that there are other alternatives by which to achieve desired objectives. If inconvenience and inequities become sufficiently irksome, much can be done to overcome them by enlightened voluntary cooperation which, though it may lack the directness and simplicity of clear-cut national control, can accomplish many of the same ends. Moreover, such cooperation has the distinct advantage of arising from local realization of need, which, while sometimes long delayed, wins stronger support when it finally comes to focus.

One approach to greater consistency may be observed in the general field of legislation. During the first century of national growth, the creation of new states, each with its own legal system, led to insupportable diversity in laws governing the most common business procedures. One of the first goals of the founders of the American Bar Association in 1878 was alleviation of this situation. Initial steps were taken in 1881 which led to the formation in 1892 of the National Conference of Commissioners on Uniform State Laws, composed of delegates appointed by the governors of the several states. Its function was to prepare model statutes which could be accepted or adapted by individual states. The success of this venture may be gauged by the widespread adoption of many of its proposals. The Uniform Negotiable Instruments Law, for instance, was eventually adopted in 54 jurisdictions. That the process requires time is shown by the fact that, while the Conference prepared this law in 1897, the last state to adopt it did so only in 1927.[36] Critics have pointed out that such a prolonged delay usually means that later acts often incorporate modifications based upon experience of earlier laws and that the net result is rarely real uniformity. Nevertheless, this example suggests that architects, perhaps in concert with other professions, might find it helpful to prepare, possibly with the aid of the Conference, a uniform professional licensing statute which in time could inspire modification or replacement of the heterogeneous acts now in force. The advantage of Conference assistance would derive from its established position and reputation in legislative circles.

The principle of cooperation between state boards which administer registration laws arose soon after such regulations became widespread. A national association of dental examiners was formed in 1883.[37] The Federation of State Medical Boards was established in 1892.[38] Members of state boards of law examiners from 1898 on met in conferences sponsored by the Section on Legal Education of the American Bar Association.[39] Pharmacy examiners joined in a national organization in 1904.[40] The multiplication of architectural registration acts between 1910 and 1920 likewise emphasized the need of communication and cooperation among the state boards. By the end of the decade the problem became particularly urgent for Chicago architects whose practice frequently crossed into neighboring states. The situation prompted Emery Stanford Hall, F.A.I.A., a leader in the Chicago group, and a recently appointed member of the Illinois Board, to urge an association of architectural boards. Thus, in 1920 was created the National Council of Architectural Registration Boards. During the next two decades, Hall served as secretary and contributed much to the development of the NCARB program. This program has embraced several functions. First, NCARB acts as a clearing house and forum for discussions on registration matters. Its annual meetings and proceedings have become influential means of informing board members of the principles, practice, and changing needs of the registration process. This is especially valuable because the membership of the boards undergoes constant change. A second function is the analysis and development of qualifications for registration. Third is the establishment of standards for the content, conduct, and evaluation of qualifying examinations. And fourth is the provision of machinery by which architects may obtain with minimal difficulty registration in states other than their own. Detailed comment on these operations will be given in the next section.

Thus, the inception and growth of NCARB has followed closely the pattern of professional cooperation which, in the context of American constitutional law, has been the only available means to remedy an otherwise insupportably chaotic situation. Recognition and appreciation are due, therefore, to the wisdom and vision of its founders and to those who have for 30 years contributed time and thought to its evolution. It must be emphasized that, while participation in NCARB by its member boards is purely voluntary, its influence upon them is nonetheless significant. Thus,

371

especially in its impact upon professional standards and their implications for architectural education, NCARB enjoys formidable opportunities and responsibilities. Moreover, through its representatives in NAAB, this educational influence is directly exercised. On the other hand, NCARB in turn must respond to aspirations springing from the profession, for all representatives from the boards must, as practicing architects, concern themselves with their profession's needs. It follows, therefore, that NCARB, as an integral part of the profession's organization, must seek in its future growth to infuse its program with the highest quality of professional leadership. Within this framework, the Commission urges cooperation by the profession and by all boards in working toward a more uniform and more equitable registration process (*Recommendation 32*).

6. THE DETERMINATION OF REGISTRANTS

The crux of the whole registration process rests in the definition of competence for architectural practice and the selection and administration of appropriate means to determine whether an applicant satisfies these qualifications. At first glance the solution seems easy and direct: compose a test based on self-evident requirements and demand that the applicant pass it with a certain minimum grade. Nevertheless, when closely analyzed, this simple statement raises many questions which, because qualification is a serious matter for both applicant and society, must be answered with intelligence, consistency, and justice.

The ideal qualifications of an architect have been listed in Section 3, *Chapter III*. The formulation of such ideals needs no apology, but it is obvious that, while outstanding individuals may in maturity approach them in remarkable degree, many useful persons must be content with less elevated accomplishments. The positive fostering of ideals and excellence is the special province of individual ambition and professional zeal. Licensure and registration, on the other hand, are legal devices to protect society from incompetence, misconduct, and deceit. Thus, by their nature, they are not concerned with the discovery of genius or the determination of an order of merit. The problem, therefore, resolves itself into the fixing of a reasonable minimum below which public hazard outweighs individual right to freedom of action. Despite this negative view, it should be remembered that even a minimum standard can be a worth-while gain and that, in time, public realization of the resulting benefits will bring support for progressively higher thresholds of professional qualification.

The translation of the term, *reasonable minimum,* into a definite list of objective requirements still remains. While all state registration acts must subscribe to the limitation of reasonableness, for fear of invalidation, none of them gives it explicit meaning. As is the wont of law when faced with recalcitrant terms, an oblique approach is adopted in which the desired goal is defined by the means used to attain it. Thus, to all intents and purposes, the rule of law becomes a rule of discretion and opinion. This view of course need not be taken as questioning the integrity of examiners, for under such conditions they have no choice but to perform their duties in good conscience to the best of their abilities.

Nevertheless, reasonable qualifications for the practice of architecture should be susceptible to analysis and definition. Their scope includes the possession of certain specialized knowledge, the command of certain skills, the attainment of a degree of judgment derived from thoughtful consideration of experience, and a reputation and promise of personal integrity. While no examiner can truthfully appraise integrity by only a brief encounter, independent testimonials can assist in establishing it. Unless a candidate is definitely proved to be untrustworthy, he must be presumed to be upright. Nevertheless no one can predict what hidden weakness subjection to stress or temptation will reveal. On the other hand it should be possible to state in detail the minimum knowledge, skill, and judgment which a candidate should command. This definition might begin with the assumption that public protection will be reasonably safeguarded if the candidate is capable of performing with reasonable effectiveness the professional services required in building projects of certain fixed scales, types, and construction. From this goal, a definitive inventory of the requisite knowledge, skills, and judgment could be developed, and the candidate's possession of these could then be scientifically sampled and objectively measured.

Superficially such an approach may seem to produce much the same result as present practice. Nevertheless formal definition of the scope of competence has many advantages. For the candidate, on the one hand, it provides an explicit list of items which he must master during school and candidacy. This does not mean that he should set his sights at the minimum level of accomplishment; if he does, school, adviser, and profession have dismally failed in their responsibilities. Actually the range of capacity indicated would be quite sufficient to demand serious application. Thus the process of qualifying could acquire an orderly method reinforcing academic and candidate preparation. For the examiner, on the other hand, the definition of limits would permit more systematic and objective inspection of the candidate's attainments, and do much to eliminate arbitrary selection and subjective evaluation of qualifying criteria.

The measurement of candidates against established criteria of qualification is the second stage of the registration process. As currently practiced, this stage usually consists of some combination of three devices: first, evaluation of the candidate's record of education, training, experience, and character; second, an interview or oral examination; and third, a formal written examination. The selection, character, and application of these devices vary considerably in accord with the provisions of particular acts, with the skill of examiners, and with the status of the applicant. In general, three types of candidates are distinguished: experienced architects who are in practice at the time an act is adopted; experienced practitioners who are registered in another state; and candidates for initial registration. The first two groups are commonly designated as *Senior* applicants, and the third group as *Juniors*. The latter are usually further subdivided as to their educational preparation, that is, candidates who do not hold a secondary school diploma, candidates who do hold such a diploma, and candidates who have graduated from a school of architecture acceptable to the examining board.

Most acts have provided that all resident architects who were in active practice at the time of adoption of the acts should be registered in their respective states upon application and without examination. Such registrants are usually called "grand-fathers." The reason for such a provision lies in the principle that law cannot take away the right of an individual to continue in his established and lawful occupation. To the extent that such registrants do not meet standard qualifications, the realization of the full benefits of registration is delayed until they cease to practice. The *1950 Survey* found that 13 per cent of all registered architects were registered on this basis (*Table 43*). Of this group the proportion who could not originally have met normal requirements is probably very small. Thus, the registration of "grandfathers" no longer constitutes a major problem and it is obvious that before long it will disappear altogether. In the meantime, since the right to practice on such a basis is usually recognized only by the board of the state in which the registrant resides, other boards seldom honor such credentials.

Registration by Senior Examination

As soon as an architect obtains a commission elsewhere than in his state of residence, he faces the necessity of securing registration in the state in which the project is located. The *1950 Survey* found that 35 per cent of all architects have practiced in two or more states or countries (*Table 12*); 16 per cent had practiced in 3 or more; 8 per cent in 4 or more; 4 per cent in 5 or more; and 2 per cent in 6 or more. The highest number reported by one architect was 61.[41] It has already been noted that the average number of registrations held by all architects was 1.7 (*Table 44*). Thus, while two-thirds of all architects have not been particularly concerned with the problem of additional registration, one-third has been to the number of approximately 6700 individuals. Such a group, however, is too small to argue that architectural practice is "inter-state commerce." For architects who practice in many states, the process of qualifying with each board soon becomes an intolerable burden.

When few states had registration laws, most of them granted licenses to out-of-state registered architects on the basis of *reciprocity*. In time some states with larger requirements began to demand that the applicant's home registration must be equivalent to these greater demands. This soon led most states to restrict reciprocal recognition to those states which accorded them the same courtesy. If such a relationship was lacking, the applicant had no recourse except to devote much time, expense, and effort to satisfying all qualifying tests. Most acts, however, recognized that applicants who had practiced successfully for a certain period—usually ten years—could be suitably tested by a *Senior Examination* directly related to their practice. Such an examination reviews and checks the applicant's education and professional record, samples his professional calibre by requiring an exhibit of photographs, working drawings, and

374

specifications of his recent work, and explores his capacity by an oral test. The applicant is sometimes asked to give a brief oral account of some special investigation in which he has taken an important part. A board also reserves the right to make other inquiries to satisfy itself as to the applicant's true professional status and integrity. Senior Examinations are intended to be as searching as any other investigation.

If an out-of-state applicant has obtained his initial registration by means of formal examination equivalent to that demanded by the other, he can ask that its scope be certified by his home-state board. If equivalence is proved, out-of-state boards are often willing to accept it and grant the requested registration. If the original examination is not equivalent, supplementary tests are usually required.

Nevertheless, even with the provision of Senior Examinations, inconvenience, the cost in time and effort, and inevitable delays caused mounting discontent. Amelioration of these difficulties was the primary objective of the founders of NCARB. Two methods were developed for this purpose. First was the NCARB *Certificate* which was made available to those architects who satisfy the requirements of the *Standard NCARB Examinations*. One of these requirements is the submission of personal and professional data, with references, which after thorough investigation become the applicant's *Council Record*. The Senior Examination is available for architects with a record of ten years of practice as a principal; other candidates take the Junior Examination. The examinations, themselves, while posed and administered by the applicant's own state board, conform to NCARB specifications which ensure that the level of difficulty is at least equal to that required by any other board. If the applicant has been registered by virtue of an examination of lesser extent, he can take such supplementary tests as are necessary to satisfy the Standard NCARB Examinations. Almost all state boards now recognize the NCARB Certificate as satisfying their own qualifications for registration, and architects holding the Certificate can obtain such registration with minimum effort and delay. Two states register only those out-of-state architects who hold NCARB Certificates. In 1950, 1280 architects held NCARB Certificates.[42] The *1950 Survey* revealed that certificate holders had used them to obtain additional registrations in an average of 2.5 states (*Table 46 B*).

The second method was developed for architects who do not hold NCARB Certificates. It consists of the preparation and filing of an *NCARB Council Record,* as already described, which upon request of the holder is made available to any board from which he seeks registration. Because such a Council Record constitutes a transcript of all pertinent data and references, compiled with painstaking and disinterested care, and is certified by NCARB, most state boards accept it as an accurate record which makes further local checking unnecessary. Thus the use of a Council Record can save the applicant much time in preparing new applications and by securing action by the examining board as promptly as possible. Ten state boards now consider out-of-state applications only when accompanied by a Council Record. The use of the Council Record system has grown remarkably. Initiated in 1921, by 1931 572 records had been prepared; 865 were added by 1941; and by 1951 2070 more were on file, bringing the grand total to 3507.[43]

In view of this extensive use of its services, it would be surprising if NCARB had not been subjected to criticism. The second section of the Houston resolution of 1949 read:

"Resolved: . . . that a further study be made of the manner in which the NCARB is operating so that improvements may be suggested tending toward further expediting the functioning and service of NCARB to the profession."

It should be noted that criticism has been directed, not against the theory of the NCARB program, but rather toward the mechanics of its operation.

The most common complaint has been the length of time it sometimes takes NCARB to render its services. Although few agencies are always perfectly efficient and procedural improvements are always possible, it is only fair that critics of NCARB should also make allowance for certain factors which impose unavoidable delays. In the early 30's the maximum number of Council Records prepared in a single year was 61 and in 1936 only 24 were processed. Immediately after the war the upsurge of construction was immediately reflected in the 328 and 344 Council Records completed during 1945 and 1946. Although these peak loads subsided to 241 in 1950, this still meant an average of about one record per working day. In the same year, 142 Certificates—each an involved task—were issued.[44] The number of referrals of Council Records to state boards likewise mounted. Unfortunately, requests for services are seldom evenly spaced and at times they inevitably accumulate. It has not been possible to finance a staff proportioned to abnormal volumes, and if this were to be done the cost would have to be met by a considerable increase in the size of fees. A major source of delay, however, has been the difficulty of eliciting replies from persons named as references. Not infrequently several follow-up letters, and even telegrams, are necessary in order to complete a file. Nevertheless, even under the most favorable circumstances, such procedures take time. For this reason, NCARB has always been careful to advise prospective applicants to allow four to six weeks for normal processing and it has repeatedly stressed the desirability of initiating proceedings as normal, rather than as emergency, measures. Architects who wait until an actual out-of-state commission is secured naturally become eager to obtain NCARB assistance, but unfortunately they are also apt to be impatient and critical.

One further source of delay must be mentioned. In its early years, NCARB delegated many decisions to its secretary. At times some applicants have apparently felt that rulings in their cases were inequitable. As the use of NCARB grew, experience suggested the establishment of a Board of Review whose functions include the evaluation of each applicant's eligibility with respect to "good moral character," and the determination of the equivalence of the applicant's educational and experience record to NCARB standard requirements. This Board of Review, composed of members serving voluntarily and without recompense, meets at stated intervals. Thus, reasonable time must be allowed to secure its decisions on these matters.

It is clear that any benefits provided by NCARB services are contingent upon the extent of voluntary cooperation accorded by the several states. Fortunately the record has been very gratifying. The most flagrant withholding of cooperation has been in the state of Illinois, and it was no accident that the Houston resolution was initiated by the Chicago Chapter of The AIA. The reason for this situation is reported to lie in the fact that the administrative agency of the Illinois act, the state's Department of Registration and Education, has arbitrarily chosen to adopt a narrow interpretation of the Illinois act and so not only refuses to recognize NCARB Certificates and Council Records, but also declines to certify its registrants to NCARB or to conduct NCARB examinations for Illinois residents. Although the act provides an Examining Committee composed of five architects appointed by the Director of the Department, and although the act stipulates that the Director can perform his duties only after receiving advice from the Committee, the final determination of policy is his decision. Thus, however disposed the examiners may be to cooperate in the NCARB program, they are without power to carry it into effect. This impass has created extensive and wholly unnecessary handicaps for more than 1400 Illinois architects in the conduct of their practices, but to some extent they themselves must share the blame. In ordinary circumstances, bureau officials respond quickly to unified protest. Unfortunately, however, for the time being conditions within the profession in Illinois are such as to prevent concerted action. Until this can be remedied, there appears to be little likelihood of solving this and other aggravating situations. As a temporary expedient, Illinois architects who wish to obtain NCARB Certificates are forced to work through the boards of neighboring states. In a negative way this Illinois experience gives new appreciation of the general progress and benefits which enlightened cooperation has won in other states.

The Commission believes that the methods developed by NCARB for the amelioration of the process of out-of-state registration have proved to be well conceived and that the past accomplishments of NCARB in such matters comprise a most enviable record of service to the profession. In addition, the Commission believes that those who administer NCARB should maintain constant vigilance in seeking the highest order of accuracy in the records which it prepares, in developing the most felicitous organization of its work which will promote prompt and effective services, and in exploring new methods and refinements for the perfecting of its functions. These are duties which should guide all such agencies, but in a very special way the future success of NCARB will depend upon its imaginative execution of them. The fact that its work must be accomplished through the voluntary participation of its members should aid, rather than deter, their fulfillment.

Registration by Junior Examination

For Junior candidates—those seeking initial registration—qualification is normally based on: age, citizenship, education, candidacy training, character, and formal tests intended to reveal command of at least the established standard of professional competence. A check conducted by the Commission revealed that 39 acts declare mini-

377

mum age requirements; 10 set 25 years, and 28 give 21 years.[45] Twenty-nine acts register only U. S. citizens or those who have initiated naturalization proceedings. Thirty-two acts state specifically that "good moral character" is a prerequisite for registration.

With respect to education, candidacy, and the use of examinations, the Commission analyzed the requirements of 44 acts and found a most bewildering diversity, bordering on anarchy:[46]

Requirements for Initial Registration in 44 States, 1949

No. of States	Education Required			Years of Office Experience Required		Board Exams Req'd.		
	NONE STATED	HIGH SCH. DIPLOMA	ARCHIT. DEGREE	RANGE	MEDIAN	Written FULL	BRIEF	Oral
5	X					X		
18	X			3–15	8	X		
9		X				X		
31		X		3–12	8	X		
1		X		15				X
1		2 yr. College		3		X		
1		2 yr. Arch. Sch.		5		X		
1			X					
11			X	2–5	3			
1			X				X	
1			X	3 (+ evidence of knowledge of practice)				
3			X			X		
21			X	1–3	3	X		

Thus 9 different states confer registration solely by written examination without any specification of educational or practical experience requirements in architecture whatsoever. At the other extreme, 4 states register only those who are graduates of accredited schools of architecture, who have had 1 to 3 years of office experience, and who pass an extended written examination. In the 18 states which demand only a term of office experience for admission to the examination, the amount of experience required varies 500 per cent—from 3 to 15 years. For high school graduates, the professional examination may be taken in one eastern state without any office training at all, while in an adjoining state 12 years of such experience are necessary for admission to the examination. It is hard to escape the conclusion that only a few of these regulations can have been the result of any rational analysis of what constitutes a desirable or reasonable preparation for the practice of architecture.

It is of interest to note the percentages of architects who have been affected by these alternate methods of initial qualification (*Table 43*). Although 9 acts allow examinations to candidates without experience, it appears that only one per cent—and probably less—have overcome this handicap and gained registration. The use of the various types of qualifications is shown in the tabulation on the next page.

Qualification Pattern	% in Pattern	Non-Degree Educ.	Profess. Degree	Office Experience	Examination	
					WRITTEN	ORAL
A	10.3%	—%	10.3%	10.3%	10.3%	10.3%
B	9.3	—	9.3	9.3	—	9.3
C	29.2	—	29.2	29.2	29.2	—
D	10.8	—	10.8	10.8	—	—
E	5.2	5.2	—	5.2	5.2	5.2
F	7.3	7.3	—	7.3	—	7.3
G	13.8	13.8	—	13.8	13.8	—
% AFFECTED		26.3	59.6	85.9	58.5	32.1
H	13.0	GRANDFATHER		13.0		
I	1.1	OTHER BASES		?		

The educational and experience qualifications for admission to the Standard NCARB Examinations comprise the only organized attempt to bring some order out of this chaotic situation. NCARB admits to its examinations applicants with degrees from accredited schools of architecture and three years of practical experience under a registered architect, and also those applicants who are judged by its Board of Review to have equivalent preparation. Equivalence is defined to mean that candidates holding only high school diplomas and graduates of unaccredited schools of architecture must prove a degree of training equal to that received in an accredited school of architecture and, in addition, present proof of at least 9 years of employment under a practicing architect. Candidates who do not hold high school diplomas must conform to the same standard, except that the minimum length of office experience is 12 years. Since NCARB follows the principle that its standards should equal the greatest demands of any existing act—although for high school graduates it asks 1 and 3 years less than prevails in two states, it is clear that NCARB requirements rest on the same empirical basis as those of individual states. Therefore they cannot be said to have arisen from any inherent needs of a systematic program of candidate training. The facts that 23 states do demand 3 years of practical experience for graduate candidates, or that architects have expressed opinions averaging 3.6 years (*Table 47*), do not necessarily change the pragmatic character of these demands.

The requirements of NCARB and most states, with respect to graduate candidates, were established when four-year collegiate curricula were acceptable. At that time the total length of formal education and training for graduates was 19 years and for high school graduates 21 years. Thus by recognizing a two-year advantage in a preparation involving a professional degree, NCARB and these several states tacitly equated 1½ years of academic study with one year of office training.[47] Many states, however, allowed only a one-to-one correspondence. The mandatory extension of collegiate curricula to 5 years has not been compensated by any reduction of the length of office experience, so that the graduate candidate in many states and under NCARB rules now benefits by only one year over non-graduates. In addition, acts which admit candidates with 15 years of office training but no general educational accomplishment thus maintain a total stated requirement 5 years shorter than graduate candidates and 6 years below candidates holding high school diplomas. While it is probably reasonable to assume that most candidates will have had at least elementary schooling, 23 acts do not in fact require it. Although most architects agree that it is undesirable to restrict the profession to a single avenue of approach, these acts seem over-generous to non-graduate candidates to the point of weakness. Medicine, law, and several other professions have taken a more rigorous stand on this "poor-boy" question.

The process of initial qualification is thus seen to be characterized at present by a great diversity of conditions: lack of well-defined goals; absence of a systematic program of candidate training; and heterogeneous mandatory requirements. In such a state, it is small wonder that many acts resort to such phrases as "equivalents as may be acceptable to the board" or "such requirements as the board may determine." It must be recognized, of course, that the evaluation of human beings by other human beings can never become a mathematical procedure and that the administration of all social regulations must be exercised by enlightened and responsible officials. Nevertheless it seems certain that the registration process is susceptible to a higher degree of the application of orderly principles than it now exhibits. It is difficult to take seriously a situation in which artificial geographical boundary lines change completely both the definition of the minimum architectural competence demanded for public protection and welfare and the means of determining such competence.

Certain approaches to a more logical solution of this problem have already been suggested. A detailed statement of the minimum of knowledge and skills requisite for such protection in the conduct of normal practices can and should be formulated in order that the public, the examiners, and the candidates alike can know what is expected. Secondly, such a definition, in turn, can form a controlling program to establish the length and content of candidate training as described in *Chapter VIII*. And, third, once these limits are fixed, the optimum method of determining a candidate's satisfaction of them can be solved by carefully validated experiments. Perhaps it will be objected that the accomplishment of such codification would not ensure acceptance by the several boards. This is true, but in the long run the boards will certainly be more inclined to respond voluntarily to criteria based on logic and demonstrated effectiveness than on a welter of conflicting, arbitrary, and untested opinion. Moreover, public declaration of the criteria thus determined could do much to strengthen appreciation of architectural services, which in turn would promote wider acceptance of registration and, consequently, firmer support for its enforcement.

As already noted, investigation of candidates' qualifications may be made by means of personal records, interviews, and formal examinations. Since each of these devices has its inherent advantages and shortcomings, some combination of them is usually employed. All boards require candidates to submit with their applications attested records of age, citizenship, education, office and other experience. Examples of architectural drawings executed by the candidate are sometimes requested. Most states require letters of reference from architects and laymen. In evaluating these records, statements of fact are usually subjected to independent check. The importance of testimonials, however, varies greatly since all applicants naturally endeavor to select favorable references. In the NCARB Junior Examination the candidate's personal record—Examination A: Natural Aptitude and Theoretical and Practical Training—counts a maximum of 100 out of the total of 1000 grade points.

Candidate interviews vary as to character and scheduling according to the boards' procedures. The function of the interview may range from a mere personal introduction to a full-scale oral examination. It may be scheduled before or after a written examination. 16 of 31 responding board secretaries reported the use of interviews or oral examinations for Junior applicants. Members of 38 boards, however, voiced widely differing opinions as to the real value of interviews. Only 17 out of 92 responding members thought them "very effective," but only from 3 boards were two or more such opinions forthcoming. Fifty-one members considered interviews to be "worth while," but only from 12 boards did two or more express themselves thus. Twenty-four members regarded interviews as "of little value." Four boards were represented by two or more such opinions.

Interviews

The usefulness of interviews has also received prolonged attention by NCARB, which requires a *Personal Audience* as Section B of its Standard Examination for juniors

"so that (the board) may have an opportunity to judge (the candidate's) natural endowments for the practice of architecture, his ethical standards, and by questions, gain further knowledge of his fitness."

This section is assigned 100 of the 1000 grade points of the whole NCARB examination. The principle of the interview has been questioned by Professor Ralph E. Winslow, then President of the New York State Board, who stated, at the 1951 NCARB Convention, that:

"It is apparent that this examination is also a scrutiny—a visual and auditory appraisal—and it is my belief that, as such, it is also lacking in both validity and reliability. The well-dressed, well-poised young man who talks with a quiet air of self-assurance may be less well endowed for the practice of architecture and possessed of far lower standards of ethics than the tense and nervous chap with the rasping voice who spent the previous night sleeping in a coach seat of a railway car. Can we really judge, with any degree of reliability, in the manner described in the Syllabus, a candidate's 'natural endowments for the practice of architecture'? By what questions, without giving an extensive, carefully prepared examination, can we 'gain further knowledge of his fitness'? May we presume, on the basis of what must be a comparatively short period of time, to determine and evaluate a man's ethical standards?"[48]

Others have questioned the legality of a board judging "natural endowments," or of refusing to register a candidate on the basis of an interview when he has already passed a written examination, or of barring him from the written examination as the result of an interview.[49]

If interviews are in reality oral examinations, great care must be exercised in order to make sure that they are conducted fairly. Some boards use such oral examinations as a check on written examinations or, in some cases, as a check on those whose grades on the written examination fall near the passing mark. The difficulty of achieving valid grades under such conditions is well known, and arises from the chances that oral questions may or may not be clearly pointed and expressed, and that oral answers may be conditioned by their spur-of-the-minute nature, the fluency of the candidate, and the subjective character of the whole situation. Attempts have been made to guard against such defects. The New York State Board, for example, prepares questions in advance and derives grades by combining each member's independent mark for each answer. In the *1950 Survey of Board Members,* however, the six members of the New York Board split half-and-half in considering interviews as "worth while" and as "of little value."

Professor Winslow has suggested that interviews could be appropriately and profitably used to explore the range and depth of candidacy experience. This shift of character would be especially desirable as the more clearly focused candidate training program proposed in *Chapter VIII* becomes a reality. Under such conditions the interview could be conducted as a friendly review of the candidate's logbook which would give members of the board an opportunity to investigate and advise him as to his background and progress. Thus the assignment of a definite and valuable function to the interview would give it point and meaning from the standpoints of both board and candidate, and do much to transform the relationship between them from one of potential coolness to one of mutual respect and positive helpfulness. The Commission believes that such a development is highly desirable.

Written Examinations

The third method of ascertaining a candidate's qualifications is by formal written examination, which is based on the theory that capacity and achievement can be measured by evaluating examinees' written responses to sample questions posed by the examiner. Examinations can have one of these possible goals: first, the establishment of an order of ranking among the examinees; second, the determination of a limited number of the most qualified examinees; and, third, the separation of qualified and unqualified members of a group. Since architectural registration is concerned only with the latter function, its examinations are consequently simple pass-or-fail tests. In theory the dividing line should be determined by an absolute standard representing the minimum competence compatible with public safety and welfare.

It is obvious that, if such a process is to accomplish its purpose, it must be both valid and reliable. Validity means that it does in fact measure the specific abilities it purports to judge. Reliability means that any variation in final marks must result solely from real differences in the abilities of the examinees even when different examiners administer the test, or when different groups take it, or whenever it is repeated. The attainment of such consistency depends on the skill of the examiner in selecting an equitable sample of the field to be probed, in posing questions so that there can be no misunderstanding of their meaning and intent, in controlling the taking of the test so that all candidates are treated identically and are encouraged to put forth their best efforts, and in evaluating justly the answers received. If these conditions do not prevail, the resulting scores will measure inextricably both examinee and examiner and the very purpose of the process is vitiated. The conduct of examinations is, therefore, a serious and highly specialized technique.

Faith in the ability of formal examinations to accomplish their intended purposes is very old. Many early licensing systems included such tests. The universities of medieval Europe, newly founded to train theologians, lawyers, and physicians, awarded their degrees to scholars who passed oral tests on prescribed texts and withstood the trial of disputation before their teachers and fellow students. Not until about 1800 did the universities generally require written examinations. Admission to the guilds was also controlled by questionings and practical demonstrations. Gradually, during the nineteenth century, these traditions coalesced to form the qualifying examinations on which the new professional societies based the admission of candidates to membership. With the appearance of professional schools, however, certification of successful completion of the prescribed curriculum was soon considered to make further examination unnecessary. In France, for example, the architectural diploma of the *Ecole des beaux-arts* was recognized as satisfying all registration requirements, and in Great Britain the RIBA likewise came to accept graduation from an approved school in lieu of all but one portion of its tests. In Prussia, although the awarding of professional status depended upon examination by the Royal Department of Public Works, its direct connection with the *Bau-Akademie* ensured an intimate link between test and educational program.

The administration of architectural registration in the United States by 49 state acts and boards has led to great diversity in the requirement of the formal examination. All acts demand that all non-graduate candidates must pass formal written and practical tests. Twenty-four also require all graduate candidates to pass the same examination. Diversity in the character and depth of examinations has also arisen from the same dispersal of authority. As in other aspects of the registration process, NCARB has attempted to mitigate this situation by formulating the *Junior Examination Syllabus* which establishes mandatory standards for all candidates who seek its Certificate, but which are otherwise only advisory for the local tests conducted by individual boards. It must be emphasized that NCARB does not itself prepare or give any actual examinations, delegating this responsibility to the boards. Thus, even those examinations which it accepts for its Certificate, though based on its standards and syllabus, vary markedly by being posed and graded by the local boards.

Registration acts define the objective of the formal examination only in the most general terms, or, as previously noted, by describing the general content of the examination itself. The best such statement of objectives is that expressed in the NCARB Syllabus:[50]

"The Junior Examinations shall be given under conditions as nearly like those under which an architect works in his own office as is practicable. . . . By virtue of the Candidate's eligibility to be examined, it is presumed that he is well grounded in the theory of the different branches of architectural practice and that he either has the necessary factual knowledge or knows where to find it. It remains then for the examiners to ascertain with what ability and skill the candidate is able to apply his theoretical and factual groundwork to the actual problems of practice. This is the essence of the Junior Examinations. In preparing the questions, the examiners should keep this constantly in mind, confining the requirements to problems of practical application and avoiding those of theory and fact."

A decade ago the scope and length of board examinations varied considerably, but gradually NCARB standards have been adopted by many states. Previous to 1953, the NCARB Syllabus divided the written examination into 4 divisions and 10 sections, as follows:

Division	Subject	Points	Pass	Length
I. A.	Natural Aptitude and Theoretical and Practical Training	100	60	
B.	Personal Audience	100	60	
II. C.	Structural Design	75	45	3 hrs.
D.	Truss Design	50	30	2
E.	The Selection and Use of Materials	75	45	3
III. F.	Mechanical Equipment of Buildings	75	45	3
G.	Counseling and Administration	75	45	3
H.	Supervision	50	30	2
IV. I.	Miscellaneous (Selected by the examining board, but Analysis, or Urban Planning are suggested)	50	30	2
J.	History and Theory of Architecture	50	30	2
K.	Architectural Composition	100	60	4
V. L.	Design Problem	200	150	12
	Totals........................	1000	750	36

Although a passing mark of 60 per cent was required in each section, 75 per cent was demanded for the whole examination.

In 1953, NCARB issued, after long discussion, a revised Syllabus (*Circular of Advice, No. 3-53*) which modifies and regroups the examinations as follows:

Division	Subject	Points	Pass	Length
A.	Academic and Practical Training	100	75	
B.	Personal Audience	100	75	
C.	History and Theory of Architecture	100	75	3 hours
D.	Site Planning	100	75	5
E.	Architectural Design	200	150	12
F.	Building Construction	100	75	3
G.	Structural Design	100	75	5
H.	Professional Administration	100	75	3
I.	Building Equipment	100	75	5

It is interesting to note that history and theory have regained the hour previously dropped, that Composition and the Miscellaneous examinations have been transformed into Site Planning, that Supervision has been integrated with the Selection and Use of Materials into Building Construction, and that the 2 hours thus freed have been assigned to Building Equipment.

The *1950 Survey* queried registered architects as to their opinion of the formal examinations by which 75 per cent of them had been qualified. *Table 43* reveals that, of this group, 78 per cent took written examinations—including 21 per cent who also underwent additional oral tests. The remaining 22 per cent had only oral questioning. *Table 50* indicates that a considerable proportion of these successful examinees considered their examinations to have been adequate in coverage. This general satisfaction is somewhat surprising in view of perennial complaints, but it should be remembered that the *1950 Survey* included only successful examinees, that time may have mellowed many memories, and that opinions are not always based on considered analysis. Under such circumstances, exceptional opinions take on added significance. 15 per cent of the responders felt that emphasis on structural design was excessive, and 25 per cent held similar views with regard to history of architecture. Conversely, 10 per cent regarded the testing of draftsmanship as inadequate and 23 per cent thought likewise about mechanical equipment. Twenty-one per cent believed that not enough stress was placed on ability to use English effectively. The *1950 Survey* also investigated architects' opinions as to the relative importance of ten areas usually covered by examinations (*Table 51*). Again, the status quo was strikingly approved; 94 to 99 per cent of the responders believed the inclusion of nine areas to be important or desirable; 80 per cent voiced the same opinion about the tenth, the history of architecture.

In contrast to the opinions of architects, examiners themselves are sometimes more critical. In 1951 in a review of examinations, J. Woolson Brooks, then president of the Iowa State Board, pointed out the need of an equitable balance between the several areas:

"It does not make sense to license an architect on a grade of 75 per cent in design

. . . and at the same time to require him to solve involved structural problems which represent more nearly 125 per cent on the same scale (of difficulty)."[51]

The question of proper content and balance will be resumed later in this section.

The scope of registration examinations is closely linked with their length. A check of 44 acts, already noted, has revealed that 27, of 30 which stated the length of their examinations, conformed to the 36-hour, 4-day NCARB standard. Many also follow the NCARB outline of content; 3 states required 3 instead of 4 days, or a total of about 28 hours. Two acts, which did not stipulate length, indicated a shorter period by their reduced content. In one of these states only structural design and administrative practice were examined; in the other the NCARB Syllabus was used, but no design problems or questions on reinforced concrete or trusses were given. Looking back upon their own examinations, 84 per cent of all registered architects remembered them as satisfactory in length; 4 per cent thought them too short; and 12 per cent complained that they were too long (*Table 50*).

Although many registration acts specify the general areas in which applicants must be examined, the *1950 Survey of Board Secretaries* found that 30 of the 31 responding boards have authority to determine the character of the examination questions. One board considered that it would need legislative sanction to modify its examination, but obviously it too had the power to determine the details of its questions. In carrying out this responsibility, the formulation of the examination questions is usually performed by members of the boards. Of the 32 responding boards, 26 operated in this manner while 5 reported that this task was delegated to the faculty of a local school of architecture. The more complete *1950 School Survey* revealed that, in reality, 10 schools prepare and conduct the whole examination, and that 11 schools assist their boards in drafting examination questions. In one state, two board members joined with teachers to prepare examinations. In another, questions were written by the board's secretary and were subsequently reviewed by the board. In still another, the secretary took the entire responsibility. Two boards received assistance from other architects; another board retained a consulting engineer to prepare questions in structural design and graphic statics.

Examinations for architectural registration normally use three types of questions: first, the design problem which is intended to reveal ability to solve creatively the requirements of a building of moderate complexity; second, the operative problem which probes ability to apply scientific and mathematical techniques to structural and equipment situations; and, third, the essay question which provides the applicant with an opportunity to prove his possession of data and principles and his ability to organize, interpret, and apply them effectively to common building problems. It is widely recognized that only a few individuals will respond uniformly to all of these methods; but, since the three approaches are essentially complementary, they do serve to explore both the strengths and weaknesses of candidates.

Twenty-five boards reported they base their examinations on the NCARB Syllabus, implying a degree of uniformity in their questioning. It should be noted, however, that the Syllabus is a very general statement. The section describing the test in Mechanical Equipment is typical:

"The candidate may be asked questions to determine his knowledge and judgment on the installation and use of heating, ventilating, and air-conditioning systems; electrical equipment, including kinds of current, wiring, distribution systems, lighting fixtures, generators, motors, and private power plants; plumbing, including supply and waste systems, sewage disposal, sprinkler systems, and fire protection equipment; elevators, including location, type, speeds for various uses, safety devices, etc."

When such a generalized account is interpreted by 49 boards, it is apparent that the content and the actual location of the passing threshold of any examination based on it can spread over a wide range. Altogether, the Syllabus adds up to a comprehensive definition of architecture and practice which in reality leaves each board free to follow its own devices as to examination content—which of course their legal independence permits—but the coverage of the Syllabus is so broad as to be of only limited service to a candidate concerned with preparation for the examination, or to an examiner faced with selecting a specific sampling.

This handicap is softened to some extent by those boards which give some advice to prospective candidates. Candidates are informed by 28 boards that examinations will be based on a syllabus, but in most cases this meant the general statement provided by NCARB. Several acts do contain similar outlines, but, since all are briefer than the NCARB Syllabus, they are even more generalized. Sample examination questions are provided by 2 boards, while 13 boards allow official access to entire sets of previous questions. It is highly probable, however, that such data are widely circulated in other states as well; 16 boards reported that the type of building selected for the design examination was announced some time before the test. More effective preparation of candidates regarding the objectives, nature, and coverage of the examinations would seem to be an important duty of each board or of all boards acting together through NCARB. The Commission considers that such a function could be profitably linked with the candidate guidance manual suggested in *Chapter VIII*. In any case, the Commission believes that some means of acquainting prospective candidates with the nature, range, and form of examination questions applies a sound pedagogical principle which would do much to eliminate fortuitous tensions and create an atmosphere conducive to achieving the real purposes of the examination (*Recommendation 33*).

It has been emphasized that the construction of a valid and reliable examination demands considerable skill and experience. It involves the determination of a judicious sampling of the subject field. The character and type of questions must fulfill the objectives of the testing process. They must be carefully designed to provide the necessary conditions required to arrive at the desired response, phrased with maximum clarity to avoid ambiguity and the possibility of misinterpretation, and so devised as to be achievable within the allotted time schedule. Basic and obvious as these factors may seem to be, too many examinations neglect to take them into account.

President Brooks of the Iowa Board has stressed particularly the necessity of clear, straightforward questions which are vitally related to architectural practice and which are capable of being answered directly and definitely. He has noted that:

"nothing impairs the authority of a Board more than trick or catch questions, unless it be questions of opinion in which the applicant's answer is heavily discounted because it disagrees with the prejudices of the member who corrects the papers."[52]

The fact that 8 per cent of the responders to the *1950 Survey* had found the statement of questions to be ambiguous suggests that such criticisms are not irrelevant. Some boards have sought to safeguard their examinations from such defects by trying them out on their members, but such a check does not always fulfill its purpose because the advanced experience of board members and their general familiarity with such questions introduce abnormal factors into the trial.

As to places in which examinations are held, the *1950 Survey of Board Secretaries* reported that 16 were conducted in various public buildings, 15 in schools of architecture, one in a school of engineering, another in a school of art, 7 in hotels, one in a private club, and 2 in architectural offices.

The grading of examinations is usually accomplished by the members of the boards. For 29 of 33 responding boards design problems are judged by the whole board acting as a jury; 16 do likewise in evaluating other sections of the examination. For 17 boards, members grade such sections individually, and for 3 boards, teacher-members grade these parts. Five boards delegate grading to school faculties, but the *1950 School Survey,* with a more complete response, reports that 16 schools perform grading duties, although this probably includes the 10 that conduct complete examinations. For 3 other boards grading assistance is recruited from among local architects. The board for which a consulting engineer wrote the structural questions also employed him to grade these sections. Secretaries in 30 cases reported that their boards have authority to determine the basis of grading examinations. Two boards reported that such modifications could only be attained by legislative action.

The *1950 Survey of Board Secretaries* obtained data from 23 states on the average total number of examinees per year for the three years 1948, 1949, and 1950. The results were as follows:

Arkansas	10	Maryland	102	North Carolina	25
Connecticut	35	Michigan	12	Ohio	92
D. Columbia	20	Minnesota	35	Pennsylvania	225
Florida	75	Mississippi	5	Rhode Island	3
Illinois	120	Missouri	45	South Dakota	2
Kansas	1/3*	Montana	10	Tennessee	17
Kentucky	25	Nebraska	5	Texas	60
* Act passed 1949		New Jersey	35	Utah	3

Even these partial data are of little use, because many examinees were repeating all or part of the examinations. It is an unhappy fact that the architectural profession has thus far not been sufficiently interested in the registration process to ascertain the number of candidates who seek or gain admission to it and their record in undergoing it. Such statistics would be useful in many ways, as those which have for years been compiled annually for medicine, pharmacy, law, accounting, and many other professions amply prove. Both The AIA and NCARB, each of which has a vital interest in such knowledge, must share the charge of negligence in this matter. In 1953, NCARB at last appointed a committee to assemble such data, but the boards have been extremely slow in cooperating, and a year later no report had yet been issued. The Commission urges The Institute to see that such studies are placed immediately on a continuing basis (*Recommendation 34*).

Information regarding the success or failure of examinees is even more fragmentary. Such data are published as a routine matter by the professions just mentioned. The *1950 Survey of Board Secretaries* obtained responses from 25 boards with the following results:

Per cent of Candidates Passing Examination in 25 States, by Number of Tries

	NO. EXAMS TO PASS			
	1	2	3	4+
S n	77.3%	1.8%		
S	75	50		
S n ua	75	15	10	
S n ua	70	90	100	
S n a	65	85	100	
S n a	62	31	7	
S a	60	80	90	
S n a	55			

	NO. EXAMS TO PASS			
	1	2	3	4+
M n a	52%	25%	1%	00.02%
S n	50	90		
M n a	50	75	90	
L a	35	44	70	50
M n a	33	83	52	
S a	33	50		
S n a	30	50		
L n a	26	22	8	6
S n	25	95		

	NO. EXAMS TO PASS			
	1	2	3	4+
L a	25%	50%	85%	90%
M n a	25	29	5	4
L n a	20	50		
S n a	18	50	22	10
L n a	12	29		
L n a	8	25	14	3
S n a	5	20	30	45
S n	1.4	8.2	2.7	13.7

$$L = 75+$$
$$M = 26\text{-}74 \quad \text{No. of Candidates}$$
$$S = 25-$$

n = Exam reported to be based on NCARB Syllabus
a = State with accredited school or schools
ua = State with unaccredited school

It is apparent that, while some of these figures derive from careful study of board records, others are rough estimates. Moreover, some represent per cents of all successful candidates, while some are per cents of all candidates repeating the examination. Thus, only the initial figures are strictly comparable. The wide range of initial passes can be explained only by assuming either great differences in the stringency of the tests or by the adequacy or inadequacy of the examinees' preparation. For example, several boards are required by law to admit to their examinations high school graduates who need not have had any architectural experience whatsoever, either academic or practical. Nevertheless, in the table above, these states do not by any means show

1. Passing Record of Candidates in Examinations in State "A," 1944–1948

	Number						Per cent of All Candidates						Per cent of Total Passed				
	ALL CANDIDATES	PASSED					ALL CANDIDATES	PASSED									
		TOTAL	1ST TRY	2ND TRY	3RD TRY	4+ TRIES		TOTAL	1ST TRY	2ND TRY	3RD TRY	4+ TRIES	TOTAL	1ST TRY	2ND TRY	3RD TRY	4+ TRIES
Total	538	337	141	118	44	34	100	63	26	22	8	6	100	42	35	13	10
*Non-Graduates	188	99	32	38	19	10	100	53	17	20	10	5	100	32	38	19	10
Graduates Total	350	238	107	75	30	26	100	68	31	21	9	7	100	45	31	13	11
4-yr. Degree	53	29	14	8	2	5	100	55	26	15	4	9	100	48	28	7	17
5-yr. Degree	262	181	76	61	25	19	100	69	29	23	10	7	100	42	34	14	10
6-yr. Degree	11	11	5	4	1	1	100	100	45	36	9	9	100	45	36	9	9
7½-yr. Degree	24	17	12	2	2	1	100	71	50	8	8	4	100	70	12	12	6

Comparison of Schools Represented by 10 or More Graduates

4-yr. school	17	14	6	5	—	3	100	82	35	29	—	18	100	43	36	—	21
5-yr. schools																	
A	63	40	12	15	12	1	100	63	19	24	19	2	100	30	37	30	3
B	43	32	16	8	5	3	100	74	37	19	12	7	100	50	25	16	9
C	32	23	11	4	2	6	100	72	34	13	6	19	100	48	17	9	26
D	31	20	7	7	2	4	100	65	23	23	6	13	100	35	35	10	20
E	20	16	6	9	—	1	100	80	30	45	—	5	100	38	56	—	6
F	17	9	4	1	3	1	100	53	24	6	18	6	100	44	11	33	11
G	15	12	7	3	—	2	100	80	47	20	—	13	100	58	25	—	17
H	14	9	3	6	—	—	100	64	21	42	—	—	100	33	67	—	—
I	11	8	5	3	—	—	100	72	45	27	—	—	100	62	38	—	—

* Non-graduates must hold high school diploma and have 12 years of office training.

2. Passing Record of Candidates in Examinations in State "B," 1945–1949

Total	130	75	25	38	7	5	100	57	19	29	5	4	100	33	50	10	7
**Non-Graduates	29	14	3	9	1	1	100	48	10	31	3	3	100	21	64	7	7
Graduates Total	101	61	22	29	6	4	100	60	22	28	6	4	100	36	48	10	6
4-yr. Degree	72	42	14	21	4	3	100	58	19	29	6	4	100	33	50	10	7
5-yr. Degree	29	19	8	8	2	1	100	66	28	28	7	3	100	42	42	11	5

** Non-graduates must hold high school diploma, but no office training is required.

the highest percentages of failures. Since the data are well distributed across the country and between states with and without schools, this diversity of results is far too great to be explained in any large part by differences between schools. It is all the more remarkable when 20 of the 25 boards state that their examinations are based on the NCARB Syllabus! There seems to be some correlation between the number of candidates per year and the percentage of initial passes. Small groups tend to be more successful than large groups. On the whole, however, it is difficult to escape the conclusion that the levels of difficulty of the examinations varied so broadly that they indicate a completely irrational range of definitions of competency. In any case, accurate and complete statistical studies should be made immediately.

The Commission had access to comparable detailed analyses of candidate performance in only two states. Unfortunately the period covered involved profound dislocations so that the data obtained cannot be accepted as typical. Nevertheless, as shown on page 390, results indicate fully the desirability of a nation-wide study.

If it is assumed that the examinations in both states were of equal difficulty, these data reveal surprisingly comparable over-all results. The proportions of all passes and of initial and later passes correspond to a remarkable degree. The slightly lower figures for State "B" are due, no doubt, to the failures of candidates who offer the lower minimum of education and experience. On the other hand, the correlation between the two sets of non-graduate candidates raises the question as to whether the long experience requirement of State "A" has real value, or whether, in State "B," most such candidates had voluntarily waited to apply until they had acquired comparable experience. The similarity of the ratios for graduate candidates—total, 4-year degree, and 5-year degree—seems well within the range of personal variation of individual candidates, although State "B" ratios are again slightly lower, due perhaps to lower requirements. The smallness of the difference might also be interpreted as indicating little advantage to the 3-year experience period demanded by State "A," but it is more probable that graduate candidates in State "B" voluntarily obtained equivalent experience before applying for registration.

The *1950 Survey of Board Secretaries* secured some data on the examination areas which have accounted for the largest number of failures; 24 responses yielded 35 items. One mention each cited history, composition, supervision, and "planning for safety," while two noted construction. The greatest stumbling blocks, by all odds, were architectural design with 12 mentions and structural design with 19. One secretary observed what must be almost universal experience that, "we find that usually an applicant who is strong in one is weak in the other." The analyses of States "A" and "B"—quoted above—reported the per cent of passes in the four major divisions of their examination (these data are tabulated on the next page). In contrast to survey data, both states reveal more failures in architectural design than in structures.

This analysis of division passes provided the only data by which the Commission could study the long-term reliability of examinations. In general, the record of State "A" appears to be remarkably consistent as measured by the percentage of passes in successive groups. In all but a few cases the range of pass percentages seems within

Division Passes in % of All Taking Each Division, Including First and Repeat Tries
State "A" (1944–1949)

SUBJECT	OVER-ALL	SEMI-ANNUAL EXAMS											
		A	B	C	D	E	F	G	H	I	J	K	L
Archit. Design	48	23	48	43	46	49	44	70	46	37	43	58	40
History-Theory	68	75	46	79	57	42	69	67	56	58	89	71	84
Structures	66	45	59	71	81	55	66	78	76	62	51	67	71
Practice-Equip.	76	67	92	92	78	73	76	64	83	57	87	83	67
Total	64	52	61	71	64	54	64	70	65	53	67	70	65

State "B" (1945–1949)

SUBJECT	OVER-ALL	A	B	C	D	E	F	G	H	I
Archit. Design	40	50	83	67	43	55	55	50	18	20
History-Theory	52	100	100	100	88	69	58	26	38	30
Structures	45	80	40	62	35	43	41	44	53	26
Practice-Equip.	68	75	60	58	85	71	57	59	63	87
Total	50	75	70	70	61	57	52	45	43	37

the variation of candidate abilities to be expected in different groups. On the other hand, State "B" illustrates a marked variety in pass percentages and a general decline in the design and history-theory divisions. This contrast emphasizes the necessity of continuing checks on all examinations to ensure a high degree of reliability.

This review of current written examinations for architectural registration raises many questions in the minds of all thoughtful architects and teachers. If such examinations are to be continued as a major determinant of professional qualification, it is obviously necessary to take all possible precautions to make them consistent with the objectives of social control, the nature of professional practice, and fair treatment of the examinees. The Commission believes that these goals are universally accepted at the present time, but it has been unable to procure enough positive data to judge precisely whether the results achieved fulfill these excellent intentions. In view of the apparent wide diversity of interpretation of the NCARB Syllabus, the wide range of coverage, the disuse of modern testing controls which could help to improve validity and reliability, and the total absence of any thoroughgoing check—statistical or otherwise—of current operations, no informed judgment is now possible.

The Commission emphatically does not wish to have this opinion interpreted as a denunciation of the several boards or of the NCARB. It believes that the profession owes a large debt to the many devoted architects who at considerable personal sacrifice worked to establish and now work to administer the registration process which is so important to the American people and the profession. Nevertheless, the Commission firmly believes that the time is past due for a thorough reconsideration of the procedure of designing, preparing, conducting, and grading registration examinations. Because the Commission has not been able to procure sufficient facts, it does not now feel justified in offering a definitive solution, but it does suggest a number of approaches that should be closely studied by all who are concerned with such matters.

It is obvious that any analysis of these questions must start with the basic questions, *What is competence in terms of the performance of architectural services?*, and *What degree of competence should be established as the legal qualification for practice?* Answers which are expressed in broad generalities alone cannot suffice; the final definition must be precisely stated in terms of specific functional abilities and capacities. The formulation of such objectives must, of course, come from the profession of architecture, but the profession should also seek the aid of other disciplines which have had experience in such endeavors.

The NCARB Syllabus forms an excellent starting point for such an analysis because of the wide acceptance which its outline of examination areas and methods has received. In architectural design, the examination calls for the solution of a building project of intermediate size and complexity, without highly specialized features, and of a type normal to ordinary practice. It has been suggested that the problem should contain some special feature which, because it would prevent the introduction of memorized solutions, would reveal the candidate's capacity for independent and creative thought. The type of project chosen should be announced well in advance. The program should include such data as an architect usually assembles preparatory to beginning design. Design examinations last for 12 hours and are conducted *en loge*. The final presentation should be small enough to be prepared in a maximum of three hours by a candidate having reasonable skill. The grading of such design problems usually follows such criteria and values as:[53]

1. Planning for convenience, safety, and efficient operation.....50 per cent
2. Constructability......................................20
3. Effective exploitation of site possibilities...................10
4. Attractiveness of aesthetic organization....................10
5. Facility of presentation................................10

The examination in structural design absorbs 5 hours. It samples the candidate's ability to apply structural theory to problems met in actual practice, to arrange and design structural elements in timber, steel, and reinforced concrete with regard to stability, economy, and fitness, and to advise clients in the choice of an appropriate structural system. Problems involving rigid frames and secondary stresses may be considered for inclusion, but only if advance notice has been given. A portion of the examination is usually devoted to truss analysis and design, which, while too short a time to solve a complete unit, can reveal the candidate's real understanding of stresses and strains in structures. Choice of graphic or algebraic methods is usually permitted, and the use of handbooks is allowed.

The 3-hour examination in Building Construction is intended to test the candidate's knowledge of the selection and use of materials, and especially his judgment in such

393

applications, rather than his memory of a textbook recommendation. Most examiners discourage the employment of obscure expressions drawn from specifications and prefer clear discussions of the reasons underlying the selection of materials. Sketches illustrating good practice in the use of materials in combination are welcomed. The examination also deals with the supervision of construction.

The Professional Administration examination explores in its allotted 3 hours many subjects on which an architect must advise clients. These include: cost estimates, the financing of building projects, investment aspects, the selection of contractors, construction contracts, bonds, and the relations and responsibilities of owner, contractor, and architect.

Five hours are devoted to Building Equipment—heating, ventilation, sanitation, illumination, and electrical installations—in order to probe command of basic scientific principles, ability to solve simple requirements, and understanding of more complicated problems. The candidate should demonstrate capacity to plan the equipment needed for simple buildings and to collaborate intelligently with engineers in determining and incorporating installations in larger projects.

The examination in the History and Theory of Architecture has recently been re-alloted 3 hours. The appropriateness of a history test has been questioned, but, as previously noted, the *1950 Survey* showed that 80 per cent of all responding architects thought its inclusion important or desirable. Only 2 of 105 board members wished to abandon it; one wished to excuse graduate candidates from taking it; and another thought the time allotted to history should be increased. The purpose of the examination in history is to ensure that architects understand and appreciate the relationship between architecture and the social conditions from which it grows. It is difficult to see how current problems can be solved intelligently if architects are ignorant of the past whence these have sprung. Many progressive architects hold that a firm foundation in history is now more than ever necessary to sound practice. While lack of history would not endanger public safety, architects would be much less effective in many aspects of their service if such background were lacking. The examination affirms these views by emphasizing a critical knowledge of architectural masterworks as seen against their social contexts.

In the revised Syllabus, 5 hours are assigned to the examination in Site Planning. This comprises a short design problem involving a group of buildings, the solution of which is intended to test the candidate's ability to advise a client soundly with respect to considerations of land values, obsolescence, the handling of traffic, and the functional and aesthetic interrelationships of juxtaposed structures.

Underlying this general program of examination, the Syllabus assumes a tacit definition of minimum competence. Its usefulness would be greatly enhanced, however, if it could be made to indicate more precisely the level of development which is expected in each area. Such a statement would place both candidate and examiner on common ground and forestall suspicions that definitions of competence are consciously or subconsciously kept nebulous in order to preserve leeway for intuitive judgments. It will take much serious and clear-headed thought to reach specific defi-

394

nitions, but there does not seem to be any inherent reason preventing their attainment.

Once objectives and scope are determined, the means of testing must be reviewed. This immediately raises the problem of length. The present 36-hour schedule, concentrated within four days, has met with considerable criticism as constituting a trial of physical endurance, rather than a demonstration of professional skills. This could be relieved by less thorough sampling, by exploring fewer areas, by using types of questions capable of quick answers, or by subdividing the long examination into a series given at different times. All of these solutions will provoke heated opposition. The choice of 36 hours was originally an empirical decision on the part of one state, but its adoption by NCARB, because it was then the longest requirement, has now made it the standard regardless of whether or not it originally was valid. Such matters have a way of self-aggrandizement which makes reassessment very difficult. In this case, those states which have refused thus far to increase their own 28-hour program have come to be denounced for "easy" examinations. The idea that additional time is unnecessary is, of course, heretical. Yet no controlled studies have been carried out to correlate the length or extent of testing with the measurement of competence. Since the Commission believes that such studies might well discover testing methods which would be at once speedier and more reliable, it urges that they be initiated as soon as possible (*Recommendation 35*). Until such an analysis is available, the Commission recognizes that the 36-hour examination should be retained simply because it is one of the few points of agreement in an otherwise heterogeneous situation.

The special nature of the examination in architectural design will probably prevent any significant modification of its administration. Problems demanding demonstration of structural and equipment calculations cannot be much reduced, although many time-saving devices could be introduced. The Virginia board, for example, issues printed problems in graphic form in which the candidate only needs to complete the missing parts. For all other examinations, however, the primary method is the essay or free-response question, in which the examinee supplies, composes, and writes the materials of his answer. The essay question is often preferred because it is thought to be the only means of testing the candidate's ability to handle his material creatively.

The Commission submitted a number of recent board examinations to Dr. Henry Chauncey, president of the Educational Testing Service, an organization which, in addition to many other activities, prepares and administers the College Entrance Examination Board Tests, the entrance examinations for four armed services' academies, the Selective Service College Qualification Test, and the Law School and Medical College Admissions Tests. Dr. Chauncey noted the widespread use of essay questions in these board examinations and remarked that, although their expression was clear and concise, this type of question has proved so unreliable that its use has greatly declined. This unreliability is due both to examinee and examiner. Since each essay answer consumes considerable time, the test must be restricted to only a few questions and, in turn, the chance that the range of questions will sample the candidate's real knowledge declines sharply. This is particularly unhappy in a pass-or-fail test because it does not discriminate sufficiently among the group whose performance falls near the established passing threshold. Furthermore, legitimate variations of interpretation and opinion can insinuate themselves, and an initial misconception may be discovered too late for rewriting. Then, too, answers will vary widely in the impression given due to technically extraneous factors such as facility in rhetoric, handwriting, and willingness to go beyond a minimum response. From the standpoint of grading, essay answers are subject too largely to subjective factors. Different graders seldom give identical marks to the same paper, and even the same grader marks differently on different occasions. Grading fatigue is a serious hazard. If essay questions are employed, equitable marks can only be secured by an elaborate system of cross-checking.

Dr. Chauncey stated that the development of objective tests has eliminated most of these difficulties. In these tests, the question is framed to require only one response which must be definitely right or wrong. In its earliest form, this meant the true-or-false question, but other types have been developed, of which the multiple-choice question is the most familiar. The examinee simply checks the correct answer in the proper spot. Increased speed of answering thus permits the number of questions assigned to a particular period to be multiplied many fold, from 20 to 25 as against one essay question. This permits more extended sampling of the candidate's command of the field and greatly reduces the element of luck with respect to knowing a particular question. Controls to discount guessing are easily provided. Unusual questions, which cannot be justified when few are available, may be included, and questions of varying difficulty can be introduced to provide maximum discrimination at any critical point. While widely thought to be limited to factual information, objective tests have been so developed as to measure accurately mental processes, values, and judgment. Then, too, objective tests can be scored mechanically with perfect accuracy and great speed. Experience over many years has amply proved that these tests are much more reliable measures of candidate response than the older essay type. Moreover, in successive examinations over a period of years, consistent standards of difficulty can be maintained. Because of these advantages, the Commission urges examiners to study their application in architecture (*Recommendation 36*).

Regardless of the type of questions used, the preparation and administration of examinations of proven validity and reliability demand the services of expert examiners. For professional examinations on which public safety and individual careers hinge, these qualities are mandatory. Unfortunately the provision of expert services is not feasible unless the volume of work is large enough to keep unit costs within reasonable bounds. It is obvious, therefore, that not even the largest group of architectural candidates of a single state could support such services. This readily explains why older examination methods have continued to persist and why the exploration of improved methods has been so long delayed. As long as the whole group of architectural candidates is dispersed among 49 boards, present procedures will probably remain inviolate.

Nevertheless, two examples, comparable to architecture, can be cited to prove that the preservation of state authority is not incompatible with a cooperative solution. In 1915 the National Board of Medical Examiners was organized to develop and conduct a national medical examination which could be accepted by the individual state boards as equivalent to their own separate examinations. By 1932 the NBME certificate had been recognized by 41 states and 3 territories, and in the previous year 9 per cent of all medical graduates obtained it.[54] In 1953 all but two boards had accepted it, although 5 boards still require a supplemental oral examination and one board demands a supplemental written examination. NBME conducts its examination in three parts. The first is a written examination on 6 basic medical sciences and is given at the end of the second year of the medical curriculum. The second written part covers 5 divisions of medical practice and is given at the end of internship. Both are conducted at any approved medical school when 5 or more applicants are available. The third is a clinical and practical examination conducted before committees of practitioners in 25 centers.[55] NBME has recently obtained the assistance of the Educational Testing Service in preparing and scoring its two written examinations and at the same time has adopted, after stringent trials, the objective type of questions.[56]

The second example is furnished by the uniform examination for certified public accountants conducted by the Board of Examiners of the American Institute of Accountants. This society maintains an Educational Office the staff of which prepares the 3-day examination, conducts trial-runs on recently successful candidates, marks the papers of more than 5000 candidates, and recommends grades to the state boards.[57] This centralized service was begun in the early 1930's and is now used by all states. Some states have ruled that their boards can use the society's questions, but that the local boards must perform the grading. For most boards, however, review and acceptance of a national grade makes it the boards' own mark.

These two examples immediately suggest an investigation of a nation-wide uniform examination for architecture, which would not only be desirable in itself, but possibly would also support the assistance of expert examiners. Unfortunately the number of candidates per year can only be approximated; perhaps there would be in the immediate future about 600–800. Although this group would be much smaller than those in medicine and accountancy, it might be large enough to justify a unified examination. The potential advantages include the attainment of much higher reliability due to the use of modern techniques of standardization and the use of objective questions, improved grading, and, not least, the relief of board members from much unfamiliar and routine labor. On the other hand, the boards probably would still wish to conduct the examination in architectural design, even though a uniform program might be used. Uniform structural problems, though susceptible to objective tests, might likewise be administered locally. These, together with the oral interviews on candidacy training, and the review and legal approval of the suggested national grade should satisfy fully the responsibility of a board to carry out the mandate of its act. The Commission recommends that The Institute explore such a plan (*Recommendation 37*).

The question at once arises as to the appropriate agency to conduct national architectural examinations. It might seem at first glance that NCARB should do so. Many years ago, NCARB did consider such a role, but declined to accept it. At that time the number of examinees was very small and a centralized system would have been uneconomical. Today, however, with greatly increased volume, the situation is very different, and NCARB might well reconsider its position. It should be noted, on the other hand, that in both the medical and accountancy fields national examinations have been assigned, not to state board associations, but to independent national agencies. NBME is a separate agency; and the accountants' Board of Examiners is a section of their professional society. It may prove preferable, therefore, to assign this function to a new agency, perhaps within The AIA itself. It may be argued that the cost of a mass operation will require the substitution of paid assistance in place of present volunteer efforts. In the light of the modest examination fees and balanced budgets which prevail in both medicine and accountancy, it is probable that some feasible financial solution could be found for architecture as well.

It should not be overlooked that accumulation of experience with national objective examinations could easily lead to the discovery that competence could be accurately measured, perhaps even more effectively by a combination of short key tests designed to cover mental capacity as well as subject fields. It is conceivable that such a combination might prove to be so critical that the total examination could be considerably shortened. Such a development would be a long-term affair, but the problem of recruiting the best available talent is of such importance to the profession that no refinement which promises greater effectiveness should be left unexplored.

The *1950 Survey of Board Secretaries* investigated whether simultaneous and identical, i.e., national, examinations would be possible under existing registration acts. Of 31 responses, 25 answered affirmatively, 2 considered that it might be possible, one thought it could be arranged by a minor revision of the act, 2 were doubtful, and 4 said no. The *Survey of Board Members* asked whether such an arrangement would be acceptable. Sixty-three out of 105 members—60 per cent—favored it; 35 members —33 per cent—did not; 7 did not offer an opinion. When these reactions are tabulated by boards, 27 approved, 3 boards were evenly split, and 10 disapproved. Since the survey question was posed without discussion, it is probable that after successful demonstration of the plan's mechanics and advantages, its adoption would become general. This would also seem to be promised by past experience in the medical and accounting professions.

The Commission also discussed immediate improvements in current examining techniques. One suggestion proposes that a central file of test questions be established—a "blood bank" of problems—to which the individual boards would send a copy of each examination, together with comments as to the results obtained. From this file, selections of particularly successful questions would be drawn to compose an anthology which could be inexpensively duplicated and circulated to all boards. In addition, it would be helpful to have national committees of practitioners for each examination field to advise regarding coverage, prepare suitable questions, and develop new types of questions. Because board memberships change, such a handbook and such advice would greatly speed the indoctrination of new examiners and stimulate all to explore new developments and refinements. The Commission believes that The Institute should urge NCARB to study such a plan (*Recommendation 38*).

Another proposal concerns the character of questions used in most examinations. It has been noted that the NCARB Syllabus stresses questions designed to reveal the candidate's ability to apply his knowledge, skill, and judgment to actual situations that might occur in practice. The theory is that possession of basic facts and skills is presumed to have been accomplished by the beginning of candidacy and that the licensing examination is concerned only with the ability to use them in an effective manner. Thus, many examiners seem to make a clean-cut line of demarcation between "school questions" and "practical questions." While the Commission has not made a statistical study of whether current examinations actually differ in any significant degree from "school questions," it is of the opinion—which many practitioners and teachers also hold—that a large proportion of the boards' "practical questions" are indistinguishable from questions asked in school examinations. The reason is twofold: first, school instruction in professional subjects is meaningless unless practical applications are continuously used to illustrate the operation of principles and theory—in other words, no sound "school question" can be purely theoretical; and, second, since most examiners come to their task with little pedagogical experience, they tend to revert to types of questions which they themselves have answered in school. A comparison of school and board questions would be a revealing study.

Nevertheless, the Commission believes that the point of view contained in the NCARB Syllabus is well taken, and that examiners should make a concerted effort to develop types of questions which would actually conform to its precept. By this means, the registration examination might become a logical and meaningful culmination of the enriched candidacy program envisioned in *Chapter VIII*. One suggestion toward this end has proposed that the entire registration examination should be organized around a single building project and the professional services it would require. No doubt intensive study would reveal many other possibilities.

Recommendation by the Commission of an organized program of candidate training raises other questions regarding its proper relationship to the registration process. It has been suggested in Section 2, *Chapter VII,* that, with more efficient use of the candidate period, its present average length of three years might be safely reduced to two. Again, although admission to candidate enrollment and the issuing of the candidate logbook has been proposed in *Chapter VIII* as automatic for school graduates and by adviser-chapter committee recommendation for others, an alternative is admission by examination. The function of such a test would be to introduce an additional screening process which would bar or discourage those youths who do not meet some new standard of qualification. It might be scheduled at a level equivalent to graduation from architectural school or, like the NBME first written examination, at a level equivalent to the end of the second year of the architectural curriculum.

In the latter case, the fact that most curricula include a very limited amount of professional work in the first two years would mean that the test would have to be based on a combination of beginning technical courses, non-professional general courses, and aptitude tests. This situation thus differs from the basic medical examination which comes after at least 5 years of schooling and is devoted to definite professional courses, such as anatomy, physiology, bacteriology, etc. For applicants who are attending architectural schools, an examination in course work would probably require the gradual standardization of present widely-varying programs in those years. This would be a decided reversal of the policy of non-interference which the profession has thus far maintained in its handling of accrediting. Moreover, if a test on schoolwork is made mandatory, it implies that the examinations conducted in these courses by the schools themselves are, despite accrediting, untrustworthy screening devices which must be reexamined by outside agencies. If the examination minimizes course materials, it would be forced to depend on aptitude tests, the validity of which for architecture has yet to be established. Even if valid aptitude tests can be developed, it would be dangerous to set them up as positive barriers, but, on an advisory basis, as suggested in Section 2, *Chapter VII,* they should prove to be valuable aids. While a formal examination could be used to channel some students into a terminal third year, as described in the same section, it is probable that a more equitable determination would result from careful faculty counseling. Considering all of these points, it would seem preferable to follow the proposal made in the same section, that logbooks be issued and probationary status be granted automatically to all students who are in good standing and ready to enter the third year of an accredited curriculum. For prospective candidates not attending schools, the attainment of an equivalent level of preparation could be controlled by certification by an employer-adviser, or by an appropriate Committee of an AIA chapter. If completion of an organized candidate training program were to be made a board requirement, opportunity of appeal to the board would probably have to be provided so that unofficial professional agencies would not monopolize control of admission to candidacy. In this case, a board might conduct some kind of examination to establish qualification for candidacy.

If a formal examination for admission to candidacy is scheduled after graduation from an accredited school, it has been suggested that board examinations might be safely reduced in content and length. This is represented as feasible because part of the screening function of the board examinations would be transferred to the candidacy admission test. If such an arrangement were to be made mandatory, the results would have to be accepted by the registration boards whether or not they administer the admission test. Thus, the outcome is in reality a *two-stage examination,* a plan which has received considerable attention in recent years. Proponents of the two-stage examination cite the advantages of testing certain subjects as soon as possible after corresponding school courses are completed. In theory, of course, board examinations assume that all of their questions test both theory and the results of practical office experience. Since, however, board questions are so frequently equivalent to those found in school examinations, the distinction and objection now have little significance. Objection is also raised that boards must certify competence as of the date of admission to practice. Since at least 12 acts do not require any written examination at all of graduate applicants, the demand for certification at a particular moment does not seem to arise from any fundamental legal principle, but only from the provisions of the act itself. Indeed, all of the 46 states which accept the NBME certificate, which is based in part on a test given at least 3 years prior to registration, emphatically deny any such legal principle.

The *1950 Survey of Board Members* sounded opinion on these problems. The omission of parts of the registration examination for candidates who had undergone a controlled experience program was opposed by 65 and favored by 44. Of the latter, 10 suggested deletion of questions on practice; 6, history; 5, specifications; and 4, counseling and administration. Of 95 responses, 54 favored requiring an admission examination for all candidates. Twenty-nine favored exempting all candidates who had had 9 or more years of uncontrolled office experience; 30 members favored the exemption of all graduates of accredited schools. As to the two-stage plan, the opinion of registered architects was obtained with regard to the desirable time for examinations in specific subjects. *Table 52* shows that from 83 to 94 per cent of responders thought that examinations in the selection and use of materials, supervision, counseling and administration, and mechanical equipment should be taken after gaining office experience. While 65 per cent held the same opinion with regard to architectural design, 33 would like to require it just after graduation. For structural design, architectural composition, and truss design, 42 per cent called for examinations immediately upon graduation. For history, 64 per cent held the same view. Thus, while all subjects except trusses and history displayed a majority in favor of the status quo and a natural disinclination to change, strong minorities thought earlier tests desirable for architectural and structural design, composition, trusses, and history.

Nevertheless the Commission, by majority vote, favored the retention of a single, post-experience examination, for reasons given in the following resolution, prepared by a special committee after a detailed study of the problem:

"*Whereas,* your committee believes the simple objective of this Commission to be the discovery and recommendation of proposals to improve the professional competence of architects, and,

"*Whereas,* we have considered the experience of the single examination for registration, as well as the implications of the two-stage examination, and find the latter justified only by the convenience of the candidate, and,

"*Whereas,* we believe that this question must be resolved independently of the length of registration examinations, their present quality, or their content,

"*Be It Resolved, Therefore,* that this Commission endorse the single examination for registration that follows a required period of practical experience." (*Recommendation 39*).

It remains to note one other solution which was favored by a minority of at least two members of the Commission. This plan would accept the diploma of an accredited school of architecture as satisfying all written board examinations except one which would deal with such new knowledge and skills as are acquired during an organized program of candidate training. Although this proposal was rejected by the Commission, a summary of the minority position should be of interest in rounding out this analysis of the examination process.

The proposers maintained that, despite the policy announced by the NCARB Syllabus, a large proportion of present board examination questions are directly equivalent and often identical to those contained in examinations conducted within the accredited schools. This view is supported by the large number of practitioners who believe that many parts of registration examinations should be scheduled immediately after graduation (*Table* 52). Since the time allotted to examinations in professional courses in accredited curricula totals from 120 to 140 hours, and since school grades are also based on prolonged faculty observation of students' performances, it is difficult to believe that a more trustworthy appraisal of performance in these same subjects can be obtained by a cursory investigation lasting for a total of only 36 hours. It seems logical to conclude that by giving scant attention and weight to the candidate's academic record—the NCARB Syllabus allots to this record only a part of the 100 points assigned to the personal record section and this in turn constitutes only a tenth of the total of 1000 points assigned to the whole examination—most boards have neglected an index of candidate accomplishment which has higher reliability than their own examinations.

Several objections are usually raised against such a proposal. The claim that a candidate must prove competence at the moment of licensing has already been shown to be controverted by the acceptance of NBME certificates by 46 state medical boards. The argument that board examinations force candidates to make beneficial reviews of school subjects implies that all practitioners should be required to undergo periodic reexaminations for the same reason. The charge that schools vary so markedly in quality that their graduates must be screened by independent tests obviously suggests the untenable conclusion that the accrediting process sponsored by The AIA, ACSA, and NCARB has achieved no validity whatsoever. In reality, no school can be or is now accredited unless its program goes far beyond the level of minimum competence which boards must maintain in order to come within the reasonable limits prescribed by law. The fear that such a plan would impose upon the schools such legal responsibility as to distort their teaching and impair their freedom of approach constitutes an inadmissible suggestion that the schools do not now have, recognize, or fulfill their inescapable obligations to students, the profession, and the community. Finally, the claim is made that the proposal would confer upon graduate-candidates a privileged status inimical to democratic ideas. Actually most acts are heavily weighted in favor of non-graduates who are permitted to count unsystematic employment as the full year-to-year equivalent of the rigorous academic studies in which graduates invest considerable time, effort, and personal funds. The only privilege which graduates are now accorded is to take one-to-three years sooner an examination primarily designed to screen non-graduates.

Such a plan is not new. It has been the basis of British licensure for 70 years. By including an examination on candidacy experience, it exceeds the demands of French registration law and the laws of the 12 American states which register graduates without examination, although usually after a stated period of experience. Moreover, it parallels the conclusion of the Commission on Medical Education that:

"the license to practice should be granted directly on the basis of graduation from a medical school which provides an adequate standard of education and on completion of a satisfactory internship. Such a procedure would be in keeping with present practice in most countries of the world. Adequate safeguards for the protection of educational standards can be provided through inspections and visits to the schools by competent observers and by other devices."[58]

The attitude toward graduates exhibited by most present-day registration laws was already established in Dankmar Adler's first draft of a model act in 1885. At that time, schools and graduates were so few that the possibility of recognizing academic training probably never occurred to him, especially since he himself and all of his colleagues had never experienced such studies. In medicine and law, the early direct licensing of graduates had by that time been abandoned due to the rise of proprietary schools which had become "diploma mills." With the maturing of the schools, graduates have come to outnumber non-graduates, and with the advent of accrediting, academic bargain-basements have been eliminated. Nevertheless, the attitude itself, already embedded in law, still survives in most architectural acts, sustained by tradition and its own momentum.

The *1950 Survey of Board Members* reveals how widely this attitude has persisted. Of 101 responders, 95 thought that their 40 boards give sufficient recognition to graduates. If those states who do not require full examinations of graduates are omitted, 78 members of 31 boards remain. A similar response met the proposal, already noted, to exempt graduates from a candidacy admission examination. In 31 states requiring full licensing examinations, 57 members in 29 states disapproved this suggestion, and only 23 in 15 states accepted it.

It would naturally be supposed that a statistical study of the success of graduates in current board examinations would assist in making a just decision. Data on two states, "A" and "B," have been previously noted, but since they are drawn from an abnormal period, 1944–1949, they cannot be accepted as typical. The *1950 Survey of Board Secretaries* sought the same information and was subject to the same limitations. Of 23 boards which yielded definite replies, 6 observed no difference between the performances of graduates and non-graduates. One of these came from State "A" whose detailed analysis showed that 77 per cent of all passes were earned by graduates, and that 68 per cent of the graduates passed as against 53 per cent of the non-graduates. The responding secretary probably had not seen the actual figures. Seventeen boards observed greater success on the part of graduates, in some states to a remarkable degree, but in only a few cases did replies seem to be other than rough estimates. In any case, confirmation pro or con would involve the establishment of the reliability of the examinations upon which the data are based, and, in addition, the assurance that candidates had received adequate and comparable training during candidacy.

In the context of the present climate of professional opinion, it is hardly to be expected that reorientation of viewpoints upon such a proposal can be rapid. Indeed, any such shift can come about only after prolonged inspection, analysis, and debate. What is important is to remember that the registration process is not an end in itself, but a process which by continuous refinement can be brought to serve that social need which is its only sanction. In carrying out this mandate, the profession is inevitably confronted by many perplexities inherent in all attempts to relate daily life to just principles. It will always be that current frictions tend to cloud perception and appreciation of progress already gained. Despite lingering imperfections, the contribution of registration procedures to public weal has over the past half-century grown steadily. Now that all states have subscribed to its principle, it will at last have the opportunity during the coming decades to prove its utility and wisdom on a continental scale.

NOTES: CHAPTER NINE

[1] Will Durant: *The Story of Civilization*, vol. 1, *Our Oriental Heritage*, 1935, p. 782. Under the Han Dynasty of the 2nd century, B.C., the same examination procedure was extended to the selection of governmental officials (*Ibid.*, pp. 800–801).

[2] A. Castiglione: *History of Medicine*, 1941, pp. 233, 240.

[3] Durant: *op. cit.*, vol. 3, *The Age of Faith*, 1950, p. 246.

[4] E. Kantorowicz: *Frederick the Second*, 1931, p. 356.

[5] Assoc. of American Medical Colleges: *Final Report of the Commission on Medical Education*, 1932, pp. 151, 289.

[6] Adolphe Lance: *Du diplôme d'architecte*, 1855, cited in J. W. Papworth, "An abridgment of M. Lance's Essay, entitled 'On a Diploma in Architecture' with Remarks and Suggestions." (*RIBA Papers*, Session 1855–56, p. 24.)

[7] W. Tite, "Some Remarks on the Present Condition and Future Prospects of Architecture in England" (*Ibid.*, pp. 5–10).

[8] Papworth, *loc. cit.*, p. 25 ff.

[9] R. Rhéné Spiers, "The French Diplôme Architecte and the German System of Architectural Education." (*RIBA Transactions*, 1883–1884, p. 121 ff.)

[10] J. A. Gotch: *The Growth and Work of the RIBA*, 1934.

[11] AAMC: *op. cit.*, pp. 290–291.

[12] Gotch: *op. cit.*

[13] AAMC: *op. cit.*, pp. 153–154; Lester W. Bartlett and Mildred B. Neel: *Compensation in the Professions*, 1933, p. 17.

[14] William Frederick Norwood: *Medical Education in the United States before the Civil War*, 1944, p. 406.

[15] Illinois State Board of Health: *Medical Education and Medical Colleges in the United States and Canada*, 1886, p. 6.

[16] Glenn Sonnendecker and George Urdang, "Pharmaceutical Education" (*Higher Education*, vol. 9, no. 12, February 15, 1953, p. 134).

[17] Illinois State Board of Health: *op. cit.*, p. 6; Milton Friedman and Simon Kuznets: *Income from Independent Professional Practice*, 1945, pp. 8, 21.

18 *Encyclopædia Britannica,* 14th edition, art. "Medical Education," sect. III.

19 AAMC: *op. cit.,* p. 155.

20 Daniel H. Burnham, "What an Architectural Association Should Be." (*Inland Architect and Builder,* vol. 5, no. 2, March, 1885, pp. 20–21); tentative interest in some form of legal control had appeared in editorial comments as early as November and December, 1884 (*Ibid.,* vol. 4, no. 4, p. 49; no. 5, p. 61); at the second meeting of the Illinois State Association, January 23, 1885, Henry Ives Cobb stated: "Before a lawyer is allowed to practice, he must be admitted to the bar, and I hope some day that before an architect is allowed to practice, he will be obliged to be admitted to some bar," to which Adler's reply included the phrase "a person, in order to obtain a license to practice as an architect, must pass an examination . . ." (*Ibid.,* vol. 5, no. 1, February, 1885, p. 6). Adler also observed European laws directly for, during the remodeling of the Exposition Building as an opera house in 1884, or in the first stages of planning the Auditorium in 1886, he visited Europe to study the latest developments in theater design (Thomas E. Tallmadge: *Architecture in Old Chicago.* 1941, pp. 161–162). In 1892, when, as AIA secretary, he defended the attempt to obtain a registration act in New York, he cited the central European acts he had observed. Thus, depending upon the date of this European trip, he was either inspired or reinforced by these European laws.

21 *Ibid,* vol. 6, no. 7, January, 1886, p. 115. This item had not been noted in 1885.

22 *Ibid,* vol. 6, no. 5, November, 1885, pp. 72, 82–83.

23 *Ibid,* vol. 6, no. 8, January, 1886 (intermediate news number), pp. 127–129.

24 State of Illinois: *1st Biennial Report of the Board of Examiners of Architects,* 1899, pp. 4, 7, 9.

25 State of Illinois: *3rd Biennial Report of the Board of Examiners of Architects,* 1903, p. 7.

26 State of Illinois: *5th Biennial Report of the Board of Examiners of Architects,* 1907, p. 11.

27 Data from: Clinton H. Cowgill and Ben J. Small: *Architectural Practice,* 1949 (revised edition), pp. 288–289; dates since 1949 communicated by Fred. L. Markham.

28 F. J. Ludes and H. J. Gilbert: *Corpus Juris Secundum,* 1951, vol. 16, art. "Constitutional Law," Sect. 181; Ernst Freund: *Police Power, Public Policy, and Constitutional Rights,* 1904.

29 As is later noted, 140 board members failed to respond. Seven states were not represented at all.

30 The acts of Vermont and Wyoming became law only in 1951. The secretaries of the following 14 states did not respond: Alabama, Arizona, California, Colorado, Georgia, Idaho, Indiana, Louisiana, Maine, Massachusetts, New Hampshire, North Dakota, Oregon, and West Virginia. No replies were received from board members of the following 7 states: Arizona, Connecticut, Georgia, Idaho, North Dakota, Pennsylvania, and Wisconsin. The states of Arizona, Georgia, Idaho, and North Dakota remained, therefore, entirely unrepresented in the data received.

31 In America, licensure and registration are often used interchangeably, because the process is unified under a single agency. In Great Britain, on the other hand, licensure in the past was performed by the professional college or examining agency, but registration was a governmental function. Licensure is thus the issuing of a permit to practice and/or to use the professional title. Registration is recording of licensees upon an official register.

32 14 secretaries reported such requirements at the state level, but only 2 noted them at the county level. The general absence of county building codes may explain this low figure. 15 secretaries thought compliance was good at the state level, and only 1 was of the same opinion at the county level.

33 The states are: Michigan, Minnesota, South Dakota, Nebraska, Missouri, Virginia, and Tennessee.

34 The number of members were: 9 in Minnesota (the largest reported); 7 in Michigan and Missouri; 6 in Tennessee; and 5 in Nebraska and South Dakota.

35 Kentucky also reported such a provision, but is not included because the state does not have a school offering a professional curriculum. Although Alabama did not respond to the Survey, it is known that the Dean of the School of Architecture and the Arts of the Alabama Polytechnic Institute is by law an ex officio member of the state's registration board.

36 *Encyclopædia Britannica* (14th edition), arts. "Judicial Reform," "Bill of Exchange."

37 Bartlett and Neel, *op. cit.,* p. 15.

38 The Federation should not be confused with the National Board of Medical Examiners which will be discussed later in this Section.

39 Albert J. Harno: *Legal Education in the United States,* 1953, p. 88. These conferences led, in 1931, to the establishment of the National Conference of Bar Examiners (*Ibid.*).

40 Bartlett and Neel, *op. cit.,* p. 15.

41 AIA: *Progress Report, 1950 Survey of the Architectural Profession,* 1951, p. 21.

42 NCARB: *30th Annual Report,* 1951, p. 37. This would be 6.7 per cent of all registered architects in 1950, but the NCARB figure apparently refers to the total number of certificates issued since the establishment of the Council, and does not delete those lapsed by death or other causes, although this number is probably very small. Nevertheless, the true national ratio must be somewhat lower. The *1950 Survey,* however, reported 991 certificate holders among 6605 responders, which gives a ratio of 15 per cent (*Table 46 A*). These 991 certificates were 77 per cent of the NCARB figure. Thus, it seems clear that the 35 per cent sample of the Survey was not as representative in this case as in other aspects of practice.

43 *Ibid.,* pp. 34–35. This grand total gives a national ratio of 18.3 per cent, as against the 23 per cent shown in *Table 45* of the Survey. Although the reservations listed in *Note 42* also apply here, the difference of the ratios is much smaller.

44 *Ibid.*

45 These counts combine data from the *1950 Survey of Board Secretaries* and the 44 acts published in Cowgill and Small (*op. cit.,* pp. 289–345). Michigan reported the inclusion of an age limit, but did not state what it is.

46 The acts used were those published in Cowgill and Small (*Ibid*). The five states omitted were those which had in 1949 not yet enacted registration laws: Kansas, Nevada, New Hampshire, Vermont, and Wyoming. The Kansas act of 1949 does not require a qualifying examination.

47 At least two states—Alabama and Utah—state officially that one year of professional schooling is counted as 1½ years of office training.

48 NCARB: *30th Annual Report,* 1951, pp. 12–13.

49 *Ibid.,* pp. 13–18.

50 NCARB: *Circular of Advice, No. 3,* Part II, Sect. 3.

51 NCARB: *30th Annual Report,* 1951, pp. 38–39.

52 *Ibid.*

53 The criteria listed are used by the Ohio board (NCARB: *30th Annual Report,* 1951, p. 41).

54 AAMC: *op. cit.,* p. 157.

55 *American Medical Directory,* 1950, pp. 107–108.

56 See also Francis T. H'Doubler, "Multiple choice-objective examination. Experience of the Missouri Board of Medical Examiners" (*Proceedings of the 49th Annual Congress on Medical Education and Licensure,* 1953, pp. 52–54).

57 Robert D. Haun and Leo Herbert, "Grading the American Institute of Accountants Examination Papers" (*Accounting Review,* October, 1952, pp. 523–529).

58 AAMC, *op. cit.,* p. 169.

CHAPTER X

Expanding Professional Resources

1. NEW HORIZONS IN PROFESSIONAL COMPETENCE

Preceding chapters of this report have dealt with two of the primary obligations of the profession of architecture: the replenishment of personnel through a well-conceived and systematic program of education, and the attainment of conditions of service under which architects can render most effectively their unique contributions to society. It remains to consider a third responsibility, fully as critical, that of increasing the quality and volume of these contributions by conscious and persistent enhancement of the professional competence of each of its members.

This mandate obviously springs from a strong belief in the necessity, possibility, and opportunity of expanding personal capacity. Architects are particularly sensitive to such a view because the always fresh creative potentialities inherent in the determination of each new plan, structure, and expressive form constitute a constant challenge and incentive to grow in insight and ability. In fact, this is the source of that special appeal which architecture holds for its practitioners.

The improvement of competence has been a recurring theme among architects. In large part, it motivated the formation of professional societies to stimulate, exchange, and spread new ideas. The need for such a forum had become imperative in the early 19th century because isolated practitioners could no longer cope with the problems posed by an architecture and profession which were expanding so rapidly in scope, knowledge, and techniques. It was no accident, therefore, that, as the modern concept of a profession grew, it firmly embraced the obligation of professional growth through collaborative enterprise. Today these same influences are even more compelling. No single individual can hope to master even the most common techniques if he works alone; indeed, the requirement of candidacy is conceived as a safeguard against even the attempt. It follows, therefore, that, since each is nourished by the profession, each in turn owes to it a debt which only personal cooperative participation can repay. This is a fundamental point because a profession exists only in its members.

The basis of growth in competence is twofold. First is the advancement of knowledge and the apprehension of hitherto unsuspected principles. Second is the dissemination of these discoveries so that they can extend the equipment, insight, and capacity of all practitioners and thus be promptly and widely applied to the practical solution of social needs. It is this aspect of professional growth which comprises that wider definition, already noted, of education for practice as a continuing process far transcending the initiation and disciplining of raw recruits. In an era and civilization which have embraced so thoroughly the pursuit and application of innovations and which reveal so clearly the results of dynamic attitudes, architects must likewise explore new frontiers if they are to serve as profoundly as possible their time and their society. The alternative is to surrender architecture to the forces of unimaginative reaction and relinquish its ancient role as a creative and meaningful adventure of the human spirit.

2. RESEARCH IN ARCHITECTURE

The discovery of new knowledge and the formulation of new principles occurs whenever experience is interpreted and organized by intuition or intellection for the purpose of deepening understanding, sharpening sensitivity, and guiding future action. The results may range from casual observation to the construction of a system synthecizing in a single law whole congeries of complex data. The validity of these findings is considered to be established when application under identical conditions produces identical results. In its earliest crude form, this process produced the innumerable rules of thumb which comprised the stock in trade of ancient crafts. In its most potent modern expression, it employs the scientific method in well-planned programs of organized research. Between these extremes lie many gradations of endeavor, none of which should be neglected in the search for insight and capacity.

The application of this process to the realm of architecture began with the first primitive observations of the nature of materials. With the accumulation of experience, it undergirded the structural solutions of such feats as the Roman Pantheon and the intricately vaulted cathedrals of the Middle Ages. The apprehension of the principles of mechanics, first seen in the extensive notebooks of Leonardo and first proved in experiments by Galileo, led to a comprehensive theory by which, with the use of certain assumptions, the future performance of a structural system could be calculated with increasing precision. Architects were quick to employ such discoveries and, on occasion, themselves contributed to knowledge. Soufflot, confronted by imminent failure of the piers of his Paris Pantheon—due to his bold ambition to combine antique grandeur with Gothic litheness—set up beneath its portico the earliest material testing apparatus in order to learn the crushing point of stone. Thomas Ustick Walter, during the construction of Girard College, satisfied himself by careful tests that the introduction of bonding irons in brickwork involved no destructive hazard. The tangibility of construction thus promoted attention to architectural research.

In other respects, architecture resisted such methods. Though formerly buildings were often well designed to accommodate intended use, the needs themselves were usually defined in only the most general terms and building plans were guided by only limited generalized principles. The first great step toward modern planning emerged in the principles of circulation which formed such an important part of the teaching of the *Ecole des beaux-arts*. Gradually, experience in industrial planning gave rise to means of measuring the physical efficiency of buildings, and by World War I these ideas began to be transferred to other building types as well. More recently, the formulation of planning standards has grown apace, and, when logically determined by careful and enlightened research, has greatly increased the utility of buildings.

Even in the aesthetic field, architects have long sought to replace intuition by law. Pythagorean mysticism with its rule of number and proportion has had recurrent applications from Iktinos' vanished treatise to the latest *Modulor*. Belief in such authoritarian doctrines—widespread though they have been—is an act of faith; they have not, and perhaps cannot be demonstrated to possess, ultimate validity. Their very transitoriness has prompted many to deny that aesthetic phenomena can be subjected successfully to analysis and experimental proof. Nevertheless, granting the perhaps unfathomable complexity of the creative act, the effect of the product is most certainly influenced by definite factors susceptible to psychological investigation. From Lipps to Ames, aestheticians and psychologists have made some progress in the general aspects of such situations, but architects have yet to fuse or interpret these findings with their own special knowledge of the process of design.

There are those who feel that the nature of architecture is such that, while it may draw upon other basic disciplines for whatever results of research they can give, it itself does not yield to research methods. It is true that the scope of architecture is so broad that it touches almost every field of knowledge, and architects themselves cannot expect to conduct investigations in each of these fields on a professional level. By the same token, experts in these fields can seldom translate their findings into architectural terms. The solution of this impass is not to forego such assistance, but by joint action endeavor to bridge the gap. Unfortunately, such a cooperative approach has rarely been utilized.

Notwithstanding, there exist some problems which are characteristically architectural in nature, and with which no other discipline is directly concerned. Here, almost entirely, the state of the art remains on an intuitive basis, for the strongly individualistic temper of the profession, its habituation to quick generalization and empirical rationalizations, its correctly conservative attitude toward clients' funds, and its subjection to a pace of performance inimical to preliminary or fundamental experiments have all discouraged the adoption of orderly and comprehensive investigation. Thus, it is that those who see no potential benefits from architectural research argue a priori that architecture—so similar in many ways to the technologies—must stand apart from one of the most potent resources of contemporary experience.

Another cause of resistance may be the fear that criteria born of logic might become an intolerable straitjacket to inspiration. Although some enthusiasts seem to desire to transform design into a mathematical calculation, this is impossible. The thoughtful protagonist of architectural research has never fallen into such a pitfall. Far from envisioning any curtailment of creative synthesis—that mysterious, ultimate act which must remain the province of the designer's intuition, research is intended to clarify and order those preparatory considerations upon which this intuition acts. In short, research is not an end in itself, but rather a valuable reinforcement and stimulus to design. There is always danger, of course, that a little research will stir such enthusiasm as to seduce common sense. It is also true that pretentious mountains of reports have labored to bring forth such gems as: "a tree is a useful *brise-soleil*," or "kitchens should adjoin dining spaces." Nevertheless there is hardly a question arising in daily practice which could not be more effectively answered if subjected to systematic study.

Research in architecture, as in other fields, may concern itself with different types of problems. Walter A. Taylor, Director of Education and Research of The AIA, has presented them clearly:[1]

A. Research in the Basic Sciences

Such research seeks additional basic principles, and its projects are usually confined to one discipline, or closely related disciplines.

B. Research in the Applied Sciences

This type studies the application of a basic science to practical, but usually generalized, problems.

C. Product Development

This type of research aims to solve problems connected with the manufacture and marketing of a specific proprietary product of a single company or of a trade association. It usually combines the solution of manufacturing difficulties, the testing and control of the product, and its design to facilitate sales.

D. Testing

Such research establishes the properties of materials to supply design criteria and maintain controls. On occasion, it serves the other types of research projects.

E. Surveys

This type deals with data gathered from a whole field or from representative samples of a large field. It is widely used in ascertaining data, opinions, or preferences from large groups of people.

F. Documentation Research

This type refers to the organizing of the literature of research to facilitate its use. The assembly of data, its classification, and the preparation and publication of catalogs, bibliographies, and abstracts are characteristic forms.

Mr. Taylor suggests one additional category, entitled *Type X, Composite Research,* which investigates in a problem the interaction of factors involving two or more basic fields or two or more products in combination. In such studies, the effects of variables in one field are observed in others in order to discover an optimal relationship. He emphasizes especially that such a framework would permit and encourage the inclusion of the social sciences on which the architect must draw to ensure that his work will attain validity in human values. He notes that in one sense this is a process very similar to design, and that it is often claimed that "every design problem is a research project." The difference is, however, that "very few projects can afford particularized research in advance of design" and that "there is little reliable carry-over from one project to another."

All of these types can make valuable contributions to architectural knowledge, and none should be neglected. Mr. Taylor discerns in Composite Research particular adaptability to characteristic architectural problems. For all, however, he believes that architects must play a vital threefold role in initiating the questions which research should investigate, in reporting experience from the field, and in applying promptly the answers which thorough investigations yield. He states,

"The architect's greatest responsibility in research is, as in practice, to bridge the gap between the social and physical sciences. He alone is in a position to analyze and report unsatisfactory solutions which may be satisfactory technologically, but fail in terms of human use and reaction . . . The building industry, a craft industry as old as civilization, has accommodated within itself, with a fair degree of success, modern science and technology, but it has been a grafting and remodeling operation. In contrast, the automotive and electronic industries were born full-fledged out of the age of science and the industrial revolution, and have normally and naturally based their evolution on research. Our most important objective is to complete the conversion of our industry into a 20th-century industry, in which research is not a fortuitous adjunct, diversion, or happenstance, but a basic tool and a top priority investment."

It should be noted that the research process remains incomplete until its findings are published for all to see. Without this step, whatever is discovered does not become an integral part of the professional body of knowledge nor can it be subjected to independent analysis and check. In the physical sciences and in many technical fields, particularly in engineering, the obligation to publish the findings of research and field experience has long been recognized. Unfortunately, this aspect of professional responsibility has still to be impressed on architects. This is the reason that, if the performance of architectural services involves investigation and analysis similar to research, it does not achieve the status of genuine research until its reasoning and conclusions are reported for all to study. This demand cannot be satisfied by a glamorized publicity spread or a discretely laudatory magazine presentation which, if taken at face value, would seem to indicate that Olympian omniscience presides over all architectural design. It has been stated that "the world's best research laboratory for building is the composite experience of the architectural profession," but until such experience is made available to the whole profession, it remains a private secret of strictly limited import.

If product research and testing are excepted, architectural research has long been dependent upon the occasional efforts of individuals or special groups. From 1835 on, the Associated Factory Mutual Fire Insurance Companies of New England evolved the first comprehensive program of fire-loss prevention, a body of principles which underlies all present precautionary systems.[2] It was a Chicago architect, Frederick Baumann, who in 1873 first placed the design of foundations on a scientific basis.[3] While skeleton construction goes far back into history, it was W. L. B. Jenney who first achieved its thoroughgoing application in an iron-framed skyscraper. It is on these and many similar American and European contributions that the fundamental bases of modern architecture rest.

Nevertheless, the realization that research must be organized on a permanent and systematic program gradually took form. In 1886, the New England Mutuals opened the first laboratory for research in fire protection.[4] In 1903, Columbia University established the first permanent Fire Testing Station.[5] The logical conclusion, however, was reached in 1920 when Great Britain formed the Building Research Board whose Station since 1925 has been located at Garston, near Watford.[6] The steady flow of able reports on construction and design criteria which it has maintained for more than three decades is the outstanding proof of the value of a concerted attack upon the frontiers of architectural knowledge. Its example has been adopted in many European countries and as far distant as Japan. Most of these programs are supported by government appropriations.

No comparable comprehensive attack on the problem of architectural research has appeared in the United States. The closest approach was the short-lived program of the Housing and Home Finance Agency which in a typical American "emergency" was overnight assigned the Gargantuan task of starting full-blown a vast series of contract research projects on home construction and design. Then, with the same suddenness, the effort was abandoned. The disorganized character of the American building industry has obstructed any coordinated plan of self-supported research. The result has been that such work has devolved on a few privately-financed foundations, contract laboratories, and universities, all supported with precarious and minuscule budgets. Their projects, though limited in scope and scale, have enjoyed considerable influence and amply prove the desirability of a comprehensive program commensurate with the volume of American building operations.

In recent years, there are some indications that American architects are growing restive and that they are coming to the point of demanding methodical correction of this situation. The establishment in 1946 of the Department of Education and Research within The AIA itself was the first overt sign of a new spirit of concern. The formation of the Building Research Advisory Board as a coordinating agency was another. Unfortunately, neither of these agencies commands resources capable of sponsoring or conducting actual research operations. Thus handicapped, each is forced to be content with cooperating, through committees, with other agencies which for the most part are similarly plagued by poverty. The composite picture reveals a stage of development equivalent to that which existed in agriculture, engineering, medicine, and industry more than two generations ago.

The Gordian knot, of course, is finance. It is often suggested that the resources of the manufacturers of building materials and equipment be enlisted. Many of these companies have spent considerable sums in product development, but, important as their work has been, it is futile to expect them to underwrite the kind of comprehensive program of basic investigations that the profession needs. The answer to this dilemma is twofold. First, society itself should be led to recognize the benefits to be derived from building research adequately supported from state and federal revenues. This principle has been fully accepted for more than 70 years in agriculture, for 50 years in engineering, and for 40 years in medicine. Since building surpasses agriculture in dollar volume, increased efficiency in the constructon and design of buildings is at least as important for public welfare as another bushel of corn per acre. If building construction continues in present proportions during the next 15 years, the American people will invest in new buildings alone a sum equal to the average annual Gross National Product for that period. If building expenditures persist at the 1952 level, by 1964 they will total more than the present entire gross public debt. Industries operating at only a small fraction of such a scale are considered hopelessly negligent if they fail to apply the best research techniques to the design, testing, and perfecting of their products. It seems obvious that the American public should take equal precautions to safeguard the quality of the product in which they will invest such enormous sums.

A second source of substantial support should be the whole building industry— architects, builders, the trades, material manufacturers, and investment agencies. The fortunes of all of these groups are closely linked to the effectiveness and worth of their product—the buildings which together they produce. The fact of this compelling common interest might indeed become a catalyst in securing real unity of cooperative effort and support. Since it is a widely accepted practice of proven wisdom for trade associations to finance research by collecting from their members contributions proportional to their gross operations, it is tempting to speculate what would result if this method were applied by the building industry as a whole. In 1952, the national expenditure for new buildings totaled $23¼ billions. If the industry had collected a research levy of one-fifth of one per cent on this sum, it would have secured for that year a research fund of more than $46 millions. The rate of such a levy would be considerably lower than that voluntarily imposed by many trade associations.

Over a period of years, research conducted at such a scale would do much to make empirical and intuitive methods obsolete, provide a body of proven data and principles on which sound design could be based, and raise the quality of the product to new and unprecedented worth. If the improved techniques thus discovered would increase the value or secure a saving of only one penny for each $5 spent, the entire expense would be repaid within a single year and would thus cost exactly nothing. Thereafter, these same technical improvements would continue to yield the same dividends year after year without any additional outlay. While such a prospect seems at first glance fantastically utopian, it is interesting to note that Sweden has already partially applied this principle by imposing on all construction a research levy proportioned to the cost of building labor.

It is obvious that it would be a tremendous task to rally the currently disorganized and sprawling American building industry to such a program of self-financed research, but the potential returns—clearly obtainable if the experience of modern technology means anything at all—certainly make it a worthwhile goal to pursue. The architectural profession is the only possible leader for such a program. The opportunity to urge it constitutes a challenge for every architect, for its promotion combines enlightened self-interest, the enhancement of professional competence as a whole, and, most important, improved service to society. Moreover, for those architects who will master the results of research, there is every reason to suppose that increased capabilities will stimulate wider public confidence and multiply opportunities for service. If present complaints of public indifference to the profession are justified, growth in competence constitutes the best possible means toward improved public relations. This is to emphasize once again that the profession and each of its members can and must make signal contributions to social objectives by carrying out its obligation to raise professional knowledge, skill, and competence to new heights. In no other way can the creativeness which architects profess be also applied to professional life itself.

The Commission regards the development of an active policy fostering architectural research as of paramount importance to the profession's future growth in competence. It believes that The Institute should take immediate steps to formulate such a policy and furnish leadership in its implementation (*Recommendation 40*).

3. PROGRAMS FOR PROFESSIONAL GROWTH

The accumulation of research findings will remain of small influence unless they are quickly absorbed and utilized by all professional personnel. Therefore the provision of effective means of disseminating pertinent knowledge is of prime importance in the advancement of competence and a necessary and proper concern of the profession itself. In a very real sense, the problem becomes one of fostering professional education at advanced levels in the belief that no practitioner can hope to fulfill his best potentialities if he terminates systematic study upon graduation or registration. Mere experiencing of daily practice is not enough; to be instructive the lessons of practice must be systematically reviewed and organized in the light of all available knowledge.

Such a program of advanced professional education must be designed to satisfy several needs. First, it must draw upon all sources of pertinent data—field, office, and laboratory. Second, it should employ all methods to distribute them—from formal courses to informal discussions. Third, it must be gauged for several levels of participation, i.e., candidates, practitioners beginning to take part, and architects prepared for expansion into the most advanced subjects. And, fourth, it should be possible to participate in large or small groups, or on an individual basis.

A number of methods may be suggested for such a comprehensive and flexible program. The well-organized lecture series—accidentally mislabeled *seminars*—provided at recent AIA conventions have presented numerous topics effectively and palatably.

The appeal of this medium has been amply proven by its prompt adoption for regional and state association meetings. Much of this success has been due to the initiative and assistance of The AIA's Department of Education and Research in selecting timely subjects and in seeking out able speakers. It must be recognized, however, that the mixed character of convention audiences, the pressure of brief schedules, and the inevitable commotion attendant on large meetings tend to restrict these lectures to broad general outlines. Despite such handicaps, these series serve a particularly useful function by opening vistas to areas and ideas which might otherwise have escaped notice. Thus they should not only be continued, but also expanded in range and depth.

Local chapter meetings offer equally important educational opportunities, but too often routine business is permitted to crowd out any constructive exploration of new topics. Large chapters have benefited by their greater resources and many have succeeded in maintaining an excellent record of stimulating meetings. Small chapters, however, laboring under restricted budgets which make it difficult to procure wellknown speakers, frequently neglect to transform their special character into positive advantage. Group discussions of apposite subjects led by a few members each assigned a special aspect of the question, or clinical reports of field or office experiences show what a resourceful program chairman can provide. Under such circumstances, the attitude that every meeting to be worth while must present a titilating exposition of some epoch-making subject can be replaced by an exhilarating cooperative discussion in which each participant can contribute to the group effort. No doubt, The AIA could furnish effective aid toward such a development by suggesting topics, syllabi, bibliographies, slide kits, and even library loans for series of coordinated chapter programs. As the results of research become available, such means of dissemination and study can become increasingly important.

The enthusiastic reception of convention lectures suggests the need for organizing special meetings, or *short courses,* to provide more extended and concentrated study of particular phases of architecture and practice. Such short courses have been introduced in many fields and participation in them has mounted in recent years. The medical profession, for example, in a recent year held 720 different specialized courses some of which required tuition fees as high as $1000. Lawyers have likewise found such courses profitable. The annual 3-day Builders' Short Course, conducted since 1945 by the Small Homes Council of the University of Illinois, recently attracted more than 400 contractors, builders, and material dealers from 17 states and Canada. A few such courses have been organized for architects. Those conducted at MIT have met with excellent response, and seem to indicate that the idea should win general support. All schools of architecture are ready to cooperate with professional groups in developing such programs.

In large centers, especially those in which schools of architecture are situated, the opportunity to participate in formal courses on advanced professional topics is often already provided or can be organized. Columbia University has been particularly active in this type of program. Other schools have expressed willingness to cooperate, if sufficient demand is manifested. The presence of a considerable number of like-minded professional men in a large center can also lead to informal groups—more or less permanent—for the purpose of cooperative study. The architectural clubs, such as have long flourished in Boston, Philadelphia, and Pittsburgh, conduct excellent educational programs which, while primarily intended for draftsmen, could easily be expanded to more advanced levels for practitioners. Such a program for young practitioners, organized by the Chicago Chapter of The AIA at monthly sessions, has enjoyed great success.

Outside these centers, the possibility of organizing group studies, while less easy, is far from impossible. The promotion of special study groups might well be a function of AIA chapters. Monthly or semimonthly sessions would probably be feasible in most sections. If a school of architecture is convenient within the area of demand, it might well take the initiative in organizing and administering such courses. Since many universities regularly provide off-campus extension courses by sending faculty members to centers of demand, this, too, presents a feasible solution.

Finally, for those who are completely isolated or for those who prefer individual study, correspondence courses could be arranged. Although some institutions already supply a wide variety of subjects on this basis, technical education of this type has been limited almost entirely to a few proprietary schools, and these operate wholly at an elementary level. Nevertheless, if a well-conceived series of advanced correspondence courses were to be offered, it is highly probable that sufficient demand would be forthcoming to justify the effort. It would seem that The AIA is the appropriate center to take the initiative in such a program, but further investigation may indicate that actual preparation might be contracted for with a school of architecture or with an established proprietary school.

It is patent that the methods just described are equally adaptable to serving the needs of the different classes of professional personnel. For candidates, many phases of office experience could be reinforced by organized study and the pursuit of advanced phases of practice could be fostered. For draftsmen, deficiencies in academic training could be partially remedied. Applicants for registration could join in reviews of previous studies in preparation for examinations. Young practitioners could explore the theory and use of advanced aspects of their art, and mature architects could secure the stimulus of joint discussions of new discoveries found in field and laboratory. It is not difficult to predict the tremendous impact which such a program could have toward raising the general level of competence of the whole profession.

It remains to note another avenue of professional growth—that of purposeful travel. Architects have for centuries been fully aware of the benefits of inspecting outstanding buildings, of studying at first hand their technical features, and of absorbing directly their aesthetic qualities of form and expression. The *1950 Survey* clearly revealed that American architects had sought such experiences energetically both at home and abroad. The rewards of such efforts could be greatly enhanced, however, if the discovery of worthwhile examples could be placed on a less accidental basis and if technical descriptions could be made available to facilitate observation. The local guides[7] issued in connection with the New York and Seattle conventions of The AIA show

416

what can be accomplished. Since such books and pamphlets have a wide public appeal as well, other Institute chapters might find similar publications to be economically practicable and an excellent means of public relations. For certain buildings which naturally attract numerous visitors, individual leaflets setting forth architectural features could serve both public and professional needs.

Any discussion of spreading new architectural knowledge must emphasize the crucial role of the architectural press. In general, news coverage of projects and developments is promptly and effectively reported by American journals. For many types of buildings, special periodicals present innovations and valuable data. Following World War II, publication of new architectural books got under way in the United States, and at present a large variety is available. The greatest number of such books are of a practical nature because books on architectural history, criticism, and philosophy have such limited markets. Such books are expensive to produce, since they must be well illustrated to appeal to architects. Despite this and the fact that trained architectural writers are few and far between, probably 3 to 7 books on criticism and philosophy are published each year by commercial publishers and university presses. The largest gap in architectural publications, in fact, is in the area of technical papers devoted to systematic comprehensive presentation of the design and construction of complete projects and to theoretical and research topics. The profession lacks entirely any medium comparable to the *proceedings* which form such valuable repositories of technical knowledge in the sciences and technologies. Without such means of recording methodically the accumulated experience of the profession, it is difficult to understand how a sound basis of future growth can be obtained.

The Commission believes that the general problem of advanced professional education by which the findings of research can be made familiar to all members of the profession is one of the most important now facing American architects. It also believes that leadership in developing such a systematic and comprehensive program is peculiarly the responsibility of The AIA. It urges that The Institute develop such a program immediately (*Recommendation 41*).

4. GRADUATE STUDIES IN ARCHITECTURE

The foregoing discussions of research and advanced architectural education have emphasized direct solutions organized by the profession itself. It remains to consider what could become the most effective aid to these professional objectives, that is, the development of graduate studies in the schools of architecture. The importance of graduate work in the sciences and technologies is now thoroughly recognized, and its intimate relationship with the rise and prosecution of research in these fields is widely appreciated. Unfortunately, in architecture, the situation is exactly reversed. It is, therefore, necessary to investigate the causes of this neglect, outline the character of an appropriate program, and trace the potential benefits to society, the profession, and the schools.

417

A. Background

The inception of American collegiate architectural education—MIT, 1868; the University of Illinois, 1870; Cornell University, 1871; Syracuse University, 1873; the University of Pennsylvania, 1874; and Columbia University, 1881—coincided with the beginning of a remarkable expansion of graduate studies in American universities. In 1871, there was a total of only 198 graduate students enrolled in the whole United States, but by 1897 this had risen to 4392, by 1926 to 32,500, and by 1948 to 174,432. This extraordinary growth reflected the increasing emphasis placed in almost all phases of modern life upon the organized enhancement of knowledge and the acquisition of more effective skills in its application.

Several factors should have encouraged a parallel development of graduate studies in architecture. The first undergraduate curricula in architecture conformed to the four-year length traditional for liberal arts since the Middle Ages. Students brought to their architectural studies a secondary-school preparation which was often of indifferent quality, dominated by the traditional classical literary bias, and often wholly innocent of mathematics and the basic sciences. The content of early undergraduate curricula in architecture was determined, therefore, not by any standard set by the needs of professional practice, but by the immaturity of the entering student and the arbitrary length of the program.

Almost immediately MIT, Illinois, Pennsylvania, and Cornell recognized the need and attempted to satisfy it. In 1872, Professor William R. Ware, head of the department at MIT, wrote in his annual Report,

"the proposed establishment in the School (MIT), of Post-Graduate courses of study, will be of special advantages to this Department . . . As the professional course in the other Departments of the School is accomplished during the Third and Fourth (undergraduate) Years, we have hitherto, in order to conform to them, had to set down the architectural work also, under the form of a two years' course; but to give notice that hardly in any instance could two years suffice to complete it. The extension of the period of study for an indefinite term after the regular course is finished will relieve us from this embarrassment. It will now be possible by exacting a certain amount of vacation-work and somewhat diminishing the work set down to be done in connection with the classes in Civil Engineering, to give the regular students of these two years a sufficient knowledge of the elements of Architecture not to discredit the school —not enough to make them architects, even in the sense in which their fellows become at once Chemists and Civil Engineers,—but enough for Bachelors of Science, enough to enable them to pursue their further studies, in offices and in this Department, to the best advantage. This undergraduate work will thus be complete in itself, including all that relates to the scientific basis of the profession, giving all that an architect needs to know of Mathematics, Chemistry, Physics, Geology, and Engineering, with as much of Architectural Drawing and of Architectural Design as can reasonably be compressed within the regular curriculum of a school of science.

418

"The Post-Graduate course will then take up such special scientific topics as may prove desirable, with something of Practice; but it will be chiefly occupied with advanced work of composition and design, in continuation of that begun in the Third and Fourth (undergraduate) Years. This work is perhaps more germane to a school of Art than to a school of Science. But it is a work greatly in demand, and one which we may ourselves take in hand with great advantage to our own undergraduates, to more advanced students, wherever trained, and to the community. . . .

"But for the main work of the Post-Graduate course, the study of Architecture as a branch of the Fine Arts, no period of time can be fixed, and no special curriculum assigned. Architecture in this respect is not an exact science, and the methods appropriate to a school of science are less pertinent to this part of the work than those of a school of art. Still it may be possible, without attempting to set any limit of time, nor to fix upon any course of study as in itself sufficient, to prescribe certain tests of attainment, as is done at the *Ecole des beaux-arts,* by which the further honors of the schools shall be governed. Just what these honors shall be, and by what rules they shall be awarded, may best be left for time and experience to determine."[8]

Ware's pioneering statement was surprisingly comprehensive, but the program he envisaged did not mature for many years. In 1877-78, the MIT catalog listed five graduate students in architecture, four of whom held undergraduate degrees from Harvard. Three had entered MIT in 1876. None attained a degree in architecture, and they were probably engaged in elementary professional courses to supplement their training in liberal arts at Harvard. The only graduate degree offered at MIT in the 1870's was that of Doctor of Science.

The first graduate degree in architecture in the United States was awarded by Cornell in 1876. The recipient was George Holt Berry, who had obtained his baccalaureate in 1874. The graduate degree was "Architect," comparable in terminology to those conferred by departments of engineering, and it called for a two-year program of study beyond the baccalaureate. No details of the component courses were carried in the early catalogs. Despite his priority in graduate work in architecture, Berry became in 1876-78 Superintendent of Schools and high school principal in Duluth, Minnesota, then turned to farming, and finally established himself as a merchant in Harriman, Tennessee.[9]

In 1876 the Department of Drawing and Architecture of the University of Pennsylvania published a two-year curriculum in architecture leading to a Master of Science degree. The undergraduate curriculum had been established in 1874 in the Department of Science under Thomas W. Richards, a Philadelphia architect. In the following year, upon receipt of a handsome endowment, the department became the Towne Scientific School and its educational program was immediately expanded. The description of the graduate curriculum in architecture read:

"Freehand sketching of executed works and buildings under course of erection—Measuring and description—original designs, with plans, elevations, sections, and perspective drawings in different styles of architecture—specifications—description of plans, indicating the advantages and reasons for specific arrangements—full-size working drawings of original designs—estimates and contracts—quality of material—heating and ventilating."

Since the undergraduate curriculum provided design exercises only in the fourth year, it is evident that the graduate program was intended primarily as an extension of this phase of the work. The emphasis on plan analysis was prophetic. Review of the university's annual catalogs reveals that, up to the reorganization of architectural instruction in 1890, only a handful of students enrolled for undergraduate work and that none at all entered the graduate program.

The second and third graduate degrees were conferred by the University of Illinois, in 1878 on Nathan Clifford Ricker, and in 1880 on Clarence H. Blackall. Ricker had completed his undergraduate curriculum in February, 1873, and had thus become the first architectural graduate in the United States. Blackall had received his undergraduate degree in 1878. Both graduate degrees were designated "Master of Architecture," as provided by action of the Board of Trustees in 1877. The requirements for this degree, like those in engineering, could be satisfied either by a one-year program in residence, or by a term of successful practical experience, the completion of an approved program of non-resident study, and the submission of an acceptable thesis. This latter option, which both Ricker and Blackall elected, was intended to stimulate and reward the continuation of organized studies as the graduate began active participation in the field. It thus established the precedent for the later "professional degrees," so widely used in engineering, and so called to distinguish them from the normal academic graduate degree earned in residence. While the administration of such degrees has presented difficulties that have tended to diminish their use in recent years, they long served as useful devices to encourage graduates to plan for professional growth under academic guidance.

Neither Syracuse or Columbia attempted graduate work in their early years.

Despite these tentative beginnings, there were a number of factors which long prevented American architectural schools from exploiting the idea of professional studies at the graduate level. Gradual improvement in secondary-school preparation reduced somewhat the delay in beginning professional subjects. The undergraduate curriculum was slowly freed of courses extraneous to the needs of architects, permitting the inclusion of more professional work, and thus relieving the immediate pressure for a graduate year. More than this, however, meager budgets, inadequate for even the undergraduate program, could not provide the additional staff or facilities required for advanced work. Few, if any, students could afford the extra cost of graduate training. The most potent factor of all, however, was the absence of any tradition of graduate study. Indeed, the idea of even undergraduate training in architecture was at this time hardly accepted by architects. Ware, in his report, had cited the only possible precedent, oblique as it was, in the practice at the *Ecole des beaux-arts* of students continuing to take design *projets* long after satisfying the school's minimum requirements. But the *Ecole* sponsored no advanced courses to carry the students beyond their basic undergraduate courses, nor did it recognize additional effort except by listing the student's awards upon his permanent record. Motivation was supplied by hopes of success in the competition for the *Grand Prix de Rome*. Finally, the avowed aim of American architectural schools of preparing students to begin practical experience in actual offices as soon as possible discouraged prolongation of school days. Contemporary practitioners viewed graduates with suspicion, and four years of school training were deemed a maximum indulgence. In this they expressed, in common with engineers, a characteristic reverence for practical experience, and the administrative association of most of the early architectural departments with schools of engineering naturally emphasized this point of view.

During the ten-year interval from 1880 to 1891, no further graduate degrees were awarded at Cornell or Illinois, nor did MIT, Columbia, or Pennsylvania yet confer their first. Beginning in 1891, however, the idea of graduate study began to take hold. In that year, Cornell awarded an M.S. in Architecture to F. L. Robinson, who later

	Cornell	Illinois Resident	Prof.	MIT	Columbia	Penn.	Total
1891	1				1		2
1892	—				1		1
1893	—			1	—		1
1894	1		2		1		4
1895	1		1	1	—		3
1896	1		—	2	—		3
1897	1		1	2	1		5
1898	—		1	1	—		2
1899	—		—	1	1		2
1900	—	1	—	—			1
1901	—		—	1			1
1902	—		—	3	1	1	5
1903	1		2	5	—	—	8
1904	1		1	4	1	—	7
1905	1		1	9	1	—	12
1906	1		1	3	2	—	7
1907	1		—	5	1	1	8
1908	3		1	—	1	—	5
1909	1		2	6	—	—	9
1910	—	1	3	5	—	—	9
1911	—	—		5	—	5	10
1912	2	1		4	—	6	13
1913	1	1		4	—	8	14
1914	1	2	2	3	—	10	18
Total	18	6	18	65	12	31	150

24

practiced in New York City, and in the same year Columbia conferred its first graduate degree in architecture, a Master of Arts, to John Storm Appleby. In 1893, MIT gave its first architectural Master of Science degree to P. A. Hopkins. Also in 1893, Illinois announced a comprehensive program of resident graduate study and in the following year revived in a more vigorous manner the use of the professional degree, Master of Architecture. Likewise in 1894 George Washington University initiated graduate work. In 1897 Pennsylvania introduced its first graduate curriculum. The subsequent growth of graduate studies at these institutions is clearly seen in the table, shown on the preceding page, of graduate degrees awarded from 1891 to 1914.

Between 1900 and 1914, nine more schools of architecture began to offer graduate curricula: Harvard and Washington, 1902; Armour, 1904; Syracuse, a "professional degree," 1906; Notre Dame, 1908; Texas, 1909; Ohio State, 1912; California, 1913; and Michigan, 1914. In 1906, Harvard placed its professional curriculum entirely on a graduate level, giving the Master of Architecture as a first professional degree. The change ensured that students entering professional studies would have a strong background of general education, but it did not affect the character of graduate professional studies themselves. A similar, but more complicated, plan was adopted at California in 1913.

No detailed statement of the content of the graduate curriculum at Cornell appeared in its catalogs during the 1890's. The Illinois plan for resident graduate study, published in 1893, listed the following topics from which the student's program was to be selected:

Majors
1. Construction of Extensive Wooden Buildings.
2. Recent Uses of Stone, Brick, and Terra Cotta in Architecture.
3. Metallic Skeleton Buildings.
4. Fire-resisting and Fireproof Buildings.
5. Sanitation of Public and Semi-public Buildings.
6. Researches on the Evolution of Architectural Styles.
7. Higher Application of Graphic Statics.
8. Heating and Ventilation of Large Buildings.
9. Higher Studies in Architectural Design.
10. Researches and Experiments in Applied Esthetics.
11. Translation of an Approved Technical Architectural Work from French or German original.

Minors
1. Stereotomy Applied to American Problems.
2. Examinations of Heating and Ventilation of Buildings.
3. Higher Workshop Practice.
4. Photography for Architects.
5. Methods of Reproducing Drawings, Specifications, etc., for Architects.
6. Higher Problems and Methods in Perspective.

7. Practice in Estimating, Specifications, etc. for Large Buildings.
8. Higher Industrial Design.
9. Advanced Water Color Painting.
10. Study of Office Methods and Arrangements.
11. Any Major offered in the College of Engineering.

The variety and contemporary pertinence of these topics is striking, and they reflected the life-long devotion of Ricker to architectural scholarship. Notwithstanding its ambitious character, it was seven years before Ralph W. Weirick graduated in this program in 1900.

The Illinois curriculum was reorganized in 1906 by establishing a number of courses treating subjects previously listed as majors. Active promotion of the program awaited the arrival in 1910 of Frederick M. Mann, who succeeded Ricker as head of the department. Mann had received his Master of Science degree at MIT in 1895, the second such degree awarded there, and, in his four years at Illinois, he turned the emphasis from the "professional degree" to resident graduate studies. This direction was continued after 1914 under L. H. Provine, who became head of the department when Mann returned to the University of Minnesota.

At MIT, the introduction of graduate studies, foreseen by Ware, was finally achieved under Frank Ward Chandler, who had risen from Ware's assistant to head the school in 1888.[10] Some indication of the nature of the graduate program carried by six of the first eight students between 1893 and 1899 is indicated by the subjects of their theses. One dealt with building materials, a second with steel-framed domes, and four with historical topics. Beginning in 1901, however, the graduate program was reoriented almost wholly to design, and all theses consisted of large-scale problems in design. The revised graduate program was published for the first time in the Annual Catalogue for 1902–03, as follows:

First Term	*Second Term*
History and Art of the Italian Renaissance	Advanced Architectural Design: Thesis
Advanced Architectural Design	Philosophy of Art
Advanced Composition	History and Archaeology
Advanced Construction Design	Advanced Decorative Design: Life Class
Building Laws and Contracts	Composition in Rendering
Advanced Decorative Design: Life Class	
Composition in Rendering	
Aesthetics	

No doubt the establishment of this new curriculum was strongly influenced by the presence and brilliance of Desiré Despradelle, who had succeeded Létang in 1892 as chief critic in design.

423

The pattern of the graduate curriculum at the University of Pennsylvania first appeared in the catalog of 1897–98. It consisted of:

	1st Term	2nd Term
Antique (drawing)	4 hrs.	4 hrs.
Water Color Rendering	6	6
Ornament	9	6
Design	30	30

This arrangement continued with slight modifications until 1912, when the program was elaborated to include other areas of interest. As described in the 1913 catalog, it provided four graduate options:

I. *Architectural Design*
    Majors: Design, Life Drawing, Water Color Rendering
    Minors: History of Architecture, History of the Fine Arts, Construction

II. *Architectural History and Criticism*
    History of Architecture, Painting, and Sculpture
    Philosophy of Architecture
    Ancient Languages and History
    Life Drawing
    Water Color

III. *Architectural Construction* (for students who had taken the undergraduate option in Design)
    Major: Construction
    Minor: Materials of Construction, Testing Laboratory.

IV. *Architectural Construction* (for students who had taken the undergraduate option in Construction)
    Major: Construction
    Minor: Design, or History of Architecture

The third and fourth options no doubt witness the influence of Thomas Nolan, who in 1904 had inaugurated the undergraduate option in Architectural Engineering. Unfortunately, no records are easily available to reveal the popularity of these options, but no doubt the design option remained by far the most favored. Pennsylvania's expanded offerings at the graduate level, the renown of Paul Cret as critic in design, and especially the establishment of three graduate fellowships in 1911, all combined to raise Pennsylvania into an outstanding graduate center in the second decade of the 20th century.

Columbia, like Cornell, offered no fixed curriculum at the graduate level, preferring to adjust the program to the individual student. It is surprising, however, that despite Ware's long-expressed interest in graduate studies and the metropolitan location of the school, Columbia during this period attracted relatively few graduate students. On the other hand, Columbia was unique among the schools in offering the opportunity for a program of studies leading to the Doctor of Philosophy degree. Two candidates enrolled in this program, Charles T. Mathews in 1895–96 and 1896–97, and Alexander R. McKim in 1897–98, but neither completed the requirements for the degree.

Thus, the later pattern of American architectural education at the graduate level was set during the two decades, 1891–1914. Except in the history and construction options offered at Pennsylvania, the graduate year was dominated by work in advanced design. Some auxiliary studies in drawing, history, and construction were usually included, but the demands of design left little time for real graduate scholarship in these fields. Essentially, the function of the program was to extend and intensify the student's undergraduate experience in design, free of the distractions crowding the baccalaureate schedule, and concentrating every effort to solving creative exercises of large scope and ambitious style. Just as the advanced student at the *Ecole* dreamed of the *Grand Prix,* so the American graduate student was encouraged to regard graduate design as a preparation for the Paris and Rome prize competitions. The refinement of skills necessary to this kind of design—the digestion of programs, the selection of *parti,* the working out of details of plan and elevation, and facile delineation—was valued alike by student and practitioner. Nevertheless, despite these contributions, this concept of the potentialities of graduate studies was unnecessarily narrow.

Some indication of the state of graduate studies in American architectural schools in 1930 is obtained from the Bosworth-Jones report of that year.[11] Twenty-two of the 52 existing schools listed a total of 194 candidates for the master's degree. This included, however, some 86 students at Harvard, Princeton, and California, for whom the master's degree would be a first professional degree. The total number of graduate students, in the normal sense of the term, that is, those who are candidates for a second professional degree, was 108. This was 1.84 per cent of the total of 5890 candidates for the first degree in architecture and architectural engineering. The largest graduate enrollments were: Illinois, 26; MIT, 16; Columbia, 15; Pennsylvania, 7; Washington University, 7; and Oregon, 6. At twelve of the 22 schools, the graduate program constituted a sixth year following a five-year undergraduate curriculum. At the other 10 schools, it formed a fifth year, but in these schools most of the graduate students had received their baccalaureates from the same school so that in effect the graduate year was more or less the equivalent of the senior year of the five-year curricula. Bosworth and Jones noted that those schools which had adopted five-year undergraduate curricula believed that their graduate enrollment had declined as a result of the change.[12]

In characterizing the graduate work of the period, Bosworth and Jones stated that "The terms 'advanced study and research' are a little misleading if understood with the connotation such terms usually have when used by the academic scholar. Research work is sometimes carried on, but for the most part the work of the architectural post-graduate differs only slightly from that of the regular fifth-year undergraduate. He usually does the same problems. He is expected to do them better . . ."

During the 1930's, the emphasis on design in the graduate year was heightened by the appointment at Harvard of Walter Gropius, who organized a master class which absorbed the students' entire program. Design, in this case, was interpreted in its broad sense and included extensive program analyses and construction studies. Gropius devoted all his own teaching to the graduate class of 16 students. A similar situation developed at the Illinois Institute of Technology under the leadership of Mies van der Rohe.

Another development in the 1930's was the new enthusiasm for planning as an extension of the older field of city planning and civic design. In embracing this new program many schools diverted graduate students who had formerly continued their architectural studies. In view of the intimate connection between architecture and planning, this new educational fashion produced much good, but the growth of direct graduate studies in architecture itself was not facilitated.

World War II brought all architectural education to a virtual halt, but after its cessation veteran educational subsidies not only deluged undergraduate curricula, but also encouraged many graduates to enter graduate school, both to refresh their professional skills and to extend their competence to higher levels. The total graduate enrollment approximately doubled, and would no doubt have reached higher levels but for restrictions imposed by the limited staff and facilities available in the emergency. In 1951, although the crest of the veteran wave had passed, the total number of graduate students in the 29 schools reporting such work in architecture and architectural engineering was 239. This was 1.9 per cent of the candidates for the first professional degree, an increase in the ratio of only 3.5 per cent over 1930. In 1949, the ratio of graduate to undergraduate students in engineering was 8.8 per cent, more than 4½ times the ratio for architecture. Of the 239 architectural graduate students, the University of Illinois had 27, the Illinois Institute of Technology 24, MIT 18, Harvard 16, Florida 12, Houston 12, Yale 11, and Columbia 10. In all these schools, design formed the principal core of almost all student programs, but in some of them additional courses dealt with other phases of the profession. At Columbia, Talbot Hamlin's course in the Literature of Architectural Theory is an outstanding vehicle for strengthening the student's intellectual understanding by analyses of the historic systems of architectural thinking. At MIT, the graduate course in architectural acoustics under R. H. Bolt provides important technical knowledge usually neglected in undergraduate years. At Harvard, outstanding graduate courses in architectural history are available. And at Illinois, graduate courses in Advanced Planning Principles, Urban Housing, Advanced Structural Theory, and Building Construction enrich the students' experience.

It remains to note the occasional use of graduate studies in architecture for the doctoral type of program. Such curricula, inspired by those developed in the fields of liberal arts, science, and the technologies, have been largely confined, for architecture, to historical investigations. The use of the degree for creative work in the arts has been accepted by very few institutions, and only once in architectural design. Three Ph.D.'s have been conferred by Catholic University for studies tracing the development of some type of building, usually religious. Columbia conferred a Ph.D. in 1929 for a study tracing the development of architectural theory, and in 1941 for a history of collegiate architectural education in the United States. Harvard inaugurated a program in 1942 to be administered by the Department of Architecture. Two degrees were conferred. Although the program was not intended to be restricted to historical topics, and several candidates began non-historical dissertations, the two dissertations completed under its aegis dealt with the use of iron in building construction and the development of railroad stations. Unfortunately, for various reasons the program was permitted to lapse. In most universities, when doctoral programs are proposed on professional architectural topics, the programs must be taken in academic divisions alien and often unsympathetic to the needs and methods of architecture. Although there are innumerable architectural problems investigations of which would promise important contributions to professional knowledge, these opportunities have been almost wholly neglected by schools of architecture due to their exclusive preoccupation with only one phase of professional work, design. This situation needs serious consideration.

The *1950 Survey* revealed that 10 per cent of all registered architects of the United States hold a second professional degree. The highest rankings among those institutions which granted these second degrees were:

MIT	12.6%	California	5.9%	Washington U.	3.0%
Harvard	11.5	Princeton	5.1	Yale	2.9
Pennsylvania	10.7	U. Illinois	5.0	Rice	2.7
Columbia	6.2	Cornell	4.1	Carnegie	2.3
				Georgia Tech	2.3

In the field of engineering, 13.35 per cent of all personnel hold master's degrees and 3.05 per cent hold doctoral degrees.

B. The Aims of Graduate Studies in Architecture

Programs of graduate studies in architecture necessarily demand considerable expenditures of effort and funds on the part of both students and schools. Such programs must therefore return substantial benefits to student, school, and the profession, if they are to succeed. Well-defined aims and functions will do much to encourage future growth.

The most obvious aim of graduate study is the long-accepted function of extending the undergraduate preparation for professional practice. Even with undergraduate curricula now standardized at five years, the schedule is inevitably inadequate to compass the expanding skills and knowledge demanded by a rapidly changing profession. Preparation for life can never be mastered in a few years; it must continue throughout life. It may be argued, of course, that the five-year undergraduate program is a sufficient term to spend in the artificial climate of school, and that upon completing it the student would best begin active participation in actual office work. This is the same argument used long ago by practical men who then opposed the first undergraduate schools. It is acknowledged that, for many graduates, undergraduate courses will provide all that they can absorb or apply for many years to come. Nevertheless, there are also those who can take advantage of further academic training. Just as formal education at the undergraduate level is more efficient in time and effort than unorganized practical experience, so, for those who are ready to profit from them, graduate studies can carry them faster and more directly to advanced knowledge and skills. For them, the additional time required for graduate work will mean more rapid progress in practice later on. Thus, the function of graduate study as further preparation for practice can be easily accepted.

Secondly, graduate study is an invaluable method of training teachers for the professional schools. The validity of this practice does not lie in the acquisition of a graduate degree with which to ornament the school catalog or enrich an accrediting questionnaire. It rests in the proven principle that a skillful teacher must know and understand as much as possible about both his special subject and the general field of which it is a part. A teacher must master more than just the facts and principles he will teach in a specific course. He must command a wider range from and by which he can draw a fresh, pertinent, and organized selection of the materials which comprise the subject at hand. This is the skill which distinguishes an able and inspiring teacher from the dull drill-master who is only a page or two ahead of his class in a cut-and-dried textbook. Since the recruitment of teachers for professional courses must usually be from the profession itself, and not from personnel especially pre-trained for educational duties, it follows that the preparation of architectural teachers must often be concurrent with their teaching. There will, therefore, be a continuing need for graduate programs which can assist these teachers to grow in knowledge and pedagogical skills. This does not mean that professional teachers can forego direct experience in the profession they serve, but it does signify that such direct experience does not guarantee a fully satisfactory teaching performance, and it suggests that every teacher could benefit from an appropriate program of graduate studies.

A third area in which graduate programs can serve the advancement of architecture is by fostering investigations from which new knowledge can be gained, and by training the personnel required to carry out such investigations. In a nation which accepts in almost every other field the principle of specialized research, architecture has in most of its aspects remained stolidly aloof on the ground that judgment based on systematic analysis is inferior to free-wheeling intuition. Fortunately, this diffidence has been somewhat masked by adopting the results of research done by others. Architects have used and will no doubt continue to use the new materials, structural systems, and equipment developed by structural, mechanical, and electrical engineers, but architectural progress, even in such material aspects, would be more direct and effective if the architect's point of view helped to guide and control such developments. In other types of problems, not susceptible of commercial exploitation, research has been conspicuous by its absence. There is hardly a so-called basic principle that has been demonstrated unequivocally or that does not demand concentrated analysis, experiment, and systematic testing. It is difficult to understand how so essential and widespread an endeavor as architecture has so long escaped the most fruitful discipline of our present civilization.

Some signs of awakening are now current. The investigation of natural lighting and ventilation in schools being pursued at the A. and M. College of Texas, the study at Illinois of various problems centering around the single-family detached dwelling, the work at MIT on architectural acoustics, and a few other examples indicate that the turning point has been reached. Not only have these projects proved the value of the results of research, but they also have revealed the urgent need for personnel trained to conduct such investigations. Moreover, it is increasingly clear that, if this unfortunate situation is to be corrected promptly, the profession must press for architectural research programs centered at leading architectural schools, following the long-established precedent of engineering and agricultural experiment stations. It is ironical that it was an architect, Nathan Clifford Ricker, who, as Dean of the College of Engineering at Illinois, established in 1903 the first engineering experiment station in the United States. Half a century later, architecture still lacks a program, facilities, and personnel to answer fundamental questions. The solution is intimately linked with the development of graduate studies in architecture.

In considering the three aims just stated, a question may arise regarding the degree to which graduate architectural students should be permitted to follow specialized studies. Some critics will object that a high degree of specialization will contribute little to general competence in practice. It is clear, of course, that, if the sole aim of graduate study is further preparation of the individual student for practice, a general approach must be stressed. It is for this reason that existing graduate programs are so thoroughly dominated by courses in design. But even in these courses, design is studied, not in abstractions, but in exercises dealing with specific problems and types of buildings. Further, the frequent use of specific subject-matter courses, for example, in housing, indicates that detailed study of a particular type of building does not endanger the student's general competence, but, on the contrary, improves it by giving him the valuable experience of a deeper and more comprehensive consideration of the subject than is possible in the usual limited design problem. It should also be noted that, if a design course concentrates on a single problem over a whole semester, it becomes in effect a course on the type selected. Moreover, when special subject-matter courses are available, it is perfectly possible and indeed highly advantageous to correlate the work in design with them. In this way design can be supplemented and reinforced, and, by being relieved of the burden of dealing with most of the theory of the problem at hand, it can emphasize more fully other phases of the work.

Despite the importance of graduate study as preparation for practice, and this aspect will probably continue to be selected by most students, it should be recognized that the other aims described above are legitimate functions which should be provided for in any well-rounded graduate program. For these aims, special knowledge and skill are their *raison d'etre*. Even though a teacher can use and should have all the general competence he can acquire, he also needs opportunity to enlarge his command of his special field. For those who will enter research work as a vocation, specialization is the essence of their calling. There is no such thing as "general research." To find the answer to a specific question requires sharp concentration on its conditions and factors. It is the need of the general practitioner for such specific knowledge, and his own lack of time and facilities to seek it out, that creates the necessity for specialized personnel.

The graduate program, therefore, cannot be directed exclusively to either general practice or specialization. Rather it must provide for both. In doing so, however, both types of students, by contacts with their fellows, should absorb something of the other approach and thus escape the narrowness which exclusive preoccupation with either surely imposes.

C. Graduate Curricula in Architecture

Fulfillment of the three functions of graduate studies just described suggests two types of graduate curricula.

First is the advanced subject-matter and higher skills level characteristic of present curricula leading to the Master's degree. This program should be designed to build new knowledge and new techniques upon a solid foundation of undergraduate training and some practical experience. It should provide a number of options in order to meet the needs of future practice and of teachers, and it should expose all candidates to some preliminary training in research, for it in turn will serve as the recruiting ground for research personnel. While it is probable that for various reasons, personal and financial, the normal length of the master's program must, for the present time, be kept at one academic year, it is also possible that some students will find it advantageous to complete more than one option, or that some practitioners will return to acquire competence in some phase, either newly developed or newly needed. To ease the problem of attendance by candidates and practitioners, it is possible to conduct some courses at times and places convenient to these participants. For schools located in metropolitan centers no difficulties would be encountered. Indeed, some schools, like Columbia, already offer a number of courses of this kind. But even more secluded schools could meet the problem by the extension course method commonly used by schools of engineering, education, and agriculture. Once the value of such courses is demonstrated, adequate participation will be forthcoming, and it is entirely possible that some of these extension students will be led to undertake a full program of resident graduate study. If the educational needs of professional teachers are to be satisfied, provision for summer graduate courses in the several subject fields should be made, similar to those conducted at Harvard in the late 30's for teachers of architectural history. The stimulus to be derived not only from top-quality courses, but also

430

from free discussion with colleagues, can be a most exhilarating and beneficial experience.

Options in the master's curriculum should include majors in advanced design, advanced structural theory, building construction, building equipment, theory, and history. A planning option might be added. A course in the philosophy and methods of architectural education would be useful for teachers. Minors in each option could be selected from one or more of the other options.

The second type of graduate curriculum provides an extended and intense training in the methods and materials of architectural research. In general, such a curriculum would presuppose completion of a master's program and would correspond in character to the Ph.D. program developed in the liberal arts, sciences, and technologies. Like such programs, it would normally include three stages. After the general area of investigation is selected, the candidate would first fill in gaps in his equipment with additional courses, in architecture or other disciplines, which are essential to his research. In the second phase, he would gain experience in the research process by undertaking a series of limited problems. These problems may or may not, at the discretion of his adviser, relate directly to his ultimate research project, but in handling smaller topics he should gain the skill and judgment he must have for more complex problems. Finally, in the third phase, he would take up an original investigation calculated to demonstrate his ability to analyze a problem; collect, weigh, and interpret authentic evidence; reach a valid conclusion; and present his findings in a lucid report. Although undergraduate and master's themes and reports have the same basic aim, the extension of the process to the grand scale of an original contribution raises the doctoral problem to major proportions. Successful completion of the project should indicate that the candidate is capable of carrying out further research independent of advice or supervision, a capacity which is the accepted goal of the doctoral program. The program would usually require a period of two years beyond the master's degree, but under special circumstances a shorter or longer schedule might be more feasible.

D. Graduate Courses

To implement the curricula just described will require a considerable expansion beyond present graduate course offerings. For the full program five types of courses suggest themselves.

I. Advanced "subject-matter" courses.

In these courses or course sequences, various phases of architecture would be dealt with at a much more intensive scale and comprehensive scope than is possible at the undergraduate level. The aim is to add to the student's understanding, expand his horizons, and encourage rigorous thought on the problems at hand. In general, in the first courses in each sequence, the instructor would organize and present the material, but in the later courses the use of the seminar method would place increasing responsibility upon the individual students.

431

Course sequences should include the following areas:
a. Theory
b. Various building types
c. Advanced building construction
d. Structural theory
e. Building equipment
f. Architectural and decorative composition
g. History
h. Practice
i. Materials and methods of architectural research
j. Teaching methods

While each sequence should extend over at least one year, it would be possible to vary the offering by scheduling certain courses in alternate years.

Some of the courses would profit by the use of visiting specialists, from the architectural profession, related vocations, or from other divisions of the university. In certain courses, laboratory demonstrations or group experiments should be used as direct teaching devices for the problems and methods under consideration.

Subject-matter courses are of particular importance in the master's curriculum.

II. Advanced Design Courses

This type of course is the most widely used in graduate study today. In most institutions, it varies little from the work of the fifth undergraduate year, but in a few instances it has been given special graduate character. Occasionally, this means a close approximation of design as practiced under office conditions. Frequently, this means in turn that "design" is taken in its broadest sense as including working drawings, details, and specifications. This is especially true of the final term which is often devoted to a design "thesis." If, however, as will be discussed later, applicants for the graduate program are encouraged to acquire some office experience before returning to school, the inclusion of office practice in the graduate design course can be greatly diminished and greater emphasis can be devoted to exploring advanced principles and methods. In any case, the standard of performance in graduate design should approach more and more that of professional practice.

III. Graduate Seminars and Core Courses

In providing a number of curricular options and course sequences from which the individual student may select according to his particular talents, interests, and ambitions, there is some danger that the valuable experience of being an intimate part of the whole graduate group may be obscured. The stimulation derived from discussion with one's fellows is often an important, and always an enjoyable, means of relating oneself to the whole field. For this reason, graduate curricula in architecture might well adopt the idea of the graduate seminar, which has been used so effectively in other disciplines. In it, on an informal or formal basis, occasion is provided for students to hear a fellow expound his own particular project and join in discussing it. In time, all students can thus become familiar with what each member of the group is doing. Such a seminar also gives opportunity to discuss various isolated topics with faculty or visiting lecturers.

Another device to foster cohesiveness is the practice of requiring all students to take one or more core courses. By this means a degree of unity in point of view might be encouraged among the group, although the promulgating of doctrines should be avoided. Courses, such as Materials and Methods of Architectural Research, already mentioned, or the Development of Contemporary Architectural Thought, might serve this function. This core should not be too extensive, else the result becomes a fixed and rigid curriculum and thus loses the flexibility provided by the concept of options.

IV. Directed Project Courses

In the later part of the master's curriculum and, to a larger extent, in the first part of the doctoral program, the graduate student should be given opportunity to undertake under guidance the study of one or more individual problems. This arrangement serves several functions. It permits some adjustment of the program to the student's individual interests and needs. This is especially useful when the topic selected is too particularized or too infrequently needed to justify a full subject-matter course. Not only will such project courses provide additional content, but they also serve as exercises in applying research techniques. In this way they can aid the prospective doctoral candidate in focusing his attention within his special field, and prepare him to undertake his final investigation and dissertation. If the selection of the subject of his final investigation can be decided upon at an early date, it is perfectly feasible to permit parts of it to serve as topics for the projects course.

V. Thesis Courses

In the final year of the doctoral curriculum, the student will need to devote his whole energy to his original research program. While not mandatory, it is helpful to both the student and his teacher-adviser if this work can be formalized in a sequence of specific courses. Naturally, their character would be similar to the directed project courses, but their intensity would be increased and the role of the teacher would become more that of a colleague and adviser, than that of a director.

E. The Graduate Student

The extension of professional education by graduate studies raises a number of difficult problems for the prospective student. Supplying motivation is not one of these problems, since the three basic aims of the program are derived from professional opportunities that will naturally challenge and attract energetic, talented, and ambitious undergraduates. Given the availability of a rich and varied program, there can be no doubt that, other factors being favorable, the present graduate enrollment would increase to a ratio comparable to that found in graduate curricula in engineering.

One of the problems that immediately appears is the further delay in entering upon professional and adult social life. Completion of the master's program, that is, the sixth year of professional education, would normally come at age 24. If compulsory military service intervenes, this would become at least 25. If a year or two of candidacy were gained before undertaking the master's program, age at graduation would be 26 or 27 years. The addition of two more years for the doctoral program would bring the graduate to age 28 or 29.

Nevertheless, this picture, when compared with that in other disciplines, is less formidable than it first appears. The only major educational difference is the fifth undergraduate year now universally required in architecture. Moreover, candidacy should not enter into the question of formal education because it is a period of earning power. It is also worth noting that age and cost factors did not discourage the enrollment in other fields in 1948 of more than 174,000 graduate students. Thus, the real question is whether graduate study is less beneficial for architecture than for other professions. No serious critic of the present state of architectural knowledge and professional education will support such an unrealistic view. Indeed, in the opinion of most such critics, it is the lack of a vigorous pursuit of new architectural knowledge which constitutes the profession's greatest barrier to progress. In no other major field of endeavor are the potentialities of a concerted graduate program so open to exploitation or of such exciting promise.

The selection of graduate students presents no great problem. Unlike the review of high school applicants for whom only general scholastic records are available, the graduate can present the evidence of a five-year undergraduate program of professional studies. To this may or may not be added his internship record. Nevertheless, final selection demands careful consideration. The chief criteria for admission should be capacity to benefit from advanced training and an indication of strong motives and promise to do so. Care should be taken to discover those applicants who have been slow in developing in their undergraduate years, but notwithstanding have finally gained real promise. In the beginning stages of graduate expansion, however, the limited facilities available for graduate programs will necessarily produce keen competition among applicants and perhaps a temporarily excessive premiation of the highest undergraduate academic records.

As in other disciplines, the greatest single deterrent to student participation will be the financial burden on the individual. Two current ameliorants can be adopted. First, graduate fellowships covering all or part of the cost should be provided. Second, to aid the undergraduate, graduate, and research faculties, graduate students can be employed as part-time assistants. The establishment of fellowships should be particularly attractive to companies manufacturing building products because they could naturally regard the graduate program as a recruiting center for research personnel.

While these problems are very real, it must be remembered that they are not peculiar to architecture. That they have been met successfully in other fields is proof that they can be solved for the architectural program.

F. The Graduate Faculty

The key to the successful development of graduate studies in architecture is the faculty assembled to implement it. With the graduate staff rest the responsibilities of formulating the specific program, organizing the component courses, setting standards of scholarship, morale, vision, and industry, leading students to grow in knowledge, skill, and judgment, and at the same time foreseeing and guiding the direction in which architecture itself should evolve. To an unusual degree, therefore, the graduate faculty must embody the ideal attributes of breadth, wisdom, imagination, and devotion.

The discovery of not one, but a whole group of such teachers who can and will cooperate wholeheartedly in a unified program presents formidable problems. The limited scope of graduate architectural programs in the past has trained few individuals to undertake such duties. Since the qualities sought are identical with those which ensure the highest success in practice itself, and since practice has rightly been, by definition, the goal of professional education, and since even the most affluent educational institution has been unable to compete with the financial rewards of private enterprise, it is not surprising that no large body of candidates stands ready for appointment to graduate faculties. Such candidates must be sought diligently and long and it must be the different, but unprecedented, opportunity and challenge, rather than competition with practice on its own terms, that will in the end attract their participation.

If graduate study is to be a dynamic endeavor, the graduate center must itself lead the search for new knowledge. This means that the graduate faculty must take an active part in investigations of all kinds; indeed, the faculty must become both a graduate and a research faculty. Here, too, there is little precedent and tradition in schools of architecture. In the past, architecture has relied almost exclusively on intuitive analysis and empirical creativeness. The difficulty of dealing with extremely complex groups of factors, such as physical efficiency, structural economy, and aesthetic attractiveness, has tended to discourage systematic analyses. Even after acknowledging the intuitive character of creative synthesis, which in its narrow sense is the act of design, there remain many considerations preparatory to this act which are quite susceptible of methodical inquiry. In fact, if answers to such problems were at hand, the act of creation would be much facilitated. These, then, are appropriate investigations in which graduate teachers could perfect and demonstrate the techniques of research and, at the same time, make positive contributions to the resources of the profession. The addition of ability to perform research to the other qualifications desired in graduate teachers, further limits the roster of candidates. It comprises a difficult dilemma which can probably be solved only by selecting appointees capable of pioneering and self-training.

It is obvious that, for the kind of graduate program herein described, with its comprehensive scope, its definite aims, and its specific methods, the usual practice of

435

imposing the responsibility for its operation upon the undergraduate staff with little or no relief from regular duties becomes indefensible. There can be no objection, of course, if properly qualified teachers are assigned to both undergraduate and graduate instruction, provided adequate time is allotted for the effective development of each phase of the program. Indeed, positive advantages could be gained not only because of the cross-fertilization of both phases and the stimulating effect upon the instructor, but also because undergraduates would surely gain some knowledge of the graduate program through normal contact with the staff, with the result that they might be motivated to participate in it later on. On the other hand, undergraduate teachers should not attempt graduate courses unless adequate recognition is given in load calculations to the time required to conduct such instruction on an authentic graduate level.

In building a graduate faculty in architecture, the question will soon be raised concerning the possession of graduate degrees as a qualification to teach graduate courses. In other departments of a university it is almost always mandatory that a teacher must hold a degree at least equal to that of the curriculum in which he is teaching. For the master's program in architecture this policy will rarely constitute an obstacle, for the *1950 Survey* revealed that 48 per cent of all architectural teachers, who were also registered for practice, held graduate degrees. Nevertheless, inflexible adherence to such a policy would eliminate a number of teachers who are otherwise well qualified by reason of excellent experience in practice and marked ability in teaching. It would be ridiculous to deprive the program of their assistance for such an arbitrary reason. Indeed, if their level of experience, thinking, and instructional capabilities will contribute significantly to the graduate program, it might well be argued that the institution in which they teach should confer on them a master's degree on the basis of evident professional accomplishment over a term greatly exceeding the length of an academic curriculum.

For the doctoral program especially, only a tiny handful of holders of this degree have been produced, and in all instances their special training has been in history. Clearly, it will be impossible to restrict the faculty charged with administering this program to doctoral graduates. It will be necessary to select for this program those teachers who, regardless of academic recognition, display a real understanding of the needs, character, content, and potentialities of the program. As graduate studies in architecture evolve over the coming decades, the critical situation can gradually be transformed into one more consonant with normal academic procedures.

G. The Graduate School and its Budget

Provision of the opportunity for qualified candidates to pursue graduate studies in architecture of the scope described above implies the establishment in one or more American universities of an outstanding faculty and adequate facilities with which to conduct the program.

Some idea of the possible national scale which such studies might reasonably attain

436

if energetically developed is indicated by the fact that, if graduate enrollment in architecture, now 239, grew to the intensity now present in engineering, there would be 1100 graduate students in architecture. Such an enrollment would constitute 8.8 per cent of the total undergraduate enrollment and accordingly would accommodate almost the whole group which normally earns the highest academic records in undergraduate work.

No economic studies of graduate programs in architecture are available. It is estimated, however, that for a minimum program of the type here envisioned, the enrollment in any one institution should be approximately 50 students. For this group, a faculty of nine would be required, and their teaching loads would conform to normal academic standards for graduate instruction. If an average salary of $9000 is assumed, and this figure is modest in view of the quality required, the yearly teaching budget would total $81,000. To this must be added a minimum of $5000 per year for secretarial assistance, bringing the total to $86,000, or $1720 per student per year.

Any program of graduate study, in order to approach equal opportunity for participation and minimize the barrier of inadequate personal funds, should provide a number of graduate fellowships with which to subsidize carefully selected students. This is especially important in the early years of the program, when the tradition and standards are being established. Assuming ten such fellowships at a common $1200 per year, the annual cost would be $12,000. In addition, graduate assistantships, to aid either the graduate faculty in research projects or the undergraduate staff as graders, readers, monitors, etc., would make it possible for others to take part.

If the basis for estimating is raised to 100 graduate students, the faculty required would not increase in direct proportion. For a group of this size, a faculty of twelve would probably suffice. This would, in turn, reduce the annual cost per student to about $1130.

The physical facilities required by such a program depend so much upon its specific development by a particular faculty that only a very general indication can be given. Certain facilities could be shared with the undergraduate program, such as a space design laboratory, a structural laboratory and computing room, photographic laboratory, and exhibit and judgment rooms. The difficulty is that, all too frequently, these facilities are lacking, even for undergraduates. The graduate group will require for their exclusive use, the usual complement of drafting, seminar, and class rooms, a model-making shop, a mockup laboratory in which to test full-size details, at least two research laboratories, and the usual faculty and clerical offices. Altogether, a minimum of about 12,000 net square feet would be required for an enrollment of 50.

It is clear that the total graduate budget on a national scale will be of considerable magnitude. Even in units of 100 students, the annual teaching budget would come to a million and a quarter dollars. Nevertheless, architects should remember that other groups—engineers, farmers, doctors, scientists, educationalists, veterinarians, etc., etc., etc.,—have long ago demanded and received vast funds for graduate training and research. The inevitable conclusion must be that architecture and building, one of the largest enterprises in the nation, have no need for greater knowledge or skill, have no potentialities for further development, or are activities of inferior quality. No architect can afford to admit such an allegation, nor will he do so. The remedy is realization of the need and a will to satisfy it. Once architects become aware of the benefits of such a program and make their voices heard, funds will be found. Once the results begin to appear, the program will grow at a cumulative rate.

Obviously, no one institution can become an exclusive national center for graduate study in architecture. On the other hand, unless the provision of funds for graduate study becomes much more uniform than funds for undergraduate study have hitherto appeared, graduate programs will naturally be concentrated in a relatively few schools. It is to be hoped, and no doubt expected, that these graduate centers will distribute themselves regionally so that they may serve more closely the students and the problems near at hand. A reasonable immediate goal would be the achievement of a full graduate program in four or five strategic institutions by 1960. Over a longer term, this initial group should grow to ten or twelve.

The program here envisioned cannot be achieved overnight, but it is of the utmost importance to make an immediate beginning by bringing to bear the whole weight of the profession to emphasize the urgency of the need and the vast potentialities to be derived from its satisfaction. If the members of The AIA are themselves convinced of its necessity, it should be possible for The Institute to organize a vigorous campaign to secure sufficient funds for operation during the first few years. The dynamic character of the program should have great appeal for forward-looking foundations, progressive manufacturers of building products, and all agencies concerned with the conduct of construction programs. Architects themselves could pool their own resources in the American Architectural Foundation and solicit other contributions to swell its endowment. Considerations of the possibilities of such a program could indeed prompt Institute members to earmark a special increase of dues for the inauguration of a first unit of the program. An annual contribution of $10 per member would produce at present almost $100,000, the equivalent of an endowment of $2½ millions. It would seem that a program so vital to the future of the profession should certainly receive as much support as the conduct of public relations. Moreover, it should not be overlooked that a graduate and research program supported by The AIA would be a perennial source of the finest type of public relations. In short, there seems to be no significant reason to postpone action if the program is judged to be advantageous.

The problem of locating such a beginning will inevitably arise. Many schools would no doubt be eager to be designated as a graduate center, and it would be very difficult for The AIA to select a single institution. This problem might be escaped by the formation of an independent graduate school directly sponsored by The Institute. This solution, however, would require additional expenditure to assemble a suitable graduate library and to secure and maintain appropriate facilities. If this proves unwise, the choice of an initial school might be based on two major factors: first, a preliminary survey and recommendation conducted by a joint commission of representatives of The Institute, ACSA, and NAAB; and second, the willingness and ability of schools desiring such designation to provide a substantial contribution in facilities and funds. Although the accrediting of graduate programs has already been suggested, it seems wiser at the present time to defer such decisions until such a commission could make recommendations.

The Commission believes emphatically that the realization of a strong program of graduate study and research in architecture has high priority in any campaign to enlarge the resources and raise the competence of the profession. It considers that the possibility of such a program constitutes one of the profession's greatest opportunities during the next generation. Therefore it urges The Institute, ACSA, and the schools to begin immediately to develop and implement such a program (*Recommendation 42*).

NOTES: CHAPTER TEN

[1] Walter A. Taylor, "Research, the Building Industry, and the Architect" (*Bulletin of The AIA*, September–October, 1953, pp. 145–148).

[2] Manufacturers Mutual Fire Insurance Co.: *The Factory Mutuals, 1835–1935*, 1935, passim.

[3] Ralph B. Peck: *History of Building Foundations in Chicago*, 1948 (University of Illinois, Engineering Experiment Station, Bul. No. 373), p. 15.

[4] *The Factory Mutuals*, p. 98.

[5] J. K. Freitag: *Fire Prevention and Fire Protection*, 1921 (2nd edition), p. 125.

[6] Dept. of Scientific and Industrial Research: *Report of the Building Research Board, 1926*, p. 1.

[7] Huson Jackson: *A Guide to New York Architecture 1650–1952*, 1952. Victor Steinbrueck: *A Guide to Seattle Architecture 1850–1953*, 1953. These two guides and the new one, Henry-Russell Hitchcock's *A Guide to Boston Architecture 1637–1954*, were issued in connection with the 84th, 85th, and 86th Conventions of The American Institute of Architects and presented to the delegates by Reinhold Publishing Corporation's Book Division and *Progressive Architecture* division. In all three cases the local chapters provided the publisher with a completed manuscript including illustrations. In the case of the Seattle and Boston guides the chapters received financial help from the Institute.

[8] MIT: *Reports of the President, Secretary, and Departments*, 1871–1872, pp. 44–47.

[9] *Ten-Year Book of Cornell University*, vol. 4, 1868–1908.

[10] *Technology Review*, vol. 29, no. 1, November, 1926, pp. 16–17.

[11] F. H. Bosworth, Jr., and Roy Childs Jones: *A Study of Architectural Schools*, 1932, pp. 188–189.

[12] *Ibid.*, p. 96.

CHAPTER XI

The Commission's Recommendations

1. GENERAL CONCLUSIONS

The Commission was charged to review and make recommendations regarding the content, methods, operation, and results of architectural education and registration, but it soon became apparent that such a task involved certain basic assumptions and procedures. First, the Commission affirmed its conviction that architecture is "an art for all men" and that the profession of architecture must be conceived as an integral part of the fabric of the nation. It followed that the sole purpose of the profession is to ensure in adequate quantity and the highest quality the performance of those services which social purposes require. Next, the Commission deduced from the complex nature of architecture and its all-pervading influence upon society that quality services cannot possibly be supplied by mere technicians, but that they demand practitioners who are at once outstanding professionals and enlightened citizens.

The attainment of such qualities and capacities is clearly a never-ending task, and from this fact arose the conviction that professional education for the practice of architecture is an integrated process continuing from recruitment to retirement. It was with this belief that the Commission approached its analysis of educational content, methods, and results. In order to escape the hazards of opinion and preconceptions, the Commission conducted a survey of the profession, the schools, the registration boards, and representative laymen from all of whom an unprecedented wealth of information was obtained. Detailed consideration of these data served as the starting point of all of the Commission's deliberations. In addition, the Commission reviewed the evolutionary background of the problems confronting it in order to gain insight into the operation of causal factors. Finally, it endeavored to achieve thorough functional analyses of current relationships fundamental to creative and imaginative re-synthesis. The complexity of these problems and the need to present and document these deliberative processes explain and justify the extent of this Report.

In general, the Commission found that existing over-all programs of architectural education and registration are soundly conceived and, on the whole, effective in terms of familiar criteria. No revolutionary change seems to be demanded. On the other hand, the Commission is convinced that what is needed throughout is intensification, systematization, refinement, and deepening. Such measures are needed because professional education, like architecture and practice themselves, has reached a stage in its evolution in which new demands for functional efficiency make evaluation and integration imperative. While certainly rigid formulization should be avoided, it is also true that the day of laissez-faire should be definitely ended.

This process of renewal should be directed toward all phases of education for practice. Recruitment needs validated aptitude tests and preliminary guidance. The professional schools need to raise the effectiveness of their instruction by improved teaching methods, aids, and facilities, by intensifying content and coverage, and by firmer integration of content and methods both within the curriculum and with regard to candidacy and practice. These objectives imply a more highly trained and specialized faculty, operating under more equitable teaching loads. This, in turn, raises the problem of increased resources based on larger budgets and on more economical units of enrollments. Candidate training must likewise be given real efficiency. Licensing and registration need similar measures. The degree of competence to be demanded for initial licensure requires explicit definition. Licensing examinations need close study with regard to the validity and reliability of their content and administration. Finally, the profession must undertake a thorough, comprehensive, and continuing program designed to expand the capacities of all its members through new knowledge won by research and disseminated by effective organization of advanced professional education.

The Commission is well aware that such a vision will demand a quality of thought, a contribution of effort, and a degree of financial support wholly unprecedented in the annals of the profession. To those who may regard such a vision as merely visionary, the Commission responds with D. H. Burnham's famed counsel to "make no little plans." While it is patent that sound growth evolves gradually, it is equally true that without vision growth will be only spasmodic and capricious. It would indeed be ironic if a profession dedicated to the planning of vast enterprises proves too timid to control its own future.

2. SPECIFIC RECOMMENDATIONS

The general tenor of this Report, just recapitulated, is accompanied by a long series of specific recommendations addressed to The American Institute of Architects. Some deal with detailed suggestions for the solution of particular and immediate problems. Many, on the other hand, recommend only general directions of approach or further study by appropriate agencies. All are offered with the realization that progress is more certain if it can be induced to spring from the best of current practice. For each item, reference is provided to appropriate discussion in the body of the Report.

R–1: Comprehensive Study of Office Administration (p. 32)

The Commission recommends that The AIA conduct a detailed survey of administrative conditions and procedures now used in the practice of architecture. Such a survey should investigate in greater detail than was possible in the *1950 Survey* all aspects of office operation and study the possibility of developing criteria with which to judge the efficacy of various methods.

R–2: Continuing Statistical Studies of the Profession (p. 63)

The Commission recommends that The AIA undertake annual statistical studies of the size, composition, character, and distribution of the profession. It believes that up-to-date and accurate data on the country's registered architects are essential to the wise determination of many problems of the profession, and, when combined with data on enrollments, graduations, registrations, and retirements, would provide a most useful picture of professional conditions. Further, a current unduplicated list of architects would serve many useful purposes. Finally, study should be given to means of ascertaining the current actual number of architectural firms and the number of architectural employees of different types.

R–3: Aptitude Tests for Prospective Architects (p. 134)

The Commission recommends that The AIA, in conjunction with ACSA, investigate the development of a reliable aptitude test to discover those who may be suited for professional training. Such a study should include consultation with successful testing agencies, preparation and validation of experimental tests, and the eventual promotion of such tests if they prove trustworthy.

R–4: Guidance Manual for Counsellors and Students (p. 135)

The Commission recommends that The AIA, in conjunction with ACSA, cause to be prepared and circulated an up-to-date manual which will present to vocational counsellors and students of secondary schools the opportunities, nature, and qualifications of careers in architecture. Such a manual might also serve as an introduction for beginning trainees in schools and offices.

R–5: Chapter Guidance and Preliminary Office Experience (p. 135)

The Commission recommends that The AIA urge each of its chapters to maintain a committee charged with cooperating with secondary schools in its area for the purpose of presenting general information to secondary-school students regarding careers in architecture, advising interested students as to their probable suitability for such careers, and arranging trial experiences in architectural offices. The operation of such a program will require a chapter guidance training manual to instruct the committees as to the proper performance of their duties.

R–6: Architectural Workbooks for Elementary and Secondary Schools (p. 137)

The Commission recommends that The AIA investigate the feasibility of preparing project workbooks for use in elementary and secondary school classes, designed to familiarize all such students with the importance, influence, and appeal of good architecture in community life. These workbooks should also explain the work and contributions which architects provide in attaining a convenient and attractive community. Besides the establishment of architecture and architects in the minds of all students, such workbooks would cultivate in some students an interest in architectural careers.

R–7: Student Inspection Trips during Vacations (p. 154)

The Commission recommends that The AIA, in conjunction with ACSA and representatives of student chapters, investigate the feasibility of minimum-cost summer inspection trips designed to provide architectural students with guided access to outstanding works in a number of centers. It is also envisioned that such trips would be augmented by visits to architectural offices and discussion sessions with prominent architects.

R–8: Modification of Fulbright Rules for Architectural Appointees (p. 154)

The Commission recommends that The AIA endeavor to secure an adjustment of the rules governing Fulbright grants for foreign study so that architects, architectural students, and teachers need not confine their programs to a single country, but can obtain funds in several countries for travel devoted to serious professional study.

R–9: On-Site Experience during Candidacy (p. 155)

The Commission recommends that The AIA urge NCARB and all registration boards, which require of graduate candidates two or more years of architectural experience, to permit such candidates to count on-site employment by an acceptable contractor in full up to approximately one-fifth of the total time required. While the Commission recognizes that the benefits of on-site training are also attainable in other ways, and while it does not feel that on-site training need be made mandatory, it believes that those who elect to secure such experience should be allowed to count it providing a reasonable amount of direct office training is also obtained.

R–10: Buildings for Schools of Architecture (p. 215)

The Commission recommends that The AIA urge and call upon all chapters and members to demand that the profession's schools be provided with buildings of such size, character, and attractiveness as are needed to accommodate teaching programs of high quality. The Commission regards a large proportion of the space allotted to these schools as barriers to essential instructional facilities and as affronts to the profession and to the faculties and students occupying them. It further suggests that The Institute consult with NAAB as to the desirability of emphasizing this matter through the accrediting process.

R–11: Textbooks for Architectural Courses (p. 221)

The Commission recommends that The AIA undertake, in conjunction with ACSA, an intensive study of ways and means to make suitable textbooks available for use in various architectural courses.

R–12: Student Guidance by AIA Chapters (p. 225)

The Commission recommends that The AIA urge its Chapters to offer to schools of architecture the services of appropriate committees to make periodic visits to the schools so that interested students can secure such counsel and guidance as the committeemen can contribute as practicing architects.

R–13: Intensification of AIA Student Chapter Program (p. 227)

444

The Commission recommends that The AIA, in consultation with ACSA, intensify its efforts to promote, extend, and refine its student chapter program. The Commission regards the progress already made as significant, but since it believes this program to be of great importance for the future of the profession it urges that every opportunity be exploited to strengthen it.

R–14: Shortened Education and Training for Selected Candidates (p. 234)

The Commission recommends that The AIA urge NAAB, ACSA, and NCARB to join in a study of a proposal to: admit selected students to professional curricula after the completion of third year of secondary school; screen all professional students at the end of the second year of architectural curricula; provide a year of terminal training for those judged unsuited to full professional education; intensify the upper three years of professional education; and reduce candidate training for such graduates to two years.

R–15: Professional Practice by Teachers of Architecture (p. 249)

The Commission recommends that The AIA adopt a formal policy recognizing the fundamental necessity of continuing experience in practice for all teachers of architecture who are registered architects, provided that such teachers discharge their academic duties in a manner satisfactory to the employing institution and so as to maintain high quality in the total educational program.

R–16: Periodic Studies of Teachers' Salaries (p. 260)

The Commission recommends that The AIA urge ACSA to conduct at regular intervals surveys of the salaries of architectural teachers to the end that the economic status of this group and the schools' ability to recruit qualified personnel can be justly appraised. Such studies should secure data to provide accurate comparison with salaries in other academic fields.

R–17: Establishment of Study Institutes for Architectural Teachers (p. 267)

The Commission recommends that The AIA urge ACSA, and offer its aid and cooperation, to develop, inaugurate, and maintain regular study institutes in which architectural teachers in the various subject areas can meet for cooperative discussion of course content, treatment, methods of presentation, evaluation of student performance, and other aspects of instruction.

R–18: Citations for Excellence in Architectural Teaching (p. 269)

The Commission recommends that The AIA, in consultation with ACSA, develop and establish a system of citation awards by which The Institute can recognize outstanding effectiveness in teaching and thereby testify to the high value which it—in the name of the profession—ascribes to superior service in this important field.

R–19: Structural Options of Architectural Curricula (p. 271; see also *R–24*)

The Commission recommends that The AIA reaffirm its position that any curriculum intended to train students for the practice of architecture should, as well as its degree, be entitled *Architecture,* and that if such a curriculum permits a concentration of advanced studies, such as structural design, it should be designated as an *option* of the curriculum in *Architecture.*

R–20: Architectural Courses for Non-architectural Students (p. 273)

The Commission recommends that The AIA urge ACSA and the schools to develop course offerings through which non-architectural students of their institutions can have opportunity to study, understand, and appreciate the character, values, and importance of architecture of high quality, and the manifold and essential contributions which it makes to satisfactory living.

R-21: Administrative Status of Architectural Schools (p. 277)

The Commission recommends that The AIA, in conjunction with ACSA and NAAB, urge and assist all schools of architecture to seek an administrative status which assures direct access to the chief executive officer of their respective institutions, and which recognizes architecture as a primary and homogeneous discipline. The Commission further suggests serious consideration of making such status a mandatory criterion for accreditation.

R-22: Expansion of Schools to Serve the Building Industry (p. 279)

The Commission recommends that The AIA urge all schools of architecture to expand their scope and objectives in order to serve the professional educational needs of the whole building industry. The Commission believes that The AIA should enlist the interest and support of all divisions of the industry in the development of such a plan.

R-23: Advice on Partial and Non-Professional Instruction in Architecture (p. 282; see also *R-25*)

The Commission recommends that The AIA, in conjunction with ACSA and NAAB, offer to assist the American Association of Junior Colleges and the National Council of Technical Schools in fixing appropriate objectives and standards for any partial or non-professional courses intended to train architectural personnel. Further, the Commission recommends that The AIA urge its chapters to observe and report any such programs which exist in their respective areas.

R-24: Designation of Non-Architectural Curricula (p. 289; see also *R-19*)

The Commission recommends that The AIA adopt as its official policy that the use of the designations *Architecture* or *Architectural* is applicable only to curricula intended to educate students for the professional practice of architecture, and that other curricula, not so intended, but providing instruction in certain specialized phases of building should be designated as *Building Engineering,* or a similar title which accurately describes its objective. The Commission further recommends that The AIA work to secure the complete abandonment of any use of the misleading title *Architectural Engineering.*

R-25: Observation of Technical Institute Developments (p. 290; see also *R-23*)

The Commission recommends that The AIA, in conjunction with NAAB, follow closely the development of technical institutes which offer vocational instruction in architectural subjects, and that, if in the future the number and impact of these courses indicate need of control, appropriate measures be instituted to do so by a system of accrediting.

R-26: Financial Support of NAAB (p. 291)

The Commission recommends that The AIA, in conjunction with ACSA, NCARB, and NAAB, formulate a plan of financial support for NAAB which will permit NAAB to perform its accrediting functions on an appropriate scope. The Commission further recommends that The AIA urge NCARB to acknowledge the usefulness of accrediting to its member registration boards by contributing or obtaining contributions for such support in proportion to its representation and participation in NAAB.

R–27: Expansion of NAAB Membership (p. 291)

The Commission recommends that The AIA, in collaboration with ACSA, NCARB, and NAAB, study the feasibility, advantages, and implications of increasing the membership of NAAB to twelve appointees, with four representatives each from The AIA, ACSA, and NCARB, and at the same time comprising one representative from each of the twelve AIA regions.

R–28: Periodic Review of NAAB Procedures (p. 292)

The Commission recommends that The AIA urge NAAB to review its procedures at regular intervals in consultation with The AIA, ACSA, and NCARB, and introduce such modifications as will eliminate sources of friction in the accrediting process and permit maximum cooperation by the schools.

R–29: Establishment and Location of New Schools (p. 322)

The Commission recommends that The AIA assume sole responsibility for determining the profession's need for the establishment of any new school of architecture. The Commission suggests that this function be exercised through the AIA Committee on Education, augmented by The Institute's Director of Education and Research and by the AIA director from the region in which a new school is proposed, and that the Committee should consult freely with officers of NAAB and ACSA. The Commission further recommends that decisions in such matters be guided by a general policy of concentrating enrollments in units of optimal size to support educational programs of high quality.

R–30: Systematization of Candidate Training (p. 342)

The Commission recommends that The AIA, enlisting the support of ACSA, NCARB, and NAAB, develop and establish an *AIA Candidate Training Program*. The Commission further recommends that this program include the following provisions:

a. A minimum period of 3 years of experience (except as may be modified by *R–14*) in the office or offices of registered architects who maintain practices of acceptable quality.

b. Participation by the candidate in all phases of professional service in several project cycles of varying types.

c. Recording in detail by the candidate in a Logbook of Experience of all phases of his training.

d. Periodic advisement of the candidate by an adviser, who may be the candidate's employer or another architect.

e. Periodic advisement of the candidate and review of his Logbook by an appropriate committee of an AIA chapter.

f. Admission to candidacy and the issuing of the Logbook by The AIA, on the basis of graduation from an accredited school of architecture, or upon certification by a Chapter Advisement Committee that the candidate has achieved a level of attainment equivalent to such graduation.

g. Maintenance of candidate status by evidence of acceptable progress, and termination of such status at registration, or upon evidence of lack of progress.

h. Regular reports by the advising chapter committee to The AIA regarding the status of candidates in its care.

The Commission further recommends the preparation of suitable guidance manuals for candidates, advisers, and advising committees.

R–31: Architect-in-Training as Title of Candidate (p. 344)

The Commission recommends that The AIA accord all candidates enrolled in its AIA Candidate Training Program the title *Architect-in-Training*.

R–32: Cooperation in NCARB toward Uniform Registration Laws (p. 372)

The Commission recommends that The AIA reaffirm its position that the profession and all registration boards should work toward a more uniform and more equitable process of architectural registration and that all such efforts be guided by and use the facilities of NCARB.

R–33: Candidate Access to Sample Registration Examinations (p. 387)

The Commission recommends that The AIA urge all state registration boards to make available to their candidates copies of representative previous examinations or examination questions in order to acquaint them with the general character and scope of these tests.

R–34: Statistical Studies of Registration Examining (p. 389)

The Commission recommends that The AIA urge NCARB to gather, analyze, and report annually the statistics of the examining process in order to keep the profession informed as to the number of applicants, admissions, and the operation of the process. The Commission further recommends that The AIA urge all state boards to cooperate in such studies.

R–35: Investigation of Validity and Reliability of Registration Examinations (p. 395)

The Commission recommends that The AIA, in cooperation with NCARB, undertake, with the assistance of expert and experienced testing agencies, a thorough investigation of current methods used in registration examinations in order to determine their validity and reliability in establishing competence to practice architecture, and to ascertain whether and what improvements should be introduced into the examining process to secure more trustworthy results.

R–36: Study of Objective Methods for Registration Examinations (p. 396)

The Commission recommends that The AIA, in cooperation with NCARB, undertake, with the assistance of expert and experienced testing agencies, a thorough investigation of the adaptability of objective methods to registration examinations, and conduct such trials as may be necessary to ascertain their feasibility and merits. The Commission further recommends that, if such methods prove to be advantageous, The AIA urge their appropriate use in all registration examinations.

R–37: Investigation of a National Registration Examination (p. 397)

The Commission recommends that The AIA, in cooperation with NCARB, ACSA, and NAAB, explore the operation and results of existing national examining agencies with a view to the development and establishment of a comparable system for the profession of architecture.

R–38: Anthology of Examination Questions (p. 399)

The Commission recommends that The AIA urge NCARB to seek the cooperation of all registration boards in gathering, collating, and circulating an anthology of suitable and successful questions used in registration examinations. The Commission further recommends that The AIA urge NCARB to establish for each area of examination a national committee whose function would be to render advice regarding the character, scope, and statement of examination questions, to prepare suitable questions to be included in the anthology, and to develop new types of questions.

R–39: Endorsement of Single Registration Examination (p. 401)

The Commission endorses and recommends that The AIA endorse the principle of a one-stage examination for registration and that this be administered only to candidates who have completed a required period of practical experience.

R–40: Concerted and Comprehensive Support for Architectural Research (p. 414)

The Commission recommends that The AIA devote its most serious thought and its most sustained effort to develop, implement, and lead a comprehensive and effective program of organized research in all phases of architecture, building, and practice; that it enlist all possible means and agencies to join in a concerted campaign to expand the boundaries of architectural knowledge; and that it work with utmost energy to secure ample and continuing support for the conduct of such research; all to the end that the profession of architecture and the building industry can better fulfill the building needs of the American people.

R–41: Development of Advanced Professional Education (p. 417)

The Commission recommends that The AIA expand its program of stimulating the professional growth and stature of all members of the profession by developing and conducting a comprehensive program of advanced professional education suited to needs of all candidates, employees, and practitioners.

R–42: Development of Graduate Studies in Architecture (p. 439)

The Commission recommends that The AIA recognize officially the paramount contribution to the advancement of architectural research and to the increased competence of the profession which a comprehensive program of graduate studies could provide; and that The AIA, in collaboration with ACSA, undertake immediately to stimulate and support by all possible means the expansion and maturing of such programs; and that as an initial step The AIA seek and actively assist the immediate establishment of a full-scale program in an appropriate institution or agency.

R–43: Future Surveys

The Commission recommends that The AIA adopt an official policy of conducting decennial surveys of the profession in order to secure accurate data on trends in its character, composition, distribution, techniques, facilities, and activities, the knowledge of which can be used to guide its future development. The Commission further recommends that the next survey be conducted in 1961 so that its findings can be correlated with national census data.

CHAPTER XII

The Role of The AIA

1. THE AIA, MEDIUM OF PROFESSIONAL COOPERATION

In 1857 the Articles of Incorporation of The American Institute of Architects stated:

"The object of this Society is to elevate the architectural profession as such, and to perfect its members practically and scientifically."

Today The Institute's By-Laws give fuller definition:

"The objects of The American Institute of Architects shall be to organize and unite in fellowship the architects of the United States of America; to combine their efforts so as to promote the aesthetic, scientific, and practical efficiency of the profession; to advance the science and art of planning and building by advancing the standards of architectural education, training, and practice; to coordinate the building industry and the profession of architecture to insure the advancement of the living standards of our people through their improved environment; and to make the profession of ever increasing service to society."

During the past century, The Institute has become in fact the medium through which American architects accomplish their professional purposes. From its birthplace on the Atlantic seaboard, it now extends across a continent. Its original roster of a few struggling chapters has multiplied to more than a hundred. The unification movement of the early 40's integrated within its structure numerous state associations. From an initial roll of 13, its membership is now approaching 10,000, a majority of all U. S. registered architects. Thus, as a democratic organization within a democratic society, The Institute stands as the sole national agency, geographically comprehensive and professionally representative, uniting all whose concern is the science and art of architecture.

Time was when individual efforts sufficed for a practice of architecture which involved only personal and private decisions. The rise of group action throughout American life has introduced new factors against which it is difficult for isolated individuals to contend. In such a situation, architects themselves have joined together to safeguard the channels through which they can serve social needs. For this reason, too, they must cooperate in a well-disciplined profession capable of commanding respect and attention in national, state, and local councils.

Nevertheless, The AIA is not an impersonal entity in itself. It does not determine policies, promulgate rules, or impose conditions. The Institute is rather a society of individual members who cooperate voluntarily in seeking common goals. Chapters, associations, officers, directors, committees, and secretariat are but the necessary agencies by which policies agreed upon by individual members can be effectively combined in harmonious performance. The work of the profession remains, as it must in every democratic institution, the responsibility of the individual member. Accomplishment depends upon his high aim, good will, and personal devotion to the task. Although this Report presents many recommendations to The AIA for action at national, regional, state, and chapter levels, all are inevitably addressed to each individual member of The Institute, for it is he who must accept its conclusions and join with his fellow members to fulfill their aims.

2. OPPORTUNITIES AND RESPONSIBILITIES AT THE NATIONAL LEVEL

In 1946 the structural reorganization of The AIA was predicated on the following goal:

"The AIA should so organize as to furnish adequate, inspiring leadership and service to the public, to the profession, and to professional education through the development of long-range objectives so that the architect may occupy himself with every phase of life in the civilization of which he is a part and thus may improve the physical framework of our living."

The long-term objectives, adopted at that time, embraced:

a. A thoroughly unified profession.
b. Education for the profession
c. Adequate professional training more closely allied to and functioning with the profession
d. Adequate research, study, and correlation of data on technical matters, materials, and methods.
e. Adequate and proper public relations.
f. Adequate professional relations.
g. Journalism with vitality to develop progress within the profession.
h. Properly organized and staffed national headquarters so to conduct affairs that the basic objectives may be obtained.

Notable progress toward fulfilling these aims has already been made, and, while much remains to be done, every member has come to realize the importance of a strong national program.

The unification of the profession within the framework of The AIA has been largely accomplished from a structural point of view. The *1950 Survey* revealed, however, that only 44 per cent of all U. S. registered architects held Institute membership. This percentage has continued to rise, but many more should be drawn to participate in the Institute program if maximum strength and comprehensiveness are to be attained. The *Survey* suggested that the group of architect-employees of practitioners could be a potential source of members. Greater emphasis on Student Associates and their regular progression to Junior Associateship and Associateship, would no doubt encourage more certainly and more promptly the entrance of such employees into full and active adherence to The Institute. The *Survey* also found a large group of registered architects in public employment. Those qualified for Institute membership should certainly be enlisted, since any view that public employment excuses the obligation to participate in the profession's national society should be immediately scotched. The Commission believes that The Institute's Committee on Membership should study the *Survey's* disclosures and investigate these potential sources of new members. Moreover, the Commission suggests that the effort of this Committee might well be concentrated first in those areas where membership ratios now fall much below the national average. Another group consists of architects holding out-of-state certificates, but not in-state registration. If it is assumed that half of the 10,000 non-AIA architects in 1950 were by occupational and personal qualifications eligible for Institute membership, this addition of 5000 would have enlarged its roster by 59 per cent to a total of 13,500.

Through strong national organization, individual members can join to play an influential role in the solution of many public problems. They can thus exercise effective leadership in the building industry and unite with other agencies to achieve common goals, as in the Building Research Advisory Board. Then, too, collaboration with other professions at the national level can encourage cooperation in local echelons, with the result that many sources of friction arising in local rivalries can be forestalled or minimized. Furthermore, a strong national organization can keep clear essential avenues of service. If The Institute had enjoyed such strength at the outbreak of World War II, it would have been much easier to break through that ignorance and prejudice which often refused to apply the profession's valuable capabilities to problems of the emergency. Within the profession itself, national organization forms a common meeting ground encouraging that mutual respect which facilitates resolution of sectional and parochial suspicions. Through the pooling of resources, objectives which no local group could afford become capable of realization. In some of these matters, the tangible benefits to be realized from cooperation have only recently begun to be explored and exploited.

The advantages of national strength and cooperative effort are basic to many of the Commission's recommendations. Indeed, the very envisioning of some possibilities would have never emerged but for the stimulation that nation-wide exchange of ideas excites. Some proposals will entail wise, but large expenditures, for example, the development of valid aptitude tests or the promotion of research and graduate studies, which even at the national level will be hard to fund. Others, such as excessive variation in requirements for registration, can only be ameliorated by a wider consciousness that geographical boundaries cannot alter basic needs and principles and that logic demands harmonious solutions to identical problems. The development of a national registration examination would be unthinkable without presupposing a central rallying point. It is unnecessary to repeat those matters respecting education and registration which will demand consideration and action at the national level.

The hazard of a national organization is the temptation to accord it independent and determinating status. Distance precludes intimate observation of its mechanics and under the aura of national prestige it may seduce the provinces to passive waiting for authoritarian directives, thus withering the very grassroots of its vitality. Such a perversion need not arise if individual members remain alert. Nevertheless, a reverse risk is also present, for if individual participation fails to be self-disciplined and constructive and subsides into habitual complaint, cooperation is vitiated and action is subverted. Thus, while power resides in the membership, it becomes the duty of those who exercise it to do so with intelligence and wisdom. If such conditions do prevail, accomplishment can be certain and sound.

Fortunately, the governance of The Institute provides ample safeguards to ensure both responsibility and responsiveness. The authority of the Board stems from chapter-elected delegates. In turn, the scope of The Institute's program demands that most of its work must be accomplished by voluntary committees. The secretariat assists the committees and administers the decisions of the Board. Thus, as should be, The Institute is a democratic agency and as such emphasizes once more the dependence of the profession upon an active and enlightened membership.

For these reasons and upon this theory, the Commission recommends that the role of The Institute be at all levels and at all times one of strong leadership.

3. OPPORTUNITIES AND RESPONSIBILITIES AT THE STATE LEVEL

The state associations and state chapters have sufficient in common to suggest combining recommendations at the state level. This is likewise true of district associations of chapters within the larger states.

A. EDUCATION

To the state organization must go the responsibility of maintaining cooperation between the profession and the professional schools. While local chapters and individual members may assist, counsel, and advise with the school personnel, it is the state-wide organization which must speak authentically with the school administration on matters of professional policy and procedures. The state association or chapter should gear its organizational machinery to assume this task.

The professional organization must be careful in its approach to this task, however. Theirs is the function of defining the product of the schools, not the means by which that product is developed. The curriculum, its content, and its organization are the specific responsibilities of the educator. He may, and perhaps should, discuss his problems with the professional committees, but the final decisions are his to make.

The assignment of visiting committees, furnishing in-practice critics and instructors, directing attention to outstanding teacher talent, encouraging joint chapter and school meetings, exhibits, and socials are all proper activities at this level of organization.

Student Chapters

The state associations or state chapters should guide the student chapter in the local schools. The state associations will no doubt find it advisable to delegate the direction of specific student chapters to local chapters in the immediate vicinity of the schools, but such delegation should not relieve the state association of interest or responsibility in the proper functioning of the individual student chapters. The state chapter will of course assume necessary responsibility for the school chapters within the state.

School Locations

The state associations or state chapter should assume with The Institute the responsibility for encouraging a sufficient number of schools to provide training in all regions of the nation. This responsibility should not be used to reduce the number of schools or graduates to the point that the profession will be accused of contributing wilfully to a professional shortage. Nor should schools be encouraged in impractical expansion.

When the establishment or expansion of an architectural school is contemplated, the local professional body, knowing the immediate circumstances, should conduct careful investigation on as objective a basis as possible, and be prepared to make intelligent recommendations to the national body when required. Since such movements are generally known some time in advance of actual implementation, the local body should keep advised on the ambitions of all growing institutions within their state and be prepared to advise local school authorities before commitments are made which can be altered only with difficulty and embarrassment.

In-Practice Education

As the national conventions of The AIA continue to grow in size, it is becoming increasingly evident that the educational process found in the seminar, the open discussion and the more intimate informative lectures are more amenable to the smaller attendance possible in regional sessions or the state association or chapter meetings.

455

It is certain that on the state level much good can be accomplished by exhibits, building clinics, a general exchange of ideas, or consideration of specific problems of local application. It should be the task of the association or chapter education committees to implement such activities.

Specific courses of study should be inaugurated in conjunction with the local school of architecture. These may be on a classroom or correspondence basis, but should be carefully considered in advance to insure wide participation and pertinent content.

B. REGISTRATION

In general, the most specific responsibility of the state associations and the state chapters lies in their relationship to registration. This is due to the nature of registration as a function of the individual states. Only an organization set within state lines is able to speak with authority and with hope of influencing state legislation or administration. The local chapter lacks the force of state-wide appeal, the national organization is a foreigner.

Legislation

The proper committees of the association or state chapter should maintain constant surveillance of the application of all state laws governing registration. With this background and the suggested legal provisions of this *Survey,* recommendations should be made periodically to the association or chapter outlining the changes to the local law, which should be requested of the state legislature. The professional body should then assume its responsibility to have such recommendations enacted into law.

Enforcement

State associations and state chapters should assume the task of policing unofficially the administration and enforcement of the registration law. If the law is well written and sufficiently definite in spelling out its enforcement, little will be required of the professional body; but vigilant committees of the association can render great service to the public with even a poorly written law. The profession must undertake this task, not in the spirit of protecting a professional right or concession, but in the spirit of protecting the public against unsound structures, inconvenient planning, dangerous sanitation, or a wasteful use of materials providing unaesthetic appearance.

Examination

The state association or state chapter through its proper committee should with the consent and cooperation of the state board conduct a periodical review of the licensing examinations. In this review it should compare such examinations with those given in other states similarly situated.

In a spirit of cooperative helpfulness this committee should make such recommendations as it feels are advisable to the board. In particular, it should call to attention any special conditions of practice within the state requiring particularized examination content. It should familiarize itself with any recommendations from the national body relating to the basic nature of professional practice which shall serve as a guide to the subject matter proper in an examination and the use of new testing methods or devices. Such committee may well be the training ground for future membership to the Boards of Examiners. This friendly check upon the activity of the Board of Examiners can do much to build a sound examining procedure and give a wider appreciation of state registration problems.

4. OPPORTUNITIES AND RESPONSIBILITIES OF THE LOCAL CHAPTER

Some of the tasks of the local chapter which is organized on state basis have been outlined in the previous division. There are many other responsibilities which must devolve upon the chapter group.

Local chapters can do much to direct the attention of public school administrators to the proper secondary training essential to professional study. Educators are generally sensitive to intelligent, carefully considered recommendations from interested citizen groups. The recommendations contained herein relative to secondary school preparation, revised to adapt them to local situations may serve as a stimulant to improving the curricula of schools in the chapter's area.

The local chapters should assist individual members in the encouragement of aspiring youngsters, by offering scholarships, awards, and other stimulants to effort.

The greatest educational service within the chapter, however, is its work with the individual membership. To too great a degree there exists within the profession tight in-fighting between members when commissions are being awarded. It is possible that chapters will always be disturbed by such contests and occasionally by hard feelings and enmities arising therefrom. The chapter must assume the tremendous task of reconciling the profession to itself, of establishing in its membership the simple rudiments of ethical action, basic honesty, mutual regard, and charity. Such a situation may be helped in various ways not the least important of which is simple, straight-from-the-shoulder talks. That chapter is fortunate who numbers within its membership an individual gifted with the art of plain speaking.

To teach men how to accept success gracefully; to stand up to criticism with a courageously open mind; to defend one's convictions without equivocation; and to endure defeat without bitterness or recrimination is a big order for any group organization, but that is the realistic task facing the local chapter. It is in this close personal, professional relationship that all that is anti-social within the individual comes out. A friendly, courteous spirit developed in a chapter can be the candle which may enlighten the community, state, and the nation. How this may be accomplished will vary with each situation and group, but, generally, the task resides within the chapter.

The local chapter may do much to implement the technical education of its membership, the principal burden of which is carried at the state level. Local study classes, meetings devoted to discussion of mutual problems, exchange of library facilities, etc., are all possible areas of activity.

At the local chapter level it is possible to make intelligent studies of the demands of the profession, in terms of abilities, technical knowledge, and personal qualifications. Here should be made the close studies of the architectural profession: What does the practitioner do with his time? How does the use of time differ in the large and the small office? To what extent and how are consultants being utilized? Each chapter should periodically make an analysis of its membership for its own use and to induce a stream of information into AIA headquarters which may make unnecessary the expensive questionnaire technique required for the current *Survey*.

Such information, while of great value to the educational institutions serving the profession, may be of even more value to the state boards of examiners in selecting the most pertinent content for licensing examinations.

The policing of the area served by the chapter, to insure proper respect for and enforcement of the registration statute, must also be a major task of the group.

5. OPPORTUNITIES AND RESPONSIBILITIES OF THE INDIVIDUAL ARCHITECT

With all that has been written of architects as organized groups, what remains to be said for the responsibility of the individual practitioner? That his task is vital is emphasized in the opening paragraphs of this chapter. Its importance is founded upon the simple fact that architectural service, in spite of some recent trend to large organizations, is still a personal service. It is the client asking and accepting advice from a professional adviser of his own choice. The client's reaction to the advice received, and its subsequent structural fruition, his satisfaction with its success, or his dissatisfaction with its failure not only determines his response to his adviser, but invariably conditions his response to the entire profession.

A. EDUCATION

Every architect should recognize the need for continued study of all subjects and areas of knowledge, but especially of those which pertain to his professional improvement. Beyond this recognition, he must actively engage himself in a vigorous, continuing self-educational process throughout his lifetime.

In-Practice Education

He should be willing to maintain frequent contact with his local chapter group, con-

458

tributing his time and means to its improvement and expansion; assume his individual responsibilities on chapter committees and in its official organization, when so selected. He should in particular participate in the organized educational activities of the group. This participation should not be confined solely to those activities instituted by others; but he should introduce and open up new fields of study and the means whereby these may be explored.

Secondary Education

He should participate actively in the civic affairs of his community. Especially should he acquaint himself with the educational system under which the youth of his community are being trained. By calling attention of local educators to the needs of later professional study, he may so influence primary and secondary school curricula as to provide a more substantial base for such careers.

Recruitment

He should concern himself with the encouragement and development of the future members of the architectural profession, giving his time freely to advise, counsel, and instruct young men and women who demonstrate an intelligent interest therein.

Assistance to Architectural Schools

If there is a nearby architectural school, he should familiarize himself with its operations and cooperate in whatever way is open to him to insure its success and the proper training of its students. This may suggest part-time instruction, lectures, library donations, participation in exhibits, use of students in offices, service on juries and as a critic.

Setting Professional Standards

He should intelligently analyze his own office operations and cooperate with his chapter and The Institute in making available that information which will more clearly define the detailed activities of his profession and thus lead to a clearer understanding of the necessary educational demands.

B. REGISTRATION

In all of his contacts with the public, the individual practitioner should so speak and act that the public may understand that registration and licensing are not instituted to give special privilege to the select few and protect them therein, but are for the purpose of protecting the building public against the fraudulent, the unprepared, and the incompetent.

Licensed Competence

He should so practice that his competence is clearly evident from his work. Nothing breaks down the confidence of the public in licensing procedure so quickly or surely as to have the licensed practitioner caught by his own carelessness, neglect, or ignorance.

Insistence upon perfection; the ability and willingness to demand good craftsmanship; absolute objectivity in giving advice; intelligent orientation in the sound use of local building materials and methods; basic concern with the best interest of the client, often including protection from his own extravagances, are a few of the key practices which will engender public confidence in the architectural profession.

Examiner Board Services

Each architect should prepare himself so that he may accept the responsibility of acting as a member of the board of examiners of his home state. If offered such responsibility, he should accept and serve therein to the best of his ability.

National Council Certification

He should secure at the earliest convenient time an NCARB Council Certificate which may be used in securing registration expeditiously in other states. Many practitioners delay this procedure until confronted with an immediate commission and are then impatient and critical at seeming delay. Since the certification process is involved and time-consuming, the wise practitioner will make early provision, even though practice across state lines is not an immediate prospect.

Law Enforcement

As he conducts his business from day to day, the practitioner should note any tendency on the part of others to disregard the laws relating to building generally, and call attention thereof to the proper officials. If, in his capacity as "master builder," an architect interests himself in all regulations relating to construction and their proper enforcement, and becomes recognized for such surveillance, it comes as an accepted part of his self-imposed policing duty to check malpractice of the licensing law. Such activity is wholly consonant with the character of the professional responsibility assumed by the architect and if used judiciously cannot but build public confidence in the practitioner and the profession.

Summary

The work of the profession in any part and at any level will not be accomplished unless the individual members collectively do it. Each member can fit himself into the program according to his present relation to The Institute and carry on from there. His contribution of thought, time, and effort, added to that of all other individual members, can accomplish the task. What he can do is enough to challenge any man, whether he have one talent or ten. The discipline of Architecture demands all of a man's mind, to comprehend and assimilate; all of a man's skill and ability, to practice; all of a man's spirit, honorably to account for its stewardship. It demands integrity, industry, intelligence, imagination, initiative, and likewise courage, perseverance, sacrifice, and constant striving.

We are free men—by the grace of God and our heritage. Conjoined with our freedom, and not to be dissociated from it, is our responsibility. Socially responsible practice of our profession demands that the architect be a "whole man"—gentleman, scholar, citizen, philosopher. Out of his productive time and income he should give a tithe to the betterment of his community and the society to which he owes his life and his living. Nothing less than a lifetime dedication to the ideals of his profession will suffice for his ultimate satisfaction and happiness.

There is one aspect of our responsibility that no one else can discharge for us. Where we as individuals live and practice our profession, we are the profession. The profession and all architects are judged by us. No program of national publicity or public relations will avail if in our own community we fail to do a good job. Here is a responsibility we cannot transfer or shirk. Upon us personally and individually rests the yoke of the discipline of our profession. Of each of us is demanded the most meticulous care in the handling of each commission entrusted to us.

It is fitting, therefore, that in the enjoyment of these opportunities and in the discharge of these responsibilities, the Oath of the Architect should be:

Humbly and proudly I profess my competence under the discipline of architecture.

Upon my honor I promise unending devotion to the task of continually studying, learning, seeking, experimenting, that I may become ever better educated and trained for my work.

Upon my honor I promise to my community undeviating adherence to the ideal of service to my fellow men, as the goal of my effort, that I may honestly and fully earn my living—my right to live among them.

Upon my honor I promise to maintain that integrity in practice which will insure to each client the finest possible stewardship of his interest.

Upon my honor I promise in the execution of every commission to strive to create beauty as well as order, character as well as safety, spiritual value as well as convenience.

Upon my honor I promise to join with my fellow architects to make our profession of the greatest possible usefulness and benefit to our society, to share and disseminate all valuable professional knowledge, and to pass on to the succeeding generation the full and fine discipline of our profession, enriched because of my dedication.

Appendices

Glossary of Abbreviations

Index

Tables

Appendix A: The Survey Documents

The 1950 Survey of the Architectural Profession

**The Commission for the Survey of Education and Registration of the American Institute of Architects,
Department of Education and Research**

A. PROFESSIONAL HISTORY AND PRACTICE

1. Age last birthday....................................___

2. Sex.........................Male____1 Female____2

3. Age at which you first registered as an architect.....___

4. Have you continuously maintained employee status in architectural practice?.............Yes____1 No____2

5. Age at which you first entered into practice as an independent architect or principal?...............___

6. Have you continuously maintained this independent status? (Exclude Armed Forces Service)....Yes____1 No____2

7. If your answer to question 6 was no, was the change in status necessitated by general economic conditions? (Exclude Armed Forces Service) ....Yes____1 No____2

8. Check below in column 8 the State in which you were employed or conducted your practice for the major part of 1950.

9. Check below in column 9 the home State in which you were resident at the time of graduation from secondary or high school.

10. Check below in column 10 the State in which you were first registered.

State	8	9	10
Alabama...............73____	73____	73____
Arizona...............96____	96____	96____
Arkansas..............61____	61____	61____
California.............43____	43____	43____
Colorado..............94____	94____	94____
Connecticut...........36____	36____	36____
Delaware..............21____	21____	21____
District of Columbia.......89____	89____	89____
Florida...............28____	28____	28____
Georgia...............27____	27____	27____
Idaho................92____	92____	92____
Illinois...............13____	13____	13____
Indiana...............12____	12____	12____
Iowa.................52____	52____	52____
Kansas...............57____	57____	57____
Kentucky.............71____	71____	71____
Louisiana.............62____	62____	62____
Maine................31____	31____	31____
Maryland.............22____	22____	22____
Massachusetts.........34____	34____	34____
Michigan... ....14____	14____	14____
Minnesota............51____	51____	51____
Mississippi...........74____	74____	74____
Missouri.............53____	53____	53____
Montana.............91____	91____	91____
Nebraska... ....56____	56____	56____
Nevada..............98____	98____	98____
New Hampshire........32____	32____	32____
New Jersey...........02____	02____	02____
New Mexico..........95____	95____	95____
New York............01____	01____	01____
North Carolina........25____	25____	25____
North Dakota.........54____	54____	54____
Ohio................11____	11____	11____
Oklahoma............63____	63____	63____
Oregon..............42____	42____	42____
Pennsylvania.........08____	08____	08____
Rhode Island.........35____	35____	35____
South Carolina........26____	26____	26____
South Dakota.........55____	55____	55____
Tennessee............72____	72____	72____
Texas...............64____	64____	64____
Utah................97____	97____	97____
Vermont.............33____	33____	33____
Virginia..............23____	23____	23____
Washington...........41____	41____	41____
West Virginia.........24____	24____	24____
Wisconsin............15____	15____	15____
Wyoming.............93____	93____	93____
U. S. Territ. and Possess.....X6____	X6____	X6____
Foreign Countries.......R7____	R7____	R7____

11. In how many domestic states and foreign countries have you been located for the practice of architecture?....___

12. Check below the current population which corresponds to that of the community, city or metropolitan area in which you were employed or in which your office was located for the major part of 1950.

Current Population	Check
Under 5,000................................1____
5,000 to 10,000............................2____
10,000 to 25,000...........................3____
25,000 to 50,000...........................4____
50,000 to 100,000..........................5____
100,000 to 500,000.........................6____
500,000 and over..........................7____

13. Check below the one appropriate item that corresponds to your primary status of employment for the major part of 1950.

Item	Check
Engaged in architecture as:	
Individual practitioner.......................01____
Principal in firm sharing in financial responsibility.....02____
Associate not sharing in financial responsibility........03____
Consultant.................................04____
Teacher (architectural faculty only).................11____
Employee of an *architectural* organization on a salary or wage basis..........21____
Employee of *non-architectural* firm, organization or institution (exclude private consulting work or teaching)........22____
Employee of Federal Government.................31____
Employee of State Government..................32____
Employee of County Government................33____
Employee of Municipal Government..............34____
Employee of other public authority.................35____
Member of Armed Forces......................36____
Engaged in non-architectural work.................41____
Retired...................................51____
Unemployed...............................61____

14. Check below the income bracket that represents your personal net annual income before taxes from fees and/or salaries received for architectural work only during 1949.

Item	Check
Under $3,000..............................0____
$3,000 and under $4,000.....................1____
$4,000 and under $6,000......................2____
$6,000 and under $8,000......................3____
$8,000 and under $10,000.....................4____
$10,000 and under $12,000....................5____
$12,000 and under $15,000....................6____
$15,000 and under $18,000....................7____
$18,000 and under $25,000....................8____
$25,000 and over...........................9____

15. Check below the types of organized program or suggested field of study in which you as an architect would participate if such were available.

Organized program:	Check
Advanced courses in architectural schools.............1____
Courses of study published regularly in current periodicals................................2____
Printed courses of study prepared and distributed by a central agency.......................3____
Refresher courses in architectural schools.............4____
Seminars on a state or regional basis.................5____
Short (two-week) intensified institutes conducted by architectural schools.......................6____
Visiting lecturers..............................7____
Prefer no organized activity.....................8____

Suggested field of study:	
Advanced construction techniques....................1____
Chemical properties of building materials..............2____
Construction problems arising from atomic developments.3____
Contemporary aesthetics..........................4____
Design to satisfy physiological demands of human life...5____
Economics and business of construction...............6____
Law as related to building construction................7____
Non-selling analysis of new materials.................8____
Planning of special type buildings (schools, hospitals, etc.)....................................9____
Real estate...................................0____

A. Professional History and Practice (Continued)

16. With respect to the activities listed below check in the boxes representing units of 10 percent the distribution of your professional time for the major part of 1950 to total 100 percent.

Check to total 100 Percent repeating check marks opposite such activities as may be necessary.

Activity	10	10	10	10	10	10	10	10	10	10
Administration and office management............01										
Client relations............02										
Construction, supervision in field and inspection............03										
Consulting............04										
Design, architectural............05										
Drafting and development of working drawings............06										
Engineering, electrical............07										
" mechanical............08										
" sanitary............09										
" structural............10										
Estimating............11										
Overall activities of general practitioner............12										
Planning, city or site............13										
Specification writing............14										
Building code administration............15										
Contractor, general............16										
Editing, writing, research............17										
Engineering, general............18										
Industrial product design............19										
Interior design or furniture............20										
Landscape design............21										
Maintenance of buildings............22										
Personnel and labor problems............23										
Sales of building products............24										
Teaching (architectural faculty only)............25										
Other activities not listed............26										
Retired............27										
Unemployed............28										

NOTE.—Questions 17 to 27 below are to be answered only by one of the principals or owners of the architectural firm or office, or top-ranking salaried architect who functions as a principal in a government agency, private organization or institution.

17. Check below the one means you most generally utilize to handle each of the services listed.

Service	Self (1)	Partner (2)	Full-time employee (3)	Consultant (4)
Structural engineering	1___	1___	1___	1___
Mechanical engineering including sanitary, heating and ventilating	2___	2___	2___	2___
Electrical engineering	3___	3___	3___	3___
Interior design	4___	4___	4___	4___
Landscape architecture	5___	5___	5___	5___

18. Check below the estimated total cost of projects actually contracted for with clients by your firm during 1949.

Cost of Projects	Check
Under $100,000	1___
$100,000 and under $500,000	2___
$500,000 and under $1,000,000	3___
$1,000,000 and under $2,000,000	4___
$2,000,000 and under $5,000,000	5___
Over $5,000,000	6___

19. Check below in order of frequency or volume the three building types which customarily constitute the greatest volume of your firm's work.

Building Type	First (1)	Second (2)	Third (3)
Churches	1___	1___	1___
Commercial	2___	2___	2___
Community Planning	3___	3___	3___
Educational	4___	4___	4___
Hospitals	5___	5___	5___
Industrial	6___	6___	6___
Public (Incl. housing)	7___	7___	7___
Recreational	8___	8___	8___
Residential	9___	9___	9___
Other	0___	0___	0___

20. If your office claims to be specialists in any single building type insert the code number from Question 19 for that type here.................

21. Does your office associate with other architects as consulting expert or specialist?.........Yes___1 No___2

22. How many principals or partners are in your firm?....___

23. What is the total number of employees in your organization? (Exclude partners and principals).................

24. What is the distribution of this total number of employees among the following categories?

Category	Number of employees
Administrators and office managers	1___
Designers	2___
Project managers, job captains, squad bosses	3___
Draftsmen	4___
Engineering personnel	5___
Research personnel	6___
Specification writers	7___
Outside superintendents	8___
Stenographers, clerks, accountants and all others	9___

25. How many of your employees are graduates of architectural schools?.................

26. How many of your employees are registered as architects?.................

27. How many of your employees are candidates for registration?.................

466

B.   EDUCATION FOR PRACTICE

28. To answer this question please refer to the "Code List of Architectural Schools" printed on the back of the covering letter to this questionnaire and insert below the code number or numbers that may apply to you with respect to the information requested.

First school attended (1)	Second school attended (2)	School of first degree in architecture (3)	School o, second degree in architecture (4)	School of architectural engineering degree (5)	School in which was completed a "special course" (non-degree) in architecture (6)
___	___	___	___	___	___

29. Since you graduated from high school how many years have you devoted to?
Professional architectural education at college level.___
All other college level education.................___

30. Do you hold a degree in engineering other than architectural engineering?.................Yes___1 No___2

31. Do you hold a degree or degrees in Liberal Arts?
Yes___1 No___2

32. Do you hold a degree or degrees in any other field of non-architectural education?............Yes___1 No___2

33. Did you ever receive a certificate in architecture from a trade school, technical institute, or non-degree college level institution?.................Yes___1 No___2

34. Was your entire training obtained in architectural offices?
Yes___1 No___2

35. Have you studied architecture in a foreign country?
Yes___1 No___2

36. Have you been the recipient of a fellowship or grant for advanced study, research or travel?..Yes___1 No___2

37. Check below the courses with which you have supplemented your education other than that required by your formal architectural education.

Course	Check
Business and economics	1___
City Planning	2___
Engineering	3___
Fine Arts	4___
Landscape Architecture	5___
Law	6___
Liberal Arts	7___
Real Estate	8___
Social Sciences	9___
Other unspecified courses	0___

38. Based upon your experience in practice, check below the one appropriate column for each of the items listed to indicate your opinion of the effective content of an architectural curriculum.

Item	Important (1)	Desirable (2)	Of Minor Importance (3)
Professional:			
Applied science (light, color, sound)	01.___	01.___	01.___
Architectural design	02.___	02.___	02.___
Building codes, law and real estate	03.___	03.___	03.___
Building materials and methods	04.___	04.___	04.___
Community and city planning	05.___	05.___	05.___
Freehand drawing	06.___	06.___	06.___
Graphics (descriptive geometry, shades and shadows, perspective and presentation)	07.___	07.___	07.___
History of architecture	08.___	08.___	08.___
Interior design, decoration and furniture	09.___	09.___	09.___
Landscape design	10.___	10.___	10.___
Mechanical, electrical and sanitary installations	11.___	11.___	11.___
Office administration	12.___	12.___	12.___
Professional relations and ethics	13.___	13.___	13.___
Site engineering	14.___	14.___	14.___
Specifications	15.___	15.___	15.___
Structural design	16.___	16.___	16.___
Theory of architecture and composition (including basic design)	17.___	17.___	17.___
Working drawings	18.___	18.___	18.___
Academic:			
Chemistry	19.___	19.___	19.___
English	20.___	20.___	20.___
Fine arts	21.___	21.___	21.___
Foreign language	22.___	22.___	22.___
Mathematics	23.___	23.___	23.___
Physics	24.___	24.___	24.___
Psychology and human relations	25.___	25.___	25.___
Social sciences and philosophy (Economics, political science, sociology, history, anthropology, etc.)	26.___	26.___	26.___

467

C. REGISTRATION AND EXAMINATIONS

39. Check below the one item that covers the basis upon which you first became a registered architect.

Item	Check
Degree plus experience plus oral examination	1___
Degree plus experience plus written examination	2___
Degree plus experience plus written plus oral	3___
Degree plus experience	4___
Experience including non-degree education plus oral examinations	5___
Experience including non-degree education plus written examinations	6___
Experience including non-degree education plus written plus oral examinations	7___
Automatic or "grandfather" (engaged in practice at the time legislation came into effect)	8___
Other basis unspecified	9___

40. Have you a "Council Record" filed with the National Council of Architectural Registration Boards? Yes___1 No___2

41. If you have been certified by the NCARB, check below the appropriate item or items.

Item	Check
Junior Examination	1___
Senior Examination	2___
Both Junior and Senior Examinations	3___

42. In how many states are you currently registered? ___

43. In how many states did you utilize NCARB Standard Junior or Senior Examination as an aid in achieving registration (active and lapsed)? ___

44. Evaluate by a check mark in the one appropriate column your pre-registration experience in architectural practice for the items listed.

Item	Adequate (1)	Inadequate (2)	No Experience (3)
Administration	1___	1___	1___
Client relations	2___	2___	2___
Design, general architectural	3___	3___	3___
Design, mechanical	4___	4___	4___
Design, structural	5___	5___	5___
Direct experience on a construction job	6___	6___	6___
Drafting, working drawings and details	7___	7___	7___
Field supervision	8___	8___	8___
Preparation of specifications	9___	9___	9___
Site planning	0___	0___	0___

45. Check in the one appropriate column or section to indicate your opinion of your examination for registration with respect to the items listed below.

Item	Excessive (1)	Adequate (2)	Inadequate (3)
Emphasis on:			
Factual knowledge	1___	1___	1___
Skill in draftsmanship	2___	2___	2___
Facility in use of English	3___	3___	3___
History of architecture	4___	4___	4___
Architectural design	5___	5___	5___
Structural design	6___	6___	6___
Mechanical equipment	7___	7___	7___
Length	8. Too long___	8. Satisfactory___	8. Too short___
Character	9. Too difficult___	9. Satisfactory___	9. Too easy___
Statements of questions	0. Clear___	0. Satisfactory___	0. Ambiguous___

46. To answer this question please review "Outline Statement of Qualifications for the Practice of Architecture" on the back of the covering letter to this questionnaire and then check below in the one appropriate column to indicate your opinion of the importance of the items for inclusion in an examination for registration.

Item	Important (1)	Desirable (2)	Of Minor Importance (3)
Administration	1___	1___	1___
Architectural design	2___	2___	2___
Composition and theory	3___	3___	3___
History of architecture	4___	4___	4___
Materials	5___	5___	5___
Mechanical equipment	6___	6___	6___
Professional relations and ethics	7___	7___	7___
Site engineering	8___	8___	8___
Specifications	9___	9___	9___
Structural design	0___	0___	0___

47. Check below in the one appropriate column to indicate your opinion as to when the candidate for registration should be examined in the following subjects.

Subject	Immediately after completion of college work (1)	Upon completion of required office experience (2)	No examination on this subject should be given (3)
Architectural Composition	1___	1___	1___
Counselling and Administration	2___	2___	2___
Design Problem	3___	3___	3___
History of Architecture	4___	4___	4___
Mechanical Equipment of Buildings	5___	5___	5___
Natural Aptitude and Theoretical and Practical Training	6___	6___	6___
Selection and Use of Materials	7___	7___	7___
Supervision	8___	8___	8___
Structural Design	9___	9___	9___
Truss Design	0___	0___	0___

48. In your opinion how many years of office experience should an applicant have after graduation from an accredited school of architecture to be qualified for admission to the examination for registration? ___

49. Would you consider experience with a general contractor (up to a year) equivalent to experience in an architect's office in the preparation of young men for the practice of architecture? Yes___1 No___2

1. **Did you serve in the Armed Forces of the U. S. in World War II?**
   Yes———1 No———2

2. **Check the branch of the Service in which you served.** Army——1 Navy——2
   Air Force——3 Marine Corps——4 Coast Guard——5

3. **If commissioned, check rank held at separation.**

Brigadier General or higher ———— 1	Commodore or higher ———— 8
Colonel ———— 2	Captain ———— 9
Lt. Colonel ———— 3	Commander ————10
Major ———— 4	Lt. Commander ————11
Captain ———— 5	Lieutenant ————12
1st Lieutenant ———— 6	Lieutenant (jg) ————13
2nd Lieutenant ———— 7	Ensign ————14

4. **Do you hold reserve commission?** .... Yes——1 No——2

5a. **Were your duties with the Armed Forces of a professional character**
    (architecture, engineering)? .... Yes——1 No——2

5b. **If, in your opinion, your architectural training qualified you specially for non-**
    architectural work in the Armed Forces, briefly describe that work..............
    ....

6. **Were your duties as a wartime *civilian* worker of a professional character**
   (architecture, engineering)? .... Yes——1 No——2

7. **Check below to indicate your specific contribution as a wartime *civilian* worker.**
   Formally attached to one of the services or a government agency ————————1
   In industry engaged on wartime contracts ————2
   In professional practice as architect and/or engineer ————3
   Teaching: A.S.T.P., or other servicemen: E.S.M.W.T., etc. ————4

8. **Age last birthday**..——

Name   *City & State*   *(Please letter legibly)*

The 1950 Survey of Schools of Architecture

DEFINITIONS

Throughout this Report the following definitions apply: The _Institution_ is the university, college, institute or other parent institution to which the School is attached. The _School_ is the unit which directly administers the Curriculum in Architecture.

1. NAME OF INSTITUTION.

_____

2. TITLE OF ADMINISTRATIVE DIVISION, if any, of which School is a part.

_____

3. TITLE OF SCHOOL.

_____

Address: _____

_____

4. SUBMITTED FOR THE CURRENT ACADEMIC YEAR ENDING:
Month_____ Year ____

Name _____

Signature _____

Title _____

Date _____

5. TYPE OF INSTITUTION.
Privately endowed or supported ☐ State supported ☐ Municipally supported ☐ Denominational ☐
If other, describe _____
_____

6. ADMINISTRATIVE SET-UP OF SCHOOL.
a. The School is a: College ☐ School ☐ Department ☐ Course or Curriculum only ☐
b. Which is: Once, ☐ Twice, ☐ Thrice, ☐ administratively removed from chief authorities of the Institution (e.g., a department in a college of engineering, or fine arts, of a university would be twice removed).
c. As a single unit of one of the following: The Institution ☐ An administrative division composed of kindred departments (architecture, city planning, landscape architecture and the like) ☐ A technology division ☐ A fine arts division ☐ An engineering division ☐ Other (specify) _____

7. CURRICULA, DEGREES, ENROLLMENT.

Note: New students admitted should include all students enrolled for the first time in the specific curriculum. 1st Degree students in Architecture are those enrolled in a curriculum leading to the first degree which is usually a Bachelor's degree, but in some cases may be a Master's degree.

New students and enrollments listed below for the current academic year may be increased by the estimated additional number whose admission is expected in the remaining terms of the year if mid-year admissions are significant in number.

Give the actual number of enrolled students on the date of this report, or if this figure is not representative of the average enrollment during the complete academic year, give the estimated average for the terms of the complete academic year.

Number of new students admitted during current academic year who are candidates for:

	1st Degree	2nd Degree

Note: Please include and distribute new student figures in the table below.

CURRICULA	Title of		Check below if certificate only is awarded	years required to complete curriculum for		students enrolled during current academic year who are candidates for		students expected to graduate during current academic year with	
	1st Degree	2nd Degree		1st Degree	2nd Degree	1st Degree	2nd Degree	1st Degree	2nd Degree
Architecture									
Architectural Engineering									
Others related to Architecture (list below)									

8. TUITION AND FEES.

Annual Tuition for normal academic year $_____

Resident $_____ Non-Resident $_____

Additional Special Fees (Annual Average)
$_____

9. SCHOOL TERMS AND CREDIT UNITS.

a. Length of School Term:
Semester ☐ (weeks), Quarter ☐ (weeks), Other (describe)_____
b. Standard credit hour as used by this School means 3 clock hours per week per term in class and preparation, laboratory or drafting rooms.
Yes ☐ No ☐
If other, describe_____

_____

10. OBJECTIVES.

Check which one or more of the following describes the objectives which the training offered by the School is intended to serve:

a. Vocational training for architectural draftsmen, designers, superintendents, etc. as distinguished from registered architects. ☐

b. Pre-professional training providing general and technical studies acceptable in partial fulfillment of the requirements of Professional Curricula in Architecture or related fields at the same school or elsewhere. ☐

c. Does the work described in b. above constitute a field of concentration, or major, accepted by the Institution for a liberal arts degree? Yes ☐ No ☐

d. Professional training providing the general and technical studies required of candidates for registration as practicing architects. ☐

e. Post-graduate training providing special advanced study and research for graduates of schools offering complete professional training as described in d. above. Only ☐ Largely ☐ Partially ☐ Rarely ☐ Not at all ☐

f. Training for a special type of student. Yes ☐ No ☐ If yes, explain _____

g. Training for students from a limited geographical area. Yes ☐ No ☐ If yes, explain _____

h. Students whose vocational objective is limited to certain special phases of architectural practice. Yes ☐ No ☐ If Yes, explain _____

i. Describe other special objectives to which attention should be called. _____

11. METHODS OF REPORTING BUDGET AND FACULTY.

In order that this Report may reveal as nearly as possible the budget and faculty available to carry on the Curriculum in Architecture under the diverse conditions prevailing in different schools, one of the following two methods of reporting should be used:

Method 1

For many schools, budget and faculty may be reported in toto. When this is done, Item 21 should be answered as accurately as possible to show what the reported budget and faculty do or do not contribute to the teaching and administration of the Curriculum in Architecture. If this method has been used, check here. ☐

Method 2

Certain schools which offer several curricula in addition to a Curriculum in Architecture, but which operate as single administrative units with a unified budget and faculty, will present a more accurate picture of their situation if they report the pro rata share of budget and faculty which is devoted to the teaching and administration of their Curricula in Architecture. If this method has been used, check here. ☐

12. BUDGET.

a. 1) Total number of individual Budget-Teachers ____
2) Full-time equivalent number of Budget-Teachers (Use school's own definition of what constitutes full- and part-time. A Budget-Teacher is one who is regularly appointed to the School Faculty and whose salary is paid from the Teaching Budget)

b. Percent of total number of individual Budget-Teachers who are on full-time appointment ____

c. Teaching Budget:
1) Regular Teaching Budget (The total of salaries allotted to Budget-Teachers reported in a.) $ _____

2) Supplementary Teaching Budget (The total of fees allotted for visiting lecturers and critics not reported as Budget-Teachers in a.) $ _____
Total Teaching Budget $ _____

d. Administrative Budget (The total of allotments for: 1) wages or salaries of clerical, library, and other non-academic employees; 2) supplies, equipment, and miscellaneous expense; 3) faculty travel allowances, etc. If Teaching Budget is pro-rated according to Item 11, the administrative budget should be similarly pro-rated.) $ _____

Note: The following items should not be included in the Budget allotments reported above: 1) expenditures for scholarships, prizes, and student aid; 2) retirement allowances; 3) light, heat, or janitor services; 4) capital expenditures for buildings, permanent equipment, or library books.

e. Average Teacher's Salary: Item c.1) divided by Item a.2). Do not deduct from salaries T.I.A.A. and other annuity participation. $ _____

13. GEOGRAPHIC DISTRIBUTION OF STUDENTS.

Give the geographic distribution of home state of residence of all architectural students currently enrolled. Insert number of students:

Alabama	____	Idaho	____	Michigan	____	New York	____	Tennessee	____
Arizona	____	Illinois	____	Minnesota	____	North Carolina	____	Texas	____
Arkansas	____	Indiana	____	Mississippi	____	North Dakota	____	Utah	____
California	____	Iowa	____	Missouri	____	Ohio	____	Vermont	____
Colorado	____	Kansas	____	Montana	____	Oklahoma	____	Virginia	____
Connecticut	____	Kentucky	____	Nebraska	____	Oregon	____	Washington	____
Delaware	____	Louisiana	____	Nevada	____	Pennsylvania	____	West Virginia	____
Dist. of Columbia	____	Maine	____	New Hampshire	____	Rhode Island	____	Wisconsin	____
Florida	____	Maryland	____	New Jersey	____	South Carolina	____	U.S. Terr.& Poss.	____
Georgia	____	Massachusetts	____	New Mexico	____	South Dakota	____	Foreign	____

14. CURRICULUM IN ARCHITECTURE.

List below in the appropriate group of studies, the School's own credit units required for the 1st Degree in Architecture (including options, if any) together with all other requirements for graduation.

STUDIES	CREDIT UNITS REQUIRED	
	Option 1 – Title	Option 2 – Title
a.General Studies		
1)Specified courses in physical and social sciences, language, mathematics (include algebra and trigonometry only; list additional higher mathematics under Technical Studies) and other subjects not included under Technical Study groups listed below.		
2)Elective courses specified to be chosen from the General Studies listed above.		
3)Two-thirds of all unspecified pre-professional or free elective courses.		
Total General Studies		
b.Technical Studies		
1)Design (To include basic design, architectural design and thesis)		
2)Construction and Equipment		
a)Structural Theory (To include analytic geometry, calculus, mechanics, strength of materials, statics, structural design in masonry, wood, steel, and concrete).		
b)Building Materials and Methods (To include technology of building materials, building methods, working drawings, construction details, etc.).		
c)Building Equipment (To include mechanical, electrical, illuminating, sanitary, and acoustical equipment of buildings).		
3)History, Theory and Professional Relations		
a)History of Architecture and related arts.		
b)General Theory of architectural design, composition, color, planning and requirements of buildings, etc.		
c)Professional Relations, ethics, contracts, office organization and procedures, specifications, business law, etc.		
4)Drawing		
a)Graphics (To include descriptive geometry, projections, shades and shadows, perspective, and all forms of training in architectural representation).		
b)Freehand Drawing, Painting and Modeling.		
5)Related Fields		
a)Community and City Planning.		
b)Landscape Design.		
c)Furniture and Decoration.		
d)Other.		
6)Elective courses specified to be chosen from the above groups of Technical Studies		
7)One-third of all unspecified, free elective courses		
Total Technical Studies		
c.Total credit units required for degree.		

d.If there are other requirements for graduation not covered by
  a. and b., add a second sheet to describe them.

15. ENTRANCE REQUIREMENTS.

a.Secondary School Requirements

College Board exams	Required☐Optional ☐
State Board exams	Required☐Optional ☐
Institution's own exams	Required☐Optional ☐
Certificate from approved secondary School	Required☐Optional ☐

What are your definite requirements at Secondary School level?

    Subject   Unit Value

_____ _____

_____ _____

_____ _____

_____ _____

b.Pre-Architectural College Work Requirements:
Specify amounts in years _____

c.Additional Qualitative or Selective Requirements: Secondary school ranking (specify minimum requirements)____ College aptitude test (specify minimum score required)____ Architectural aptitude tests, specify_____

_____

Other, describe _____

_____

16. STUDENT AID.

a. Give average of last three year's funds awarded to Undergraduate Architectural Students for prizes, scholarships and other financial aid.
            $_____

b. Give average of last three year's funds awarded to Graduate Architectural Students for prizes, scholarships, and other financial aid. (Include graduating thesis scholarships). $_____

17. STUDENT MORTALITY.
   a. Have you made a study recently of student mortality in your architectural school? Yes ☐ No ☐
   b. If so, what percentage of new students continued into <u>second</u> year? _____ %
   c. What percentage of new students continued until graduation? _____ %

18. TRANSFER STUDENTS.
   a. How many new students during 1949-50 entered from technical or vocational institutes? _____
   b. Do you exercise any control over the architectural courses offered in these institutes from which you attract applicants? formal control ☐ ; informal advice ☐ ; none ☐
   c. During 1949-1950 what percentage of new students entered architecture with previous pre-professional college work? _____ %

19. OCCUPATIONS OF GRADUATES.
   a. Do you have reliable data on the occupations of graduates? Yes ☐ No ☐ If your answer is Yes;
   b. What is the number of graduates whose present occupation is known? _____
   c. This number is approximately___% of the total number of graduates.
   d. General occupations of known graduates are as follows:
      1) Number in professional architectural work _____
      2) Number in non-professional work in the building industry _____
      3) Number in related design fields _____
      4) Number in occupations unrelated to architecture, building or design _____

20. GRADUATE INSTRUCTION.
   a. Curricula

Title of curriculum	Title of 2nd degree	Normal length	1949-50 enrollment	Title of 3rd degree	Normal length	1949-50 enrollment

b. Describe your admission requirements to graduate curriculum. _____

_____

c. Fields of concentration offered (mark M for master's level, D for doctoral)
   1) Design ___ ___
   2) Special types of buildings

_____

_____

   3) City planning ___ ___
   4) Structural theory and design ___ ___
   5) History ___ ___
      Special periods_____ ___ ___

_____

   6) Materials and methods of construction ___ ___
   7) Other_____ ___ ___

_____

d. Fields of concentration permitted in other divisions of Institution: (mark m if for minor only)
   1) Sociology ___ ___

   2) Climatology ___ ___

   3) Geography ___ ___

   4) Aesthetics ___ ___

   5) Structural Engineering ___ ___

   6) Mechanical Engineering ___ ___

   7) Other_____

e. Graduate staff:
   1) Number of School's staff entirely assigned to graduate courses _____
   2) Number of School's staff assigned to graduate courses <u>and</u> research _____
   3) Number of School's staff teaching both undergraduate and graduate courses _____
f. What percentage of School's budget is devoted to graduate instruction? _____ %
g. Graduate assistantships: 1) Number available ___
   2) Average stipend___; top stipend___; smallest _____; Half-time stipend: average___; top ___; smallest _____.
   3) Duties chiefly in: undergraduate teaching ☐; departmental work ☐; research assistance ☐; other _____
h. Fellowships available to graduate students:
   1) Number available _____
   2) Awarded by design competition ☐ ; academic record ☐ ; professional record ☐ ; other ☐
   3) Stipends_____ 4) Time required _____
   5) If for travel, to what countries _____

   _____

   6) Other comments _____

j. Instruction space for graduates:
   1) Desk for each in graduate students' room? ☐
   2) Own drafting table for each? ☐
   3) Carrel provided in School library? ☐
21. EFFORT TO OTHERS.
   a. Percentage of Budget-Teachers effort diverted from the teaching and administration of the Technical Studies reported in Item 14-b.
      1) Specific duties to the Institution rather than to the School, such as administration, architectural services, etc. _____ %
      2) To non-professional students (the percentage reported should preferably be based on the proportion of non-professional student credits taught to the total student credit units taught. If such data is not available, use any other method of computation or the best judgment obtainable). _____ %
   b. Percent of Technical Studies listed in Item 14-b. taught by Budget-Teachers _____ %

22. FACULTY IMPROVEMENT.
    a. Does your school conduct a special program to improve faculty teaching competence? ☐, on organized basis ☐, on informal basis ☐, on institution-wide basis ☐ Other, describe

    _____

    b. Would your school favor participation in a program to improve the teaching of technical subjects? Yes ☐ No ☐ ;through occasional teaching institutes? Yes ☐ No ☐ ;through special summer courses? Yes ☐ No ☐ ;these courses to be approximately 2 weeks long ☐ 4 weeks long ☐ ; full summer session with academic credit ☐ ;would your school assist teachers financially to take part? Yes ☐ No ☐
    c. Would your school favor an organized program to place teachers in progressive architectural offices for limited periods? Yes ☐ No ☐
    d. Would your school favor a program of visiting professorships? Yes ☐ No ☐ ; of exchange professorships? Yes ☐ No ☐ .
    e. Does your school carry on an active program of sabbatical leaves? Yes ☐ No ☐ . How many such leaves (exclusive of military leaves) have been taken during the past 15 years? _____How many leaves without pay have been taken in order to participate in professional activities? _____

23. PROFESSIONAL PRACTICE BY FACULTY: What is your School's policy on Professional Practice by full-time Faculty?   a. No limitations ☐
    b. Encouraged to extent compatible with teaching duties ☐ . c. Approval required for specific projects: By School Head ☐ . By higher administrative authority ☐ . d. Allowable only for part-time staff ☐ . e. Tolerated, but not encouraged ☐ . f. Entirely forbidden ☐ ; or forbidden due to opposition of architects ☐ ; or due to possible neglect of teaching ☐
    g. Other(comments)_____
    h. Are architectural teachers expected to provide architectural services, other than advisory, to the Institution as a part of their normal duties? Yes ☐ No ☐ ;at extra compensation? Yes ☐ No ☐ .
    j. Are full-time teachers permitted and encouraged to perform professional architectural services for the Institution on private commissions? Yes ☐ No ☐ .
    k. Are part-time teachers permitted and encouraged to perform professional architectural services for the Institution on private commissions? Yes ☐ No ☐ .
    l. Do any members of the faculty advise the Institution on its architectural problems: By formal appointment? Yes ☐ No ☐ ;with compensation in the form of reduced teaching duties? Yes ☐ No ☐ ;extra compensation? Yes ☐ No ☐ ;by informal arrangement? Yes ☐ No ☐ .

24. RESEARCH.

Architectural research is here understood to be the investigation and analysis of phenomena, principles, applications, or methods of procedure relating to the design and construction of buildings, the reports of which are to be published for the enhancement of the profession's technical resources.

a. Participation of staff (give number carrying on bona-fide systematic research projects): undergraduate teachers ____; graduate teachers ____; research staff ____.
b. Projects, 1945 to date: 1)Total number begun ____; 2)Number of projects taken on contract____;3)Total number of projects completed, but not published____; 4)Total number of projects completed and published____.
c. Project subjects, 1945 to date (mark C if on contract):_____

_____
_____

d. List any architectural research projects done independently by staff or other divisions of your Institution:_____

_____
_____

e. List architectural research projects in which the School staff collaborated with other divisions in your Institution:_____

_____

f. Describe briefly any special research facilities administered by the School: _____

_____
_____

g. 1949-50 School Budget for Research:
   1) Total expenditures for architectural research $_____
   2) Expenditures reimbursed by research contracts $_____
   3) Net cost or profit to School for research $_____
h. Research projects proposed for the near future: _____

_____
_____
_____

25. SCHOOL'S SERVICE TO THE PROFESSION, 1949-1950.

a. Number of staff speaking before groups of architects ___; number of talks ___; number of staff speaking before other groups in the building industry___; number of talks___.

b. Number of technical programs (seminars, etc.) organized by staff for professional groups ___.

c. Number of refresher courses organized by School for those preparing for registration examinations ____; total enrollment____.

d. Number of advanced technical courses offered for architects:

Courses	Enrollment

e. Other services to the profession: _____

26. NATIONAL ARCHITECTURAL ACCREDITING BOARD.

a. Has your School undergone NAAB inspection? Yes ☐ No ☐

b. Did the Pattern Map prepared from your Factual Report constitute a helpful appraisal of the School's facilities and general situation? Yes ☐ No ☐
Suggested improvements: _____

c. Did you feel that the personnel of the visiting Inspection Team was qualified to evaluate your progress, work, and situation? Yes ☐ No ☐ ; did they show a proper interest and understanding with respect to organization of your curriculum? Yes ☐ No ☐ ; the organization, content, and methods used in the specific courses? Yes ☐ No ☐ ; in the qualifications of your teachers? Yes ☐ No ☐ ; in student opinion and morale? Yes ☐ No ☐ ; in administrative problems? Yes ☐ No ☐ . Suggested improvements: _____

d. Did your School receive any benefit or assistance due to the inspection which ameliorated a difficult local situation? Yes ☐ No ☐ .

e. Other comments _____

27. REGISTRATION PROCEDURE.

Does your School conduct the examination for any state registration Board? Yes ☐ No ☐ ; assist in drafting the questions? Yes ☐ No ☐ Grade the examinations? Yes ☐ No ☐

28. CATALOGUE.

Please supplement this report by sending two copies of your most recent catalogue or bulletin of information which contains information concerning your School.

The 1950 Survey of the Architectural Profession

The Commission for the Survey of Education and Registration of the American Institute of Architects,

Department of Education and Research

1741 NEW YORK AVENUE, N. W.

WASHINGTON 6, D. C.

FACULTY QUESTIONNAIRE

1. Name _____

2. Rank _____ Year of birth _____
   Percent of full-time for which appointed.___%
   List part-time at percentage as determined by
   institution practise. A teacher who is called
   by the institution a full-time teacher should
   report 100% even though he may engage in private practise,etc., in addition to teaching load.

3. GENERAL EDUCATION. Give years of formal training at college level. Count one year of a 4 or
   5-year, and two years of a 6-year Professional
   Curriculum in Architecture as General Education.

Institutions	No. of years	Degrees earned

4. TECHNICAL EDUCATION. Give years of formal training at college level. Count three years of a
   4-year, and four years of a 5 or 6-year Professional Curriculum in Architecture as Technical Education. Count additional graduate years
   of technical study at full value.

Institutions	No. of years	Degrees earned

5. ACADEMIC DISTINCTIONS AND FELLOWSHIPS HELD FOR
   RESEARCH, TRAVEL, ETC. _____

6. TRAVEL EXPERIENCE. Give number of months spent
   on specific travel expeditions -
   For serious study.   Foreign __ Domestic __
   Not for serious study. Foreign __ Domestic __
   For practise only.   Foreign __ Domestic __

7. TEACHING EXPERIENCE AT COLLEGE LEVEL.

Institution	No. of years	Teaching load Full time 1/4	1/2	3/4

8. REGISTRATION FOR PRACTICE
   As Architect ___ In what states_____
   As Engineer ___ In what states_____
   Do you hold senior NCARB certificate? Yes_No__
   Do you hold junior NCARB certificate? Yes_No__

9. SERVICE TO INSTITUTION.
   What percentage (if any) of your total effort
   is normally given to architectural practise
   for the institution? _____%
   Does this work carry compensation outside of
   Budget provisions for salary?   Yes ___ No __
   Percentage of teaching salary_%

10. EXPERIENCE IN PRACTISE.
    Principal means an individual who is singly
    responsible, or equally responsible with others
    for the conduct of professional services.
    Associate means an employee who is permanently
    identified with a firm, and who bears suffic-
    ient responsibility to have a financial inter-
    est in the firm or his name on its letterhead.
    Calculate number of years for part-time or oc-
    casional practise at estimated equivalent to
    full-time engagement in the three fields des-
    ignated below:

	Number of years engaged as:				
	To-tal	Em-ployee	Asso-ciate	Prin-cipal	Con-sultant
Architecture					
Full-time					
Part-time or occasional					
Engineering					
Full-time					
Part-time or occasional					
Related fields					
Full-time					
Part-time or occasional					

11. PROFESSIONAL WORK. Describe briefly below the
    most important professional work for which you
    have been responsible and indicate Yes___ or
    No___ if this work was the design of a build-
    ing for which you were the architect.

    _____
    _____
    _____
    _____

12. CREATIVE ACTIVITIES. List accomplishment in
    respect to research, publications, exhibitions,
    competitions, buildings, etc.

    _____
    _____
    _____

13. MEMBERSHIP IN PROFESSIONAL SOCIETIES.
    American Institute of Architects.
                    Associate Member _____
                    Corporate Member _____
                    Fellow
    Other comparable professional societies:

    _____

14. OFFICES AND DISTINCTIONS. Offices held, committee or board memberships, etc. in professional societies and activities. _____

_____

_____

Special distinctions, including fellowships in professional societies, listing in Who's Who in America, prizes, medals, competition awards, etc. Do not include any school honors or awards.

_____

_____

15. ADMINISTRATIVE DUTIES. Describe briefly.

_____

_____

16. TEACHING. Enter below the appropriate information re the courses you are teaching this semester.

Course Title	Students (Number)			Hours (Per Week)			
	Undergraduate architectural	Graduate architectural	Others	Lecture or recitation contact hours	Drafting Room or Studio contact hours	Seminar hours	No. of sections

17. METHODS. Describe briefly any unusual teaching methods, devices, or aids that you have found particularly effective in any or all of the above courses. _____

_____

18. ASSISTANCE. How much assistance is provided to you for secretarial, clerical, grading, etc.? Total hours per week _____

19. TRENDS. Generally speaking, programs of architectural education are different from what they were 20 years ago. What significant trends have you noted in development of architectural education during these 20 years in schools with which you have been associated?

_____

_____

_____

What significant changes (if any) in architectural education would you predict for the next 20 years? _____

_____

_____

_____

20. SELECTION OF STUDENTS. How would you suggest that the selection of students admitted to architecture could be made more effective?

_____

_____

21. TEACHER DEVELOPMENT.
a) How many schools of architecture have you visited and observed since Jan. 1, 1947? _____
b) Did your school pay all or part of your expenses for such visits? All ___ Part ___ None ___
c) Would you favor an organized program to place teachers in progressive architectural offices for limited periods? Yes ____ No ____
d) Would you favor an organized program of visiting or exchange professorships? Yes ___ No ___
e) Would you favor a program for the exchange of opinion through occasional teaching institutes for architectural faculty? Yes ___ No ___
f) Would you consider participation at your own expense in a teaching institute held within 500 miles of your school for: 1 week long Yes ___ No ___
2 weeks long Yes ___ No ___
4 weeks long Yes ___ No ___
g) If your answer to f) is "no", would you consider participation in a teaching institute if your school paid part or all of the expense? Yes ___ No ____ What percentage of expenses would you hope to have paid by your school? _____ %
h) How could your school assist you in increasing your effectiveness as a teacher?

_____

_____

22. RESEARCH. Architectural research is here understood to be the investigation or analysis of phenomena, principles, applications or methods of procedure relating to the design and construction of buildings, the reports of which are to be published for the enlargement of the profession's technical resources.
a) What research projects are you pursuing? List and describe briefly. _____

_____

b) What research projects have you completed? List and describe briefly. _____

_____

23. COMMUNITY ACTIVITIES. In what voluntary or civic activities are you now actively participating?

_____

24. A.I.A. How could The American Institute of Architects assist you in increasing your effectiveness as:
a) a teacher? _____

_____

b) a practising architect?

_____

_____

_____

_____

The 1950 Survey of the Architectural Profession

The Commission for the Survey of Education and Registration of the American Institute of Architects,

Department of Education and Research

1741 NEW YORK AVENUE, N. W.

WASHINGTON 6, D. C.

QUESTIONNAIRE FOR SECRETARIES OF ARCHITECTURAL REGISTRATION BOARDS

A. The Registration Law

1. In what year was the architectural registration law passed in your state? _____

2. Has this law been amended since its original passing? Yes __ No __; if yes, did the amendments improve the law? Yes ____ No ____

3. a) Have you attempted unsuccessfully to amend your law? Yes ____ No ____
   b) If the answer is yes, wherein did you find your opposition? _____
   _____
   _____
   _____

4. What is your status as secretary?
   a) full-time for the architectural board ____
   b) part-time " " " " ____
   c) serve joint architectural, engineering, and land surveying board ____
   d) serve bureau for all professional registration ____
   e) other (describe) _____
   _____
   _____

5. Does the Board have authority to make the following changes without legislative action?
   a) qualifications for admission to examinations Yes ____ No ____
   b) character of examination questions Yes ____ No ____
   c) basis for grading examinations Yes ____ No ____

6. a) Does the way in which the practice of architecture is defined in your law limit its application to matters of public safety (life, health, morals)? Yes ____ No ____
   b) Does it include matters of general welfare, aesthetics, etc.? Yes ____ No ____

7. a) Does your law place restrictions on:
      use of the term "architect"? Yes __ No __
      practice of architecture? Yes __ No __
   b) If permissive, but not mandatory, quote pertinent section. _____
   _____
   _____
   c) If "designer" may practice, quote pertinent section. _____
   _____
   _____

8. What buildings are exempted from the provision of the law?
   a) farm buildings ____
   b) single family houses ____
   c) two-family houses ____
   d) State limit of area _____ sq. ft.
   e) State limit of cost $_____
   f) other_____

9. Describe provisions of other legislation which affects the operation of the registration law.
   _____
   _____

10. a) Do building officials require that names of registered architects (or engineers) appear on drawings, etc., submitted with applications for permits?
    b) Are permits issued without this requirement being fulfilled?
    c) Is a certification required that buildings conform with requirements of law required of architects (or engineers)?

	City		County		State	
	Yes	No	Yes	No	Yes	No

   d) Is this a requirement of your registration law?__ state building code?__ judicial order?__ local building codes? ____

B. The Board

11. What is the number of members of your Board?__

12. What is the term of office? _____

13. What are the restrictions on re-appointment?
    a) None ____
    b) Limited to __ terms
    c) Other _____

14. What is the manner of selection of Board members?
    a) By Governor without consultation _____
    b) On recommendations by Board _____
    c) Through organized recommendation by the architectural profession _____
    d) Through casual recommendation by individual architects _____
    e) Other_____

15. What are the qualifications for Board membership?
    a) Age _____ years
    b) Professional practice _____ years
    c) Residence in State _____ years
    d) Other_____
    _____
    _____

16. What is the manner of selection of chairman (or equivalent officer)?
    a) Election by Board ____
    b) Appointment by Governor ____
    c) Other_____

17. Do architectural school faculty members serve as regular members of the Board?
    a) As a requirement of the law _____
    b) By custom _____

18. Is the inclusion of architectural school faculty members opposed?
    a) By members of the Board _____
    b) By the architectural profession _____

19. If Board members are paid for service, how are they paid?
    a) Per diem ____
    b) Per meeting ____
    c) Annual ____
    d) No remuneration ____

478

C. Examinations

20. What are the regular times at which examinations are given? _____

21. What is the limit to the number of times a candidate may re-take examinations?
    a) without payment of additional fees _____
    b) with payment of additional fees _____

22. What information concerning examinations is available to candidates?
    a) Syllabus _____ b) Sample questions _____
    c) Complete drafts of past exams _____
    d) Type of building to be the subject of the design problem _____

23. Who prepares examination questions?
    a) All Board members by assignment of parts _____
    b) Selected Board members:
       1. Members of a school faculty _____
       2. Other (explain): _____
    _____
    _____
    _____

24. Who grades examinations?
    a) All Board members as a jury, -
       1. design examinations _____
       2. other examinations _____
    b) Individual Board members for separate parts _____
    c) Selected Board members, -
       1. members of school faculty _____
       2. other _____
    d) State agency not controlled by Board _____
    e) Other than Board members, -
       1. members of school faculty _____
       2. other (explain) _____
    _____

25. Does the Board follow the NCARB Syllabus and grading system? Yes _____ No _____

26. Where are the examinations held?
    a) In a State building _____
    b) At an architectural school _____
    c) At a hotel _____
    d) In an architect's office _____
    e) Other _____,

27. What are the qualifications for admission to the Junior Examinations?
    a) Age _____
    b) Citizenship _____
    c) Architectural education _____
    d) Years of experience _____

28. From what parts of the examinations (if any) are graduates of accredited schools exempted? _____
    _____
    _____

29. What significant changes in examinations have been made by your Board during the past 3 years? _____
    _____
    _____

30. Does your Board try to measure personality characteristics in candidates? Yes ___ No _____
    If so, please describe method. _____
    _____
    _____
    _____

31. If study should indicate that it were feasible for most State Boards to give simultaneous examinations, using the same questions, could your Board do so?
    a) Under present law _____
    b) With minor revisions of your law _____

32. Does your Board include an interview (or oral examination) in the examinations for Junior Applicants, -
    a) who are exempted from written examinations?
       Yes _____ No _____
    b) whose grades on written examinations are marginal? Yes _____ No _____
    c) others _____

33. Over the past three years what percentage of applicants has passed, -
    a) the first time? ___ b) the second time? ___
    c) the third time? ___ d) later than 3rd time? ___

34. In what subject are the greatest number of failures? _____

D. Operational Policies

35. What are the fees, -
    a) for original application and examination?
       _____
    b) for reinstatement? _____
    c) refund to those withdrawing applications?
       _____
    d) refund to those failing examinations? ____
    e) for annual registration renewals? _____
    f) for biennial registration renewals? _____

36. Who receives fees?
    a) Secretary of Board _____
    b) Other State official _____

37. What is the disposition of fees?
    a) Under control of Board _____
    b) In general fund of State _____
    c) Surplus to general fund _____
    d) Part of surplus to general fund
       Percent _____

38. Are annual reports sent to, -
    a) Board members? _____
    b) State officials? _____
    c) all architects registered in State? _____

39. Does your Board maintain reciprocal relations with, -
    a) adjoining State Boards? _____
    b) states with equal requirements? _____
    c) any state? _____

40. Does your Board require deficiency examination of applicants previously licensed in states with inferior requirements?
    1. partial _____ 2. complete _____

41. Does your Board require applicants registered in other states. -
    a) to submit an NCARB record? _____
    b) to submit an NCARB certificate? _____

42. a) What is the average number of Junior candidates over the past 3 years? _____
    b) Approximately what % of these are graduates of accredited architectural schools? _____

43. If you have noted any difference, are graduates of accredited architectural schools more successful in examinations than others? (Please give data if available, otherwise your opinion.) _____
    _____
    _____
    _____
    _____

The 1950 Survey of Registration Board Members

1. In your opinion, how many architects in your state are satisfied with:
   a) Your Registration Law.
      1. Majority _____ 2. Half _____ 3. Few _____
   b) Its operation?
      1. Majority _____ 2. Half _____ 3. Few _____

2. In your opinion, does architectural registration in your state:
   a) Unduly restrict the number entering practice?
      Yes _____ No _____
   b) Admit unqualified persons to practice?
      Yes _____ No _____
   c) Give sufficient recognition to graduates of accredited architectural schools? Yes___No___
   d) Give sufficient recognition to potential applicants,
      1. Who have had especially favorable experience? Yes _____ No _____
      2. Who have unusual natural ability?
         Yes _____ No _____

3. If you would like to change your law, please outline changes you would suggest:

   _____
   _____
   _____
   _____
   _____

4. If you know of weaknesses in Registration Law of other states, please indicate:

   _____
   _____
   _____
   _____

5. If your Board required interviews (or oral examinations) of Junior Applicants, do you think them: a. very effective ___ b. worth while ___
   c. of little value ___

6. If provisions were made for applicants to receive a satisfactory controlled office experience under the guidance of qualified architects and were required to submit a certified log book reporting this experience:
   a) What portions, if any, of your present examinations would you be willing to omit?

   _____
   _____
   _____
   _____
   _____

   b) Would this procedure facilitate passing upon candidates?

   _____
   _____

   c) If, in addition, candidates were required to submit samples of work done during the controlled experience period, would decisions regarding their status be facilitated?

   _____

7. Would you favor an examination for admission to a controlled experience period:
   a) required of all candidates? Yes ___ No ___
   b) exempting candidates with nine or more years of uncontrolled office experience?
      Yes ___ No ___
   c) exempting graduates of accredited architectural schools? Yes ___ No ___

8. What suggestions, if any, would you offer:
   a) for the revision of the NCARB Syllabus?

   _____
   _____
   _____
   _____
   _____
   _____
   _____
   _____

   b) for the procedure of the NCARB?

   _____
   _____
   _____
   _____

9. Would the preparation of a "model" architectural registration law be beneficial in guiding and influencing future amendments of your law?

   _____
   _____
   _____
   _____
   _____
   _____
   _____
   _____
   _____
   _____

10. If study should indicate that it was feasible for most state Boards to give simultaneous Junior Examinations using the same questions, would you favor doing so? Yes ___ No ___

11. How many years have you served as a member of your Board? _____ years.

12. What do you consider to be the optimum period of service? _____ years.

13. Which, if any, of the above statements may be quoted?

   _____

Appendix B: The Statistical Basis of the Survey

A. INTRODUCTION

1. *Range and magnitude of the data sources.* Throughout its numerous deliberations the Survey Commission ever kept in mind that its report on the *1950 Survey of the Architectural Profession* had to be based on more than mere fact finding. With this as its unique thesis, therefore, every topic compatible with the Survey charter was so designed in respect of its question content to be a judicious mixture of fact and opinion. And to obtain the responses to these major questions, many of which had numerous subdivisions, the following separate and distinct sources were used.

	Number		Major
	Mailed	Returned	Questions
1. Individual Registered Architects:			
a. General Questionnaire..................	19,137	6,605(35%)	49
AIA members.........................	8,461	3,744(44%)	
Non-AIA members....................	10,676	2,861(27%)	
b. War Service Questionnaire..............	19,137	8,851(46%)	8
AIA members.........................	8,461	4,649(55%)	
Non-AIA members....................	10,676	4,202(39%)	
2. Registration Board Questionnaires:			
a. To Secretaries........................	49	33	43
b. To Individual Board Members..........	193	105	13
3. School Questionnaires:			
a. To Deans and Directors of Architectural Schools.............................	65	59	28
b. To Faculty Members..................	900	436	24
4. Questionnaires to AIA Chapter Secretaries:			
a. To test AIA membership characteristics...	32	23	8
b. To test characteristics of AIA and Non-AIA non-respondents........................	47	41	8
5. Regional Conferences with nearly 100 non-architects.................................	—	—	3
6. Opinions from Fellows of AIA..............	343	68	2
7. Opinions from Honorary Corresponding Members in foreign countries..............	46	11	2

2. *Mailing schedule and general status of returns.* Two other unique features of the survey procedures warrant comment at this time. The two basic questionnaires to individual architects were all in the mail by September 1, 1950 and closed out as regards returns by November 30. By January 31, 1951 the "special questionnaires" to registra-

481

tion boards, faculty members and the deans and directors of architectural schools and colleges had been mailed. And from January to April 1951 all basic work had been completed on the collection of data to test the registered architects' responses; all regional conferences had been held: and the letters from Honorary Corresponding Members had been received and summarized.

The second notable feature is the unusually high ratio of returns as indicated above. The returns from the individual registered architects were particularly gratifying, and, as the ensuing discussion makes clear, these may be accepted as being representative of either the entire profession or its two separate components of AIA and Non-AIA registered architects especially with respect to their geographical location and employment status distributions. However, age characteristics are slightly biased in favor of younger architects. The starting point of this discussion is the unduplicated mailing list.

3. *The unduplicated mailing list.* The unduplicated mailing list of 19,137 registered architects was compiled from two separate sources: The roster of 8,461 AIA members as of July 1950, and 10,676 names of Non-AIA architects which were obtained from the latest lists in the files of every registration board in the country.

In these regards valued and essential cooperation was provided by architectural registration boards and similar remarks apply to the AIA Chapters throughout the country, which were called upon to furnish the information required to make independent checks of the AIA members in their chapters and of the non-responding architects located in their particular areas.

Despite the formidable task involved in compiling the unduplicated mailing list, the high standard of accuracy maintained in its preparation is reflected in the fact that subsequent corrections based on the War Service Questionnaire returns, since it was issued prior to the General Questionnaire, were relatively few in number. It was inevitable that some recipients of the questionnaire would indicate a change of address. In the case of the AIA members only 37 transfers were recorded and only 81 of the Non-AIA architects. The majority of these transfers involved contiguous states.

The other correction factors to the initial mailing list that may be noted are: 52 were reported deceased, 103 had received two questionnaires, 45 were discarded because responses were too few in number or were returned blank as having been retired or in non-architectural work, 27 returned cards unanswered and only 38 were returned by the post office department as "unclaimed."

In other words, the grand total of corrections did not exceed 160 individual architects after allowing for duplication. No attempt was made, however, to adjust the initial mailing list of 19,137 architects for these factors. To say, for example, that only 52 were deceased would be a completely erroneous assumption. The principal thing to be noted is that, based on a 46 per cent return, corrections of the order of 2 per cent would effect at most the same proportion in the total mailing list of 19,137 or 380 individuals, a negligible number indeed in view of the fact that these 380 individuals in all likelihood would distribute themselves over the 48 states and the District of Columbia in proportions similar to the general distributions of the actual returns received.

4. *Women architects.* Another aspect of the data to be noted at this time is the extent to which they include women as practicing architects. Actually, only 71 questionnaires (37 AIA and 34 Non-AIA) members were returned by women architects, and, being too few to warrant separate tabulation they have been included throughout with those from male respondents who overwhelmingly predominate in the architectural profession.

B. REPRESENTATIVENESS OF THE GENERAL QUESTIONNAIRE RETURNS

1. *The characteristics to be tested.* The need to test the characteristics of the returns results from the fact that the general questionnaire data have been derived from a 35 per cent sample of the entire unduplicated mailing list, which, as indicated above is a composite of a 44 per cent sample of the AIA architects and a 27 per cent sample of the Non-AIA architects. The characteristics to be tested may be summarized as follows: At the time the data were collected the individual architect had one specific location and a particular employment status and age. Being of a particular age, his earnings' capacity would in most cases differ from architects older or younger than he not only because earnings of professional workers do increase with age, but also because his earnings would vary with the way in which he earned his livelihood. For in that specific geographical location he did obtain his living as an architect in one of four ways: As an individual practitioner, as a teacher, or as a private or public employee architect. As an employee architect his specific duties would have been one of several possibilities: designer, draftsman, outside superintendent, etc. For survey purposes, too, he could have reported he was engaged in non-architectural work, was employed or had retired from the profession.

2. *Size of sample and cross-classifications.* It may also be observed that in surveys of any group of professional workers, it is not only vitally important that the sample of returns be large enough to check a wide range of characteristics, but the sample also must be large enough to allow of making the greatest number of cross-classifications among the widest possible range of variables within the questionnaire itself. Were this survey based, for example, on a 10 per cent sample selected from the unduplicated mailing list, that is, approximately 2,000 architects instead of the 6,605 who actually returned the General Questionnaire, very severe limitations would have been imposed on the number of cross-classifications that could have been derived, e.g., age with income, age by employment status, plus the very important fact that comparisons of state or regional data for selected variables would not have been obtained because of lack of density in the number of returns. With respect to the 49 questions in the general questionnaire the optimum number of cross-classifications have been derived from the 6,605 returns.

3. *The testing procedures.* To establish the representativeness of the General Questionnaire returns, the following procedures have been adopted as regards three of the

483

basic characteristics of the data. In the case of geographical location it is necessary first to be assured that the proportions of returns do not differ significantly from the proportions for the corresponding 49 locations in the unduplicated mailing list, i.e., 48 states and the District of Columbia. In these particular comparisons it is possible to contrast the distributions for both the General and War Service Questionnaires which, essentially, are two different samples drawn from the same universe. Similar contrasts are possible with regard to their respective age characteristics which is followed by the discussion of employment statuses that derives, of course, only from the General Questionnaire.

To test the age characteristics and the employment status distributions, 41 of the AIA chapter secretaries were asked to obtain the information by telephone from a selected group of AIA and Non-AIA architects who had not returned the General Questionnaire. An independent check on the employment status distributions of AIA architects only was also made among 20 AIA chapters who furnished this information about their own chapter memberships.

4. *Geographical location characteristics.* Despite the fact that 8,851 or 46 per cent of the 19,137 registered architects returned the War Service Questionnaire and only 6,605 or 35 per cent of the same 19,137 architects returned the General Questionnaire, *Table I* clearly indicates that the incidence of return among each of the 49 locations is not only parallel to the location distribution of the combined unduplicated mailing list, but exactly similar conditions exist among AIA and Non-AIA architects when they are dealt with as separate entities.

Because there are no underlying differences among the 49 locations from which the sample data were returned, and because they do parallel in every instance their respective population distributions, either or both sets of returns may be accepted as representative of the geographical distribution of the architectural profession throughout the country.

5. *Age characteristics.* The first observation to be made about the age characteristics of the architectural profession is that they differ but slightly from one location to another (*Table I*). The general pattern, therefore, of this characteristic is indicated by the returns for the country as a whole.

In 1950 the data reveal that the 4,649 AIA members who returned War Service Questionnaires had a median age of 47.2 years (i.e., 50 per cent of the group were above and 50 per cent were below this particular age). This median age differs but slightly from the median age of 46.5 years for the 3,744 AIA members who returned the General Questionnaire. In the case of the Non-AIA architects, the corresponding median ages are 46.7 and 44.5 years.

The extent to which these age characteristics are representative of the profession will be indicated in a subsequent discussion of the non-response data. This particular discussion is preceded, however, by one that deals with the pattern of employment statuses as derived from the General Questionnaire.

6. *Employment status characteristics.* According to the data presented in *Table 2* the employment status characteristics of the profession, like the age characteristics,

show similar distributions as between one geographical location and another. Such differences as do exist merely reflect the varying possibilities in employment opportunities particularly for the private employee architects. Selecting, therefore, the national distribution it shows that the architectural profession is predominated by individual practitioners, who, in the case of the AIA members, comprise 81 per cent of their group in contrast to only 56 per cent in the case of the Non-AIA members. Second in order of importance come private and public employee architects that cover 14 per cent and 37 per cent, respectively, of the AIA and Non-AIA architects. The remaining 6 per cent of the Institute members includes 4 per cent as teachers and 2 per cent who indicated they were engaged in non-architectural work or had retired. The remaining 7 per cent of the Non-Institute architects on the other hand includes only 2 per cent as teachers and 5 per cent classified as being in non-architectural work, retired, or unemployed.

7. Independent tests of the survey data.

(a) *AIA chapter memberships.* To establish whether or not the employment status distributions of the survey data are typical of the profession, two tests have been applied. First, in the case only of the AIA architects, 20 AIA chapter secretaries were requested to furnish the Commission with the breakdown of their memberships by the same employment status categories used in the General Questionnaire. These 20 chapters were selected to insure that they represented the following five main types of areas of professional activity: Urban, urban-rural, densely populated states, sparsely populated states, and suburban areas. The states involved in these chapter distributions are as follows:

	Total								
State	14	CAL.	CONN.	DEL.	FLA.	LA.	MISS.	MO.	N. Y
No. of Chapters	20	3	1	1	1	2	1	1	3
Architects Reported	1,747	357	141	33	59	58	52	149	243

State	OHIO	ORE.	PA.	TEX.	UTAH	W. VA.
No. of Chapters	1	1	2	1	1	1
Architects Reported	76	106	196	178	52	47

Insofar as the separate states are concerned, it was hardly to be expected that even the combined chapter returns would match in all respects the employment statuses of the General Questionnaire data. What had really to be determined was whether or not a reasonable consistency in order of magnitude existed among the several distributions. That this requirement was met is revealed when the state data are combined for AIA regional districts as shown in *Table 3*. Here it is clearly indicated that individual practitioners still predominate, are followed in turn by private and public employee architects, teachers, architects engaged in non-architectural work, and those who had returned or were unemployed. For this characteristic of the data, similar conditions also were found to exist among non-responding architects.

b. *Characteristics of non-responding architects.* To collect the non-response information the Survey Commission received the unqualified cooperation of 41 of the

AIA chapter secretaries who were called upon to contact by telephone varying groups of registered architects and to obtain directly from them their ages at last birthday and their employment status in 1950.

Insofar as totals only are concerned (*Table 4*), it may be noted that the 382 AIA non-respondents represent 12.8 per cent of their particular universe, and of this number information was obtained from 333, or an 11.5 per cent sample of all the AIA non-respondents. The corresponding figures for the Non-AIA architects are: 714 selected, or 12 per cent of their universe, and of these 379 or 6.4 per cent were individually contacted by AIA chapter secretaries. As for the six distributions in *Table 4* the significant feature of them is their general parallelism, particularly as regards those for the AIA non-respondents.

Insofar as the non-respondents' employment statuses are concerned, *Table 6* shows these particular data grouped and compared with the corresponding figures for the same 9 states for the responses to the General Questionnaire. The close correspondence that exists between the several proportions for each employment status leads to the conclusion that the General Questionnaire returns may be accepted as being representative of both AIA and Non-AIA architects for the 9 particular states concerned. But since these 9 states represent 60 per cent of the entire profession it also is reasonable to assume that these distributions may be accepted as representing the employment status distributions of the entire profession.

As regards the age characteristics of the non-responding architects, complete comparisons of median ages among all of the 9 states was possible only for individual practitioners. This is accounted for by the fact that for each of the other employment statuses too many states included fewer than 10 architects and for these no median ages were computed.

From the comparisons of median ages shown in *Table 5* it is clear that those for non-respondents are generally higher than those of respondents. From this situation it can only be concluded that the general questionnaire returns, insofar as age is concerned, are generally biased in favor of younger architects. The fact, however, that the median age differentials are not excessively great for all of the 9 states leads to the belief that a similar situation would be found to exist among the remaining states which would offset to some extent those instances where differentials were excessive. Despite the presence of this bias no attempt has been made to adjust the data because there are innumerable factors to be assessed with respect to the proper weighting factors that should be used. In any event the single principal variable that would be affected would be the annual incomes, which, in this survey were reported for the year 1949.

8. *The analyses of the data outlined.* With the knowledge that a high degree of reliability attaches to the general questionnaire data, it is with a similar degree of assurance that the analyses of the entire data may now be approached to evaluate the status of the architectural profession with respect to its education, practice activities, and registration.

Andrew Fraser, SURVEY CONSULTANT

Appendix C: Statement of Elements for an Architectural Registration Act

INTRODUCTORY NOTE

The *1950 Survey of Board Members* disclosed a general opinion that the preparation of a model architects' registration act would be a useful service in providing a standard of comparison whenever amendments or new substitute bills are contemplated. The Commission acknowledged this need and requested two of its members, Clinton H. Cowgill, then president of NCARB, and Fred L. Markham, vice-president of NCARB, who both had had extensive experience in this field, to study the problem. After discussing successive drafts, it was decided that no model act could be phrased to satisfy all the variations of conditions and legal procedures which control the framing of legislation in the several states. For this reason, therefore, the original plan was modified to produce a statement of the functional elements, or provisions, which experience has proved necessary for the effective operation of such acts. Under each element is quoted an appropriate section, chosen for its satisfactory content and felicitous expression. Whenever possible, these statements have also been selected from sections which have successfully met judicial test. In several cases, alternative sections are also given, some of which incorporate slightly different conceptions of content, procedure, or form. It is hoped that this arrangement will aid in the analysis and improvement of existing acts and assist in time in the attainment of an acceptable degree of general uniformity among the statutes of the various states. In addition, an outline of sections for a complete act is also provided.

I. OUTLINE OF SECTIONS FOR AN ARCHITECTS' REGISTRATION ACT

1 Purpose and Scope
2 Definitions
3 Administrative Body
4 Powers and Duties of the Administrative Body
5 Income and Expenditures of the Administrative Body
6 Mandatory Records of the Administrative Body
7 Applications for Registration
8 Fees
9 Qualifications
10 Examinations
11 Certificates and Seals
12 Renewals
13 Re-registration under this Act

II. THE ELEMENTS OF AN ARCHITECTS' REGISTRATION ACT

1. *TO ESTABLISH THE BASIC CONSTITUTIONAL JUSTIFICATION FOR THE ACT AND OUTLINE ITS SCOPE*

"In order to safeguard life, health, and property, and to promote the public welfare, any person practicing or offering to practice architecture, shall hereafter be required to submit evidence that he is qualified so to practice and shall be registered as hereinafter provided; and it shall be unlawful for any person to practice or to offer to practice architecture in this state as defined in the provisions of this Act, or to use in connection with his name or otherwise assume, use, or advertise any title or description tending to convey the impression that he is an architect unless such person has been duly registered under the provisions of this Act."

From New York Law:

"In order to safeguard life, health and property, no person shall practice architecture in this state, or use the title architect or any title, sign, card or device to indicate that such person is practicing architecture or is an architect, unless such persons shall have secured from the regents a license or temporary permit as architect, in the manner hereinafter provided, and shall thereafter comply with the provisions of this article. A certificate of registration as registered architect, heretofore duly issued under the laws of this state, shall serve the same purpose as, and is hereby declared to be, the license required by this article. Every holder of a license shall display it in a conspicuous place in his principal office, place of business or employment."

2. *TO DEFINE THE KEY TERMS USED IN THE WRITING OF THE ACT*

"The terms as used in this Act are defined as follows:

"An architect is one who designs, prepares working drawings and specifications, or supervises the construction, enlargement or alteration of buildings, or parts thereof, to be constructed for others. The practice of architecture is the professional service of an architect as defined above. The term *Board* as used in this Act shall mean the State Board of _____ _____ _____ provided for by this Act.

"A building is normally composed of walls (or columns), floors (or floor), and roof, with or without other elements."

From New York Law:

"*Board* means the State Board of Examiners of Architects of the State of New York. *Architect* means a person who engages in the practice of architecture as hereinafter defined. A person practices architecture within the meaning and intent of this article, who holds himself out as able to perform or who does perform any professional service such as consultation, investigation, evaluation, planning, design, including aesthetic and structural design, or responsible supervision of construction, in connection with any private or public buildings, structures or projects, or the equipment or utilities thereof, or the accessories thereto, wherein the safeguarding of life, health or property is concerned or involved, when such professional service requires the application of the art and science of construction based upon the principles of mathematics, aesthetics and the physical sciences."

3. *TO PROVIDE AN ADMINISTRATIVE BODY TO CARRY OUT THE PURPOSE OF THE ACT*

(This will vary widely, depending upon the basic administrative structure in the state government. The outline here given will need broad interpretation in its application to a particular state.)

"A State Board of _____ is hereby created whose duty it shall be to administer the provisions of this Act. The Board shall consist of _____ members appointed by the Governor, and who shall have the qualifications required elsewhere herein.

"Appointments to the Board shall be for a term of _____ years. One appointment shall be made for a _____-year term ending _____. One appointment shall be made for a _____-year term ending _____. Appointments to the Board shall be limited to two successive terms of office. Vacancies in the membership of the Board, however created, shall be filled by appointment by the Governor for the unexpired term. Every member appointed to the Board shall receive a certificate of his appointment from the Governor and before beginning the term of office shall file with the Secretary of State his written oath or affirmation for the faithful discharge of his official duty. Each Board member shall hold office until the expiration of the term for which he is appointed or until a successor shall have been duly appointed and shall have qualified.

"Each member of the Board shall be a citizen of the United States and a resident of this state, and shall have been engaged in the practice of architecture for at least 15 years.

"Each member of the Board shall serve thereon without compensation, provided that he shall be reimbursed for all actual traveling, incidental, and clerical expenses necessarily incurred in carrying out the provisions of this Act, and in addition $_____ per diem for attending meetings.

"The Governor may remove any member of the Board for misconduct, incompetency, neglect of duty, or for any other sufficient cause.

"The Board shall hold a meeting within thirty days after the passage of this

Act, and thereafter shall hold regular meetings as established by the rules and by-laws of the Board. The Board shall elect annually a chairman and a vice-chairman. A quorum of the Board shall consist of not less than _____ members."

4. *TO OUTLINE POWERS, DUTIES AND RESPONSIBILITIES OF THE ADMINISTRATIVE BODY*

"The Board shall have the power to adopt and amend all by-laws and rules of procedure, not inconsistent with the constitution and laws of this state, which may be reasonably necessary for the proper performance of its duties and the regulations of the proceedings before it,—fixing the nature, content, and extent of examinations, and the time of filing applications. The Board shall adopt and have an official seal.

"In carrying into effect the provisions of this Act, the Board, under the hand of its chairman and the seal of the Board, may subpoena witnesses and compel their attendance, and also may require the production of books, papers, and documents, in a case involving the revocation of registration or practicing or offering to practice without registration; provided, however, that in no case may said Board require the testimony or production of books, papers and documents of the client of any architect whose registration is being sought to be revoked without the consent of said client. Any member of the Board may administer oaths or affirmations to witnesses appearing before the Board. Except as provided above, if any person shall refuse to obey any subpoena so issued, or shall refuse to testify or produce any books, papers, or documents, the Board may present its petition to such district court as may have jurisdiction, setting forth the facts, and thereupon such district court shall, in a proper case, issue its subpoena to such person, requiring his attendance before such court and there to testify or to produce such books, papers, and documents, as may be deemed necessary and pertinent by the Board. Any person failing or refusing to obey the subpoena or order of the said court may be proceeded against in the same manner as for refusal to obey any other subpoena or order of the court."

5. *TO SPECIFY THE MANDATORY RECORDS OF THE ADMINISTRATIVE BODY*

"The Board shall keep a record of its proceedings and a register of all applications for registration, which register shall show (a) the name, age, and residence of each applicant; (b) the date of application; (c) the place of business of such applicant; (d) his educational and other qualifications; (e) whether or not an examination was required; (f) whether the applicant was rejected; (g) whether a certificate of registration was granted; (h) the date of the action of the Board; and (i) such other information as may be deemed necessary by the Board.

"The records of the Board shall be prima facie evidence of the proceedings of the Board set forth therein, and a transcript thereof, duly certified by the Secretary of the Board under seal, shall be admissible in evidence with the same force and effect as if the original were produced.

"Annually, before _____ the Board shall submit to the Governor a report of its transactions of the preceding year, and shall also transmit to him a complete statement of the receipts and expenditures of the Board, attested by the affidavits of its chairman and its secretary, and shall file a copy thereof with the _____."

"A roster shall be published by the Secretary of the Board during the month of _____ of each year showing the names and places of business of all registered architects. Copies of this roster shall be mailed to each person so registered, placed on file with the _____ and all building officials in the State, and furnished to the public on request."

6. *TO ESTABLISH LICENSING AS BETWEEN THE STATE AND THE INDIVIDUAL CITIZEN*

"No corporation shall practice architecture in the state or be granted a license under this Act."

"Nothing in this article shall be construed as prohibiting a joint enterprise, partnership or association between one or several professional engineers and one or several architects, all duly licensed under the respective provisions of this article, and it shall be lawful for such partnership, joint enterprise or association to use in its title the words "architects and engineers" or "engineers and architects," provided, however, that all announcements, cards, stationery, printed matter and listings of such partnership, joint enterprise or association shall indicate as to each member whether he be a licensed architect or a licensed engineer."

From New York Law:

"Nothing in this article shall be construed to prohibit an individual, or a joint enterprise, partnership or association of architects and/or professional engineers, all duly licensed and all formed by a group of former employees of a firm of architects or professional engineers from using the name of such firm, where each of such employees has been employed continuously by the firm for a period of not less than fifteen years and the retired members and the executors of the estates of any deceased former members, of the firm, have consented to such use."

"A partnership may engage in the practice of architecture in this state, provided the person or persons connected with such partnership in charge of the designing or supervision which constitutes such practice is or are registered as herein required. The same exemptions shall apply to partnerships as apply to individuals under this Act."

7. *TO ESTABLISH MEANS OF IDENTIFYING REGISTRANT AND PROVIDING FOR A SEAL*

"The Board shall issue a certificate of registration upon payment of registration fee as provided for in this Act, to any applicant who, in the opinion of the Board, has satisfactorily met all the requirements of this Act. The issuance of a certificate of registration by this Board shall be prima facie evidence that the person named therein is entitled to all the rights and privileges of a registered architect while the said certificate remains unrevoked or unexpired.

"Each registrant hereunder shall upon registration obtain a seal of the design authorized by the Board, bearing the registrant's name. Plans, specifications, and reports prepared by a registrant shall be stamped with the said seal when filed with public authorities, during the life of the registrant's certificate, but it shall be unlawful for anyone to stamp or seal any documents with said seal after the certificate of the registrant named thereon has expired or has been revoked, unless said certificate shall have been renewed or reissued."

8. *TO ESTABLISH POWERS AND PROCEDURES FOR REVOCATION OF LICENSE*

"The Board shall have the power to revoke the certificate of registration of any registrant who is found guilty of:

    (a) The practice of any fraud or deceit in obtaining a certificate of registration;

    (b) Any gross negligence, incompetency, or misconduct in the practice of architecture.

"Any person may prefer charges of fraud, deceit, gross negligence, incompetency, or misconduct against any registrant. Such charges shall be in writing, and shall be sworn to by the person making them and shall be filed with the Secretary of the Board. All charges, unless dismissed by the Board as unfounded or trivial, shall be heard by the Board within three months after the date on which they shall have been preferred. The time and place for said hearing shall be fixed by the Board, and a copy of the charges, together with a notice of the time and place of the hearing, shall be personally served on or mailed to the last known address of such registrant, at least thirty days before the date fixed for the hearing. At any hearing, the accused registrant shall have the right to appear personally and by counsel, to cross-examine witnesses appearing against him, and to produce evidence and witnesses in his own defense. If, after such hearing, upon a majority vote of the entire Board the accused is found guilty, the Board shall revoke the Certificate of Registration. The Board, for reasons it may deem sufficient, may reissue a certificate of registration to any person whose certificate has been revoked, providing three or more members of the Board vote in favor of such reissuance. A new certificate of registration, to replace any certificate revoked, lost, destroyed, or mutilated, may be issued, subject to the rules of the Board, and a charge of Three Dollars ($3.00) shall be made for such issuance. Any person who shall feel aggrieved by an action of the Board in denying or revoking his certificate of registration may appeal therefrom to the district court and, after full hearing, said court shall make such decree sustaining or reversing the action of the Board as to it may seem just and proper."

9. *TO ESTABLISH VIOLATION OF LAW AS A MISDEMEANOR*

"Any person who shall practice, or offer to practice architecture in this state, without being registered in accordance with the provisions of the Act, or any person presenting or attempting to use as his own the certificate of registration or the seal of another, or any person who shall give any false or forged evidence of any kind to the Board or to any member thereof in obtaining a certificate of registration, or any person who shall falsely impersonate any other registrant of like or different name, or any person who shall attempt to use an expired or revoked certificate of registration, or any person who shall violate any of the provisions of this Act, shall be guilty of misdemeanor, and shall, upon conviction, be sentenced to pay a fine of not less than _____, nor more than _____ or suffer imprisonment for a period not exceeding three months, or both."

10. *TO ESTABLISH POWER OF INJUNCTION IN CASE OF VIOLATION*

"If any person shall carry on or practice as an architect as herein defined in violation of the provisions of this Act, the carrying on or practicing as such shall be deemed a nuisance, and may be restrained and abated by injunction as hereinafter provided.

"It shall be optional with the district attorney in all cases of a violation of any of the provisions of this Act to proceed by complaint and information against any violator, or to institute proceedings by injunction in any court of competent jurisdiction in the county in which such violation occurs, to abate and restrain such nuisance.

"When the district attorney elects to proceed by injunction in any case mentioned in the last preceding paragraph, such election shall operate as a bar to any criminal proceedings provided for the violation of the provisions of this Act when such violation occurs prior to the hearing on such injunctive proceeding and no testimony given by the defendant shall be admissible against him in any criminal proceeding instituted for any violation occurring subsequent to the hearing on such injunctive proceedings."

11. *TO ESTABLISH STATES ATTORNEY GENERAL AS COUNSEL FOR ADMINISTRATIVE BODY*

"The attorney general of the state or his assistant shall act as legal adviser of the Board and render such legal assistance as may be necessary in carrying out the provisions of this Act."

12. *TO BIND THE STATE IN ALL ITS DEPARTMENTS AND POLITICAL SUBDIVISIONS TO CONFORMITY WITH THE ACT*

"All buildings erected by the State and political subdivisions thereof shall be designed by and their construction shall be supervised by architects registered as provided by this Act."

13. *TO REQUIRE ALL OFFICERS OF THE STATE AND ITS POLITICAL SUBDIVISIONS TO ENFORCE THE ACT*

"It shall be the duty of all duly constituted officers of the law of this state, or any political subdivision thereof, to enforce the provisions of the Act and to prosecute any persons violating same."

From New York Law:

"No official of this state, or of any city, town or village therein, charged with the enforcement of laws, ordinances or regulations relating to the construction or alteration of buildings or structures, shall accept or approve any plans or specifications that are not stamped with the seal of a licensed architect or a licensed professional engineer."

493

14. *TO ESTABLISH EXCEPTIONS TO THE APPLICATION OF THE ACT*

"Nothing in this Act shall be construed as curtailing or extending the rights of any other legally recognized profession or craft. This Act shall not be construed to prevent:

"(a) The practice of a person not a resident of and having no established place of business in this state, practicing or offering to practice herein the profession of architecture, when such practice does not exceed in the aggregate more than _____ days in any calendar year; provided such person is legally qualified by registration to practice the said profession in his own state, territory, possession or district of the United States or country in which the requirements and qualifications for obtaining a certificate of registration are not lower than those specified in this Act; or

"(b) The practice of a person not a resident of and having no established place of business in this state, or who has recently become a resident thereof, practicing or offering to practice architecture herein for more than _____ days in any calendar year, if he shall have filed with the Board an application for a certificate of registration and shall have paid the fee required by this Act; provided that such a person is legally qualified by registration to practice architecture in his own state or country in which the requirements and qualifications for obtaining a certificate of registration are not lower than those specified in this Act. Such practice shall continue only for such time as the Board requires for the consideration of the application for registration; or

"(c) The work of an employee or a subordinate of a person holding a certificate of registration under this Act, or an employee of a person practicing lawfully under Paragraph (a) or (b) of this Section; provided such work does not include final designs or decisions and is done under the direct responsibility, checking, and supervision of a person holding a certificate of registration under this Act or a person practicing lawfully under Paragraphs (a) or (b) of this Section; or

"(d) The practice of officers and employees of the Government of the United States while engaged within this state in the practice of architecture for said government; or

"(e) The preparation or use of working drawings and specifications by anyone, for farm buildings, single family houses or for work the cost of which does not exceed $_____; or

"(f) The design, preparation of working drawings and specifications, and supervision of construction by Registered Professional Engineers, of or for buildings devoted largely to manufacturing, processing or storage, including warehouses, public garages, factories, power houses, refineries, packing plants, refrigeration plants, dying and cleaning plants, laundries, freight depots, grain, coal, and mineral elevators, water works buildings, and sewage disposal plant buildings."

15. *TO ESTABLISH THE BASIS FOR ADMITTANCE TO EXAMINATION*

"The following shall be considered as minimum evidence satisfactory to the

Board that the applicant is qualified for registration as an architect:

"(a) Graduation in an approved curriculum from a school or college approved by the Board (or the equivalent); and a specific record of an additional three years or more of experience in work of a character satisfactory to the Board, and indicating that the applicant is competent to practice; and successfully passing written, or written and oral, examinations; or

"(b) Graduation in an approved curriculum from a school or college approved by the Board (or the equivalent), and a specific record of ten years or more of lawful practice as a principal of a character satisfactory to the Board and indicating that the applicant is competent to practice, and successfully passing an oral examination with exhibits and report on research."

From New York Law:

"Any citizen of the United States, or any person who has duly declared his intention of becoming such citizen, who is at least twenty-five years of age and of good moral character, may apply for license under this article. He shall submit evidence satisfactory to the department of having completed an approved four year high school course of study or the equivalent thereof as determined by the department. He shall submit evidence that he graduated from a college or school of architecture registered by the department as maintaining satisfactory standards. He shall also submit evidence of practical experience in architectural work of a grade and character satisfactory to the board. Each complete year of study in the registered college or school of architecture may be accepted in lieu of one year of such experience and the applicant must submit evidence of sufficient additional experience to give him a total of eight years. In lieu of graduation from a registered college or school of architecture and the practical experience in addition thereto an applicant may submit evidence of twelve years' practical experience in architectural work of a grade and character satisfactory to the Board."

16. *TO ESTABLISH DETAILS CONCERNING EXAMINATION*

"Examinations shall be held at such time and place as the Board shall determine.

"The scope of the examinations and the methods of procedure shall be prescribed by the Board with special reference to the applicant's ability to design and supervise so as to insure the safety of life, health, and property. A candidate failing on examination may apply for re-examination at the expiration of six months and not later than thirteen months and will be reexamined without payment of additional fee. Subsequent examination will be granted upon payment of a fee to be determined by the Board."

From New York Law:

"Upon complying with these requirements, he shall pass a written examination, in such technical and professional subjects as are prescribed by the Board, to establish his competency to plan, structurally design and supervise the construction of buildings and similar structures. Each written examination may be supplemented by such oral examination as the department may determine upon recommendation of the Board."

17. *TO ESTABLISH AUTHORITY TO ACCEPT LICENSES AND EXAMI-
NATIONS OF OTHER STATES OR OTHER ADMINISTRATIVE
BODIES*

"The Board may, upon application therefore, and the payment of a fee of Ten
Dollars ($10.00), issue a certificate of registration to any person who holds a
certificate of qualification or registration issued to him by proper authority of the
National Council of Architectural Registration Boards, or of any country, provided that the applicant's qualifications meet the requirements of this Act and
the rules established by the Board."

From New York Law:

"Upon the recommendation of the board the department may exempt from
examination an applicant for license as architect who holds a license or certificate
to practice architecture issued to him upon examination by a legally constituted
board of examiners in any other state or political subdivision of the United States
provided the requirement for such license or certificate was the full equivalent of
the requirement in this state at the time it was issued and provided, further, that
the applicant's record fully met the requirements of this state in all respects other
than examination.

"Any architect who has lawfully practiced architecture for a period of more
than ten years without the state may be granted a license upon passing a practical
examination the character of which shall be determined by the Board."

18. *TO PROTECT INDIVIDUAL PROVISIONS OF THE ACT IN THE
EVENT OF ATTACK FOR UNCONSTITUTIONALITY*

"If any section or sections of this Act shall be declared unconstitutional or in-
valid, this shall not invalidate any other sections of this Act."

19. *TO PROVIDE FOR REPEAL OF LAWS IN CONFLICT*

"All laws or parts of laws in conflict with the provisions of this Act shall be,
and the same are, hereby repealed, and _____
are expressly repealed."

20. *ENACTMENT CLAUSE*

"The General Assembly hereby finds, determines and declares that this Act is
necessary for the immediate preservation of the public peace, health and safety."

TO BE INCLUDED AS PART OF BYLAWS AND RULES

1. The detailed procedure of filing and processing applications.
2. The details of examination procedure and grading.
3. Meetings of the Board.

Glossary of Abbreviations

AAU	Association of American Universities
ACSA	Association of Collegiate Schools of Architecture
AIA	American Institute of Architects
ASEE	American Society for Engineering Education
ASLA	American Society of Landscape Architects
BAID	Beaux-Arts Institute of Design
ECPD	Engineers Council for Professional Development
ETS	Educational Testing Service
FAIA	Fellow of American Institute of Architects
IIT	Illinois Institute of Technology
MIT	Massachusetts Institute of Technology
NAAB	National Architectural Accrediting Board
NBME	National Board of Medical Examiners
NCARB	National Council of Architectural Registration Boards
RIBA	Royal Institute of British Architects
SPEE	Society for the Promotion of Engineering Education
SSA	Social Security Administration
WAA	Western Association of Architects

Index

498

TABLE I: U·S· REGISTERED ARCHITECTS · THEIR RESPONSES TO 1950 SURVEY QUESTIONNAIRES · & THEIR MEDIAN AGES · 1950 · By States & A·I·A Regions

TABLE I

Column groups: **Number of Architects — Total Mailings** (Total / AIA / NonAIA) · **Number of Responses — War Service Quest. (WSQ)** and **General Quest. (GQ)** (Tot / AIA / NonA) · **% of Architects — Total Mailings** (Tot / AIA / NonA) · **% of Responses to U·S· Totals — WSQ / GQ** (Tot / AIA / NonA) · **% of Responses to State Totals — WSQ / GQ** (Tot / AIA / NonA) · **% of State Archts in A·I·A** · **Median Ages — A·I·A** (WSQ / GQ) and **Non A·I·A** (WSQ / GQ)

Region / State	TM Tot	TM AIA	TM Non	WSQ Tot	WSQ AIA	WSQ Non	GQ Tot	GQ AIA	GQ Non	%TM Tot	%TM AIA	%TM Non	%US WSQ Tot	%US WSQ AIA	%US WSQ Non	%US GQ Tot	%US GQ AIA	%US GQ Non	%St WSQ Tot	%St WSQ AIA	%St WSQ Non	%St GQ Tot	%St GQ AIA	%St GQ Non	%St AIA	Med AIA WSQ	Med AIA GQ	Med Non WSQ	Med Non GQ
U·S	19,137	8,461	10,676	8,851	4,649	4,202	6,605	3,744	2,861	100	100	100	100	100	100	100	100	100	46	55	39	35	44	27	44	47.2	46.5	46.7	44.5
New England	1504	571	933	617	285	332	468	246	222	7.9	6.7	8.7	7.0	6.1	7.9	7.1	6.6	7.8	41	50	36	31	43	24	38	44.5	47.9	47.9	45.9
Maine	55	21	34	32	15	17	24	13	11	0.3	0.2	0.3	0.4	0.3	0.4	0.4	0.3	0.4	58	71	50	44	62	32	38	53.3	49.2	52.5	44.5
New Hampshire	58	29	29	27	15	12	27	15	12	0.3	0.3	0.3	0.3	0.3	0.3	0.4	0.4	0.4	47	52	41	47	52	41	50	45.0	47.5	42.5	44.5
Vermont	29	17	12	15	10	5	15	11	4	0.2	0.2	0.1	0.2	0.2	0.1	0.2	0.3	0.1	52	59	42	52	65	33	59	—	—	—	—
Massachusetts	770	298	472	293	143	150	224	125	99	4.0	3.5	4.4	3.3	3.1	3.6	3.4	3.3	3.5	38	48	32	29	42	21	39	50.2	48.6	49.7	49.5
Rhode Island	115	57	58	45	23	22	28	20	8	0.6	0.7	0.5	0.5	0.5	0.5	0.4	0.5	0.3	39	40	38	24	35	14	50	48.3	47.1	48.7	48.7
Connecticut	477	149	328	205	79	126	150	62	88	2.5	1.8	3.1	2.3	1.7	3.0	2.3	1.7	3.1	43	53	38	31	42	27	31	45.3	45.3	46.2	43.8
New York	2945	1251	1694	1146	630	516	896	512	384	15.4	14.8	15.9	12.9	13.5	12.3	13.6	13.7	13.4	39	50	30	30	41	23	42	49.5	48.2	53.7	49.8
Mid-Atlantic	3396	1381	2015	1595	782	813	1074	586	488	17.7	16.3	18.9	18.0	16.8	19.3	16.3	15.7	17.1	47	57	40	32	42	24	41	48.5	47.6	48.5	46.6
New Jersey	1031	183	848	420	108	312	235	82	153	5.4	2.2	7.9	4.7	2.3	7.4	3.6	2.2	5.3	41	59	37	23	45	18	18	48.9	48.4	49.9	51.5
Pennsylvania	1230	613	617	606	339	267	430	244	186	6.4	7.2	5.8	6.8	7.3	6.3	6.5	6.5	6.5	49	55	43	35	40	30	50	49.2	48.8	49.2	45.1
Delaware	40	30	10	26	21	5	14	14	0	0.2	0.4	0.1	0.3	0.5	0.1	0.2	0.4	0.0	65	70	50	35	47	0	75	52.1	50.5	50.5	—
Maryland	337	171	166	160	90	70	88	62	26	1.8	2.0	1.6	1.8	1.9	1.7	1.3	1.7	0.9	47	53	42	26	36	16	51	46.2	48.5	46.8	43.9
District Columbia	333	166	167	155	85	70	158	88	70	1.7	2.0	1.6	1.8	1.8	1.7	2.4	2.4	2.4	47	53	45	47	53	42	50	48.2	48.5	48.0	46.1
Virginia	344	171	173	181	114	67	115	78	37	1.8	2.0	1.6	2.0	2.5	1.6	1.7	2.1	1.3	53	66	39	33	45	21	50	44.7	48.5	43.9	43.9
West Virginia	81	45	36	47	25	22	32	18	14	0.4	0.5	0.3	0.5	0.5	0.5	0.5	0.5	0.5	58	56	61	39	40	39	56	53.5	49.5	50.0	42.5
Great Lakes	2019	1077	942	944	556	388	702	433	269	10.5	12.7	8.8	10.7	12.0	9.2	10.6	11.6	9.4	47	52	41	35	40	29	53	47.6	46.8	46.1	43.1
Ohio	945	438	507	485	262	223	355	174	181	4.9	5.2	4.7	5.5	5.6	5.3	5.4	4.6	6.3	51	60	44	38	40	36	46	47.6	47.7	48.1	40.2
Indiana	260	141	119	136	77	59	105	63	42	1.4	1.7	1.1	1.5	1.7	1.4	1.6	1.7	1.5	52	55	50	40	45	35	54	48.9	47.7	48.2	47.0
Michigan	633	455	178	262	222	40	203	173	30	3.3	5.4	1.7	3.0	4.8	1.0	3.1	4.6	1.0	41	49	22	32	38	17	72	48.8	46.5	56.7	51.9
Kentucky	131	53	78	61	34	27	39	23	16	0.7	0.6	0.7	0.7	0.7	0.6	0.6	0.6	0.6	47	64	35	30	43	21	40	45.0	46.5	46.9	47.5
North Central	2084	802	1282	930	442	488	737	378	359	10.9	9.5	12.0	10.5	9.5	11.6	11.2	10.1	12.5	45	55	38	35	47	28	38	46.8	46.4	46.5	46.3
Illinois	1433	530	903	616	273	343	509	231	278	7.5	6.3	8.5	7.0	5.9	8.2	7.7	6.2	9.7	43	52	38	36	44	31	37	45.6	45.3	45.3	45.1
Wisconsin	337	131	206	154	81	73	106	73	33	1.8	1.5	1.9	1.7	1.7	1.7	1.6	2.0	1.2	46	62	35	31	56	16	39	45.1	47.2	51.6	49.0
Minnesota	271	130	141	135	79	56	106	72	34	1.4	1.5	1.3	1.5	1.7	1.3	1.6	1.9	1.2	50	61	40	39	55	24	48	45.0	42.1	55.6	54.5
North Dakota	17	5	12	16	4	12	9	4	5	0.1	0.1	0.1	0.2	0.1	0.3	0.1	0.1	0.2	94	80	100	53	80	42	29	—	—	—	—
South Dakota	26	6	20	9	5	4	7	5	2	0.1	0.1	0.2	0.1	0.1	0.1	0.1	0.1	0.1	35	—	—	27	—	—	19	45.7	—	55.0	—
Central	1164	488	676	575	282	293	379	202	177	6.1	5.8	6.3	6.5	6.1	7.0	5.7	5.4	6.2	49	58	43	33	41	26	42	48.4	47.1	48.4	45.5
Iowa	164	69	95	92	41	51	58	7	51	0.9	0.8	0.9	1.0	0.9	1.2	0.9	0.2	1.8	56	59	54	35	10	54	42	55.2	48.2	43.7	44.7
Missouri	569	195	374	261	106	155	156	120	36	3.0	2.3	3.5	2.9	2.3	3.7	2.4	3.2	1.3	46	54	41	27	62	10	34	50.0	42.5	46.4	44.7
Nebraska	102	48	54	52	33	19	52	21	31	0.5	0.6	0.5	0.6	0.7	0.5	0.8	0.6	1.1	51	69	35	51	44	57	47	47.5	44.6	46.4	48.8
Kansas	191	90	101	96	51	45	68	19	49	1.0	1.1	0.9	1.1	1.1	1.1	1.0	0.5	1.7	50	57	45	36	21	49	47	46.8	45.4	45.8	45.8
Oklahoma	138	86	52	74	51	23	45	35	10	0.7	1.0	0.5	0.8	1.1	0.5	0.7	0.9	0.3	54	59	44	33	41	19	62	44.8	45.4	33.7	44.2
South Atlantic	1128	572	556	584	345	239	456	289	167	5.9	6.8	5.2	6.6	7.4	5.7	6.9	7.7	5.8	52	60	43	40	51	30	51	44.3	43.6	44.3	41.7
North Carolina	207	124	83	124	72	52	84	31	53	1.1	1.5	0.8	1.4	1.5	1.2	1.3	0.8	1.9	60	58	63	41	25	64	60	47.3	45.5	43.5	37.5
South Carolina	126	55	71	55	38	17	39	20	19	0.7	0.7	0.7	0.6	0.8	0.4	0.6	0.5	0.7	44	69	24	31	36	27	44	41.7	43.5	44.0	42.7
Georgia	293	136	157	120	70	50	111	101	10	1.5	1.6	1.5	1.4	1.5	1.2	1.7	2.7	0.3	41	51	32	38	74	6	46	42.0	46.3	43.9	41.7
Florida	502	257	245	285	165	120	222	137	85	2.6	3.0	2.3	3.2	3.5	2.9	3.4	3.7	3.0	57	64	49	44	53	35	51	40.5	43.7	37.1	42.8
Gulf	833	437	396	426	256	170	321	195	126	4.3	5.2	3.7	4.8	5.5	4.0	4.9	5.2	4.4	51	59	43	39	45	32	52	45.9	44.2	44.5	42.8
Tennessee	229	120	109	132	73	59	98	54	44	1.2	1.4	1.0	1.5	1.6	1.4	1.5	1.4	1.5	58	61	54	43	45	40	52	47.3	45.5	43.5	40.9
Alabama	148	87	61	71	44	27	57	37	20	0.8	1.0	0.6	0.8	0.9	0.6	0.9	1.0	0.7	48	51	44	39	43	33	59	43.5	44.8	43.9	37.5
Mississippi	103	54	49	54	31	23	38	18	20	0.5	0.6	0.5	0.6	0.7	0.5	0.6	0.5	0.7	52	57	47	37	33	41	52	42.0	46.3	38.8	38.3
Arkansas	59	35	24	34	24	10	28	19	9	0.3	0.4	0.2	0.4	0.5	0.2	0.4	0.5	0.3	58	69	42	47	54	38	59	43.1	45.2	53.3	44.5
Louisiana	294	141	153	135	84	51	100	67	33	1.5	1.7	1.4	1.5	1.8	1.2	1.5	1.8	1.2	46	60	33	34	48	22	48	40.5	43.7	37.1	35.5
Texas	964	431	533	483	262	221	347	204	143	5.0	5.1	5.0	5.5	5.6	5.3	5.3	5.4	5.0	50	61	41	36	47	27	45	44.4	43.6	43.1	41.2
Western Mountain	406	216	190	226	129	97	176	102	74	2.1	2.6	1.8	2.6	2.8	2.3	2.7	2.7	2.6	56	60	51	43	47	39	53	45.9	47.0	42.2	39.5
Wyoming	19	17	2	14	13	1	14	12	2	0.1	0.2	0.0	0.2	0.3	0.0	0.2	0.3	0.1	74	76	50	63	71	100	90	44.2	46.7	41.9	37.5
Colorado	130	70	60	71	42	29	57	25	32	0.7	0.8	0.6	0.8	0.9	0.7	0.9	0.7	1.1	55	60	48	44	36	53	54	44.2	44.5	38.3	38.3
New Mexico	71	43	28	43	26	17	35	19	16	0.4	0.5	0.3	0.5	0.6	0.4	0.5	0.5	0.6	61	61	61	49	44	57	61	46.4	45.8	42.8	44.5
Arizona	108	36	72	54	30	24	38	14	24	0.6	0.4	0.7	0.6	0.6	0.6	0.6	0.4	0.8	50	83	33	35	39	33	33	51.5	58.3	54.2	—
Utah	78	50	28	44	29	15	32	25	7	0.4	0.6	0.3	0.5	0.6	0.4	0.5	0.7	0.2	56	58	54	41	50	25	64	46.3	46.5	45.0	44.5
Northwest	723	311	412	390	199	191	320	178	142	3.8	3.7	3.9	4.4	4.3	4.5	4.8	4.8	5.0	54	64	46	44	57	34	43	45.0	44.5	40.7	38.4
Montana	57	30	27	30	17	13	30	17	13	0.3	0.4	0.3	0.3	0.4	0.3	0.5	0.5	0.5	53	57	48	53	57	48	53	48.7	48.7	37.0	35.8
Idaho	25	7	18	13	12	1	10	5	5	0.1	0.1	0.2	0.1	0.3	0.0	0.2	0.1	0.2	52	—	—	40	—	28	28	36.0	28.0	—	—
Washington	430	174	256	230	103	127	180	89	91	2.2	2.1	2.4	2.6	2.2	3.0	2.7	2.4	3.2	53	59	50	42	51	36	40	44.5	43.2	40.3	38.2
Oregon	211	100	111	117	67	50	100	67	33	1.1	1.2	1.0	1.3	1.4	1.2	1.5	1.8	1.2	55	67	45	47	67	30	47	44.2	45.2	44.6	39.5
Sierra Nevada	1971	903	1068	935	491	444	729	419	310	10.3	10.7	10.0	10.6	10.6	10.6	11.0	11.2	10.8	47	54	42	37	46	29	46	46.3	46.1	44.2	44.4
Nevada	49	11	38	2	1	1	20	6	14	0.3	0.1	0.4	0.0	0.0	0.0	0.3	0.2	0.5	4	9	3	41	55	37	22	—	—	—	—
California	1922	892	1030	933	490	443	709	413	296	10.0	10.5	9.6	10.5	10.5	10.5	10.7	11.0	10.3	49	55	43	37	46	29	46	46.2	46.1	44.3	41.5

TABLE 2: EMPLOYMENT STATUS OF REGISTERED ARCHITECTS · 1950 · By A·I·A Regions & 4 Selected States

A·I·A Regions & 4 Selected States	Total No.	Total %	Individual Practitioners %	Teachers %	Private Employee Architects %	Public Employee Architects %	Others %
Totals	6605	100	70	3	19	5	3
New England	468	100	76	3	16	1	4
New York	896	100	63	3	25	6	3
Mid-Atlantic	1074	100	66	3	25	4	2
Pennsylvania	430	100	67	–	24	5	3
Great Lakes	702	100	68	2	22	5	3
Ohio	355	100	66	3	21	5	4
North Central	737	100	67	3	24	4	2
Illinois	509	100	62	4	26	5	3
Central	379	100	73	5	16	4	2
South Atlantic	456	100	80	4	9	4	3
Gulf	321	100	76	2	14	6	2
Texas	347	100	75	1	12	7	3
West-Mountain	176	100	74	4	14	4	4
Northwest	320	100	64	3	18	8	2
Sierra-Nevada							
California	729	100	68	2	18	8	4

TABLE 3: EMPLOYMENT STATUS OF MEMBERS OF 20 A·I·A CHAPTERS

Chapters Reported	Members Reported No.	Individual Practitioner %	Teachers %	Private Employee Architects %	Public Employee Architects %	Others %
20	1747	72	4	16	3	5
3	141	60	5	30	–	5
3	243	72	5	13	2	7
4	276	72	3	20	1	4
1	76					
–	149	67	7	15	5	6
3	59	90	1	4	–	2
–	110	83	2	4	1	1
1	178	71	4	15	3	4
–	52	68	7	19	3	7
3	357		2		4	7

TABLE 4: COMPARISON OF NON-RESPONDING ARCHITECTS · IN 9 SELECTED STATES

States	A·I·A Total	A·I·A Select'd	A·I·A Receiv'd	Non-A·I·A Total	Non-A·I·A Select'd	Non-A·I·A Receiv'd
No.	1902	382	333	3676	714	379
%	100	100	100	100	100	100
California	16	16	16	15	15	14
Illinois	10	10	10	14	14	16
Massachusetts	6	6	6	6	8	10
Michigan	8	10	11	4	4	3
Missouri	24	26	24	36	30	23
New York	27	26	24	30	30	23
Ohio	9	9	10	7	9	11
Pennsylvania	12	11	12	9	9	11
Texas	8	8	7	8	8	10

TABLE 5: MEDIAN AGES OF RESPONDERS & NON-RESPONDERS

States	A·I·A Genl. Ques. Responders	A·I·A Non-Responders	Non-A·I·A Genl. Ques. Responders	Non-A·I·A Non-Responders
California	46.1	50.7	42.1	56.7
Illinois	46.9	56.5	47.3	55.5
Massachusetts	50.2	61.5	52.1	58.0
Michigan	45.1	58.3	57.5	–
Missouri	48.0	52.5	46.7	–
New York	48.9	53.1	51.4	56.5
Ohio	47.1	56.5	44.2	57.0
Pennsylvania	48.4	48.5	48.5	51.7
Texas	43.6	42.5	42.0	46.3

TABLE 6: COMPARISON OF THE EMPLOYMENT STATUS OF RESPONDERS & NON-RESPONDERS IN 9 SELECTED STATES

Employment Status	Number A·I·A Genl. Quest. Resp.	Number A·I·A Non-Resp.	Number Non-A·I·A Genl. Quest. Resp.	Number Non-A·I·A Non-Resp.	% A·I·A Genl. Quest. Resp.	% A·I·A Non-Resp.	% Non-A·I·A Genl. Quest. Resp.	% Non-A·I·A Non-Resp.
Individ-Practitioners	1682	252	893	213	78	78	52	56
Teachers	79	5	36	9	4	1	3	2
Private Employees	278	47	573	130	13	13	33	24
Public Employees	79	29	172	45	4	8	10	12
Totals	2144	333	1714	379	100	100	100	100

TABLE 7: EMPLOYMENT STATUS OF REGISTERED ARCHITECTS · 1950 BY MAJOR & MINOR CATEGORIES

Employment Status	Number Total	Number A·I·A	Number Non-A	Percentages Total	Percentages A·I·A	Percentages Non-A	Median Ages A·I·A	Median Ages Non-A
Totals	6605	3744	2861	100	100	100	46.5	44.5
Practitioner Group	4635	3041	1594	70	81	56	46.5	46.0
Individual Practitioners	2652	1635	1017	40	44	35		
Principals-with financial interest	1466	1133	333	22	30	12		
Associates-no financial interest	446	237	209	7	6	7		
Consultants	71	36	35	1	1	1		
Teachers-on architectural faculty	191	136	55	3	4	2	45.5	37.0
Private Employee Architects	1230	396	834	19	11	29	43.0	40.5
With architectural firm-salary, wage	927	292	635	14	8	22		
With non-architectural organizatn (excludes private consulting or teaching)	303	104	199	5	3	7		
Public Employee Architects	362	117	245	5	3	8	49.9	49.5
Federal Government	170	50	120	3	1	5		
State Government	85	32	53	1	1	2		
County Government	10	5	5	–	–	–		
Municipal Government	72	20	52	1	1	2		
Other public authority	21	9	12	–	–	–		
Member of Armed Forces	4	1	3	–	–	–		
Others	187	54	133	3	2	5	45.5	45.5
Non-architectural work	106	24	82	2	1	3	45.5	45.5
Retired	77	30	47	1	1	1	74.0	70.0
Unemployed	4	–	4	–	–	–		

TABLE 8: AGE BY EMPLOYMENT STATUS

Age Group	U·S Tot.	A·I·A	Non-A	Individual Practitioner A·I·A	Individual Practitioner Non-A	Private Employee AIA	Private Employee NonA	Public Employee AIA	Public Employee NonA	Teachers AIA	Teachers NonA
Total Report-ing Age No.	6390	3674	2716	3027	1587	395	830	911	244	136	55
%	100	100	100	100	100	100	100	100	100	100	100
Under 20	-	-	-	-	-	-	1	-	-	-	-
20 to 25	1	-	1	-	1	1	5	-	1	-	-
25 to 30	4	1	6	1	4	5	11	3	5	1	1
30 to 35	10	8	13	7	11	16	19	9	12	10	10
35 to 40	16	16	17	16	17	18	17	21	16	20	20
40 to 45	18	20	16	21	16	19	10	18	18	18	18
45 to 50	15	17	12	17	13	14	8	16	14	20	20
50 to 55	11	12	9	12	9	12	8	16	18	7	7
55 to 60	8	12	8	12	10	8	9	10	13	11	11
60 to 65	6	8	7	8	9	5	5	7	12	7	7
65 to 75	6	5	7	5	9	2	5	5	7	6	6
75 & over	7	1	2	1	2	-	2	1	1	-	-
Median Age	45.5	46.4	44.2	46.5	46.0	43.0	40.5	49.9	49.5	45.5	37.0

TABLE 9: MEDIAN NET ANNUAL INCOME 1949. By Age Groups

Age Group	Individual Practitioners A·I·A $	Individual Practitioners NonAIA $	Private Employees A·I·A $	Private Employees NonAIA $	Public Employees A·I·A $	Public Employees NonAIA $	Teachers A·I·A $	Teachers Non-AIA $
Under 20	-	-	-	-	-	-	-	-
20 to 25	-	4900	-	4400	-	-	-	5200
25 to 30	5400	5600	5100	5300	5600	5600	6300	5200
30 to 35	6900	6800	6000	6000	6000	6700	5700	4500
35 to 40	8400	8000	6000	6500	6800	6700	7000	-
40 to 45	9800	8800	7000	6700	6900	6200	8500	-
45 to 50	11300	8300	8000	6600	6200	6900	7600	-
50 to 55	11800	9400	7900	6700	7900	5900	7300	-
55 to 60	13400	8200	7100	6300	5900	6000	-	-
60 to 65	14000	8200	-	5400	6000	5800	8600	-
65 to 75	11600	6300	-	5400	-	-	-	-
75 & over	7700	3500	-	-	-	-	-	-

TABLE 10: NET ANNUAL INCOME 1949 By brackets

Income Brackets	Tot. No.	Tot. %	Individual Practitioner A·I·A	Individual Practitioner NonA	Private Employees A·I·A	Private Employees NonA	Public Employees A·I·A	Public Employees NonA	Teachers
Total Reported No.	6200		2940	1514	390	820	114	236	186
%		100	100	100	100	100	100	100	100
Under $3000	5		4	9	3	6	3	5	5
$3 to 4000	5		3	7	3	8	2	4	6
$4 to 6000	22		12	22	31	42	26	36	33
$6 to 8000	21		15	18	34	32	41	39	27
$8 - 10,000	13		14	13	15	9	18	14	17
$10 - 12,000	9		11	11	9	2	6	2	5
$12 - 15,000	8		12	7	4	1	3	1	3
$15 - 18,000	4		8	3	2	-	1	-	2
$18 - 25,000	6		9	5	1	-	-	-	1
$25,000 & over	7		12	5	1	-	-	-	1

TABLE 11: LOCATION OF ARCHITECTS BY SIZE OF COMMUNITY

Size Groups	All Reported	Individual Practitioner	Private Employees	Public Employees
Totals No.	1819	4614	1215	352
%	100	100	100	100
Under 5000	2	2	1	1
5 to 10,000	2	2	1	2
10 - 25,000	6	7	3	2
25 - 50,000	8	9	6	4
50 - 100,000	9	10	6	7
100 - 500,000	27	28	22	30
500,000 & over	46	42	61	54

MEDIAN AGES by Sizes & Regions

A·I·A

Community Size Groups	All Reported	New England	New York	Mid-Atlantic	Great Lakes	No. Central	Central	So. Atlantic	Gulf	Texas	W. Mount'n	Northwest	SierraNev	Private Employees	Public Employees
Under 5000	45.3	-	-	45.0	-	-	-	42.5	-	-	-	-	45.0	-	-
5 to 10,000	43.2	-	-	43.0	-	-	-	42.3	-	-	-	-	41.9	-	-
10 - 25,000	44.6	44.6	47.5	46.9	42.5	43.4	45.8	42.5	44.2	39.5	-	45.0	45.0	38.3	47.5
25 - 50,000	44.9	44.6	44.4	47.5	48.8	48.3	44.0	42.3	43.8	-	46.3	45.7	41.9	36.7	48.3
50 - 100,000	46.4	48.8	52.5	49.1	43.1	50.0	50.0	43.4	43.8	40.0	48.3	-	54.2	40.0	47.5
100 - 500,000	46.2	46.9	49.0	46.7	47.3	51.7	47.0	44.6	45.0	43.5	48.1	45.3	45.6	40.2	52.8
500,000 over	49.8	51.2	48.9	48.4	47.6	46.9	49.3	43.6	47.9	45.6	-	43.6	46.3	41.2	49.7

NON - A·I·A

Community Size Groups	All Reported	New England	New York	Mid-Atlantic	Great Lakes	No. Central	Central	So. Atlantic	Gulf	Texas	W. Mount'n	Northwest	SierraNev	Private Employees	Public Employees
Under 5000	46.5	45.0	-	53.8	-	-	-	47.5	40.0	42.5	-	37.5	37.5	41.7	-
5 to 10,000	42.5	-	-	-	-	-	-	43.8	42.5	-	-	38.3	41.9	38.6	-
10 - 25,000	45.4	50.6	50.0	47.5	42.5	46.3	48.8	47.5	40.0	43.8	36.9	40.0	37.5	35.9	51.6
25 - 50,000	45.0	42.8	-	46.9	46.5	44.4	-	43.8	42.5	42.5	-	-	42.5	40.2	50.0
50 - 100,000	49.2	48.8	62.5	52.9	54.2	56.7	54.2	47.5	43.8	43.9	36.9	40.0	39.6	35.9	51.6
100 - 500,000	44.6	45.0	49.0	48.2	47.1	57.5	50.5	43.4	42.8	42.5	42.5	43.9	43.6	40.2	50.0
500,000 over	46.7	50.0	49.8	45.8	47.6	47.2	46.1	40.0	40.0	38.8	41.3	43.3	50.6	40.9	50.6

TABLE 14: ARCHITECTS IN THE ARMED FORCES

	Number			Per Cent		
	Tot.	A·I·A	NonA	Tot.	A·I·A	NonA
Totals	8806	4635	4171	100	100	100
Served in Armed Forces in World War II	2642	1350	1292	30	29	31
No service in Armed Forces in W. War II	6164	3285	2879	70	71	69

TABLE 15: BRANCH OF ARMED FORCES SERVED IN

	Number			Per Cent		
	Tot.	A·I·A	NonA	Tot.	A·I·A	NonA
Totals	2552	1302	1250	100	100	100
Army	1057	549	508	41	42	41
Navy	1011	525	486	40	40	39
Air Force	374	171	203	15	13	16
Marine Corps	58	30	28	2	2	2
Coast Guard	52	27	25	2	2	2

TABLE 17: RESERVE COMMISSIONS HELD AFTER WORLD WAR II

	Number			Per Cent		
	Tot.	A·I·A	NonA	Tot.	A·I·A	NonA
Totals	6565	3467	3098	100	100	100
Hold Reserve Comm.	1589	858	731	24	25	24
Do not hold R.Comm.	4976	2609	2367	76	75	76

TABLE 18: PROFESSIONAL DUTIES IN THE ARMED FORCE

	Number			Per Cent		
	Tot.	A·I·A	NonA	Tot.	A·I·A	NonA
Total with Armed Force service in World War II	2642	1350	1292	100	100	100
Duties professional in character	1204	651	553	46	48	43
Duties not professional in character	1360	660	700	51	49	54
No report on character of duties	78	39	39	3	3	3

TABLE 12: MOBILITY OF PRACTICE (NUMBER OF STATES & COUNTRIES WHERE ARCH'TS HAVE PRACTICED)

Number of Locations	INDIVIDUAL PRACTITIONERS						PRIVATE EMPLOYEE ARCHITECTS						PUBLIC EMPLOYEE ARCHITECTS					
	Number			Per Cent			Number			Per Cent			Number			Per Cent		
	Tot.	A·I·A	NonA	Tot.	A·I·A	NonA	Tot.	A·I·A	NonA	Tot.	A·I·A	NonA	Tot.	A·I·A	NonA	Tot.	A·I·A	NonA
Totals	3095	2064	1031	100	100	100	802	256	546	100	100	100	239	80	159	100	100	100
1	1993	1359	634	65	66	62	449	139	310	56	54	57	126	49	77	53	61	49
2	590	379	211	19	18	21	195	60	135	24	24	24	65	23	42	27	29	27
3	255	170	85	8	8	8	87	28	59	11	11	11	23	2	21	10	3	13
4	128	75	53	4	4	5	35	13	22	4	5	4	15	5	10	6	6	6
5	62	37	25	2	2	2	18	8	10	2	3	2	7	-	7	3	-	4
6 or more	67	44	23	2	2	2	18	8	10	2	3	2	3	1	2	1	-	1

TABLE 13: FLUCTUATIONS IN ARCHITECTS' PRACTICES · by A.I.A Regions

	U.S	New Eng	New York	Mid Atlan	Gt Lakes	N.Central	Central	S.Atlan	Gulf	Texas	W.Mount	Northwest	Sierra Nev
A·I·A													
Totals — Number	2933	205	371	442	339	273	163	243	156	171	91	147	332
Totals — Per Cent	100	100	100	100	100	100	100	100	100	100	100	100	100
Continuously in Independent Practice	80	81	74	81	80	84	82	82	81	78		79	78
Independent Practice interrupted	20	19	26	19	20	16	18	18	19	22		21	22
Due to General Economics Conditions	15	16	19	15	15	12	14	13	17	15		17	16
Due to other reasons	5	3	7	4	5	4	4	5	2	7		4	6
NON A·I·A													
Totals — Number	1471	139	162	233	115	199	101	101	73	82	38	83	145
Totals — Per Cent	100	100	100	100	100	100	100	100	100	100	100	100	100
Continuously in Independent Practice	77	78	74	78	77	80	76	77				76	76
Independent Practice interrupted	23	22	26	22	23	20	24	23				24	24
Due to General Economic Conditions	17	16	19	17	15	16	16	20				17	17
Due to other reasons	6	6	7	5	8	4	8	3				4	7

MEDIAN AGES

	U.S	New Eng	New York	Mid Atlan	Gt Lakes	N.Central	Central	S.Atlan	Gulf	Texas	W.Mount	Northwest	Sierra Nev
A·I·A													
Continuously in Independent-Practice	48.8	48.9	49.0	47.9	46.7	48.1	48.3	43.0	45.2	42.9	46.3	44.2	46.0
Independent-Practice interrupted	50.6	50.7	47.9	47.2	48.8	45.4	51.4	48.0	46.3	46.3	45.0	47.5	48.6
Due to General Economic Conditions		46.3		47.5	46.3	42.5		42.5	45.8				45.0
Due to other reasons													
NON A·I·A													
Continuously in Independent-Practice	47.4	51.7	49.2	47.0	48.5	48.4	44.2	42.3	41.3	40.5		38.6	39.5
Independent-Practice interrupted	46.3	55.0	50.7	50.0	47.0	52.5	47.5	46.3				50.0	55.0
Due to General Economic Conditions													43.3
Due to other reasons	47.5		39.2										

TABLE 16: COMMISSIONED RANKS HELD BY ARCHITECTS UPON DEMOBILIZATION FROM WORLD WAR II

ARMY

Rank	Number Tot	Number A-I-A	Number NonA	Per Cent Tot	Per Cent A-I-A	Per Cent NonA
Totals	729	413	316	100	100	100
Brig.General or higher	5	3	2	1	1	1
Colonel	54	40	14	7	10	4
Lt.Colonel	130	82	48	18	20	15
Major	218	139	79	30	34	25
Captain	204	99	105	28	24	33
1st Lieutenant	102	42	60	14	10	19
2nd Lieutenant	16	8	8	2	2	3

AIR FORCE

Rank	Number Tot	Number A-I-A	Number NonA	Per Cent Tot	Per Cent A-I-A	Per Cent NonA
Totals	248	120	128	100	100	100
Brig.General or higher	-	-	-	-	-	-
Colonel	10	6	4	4	5	3
Lt.Colonel	46	34	12	19	28	9
Major	65	39	26	26	33	20
Captain	56	25	31	23	21	24
1st Lieutenant	48	12	36	19	10	28
2nd Lieutenant	23	4	19	9	3	15

MARINE CORPS

Rank	Number Tot	Number A-I-A	Number NonA	Per Cent Tot	Per Cent A-I-A	Per Cent NonA
Totals	46	27	19	100	100	100
Brig.General or higher	-	-	-	-	-	-
Colonel	-	-	-	-	-	-
Lt.Colonel	1	-	1	2	-	5
Major	6	4	2	13	15	11
Captain	16	9	7	35	33	37
1st Lieutenant	22	13	9	48	48	47
2nd Lieutenant	1	1	-	2	4	-

NAVY

Rank	Number Tot	Number A-I-A	Number NonA	Per Cent Tot	Per Cent A-I-A	Per Cent NonA
Totals	835	460	375	100	100	100
Commodore or higher	3	1	2	-	-	1
Captain	1	-	1	-	-	-
Commander	48	30	18	6	7	5
Lt.Commander	198	124	74	24	27	20
Lieutenant	390	224	166	47	49	44
Lieutenant J.G.	159	68	91	19	15	24
Ensign	36	13	23	4	3	6

COAST GUARD

Rank	Number Tot	Number A-I-A	Number NonA
Totals	28	15	13
Commodore or higher	-	-	-
Captain	-	-	-
Commander	1	-	1
Lt.Commander	7	5	2
Lieutenant	7	3	4
Lieutenant J.G.	10	6	4
Ensign	3	1	2

TABLE 19: PROFESSIONAL DUTIES AS CIVILIANS

	Number Tot	A-I-A	NonA	Per Cent Tot	A-I-A	NonA
Served both as civilian and in Armed Forces in W-War II	2642	1350	1292	100	100	100
No indication of professional character of civilian work	1633	850	783	61	63	61
Civilian duties were professional in character	856	434	422	32	32	33
Civilian duties not profes.	153	66	87	7	5	7
Served only as civilians during World War II	6164	3285	2879	100	100	100
No indication on duties	789	404	385	13	12	13
Duties were professional in character	5026	2731	2295	82	83	80
Duties not professional	349	150	199	6	5	7

TABLE 20: CIVILIAN EMPLOYMENT OF ARCHITECTS DURING WORLD WAR II

	Number Tot	A-I-A	NonA	Per Cent Tot	A-I-A	NonA
Totals	6587	3521	3066	100	100	100
Formally attached to one of the services or a government agency	2021	1045	976	31	30	32
In industry engaged in war contracts	2541	1190	1351	38	34	44
In professional practice as architect and/or engineer	1914	1209	705	29	34	23
Teaching: A.S.T.P., other servicemen, E.S.M.W.T. etc.	111	77	34	2	2	1

TABLE 21: MAJOR TYPES OF DUTIES PERFORMED BY ARCHITECTS IN THE ARMED FORCES

	Number Tot	A-I-A	NonA	Per Cent Tot	A-I-A	NonA
Totals	1701	861	840	100	100	100
1. Combat, Staff, & Field Duties	797	451	346	47	52	42
2. Architecture, Engineering, & Public Wks	329	160	169	19	19	20
3. Constructn, Supervision, Contract, Matl	253	107	146	15	12	17
4. Charting, Design, Drafting, Drawing	122	49	73	7	6	9
5. Maintenance, Plant Layout, Production	47	22	25	3	3	3
6. Housing & Real Estate	18	7	11	1	1	1
7. Teaching	29	10	19	2	1	2
8. Miscellaneous	106	55	51	6	6	6

TABLE 22: DETAILED TYPES OF DUTIES PERFORMED BY ARCHITECTS IN THE ARMED FORCES

	Tot	A-I-A	NonA
Totals	1701	861	840
Combat, Staff & Field	797	451	346
Administration	54	39	15
Camouflage	77	42	35
Contracts, Negotiatn	16	9	7
Inspection	24	12	12
Intelligence	59	39	20
Interpreters	5	2	3
Meteorology	4	2	2
Military Govt.	1	1	-
Navigation	60	29	31
Ordnance	16	8	8
Organizatn, Plann'g	63	40	23
Photogra. Interpret.	75	39	36
Procurement	9	4	5
Purchasing	8	2	6
Radar	18	14	4
Research	9	6	3
Ship Repair	18	12	6
Combat, Staff, Field	175	96	79
Surveying	22	10	12
Topographical	79	42	37
Troop Training	5	3	2
Architecture, Engineering, Public Wks	329	160	169
Architecture	37	18	19
Engineering	285	138	147
Public Works	7	4	3
Construction, Supervision, Contract, Matl	253	107	146
Contractor	229	99	130
Materials	24	8	16
Charting, Design, Drafting, Drawing	122	49	73
Chart Drawing	9	6	3
Design (Architect'l), Industrial, Naval	78	36	42
Drafting	28	6	22
Drawing	7	1	6
Maintenance, Plant Layout, Production	47	22	25
Maintenance	30	14	16
Plant Layout	8	4	4
Production	9	4	5
Housing & Real Estate	18	7	11
Housing	14	6	8
Real Estate	4	1	3
Fine Arts	6	5	1
Teaching	29	10	19
Industrial Relations	4	3	1
Physically Unfit	14	3	11
Retired	-	-	-
Miscellaneous	82	44	38

TABLE 23: ARCHITECTS' EMPLOYEES by 9 groups & 3 types of firms (% of all employees in each type)

	Individ. Practi.	Comp. Dept.	Public Bur.	(continued)	Individ. Practi.	Comp. Dept.	Public Bur.
Total Number of Firms	4016	289	181				
No. reporting Employees	3377	176	98				
%	100	100	100				
Draftsmen	44	36	20	Designers	8	8	5
Stenogr., Clerks, Accounts	15	15	22	Proj.Mgrs, Job Capt. etc	8	7	17
Engineering Personnel	11	18	17	Outside Superintend's	7	6	7
				Administr.& Office Mgrs	3	2	2
				Specification Writers	2	2	2
				Research Personnel	2	1	4

TABLE 24: AVERAGE NUMBER OF PERSONNEL IN ARCHITECTURAL FIRMS

Type	Individual Practitioner Firms		Company Department Offices		Public Bureau Offices	
	A·I·A	NonAIA	A·I·A	NonAIA	A·I·A	NonAIA
Total Employment	10.0	6.2	43.2	28.2	22.5	47.8
Principals	1.8	1.5	2.1	2.0	2.0	1.9
Graduate Employees	3.1	1.8	10.4	5.5	6.0	5.7
Registered Architects	1.4	.7	4.9	3.2	3.7	4.0
Candidates for Registration	1.3	.9	2.6	2.4	2.4	2.7

TABLE 25: AVERAGE NUMBER OF PERSONNEL by A·I·A Regions — INDIVIDUAL PRACTITIONER OFFICES ONLY & EXCLUDING PRINCIPALS

A·I·A Region	Regional Distributions % A·I·A				Regional Distributions % Non A·I·A				Regional Averages A·I·A			Regional Averages Non-A·I·A		
	Offices	Graduate Employees	Registered Architects	Candidates for Registr.	Offices	Graduate Employees	Registered Architects	Candidates for Registr.	Graduate Employees	Registered Architects	Candidates for Registr.	Graduate Employees	Registered Architects	Candidates for Registr.
U·S	100	100	100	100	100	100	100	100	3.1	1.4	1.3	1.8	.7	.9
New England	7	5	6	7	7	5	5	5	2.4	1.3	1.3	1.2	.4	.5
New York	11	15	19	11	11	12	16	9	4.0	2.4	1.2	2.3	1.2	.8
Mid-Atlantic	15	12	13	11	9	13	13	14	2.6	1.2	1.0	1.4	.6	.8
Great Lakes	11	11	11	10	8	11	10	8	3.0	1.4	.9	1.6	.7	.8
No.Central	10	15	13	17	14	20	20	17	4.5	1.8	1.1	2.6	1.0	1.1
Central	6	7	6	5	6	7	5	7	3.8	1.5	1.2	1.6	.5	.9
So.Atlantic	9	8	7	8	7	6	6	6	2.7	1.1	1.2	1.8	.6	.9
Gulf	6	4	4	5	6	5	7	5	2.4	1.0	1.2	2.0	.8	.8
Texas	6	5	4	5	7	9	7	9	2.9	1.1	.7	2.5	.9	1.2
W·Mountain	3	2	3	2	3	2	3	3	2.1	.7	1.1	.9	.5	1.0
Northwest	5	5	5	6	5	6	7	6	2.9	1.4	1.3	1.3	.5	.5
Sierra Nevada	11	11	10	13	10	8	7	8	2.9	1.2	1.5	1.3	.9	1.0

TABLE 26: NUMBER OF EMPLOYEES IN INDIVIDUAL PRACTITIONER FIRMS by Per Cent of Firms in each A·I·A Region

Number of Employees	U·S Tot	U·S A·I·A	U·S NonA	New England A·I·A	New York A·I·A	Middle Atlantic Tot	Middle Atlantic A·I·A	Middle Atlantic NonA	Great Lakes A·I·A	North Central Tot	North Central A·I·A	North Central NonA	Central A·I·A	So.Atlantic A·I·A	Gulf A·I·A	Texas A·I·A	W.Mountain A·I·A	Northwest A·I·A	Sierra Nev A·I·A
Totals No.	3253	2302	951	161	267	488	339	149	256	369	233	136	132	199	126	131	78	115	265
Totals %	100	100	100	100	100	100	100	100	100	100	100	100	100	100	100	100	100	100	100
1–4	52.5	47.5	64.3	51.7	48.4	55.5	49.5	69.9	51.9	48.9	42.9	58.9	43.9	47.5	34.1	50.4	46.1	52.2	46.8
1	12.7	9.4	20.7	10.6	15.8	15.0	10.3	25.6	9.3	9.5	6.9	14.0	6.1	9.5	4.0	6.9	5.1	5.2	11.7
2	15.4	12.6	22.0	14.3	13.1	16.6	13.1	24.8	13.7	14.7	10.3	22.1	10.6	13.7	7.1	14.5	12.8	13.9	12.9
3	14.3	14.7	13.1	15.6	10.5	14.2	15.4	11.4	13.7	13.3	13.3	13.2	18.9	13.7	13.5	16.0	15.4	23.5	14.3
4	10.1	10.8	8.5	11.2	9.0	9.7	10.7	8.1	15.2	11.4	12.4	9.6	8.3	10.6	9.5	13.0	12.8	9.6	7.9
5–9	26.1	27.9	21.9	24.8	24.3	23.8	26.2	18.2	25.9	25.8	27.6	22.8	30.3	31.0	39.7	27.5	28.2	26.0	29.6
5	8.5	8.9	7.5	11.2	7.9	8.0	8.6	6.7	8.2	7.9	8.2	7.4	8.3	8.5	10.3	9.9	12.8	7.8	9.1
6	6.6	6.7	6.5	3.1	7.5	5.5	6.2	4.0	5.9	6.2	6.0	6.6	5.3	7.5	12.7	8.4	6.4	5.2	7.2
7	4.5	4.9	3.4	4.3	2.6	4.1	4.4	3.4	5.1	3.3	3.9	2.2	6.1	6.0	10.3	3.1	6.4	4.3	5.7
8	4.3	4.7	3.4	5.0	4.1	3.7	3.8	3.4	4.7	5.7	5.6	5.9	4.5	6.5	4.8	4.6	2.6	6.1	4.2
9	2.2	2.7	1.1	1.2	2.2	2.5	3.2	.7	2.0	2.7	3.9	.7	6.1	2.5	1.6	1.5	–	2.6	3.4
10–19	12.7	14.6	8.3	12.4	13.8	14.4	17.2	7.9	12.8	11.5	12.8	8.7	13.6	14.0	20.6	12.4	20.5	14.8	13.6
10	3.3	3.6	2.7	5.0	4.1	4.3	5.3	2.0	3.5	.9	.9	2.2	1.5	3.5	6.3	3.1	–	3.5	3.8
11	1.5	2.0	.4	1.2	.7	3.2	3.2	.8	2.3	.4	.3	.4	4.5	1.5	3.2	.8	2.6	2.6	1.9
12	2.0	2.0	2.1	–	1.9	2.1	2.1	2.7	1.6	3.0	3.0	2.9	2.3	2.5	1.6	2.3	3.8	2.6	1.4
13	1.0	1.2	.4	2.5	.7	.8	.8	.8	.8	1.9	2.6	.4	.8	1.5	1.6	2.3	1.3	–	.4
14	1.5	1.8	.6	3.1	1.9	1.6	2.1	.8	1.1	.4	.4	.3	1.5	1.0	1.6	3.1	3.8	.9	2.3
15–19	3.4	4.0	2.1	.6	4.5	3.7	3.7	2.9	3.5	5.5	5.5	2.9	3.0	4.0	6.3	.8	9.0	5.2	3.8
20–39	5.8	6.7	3.8	8.1	5.5	3.8	3.9	4.0	6.7	8.4	10.7	4.4	9.2	5.5	5.6	7.6	5.2	6.1	7.8
20–24	2.7	3.2	1.5	3.1	2.2	1.6	1.6	1.3	3.5	4.1	6.0	.7	3.9	2.5	2.4	4.6	1.3	4.3	3.8
25–29	1.7	2.0	1.1	1.9	1.4	1.4	1.4	–	1.6	2.4	2.6	2.2	3.8	2.0	3.2	1.5	1.4	.9	2.6
30–39	1.4	1.5	1.2	3.1	1.4	.9	.9	2.7	1.6	1.9	2.1	1.5	1.5	1.0	–	1.5	2.6	.9	1.4
40–99	2.0	2.3	1.0	1.8	6.8	2.4	–		1.1	3.3	3.4	3.0	1.5	1.5	–	2.3	–	1.8	–
40–49	1.0	1.2	.4	.6	3.5	1.2	1.8	–		1.4	1.3	–	1.5	1.0	–	1.5	3.8	.9	1.4
50–99	1.0	1.1	.6	1.2	3.3	.4	.6	–	1.1	1.9	2.1	1.5	1.5	.5	–	.8	–	–	.4
100 & more	.9	1.0	.7	1.2	1.2	.6	.8	.8	1.6	2.4	2.6	2.2	1.5	–	–	–	–	–	.4
Average	9.3	10.4	6.6	3.9	4.2	3.4	4.1		3.9	4.2	4.9	3.0	4.8	4.4	5.4	4.0	4.2	3.8	4.4
Median	3.8	4.3	2.6																

TABLE 27: DISTRIBUTION OF ARCHITECTS' TIME BY TYPES OF PROFESSIONAL ACTIVITIES

FIRST ORDER OF PREFERENCE

Activity	Individual Practitioners A.I.A	Non AIA	Private Employee Architects A.I.A	Non AIA	Public Employee Architects A.I.A	Non AIA	Teachers
Totals %	100	100	100	100	100	100	100
Design, Architectural	30	20	30	20	20	10	10
Overall Activities of a Gen'l. Practice	20	10	.	.	.	.	.
Administration & Office Managem't.	10	10	10	10	40	.	10
Client Relations	10	10	.	.	.	.	.
Drafting & Developm't of Working Dwg	10	30	50	70	20	40	.
Specification Writing	10	10	10	.	20	10	.
Construction Supervision & Inspection	10	10	.	.	10	.	.
Engineering, General	.	.	.	.	.	.	.
Consulting	.	.	.	.	.	.	.
Maintenance of Buildings	.	.	.	.	10	.	.
Teaching (Architectural Faculty only)	.	.	.	.	10	.	80
Structural Engineering	.	.	.	.	.	5	.
Editing, Writing, Research	.	.	.	.	.	5	.
Planning, City or Site	.	.	.	.	.	.	.
Estimating	.	.	.	.	.	5	.
Activities not listed in Questionnaire	.	.	.	.	.	5	.

SECOND ORDER OF PREFERENCE

Activity	Individual Practitioners A.I.A	Non AIA	Private Employee Architects A.I.A	Non AIA	Public Employee Architects A.I.A	Non AIA	Teachers
Totals %	100	100	100	100	100	100	100
Design, Architectural	10	10	30	40	20	20	20
Overall Activities of a Gen'l. Practice	10	30	10	.	.	.	.
Administration & Office Managem't.	10	20	10	10	10	10	10
Client Relations	20	20	10	10	10	10	.
Drafting & Developm't of Working Dwg	20	10	30	10	20	20	.
Specification Writing	10	10	10	10	5	.	.
Construction Supervision & Inspection	20	10	10	30	20	30	.
Engineering, General	.	.	.	.	.	.	.
Consulting	.	.	.	.	.	.	.
Maintenance of Buildings	.	.	.	.	.	.	.
Teaching (Architectural Faculty only)	.	.	.	.	.	.	.
Structural Engineering	.	.	.	.	5	5	.
Editing, Writing, Research	.	.	.	.	5	5	10
Planning, City or Site	.	.	.	.	.	.	.
Estimating	.	.	.	.	.	.	10
Activities not listed in Questionnaire	.	.	.	.	.	.	.

THIRD ORDER OF PREFERENCE

Activity	Individual Practitioners A.I.A	Non AIA	Private Employee Architects A.I.A	Non AIA	Public Employee Architects A.I.A	Non AIA	Teachers
Totals %	100	100	100	100	100	100	100
Design, Architectural	10	20	10	10	10	25	30
Overall Activities of a Gen'l. Practice	30	10	30	5	.	5	.
Administration & Office Managem't.	20	10	10	10	10	.	10
Client Relations	.	.	.	.	.	.	5
Drafting & Developm't of Working Dwg	10	10	.	10	10	10	5
Specification Writing	.	5	10	.	5	30	5
Construction Supervision & Inspection	10	20	40	35	20	.	5
Engineering, General	10	10	10	10	10	.	10
Consulting	.	.	.	.	.	20	.
Maintenance of Buildings	.	.	.	.	.	.	.
Teaching (Architectural Faculty only)	.	.	.	.	.	.	.
Structural Engineering	.	5	.	30	5	.	.
Editing, Writing, Research	.	.	.	.	.	10	.
Planning, City or Site	.	.	.	.	.	.	.
Estimating	.	.	.	.	.	.	20
Activities not listed in Questionnaire	.	.	.	.	.	.	.

TABLE 28: DISTRIBUTION OF TOTAL TIME GIVEN BY ALL RESPONDING ARCHITECTS TO 28 PROFESSIONAL ACTIVITIES

Activities	ALL	Individual Practitioners A.I.A	Non AIA	Private Employee Architects A.I.A	Non AIA	Public Employee Architects A.I.A	Non AIA	Teachers
Totals %	100	100	100	100	100	100	100	100
Design, Architectural	15.2	15.5	14.2	9.7	5.7	13.1	11.5	8.0
Overall Activities of General Practice	11.5	15.1	13.7	7.2	4.5	2.8	2.8	5.1
Drafting & Developm't of Working Dwgs.	17.9	12.8	17.3	6.9	7.8	11.0	13.8	5.6
Administration & Office Management	10.7	12.5	9.2	3.1	1.9	21.8	14.3	6.5
Client Relations	9.2	11.6	9.6	18.1	17.8	4.6	3.7	2.1
Construction Supervision & Inspection	9.7	10.9	10.3	27.4	37.3	8.9	7.4	2.0
Specification Writing	6.4	6.9	6.8	.5	.4	5.0	6.6	1.1
Consulting	3.8	4.0	4.3	.7	1.0	6.7	6.6	2.3
Engineering, Structural	2.3	1.7	2.8	.5	.4	1.1	2.4	.6
Estimating	1.8	1.5	2.0	2.3	4.0	2.7	5.4	.9
Planning, City or Site	1.3	1.2	1.1	1.4	2.0	3.4	3.9	1.8
Engineering, General	1.2	1.0	1.6	4.4	2.8	2.2	2.4	.1
Interior Design or Furniture	.9	.8	.7	1.4	1.1	.5	.9	.6
Editing, Writing, Research	.9	.6	.4	5.8	5.2	4.8	3.0	3.6
Teaching (Architectural Faculty only)	2.1	.6	.4	.2	.2	.8	.1	56.6
Engineering, Mechanical	.6	.5	.6	.4	.5	.2	.5	.3
Engineering, Sanitary	.4	.4	.5	2.4	.7	.3	.7	.1
Engineering, Electrical	.4	.4	.5	1.0	1.6	.2	.3	.1
Building Code Administration	.5	.3	.5	.3	.5	1.5	3.5	.2
Personnel & Labor Problems	.3	.2	.2	1.3	1.2	.6	.7	.2
Contractor, General	.4	.2	.7	.1	.2	-	.1	.1
Landscape Design	.2	.2	.3	1.2	1.2	.3	.4	.3
Maintenance of Buildings	.5	.1	.3	.5	.4	3.5	2.7	.1
Industrial Product Design	.2	.1	-	.8	.1	.1	.1	.1
Sales of Building Products	.1	.1	.2	.3	.2	.3	.1	-
Other activities not listed	1.1	.6	.9	1.7	1.1	3.9	6.0	1.5
Retired	.3	.1	.6	.2	.1	.2	.2	.2
Unemployed	.1	.1	.3	.2	.1	-	-	.1

TABLE 29: FREQUENCY OF BUILDING TYPES IN PRACTICE · National Distribution

FOR INDIVIDUAL PRACTITIONERS ONLY

Type	Total A·I·A	Total NonA	FIRST A·I·A	FIRST NonA	SECOND A·I·A	SECOND NonA	THIRD A·I·A	THIRD NonA
% Totals	100	100	100	100	100	100	100	100
Commercial	23	24	22	25	29	31	18	15
Residential	18	22	21	32	13	16	19	19
Educational	17	12	29	17	15	11	8	6
Churches	9	9	6	6	10	9	12	12
Industrial	9	8	5	9	10	4	11	12
Public·incl.Housing	8	8	7	5	8	14	8	6
Hospitals	7	4	6	3	8	5	6	5
Recreational	1	2	1	-	2	2	2	3
Community Planning	1	1	1	-	1	1	1	1
Other	7	10	2	2	4	7	15	21

(ORDER OF FREQUENCY: FIRST, SECOND, THIRD)

TABLE 30: FREQUENCY OF BUILDING TYPES IN PRACTICE by A·I·A Regions

FOR INDIVIDUAL PRACTITIONERS ONLY

FIRST ORDER OF FREQUENCY

Type	U.S Total A·I·A	U.S Total NonA	NewEng A·I·A	NewYork A·I·A	Middle Atlantic A·I·A	Middle Atlantic NonA	GLakes A·I·A	North Central A·I·A	North Central NonA	Central A·I·A	So.Atlan. A·I·A	Gulf A·I·A	Texas A·I·A	Northwest A·I·A	SierraNev. A·I·A
% Totals	100	100	100	100	100	100	100	100	100	100	100	100	100	100	100
Educational	29	17	23	19	28	13	35	27	19	39	21	38	33	30	30
Residential	21	32	28	23	27	31	15	19	28	10	26	13	15	14	27
Commercial	22	25	19	23	16	25	19	21	17	18	24	23	27	31	24
Public·incl.Housing	7	5	13	13	8	7	3	6	3	1	12	7	4	8	3
Industrial	5	6	4	4	4	9	6	13	19	9	5	-	6	4	3
Churches	6	6	2	7	7	7	11	6	8	12	4	4	7	6	5
Hospitals	6	3	6	5	3	3	7	4	1	10	3	11	6	8	5
Recreational	1	1	-	2	1	1	-	-	1	1	1	1	2	1	1
Community Plan'g	1	-	1	4	1	2	1	1	-	1	-	-	1	-	1
Other	2	2	4	4	2	3	1	3	1	1	4	2	-	3	2

SECOND ORDER OF FREQUENCY

Type	U.S Total A·I·A	U.S Total NonA	NewEng A·I·A	NewYork A·I·A	Middle Atlantic A·I·A	Middle Atlantic NonA	GLakes A·I·A	North Central A·I·A	North Central NonA	Central A·I·A	So.Atlan. A·I·A	Gulf A·I·A	Texas A·I·A	Northwest A·I·A	SierraNev. A·I·A
% Totals	100	100	100	100	100	100	100	100	100	100	100	100	100	100	100
Commercial	29	31	26	32	28	29	31	31	29	27	32	24	28	20	34
Educational	15	11	18	8	13	7	16	12	12	24	19	19	15	17	15
Residential	16	14	15	17	14	25	9	12	7	9	18	15	21	11	14
Public·incl.Housing	8	14	12	8	7	7	5	5	12	2	10	9	7	8	12
Churches	10	9	8	9	9	9	12	6	14	10	7	14	10	17	7
Industrial	10	4	4	14	12	11	13	14	8	13	3	5	7	7	8
Hospitals	8	5	4	5	8	3	8	15	17	14	8	11	9	9	4
Recreational	2	2	2	2	2	1	1	-	4	-	1	-	1	1	2
Community Plan'g	1	1	1	2	1	1	-	1	-	-	2	-	1	1	1
Other	4	7	4	7	6	7	5	5	5	2	2	2	2	5	3

THIRD ORDER OF FREQUENCY

Type	U.S Total A·I·A	U.S Total NonA	NewEng A·I·A	NewYork A·I·A	Middle Atlantic A·I·A	Middle Atlantic NonA	GLakes A·I·A	North Central A·I·A	North Central NonA	Central A·I·A	So.Atlan. A·I·A	Gulf A·I·A	Texas A·I·A	Northwest A·I·A	SierraNev. A·I·A
% Totals	100	100	100	100	100	100	100	100	100	100	100	100	100	100	100
Residential	19	19	22	19	16	19	24	21	14	15	23	12	19	18	15
Commercial	18	15	15	14	20	13	17	14	16	20	16	22	15	25	21
Churches	12	12	4	7	12	9	12	13	11	14	14	20	21	13	9
Industrial	11	12	14	15	12	21	10	13	11	9	9	8	13	9	9
Educational	8	6	8	6	7	6	8	13	9	12	11	7	14	8	7
Public·incl.Housing	8	6	7	10	6	8	8	9	5	7	12	13	10	5	8
Hospitals	6	5	7	4	5	6	6	6	6	12	8	8	7	5	4
Recreational	2	3	2	2	3	2	2	8	2	3	1	-	-	3	6
Community Plan'g	1	2	2	2	2	-	2	2	2	1	-	-	1	1	2
Other	15	21	19	21	16	22	13	15	24	7	10	9	10	13	20

TABLE 31: ARCHITECTS' SPECIALIZATION IN TYPES OF BUILDINGS

FOR INDIVIDUAL PRACTITIONERS ONLY

Type	Number Tot.	Number A·I·A	Number NonAIA	Per Cent Tot.	Per Cent A·I·A	Per Cent NonAIA
Totals	1715	1122	593	100	100	100
Educational	400	299	101	23	27	17
Residential	398	214	184	23	19	30
Commercial	231	146	85	14	13	14
Churches	178	114	64	11	10	11
Industrial	156	85	71	9	8	12
Hospitals	126	105	21	7	9	4
Public·incl.Housing	124	97	27	7	9	5
Recreational	39	24	15	2	2	3
Community Planning	19	12	7	1	1	1
Other	44	26	18	3	2	3

TABLE 34: MEDIAN VOLUMES OF PROJECTS CONTRACTED FOR BY FIRMS IN 1949

A·I·A Region	A·I·A No. of firms reporting	A·I·A Median volume ($1000)	Non A·I·A No. of firms reporting	Non A·I·A Median volume ($1000)
All Individ.Practit.Firms	2302	$1,082	951	$570
Gulf	126	1,500	54	962
North Central	233	1,477	136	850
West Mountain	78	1,360	23	750
New York	267	1,304	90	875
Central	132	1,190	63	517
Great Lakes	256	1,141	81	462
Texas	131	1,114	66	731
Northwest	115	1,096	53	400
Mid-Atlantic	339	1,044	149	509
South Atlantic	199	872	63	444
Sierra Nevada	265	865	90	402
New England	161	852	83	481
Company Department Offices	108	2,345	134	805
Public Bureau Offices	56	2,000	78	429

TABLE 33: FIRMS ASSOCIATING AS SPECIALISTS.

INDIVIDUAL PRACTITIONERS ONLY

A·I·A Region	Firm does Associate	Firm does not Associate
U-S	40%	60%
New York	50	50
Texas	49	51
New England	43	57
North Central	41	59
Mid-Atlantic	40	60
South Atlantic	40	60
Gulf	40	60
Central	39	61
Great Lakes	37	63
Sierra Nevada	34	66
West Mountain	32	68
Northwest	31	69

TABLE 32: PROVISION OF AUXILIARY SERVICES

Method of Providing	Structural Engineer'g	Mechanical Engineer'g	Electrical Engineer'g	Landscape Architect.	Interior Design
INDIVIDUAL PRACTITIONER FIRMS					
Total %	100	100	100	100	100
Consultant	52	77	74	66	10
Self	30	12	14	29	71
Full-time Employee	12	8	9	3	11
Partner	6	3	3	2	8
COMPANY DEPARTMENT OFFICES					
Total %	100	100	100	100	100
Consultant	40	56	56	55	9
Self	33	16	12	33	69
Full-time Employee	26	27	31	10	19
Partner	1	1	1	2	3
PUBLIC BUREAU OFFICES					
Total %	100	100	100	100	100
Consultant	36	45	49	52	15
Self	23	19	11	23	62
Full-time Employee	41	36	39	25	23
Partner	-	-	1	-	-

TABLE 36: OTHER ATTRIBUTES OF ARCHITECTS' PROFESSIONAL EDUCATION

	All Reporting Yes%	No%	Individual Practitioners Yes%	No%	Private Employee Architects Yes%	No%	Public Employee Architects Yes%	No%	Teachers Yes%	No%
Entire Training in Archit. Offices	23	77	24	76	19	81	24	76	6	94
Have studied Arch. in foreign country	20	80	21	79	14	86	19	81	38	62
Hold certificate from a trade school	16	84	15	85	16	84	25	75	13	87
Hold Liberal Arts degree	13	87	14	86	12	88	11	89	20	80
Have received fellowship or grant	10	90	9	91	6	94	8	92	44	56
Hold degree other than Arch. or Lib.Arts	4	96	4	96	3	97	7	93	11	89
Hold degree in Engineering	4	96	4	96	4	96	8	92	2	98

TABLE 35: ARCHITECTS' PROFESSIONAL EDUCATION

	ALL	Individual Practitioner	Private Employee	Public Employee	Teachers
Base Figures	6418	4635	1230	362	191
All figures are % of Column Base					
Hold first degree in Architecture	56	54	60	46	86
Hold no degrees in Architecture	44	46	40	54	14
Hold two degrees in Architecture	10	10	9	5	48
Hold degree in Archit.Engineer'g	9	7	11	13	12
Completed special course in Archit.	21	21	19	26	19
Attended one archit'l. school	66	65	70	60	87
Attended two archit'l. schools	22	21	23	24	45

TABLE 37

TABLE 37: ARCHITECTS·IN·ARCHITECTURAL·SCHOOLS: by degrees in Architecture & Architectural Engineering · Special Courses · & 1st & 2nd Attendances

The table lists the following schools in order of total of first degrees:

Univ. Illinois; U. Pennsylvania; Univ. Michigan; Cornell Univ.; Mass. Inst. Tech.; Yale Univ.; U. California; Columbia Univ.; Carnegie Inst. Tech.; Illinois Inst. Tech.; Ohio State Univ.; Georgia Sch. Tech.; Harvard Univ.; U. Minnesota; New York Univ.; U. Southern Calif.; Univ. Texas; U. Washington; Pennsylvania S.C.; Washington U.; A. & M. Col. Texas; Syracuse Univ.; Tulane Univ.; Kansas St. Col.; Univ. Kansas; Alabama Poly. Inst.; Princeton Univ.; Univ. Florida; Notre Dame U.; U. Cincinnati; Univ. Virginia; Clemson Agr. Col.; Oklahoma A. & M.; Univ. Oregon; Rice Inst.; Pratt Inst.; Iowa State Col.; Catholic Univ.; Western Reserve; No. Carolina S.C.; Rensselaer Poly. I.; St. Col. Washington; Virginia Poly. Inst.; Montana St. Col.; Cooper Inst.; Univ. Oklahoma; North Dakota A.C.; Univ. Nebraska; Miami Univ.; Univ. Detroit; Ohio Univ.; Texas Tech. Col.; Rhode Island S.D.; Univ. Colorado; Univ. Idaho; Howard Univ.; U. New Mexico; Cranbrook Acad.; Hampton Inst.; Univ. Houston; Univ. Utah; Amer. Acad. Rome; Univ. Arkansas; Univ. Denver; Ecole J.B. Arts; Unspecified

The column headings are grouped under two main sections — NUMBER and PER CENT — each subdivided into TOTAL, A.I.A., and Non·A.I.A., with sub-columns for 1st Degrees (Tot., Arch., A. Eng.), 2nd Deg., Special Courses (Cour. Ses.), and Attendances (1st, 2nd).

TABLE 38

TABLE 38: ARCHITECTS' EDUCATION, REGISTRATION, & 1950 EMPLOYMENT IN HOME STATES (State of High School Graduation)

x States with long-established schools; • other states with sch'ls

STATES & A.I.A REGIONS	1. Total Reporting High School Graduation in State	2. First Professional School Attended ALL	2. IN-STATE No.	2. %	3. Second Professional School Attended ALL	3. IN-STATE No.	3. %	4. First Architectural Degree ALL	4. IN-STATE No.	4. %	5. Degree in Architectural Engineering ALL	5. IN-STATE No.	5. %	6. Second Architectural Degree ALL	6. IN-STATE No.	6. %	7. Special Non-Degree Courses ALL	7. IN-STATE No.	7. %	8. First Registration ALL	8. IN-STATE No.	8. %	9. 1950 Employment No.	9. % of Col.1	10. Items 1,8,&9 in same State No.	10. % of Col.1	11. Preferences for Out-of-State Education
U-S Totals	6152	4113	2569	63	1399	443	32	3462	2075	60	548	336	61	639	250	39	1236	451	36	6103	3957	65	3778	61	3471	56	1-NY 36 8-NJ 8 Fla 2; 2-Pa 30 9-Wash 5 DC 2; 3-Mass 27 Wash 5 Ohio 2; 4-Ill 13 Minn 4; 5-Mich 12 Minn 4 Ind 1; 6-Calif 11 Tex 3 Kan 1; 7-Penn 9 12-SC 2 Ore 1; RI 1; Va 1
28 States with Estab. Sch'ls	4982	3446	2491	72	1119	429	38	2916	2053	71	447	330	70	517	244	47				4943	3347	68	3201	68	2492	49	
21 Other States	1170																			1160	610	53	577	49	479	41	
New England	495	285	168	59	99	46	47	240	132	55	18	10	56	46	28	61	129	56	43	477	286	60	290	59	251	51	Mass-NY-Pa
Maine	22	8						8												22	16	73	19	82	16	73	Mass-NY
New Hampshire	20	9			7			8									3			17	9	53	11	55			NY-Mass-RI
Vermont	9																							44			NY-Pa-Conn-NJ-France
Massachusetts	264	152	112	74	49	33	67	128	97	76	10	8	80	27	22	82	79	43	54	261	154	59	159	60	138	52	Mass-Conn-NY
Rhode Island	34	30	21	70	13	13	38	15	5	33	6	2	33	3	6	43	16	5	28	46	27	59	24	52	25	54	NY-Pa-DC-NJ
Connecticut	134	81	35	43	34	13	38	76	33	43	6	2	33	14	6	43	29	5	28	123	78	63	74	55	63	47	
New York	817	541	405	75	216	131	61	434	310	71	28	6	21	68	36	53	234	168	72	812	592	73	541	66	493	60	Mass-Conn-Mich
Mid-Atlantic	1012	623	307	49	190	56	29	539	297	55	55	33	60	98	50	51	236	61	26	1006	661	66	586	58	546	54	Pa-NJ-Ill
New Jersey	261	162	14	9	68	6	9	112	10	9	14	1	7	18	6	33	90			258	182	72	145	56	134	51	NY-Mass-Conn-Pa
Pennsylvania	505	317	245	77	75	41	55	298	244	82	22	17	77	57	40	70	100	55	55	505	336	67	301	60	292	58	NY-Mass-NJ-Conn-Mich
Delaware	12							4												12		50	12			42	Mass-Pa-Fla-Calif
Maryland	56	26	12	30	18	5	28	23	17	44				8	2		12			56	34	61	38	68	33	59	Pa-NJ-DC-Calif
Distr. Columbia	58	40	36	61	12	4	27	39	27	56			100	8	2	29	14	1		56	29	52	24	41	19	34	NY-Pa-Mass
Virginia	58	59			18			48			14	2		7	1	25	14	5	5	57	29	52	24	41	19	34	NY-NJ-Pa-Mass
West Virginia	27	16			12			15			3		93	9			11			22	63		14	52	33		Pa-Ohio-Va
Great Lakes	754	521	271	52	163	39	24	448	243	54	106	63	59	98	25	25	174	24	20	751	496	66	465	62	428	57	NY-Pa-Mich-Mass
Ohio	371	278	162	62	90	26	29	237	141	59	42	30	72	35	15	25	63	18	14	370	268	72	244	65	235	63	Ill-Mich-NY
Indiana	88	88	15	17	18	4	10	77	10	13	25	3	12	10	2	20	20	8		145	71	49	82	57	62	43	NY-Mass-NY
Michigan	145	123	94	76	29	9	30	107	92	86	35	21	60	17	6	66	21	8		183	122	67	110	60	104	57	Pa-Ohio-Ill-NY
Kentucky	153							27			4						14			53	35	66	30	55	27	51	
North Central	847	583	402	69	181	47	26	481	311	65	111	79	71	85	29	34	174	47	27	845	583	69	487	58	451	53	Mass-NY-Ind-Pa-Mich
Illinois	556	406	315	78	59	40	40	329	251	76	73	73	79	49	27	55	103	38	37	555	443	80	346	70	330	60	Ill-Minn-NY-Mich-Iowa-Pa
Wisconsin	127	59			17			46			8			21	2	10	32	8		127	63	53	70	55	58	46	Minn-Mass-NY
Minnesota	118	82	70	85	40	7	17	68	44	65	8	6	75	9			30	1		118	63	53	65	55	57	48	Minn-NJ-Pa-Calif
North Dakota	32	17			17			26	16	62	2			4	2		9			31	4	13	4	6	5	16	Minn-Mass-NY
South Dakota	14	14			18			18												4	3	21	4	29	3		Minn-Pa
Central	510	370	222	62	140	32	23	275	147	53	85	66	78	64	27	42	94	27	29	507	219	43	232	45	202	40	Ill-NY-Pa-Calif
Iowa	93	67	25	37	25	4	4	85	45	53	21	4	96	16	2	26	16			93	122	64	116	60	111	58	Kan-Ill-NY-Mass-Conn
Missouri	192	124	54	44	44	12	27	85	45	53	17	3	18	27	18	66	40	18		192	122	64	116	60	111	58	Ill-NY-Conn
Nebraska	45	30	22	73	19	9	30	23	10	30	23	21	60	27	2	66	17	7		45	14	31	14	31	12	31	Ill-NY-Mo
Kansas	110	92	72	78	19	9	47	56	35	74	12	2	41	13	4	24	12	4		108	37	34	47	44	32	29	Mass-Ill-Mo
Oklahoma	70	26	15	44	22	8	33	26	27	47	34		100	9	3	33	4			30	30	44	26	37			
South Atlantic	279	204	126	62	68	16	24	183	108	59	30	24	80	31	8	26	53	13	19	278	214	77	209	75	196	63	Ga-NY-Pa-Conn
North Carolina	65	46	23	24	13	1	8	34	8	24	18	15	83	5	4	12	13			65	44	68	41	63	33	47	NY-Mass-Pa-Mich
South Carolina	58	39	29	74	18	7	39	30	10	72	14	4	66	12	7	58	16	5		58	38	66	35	51	27	47	NY-Pa-Mass-SC
Georgia	71	60	48	80	18	8	33	52	43	81	3	3	100	20	12		20	4		84	53	79	52	79	50	71	NY-Pa-Mass-NY
Florida	84	39	26	44	24	5		27			5	3	60	9	2		4	1		72	30	44	56	92	63	76	Mass-NY
Gulf	268	187	88	47	64	3	5	166	77	46	20	6	45	34	4	12	36	3	8	267	183	69	170	63	157	59	Pa-Ga-Mass
Tennessee	61	33	41	68	10	3	5	27	33	70	4	5	84	14	2	20	14	2		61	40	66	41	67	35	57	NY-Mass-Pa-Mich
Alabama	70	60			17			47			6			10			13			69	40	58	38	54	33	47	Ga-La-Ill
Mississippi	25	15	2	11	8			21		16	3			9	2	20	13			29	20	69	17	59	16	55	Tex-NY-Mich-Calif
Arkansas	25	19	6	75	8			21	1		1			2			4			29	9	44	17	59	10	55	NY-Pa-Mass-Mich-Calif
Louisiana	83	60	45	75	23	3	13	59	44	75	27	4	66	12	2	17	4	1		83	72	87	64	77	63	76	Mass-NY
Texas	257	193	176	91	59	24	41	168	149	89	23	20	87	30	17	63	36	9	25	256	229	89	214	83	208	81	NY-Mich-Mass-Ill-Pa
Western Mountain	257	149	26	17	92	5	5	131	1		36	2	6	47	0	-	61	4	7	254	69	27	56	22	33	13	Calif-Minn-Mo
Wyoming	10	36	8	22	5	3	15	4			7	1	14	9	1		10	2		57	21	37	19	33	17	30	Calif-Ill-NY-Mass
Colorado	57	36	8	62	20	3		30	1	16	2			2	2	20	13			44	20	44	19	44	4		Calif-Pa-Tex
New Mexico	8	8			6			6									4			29	69		17	44			Tex-NY-Mich-Calif
Arizona		19	2	11	23		3	21						12	2	17	4	1		83	72	87	25	60	2		NY-Pa-Mass-Mich-Calif
Utah	176	100	13	13	64	2	3	87	1	4	27	1	4	33	2	25	46	2		176	41	24	25	14	5		
Northwest	239	174	143	82	54	6	11	151	100	66	22	14	64	26	2	8	30	9	30	234	171	73	166	69	157	66	Mich-Wash
Montana	31	25	16	64	6			22	12	55	14	1	56	1	2		7			31	17	55	17	55	14	45	Wash-Calif-NY
Idaho	15	10	5	50	2		15	2	1	33	2			1			3			14	3	21	3	13	2		Ore-NY-Calif-Mass-Pa
Washington	125	100	89	86	33	4	31	88	62	71	11	9	82	17	2	25	15	5		124	100	81	94	75	93	74	Pa-Mass-Wash-NY
Oregon	68	39	36	93	13	4	31	32	23	72	11	9	82	17	2	25	4			65	51	79	64	78	48		
Sierra Nevada	417	283	228	81	73	38	52	246	200	81	14	10	72	51	34	67	62	33	53	416	354	85	362	87	349	84	Pa-Wash
Nevada	6																						66				
California	411	280	228	81	72	38	53	243	200	82	14	10	72	51	34	67	62	33	53	410	350	85	358	87	345	84	NY-Pa-Wash-Mass-NJ

TABLE 39: LENGTH OF ARCHTS' COLLEGE STUDIES

Employment Status	All Reporting	Architectural Responders No.	%	Avg. Yrs.	Other Responders No.	%	Avg. Yrs.
Totals	6418	5270	82		2144	33	
Individual Practitioners	4638	3773	81	5.1	1502	32	3.0
Private Employ. Archts.	1230	1051	85	4.9	435	35	2.8
Public Employ. Archts.	362	270	75	5.0	120	33	3.0
Teachers	191	176	92	6.5	87	46	2.7

TABLE 40: ARCHTS' SUPPLEMENTARY STUDIES

Subject	All Reported	Individ Pract.	Privat Employ	Public Employ	Teach'rs
Totals (%)	100	100	100	100	100
Engineering	22	22	25	27	13
Fine Arts	14	14	14	13	17
Business & Economics	13	14	12	12	8
City Planning	9	9	8	7	16
Liberal Arts	8	8	8	6	10
Social Sciences	6	5	6	6	11
Landscape Architecture	5	6	4	4	7
Real Estate	5	5	5	5	1
Law	5	5	4	4	2
Other Unspecified Courses	13	12	15	16	15

TABLE 41: SUPPLEMENTARY STUDIES DESIRED BY ARCHITECTS

Type or Subject	All Reported	Individ Pract'rs	Private Employ	Public Employ	Teach'rs
Type of Program (%)					
Totals (%)	100	100	100	100	100
Visiting Lecturers	22	22	25	23	23
Seminars – on state or regional basis	18	18	12	16	19
Printed courses of study from central agency	13	13	16	17	7
Courses published in current journals	12	12	16	11	7
Short courses at architectural schools	10	10	12	8	16
Refresher course at archit. school	8	8	7	8	9
Advanced courses at archit. school	8	8	8	7	9
Prefer no organized activity	8	8	7	9	2
Suggested Subjects					
Totals (%)	100	100	100	100	100
Advanced Construction Techniques	20	20	21	19	19
Planning of Special Building Types	13	13	16	15	15
Economics & Business of Construction	11	11	13	12	10
Contemporary Aesthetics	11	11	11	13	9
Design to satisfy physiological demands of human life	10	10	9	11	17
Law relating to Bldg. Construction	10	10	9	11	7
Analyses of New Materials (Non-selling)	10	10	9	8	11
Constr. Problems due to Atomic Dev.	7	7	6	6	5
Real Estate	5	5	4	5	4
Chemical Properties of Bldg. Materials	3	3	3	3	2

TABLE 42: ARCHTS' OPINIONS OF IMPORTANCE OF COURSES IN THE CURRICULUM IN ARCHITECTURE

Subject	Indiv. Pract'rs Important	Desirable	Minor Import.	Teachers Important	Desirable	Minor Import.
Professional Courses						
Architectural Design	98	2	.	99	1	.
Building Materials & Methods	82	16	2	89	11	.
Theory of Arch. & Composition	78	19	3	82	16	2
Structural Design	77	21	2	88	12	.
Working Drawings	77	18	5	68	26	6
Specifications	74	21	5	56	38	6
Graphics (Desc.Geom.,Persp.,Etc)	59	34	7	70	29	1
Freehand Drawing	57	37	6	63	32	5
Prof. Relations & Ethics	55	35	10	56	35	9
Mech., Elec.,& Sanit. Install.	54	40	6	67	29	4
History of Architecture	46	39	15	58	37	5
Bldg. Codes, Law, Real Estate	44	41	15	45	43	12
Office Administration	40	41	19	32	49	19
Site Engineering	35	51	14	29	56	15
Appl'd. Science(light,color,sound)	31	55	14	47	44	9
Community & City Planning	27	56	17	47	48	5
Interior Design, Decor. & Furnit.	28	58	14	29	55	16
Landscape Design	14	60	26	19	61	20
Academic Courses						
Mathematics	78	20	2	80	18	2
English	73	22	5	88	12	.
Fine Arts	57	38	5	56	40	4
Physics	51	37	12	59	36	5
Psychology & Human Relations	42	42	16	42	46	12
Social Sci. & Philos.(Econ., Soc.)	20	49	31	41	52	7
Chemistry	14	40	46	11	44	45
Foreign Language	9	42	49	11	47	42

TABLE 43: BASES USED BY ARCHITECTS IN OBTAINING FIRST REGISTRATION FOR PRACTICE

NUMBER

Bases of Registration	All Reporting Total	Individual Pract'rs	Private Employees	Public Employees	Teachers	A.I.A. Total	Individual Pract'rs	Private Employees	Public Employees	Teachers	Non A.I.A. Total	Individual Pract'rs	Private Employees	Public Employees	Teachers
Totals	6354	4588	1224	358	184	3652	3013	396	114	129	2702	1575	828	244	55
Degree + Experience + Written Examination	1854	1237	453	94	70	1044	819	148	28	49	810	418	305	66	21
Practising when Act came into effect ("grandfather")	823	674	87	43	19	494	435	26	15	18	329	239	61	28	1
Experience incl. non-degree education + writt. exam	880	655	171	52	2	486	399	69	17	1	394	256	102	35	1
Degree + experience	685	513	109	31	32	404	335	35	10	24	281	178	74	21	8
Degree + experience + written exam + oral exam	657	449	149	37	22	370	310	38	10	12	287	139	111	27	10
Degree + experience + oral examination	594	447	92	27	28	376	313	33	12	18	218	134	59	15	10
Experience incl. non-degree educ. + oral exam	466	337	81	42	6	262	218	25	15	4	204	119	56	27	2
Experience incl. non-degree educ. + writ. + oral exams	328	238	61	26	3	189	160	19	7	3	139	78	42	19	.
Other unspecified basis	67	38	21	6	2	27	24	3	.	.	40	14	18	6	2

PER CENT

Bases of Registration	All Reporting Total	Individual Pract'rs	Private Employees	Public Employees	Teachers	A.I.A. Total	Individual Pract'rs	Private Employees	Public Employees	Teachers	Non A.I.A. Total	Individual Pract'rs	Private Employees	Public Employees	Teachers
Totals	100	100	100	100	100	100	100	100	100	100	100	100	100	100	100
Degree + Experience + Written Examination	29	27	37	26	38	29	28	37	25	38	30	27	37	27	38
Practising when Act came into effect ("grandfather")	13	15	7	12	10	13	14	7	13	14	12	15	7	12	2
Experience incl. non-degree education + writt. exam	14	14	14	14	1	13	13	17	15	1	15	16	12	14	2
Degree + experience	11	11	9	9	18	11	11	9	9	19	11	11	9	9	15
Degree + experience + written exam + oral exam	10	10	12	10	12	10	10	10	9	9	10	9	13	11	18
Degree + experience + oral examination	9	10	7	8	15	10	10	8	11	14	8	9	7	6	18
Experience incl. non-degree educ. + oral exam	7	7	6	12	3	7	7	6	13	3	7	7	7	11	4
Experience incl. non-degree educ. + writ. + oral exams	5	5	5	7	2	5	5	5	6	2	5	5	5	8	.
Other unspecified basis	1	1	2	2	1	1	1	1	.	.	1	1	2	2	4

TAB·44: AVERAGE·N°·OF·STATE REGISTRATIONS·PER·ARCHITECT

EMPLOYMENT·STATUS	AV'GE N° OF STATES
GRAND TOTAL	1.7
A·I·A TOTAL	1.9
PRIVATE·PRACTITIONERS	2.0
PRIV·EMPLOYEE·ARCH'TS	1.6
PUBLIC·EMPLOYEE·ARCH'TS	1.4
TEACHERS	1.5
NON·A·I·A TOTAL	1.5
PRIVATE·PRACTITIONERS	1.6
PRIV·EMPLOYEE·ARCH'TS	1.2
PUBLIC·EMPLOYEE·ARCH'TS	1.3
TEACHERS	1.1

TABLE·46ᴬ: ARCHITECTS·HOLDING·NCARB·CERTIFICATES — 1950

EMPLOYMENT·STATUS	NUMBER TOTAL	NUMBER JUNIOR	NUMBER SENIOR	NUMBER BOTH	PER CENT OF·TOTAL JUNIOR	PER CENT OF·TOTAL SENIOR	PER CENT OF·TOTAL BOTH	PER CENT OF·GROUP JUNIOR	PER CENT OF·GROUP SENIOR	PER CENT OF·GROUP BOTH
GRAND TOTAL	991	525	437	29	100	100	100	53	44	3
A·I·A TOTAL	692	336	335	21	64	76		49	48	3
PRIVATE·PRACTITIONERS	599	269	311	19	51	71		45	52	3
PRIV·EMPLOYEE·ARCH'TS	59	44	14	1	9	3				
PUBLIC·EMPLOYEE·ARCH'TS	12	6	5	1	1	1				
TEACHERS	22	17	5		3	1				
NON·A·I·A TOTAL	299	189	102	8	36	24		63	34	3
PRIVATE·PRACTITIONERS	201	109	86	6	21	20		54	43	3
PRIV·EMPLOYEE·ARCH'TS	66	59	7		11	2				
PUBLIC·EMPLOYEE·ARCH'TS	26	16	8	2	3	2				
TEACHERS	6	5	1		1	-				

TAB·46ᴮ: N°·OF·STATES·WHICH ARCH'TS·USED·NCARB·EXAMS

EMPLOYMENT·STATUS	AV'GE N° OF STATES
GRAND TOTAL	2.5
A·I·A TOTAL	2.6
PRIVATE·PRACTITIONERS	2.6
PRIV·EMPLOYEE·ARCH'TS	3.2
PUBLIC·EMPLOYEE·ARCH'TS	2.1
TEACHERS	2.0
NON·A·I·A TOTAL	2.3
PRIVATE·PRACTITIONERS	2.5
PRIV·EMPLOYEE·ARCH'TS	1.8
PUBLIC·EMPLOYEE·ARCH'TS	1.5
TEACHERS	1.6

TAB·48: EQUIVALENCE·OF·EXPERIENCE·OBTAINED·UNDER·A·GENERAL·CONTRACTOR

EMPLOYMENT·STATUS	NUMBER TOTAL	NUMBER YES	NUMBER NO	PER CENT YES	PER CENT NO
GRAND TOTAL	6288	3734	2354	63	37
A·I·A TOTAL	3619	2258	1361	62	38
PRIVATE·PRACTITIONERS	2983	1831	1152	61	39
PRIV·EMPLOYEE·ARCH'TS	392	251	141	64	36
PUBLIC·EMPLOYEE·ARCH'TS	114	75	39	66	34
TEACHERS	130	101	29	78	22
NON·A·I·A TOTAL	2669	1676	993	63	37
PRIVATE·PRACTITIONERS	1552	933	619	60	40
PRIV·EMPLOYEE·ARCH'TS	821	550	271	67	33
PUBLIC·EMPLOYEE·ARCH'TS	242	153	89	63	37
TEACHERS	54	40	14	-	-

TAB·47: OPINION·OF·LENGTH·OF PRE·REGISTRATION·EXPERIENCE

EMPLOYMENT·STATUS	AV'GE N° YEARS DESIRED
GRAND TOTAL	3.6
A·I·A TOTAL	3.6
PRIVATE·PRACTITIONERS	3.6
PRIV·EMPLOYEE·ARCH'TS	3.6
PUBLIC·EMPLOYEE·ARCH'TS	3.5
TEACHERS	3.1
NON·A·I·A TOTAL	3.6
PRIVATE·PRACTITIONERS	3.6
PRIV·EMPLOYEE·ARCH'TS	3.5
PUBLIC·EMPLOYEE·ARCH'TS	3.7
TEACHERS	3.1

TABLE·45: ARCHITECTS·WITH·NCARB·COUNCIL·RECORDS

EMPLOYMENT·STATUS	NUMBER TOTAL	NUMBER YES	NUMBER NO	PER CENT YES	PER CENT NO
GRAND TOTAL	5938	1367	4571	23	77
A·I·A TOTAL	3422	930	2492	27	73
PRIVATE·PRACTITIONERS	2815	804	2011	29	71
PRIV·EMPLOYEE·ARCH'TS	373	80	293	21	79
PUBLIC·EMPLOYEE·ARCH'TS	108	18	90	17	83
TEACHERS	126	28	98	22	78
NON·A·I·A TOTAL	2516	437	2079	17	83
PRIVATE·PRACTITIONERS	1449	295	1154	20	80
PRIV·EMPLOYEE·ARCH'TS	790	94	696	12	88
PUBLIC·EMPLOYEE·ARCH'TS	224	37	187	17	83
TEACHERS	53	11	42	-	-

TABLE 49: ARCHITECTS' OPINIONS OF ADEQUACY OF THEIR PRE-REGISTRATION EXPERIENCE

FIELD	AVERAGE OF 8 EMPLOYMENT GROUPS			RANGE AMONG 8 EMPLOYMENT GROUPS		
	ADEQUATE	INADEQUATE	NO EXPERIENCE	ADEQUATE	INADEQUATE	NO EXPERIENCE
Drafting Work Dwgs & Details	94	6	-	89 - 96	4 - 10	0 - 1
Design, Gen'l Architectural	87	12	1	84 - 91	8 - 15	0 - 2
Design, Structural	60	33	7	50 - 66	27 - 44	5 - 10
Direct Exper. on Construct. Job	60	31	9	51 - 72	22 - 38	4 - 15
Field Supervision	58	33	9	44 - 69	26 - 43	5 - 16
Preparation of Specifications	49	40	11	33 - 60	30 - 51	3 - 16
Client Relations	45	41	14	38 - 57	33 - 46	10 - 19
Administration	40	38	22	33 - 48	35 - 43	17 - 27
Site Planning	40	38	22	34 - 49	31 - 41	20 - 27
Design, Mechanical	37	50	13	33 - 41	46 - 57	10 - 16

TABLE 50: ARCHITECTS' OPINIONS OF ADEQUACY OF THEIR REGISTRATION EXAMINATIONS

FIELD	AVERAGE OF 8 EMPLOYMENT GROUPS			RANGE AMONG 8 EMPLOYMENT GROUPS		
	EXCESSIVE	ADEQUATE	INADEQUATE	EXCESSIVE	ADEQUATE	INADEQUATE
Skill in Draftsmanship	6	84	10	3 - 9	79 - 87	7 - 14
Factual Knowledge	10	83	7	8 - 16	80 - 85	3 - 9
Architectural Design	9	83	8	5 - 12	80 - 85	5 - 15
Structural Design	15	77	8	14 - 18	74 - 79	6 - 9
Facility in Use of English	3	76	21	2 - 5	74 - 79	19 - 24
Mechanical Equipment	7	70	23	6 - 7	68 - 76	17 - 25
History of Architecture	25	68	7	20 - 28	64 - 74	6 - 8

Character of Examination	TOO DIFFICULT	SATISFACTORY	TOO EASY	TOO DIFFICULT	SATISFACTORY	TOO EASY
	4	91	5	2 - 5	90 - 94	3 - 7

Length of Examination	TOO LONG	SATISFACTORY	TOO SHORT	TOO LONG	SATISFACTORY	TOO SHORT
	12	84	4	8 - 15	80 - 89	3 - 5

Statement of Questions	CLEAR	SATISFACTORY	AMBIGUOUS	CLEAR	SATISFACTORY	AMBIGUOUS
	26	66	8	20 - 29	63 - 69	5 - 13

TABLE 51: ARCHITECTS' OPINIONS REGARDING IMPORTANCE OF TOPICS IN REGISTRATION EXAMINATION

FIELD	AVERAGE OF 8 EMPLOYMENT GROUPS			RANGE AMONG 8 EMPLOYMENT GROUPS		
	IMPORTANT	DESIRABLE	MINOR IMPORT.	IMPORTANT	DESIRABLE	MINOR IMPORTANCE
Architectural Design	94	5	1	90 - 96	3 - 10	0 - 3
Materials of Construction	79	20	1	71 - 84	15 - 27	1 - 2
Specifications	79	20	1	68 - 85	14 - 30	1 - 2
Structural Design	70	28	2	53 - 84	15 - 44	1 - 3
Composition and Theory	68	27	5	65 - 73	23 - 31	4 - 8
Professional Relations & Ethics	62	32	6	52 - 72	24 - 40	4 - 8
Administration	60	34	6	57 - 64	31 - 36	5 - 7
History of Architecture	31	49	20	28 - 34	44 - 53	17 - 23
Site Engineering	42	49	9	38 - 48	46 - 54	6 - 11
Mechanical Equipment	46	48	6	33 - 57	38 - 58	5 - 9

TABLE 52: ARCHITECTS' OPINIONS REGARDING TIME WHEN REGISTRATION EXAM SHOULD BE GIVEN

FIELD	AVERAGE OF 8 EMPLOYMENT GROUPS			RANGE AMONG 8 EMPLOYMENT GROUPS		
	JUST AFTER GRADUATION	AFTER OFFICE EXPERIENCE	NO EXAMINATION SHOULD BE GIVEN	JUST AFTER GRADUATION	AFTER OFFICE EXPERIENCE	NO EXAMINATION SHOULD BE GIVEN
Selection & Use of Materials	4	94	2	2 - 5	92 - 96	1 - 3
Supervision	1	92	7	0 - 2	89 - 95	3 - 9
Counseling & Administration	3	84	13	1 - 8	79 - 90	9 - 18
Mechanical Equipment	11	83	6	8 - 19	79 - 86	2 - 10
Aptitude & Theor. & Pract. Train'g	16	68	16	9 - 21	59 - 72	11 - 24
Design Problem	33	65	2	29 - 40	56 - 70	1 - 4
Structural Design	42	55	3	35 - 58	41 - 63	1 - 5
Architectural Composition	42	53	5	37 - 49	43 - 59	1 - 8
Truss Design	42	43	15	36 - 54	31 - 50	14 - 17
History of Architecture	64	23	13	60 - 68	20 - 27	11 - 15

TABLE 53

TABLE 53: GROSS·NATIONAL·PRODUCT: TOTAL·NEW·CONSTRUCTION: & NEW·BUILDING·CONSTRUCTION·

	GROSS NATIONAL PRODUCT $ Millions	TOTAL·NEW CONSTRUC-TION $ Millions	% OF G·N·P	NEW·BUILD-ING· CON-STRUCTION $ Millions	% OF G·N·P	% NEW CONSTR	NEW·BUILDING CONSTRUCTION in 1947-49 Prices ($ Mil.)	% OF 1950
1915		3,262		2,178		66.8	8,407	43
16		3,849		2,663		69.2	9,312	48
17		4,569		2,913		63.8	8,351	43
18		5,118		3,008		58.8	7,113	36
19	83,700	6,296	7.5	4,315	5.2	68.5	8,812	45
1920	89,700	6,749	7.5	4,931	5.5	73.1	8,167	42
21	69,900	6,004	8.6	4,199	6.0	69.9	8,926	46
22	73,400	7,647	10.4	5,616	7.7	73.4	12,812	66
23	86,500	9,332	10.8	6,961	8.0	74.6	14,233	73
24	86,400	10,407	12.0	7,599	8.8	73.0	15,701	80
1925	91,900	11,439	12.4	8,527	9.3	74.5	17,826	91
26	96,500	12,082	12.5	9,088	9.4	75.2	18,851	96
27	95,300	12,034	12.6	8,723	9.2	72.5	18,307	94
28	98,900	11,641	11.8	8,387	8.5	72.0	17,570	90
29	104,711	10,793	10.3	7,372	7.0	68.3	15,112	77
1930	91,474	8,741	9.6	5,019	5.5	57.4	10,855	55
31	76,337	6,427	8.4	3,436	4.5	53.5	8,242	42
32	58,548	3,538	6.0	1,621	2.8	45.8	4,545	23
33	56,049	2,879	5.1	1,182	2.1	41.1	3,346	17
34	65,157	3,720	5.7	1,546	2.4	41.6	3,962	20
1935	72,602	4,232	5.8	1,978	2.7	46.7	5,090	26
36	82,981	6,497	7.8	3,239	3.9	49.9	8,069	41
37	90,929	6,999	7.7	3,860	4.2	55.2	8,458	43
38	85,334	6,980	8.2	3,687	4.3	52.8	7,983	41
39	91,197	8,198	9.0	4,797	5.3	58.5	10,279	53
1940	101,329	8,682	8.6	5,258	5.2	60.6	10,806	55
41	126,262	11,957	9.5	8,070	6.4	67.5	15,262	78
42	161,321	14,075	8.7	8,885	5.5	63.1	16,563	85
43	194,115	8,301	4.3	5,200	2.7	62.6	8,330	43
44	213,583	5,259	2.5	3,392	1.6	64.5	5,442	28
1945	215,109	5,633	2.6	3,721	1.7	66.1	5,702	29
46	211,110	12,000	5.7	9,084	4.3	75.7	11,906	61
47	233,389	16,689	7.2	11,847	5.1	71.0	12,620	65
48	259,233	21,678	8.4	15,417	5.9	71.1	14,725	75
49	258,432	22,789	8.8	15,631	6.0	68.6	15,286	78
1950	286,826	28,454	9.9	20,979	7.3	73.7	19,559	100
51	329,822	30,895	9.4	22,376	6.8	72.4	19,400	99
52	347,956	32,638	9.4	23,252	6.7	71.2	19,553	100

SOURCES: GROSS NATIONAL PRODUCT data, 1929-52, are based on U·S Dept of Commerce, Survey of Current Business, July, 1953, Table 2; note that data for 1929-49 have been adjusted by the substitution of the revised new private construction and petroleum and natural gas well drilling data from the U·S Dept. of Commerce, Construction and Building Materials, Statistical Supplement, May, 1953, Tables 1 and 24 for the new private construction figures in the Survey; this adjustment is incorporated in the Survey for subsequent years; gross national product data, 1919-28, tie into the Commerce series and are from Miles L. Colean and Robinson Newcomb: Stabilizing Construction (McGraw-Hill, 1952), pp. 200-01. CONSTRUCTION data are from Construction and Building Materials, Statistical Supplement, May, 1953, Tables 1, 2, 3, 15 & 16; building construction is comprised of private and public residential building, private and public non-residential building, farm building, 5 per cent of (private) public utility construction, and 40 per cent of military and naval construction. The Commission acknowledges the valuable assistance of Miles L. Colean, FAIA, in preparing this table.

TABLE 54

TABLE 54: ARCHITECTS-URBAN POPULATION-&-ARCHITECTS PER URBAN POPUL. :1850-1950

A·I·A REGION	1850	1860	1870	1880	1890	1900	1910	1920	1930	1940	1950
ARCHITECTS			1910-1940 includes 2% Naval Architects; 1940-50 adjusted to exclude 5% Landscape Architects								
U·S	591	1263	2,017	3,375	8,070	10,581	16,613	18,187	22,000	20,930	23,578
NEW ENGLAND	110	209	302	446	887	1292	1460	1650	1823	1752	1747
NEW YORK	181	394	470	724	1597	2321	3381	3566	4786	3705	3666
MID-ATLANTIC	137	173	294	576	1231	2067	2975	3320	4053	4347	4151
GREAT LAKES	41	108	228	448	731	1075	1639	2211	2634	2315	2458
NORTH CENTRAL	20	95	256	382	1169	1498	1823	2370	2509	2180	2380
CENTRAL	31	34	204	329	814	700	1348	1194	1217	1153	1351
SOUTH ATLANTIC	16	48	33	55	172	180	408	536	750	1059	1406
GULF	51	86	106	89	290	309	584	516	650	750	1015
TEXAS	–	8	8	52	155	187	470	495	709	927	1206
WEST-MOUNTAIN	1	5	9	59	256	200	363	319	270	359	567
NORTHWEST	–	2	6	38	341	245	913	635	585	639	943
SIERRA NEVADA	3	30	101	177	427	496	1249	1373	2016	1739	2690
URBAN POPULATION (100,000's)											
U·S	35.43	62.16	99.02	141.3	221.0	301.6	419.9	541.6	689.5	744.2	889.3
NEW ENGLAND	7.84	11.48	15.49	21.02	28.93	38.34	48.05	56.20	63.11	64.20	69.22
NEW YORK	8.73	15.24	21.89	28.68	39.10	52.98	71.88	85.88	105.2	111.6	118.9
MID-ATLANTIC	9.80	15.72	23.34	32.24	46.20	61.96	83.58	106.6	127.3	133.4	149.6
GREAT LAKES	3.88	7.34	13.62	20.71	31.86	42.79	56.90	80.33	104.0	108.0	125.8
NORTH CENTRAL	.92	3.72	8.73	14.14	27.62	40.68	54.73	68.87	86.89	91.68	103.8
CENTRAL	.89	2.73	6.58	9.58	18.30	23.39	31.94	40.20	48.74	51.90	61.37
SOUTH ATLANTIC	1.09	1.52	2.12	3.00	5.65	8.10	12.99	18.64	28.34	35.58	47.96
GULF	2.01	3.03	4.03	4.89	8.16	11.39	17.16	22.78	31.93	37.27	50.75
TEXAS	.07	.26	.54	1.46	3.49	5.20	9.38	15.12	23.89	29.11	46.13
WEST-MOUNTAIN	.04	.16	.27	1.13	2.99	4.37	7.26	9.10	11.10	13.38	19.06
NORTHWEST	–	.02	.11	.39	2.53	4.38	11.14	14.23	16.83	18.40	24.93
SIERRA NEVADA	.06	.78	2.15	3.89	6.05	7.83	14.81	23.41	41.94	49.45	71.83
NUMBER OF ARCHITECTS PER 100,000 URBAN POPULATION											
U·S	16.7	20.4	20.4	23.9	36.5	35.2	39.7	33.6	32.0	28.2	26.5
NEW ENGLAND	14.0	18.2	19.5	21.2	30.7	33.8	30.4	29.4	28.9	27.3	25.2
NEW YORK	20.8	25.8	21.4	25.3	40.9	43.9	47.1	41.6	45.5	33.2	30.8
MID-ATLANTIC	14.0	11.0	12.6	17.9	26.7	33.4	35.6	31.2	31.8	32.5	27.8
GREAT LAKES	10.6	14.7	16.7	21.6	22.9	25.2	28.9	27.6	25.3	21.4	19.6
NORTH CENTRAL	21.8	25.6	29.4	27.0	42.4	36.9	33.4	34.4	28.9	23.8	22.9
CENTRAL	34.9	12.4	31.1	34.4	44.5	30.0	42.3	29.8	25.0	22.3	22.0
SOUTH ATLANTIC	14.7	31.6	15.6	18.3	30.5	22.2	31.4	28.8	26.5	29.8	29.3
GULF	25.4	28.4	26.4	18.2	35.6	27.2	34.0	22.7	20.4	20.1	20.0
TEXAS	–	30.8	14.8	35.6	44.5	36.0	50.2	32.8	29.7	31.8	26.1
WEST-MOUNTAIN	25.0	31.3	33.3	52.4	85.7	45.8	50.0	35.0	24.3	26.8	29.8
NORTHWEST	–	100.0	54.5	97.8	135.0	56.0	82.0	44.6	34.8	34.8	37.8
SIERRA NEVADA	50.0	38.5	47.1	45.6	70.7	63.5	84.3	58.7	48.1	35.2	37.5

TABLE 55

TABLE 55: ARCHITECTURAL·FIRMS·PER·URBAN·POPULATION·&·PER·URBAN·INCOME··1950 BY A.I.A REGIONS

Column key for all sections below:

NUMBER OF EMPLOYEES	U·S TOTAL	U·S A·I·A	U·S NON A·I·A	NEW-ENGLAND A·I·A	NEW-YORK A·I·A	MID·ATLANTIC TOTAL	MID·ATLANTIC A·I·A	MID·ATLANTIC NON-AIA	GREAT-LAKES A·I·A	NORTH CENTRAL TOTAL	NORTH CENTRAL A·I·A	NORTH CENTRAL NON-AIA	CENTRAL A·I·A	SO-ATLANTIC A·I·A	GULF A·I·A	TEXAS A·I·A	W-MOUNTAIN A·I·A	NORTHWEST A·I·A	SIERRA-NEV A·I·A

FIRMS·RESPONDING·TO·THE·1950·SURVEY (from Table 26)

NUMBER OF EMPLOYEES	US TOT	US A·I·A	US NON	NEW-ENG	NEW-YORK	MID TOT	MID A·I·A	MID NON	GR-LAKES	NC TOT	NC A·I·A	NC NON	CENTRAL	SO-ATL	GULF	TEXAS	W-MTN	NW	SIERRA
1 - 4	1704	1093	611	83	129	271	167	104	133	180	100	80	58	94	43	66	36	60	124
5 - 9	850	642	208	40	65	116	89	27	66	95	64	31	40	62	50	36	22	30	78
10 - 19	415	336	79	20	37	71	59	12	33	42	30	12	18	28	26	16	16	17	36
20 - 39	191	155	36	13	15	19	13	6	17	31	25	6	12	11	7	10	4	7	21
40 - 99	64	54	10	3	18	8	8	.	3	12	8	4	2	3	.	3	.	1	5
100+	29	22	7	2	3	3	3	.	4	9	6	3	2	1	.	.	.	1	1
TOTAL	3253			246	353	488			332	369			188	266	183	198	98	172	360
A·I·A		2302		161	267		339		256		233		132	199	126	131	78	115	265
NON-AIA			951	85	86			149	76			136	57	67	57	67	19	57	95

NUMBER·OF·FIRMS·ADJUSTED·TO·ACTUAL·DISTRIBUTION·OF·ARCHITECTS

	US TOT	US A·I·A	US NON	NEW-ENG	NEW-YORK	MID TOT	MID A·I·A	MID NON	GR-LAKES	NC TOT	NC A·I·A	NC NON	CENTRAL	SO-ATL	GULF	TEXAS	W-MTN	NW	SIERRA
ADJUST. FACTOR A·I·A				102.7	108.1	104.3			110.1		93.9		106.9	90.8	99.2	93.5	93.7	77.3	95.4
ADJUST. FACTOR NON				112.6	118.2			110.7	93.8			95.7	102.3	85.8	84.2	99.9	68.8	77.7	92.3
TOTAL				261.1	390.4	518.4			353.1	348.9			199.4	238.2	172.9	189.4	86.2	133.2	340.5
A·I·A				165.4	288.7		353.5		281.8		218.8		141.1	180.7	124.9	122.5	73.1	88.9	252.8
NON-AIA				95.7	101.7			164.9	71.3			130.1	58.3	57.5	48.0	66.9	13.1	44.3	87.7

ESTIMATED TOTAL NUMBER OF FIRMS

NUMBER OF EMPLOYEES	US TOT	US A·I·A	US NON	NEW-ENG	NEW-YORK	MID TOT	MID A·I·A	MID NON	GR-LAKES	NC TOT	NC A·I·A	NC NON	CENTRAL	SO-ATL	GULF	TEXAS	W-MTN	NW	SIERRA
1 - 4	4953	2554	2399	200	327	865	408	457	343	524	220	304	146	200	100	145	79	109	277
5 - 9	2310	1493	817	96	165	337	218	119	170	259	141	118	100	132	116	79	48	54	174
10 - 19	1095	785	310	48	94	197	144	53	85	112	66	46	45	60	61	35	35	31	81
20 - 39	501	359	142	31	38	58	32	26	44	78	55	23	30	23	16	22	9	12	47
40 - 99	166	129	37	7	46	20	20	-	8	33	18	15	5	6	-	6	-	2	11
100+	77	51	26	5	7	7	7	-	10	24	13	11	5	2	-	-	-	-	2
TOTAL	9102			767	1081	1484			943	1030			563	651	483	553	223	384	940
A·I·A		5371		387	677		829		660		513		331	423	293	287	171	208	592
NON-AIA			3731	380	404			655	283			517	232	228	190	266	52	176	348

FIRMS PER 100,000 URBAN POPULATION

NUMBER OF EMPLOYEES	US TOT	US A·I·A	US NON	NEW-ENG	NEW-YORK	MID TOT	MID A·I·A	MID NON	GR-LAKES	NC TOT	NC A·I·A	NC NON	CENTRAL	SO-ATL	GULF	TEXAS	W-MTN	NW	SIERRA
URB·POPUL		889.3		69.2	118.9	149.6			125.8	103.8			61.4	48.0	50.8	46.1	19.1	24.9	71.8
1 - 4	5.57	2.86	2.70	2.89	2.75	5.78	2.73	3.06	2.73	5.05	2.12	2.93	2.38	4.17	1.97	3.14	4.14	4.37	3.86
5 - 9	2.60	1.68	.92	1.39	1.39	2.25	1.46	.80	1.35	2.49	1.36	1.14	1.63	2.75	2.29	1.71	2.52	2.17	2.42
10 - 19	1.23	.88	.35	.69	.79	1.32	.96	.35	.68	1.08	.64	.44	.73	1.25	1.20	.76	1.84	1.24	1.13
20 - 39	.56	.40	.16	.45	.32	.39	.21	.17	.35	.75	.53	.22	.49	.48	.31	.48	.47	.48	.65
40 - 99	.19	.15	.04	.10	.38	.13	.13	-	.06	.32	.17	.14	.08	.13	-	.13	-	.08	.15
100+	.09	.06	.03	.07	.06	.05	.05	-	.08	.23	.12	.11	.08	.04	-	-	-	-	.03
TOTAL	10.24			11.08	9.09	9.92			7.50	9.92			9.17	13.57	9.51	11.99	11.70	15.40	13.09
A·I·A		6.04		5.59	5.69		5.54		5.25		4.94		5.39	8.82	5.77	6.22	8.97	8.34	8.24
NON-AIA			4.20	5.49	3.40			4.38	2.25			4.98	3.78	4.75	3.74	5.77	2.73	7.06	4.85

FIRMS PER BILLION DOLLARS OF URBAN INCOME

NUMBER OF EMPLOYEES	US TOT	US A·I·A	US NON	NEW-ENG	NEW-YORK	MID TOT	MID A·I·A	MID NON	GR-LAKES	NC TOT	NC A·I·A	NC NON	CENTRAL	SO-ATL	GULF	TEXAS	W-MTN	NW	SIERRA
URB·INCOME		127.7		10.9	22.2	23.1			18.9	16.7			8.2	4.9	4.6	5.9	2.5	3.9	12.6
1 - 4	38.8	20.0	18.8	18.3	14.8	37.5	17.7	19.8	18.1	31.3	13.2	18.2	17.7	40.7	21.7	24.6	31.7	27.9	22.0
5 - 9	18.1	11.7	6.4	8.8	7.5	14.6	9.4	5.2	9.0	15.5	8.4	7.0	12.1	26.8	25.2	13.4	19.3	13.8	13.8
10 - 19	8.6	6.2	2.4	4.4	4.2	8.5	6.2	2.3	4.5	6.7	3.9	2.7	5.5	12.2	13.3	5.9	14.1	7.9	6.4
20 - 39	3.9	2.8	1.1	2.8	1.7	2.5	1.4	1.1	2.3	4.7	3.3	1.4	3.6	4.7	3.5	3.7	3.6	3.1	3.7
40 - 99	1.3	1.0	0.3	0.6	2.1	0.9	0.9	-	0.4	2.0	1.1	0.9	0.6	1.2	-	1.0	-	0.5	0.9
100+	0.6	0.4	0.2	0.5	0.3	0.3	0.3	-	0.5	1.4	0.8	0.7	0.6	0.4	-	-	-	-	0.2
TOTAL	71.3			70.8	48.8	64.3			49.8	61.6			68.4	132.4	105.0	93.8	89.6	98.1	74.7
A·I·A		42.1		35.4	30.6		35.9		34.8		30.7		40.2	86.0	63.7	48.7	68.7	53.1	47.0
NON-AIA			29.2	34.7	18.2			28.4	14.9			30.9	28.2	46.4	41.3	45.1	20.9	45.0	27.7

TABLE 56: ENROLLMENTS IN U·S SCHOOLS OF ARCHITECTURE · 1898·1911·1930·1933-53

SCHOOL	1898	1911	1930 A	1930 AE	1933	1934	1935	1936	1937	1938	1939	1940	1941	1942	1943	1944	1945	1946	1947	1948	1949	1950 A	1950 AE	1951 A	1951 AE	1952 A	1952 AE	1953 A	1953 AE
NEW·ENGL'D	107	116	275	69	192	143	122	115	145	168	165	156	112	54	75	89	149	201	281	312	321	316		290		287		274	
Harvard·U	36	36	56		35	35	32	34	49	52	58	54	39	44	48	54	115	130	136	127	126	128		102		96		100	
Mass·I·T	71	80	178	69	128	86	72	64	74	91	82	79	73	10	27	35	34	71	102	123	121	121		130		117		124	
RhodeI·S·D																			43	62	74	67		58		74		50	
U·NewHamp			41		•29	22	•18	•17	•22	•25	•25	•23																	
N·ATLANTIC	175	602	1389	96	1093	1014	939	901	844	956	1006	939	901	695	317	396	926	1499	1595	1692	1759	1737	50	1679	54	1613	89	1618	74
Yale U			105		96	96	96	96	85	70	73	65	60	43	25	19	97	145	126	118	103	114		105		90		101	
Columbia U	78	113	118		80	71	59	58	44	45	41	45	50	42	34	32	61	96	149	147	148	144		148		154		156	
Pratt·Inst										•50	•55	•60	•55	•50	48	•45	58	127	134	134	153	169		180		233		237	
N·Y·U			320		356	327	314	320	313	291	291	255	•200	62	15														
Cooper·I												•30	•40	52	29	•20	•40	•90	101	101	120	141		136		110		111	
Cornell·U	45	123	133		152	130	104	92	90	100	141	118	119	113	47	63	128	170	181	171	171	158		166		162		167	
Syracuse	11	53	69		59	51	50	59	63	64	67	60	59	49	15	32	75	109	130	142	150	159		142		140		152	
Rensselaer			63		•55	51	39	40	40	45	43	43	36	37	16	56	154	171	154	160	190	186		180		159		147	
Princeton			54		17	16	16	14	11	46	26	27	48	30	7	5	34	35	44	68	77	70		85		74		92	
U·Pennsyl.	41	216	280		96	111	105	97	78	77	92	85	70	71	36	37	142	226	267	273	280	266	20	244	12	216	14	199	14
Penn·S·C			63	96	49	46	42	35	20	83	67	55	71	58	20	47	40	170	117	170	160	130	30	95	42	90	75	90	60
Carnegie		97	184		133	115	114	90	100	95	110	96	93	88	25	40	97	160	192	208	207	200		198		185		166	
MIDWEST	72	488	947	355	752	694	575	657	750	739	798	794	731	743	207	330	1196	2041	2483	2491	2745	2674	304	2408	279	2290	333	2217	243
Miami·U													40	38	6			74	121	121	135	132		120		111		93	
Ohio·U														50	10			•20	•61	•80	•100	118	21	94	31	79	10	72	24
U·Cincin'ti			182		50	75	60	56	65	73	80	84	64	70	28	37	125	256	294	301	332	333		345		340		330	
Ohio·State		39	95	79	109	74	67	89	90	76	86	68	65	51	8	18	85	130	139	188	250	319		216		173		180	
W·Reserve			63		•45	39	•38	•44	40	42	49	48	47	49	10	18	92	89	93	13	100	87		90		79		90	
Notre·Dame		25	50	15	47	45	35	25	18	18	22	24	36	45	24	24	116	120	120	125	138	120	1	156	2	168		164	
Illinois Tech	19	98	129		102	89	27	66	81	84	82	97	78	71	30	48	•120	187	220	201	196	180		192		175		152	
U·Illinois	53	203	244	205	239	239	223	226	284	281	311	318	263	243	49	120	433	766	946	951	1001	955		854		830		874	
U·Michigan		123	184	56	160	133	125	151	172	165	168	155	138	126	42	65	225	399	489	514	493	430		341		335		262	
U·Detroit																							282		246		223		219
N·PLAINS			209	88	205	160	150	139	124	138	143	146	120	115	47	80	227	272	278	276	205	195	41	181	40	189	42	166	29
U·Minnesota			167	75	167	125	120	111	99	110	114	117	96	92	43	76	218	202	208	207	160	132		138		151		119	
N·Dakota			42	13	•38	35	•30	•28	•25	•28	•29	•29	•24	•23	4	•4	9	•70	•70	69	•75	63	41	43	40	38	42	47	29
C·PLAINS		44	298	238	284	277	233	232	259	265	266	395	398	392	110	171	675	848	1118	1286	1089	976	347	797	239	698	195	704	192
Iowa S·C				125								•140	145	•140	30	•40	263	254	349	349	221	193	32	151	30	127	17	193	18
Wash·U		44	72	43	66	64	35	32	45	49	53	51	50	61	33	44	116	131	129	178	234	237	27	235	5	189	19	155	
U·Missouri			18																										
U·Nebraska			63	18	•60	52	•50	•50	•56	•60	•60	•65	69	78	17	37	100	110	115	77	67	116	45	86	41	103	23	84	45
U·Kansas			68	6	58	60	55	59	69	71	67	64	62	55	19	18	85	180	320	407	317	215	110	167	75	157	85	158	76
Kansas S·C			77	46	100	101	93	91	89	85	86	75	72	58	11	32	111	173	205	275	250	215	133	158	88	122	51	114	53
C·ATLANTIC	8	18	189	105	85	141	70	88	118	111	120	120	284	223	76	83	284	682	863	825	746	828	162	706	154	642	123	612	106
Geo·Wash	8	9	81			64																							
Catholic·U		9	33	2	26	28	24	33	55	42	45	40	35	15	14	11	49	90	174	227	202	141	80	140	73	118	49	95	49
Howard·U			15		•12	15	•12	•15	•18	•19	•20	•20	•16	13	13	•5	27	115	199	51	21	150		130		111		101	
U·Virginia			60		•47	34	•34	•40	•45	•50	•55	•60	57	52	12	•8	•30	•100	•115	110	94	104		98		97		102	
Virginia·P·I				49									96	87	10	19	47	83	83	114	148	131	80	130	49	121	44	98	34
Hampton·I																				91	76	76		11	32	10	30	10	23
N·Car·S·C				54									80	56	27	•40	131	294	294	232	205	226	2	197		185		206	
SOUTHEAST		76	365	31	276	256	245	266	291	312	344	369	409	348	113	178	634	990	1406	1384	1398	1376	24	1205	151	1206	177	1028	215
Clemson·C			46		•45	44	•40	•35	•40	•45	•50	•60	•75	85	27	•30	144	191	•190	•190	•190	•185		175	20	148	28	97	61
Georgia Tech		42	132		65	66	60	75	93	92	102	114	129	97	30	49	160	280	370	382	415	355		285		270		244	
U·Florida			54		•50	46	•50	•52	•58	•63	•67	•65	71	56	9		120	210	396	331	325	352		325		357		260	
U·Miami																									131		149		154
Alabama·P		22	67	31	58	64	63	72	70	78	79	75	78	72	29	50	137	246	257	280	257	238		193		211		207	
U·Arkansas																			68	72	75	75	24	65		72		75	
Tulane·U		12	66		•58	36	32	32	30	34	46	55	56	38	18	49	73	63	125	129	136	171		162		148		145	
SOUTHWEST		56	364	201	405	380	407	421	453	423	492	561	589	463	216	335	745	1619	1470	1488	1560	1369	529	1233	370	1162	327	1186	411
U·Oklahoma			18	43	•60	58	•55	•60	•65	•70	•65	•65	•60	51	29	•25	143	269	274	260	300	210	22	210	45	214	24	208	15
Okla·A·M			93	4	•75	59	•60	65	79	76	71	68	66	72	16	14	79	241	125	237	252	152	56	158	50	180	45	176	←
A·M Texas			60	58	•90	85	•95	•100	•110	•120	•135	•150	147	123	26	110	186	280	215	223	218	206	132	224	140	200	140	195	121
U·Texas		56	107	59	130	135	151	147	147	172	163	158	143	121	73	125	187	565	542	348	275	325	153	263		250		256	165
Texas·Tech				37								•60	57	•45	19	•25	•75	175	221	188	190	176		135		141		143	
Rice·Inst			86		•50	43	•46	•49	•52	•55	•58	•60	56	51	53	36	74	89	93	92	108	110		108		68		95	
U·Houston																				140	217	190	113	135	92	109	80	113	73
U·New·Mex																							53		43		38		37
MOUNTAIN																			98	108	240	263	163	297	77	239	31	192	45
U·Denver																			98	108	120	120		101					
U·Colorado																						45	163	91	77	109	31	77	45
U·Utah																					120	98		105		130		115	
NORTHWEST			217	85	193	160	169	232	258	281	295	324	224	213	121	206	382	673	577	824	774	736	128	577	128	618	92	531	117
Montana S·C			29		•25	•25	•20	•24	•28	•32	•36	•40	35	39	4	•10	30	112	140	140	111	110	37	85	32	81	11	34	39
U·Idaho			21		•18	14	•14	•16	•18	•20	•25	•30	•28	25	•15	•25	•40	55	56	82	80	54		62		64		47	
U·Wash'tn			109		85	84	93	122	134	134	135	139	99	87	43	95	•155	145	123	163	167	196		168		218		209	
Wash·S·C				65																			91		96		81		78
U·Oregon			58	20	65	62	42	•70	78	95	99	115	62	62	19	76	187	361	258	439	416	376		262		255		241	
CALIFORNIA		50	369		280	241	241	230	262	285	356	327	259	134	100	668	969	997	1131	811	828	1103	170	1076	190	981	186	899	160
U·California		50	193		141	141	141	141	142	•140	181	154	141	94	50	593	579	688	781	•450	458	657		593		507		423	
U·So·Calif			176		139	100	100	89	120	145	175	173	118	40	50	75	390	309	350	361	370	415		421		410		404	
Stanford·U																						31		62		64		72	
Calif·Poly·																							170		190		186		160
TOTALS Archit.	362	1450	4622		3765	3466	3151	3281	3504	3678	3985	4131	4027	3380	1382	2536	6187	9822	11,300	11,497	11,665	11,573		10,449		9925		9427	
TOTALS Arch-Eng				1268																			1918		1682		1595		1744
TOTALS Total			5890																			13,491		12,131		11,520		11,171	
Priv·Sch'ls	309	915	2140				1238					1392									3447	3386						2893	
Public "	53	535	2482				1913					2739									8218	8187						6534	

Sources: 1898, 1911, 1934 from Weatherhead : 1930 from Bosworth & Jones; others from ACSA annual reports. Enrollments marked • are estimates.

TABLE 57

TABLE 57: RATIOS OF ENROLLMENTS IN ARCHITECTURE · ENGINEERING & LAW TO THE PROFESSIONS URBAN POPULATION & 18-21 AGE GROUP

	1900	1910	1920	1930	1940	1950	1951	1952	1953
U.S Urban Population	30,159,921 *	41,998,932	54,157,973	68,954,823	74,423,702	88,927,464	90,500,000 E	92,500,000 E	94,530,000 E
18-21 year Age Group — Census enumeration / Thompson estimates	5,930,765	7,335,453	7,343,794	9,026,741	9,753,537	8,805,020 / 8,424,165	8,227,410	8,076,441	8,001,654

ARCHITECTURE

	1900	1910	1920	1930	1940	1950	1951	1952	1953
Architects — Census enumeration / Census Archts per 100M Urb.Pop. / Registered Architects / Reg. Archts per 100M Urb.Pop.	10,581 / 35.1	16,281 / 38.8	17,823 / 32.9	21,560 / 31.3	20,512 / 27.6	23,578 / 26.5 / 19,137 / 21.5			
Architectural Students — Foreign & U.S Territories / Continental U.S / Veterans / Non-veterans	362 1898 / E / 362	1450 E / 0 / 1450		4662 E 1.5% / 4553	4131 E 1.0% / 4090	11,573 438 3.8% / 11,135 / 4,198 37.7% / 6,937	10,449 414 4.0% / 10,035 / 2,910 29.0% / 7,125	9,925 465 4.7% / 9,460 / 1,442 16.3% / 7,918	9,427 494 5.4% / 8,916 E / 963 10.8% / 7,953
Archit-Students per Architect — Census Archts / Regis. Archts	.034 1898	.089		.212	.199	.472 / .582			
Archit-Students per 100M Urb.Pp. — Continental US Veterans / Non-veterans	1.27 *1898	3.45		6.60	5.50	12.52 / 7.80	11.09 / 7.87	10.23 / 8.55	9.43 / 8.41
Architectural Students per 100,000 of 18-21 AgeGroup — Cont.US Census Thompson / Non-vet Census Thompson	6.10 1898	19.77		50.44	41.94	126.46 132.18 / 78.78 82.35	121.98 / 86.60	117.12 / 98.04	111.42 / 99.39

ARCHITECTURAL ENGINEERING

	1900	1910	1920	1930	1940	1950	1951	1952	1953
Arch.Engineering Students / Students per 100.000 Urb.Pop.				1268 / 1.82		1748 / 1.92	1682 / 1.77	1595 / 1.66	1592 / 1.63

ENGINEERING

	1900	1910	1920	1930	1940	1950	1951	1952	1953
Engineers / Engineers per 100.000 Urb.Popul.	52,896 / 175.4	84,177 / 200.5	129,939 / 239.9	215,386 / 312.4	261,428 / 351.3	400,000 E / 449.8			
Engineering Students — Total / Non-Vet.	11,415	30,337	51,908	73,386 1931	103,270	161,592 / 100,672 E	145,997		
Students per Engineer — Total / Non-Vet.	.216	.360	.399	.341	.395	.404 / .252			
Students per 100M Urb.Pop. — Total / Non-Vet.	40.2	72.2	95.8	107.3	138.8	181.7 / 113.5	161.3		
Students per 100M AgeGr. — Total / Non-Vet.	192.5	413.6	706.9	819.8	1058.9	1835.2 / 1143.2	1774.4		

LAW

	1900	1910	1920	1930	1940	1950	1951	1952	1953
Lawyers — Census enumeration / Lawyers per 100M Urban Population	107,474 / 356.3	114,704 / 273.2	122,519 / 226.2	160,605 / 232.9	180,483 / 242.5	181,226 / 203.8			
Law Students — Total E / Non-veterans / Law + Pre-Law	12,516	19,567	20,992	41,426	31,775 / 69,000 E	56,385 35,128 E / 112,580 E			
Students per Lawyer — Total / Non-veterans / Law + Pre-Law	.116	.171	.171	.258	.176 / .382	.311 .193 / .678			
Students per Urb.Pop. — Total / Non-veterans / Law + Pre-Law	41.5	46.6	38.8	60.1	42.7 / 93.2	63.4 39.5 / 137.8			
Students per Age-Gr. — Total / Non-veterans / Law + Pre-Law	211.0	266.7	285.9	458.9	325.8 / 708.0	640.4 398.9 / 1289.2			

* Urban population in 1898 estimated at 28,550,000
E denotes estimate

TABLE 58

TABLE 58: FIRST·PROFESSIONAL·DEGREES·IN·ARCHITECTURE·1930-1953: by school

SCHOOL	1930	1934	1935	1936	1937	1938	1939	1940	1941	1942	1943	1944	1945	1946	1947	1948	1949	1950 A	1950 AE	1951 A	1951 AE	1952 A	1952 AE	1953 A	1953 AE	1950% ACSA	1950% Surv
NEW·ENGL'D	58	21	19	20	18	26	26	27	20	40	19	19	14	22	43	71	77	58		94		88		64		3.2	7.1
Harvard·U	14		3	6	9	7	11	16	3	26	9	14	7	14	28	44	49	25		43		39		17		1.4	2.
Mass·I·Tech	39	21	16	14	9	19	15	11	17	14	10	5	7	8	11	24	22	22		38		33		25		1.2	4.
Rhode·I·S·D															4	24	6	11		13		16		12		0.6	0.
U·New·Hamp	5																										
N·ATLANTIC	160	196	198	154	165	149	112	134	133	101	94	41	60	144	194	310	346	367	19	262		271	6	287	9	20.0	33.3
Yale·U	27	24	26	16	22	29	16	21	15	14	9	7	1	19	21	46	28	26		36		34		23		1.4	4.
Columbia·U	15	18	28	12	12	8	6	9	9	8	2	14	8	11	12	26	25	27		21		34		25		1.5	4.
Pratt·Inst													6		41	18	26	31		5		27		37		1.7	1.
N·York·U		34	38	27	28	29	22	24	23		16																2.
Cooper·Inst															[24]	[27]	[18]	[23]		[35]		[20]		[25]			0.
Cornell·U	22	17	18	25	16	15	10	15	13	13	18	10	12	22	26	29	45	37		23		16		35		2.0	5.
Syracuse	12	9	8	8	11	8	8	9	11	8	6	1	2	9	9	14	19	40		26		27		22		2.2	5.
Rensselaer		8	15	6	9	7	9	9	9	9	2	3	7	10	19	51	43	63		81		11		32		3.5	0.
Princeton	10	7	6	3	3	3	5	7	5	7	2	2		4	11	16	12	8		9		12		12		0.4	1.
U·Pennsyl.	33	49	30	25	35	13	4	16	17	22	9	1	15	31	25	60	58	52	6	60	3	56		2.8	7.
Penn·S·C	14	11	9	8	8	18	21	10	17	10	6	5	5	11	22	26	42	37	13	28		20	3	10	9	2.0	1.
Carnegie	27	19	28	24	21	19	15	14	14	10	18	3	4	17	8	24	48	46		28		30		3.5		2.5	3.
MIDWEST	119	124	117	132	91	96	111	106	123	103	76	21	51	136	191	311	472	529	50	403	55	345	28	353	38	28.8	22.
Miami·U															7	12		19		18		11		18		1.0	0.
Ohio·U																			9		4			6			
U·Cincin'ti	10	20	14	8	7	5	12	3	7	9	10	1	1	20	16	25	33	2		53		47		43		0.1	1.
Ohio State	12	13	6	4	10	13	6	11	12	8	6	2	2	10	25	30	98	57		57		36		33		5.4	2.
W·Reserve	8					6	8	11	6	4	8	4	3	4	13	25	11	8		18		18		14		0.6	0.
Notre·Dame	10	10	10	8	4	6	8	6	4	3	4	2	6	9	10	28	8	23	2	29				16		0.4	0.
Illinois·Tech	20	17	18	21	11	9	15	14	13	15	13	2	10	11	37	37	53	42		35		30		38		2.3	3.
U·Illinois	30	40	43	42	28	35	34	44	50	30	33	12	25	61	86	138	217	211		149		112		130		11.5	7.9
U·Michigan	29	24	26	49	31	22	30	34	33	20	3	7	7	22	22	51	86	138	46	60	44	62	24	61	32	7.5	5.
U·Detroit																											0.
N·PLAINS	15	39	26	22	16	10	13	10	16	15	15	7	3	17	20	35	60	49	11	30	6	33	13	36	6	2.7	2.9
U·Minnesota	12	39	26	22	16	10	13	10	16	15	15	7	3	17	7	22	44	35	11	22		27	7	29	6	1.9	2.
N·Dakota	3														13	13	16	14		8	6	6	13	7		0.8	0.
C·PLAINS	26	31	44	35	23	31	23	29	34	24	22	13	32	38	78	195	254	171	143	170	95	113	52	119	59	9.3	4.4
Iowa·S·C																											
Wash·U	15	10	20	13	2	8	7	8	8	8	6	18	19	32	32	43	52	12	25	18	20	14	17	13	13	0.7	2.
U·Missouri												7	7	10	10	37	10	41	22	43	5	32	2	46		2.2	1.8
U·Nebraska											4	3			4	21	29	20	16	25	9	20	8	16	5	1.1	0.
U·Kansas	6	11	10	10	10	7	9	11	12	8	3	3	1	4	22	62	75	28	35	14	12	25	17	27		1.5	0.
Kansas·S·C	5	10	14	12	11	16	7	10	14	5	5		6	8	10	32	88	70	45	64	47	25	10	17	14	3.8	1.
C·ATLANTIC	15	4	3	7	1	5	9	9	7	9	22	7	7	23	40	103	162	139	59	109	39	103	32	90	33	7.6	2.7
Geo·Wash	1																										
Catholic·U	5	4	3	7	1	5	9	9	7	9		3	5	11	10	34	75	40	33	34	23	33	16	33	24	2.2	0.
Howard·U	3														4	10	21	22		14						1.1	0.
U·Virginia	6														12	30	24	22		11		11		20		1.2	1.
Virginia·P·I										22		4		4	4	12	14	24	18	15	11	15	13	17	8	0.8	0.
Hampton·I															5	12	23	1	5	1	3	1				1.3	0.
N·Car·S·C												2		8	14	18	19	23	2	23		29		20		1.0	0.
SOUTHEAST	63	22	28	23	24	28	19	24	33	26	15	14	11	46	73	123	181	173		179	7	159	18	163	34	9.4	7.9
Clemson·C	9											3	3	14	14	14	14	14		30	7	25	6	21	11	0.8	1.
Georgia Tech	20	13	18	14	8	9	5	4	12	9	1	8	3	10	20	39	35	48		43		32		32		2.6	2.
U·Florida	10												5	10	17	60	37	32		48		62				2.0	1.
U·Miami																							12		23		
Alabama·P·I	10	9		6	10	12	11	15	9	5	5	2	5	8	17	38	56	50		32		28		21		2.7	1.
U·Arkansas																	5	10		5		10		10		0.5	0.
Tulane·U	14		3	6	7	3	5	12	12	9	4		9	12	15	11	14	32		18		17				0.8	1.
SOUTHWEST	28	20	18	16	13	24	22	19	28	44	48	5	20	36	85	129	205	158	116	166	75	195	68	166	128	8.6	5.8
U·Oklahoma												5	5	13	25	30	36	11	21	20	26	5	19	10		2.0	0.
Okla·A·M	7				4	8	6	10	8	7	6	5	2	12	21	36	31	9	27	7	35	17	10		1.7	0.
A·M·Texas	10								18	21	1			12	28	28	20	25	30	30	20	25	25		1.1	1.
U·Texas	6	20	18	16	9	16	16	9	20	11	15	3	8	16	35	34	58	56	57	29	34	22	31		3.1	1.
Texas Tech																4	6	32		26		27		16			0.
Rice·Inst	5									8	6	1	2	12	9	13	16	12		17		18	14	14		0.7	1.
U·Houston																2	5	3	12	18	6	33	14	35	13	-	0.
U·New·Mex																			12		11		22		32		0.
MOUNTAIN															6	6	68	27	44	22	33	13	7			0.3	0.1
U·Denver																										0.3	
U·Colorado															6	6	68	15		44		33		7			0.
U·Utah																		12		22		13					
NORTHWEST	12	14	14	13	12	12	14	15	20	11	15	6	39	31	52	58	99	98	24	104	32	103	22	80	23	5.3	4.0
Montana·S·C	3												1		9	6	20	9	3	17		18		10	8	0.4	0.
U·Idaho	[4]														[1]	[12]	[12]	[7]		[12]		[10]		[7]			0.
U·Wash'tn	7	10	10	9	7	7	9	14	19	9	14	4	9	19	15	32	29	64		55		40		39		3.5	2.
S·C·Wash																			21		24		22		15		1.
U·Oregon	2	4	4	4	5	5	5	1	1	2	1	2	29	12	28	20	50	25		32		45		31		1.4	1.
CALIFORNIA	11	32	18	29	47	31	29	36	55	36	11	6	10	40	35	103	150	87		166	42	92	42	88	26	4.8	6.4
U·California	5	30	3	29	29	16	17	12	20	20		2		20	11	75	100	37		95		20		21		2.0	4.
U·So·Calif	6	2	15		18	15	12	24	35	16	11	4	10	20	24	28	50	50		63		55		60		2.7	2.
Stanford·U																											
Calif·Poly																		8	42			17	42	7	26		
TOTALS Archit.	507	503	485	451	410	412	378	409	469	409	337	139	247	533	811	1438	2012	1835		1710		1524		1459		100	100
Arch·Eng	178																		490		395		314		363		
Non·prof	4																		30		47		30		32		
Total	689																		2355		2152		1868		1854		

Sources: 1930 from Bosworth & Jones; others from ACSA annual reports

TABLE 59

TABLE 59 — U.S. ARCHITECTURAL STUDENTS 1933 & 1949 — BY STATES & AREAS OF ORIGIN & BY AREAS OF ATTENDANCE (ACSA survey)

Registered Architects as of 1950; Urban population as of 1950; 18–21 Age Group as of 1953, from Thompson.

TABLE 60 : INTERCHANGE·OF·U·S·ARCHITECTURAL·STUDENTS·1953· between 11 Areas (Data from 1953 ACSA Survey)

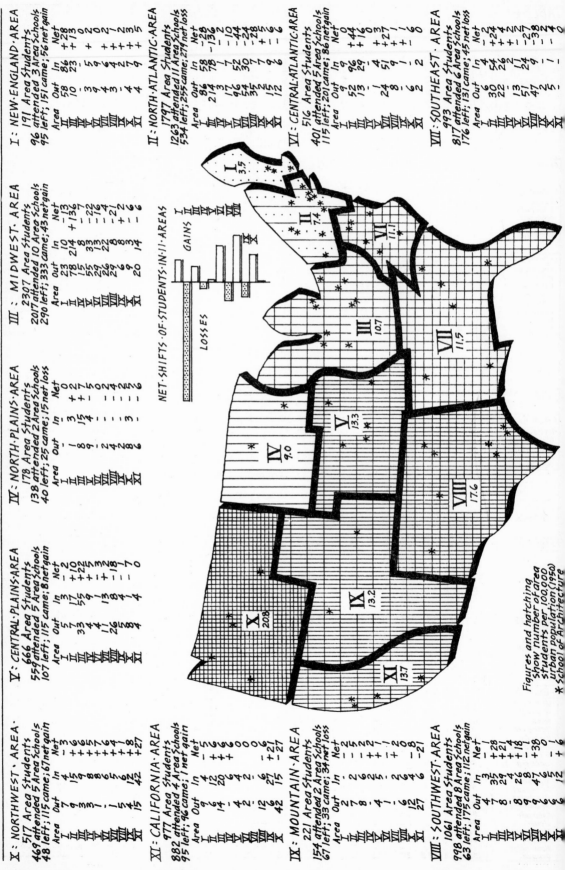

TABLE 60

X : NORTHWEST·AREA·
517 Area Students
469 attended 5 Area Schools
48 left; 115 came; 67 net gain

Area	Out	In	Net
II	7	4	– 3
III	9	15	+ 6
V	3	8	+ 5
VI	1	8	+ 7
VIII	–	6	+ 6
IX	5	9	+ 4
XI	15	42	+ 27

V : CENTRAL·PLAINS·AREA
666 Area Students
558 attended 5 Area Schools
107 left; 115 came; 8 net gain

Area	Out	In	Net
II	3	13	+ 10
III	17	17	0
IV	4	9	+ 5
VI	1	4	+ 3
VII	11	13	+ 2
VIII	26	8	– 18
IX	8	1	– 7
X	4	4	0

XI : CALIFORNIA·AREA
977 Area Students
882 attended 4 Area Schools
95 left; 96 came; 1 net gain

Area	Out	In	Net
I	–	5	+ 5
II	9	14	+ 6
III	12	20	+ 6
IV	4	4	0
V	2	2	0
VI	–	–	0
VIII	12	6	– 6
IX	6	27	+ 21
X	42	15	– 27

I : NEW·ENGLAND·AREA
191 Area Students
96 attended 3 Area Schools
95 left; 151 came; 56 net gain

Area	Out	In	Net
II	58	86	+ 28
III	10	23	+ 13
IV	3	5	+ 2
V	4	4	0
VI	4	6	+ 2
VII	3	2	– 1
VIII	–	2	+ 2
IX	2	7	+ 5
X	4	9	+ 5

II : NORTH·ATLANTIC·AREA
1797 Area Students
1263 attended 11 Area Schools
534 left; 255 came; 279 net loss

Area	Out	In	Net
I	86	58	– 28
III	214	78	– 136
IV	17	7	– 10
V	96	52	– 44
VI	54	30	– 24
VII	35	7	– 28
VIII	15	–	+ 5
IX	12	6	– 6

III : MIDWEST·AREA
2307 Area Students
2017 attended 10 Area Schools
290 left; 333 came; 43 net gain

Area	Out	In	Net
I	23	10	– 13
II	78	214	+ 136
IV	15	8	– 7
V	55	33	– 22
VI	29	13	– 16
VII	26	22	– 4
VIII	29	8	– 21
IX	6	8	+ 2
X	9	3	+ 1
XI	20	14	– 6

IV : NORTH·PLAINS·AREA
178 Area Students
138 attended 2 Area Schools
40 left; 25 came; 15 net loss

Area	Out	In	Net
I	–	1	0
II	8	15	+ 7
III	9	4	+ 5
V	4	4	0
VI	2	1	– 1
VIII	–	1	1
IX	2	3	– 2
X	8	–	6

VI : CENTRAL·ATLANTIC·AREA
516 Area Students
401 attended 5 Area Schools
115 left; 201 came; 86 net gain

Area	Out	In	Net
I	9	9	0
II	52	96	+ 44
III	13	29	+ 16
V	1	4	+ 3
VII	24	51	+ 27
VIII	8	1	+ 1
IX	6	2	+ 1
X	2	2	0

VII : SOUTHEAST·AREA
993 Area Students
817 attended 6 Area Schools
176 left; 131 came; 45 net loss

Area	Out	In	Net
I	4	2	– 2
II	36	54	+ 24
III	30	22	+ 2
IV	13	11	– 2
V	51	24	– 27
VI	47	9	– 38
VIII	5	1	– 4
IX	1	–	0

IX : MOUNTAIN·AREA
221 Area Students
154 attended 2 Area Schools
67 left; 33 came; 34 net loss

Area	Out	In	Net
I	2	–	– 2
II	7	2	– 5
III	8	1	– 7
IV	4	4	+ 2
V	5	–	– 1
VI	1	1	+ 2
VIII	6	6	– 8
X	12	27	+ 21
XI	27	6	– 21

VIII : SOUTHWEST·AREA
1061 Area Students
998 attended 8 Area Schools
63 left; 175 came; 112 net gain

Area	Out	In	Net
I	–	1	+ 1
II	7	35	+ 28
III	8	29	+ 21
IV	4	4	+ 4
V	8	26	+ 18
VII	9	47	+ 38
IX	6	5	– 1
X	6	12	+ 6

NET·SHIFTS·OF·STUDENTS·IN·11·AREAS

GAINS — I II III IV V VI VII IX

LOSSES

Figures and hatching show number of area students per 100,000 urban population (1950)
✶ School of Architecture

TABLE 61

TABLE 61: U·S ARCHITECTURAL STUDENTS · 1953 · by States of Origin; by Zones of Attendance and by Attendance at Private & Public Institutions

Groups & States	No. of Private/Public Schools	Number	% of US Total	Students per 10M Urban Popul.	Students per 100M 18-21 Age Group	Zone No. In same state	Zone No. Adjoining States	Zone No. Next-adjoining	Zone No. Other states	Zone % In same state	Zone % Adjoining States	Zone % Next-adjoining	Zone % Other states	In same state No. Private	In same state No. Public	In same state % Private	In same state % Public	Out-of-state Total Number	Out-of-state Total % of state	Out-of-state No. Private	Out-of-state No. Public	Out-of-state % Private	Out-of-state % Public	Total No. Private	Total No. Public	Total % Private	Total % Public
U·S	25/37	9424	100	10.6	117.8	6624	1435	474	891	70.3	15.2	5.0	9.5	2053	4571	33.5	66.5	2800	29.7	1259	1541	45.0	55.0	3312	6112	35.1	64.9
GROUP I: 14 States without Schools																											
GROUP I	0	519	5.5	6.2	41.6	·	318	92	109	·	61	18	21					519	100	178	341	34	66	178	341	34	66
SUB·GROUP IA: 5 Eastern States																											
S·GROUP IA	0	110	1.2	4.9	48.1	·	54	27	29	·	49	25	26					110	100	71	39	65	35	71	39	65	35
Maine		10	0.1	2.7	17.3	·	·	4	6	·	·	40	60					10	100	6	4	60	40	6	4	60	40
N-Hamps.		8	0.1	2.7	27.7	·	6	·	2	·	75	·	25					8	100	7	1	88	12	7	1	88	12
Vermont		6	0.1	4.4	25.4	·	5	·	1	·	83	·	17					6	100	6	·	100	·	6	·	100	·
Delaware		10	0.1	6.8	65.7	·	3	2	5	·	30	20	50					10	100	3	7	30	70	3	7	30	70
Maryland		76	0.8	6.0	73.3	·	40	21	15	·	52	28	20					76	100	49	27	64	36	49	27	64	36
SUB·GROUP IB: 9 Other States																											
S·GROUP IB	0	409	4.3	6.7	40.2	·	264	65	80	·	65	16	19					409	100	107	302	26	74	107	302	26	74
Wisconsin		107	1.1	5.6	54.9	·	71	15	21	·	66	14	20					107	100	28	79	26	74	28	79	26	74
W-Virginia		41	0.4	6.4	28.2	·	34	3	4	·	83	7	10					41	100	7	34	17	83	7	34	17	83
Kentucky		60	0.6	6.1	28.2	·	44	11	5	·	73	18	8					60	100	10	50	17	83	10	50	17	83
S-Dakota		19	0.2	8.8	38.8	·	7	2	10	·	37	11	52					19	100	2	17	5	95	2	17	5	95
Tennessee		90	1.0	7.1	46.7	·	53	17	20	·	59	19	22					90	100	25	65	28	72	25	65	28	72
Mississippi		56	0.6	9.3	32.5	·	33	15	8	·	59	27	14					56	100	16	40	29	71	16	40	29	71
Wyoming		9	0.1	6.2	55.5	·	3	·	6	·	33	·	67					9	100	5	4	56	44	5	4	56	44
Nevada		6	0.1	7.1	118.2	·	4	1	1	·	66	17	17					6	100	3	3	50	50	3	3	50	50
Arizona		21	0.2	7.7	69.0	·	15	1	5	·	71	5	24					21	100	11	10	52	48	11	10	52	48
GROUP II: 35 States with Schools																											
GROUP II	25/37	8905	94.5	11.1	131.9	6624	1117	382	782	74.4	12.5	4.3	8.8	2053	4571	31.0	69.0	2281	25.6	1081	1200	47.4	52.6	3134	5771	35.2	64.8
SUB·GROUP IIA: 8 States with Private Schools																											
S·GROUP IIA	14	2017	21.4	7.4	107.9	897	602	174	344	45	30	9	17	897		100		1120	55	634	486	56	44	1531	486	77	23
SUB·GROUP IIAa: 5 Eastern States																											
S·GROUP IIAa	11	1561	16.6	7.1	119.9	696	412	149	304	45	26	10	19	696		100		865	55	594	271	69	31	1290	271	83	17
Massachus'ts	2	138	1.5	3.4	56.5	52	51	6	29	38	37	4	21	52		100		86	62	70	16	81	19	122	16	88	12
Rhode Island	1	35	0.4	5.0	88.2	24	2	7	2	68	6	20	6	24		100		11	32	9	2	82	18	33	2	94	6
Connecticut	1	118	1.2	9.2	137.5	25	50	15	28	21	42	13	24	25		100		93	79	81	12	87	13	106	12	90	10
New York	6	995	10.6	8.4	139.5	578	150	68	199	58	15	7	20	578		100		417	42	217	200	52	48	795	200	80	20
New Jersey	1	275	2.9	7.2	126.3	17	159	53	46	6	58	19	17	17		100		258	96	217	41	84	16	234	41	85	15
SUB·GROUP IIAb: 3 Other States																											
S·GROUP IIAb	3	456	4.8	7.8	80.2	201	190	25	40	44	42	5	9	201		100		255	56	40	215	16	84	241	215	53	47
Indiana	1	154	1.6	7.0	78.9	19	114	6	15	12	74	4	10	19		100		135	88	19	116	14	86	38	116	25	75
Missouri	1	183	1.9	8.0	84.3	97	64	9	13	53	35	5	7	97		100		86	47	12	74	14	86	109	74	60	40
Louisiana	1	119	1.3	8.7	76.3	85	12	10	12	72	10	8	10	85		100		34	28	9	25	27	73	94	25	79	21
SUB·GROUP IIB: 8 States with Private & Public Schools																											
S·GROUP IIB	11/15	4351	46.2	11.9	165.0	3675	295	136	245	84.5	6.8	3.1	5.6	1156	2519	31.5	68.5	676	15.5	319	357	47	53	1475	2876	34	66
SUB·GROUP IIBa: 3 Eastern States																											
S·GROUP IIBa	4/4	648	6.9	7.2	77.4	458	89	40	61	71	14	6	9	229	229	50	50	190	29	112	78	59	41	341	307	53	47
Pennsylvan.	2/1	393	4.2	5.7	65.0	274	72	28	19	70	18	7	5	189	85	69	31	119	30	72	47	61	39	261	132	66	34
D-Columbia	1	85	0.9	10.6	219.5	52	5	6	22	61	6	7	26	31	21	59	41	33	39	18	15	55	45	49	36	58	42
Virginia	1/2	170	1.7	12.7	88.0	132	12	6	20	77	7	4	12	9	123	7	93	38	23	22	16	58	42	31	139	18	82
SUB·GROUP IIBb: 5 Other States																											
S·GROUP IIBb	7/11	3703	39.3	13.4	205.8	3217	206	96	184	87	6	2	5	927	2290	29	71	486	13	207	279	42	58	1134	2569	31	69
Ohio	1/4	577	6.1	10.9	155.0	461	60	29	27	80	10	5	5	79	382	17	83	116	20	85	31	73	27	164	413	28	72
Illinois	1/1	946	10.1	14.6	227.7	822	50	35	39	87	5	4	4	104	718	13	87	124	13	48	76	39	61	152	794	16	84
Michigan	1/1	422	4.4	10.3	133.3	347	21	11	43	82	5	3	10	162	185	47	53	75	18	39	36	52	48	201	221	48	52
Texas	2/3	781	8.3	17.7	193.4	705	41	6	29	90	5	8	3	160	545	23	77	76	10	12	64	16	84	172	609	22	78
California	2/2	977	10.4	13.7	335.3	882	34	15	46	90	3	2	5	422	460	48	52	95	10	23	72	24	76	445	532	46	54
SUB·GROUP IIC: 19 States with Public Schools																											
S·GROUP IIC	22	2537	26.9	15.6	113.0	2052	220	72	193	81	9	3	7		2052		100	485	19	128	357	26	74	128	2409	5	95
Minnesota	1	112	1.2	7.0	64.9	93	7	2	10	83	6	2	9		93		100	19	17	3	16	16	84	3	109	3	97
N-Dakota	1	47	0.5	28.6	90.5	37	1	·	9	79	·	2	19		37		100	10	21	1	9	10	90	1	46	2	98
Iowa	1	184	2.0	15.0	119.2	154	14	9	7	84	8	5	4		154		100	30	16	5	25	17	83	5	179	3	97
Nebraska	1	90	1.0	14.8	90.5	70	7	6	7	78	8	6	8		70		100	20	22	4	16	20	80	4	86	4	96
Kansas	2	209	2.2	23.1	177.5	174	19	3	13	83	9	1	6		174		100	35	17	5	30	14	86	5	204	2	98
N-Carolina	1	185	1.9	14.9	64.2	153	12	10	10	83	6	5	5		153		100	32	17	9	24	28	72	9	177	5	95
S-Carolina	1	98	1.0	16.1	63.9	77	10	2	9	79	10	2	9		77		100	21	21	7	14	33	67	7	91	7	93
Georgia	1	135	1.4	9.8	79.9	106	17	·	12	78	13	·	9		106		100	29	21	3	26	10	90	3	132	2	98
Florida	1	272	2.9	17.4	272.0	199	26	7	40	73	10	3	14		199		100	73	27	20	53	27	73	20	252	7	93
Alabama	1	140	1.5	11.4	61.3	126	5	1	8	90	4	1	5		126		100	14	10	5	9	36	64	5	135	4	96
Arkansas	1	83	0.9	13.4	61.3	59	17	2	5	71	21	2	6		59		100	24	29	10	14	42	58	10	73	12	88
Oklahoma	2	245	2.6	22.1	150.5	226	11	5	3	92	5	2	1		226		100	19	8	10	9	53	47	10	235	4	96
New Mexico	1	35	0.4	11.1	80.5	19	9	1	6	54	26	3	17		19		100	16	46	9	7	56	44	9	26	26	74
Colorado	1	81	0.9	10.7	124.3	51	8	5	17	63	10	6	21		51		100	30	37	12	18	40	60	12	69	15	85
Utah	1	104	1.1	25.2	226.0	96	2	4	2	92	2	4	2		96		100	8	8	3	5	38	62	3	101	3	97
Montana	1	82	0.9	32.4	231.4	66	10	5	1	80	12	6	1		66		100	16	20	3	13	19	81	3	79	4	96
Idaho	1	66	0.7	28.2	202.5	36	26	1	3	54	39	1	5		36		100	30	46	1	29	3	97	1	65	2	98
Washington	1	217	2.3	17.0	264.3	174	10	12	21	80	5	6	10		174		100	43	20	13	30	30	70	13	204	6	94
Oregon	1	152	1.6	20.8	313.8	136	8	4	4	89	5	3	3		136		100	16	11	5	11	31	69	5	147	3	97

TABLE 62

TABLE 62: SCHOOL ENROLLMENTS ·1953· by 4 Zones of Students' Origins (Data from ACSA survey)

Areas & Schools	Private Support / Public	Total of all first degree students	Total of all students from Continental US	% of US Total	Number: In-state Students	Adjoining States	Next Adjoining	Other States	Per Cent: In-state Students	Adjoining States	Next Adjoining	Other States	In-state + Adjoining	In-state + Adj + Next	No. of States Represented	Other Students: US Territories	Foreign	Total	% of Schools US Students	% US Total
U·S TOTAL	25/37	9983	9424	100	6624	1445	495	860	70.3	15.3	5.3	9.1	85.6	90.9		117	442	559	5.9	100
NEW·ENGLAND	3	274	247	2.6	76	82	24	65	30.8	33.2	9.7	26.3	64.0	73.7	31	1	26	27	11.1	4.8
Harvard·U	•	100	88	0.9	31	25	8	24	35	29	9	27	64	73	22	1	11	12	14	2.1
Mass·Inst·Tech	•	124	111	1.2	21	42	8	40	19	38	7	36	57	64	27		13	13	12	2.3
Rhode·Is·S·D	•	50	48	0.5	24	15	8	1	50	31	17	2	81	98	7		2	2	4	0.4
NORTH·ATLANTIC	10 1	1618	1518	16.1	894	417	72	135	58.9	27.5	4.7	8.9	86.4	91.1	42	12	88	100	6.6	17.9
Yale·U	•	101	96	1.0	25	41	4	26	26	43	4	27	69	73	18		5	5	5	0.9
Columbia·U	•	156	145	1.5	93	41	3	8	64	28	2	6	92	94	13		11	11	8	2.0
Pratt·Inst	•	237	236	2.5	205	26	·	5	87	11	·	2	98	98	11		1	1	5	0.2
Cooper·Inst	•	111	106	1.1	68	28	2	8	64	26	2	8	90	92	13		5	5	5	0.9
Cornell·U	•	167	149	1.6	66	39	16	28	44	26	11	19	70	81	24	1	17	18	12	3.2
Syracuse·U	•	152	137	1.5	74	51	5	7	54	37	4	5	91	95	14	6	9	15	11	2.7
Rensselaer·P·I	•	147	129	1.4	72	40	5	12	56	31	4	9	87	91	15	3	15	18	14	3.2
Princeton·U	•	92	87	0.9	17	32	14	24	20	37	16	27	57	73	24		6	6	6	0.9
U·Pennsylvania	•	199	180	1.9	97	59	12	12	54	33	7	7	87	94	20	2	17	19	11	3.4
Pennsylvania·S·C	•	90	90	1.0	85	5	11	·	95	5			100	100	12					
Carnegie·I·Tech	•	166	163	1.7	92	55	11	5	56	34	7	3	90	97	18		3	3	2	0.5
MIDWEST	4 6	2436	2350	24.9	1649	373	171	157	70.1	15.9	7.3	6.7	86.0	93.3	41	18	68	86	3.7	15.4
Miami·U	•	93	91	1.0	71	9	9	2	78	10	10	2	88	98	9		2	2	2	0.4
Ohio·U	•	72	67	0.7	37	15	15	·	55	22	22	·	77	100	5		5	5	7	0.4
U·Cincinnati	•	330	323	3.4	130	125	52	16	40	39	16	5	79	95	21		7	7	2	1.3
Ohio·State·U	•	180	173	1.8	144	13	9	7	83	8	5	4	91	96	15	2	5	7	4	1.3
Western·Reserve	•	90*	88	0.9	79	3	4	2	90	3	5	2	93	98	5		2	2	2	0.4
U·Notre Dame	•	164	155	1.6	19	57	26	53	12	37	17	34	49	66	24	1	8	9	6	1.6
Illinois·Inst·Tech	•	152*	144	1.5	104	11	6	23	72	8	4	16	80	84	19	2	6	8	6	1.4
U·Illinois	•	874	855	9.1	718	90	9	38	84	11	1	4	95	96	25	6	13	19	3	3.4
U·Michigan	•	262	248	2.6	185	26	25	12	75	10	10	5	85	95	17	5	9	14	6	2.5
U·Detroit	•	219	206	2.2	162	24	16	4	78	12	8	2	90	98	8	1	12	13	6	2.3
NORTH·PLAINS	2	166	163	1.7	130	26	4	3	79.8	15.9	2.5	1.8	95.7	98.2	9		3	3	1.8	0.5
U·Minnesota	•	119	117	1.2	93	17	4	3	79	15	3	3	94	97	7		2	2	2	0.4
North·Dakota·A·C	•	47	46	0.5	37	9	·	·	80	20	·	·	100	100	3		1	1	2	0.2
CENTRAL·PLAINS	1 4	704	672	7.2	495	114	24	41	73.4	16.9	3.6	6.1	90.3	93.9	29	15	15	30	4.5	5.4
Iowa·State·C	•	193	188	2.0	154	28	1	5	82	15	1	3	97	98	13	2	3	5	3	0.9
Washington·U	•	155	145	1.6	97	24	8	16	67	17	5	11	84	89	18	6	4	10	7	1.8
U·Nebraska	•	84	82	0.9	70	7	3	2	85	9	4	2	94	98	8		2	2	2	0.4
U·Kansas	•	158	154	1.6	93	47	5	9	60	31	3	6	91	94	14	3	1	4	3	0.7
Kansas·State·C	•	114	105	1.1	81	8	7	9	77	8	7	9	85	92	13	4	5	9	9	1.6
CENTRAL·ATLANTIC	2 4	635	602	6.4	337	76	66	123	56.0	12.6	11.0	20.4	68.6	79.6	30	9	24	33	5.5	5.9
Catholic·U	•	95	83	0.9	31	23	18	11	37	28	22	13	65	87	12	4	8	12	14	2.1
Howard·U	•	101	92	1.0	21	14	19	38	23	15	21	41	38	59	25	1	8	9	10	1.6
U·Virginia	•	102	99	1.1	54	12	12	21	55	12	12	21	67	79	16	1	2	3	3	0.5
Virginia·Poly·Inst	•	98	97	1.0	69	7	6	15	71	7	6	15	78	84	14		1	1	1	0.2
Hampton·Inst	•	33	33	0.3	9	10	7	7	27	30	21	21	57	78	13					
N·Carolina·S·C	•	206	198	2.1	153	10	4	31	77	5	2	16	82	84	15	2	6	8	4	1.4
SOUTHEAST	1 5	1028	948	10.1	652	147	48	101	68.8	15.5	5.1	10.6	84.3	89.4	35	14	66	80	8.4	14.3
Clemson·S·C	•	97	94	1.0	77	8	5	4	82	9	5	4	91	96	9	3		3	3	0.5
Georgia·Sch·Tech	•	244	224	2.4	106	49	24	45	47	22	11	20	69	80	27	4	16	20	9	3.6
U·Florida	•	260	230	2.4	199	3	4	24	87	1	2	10	87	89	15	5	25	30	5	5.4
Alabama·Poly·Inst	•	207	202	2.2	126	62	7	7	62	31	3	3	93	96	13		5	5	2	0.9
U·Arkansas	•	75	74	0.8	59	10	1	4	80	14	1	5	94	95	10		1	1	1	0.2
Tulane·U	•	145	124	1.3	85	15	7	17	69	12	6	14	81	87	16	2	19	21	17	3.8
SOUTHWEST	2 6	1223	1173	12.4	950	88	36	99	81.0	7.5	3.1	8.4	88.5	91.6	36	11	39	50	4.3	8.9
U·Oklahoma	•	208	190	2.0	108	36	14	32	57	19	7	17	76	83	29	7	11	18	9	3.2
Oklahoma·A·M	•	176	167	1.8	118	28	8	13	70	17	5	8	87	92	15		9	9	5	1.6
A·M·Col·Texas	•	195	194	2.1	185	2	2	5	95	1	1	3	96	97	7	1		1	5	0.2
U·Texas	•	256	248	2.6	227	2	2	13	92	1	1	5	94	95	14		8	8	3	1.4
Texas·Tech·Col	•	143	140	1.5	133	4	1	2	95	3	1	1	98	99	12		3	3	2	0.5
Rice·Inst	•	95	90	1.0	66	4	4	15	73	6	4	17	79	83	14	1	2	3	6	0.9
U·Houston	•	113	108	1.1	94	4	1	10	87	4	1	10	91	91	12		5	5	5	0.9
U·New Mexico	•	37	36	0.4	19	3	5	9	53	8	14	25	61	75	9		3	3	3	0.2
MOUNTAIN	2	192	187	2.0	147	12	13	15	78.6	6.4	7.0	8.0	85.0	92.0	18	3	2	5	2.7	0.9
U·Colorado	•	77	74	0.8	51	2	9	12	69	3	12	16	72	84	14	3		3	4	0.5
U·Utah	•	115	113	1.2	96	10	4	3	85	9	4	3	94	97	9		2	2	2	0.4
NORTHWEST	5	648	584	6.2	412	86	22	64	70.5	14.7	3.8	11.0	85.2	89.0	37	23	41	64	10.1	11.5
Montana·S·C	•	73	72	0.7	66	5	1	·	92	7	1	·	99	100	4		1	1	1	0.2
U·Idaho	•	47	45	0.5	36	5	2	2	80	11	4	4	91	95	6		2	2	4	0.4
U·Washington	•	209	181	1.9	123	11	14	33	68	6	8	18	74	82	30	5	23	28	15	5.0
S·C·Washington	•	78	63	0.7	51	5	1	6	81	8	1	10	89	91	9	10	5	15	24	2.7
U·Oregon	•	241	223	2.4	136	60	4	23	61	27	2	10	88	90	20	8	10	18	8	3.2
CALIFORNIA	2 2	1059	978	10.4	882	24	15	57	90.2	2.5	1.5	5.8	92.7	94.2	30	11	70	81	7.7	14.5
U·California	•	423	372	4.0	331	6	5	30	89	2	1	8	91	92	23	5	46	51	14	9.1
U·So·California	•	404	398	4.2	365	12	3	18	92	3	1	4	95	96	21	1	5	6	2	1.1
Stanford·U	•	72	67	0.7	57	2	3	5	85	3	4	8	88	92	9		5	5	2	0.9
California·Poly	•	160	141	1.5	129	4	4	4	91	3	3	3	94	97	6		14	14	13	3.4

* Report incomplete ·· 1953 total distributed according to 1951 proportions.